The Autocourse History of the Grand Prix Car 1966-1985

To everyone in Formula 1 who aimed high . . .

'There's always room at the top, and it's damned crowded down below. Why shouldn't one get there? It only needs a little more push and a little more attention to detail than the average fellow is prepared to give.' *Sir Henry O'Neil de Hane Segrave.*

THE WORLD'S BEST-SELLING CIGARETTE.

LOW TO MIDDLE TAR As defined by H.M. Government
DANGER: Government Health WARNING:
CIGARETTES CAN SERIOUSLY DAMAGE YOUR HEALTH.

The Autocourse History of
the Grand Prix Car
1966-1985

by Doug Nye

Hazleton Publishing, Richmond, Surrey

Supporting the Sport

Over the years Lucas equipped cars have been driven to more championship victories, simply because they have performed with total reliability throughout the season.

This illustrious record has been achieved by our technical support, monitoring and constant development of Lucas competition equipment which has attained a level of reliability unsurpassed in motor sport today. To pass this support on to the competitive motorist there is a nationwide network of dealers known as the "Lucas Special Section."

Lucas Electrical

Contents

PUBLISHER
Richard Poulter
EXECUTIVE PUBLISHER
Elizabeth Le Breton
PUBLISHING ASSISTANT
Jane Payton
HOUSE EDITOR
Stephen Spark
ART EDITOR
Jim Bamber

Hazleton Publishing
3 Richmond Hill, Richmond,
Surrey TW10 6RE
Printed in Holland by
drukkerij de lange/van Leer
bv, Deventer
Typesetting by C. Leggett
& Son Ltd, Mitcham, Surrey,
England.
ISBN: 0-905138-37-6

UK distribution by
Osprey Publishing Limited
12-14 Long Acre
London WC2E 9LP

Sole Distributors For North America
Motorbooks International
Publishers & Wholesalers Inc.
Osceola, Wisconsin 54020, USA ®

Title page photograph:
*'SPEED MUST NOT
EXCEED 170 MPH' reads
the dash-panel sticker
while the chassis-plate
announces this cockpit as
belonging to Repco
Brabham 'BT24-1'. These
were the last multi-tubular
spaceframe-chassised cars
to win the Formula 1
Constructors' World
Championship title (in
1967). Note grey-
enamelled chassis tube,
wrapped-over glass-fibre
body mouldings, polished
welded-aluminium strap-
in fuel tanks and clip-cover
battery box beneath the
driver's thighs . . . all
typical Sixties practice.*

Introduction

From 1966 to 1976 we could quite properly describe the contemporary Formula 1 as the '3-litre Formula'. Renault changed all that in 1977 when they pioneered exploitation of the hitherto-ignored clause which permitted use of supercharged engines of up to 1500 cc.

Renault chose to employ exhaust-driven turbocharging for their forced-induction 1500. By 1981, the normally aspirated 3-litre brigade headed by Cosworth-Ford was fighting a valiant rearguard action against the proliferation of major-manufacturer turbocharged cars then under development. By the end of 1982 the Constructors' Championship had for the first time fallen to turbocharged 1500 cc cars. No longer was this the '3-Litre Formula'.

Naturally aspirated cars fought their last battles through 1983 and into 1984 had no chance of winning, vanishing altogether during 1985.

Following a controversial ruling which banned the Cosworth engine's last redoubt, the Tyrrell team, from racing, the Austrian GP at the Österreichring on 19 August 1984 was run without a single 3-litre engine competing. In the next race, at Monza, there was not even a single 3-litre 'Cossy' in the paddock.

They would return to sing their swansong in the Tyrrell cars of early 1985 but when a Tyrrell-DFY ran in that season's German GP on 4 August, it was the end. Formula 1 was now purely 1500 cc turbocharged, and for 1986 the 3-litre naturally aspirated option was finally deleted. So the father gave way to the son, and by evolution the '3-litre Formula' had run its course, with a 20-season period to survey in these pages.

The broad subject of 'The Grand Prix Car' has been covered in the past by other learned analyses which effectively traced its development up to 1953. I make no excuses for paying tribute to the late Laurence Pomeroy's magnificent if flawed two-volume work published over 30 years ago.

Others better-qualified than I in the theoretical and academic engineering sense have since published works on the Grand Prix car to 1973 but these provided little meat for the enthusiast who memorizes the racing publications every week; the *Autocourse* reader.

As will be apparent to those who are, I am neither an engineer nor a student of engineering. However, like many fellow enthusiasts, I am fascinated by the backroom effort behind the superstars' exploits on circuit and by the design, manufacture and development of the vehicles they drive.

In the following pages I set out to record the detailed history of each of our 20 Formula 1 Constructors' Championship-winning cars from 1966 to 1985, highlighting details of their design, construction, modification and operation, while a detailed Appendix gives a reference run-down on the 331 mainstream Formula 1 races run during this period.

By definition, most racing cars are unsuccessful — there just is not enough winning to share equally. Their place is in the Team Directory section which covers every car to compete in international major-league Formula 1 during the period. Engines are covered in a similar manner.

A brief Overview provides a summary of technical progress and innovation while some topics of special interest are highlighted in boxed paragraphs placed within the text.

We have tried to avoid any easy options in compiling this survey and I hope it gives the reader as much interest as it has caused me and my publisher agonies in production.

I hope that when reading this book, you can marvel — as I always do — at the devotion and dedication of those involved in what is effectively a technological war fought at a frightening pace under incredible and unrelenting pressures. This is what enables Formula 1 racing to attract and employ such fine people — people who do not pack up and go home until the work is done, people to whom winning is reward for total effort. People I admire.

What follows is dedicated to all of them. The achievements are theirs, while the inevitable errors in a work of this magnitude are mine, and for those I apologize in advance.

Doug Nye,
Farnham, Surrey.
April 1986

Spirit of '3-Litre' Formula 1: Dan Gurney's gorgeous AAR Eagle-Weslake V12 rounding Monte Carlo's harbour-front Tabac corner during the 1967 Monaco Grand Prix meeting, Jackie Stewart's 2.1-litre BRM P261 in pursuit.

Acknowledgements

Photographs and other illustrations have been contributed by the following (listed by page): **COLOUR.** *Geoffrey Goddard,* 20, 25, 113, 114, 115 top right, 116, 117 (all), 118, 119, 120, 121, 122, 123, 124, 125, 126, 128, 209, 210, 211, 213, 216 bottom, 218 top row, 218 middle row, 218 bottom right; *Tony Matthews,* 214 middle; *Phipps Photographic,* 36, 115 bottom right, 219 top; *Renault Sport,* 218 bottom left; *Nigel Snowdon,* 212, 214 top, 215 bottom, 216 top, 217, 220, 222, 224 bottom; *TAG Turbo Engines,* 219 bottom; *John Townsend,* 224 top. **BLACK AND WHITE.** *Alfa Romeo SpA,* 147 bottom, *James Allington/Autosport,* 54; *Autocar,* 50, 60 middle; *Jim Bamber,* 91 top, 130 upper middle; *Bill Bennett/Motoring News,* 178 bottom; *Gérard Berthoud,* 164 top; *BMW Motorsport,* 148 bottom; *Charles Briscoe-Knight,* 108 bottom, 111 bottom; *Charles Briscoe-Knight/Motofoto,* 163 bottom; *BRM/Autocar,* 150; *Diana Burnett,* 104, 139 top, 141, 154 bottom, 161 bottom, 264; *Pete Coltrin,* 183 bottom; *Mike Dodson,* 94 top left; *Ferrari SpA,* 152 bottom, 250 bottom; *Ford Motor Company,* 52; *Geoffrey Goddard,* 27, 28, 29, 37 middle, 37 bottom, 41, 43, 45, 46, 48, 51, 55, 56, 57, 58 bottom, 59, 62, 64, 65 bottom, 66 top, 67, 69, 70, 71, 72, 73, 76, 78, 79 top left, 79 top right, 80, 82, 83, 84 top left, 84 top right, 85, 86, 89, 90, 91 top, 92, 93 top, 97, 99, 100, 101 top, 106 top, 108 top, 147 top, 151, 153 bottom, 155 middle, 162, 165 bottom, 167, 171, 172, 173 top, 174, 175, 176, 177 bottom, 178 top, 179, 181, 182 top, 184, 185 top, 188, 190, 200 top, 201, 203, 204 bottom, 205 top, 206 bottom, 207, 208 top, 225 top, 235, 238, 241, 243; *Robert Harmeyer Jnr,* 161 top; *Brian Hart,* 154 top; *Brian Hatton/Motor,* 58 bottom, 66 bottom, 177 top; *Michael Hewett,* 96; *Hewland Engineering,* 101 middle, 101 bottom; *Honda,* 155 top; *Jeff Hutchinson,* 133 top, 164 bottom; *David Hutson,* 160 bottom, 197 top; *International Press Agency,* 134, 139 bottom, 143 top, 148 top, 186 bottom, 193 top, 194; *John Player Team Lotus,* 196 bottom, 198 bottom left, 198 bottom right, 244, 245, 247 top, 248, 249 top; *LAT,* 130 top left, 130 top right; *Tony Matthews,* 185 bottom; *Tony Matthews/LAT,* 68, 74, 77, 88, 173 bottom, 182 bottom, 189, 202; *Matra Sports,* 63, 65 top, 66 middle, 156, 205 middle, 205 bottom; *Motor,* 58 top, 183 top; *Motor Racing Developments,* 168 top left; *Doug Nye,* 60 top, 60 bottom, 206 top; *Theo Page/Ford Motor Co.,* 47; *Phipps Photographic,* 61, 87, 130 lower middle, 166, 168 top left, 168 bottom left; *Giorgio Piola,* 33, 79 bottom, 81, 95, 98, 102, 110 bottom, 129 top, 130 bottom, 132, 163 top, 193 bottom, 197 bottom, 198 top, 208 middle, 208 bottom, 225 bottom; *Renault Sport,* 157, 158, 229; *Nigel Snowdon,* 37 top, 53, 75, 93 bottom, 105, 106 bottom, 107, 110 top, 111 top, 112, 129 bottom, 133, 135, 136, 138, 145, 146, 152 top, 153 top, 155 bottom, 160 top, 165 top, 168 bottom right, 170, 180, 187, 192, 199, 204 top, 226, 230, 232, 237, 240, 242; *STP,* 200 bottom; *TAG Turbo Engines,* 143 bottom; *Leslie Thacker,* 196 top; *Tyrrell Racing Organisation,* 246, 251; *Williams Grand Prix Engineering,* 247 bottom, 249 bottom, 250 top; *Peter Wright,* 94 top right, 94 bottom; *Leo Wybrott,* 84 middle right, 84 bottom right; *Zooom,* 186 top.

As you can imagine, the body of work presented within these pages would not have been possible without help. Any journalist is only as good as his sources and I only hope my work has been worthy of mine.

I must pay special tribute to the assistance provided by Patrick Head of Williams Grand Prix Engineering, John Barnard of McLaren International, Gordon Murray of Motor Racing Developments and Dr Harvey Postlethwaite of Ferrari for their special and decidedly expert assistance, opinion and advice.

Permission to use original factory drawings was granted by Mr Ferrari via Dr Franco Gozzi, by Peter Warr of Team Lotus, by Ken Tyrrell, and by Patrick Head of Williams Grand Prix Engineering.

Most immediate and wide-ranging help in a variety of trials, tribulations and confusions came from my friends Geoff Goddard – who took many of the photographs which follow – Denis Jenkinson of *Motor Sport,* Maurice Hamilton of *Autocourse* annual and *The Iguardna,* Alan Henry of *Motoring News* and Nigel Roebuck of *Autosport.* Matthew Carter of *Autocar* was also of great help.

Thanks also to . . . Peter Agg (Trojan), *Ing.* Giulio Alfieri (Maserati), James A. Allington (Maserati), Bert Baldwin (Goodyear), Derek Bell, Herbie Blash (Lotus and Brabham), Dr Helmuth Bott (Porsche), Sir Jack Brabham, BRM, Jimmy Buss (Hewland Engineering), Rory Byrne (Toleman), Alan Campbell (Ferodo), Michael Cane, the late Colin Chapman, Alan Charles, Denny Chrobak (Goodyear), Peter Connew, John Cooper (Goodyear), Gordon Coppuck (McLaren and Spirit), André de Cortanze (Renault), Michele Cory (BMW), Mike Costin (Cosworth Engineering), Jabby Crombac, Yvette Darcy (Renault), Gérard Ducarouge (Renault), Bernard Dudot (Renault), Eagle, Andrew Ferguson (Lotus and Vel's Parnelli), Geoff Ferris (Penske), Jack Field (Cosworth Engineering), Derek Gardner (Tyrrell), Goodyear, Dan Gurney, Brian Hart, Mr Yoshiyuki Hayashi without whose enthusiasm I would not have

been able to tackle a work of this magnitude, the late Heinz Hofer (Penske), Robin Herd (March, McLaren and Cosworth), John Judd (Repco Brabham and Engine Developments Ltd), Dr Karl Kempf (Goodyear and Tyrrell), Jean-Luc Lagardère (Matra), Lotus, Owen Maddock (Cooper), Uwe Mahla (BMW), Bob Marston (Cooper and Lola), Bob Martin (Firestone), Ted Martin (Cooper), Tony Matthews, Teddy Mayer (McLaren and Beatrice), the late Bruce McLaren, Leo Mehl (Goodyear), Hans Mezger (Porsche), Michelin, Vel Miletich (Vel's Parnelli), Andrew Nahum (Science Museum, London), Barry Needham (Alfa Romeo), John Nicholson (Nicholson-McLaren Engines), David North (Brabham), Martin Ogilvie (Lotus), Jack Oliver (Shadow and Arrows), Osella, Tim Parnell (BRM), Maurice Phillippe (Lotus, Vel's Parnelli Jones and Tyrrell), Mike Pilbeam (BRM and LEC), Raymond Playfoot (BMW), Duncan Rabagliati (Formula One Register), Alan Rees (March, Shadow and Arrows), Renault, José Rosinski, Tony Rudd (BRM and Lotus), Jean Sage (Renault), Dick Scammell (Lotus and Vel's Parnelli), Betty Sheldon (Formula One Register), Dr K. Paul Sheldon (Formula One Register), Martin Slater (Lyncar), Roger Sloman (Advanced Carbon Composites), Tony Southgate (Arrows and Shadow), Alec Stokes (BRM), John Surtees, Ron Tauranac (Motor Racing Developments, Trojan and Theodore), Len Terry (Lotus, Eagle and BRM), Theodore, John Thorpe (Safir), Sheridan Thynne (Williams Grand Prix Engineering), Mario Tozzi-Condivi (Cooper), Ken Tyrrell, Brenda Vernor (Ferrari), Neil Verweij (Alfa Romeo), Dave Wass (Arrows and Shadow), Tom Wheatcroft, founder of the Donington Collection of Single-Seater Racing Cars, Frank Williams, Aubrey Woods (BRM), Leo Wybrott (McLaren and Lotus) . . . for enabling me finally to commit this work to paper. It covers the twenty busiest seasons in Grand Prix racing history, and I hope records fairly the successes, achievements and failures of all those who pushed a little harder than the average fellow.

PARTS OF A WINNING FORMULA.

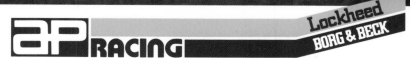

SUPERLATIVE PERFORMANCES
1966-85

Every motor race provides three opportunities for a superlative performance – race win, pole position and fastest lap.

In our 20-season period, 279 World Championship-qualifying Grand Prix races were run, supplemented by 52 non-Championship events. Individual race wins and pole positions totalled 331 each, with 337 fastest lap performances, being shared twice in Championship rounds and four times in non-Championship races. The Formula's superlative peformances thus total 999; the following table records victories, pole positions and fastest laps by chassis and by engine, in all races.

ENGINES

Engine	CHAMPIONSHIP			NON-CHAMPIONSHIP			Total
	Wins	Pole	FL	Wins	Pole	FL	
Cosworth-Ford V8	155	130	141	29	34	34	523
Ferrari	52	63	60	9	4	7	195
flat-12	37	42	44	6	2	2	
V6 t/c	12	14	12	—	—	1	
V12	3	7	4	3	2	4	
Renault V6 t/c	18	42	22	—	—	—	82
TAG Turbo V6 t/c	18	5	14	—	—	—	37
Repco V8	8	7	4	4	4	5	32
BMW 4-cyl t/c	8	13	11	—	—	—	32
Honda	6	4	6	—	—	—	16
V6 t/c	5	3	4	—	—	—	
V12	1	1	2	—	—	—	
BRM	6	2	4	3	6	5	26
V12	4	2	4	3	4	4	
H16	1	—	—	—	2	—	
1.9 V8	1	—	—	—	—	—	
2.1 V8	—	—	—	—	—	1	
Alfa Romeo	2	5	7	1	1	1	17
flat-12	2	3	6	—	1	—	
V12	—	2	1	1	—	1	
Maserati V12	2	1	2	—	—	—	5
Matra V12	3	4	5	1	1	1	15
Weslake V12	1	—	2	1	1	1	6
Hart 4-cyl t/c	—	1	2	—	—	—	3
Chevrolet V8 F5000*	—	—	—	2*	—	1	3
Coventry-Climax	—	2	1	2	1	1	7
2.7 4-cyl	—	—	—	1	1	1	
2.0 V8	—	2	1	1	—	—	
	279	279	281†	52	52	56†	999

MARQUES

Make	CHAMPIONSHIP			NON-CHAMPIONSHIP			Total
	Wins	Pole	FL	Wins	Pole	FL	
Ferrari	52	63	60	9	4	7	195
V12	3	7	4	3	2	4	
flat-12	37	42	44	6	2	2	
V6 t/c	12	14	12	—	—	1	
Lotus	51	70	41	6	11	12	191
BRM H16	1	—	—	—	—	—	
2.0 Climax V8	—	2	1	1	—	—	
Cosworth V8	47	57	36	5	11	11	
Renault V6	3	11	4	—	—	—	
2.1 BRM V8	—	—	—	—	—	1	
McLaren	48	22	34	7	4	8	123
Cosworth V8	30	17	20	7	3*	7	
TAG V6	18	5	14	—	—	—	
Chevrolet V8*	—	—	—	—	1*	1*	
Brabham	33	37	37	10	8	9	134
Repco V8	8	7	4	4	4	5	
Alfa Romeo flat-12	2	3	6	—	1	—	
Cosworth V8	15	14	16	4	2	2	
BMW 4-cyl	8	13	11	—	—	—	
Alfa V12	—	—	—	1	—	1	
2.7 Climax 4-cyl	—	—	—	1	1	1	
Tyrrell-Cosworth V8	23	14	19	1	4	2	63
Williams	22	13	21	3	1	2	62
Cosworth V8	17	10	17	3	1	2	
Honda V6	5	3	4	—	—	—	
Renault V6	15	31	17	—	—	—	63
Matra	9	4	12	3	3	3	34
Cosworth V8	9	2	9	2	2	2	
V12	—	2	3	1	1	1	
Ligier	8	9	9	—	1	—	27
Cosworth V8	5	7	6	—	1	—	
Matra V12	3	2	2	—	—	—	
Renault V6	—	—	1	—	—	—	
BRM	5	2	4	3	6	3	23
1.9 V8	1	—	—	—	—	—	
V12	4	2	4	3	4	3	
H16	—	—	—	—	2	—	
March-Cosworth V8	3	5	6	2	2	1	19
Wolf-Cosworth V8	3	1	2	—	—	—	6
Cooper-Maserati V12	2	1	2	—	—	—	5
Eagle-Weslake V12	1	—	2	1	1	1	6
Honda V12	1	1	2	—	—	—	4
Hesketh-Cosworth V8	1	—	1	1	3	2	8
Shadow-Cosworth V8	1	2	2	1	2	2	10
Surtees-Cosworth V8	—	—	3	2	2	2	9
Alfa Romeo V12	—	2	1	—	—	—	3
Toleman-Hart 4-cyl	—	1	2	—	—	—	3
Arrows-Cosworth V8	—	1	1	—	—	—	2
Ensign-Cosworth V8	—	—	1	—	—	—	1
Fittipaldi-Cosworth V8	—	—	—	—	—	1	1
Kojima-Cosworth V8	—	—	1	—	—	—	1
Parnelli-Cosworth V8	—	—	1	—	—	—	1
Penske-Cosworth V8	1	—	—	—	—	—	1
Theodore-Cosworth V8	—	—	—	1	—	—	1
Chevron-Chevrolet V8*	—	—	—	1*	—	1*	2
Lola-Chevrolet V8*	—	—	—	1*	—	—	1
	279	279	281†	52	52	56†	999

*Formula F5000 of two minor races; first F1 finishers were BRM V12- and Cosworth V8-powered.

†Two Championship and four non-Championship fastest laps were shared by different engines.

---

*Two 'Formula 1' races have been won outright by Formula 5000 cars. The Madrid GP at Jarama, 1969, was won by a Lola-Chevrolet T142, pole and fastest lap by a McLaren-Chevrolet M10A. Fastest F1 car in both practice and race as well as 'F1 class' winner was a BRM P261 V12 spl. The 1973 Race of Champions was won by a Chevron-Chevrolet B24, with a McLaren M19-Cosworth the first F1 car home. Chevron also set fastest lap in 1972 Oulton Park Gold Cup.

†These column totals are greater than the total number of races because two GP Championship and four non-Championship fastest laps have each been shared by two manufacturers.

NB: Non-Championship races include '3-litre Formula' dress rehearsal, Rand GP, Kyalami, South Africa, 4-12-1965.

▶

The cool crisp taste of
Martini Extra Dry shines through.
Once found, never lost.
It's there to be discovered.

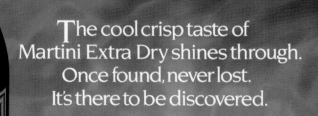

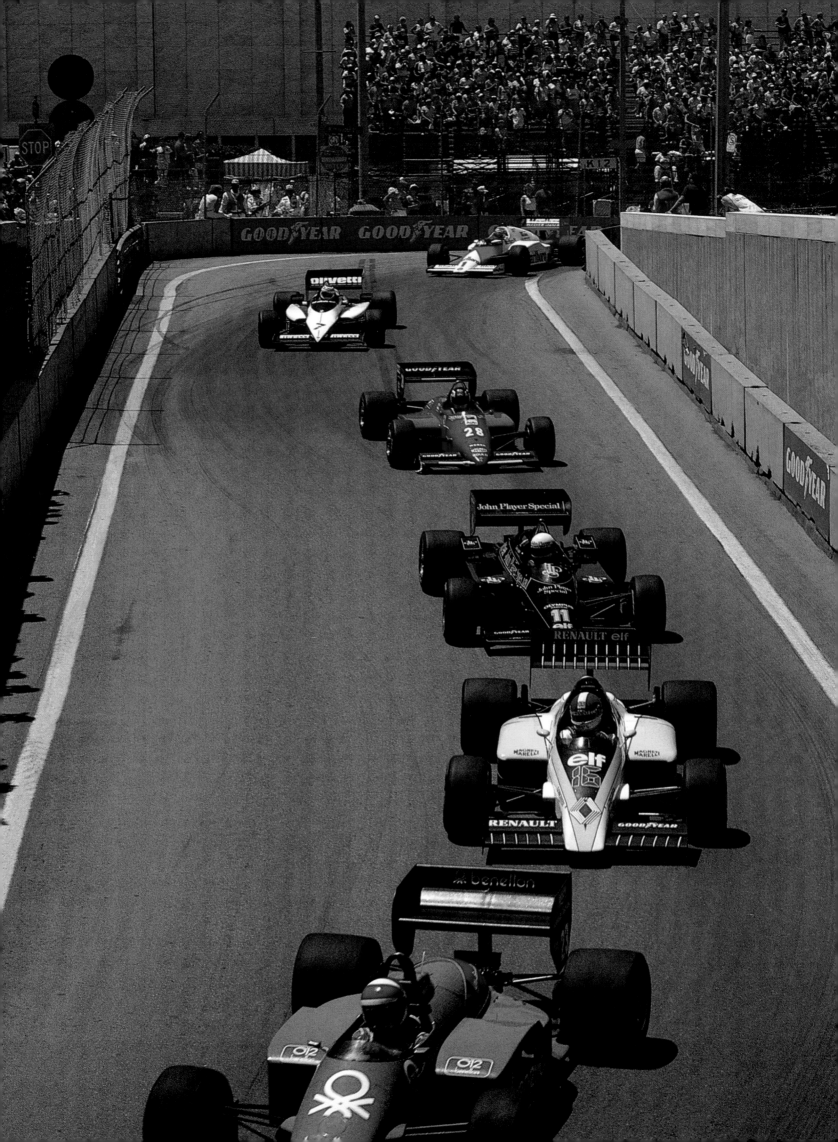

Highlights of a Racing Formula 1966-85

Inevitably, the start of any new racing Formula sees a makeshift year with lashed-up interim cars, teething-troubled new designs and nearly always the best-prepared, most practical and down-to-earth team carrying home the bacon.

This is exactly what happened in 1966 when the '3-Litre Formula' began. The modest-engined Repco Brabhams used lightweight and simple multi-tubular spaceframe chassis, BRM and Lotus followed Ferrari's 1965 lead into using the engine as a fully-stressed structural member and a number of adventurous new designs made their debut, looking to reach full development and success in 1967.

Most of their optimistic hopes were shattered that year by the emergence of the epochal Cosworth-Ford DFV V8 engine which set near-untouchable new standards of compact practical design allied to standard-setting power and torque.

When it became available to other customer teams in addition to Team Lotus in 1968, Formula 1 was thrown open to anyone and the path was cleared for the mushrooming interest and explosion of commercial sponsorship which entirely changed the superficial face of racing through the Seventies.

The emergence of such engine performance soon overwhelmed chassis and tyre capability into 1969, when some teams laid plans to overcome their traction problems by dividing drive to all four wheels instead of using just the rear pair.

These developments were effectively and neatly rendered unnecessary by the impact of aerodynamic download technology exemplified by the brief era of tall strutted wings and airfoil aids in late-1968/early-1969.

In 1969, the four-wheel drive experiments briefly flowered and died.

Come 1970, and the Lotus 72 and new flat-12 Ferrari 312B emerged. One set new standards in aerodynamic download within wing-restrictive regulations, the other greatly improved mechanical and chassis packaging, clearing airflow beneath the regulation low-level rear wing, as well as sheer horsepower.

The 72 was probably the only net front-end download car that season, all others being in varying degrees of discomfort with net aerodynamic lift around their front wheels.

An increasing rate of aerodynamic testing, pragmatic, intuitive common-sense innovation and logical thought helped shape the Grand Prix car as it went into the mid-Seventies.

Robin Herd's March outfit had been ahead of its time with its low polar moment 721X car of 1972, matched more effectively by Derek Gardner's Tyrrell 005 that same season. Mauro Forghieri's Ferrari 312B3/74 gave notice of what was to come in central mass concentration and the good rear wing performance attainable with only a knee-high flat-12 engine to obstruct flow ahead of it.

Engine and tyre performance held centre-stage through 1975-76 while Gordon Murray's intuitive genius found maturity at Brabham. In 1977, Lotus rang the changes and sparked a real aerodynamic revolution with their Type 78 and its successor the Type 79 of 1978 which established Peter Wright's ground-effects aerodynamics principle.

By harnessing airflow beneath the car in addition to airflow over the top of it, the Lotus R&D group had found a key which unlocked a whole new area of Grand Prix car performance.

All had to follow, but by this time Renault had been seduced into Formula 1 by the promotional hullabaloo now attached to it from big-sponsor exposure. It was now regarded once more as an honourable and potentially profitable arena in which a major production-car manufacturer could appear.

Renault made their first painful steps along the path towards the next revolution to overwhelm Formula 1 – the establishment of turbocharged 1500 cc engines which would have sufficient power to spare to drag huge drag-inducive high-download wings through the air, generating lap times which the naturally aspirated Cosworth brigade were increasingly hard-pressed to match.

The best Cosworth teams such as Williams and Brabham fought back brilliantly with a series of arguably ever-more dubious ploys such as lowering suspensions and post-race fillable 'brake-cooling' water-ballast reservoirs which enabled their bitter rearguard action to be fought successfully against the turbo-charged teams until 1982-83.

The sliding skirt ban of 1981 had seen lowering suspension devices introduced to retrieve workable high download ground-effects from underwing side pod tunnel sections, and as the law makers floundered about in a morass of their own making so contemporary Formula 1 cars became solid-sprung virtual 550-horsepower go-karts, subjecting their structures and drivers to fearsomely destructive jounce loads.

In 1983 underwing ground-effects sections were suddenly laid to rest once and for all as the governing body applied a new flat bottom-within-the-wheelbase regulation. As progress-ive restrictions were then placed upon avail-able race-distance fuel allowances to come into line with energy-conscious motor industry considerations, Formula 1 reached the end of two frantic decades of unremitting develop-ment effort . . . and some very fine racing.

Formula 1 in the Eighties tried to make its mark on the lucrative US scene using makeshift street circuits as here in Detroit '85. Six different makes and five different engines are represented in this bunch: Cheever's Alfa Romeo 185T V8 leads *Warwick's Renault RE60, de Angelis' Lotus-Renault 97T, Johansson's Ferrari 156/85, Piquet's Brabham-BMW BT54 and Lauda's McLaren-TAG Turbo MP4/2B.*

Williams – Honda

POWERED by
HONDA

SUMMARY

1966
New Formula introduced: widespread use of uprated 1½-litre machinery until new-generation 3-litre engines became available.

1967
Reliable Repco 3-litre V8s in ultra-light Brabham chassis took Championship while pure-bred racing engine from Cosworth-Ford set new performance standards. Gurney-Weslake V12 and BRM H16 reached respective peaks. Growing aerodynamic interest revealed by spoilers added at Spa by Brabham and Lotus, bubble cockpit canopy and gearbox shroud at Monza by Brabham.

1968
Cosworth-Ford DFV V8 engines made available for customer sale: used by McLaren and Matra International in addition to Lotus to dominate results. Small fields, strutted wing aerodynamic aids introduced by Ferrari and Brabham at Spa, developed most rapidly by Lotus thereafter. Engine power outstripped traction, Firestone YB11 tyres performed well, four-wheel drive plans were laid.

1969
500 kg minimum weight to accommodate new onboard extinguisher and roll-over bar requirements. 4WD was tried and discredited. Cosworth cars utterly dominant, led by Stewart in Tyrrell Matras. Barcelona strutted wing collapses caused hasty application of new low-wing restrictions.

1970
Bag tanks, and indirectly therefore monocoque chassis, became mandatory – end of the multi-tubular spaceframe in Formula 1, 530 kg minimum weight. Lotus 72 dominated, with luck; Ferrari flat-12 made its mark. Lotus introduced engine airbox induction scoops, Matra adopted tall airboxes, starting trend.

1971
Goodyear introduce slick tyres at Kyalami, Firestone slicker ones at Ontario (practice only) and Barcelona. Firestone introduced low-profile tyres and encountered vibration problems. Stewart dominant in new Tyrrell-Cosworth; close racing, Ferrari faltered after dominant early season. Development of front-wheel fairing bluff noses pioneered in Formula 1 by Matra, proven by Tyrrell. Lotus ran 4WD gas-turbine powered Formula 1 Type 56B.

1972
16-gauge external fuel tank sheathing required in preparation for deformable structure regulation in 1973, engines with more than 12 cylinders banned. Year of the Lotus 72 and Fittipaldi while Ferrari faltered, Stewart ulcer affected Tyrrell results until end of season.

1973
Deformable structure fuel tank protection devices mandatory from Spanish GP, along with dry-break fuel-line couplings, 250-litre maximum fuel tank capacity, 575 kg minimum weight to compensate. Stewart's Tyrrells versus Lotus twins, Fittipaldi and Peterson; all three shared honours. Far-outrigged rear wings achieved greater download; McLaren introduced Graviner breathable-air driver safety system at Belgian GP.

1974
Rear wing overhang restricted to 1 metre behind rear axle line. Ferrari resurgent with new flat-12 cars; Goodyear resources and success would force Firestone out of racing. Brabham experimented with under-car aerodynamic devices, McLaren and Tyrrell followed suit. Failure of Lotus 72 replacement Type 76 and experimental two-pedal auto-clutch system; Peterson still won three races in obsolete 72. McLaren M23 title. Harvey Postlethwaite tried rubber suspension medium on Hesketh, Gordon Murray adopted successful pullrod rising rate suspension on Brabham BT44.

1975
Ferrari flat-12s dominant for Lauda and Regazzoni, Cosworth users sought alternative engines, Brabham planned Alfa Romeo flat-12 cars. Final eclipse of classic Lotus 72s. Carbon-composite components, predominantly for wings, made F1 debut on Hesketh and Hill.

1976
New low airbox regulations introduced from Spanish GP, rear wing overhang cut from 1 metre to 80 cm, front overhang maximum 120 cm, 21 in. maximum wheel/tyre width, 13 in. maximum rear rim diameter, front rim diameter free. Maximum overall car width 215 cm. Maximum airbox height 85 cm above lowest sprung part of car. Additional forward roll-over bar mandatory, ban on oil-carrying devices behind rearmost 'casing' prevented siting of outrigged oil coolers under rear wing. 575 kg minimum weight maintained. Season-long Ferrari/McLaren battle. Increasing use of aluminium honeycomb structural panels; McLaren M26 prototype used extensive Kevlar and Nomex lightweight structural honeycomb, team also introduced compressed-air starter system at South African GP. Tyrrell introduced successful six-wheeled Project 34 cars, Brabham experimented with Dunlop carbon brakes.

1977
Airbox height now 95 cm maximum *above ground*; Lotus 78 part-honeycomb design introduced 'wing-car' ground-effects underwing technology; V8 engine unreliability allowed Ferrari first-ever Constructors' Championship hat-trick. Renault first to take advantage of turbocharged 1500 cc engine option.

1978
Single 250-litre fuel cell permitted, old maximum of 80 litres per cell rule waived. Lotus 79 wing cars destroyed all opposition, new Williams FW06 best of the rest. Gordon Murray adopted small carbon-composite structural panels in Brabham BT48 monocoque. Harvey Postlethwaite used folded aluminium-honeycomb tub in Wolf WR7-series. Maurice Phillippe and Dr Karl Kempf of Tyrrell tested 'computer-controlled' active suspension.

1979
Overall car length fixed at 5 metres, overhang limits unchanged. Ferrari flat-12 resurgent as other teams enjoyed only half-season success – Ligier early on, Williams later dominant. Renault became competitive with turbocharged engine, won first race. Aerodynamic 'porpoising' became evident, notably making Lotus 80 fail.

1980
Height of the ground-effects sliding skirted car era with Williams FW07Bs dominant but Brabham BT49s challenged later. Renault's turbocharged cars consistent and serious challengers. Ferrari announced turbocharged 1500 cc V6 car for '81.

1981
Sliding skirts banned, 6 cm ground clearance regulations enforced but sidestepped by Brabham hydropneumatic lowering suspension ploy, subsequently copied by all teams. Suspension travel minimized to ensure consistent download, compromising chassis (and driver) life. Brabham's Piquet was Drivers' Champion, Williams FW07Cs took team's second consecutive Constructors' Cup victory. John Barnard of McLaren introduced moulded carbon-composite chassis, followed by Lotus whose 'twin-chassis' Type 88 was banned. Ferrari won races in first turbocharged season. Brabham tested BMW turbocharged engine.

1982
Driver survival cell cockpit protection requirements introduced, Ferrari 126C2 turbocharged cars dominated with Renault but accidents marred season. Brabham-BMW turbocharged car won first GP, Gordon Murray introduced pit-stop refuelling and tyre-change race strategy, Renault lost Constructors' Championship to Ferrari, Drivers' title to Rosberg of Williams. Last Cosworth-powered World Champion Driver.

1983
New flat-bottom regulation applied, banning ground-effects underwing sections between wheels. Rear wing width cut from 110 cm to 100 cm, overhang cut from 80 cm to 60 cm, height raised to 100 cm for mirror visibility, minimum weight cut to 540 kg to encourage Cosworth engine users. DFY scored last 3-litre non-turbocharged engine victory. Widespread use of in-race refuelling/tyre-change tactics.

1984
Fuel volume permitted for race cut from 250 litres to 220 litres, original intention expressed to lower it further to 195 litres in 1985. In-race refuelling banned so widespread use of fuel cooling prior to filling car to reduce volume and squeeze more in. Pedal box lengths respecified. Season notable for McLaren-TAG Turbo *tour de force*, Michelin radial tyres dominant, new Goodyear radials needed to catch up.

1985
Rear wing additional winglets banned, 220-litre fuel restriction enforced for extra year, new nose-box regulations demanded crash testing before acceptance, Lotus introduced turning-vanes to reduce front-wheel drag. Fuel and engine development created massive power increase. Last 3-litre engine raced in German GP, Formula 1 all-turbocharged thereafter. Successful McLaren rearguard action retained Championship titles, BMW most powerful engine, Williams-Honda most effective combination dominating end of season. Toleman introduced effective stepped-monocoque aerodynamic device.

WE WERE IN AT THE START...

No other spark plug in the world has a record of success in motorsport like Champion. And the technology we've developed in racing has helped us produce new Champion + spark plugs. With wider based longer nosed insulators, and copper cores, you can rely on them to stay cleaner, overcome misfiring and make starting easier. That's why they are used and recommended by leading car manufacturers and engine builders throughout the world.

So when you fit a set of Champion + plugs, you can be sure of one thing. You'll start as you mean to go on.

YOU CAN'T BEAT A CHAMPION

Protection above all.

No conventional oil can meet the demands of hard driving quite like Gemini. Above all, Gemini, the latest and most advanced formula from Shell, sets new standards in protection. Through high revs and fierce temperatures Gemini stays in grade. Mile after mile, day after day, protection beyond the capabilities of conventional oils.

Technology you can trust

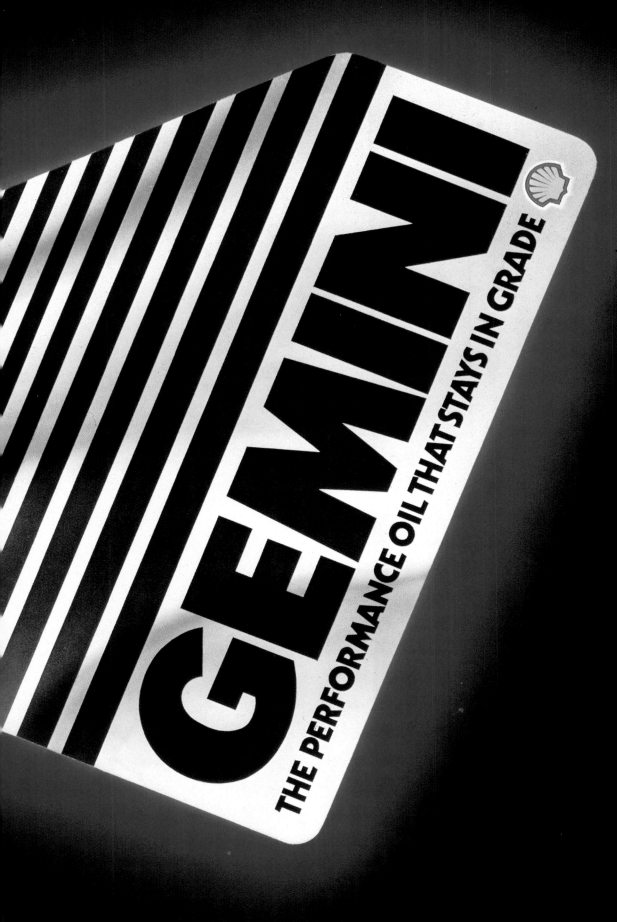

GEMINI

THE PERFORMANCE OIL THAT STAYS IN GRADE

Chapter 1

The Formula Evolves

What would become known as the '3-litre Formula', despite its inclusion right from the start of a 1500 cc supercharged option, took shape during 1963. The Monaco Grand Prix was held on 26 May that year. During that weekend beside the sea in Monte Carlo, two significant meetings were convened to tap opinion regarding a new Grand Prix Formula, due to take effect 2½ years hence, in 1966.

At that time this meeting could be seen as the contemporary Formula 1's 'mid-life crisis', for it was then 2½ years since its introduction on 1 January 1961. It had replaced the old 1954-1960 Formula, which had limited unsupercharged engines to 2.5 litres and forced supercharged units right down to only 750 cc. Under the new 1961-63 Formula – subsequently extended to the end of 1965 – the supercharged option had remained unchanged but unblown engines were straitjacketed to no more than 1.5 litres and not less than 1.3 litres. What was more, the CSI had then underlined its determination to contain speeds and prevent construction of super-light, potentially fragile racing cars by imposing for the first time a minimum weight limit. This was set at 450 kg (992.07 lb).

Under this Formula only commercially available pump petrol could be used, onboard automatic starters were mandatory for the first time, as were driver-protecting roll-over bars. Oil replenishment during the race was banned, the road wheels had to be exposed, unfaired by streamlined bodywork, and battery cut-out switches became obligatory.

After these regulations had been announced at the end of 1958 by CSI President Augustin Perouse, there was uproar amongst the British Formula 1 establishment. They muttered darkly about supporting a breakaway 3-litre InterContinental Formula which would admit existing 2½-litre machinery and also – they dreamed – attract strong US support. While they fulminated at the CSI, the European interest in GP racing, from Ferrari and now increasingly from Porsche in Germany, quietly got on with the job in hand. The upshot was that they both shone in that first '1½-litre' season of 1961 while the whingeing Brits were too late in building the engines and cars which would largely dominate the class from 1962-65. Nobody of any note adopted the 750 cc supercharged option available under this Formula.

Now, in those Monte Carlo meetings of May 1963, the Grand Prix Drivers' Association first agreed that a replacement 3-litre unblown Formula would offer much more interest for both drivers and spectators, but since only Ferrari amongst contemporary racing manufacturers was at that time building 3-litre engines (for sports and GT competition) the drivers then concluded that the best compromise would in fact be a 2-litre Formula. This would allow, they thought, existing 1½-litre Formula 1 engines to be enlarged, to offer more spectacle and a better driving challenge, while minimizing extra cost.

This was true where BRM's V8s were concerned, but there was insufficient meat on the rival Coventry Climax V8 to allow straightforward enlargement. In any case Climax's new owners, Jaguar, seemed disinclined to sanction a Climax investment in design and manufacture of a larger engine for the new class, if larger it should be. This was mainly because they were increasingly involved up to their necks in other, potentially more lucrative work. Since such leading teams as Lotus, Brabham and Cooper all used Climax engines, their future come 1966, even at this time, looked uncertain.

Immediately after this GPDA meeting, a surprisingly informal get-together was convened by the CSI under its contemporary Swiss President, Maurice Baumgartner. His heart really did seem to be in the right place, as he now canvassed the views of drivers, constructors, race organizers and even the specialist racing press. Yet, perhaps predictably, there was little agreement. Some, notably the British RAC and engine manufacturers, would have preferred to see the existing Formula continue unchanged. It would make life much simpler for them and, in the manufacturers' case, undoubtedly more profitable.

Graham Hill propounded the GPDA's 2-litre preference, adding that the jump from the proposed new 1-litre Formula 2 – which was due to commence in 1964 – to a full 3-litre Formula 1 would be too great for aspiring new drivers. Italians present smiled happily at the thought of a 3-litre Formula giving *La Ferrari* a flying start, while the French simply hoped for a Formula under which somebody, anybody, might be encouraged to construct a French-blue GP car for the first time in almost a decade.

After these naturally inconclusive Monaco meetings, further discussions continued between the CSI and the constructors, with the GPDA offering advice to anyone who would listen. During the United States GP meeting at Watkins Glen that October, another GPDA meeting briefed its delegates to recommend a 3-litre limit with a minimum weight clause of 525 kg (1157.42 lb) at the November CSI meeting in Paris, where minimum cockpit dimensions would also be suggested. That meeting, in the FIA headquarters offices at 8, Place de la Concorde, took place on Thursday and Friday, 21-22 November 1963.

There is a delightful (if probably apocryphal) story about this meeting and how the new Formula was finally decided. The British representatives had long since planned their tactics. It seemed certain the CSI was hell-bent

Crowded paddocks were a problem for the teams but undoubtedly gave Formula 1 practice periods a charming character which many now miss. Here at Spa-Francorchamps in preparation for the 1968 Belgian GP, Amon's Ferrari 312/68 '007 sports its chassis-mounted strutted wing, prompted by Chaparral out of Michael May via an unofficial Team Lotus Tasman experiment six months previously. Surtees's Honda V12 is beyond Ferrari '0011, Jochen Rindt can be seen pondering his Brabham's 4-cam Repco 860 engine and behind him is Bonnier's private yellow McLaren-BRM M5A. The more you look, the more you see . . .

Keith Duckworth—
Ford Cosworth designer.

A winner first time out—Jim Clark and the Lotus Ford 49 at Zandvoort, June 7, 1967.

Jackie Stewart won 25 of his record 27 World Championship GPs with the Ford engine plus all three World Championship Driver titles.

AFTER 155 VICTORIES WE AR

Motor racing history was created at Zandvoort on June 7, 1967, when Jim Clark captured first place in the Dutch GP and was a winner first time out with the new Ford Cosworth DFV Formula 1 engine powering his Lotus Ford 49. In the next sixteen years the Ford DFV and the DFY engines powered the winners of a record 155 World Championship Grands Prix, 12 World Championships for Formula 1 drivers and 10 World Championships for F1 constructors. They also managed to win Le Mans twice, more than 60 non-championship F1 races and in turbocharged form eight consecutive Memorial Day 500 mile events at Indianapolis. More than 540 Ford F1 engines have been built and through Formula 3000 the engine will continue to provide racing experience for future generations of F1 drivers.

TAKING A SHORT REST

One hundred not out: Jody Scheckter Wolf Ford Monaco May 22, 1977.

Detroit 1983 — Michele Alboreto (Tyrrell Ford), wins Ford's 155th Grand Prix.

155 wins on 30 circuits

SAMSON. GUARANTEED TO FLATTEN OTHER BATTERIES.

UNIPART

No topping up
Kein Nachsüllen
Pas de re-remplissage

SAMSON

Unlimited Guarantee
For as long as you own your car

Samson is made to the toughest possible specifications.

So tough we guarantee it for as long as you own your car – no matter how long you own it.

So if you keep your car for 3, 5, 10 or even 20 years, you'll never have to buy another battery.

And if you think that's amazing, here's something to really knock out the competition: Samson costs no more than other premium batteries:

Where else, but out in front.

upon ditching the existing unpopular 1½-litre class. They couldn't go to 2½ litres as that had been the preceding Formula. It seemed doubtful that they would allow the quantum performance leap to a full 3 litres. In any case this was virtually the last thing the constructors wanted, as it would render their expensive 1500s obsolete overnight and threatened almost prohibitive cost. They preferred the GPDA's original 2-litre option. It would allow conversion of existing equipment while still adding sufficient speed and power to please both spectators and drivers. But, facing the familiar caprice of the CSI, they decided instead to suggest the 3-litre limit, certain it would be rejected; whereupon, they figured, the most likely compromise would be the 2-litre class which they in fact preferred.

As it happened, when they set out their case for 3 litres the Ferrari representative, Mauro Forghieri, smiled assent, the CSI members nodded sagely, and the proposal went clean through so fast ' . . . it hardly touched the sides!'

Certainly that meeting finally agreed the new Formula 1 to take effect from 1 January 1966 and to run initially for three years to the end of 1968. It would restrict unsupercharged engines to 3 litres capacity, and supercharged units to 1500 cc, in essence allowing existing engines to be supercharged. The cars would run on commercially available fuel and the minimum weight would be 500 kg (1102.3 lb) including oil and water but excluding fuel. This compared with the 450 kg (992 lb) minimum for the existing 1500 cc Formula 1 cars.

In addition to the 3-litre unsupercharged/ 1.5-litre supercharged capacity limits, the CSI also opened the door – as predicted – to both rotary engines and to gas turbines. Rotary engines of the Wankel type would be permitted without capacity restriction but they would have to run on commercial fuel and would be restricted to minimum and maximum weight limits to be fixed at a later date. Gas turbine engines would be permitted without capacity or fuel restrictions, but with weight limitations to be applied after consultation 'with various experts' by 1 March 1964. All regulations for the existing 1500 cc Formula which had not been cancelled by these new proposals would continue to apply, which meant those onboard starters, roll-over hoops, exposed wheels, prohibited addition of oil during races, etc.

In general, these regulations were well received, although some felt that the 2.0 equivalency factor between unsupercharged and supercharged engines (3000 cc divided by 2.0 equalling 1500 cc) was too generous, since past history had demonstrated that supercharged racing engine outputs could match if not actually improve upon normally aspirated engines of three times their capacity. The gas turbine admission was thought to attract potential gas turbine car manufacturers such as Rover in the UK and Chrysler in the USA, while the Wankel clause was hoped to attract Mercedes-Benz who were involved in intensive Wankel engine research and development at that time.

In fact none of these volume car manufacturers would participate in Formula 1. BRM documents typify thinking which was probably shared by their counterparts at Ferrari. On 6 July 1964, BRM Chief Engineer Tony Rudd wrote an internal memo on the new Formula. He considered that since his existing 1.5-litre unblown V8 engines delivered 210 bhp, ' . . . we must plan for 425 hp in the first year of the new Formula. Petrol, within the definitions of the formula, will not permit the use of mean cylinder pressures above 250 lbs per sq. in. by the end of the Formula in 1969. Therefore, to obtain 425 bhp from a supercharged 1½-litre, it must turn at 26,000 rpm as it also has to

develop enough power to drive the supercharger. Such an engine is not impossible; but it would be fantastically expensive; it would have to exploit the science of metallurgy to the full; it would require heat exchangers etc, and could only be produced reliably by an organisation of the size of Ford, General Motors, Mercedes or Rolls-Royce. The alternative is the unsupercharged 3-litre.' Where Tony's typically logical memo would differ from, for example, Italian thinking in the Ferrari plant at Maranello was in his conclusion regarding his team's 3-litre Formula 1 contender . . .

'We have examined several versions', he wrote, 'and have concluded that a 16-cylinder engine would give us the best chance of success . . . the most desirable layout is an H16, we have prepared a design here at Bourne which is some 18" long, 28" wide and 14" high; this engine would weigh some 375 lbs and fit in the existing monocoque body shape . . . These cars, however, only carry 30 gallons of fuel, whereas a 3-litre engine will require at least 55 gallons, so that the cars will have to be about 1½" wider . . . These engines will cost us nearly twice as much to build; they will have to sell to private owners for between £6,000 and £7,000. The number of engines sold will obviously be less . . . the oil companies anticipated that the 3-litre engines would cost more like £10,000 each.'

We shall see shortly just how much less expensive an engine could be developed, sufficient to dominate the World Championship results in the first two seasons of the new Formula's life.

It used to be common for visiting GP teams to house their cars in garages near the circuit for overnight preparation. Here at Reims '66, casa Ferrari was wide open for inspection! The car is Bandini's pole-position 312 V12.

TEAM BARCLAY ARROWS

Marc Surer

Thierry Boutsen

BMW Turbo-Powered. Valvoline Protected.

Fast cars, great drivers and a superior motor oil—In his challenge for the 1984 World Championship, Team Barclay Arrows manager, Jackie Oliver, chose drivers Marc Surer and Thierry Boutsen for his new turbocharged BMW-powered cars. To protect his expensive, high-horsepower engines, Oliver chose Valvoline® Racing Motor Oil. The engine oil he knew would survive the severe heat build-up of Grand Prix competition,—on or off the track. Change to Valvoline for proven protection.

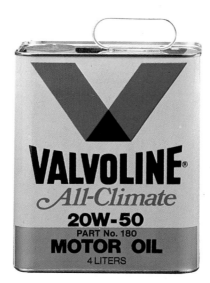

Rumours in the winter of 1964/65, with only a year to go before the new regulations took effect, included talk of Brabham almost certainly using a GM-based American V8 engine modified and developed by their financial backers, Repco of Australia. Dan Gurney, the Brabham driver, was at that time receiving a Ford retainer and was organizing a development programme in Los Angeles to build Climax 1½-litre V8 experience into an aluminium American V8. Cooper had contacted BRM for 3-litre engines, since Climax had as yet made no plans to build engines for the new class. Lotus's new engine facility was concentrating upon development of a 4.7-litre Ford Fairlane V8 engine for their Lotus 30 sports-racing car. Lotus chief Colin Chapman appeared disinterested in Climax and was thought to be working with Ford for a 1966 F1 engine. McLaren had backing from Firestone and had already obtained the exclusive European rights to the Traco Oldsmobile V8 aluminium engine, weighing 325 lb and delivering 345 bhp. It would be simple to convert this V8 to 3 litres but Bruce McLaren had already contacted BRM concerning an engine for 1966 when he would be leaving Cooper to build his own 3-litre F1 cars.

Climax were deeply involved in V12 engine development for Jaguar and had abandoned their four-valve per cylinder V8 F1 engine programme in favour of a new 1½-litre flat-16. These complex programmes left them very little spare capacity for a new 1966 3-litre engine. Chief Engineer Walter Hassan was said to want any engine they should build for 1966 to go into a four-wheel drive car, since with the tyre and chassis technology of the time this seemed the only sensible way to put 425 bhp-plus down onto the road. Climax should also either build or approve all the transmission system. This view was not shared by the client teams and appeared to be one of the reasons why Climax did not seem to be working on an engine for 1966, or so the grapevine was telling us . . .

In Germany, the Continental tyre company was thought to be working on a new racing tyre, suggesting that Mercedes-Benz could be interested in Formula 1, although these tyres might also have been for Porsche.

In Italy, Ferrari were clearly working on their 1966 F1 car and inevitably there were rumours that its 12-cylinder engine had run with a supercharger; *ergo* it had to be 1500 cc supercharged. This invoked press speculation based on the 1948 Porsche-designed Cisitalia flat-12 1500 which had used twin eccentric-vane superchargers.

Pirelli had shown racing activity and this was linked with a possible comeback by Alfa Romeo. In view of Italy's parlous financial condition, it was thought unlikely that Alfa – which was state-owned – would in fact obtain a racing budget. Several French firms were known to be working on F2 engines, but there was no sign of interest in an F1 project.

As we now know, like all rumour-mongering, some 20 per cent – maybe less – of the above had real substance, 80 per cent was pie in the sky. We shall see how competition within the 3-litre Formula shaped up in its first season and subsequently, but first we should examine how the Formula itself evolved into the longest-running Grand Prix class in history. While still maintaining the basic parameters decided by that long-gone Place de la Concorde meeting of November 1963, so many more clauses and amendments were added subsequently that the overall shape and specification of the Grand Prix car would become increasingly strait-jacketed until our period ends in 1985. This just encouraged the designers' originality to burst out through any unguarded seams to the law makers' perpetual irritation and embarrassment . . . which was, of course, always a healthy sign.

THE FIRST EXTENSION

After its initial three-year run, from 1966 to the end of 1968, the Formula was extended for a further four seasons, to the end of 1972.

During 1968 there had been a series of motor racing tragedies, which claimed the lives of Jim Clark, Mike Spence, Ludovico Scarfiotti, Lucien Bianchi and Jo Schlesser. Only Schlesser's death came in a Formula 1 car, when his brand new air-cooled Honda V8 crashed and burned during the French GP at Rouen-lès-Essarts. Nevertheless, the atmosphere of the time demanded additional safety measures to be taken, and from 1 March 1969 new F1 regulations demanded much-enlarged really practical roll-over bars and the addition of effective onboard fire extinguishing systems.

Two extinguisher circuits had to be provided, which could be fed from a single 5 kg bottle. One had to be a manually operated system which could be triggered by the driver when normally seated, the extinguishant outlets being directed towards the engine induction and injection pump. A secondary system, triggerable by the driver as well as by any helper outside the vehicle, had to discharge into the cockpit. The trigger device had to be indicated by a red-painted circle, with the letter 'E' prominently displayed.

Other changes to Formula 1 included a mandatory electric circuit breaker, which was required on all cars – single-seaters, saloons, sports and GTs – taking part in speed races from 1 January 1969. Its position had to be indicated by a blue triangle with a lightning flash emblem and had to be within easy reach from both inside and outside the car.

Rubber bag safety fuel tanks were described which would become mandatory in F1 and F2 from 1 January 1970, while short-term leak-proof tank fillers and caps which did not protrude beyond the coachwork were required from 1 March 1969. The South African GP at Kyalami opened the new season on that day, so it gave us our first sight of onboard-extinguisher F1 cars with those robust new roll-over bars and dramatic-looking circuit breaker and extinguisher trigger symbols painted on their sides.

To accommodate this extra equipment, the minimum weight limit was raised 10 kg for each system, taking the mark from 500 to 530 kg (1168.44 lb) by the start of 1970.

After the strutted wing proliferation of 1968 had culminated – as will be related – in the Spanish GP Lotus accidents of 1969, an arbitrary wing ban was applied during practice for the next GP on the calendar, at Monaco, pending formulation of new wing restriction regulations, which took effect from the Dutch GP two weeks later. Now no part of the coachwork, with the exception of the 'safety roll bar', was permitted to exceed in height a horizontal plane 80 cm (31.5 in.) above the lowest point 'of the entirely sprung structure of the car'. Behind the front wheels, coachwork was now restricted to 110 cm (43.3 in.), while maximum width ahead of the front wheels was 150 cm (59.05 in.), although any part ahead of the front wheels exceeding 110 cm in width was prohibited from extending above the height of the front wheel rims.

These more detailed dimensional restrictions upon the size, and indirectly the shape, of eligible F1 cars were the thin end of the wedge. Designers would find themselves progressively hedged about by ever-increasing legislation.

Where structures were concerned, magnesium sheet would now only be permissible if its thickness exceeded 3 mm, thinner stock representing a fire hazard. The onboard battery had to have sufficient capacity to start the engine at least twice, while teams were now permitted to start the engine in the pits or on the dummy starting grid via an external power source. From 1 January 1972 chromium plating of steel suspension members of over 45 tons per square inch tensile strength was forbidden, as it was feared the process could embrittle the material and then serve to hide incipient crack formation until too late.

DEFORMABLE STRUCTURE REGULATIONS, 1973-75

After the initial extension from 1969 to 1972, a further three-year extension was granted to the end of 1975, but by this time a maximum engine cylinder limit of 12 had been applied. Another BRM H16 would no longer be admissible, neither would such often-rumoured, ultra-expensive but potentially dominant exotica as a W24-cylinder Honda, nor an X36 Yamaha. Interested Formula 1 constructors were by this time not averse to self-protection and preservation of vested interest – Formula 1 had become increasingly a closed shop.

Now minimum weight was up to 550 kg (1212.53 lb). Minimum cockpit opening size

Lotus 49 wing collapses here at Barcelona in 1969 triggered a ban that ended the brief reign of high-strutted 'foils such as this bi-wing arrangement on Piers Courage's Frank Williams-entered Brabham BT26-Cosworth.

was 60 cm (23.62 in.) in length and 45 cm (17.72 in.) in width, maintained for a distance of 30 cm (11.81 in.) from the rearward extremity of the seat backrest towards the front.

Of more obvious significance to the appearance of the Formula 1 car, from 1 January 1972 designers were permitted to increase the overall width of the car to 130 cm (51.18 in.) on condition that the extra 10 cm (3.94 in.) on each side should form a 'deformable structure', containing no fuel, fuel lines, electrical power sources or circuitry.

In effect these new crush pads would serve to protect what were at that time still commonly midship-mounted fuel tanks. However, the rule makers prevented use of this deformable structure innovation as an excuse to add extra aerofoil aids by stipulating that any aerodynamic device situated behind the front wheels must remain within 55 cm (21.65 in.) of the car's centreline. Furthermore, any part of the structure surrounding the fuel tank which was in direct contact with the external airstream now had to include an aluminium sheet skin of at least 1.5 mm (16-gauge) thickness, the alloy specified being aluminium-magnesium with a minimum tensile strength of 14 tons per square inch and a minimum elongation of five per cent. Red rearward-facing warning lights of at least 15 watts now had to be provided for bad-weather racing, mounted as high as possible on the tail of the car and clearly visible from the rear, ready to be switched on by order of the Clerk of the Course in poor visibility.

From 1 July 1972 a clearly marked external emergency services firing handle had to be fitted, capable of being operated by emergency personnel from a distance if necessary using a hook. This emergency handle had simultaneously to trigger the onboard extinguishing systems, cut out the engine and isolate the battery. From 1 January that year a headrest capable of restraining 17 kg (37.48 lb) under a rearwards acceleration of 5G had to be fitted, so designed as to prevent the driver's head becoming trapped between the roll-over bar and the headrest itself.

By 1973 deformable structure tank protection was to become mandatory, and to accommodate it minimum weight was increased to 575 kg (1267.65 lb). From 1 January that year, overall body dimensions were modified to demand a maximum width in the area between the front and rear wheel trailing and leading edges of not more than 140 cm (55.12 in.). No oil, fuel or electrical lines should be situated beyond 60 cm (23.62 in.) either side of the car's centreline, and they must run adjacent to neither the main fuel cells nor within the crushable structure. Maximum rear wing width remained at 110 cm (43.31 in.).

Self-sealing break-away aircraft-type fuel couplings were now specified to prevent spillage in an accident, and the fuel system itself had to be arranged '. . . so that no part of it is the first object to be struck in an accident'. Total fuel tank capacity was restricted to 250 litres (54.99 Imperial gallons), of which no more than 80 litres (17.59 Imp. gall.) should be contained in any one tank. The deformable structures themselves were required from the first race of the European World Championship series, the Spanish GP.

The entire fuel tank area of the cars in direct contact with the open airstream now had to incorporate a crushable structure, which was specified as featuring sandwich construction based on a fire-resistant core of minimum crushing strength of 25 lb per sq. in. It was permissible to pass water pipes through this core, while the sandwich construction had to include two sheets of 1.5 mm thickness, one being 14 tons tensile aluminium. Minimum sandwich thickness had to be 10 mm (0.3937 in.) but the 'fore and after fuel tank area' should provide for a crushable structure at least 100 mm (3.937 in.) thick at the structure's thickest point, this situation being at the constructors' discretion, over a length of at least 35 cm (13.78 in.) after which it could gradually reduce to 10 mm (0.3937 in.).

During 1973, Formula 1 car rear wings were outrigged ever further behind the rear wheels to seek clean airflow and thus generate ever greater download. For 1974 this move was jumped upon as the regulations were rewritten to insist that '. . . nothing above the rear wheels must protrude more than 1 metre behind the axle of the rear wheels' [sic], 1 metre converting to 39.37 inches.

'THE AIRBOX RULES', 1976-77

By this time the Formula was already nine seasons old, and in its tenth season – 1975 – it was extended for a further two until the end of 1977, regulations being agreed initially for those two with little alteration. However, more significant changes were agreed to at Monza that year, to take effect from the Spanish GP on 1 May 1976.

From that date total rear overhang, beyond the rear wheels, was reduced from 1 metre to 80 cm (31.49 in.) while front overhang limit was set at 120 cm (47.24 in.). Maximum rear wheel width was fixed Imperially for Goodyear's convenience at 21 in. – the actual term used

The shapes of 1970: Ickx's Ferrari 312B (10) lines up outside Rindt's Lotus 72 with Regazzoni's Ferrari (15) and Siffert's March 701 – sans side-wing tanks on row two – Pescarolo's Matra-Simca (14) and Amon's March 701 on row three. Top-ducted radiators appear in all but the hip-radiator Lotus. Two-by-two starting grids robbed Formula 1 of some spectacle as did such sterile circuits as Hockenheim, seen here.

being 'la roue complète', or 'the complete wheel', defined by the CSI as meaning the wheel and tyre *ensemble*. Rear wheel diameter had to be 13 in. Front wheel diameter was free, but maximum width was again 21 in. Overall width of the car was now restricted to 215 cm (84.65 in.), this dimension being based upon that of the widest contemporary F1 car at the end of 1975, which was the McLaren M23. Ironically, it would be James Hunt's Spanish GP-winning McLaren M23 that May which first fell foul of this very ruling.

In preceding years, engine airboxes had been born and had flourished in variety, size and height. Now they were being restricted, brought within the 80 cm (31.49 in.) envelope measured from the lowest point of the entirely sprung structure of the car so far as the air intake orifice was concerned, while the total height of the airbox was allowed to exceed that dimension by 5 cm (1.97 in.).

To enhance driver protection, a forward roll-over bar was now specified, mounting near the dashboard in such a way that a straight line drawn to its highest point from the top of the main roll-over bar would pass above the driver's helmet when he was sitting normally within the cockpit. It was now rather vaguely specified that 'a substantial structure will extend in front of the pedals', while oil pipes and coolers were to be protected by 10 mm (0.3937 in.) thick crushable structures. This pedal protection was later defined as a structure capable of withstanding a 25G deceleration without causing the pedals to move backwards by more than 150 mm (5.91 in.) with the car carrying driver and a full fluid load. No part of the car containing oil could now be situated aft of the rearmost casing (gearbox or differential), thus banning far-outrigged underwing oil coolers etc, while the maximum height exhaust restriction was now suppressed to give free for all. Despite these changes minimum weight was unaltered at 575 kg (1267.65 lb).

In 1977 the coachwork height to the upper extremity of the airbox opening was 90 cm (35.43 in.) measured from the ground. Total airbox height could still exceed that dimension by a further 5 cm (1.97 in.)

FOURTH EXTENSION, 1978-81
Yet again a Formula extension was granted, this time for two more years, to the end of 1979 for most prescriptions, but for four more seasons, to the end of 1981, for engine specifications.

It was decided that from 1 January 1979 the cars' overall length would be limited to 5.0 metres (196.85 in.). Rear overhang limit was set at 80 cm (31.49 in.); front overhang limit was 120 cm (47.24 in.). A waiver was granted to allow total fuel capacity to be concentrated in one single cell in the new breed of narrow monocoque ground-effects cars as introduced by the Lotus 79. This single cell between cockpit and engine was considered to be so deeply protected within side pod structures, monocoque chassis and engine assemblies as to be virtually invulnerable.

By 1979 the approved FIA version of the Formula 1 regulations filled 10 close-print pages of their annual 'Yellow Book' although inevitably by the time this annual had been published each year, numerous detail changes had often been made and the only way to keep abreast of the continuing flow of gobbledy-gook from Paris was to receive and study the CSI's regular technical bulletins.

The 1979 regulations were very comprehensively and carefully framed. Overall width was still restricted to 215 cm (84.65 in.) while coachwork ahead of the front wheels could be extended to a maximum width of 150 cm (59.06 in.), though any part of that coachwork exceeding 110 cm (43.31 in.) in width should not extend above the height of the front wheel rims 'with the driver aboard seated normally and irrespective of the fuel load'.

Regulation wording was even more pernickety now where overhangs were concerned, specifying considerations such as 'Except in the case of front-wheel drive when the measurement will be taken from the centreline of the rearmost substantial load-carrying wheels, no part of the car shall be more than 80 cm behind the centre-line of the rearmost driving wheels. No part of the car shall be more than 120 cm in front of the centre-line of the foremost front wheels . . .' Six-wheelers, and talk of outrigging a pair of dummy wheels abaft the tail for wing extension purposes, had the rule makers on their toes. Interestingly, a regulation now appeared governing refuelling during the race. In the event that any fuel was added after a race start, the container from which it was drawn had to have a leak-proof coupling connecting it to the tank filler on the car, and the air vent on the container itself had to be fitted with a non-return valve.

A group of European Common Market civil servants visited one of the Formula 1 teams, to see what motor racing was all about. During lunch the conversation came round to framing the regulations. One team member declared there were far too many regulations, the Formula would be improved if they were simplified. The bureaucrats vehemently disagreed, one suspects as anyone would whose reason to exist was being challenged. 'No', they insisted, 'One should frame regulations so detailed that they cover every conceivable eventuality'. That was how it would go, though the poachers would consistently try to outwit the gamekeepers . . .

From around 1973 the Formula One Constructors' Association had effectively run Formula 1, with a relatively malleable governing body going along with most of their recommendations. This cosy state of affairs changed with the election of Frenchman Jean-Marie Balestre as CSI President. He was about to crack the whip. This is not the vehicle in which to detail the political differences between FOCA and the CSI – which changed its name to FISA (*Fédération Internationale du Sport Automobile*) in 1979. Suffice to record that the two factions fell into increasing dispute as Balestre resolved to retrieve 'the sporting power' for the governing body. FOCA, whose power had developed during the 'kit car' mid-Seventies under the dynamic guidance of Brabham team patron Bernard Ecclestone, vigorously defended its own interests.

The irresistible force and the immoveable object now clashed over a unilateral FISA decision to ban sliding aerodynamic skirts from 1 January 1981. The move was intended to reduce cornering speeds, but British teams with their Cosworth DFV engines perceived

Clothes makyth man . . . and smootheth aerodynamic flow. Revson's British GP-winning McLaren M23 sports full bodywork and tall airbox which gave ram induction and faired airflow onto that vital far-outrigged rear wing.

hidden motives designed to foster better performances from major industrial company Continental teams like Renault, which after all was now France's great white hope.

When Balestre declared – without FOCA's agreement – that FISA was indeed waiving the normal two-year stability rule to enforce this skirt ban on safety grounds, all hell broke loose. Throughout 1980 a series of disputes simmered bitterly between FOCA and FISA. It extended eventually to FISA seeking to usurp FOCA's established commercial control of Grand Prix racing. Into the winter of 1980/81 there was detailed talk of there being two parallel forms of Formula 1 racing in the coming season, one run by FISA without skirts but supported by the *Grande Costruttori* teams – notably Ferrari, Renault and Alfa Romeo – while the mere British *assemblatori* (known equally derisively as *garagisti*), typified by Williams, Brabham, Lotus or Tyrrell, would run under FOCA's own skirted rules.

FISA promptly threatened dire retribution for circuit promoters who might give FOCA races a home. Something had to give, and in January 1981 representatives from all Formula 1 teams met at Ferrari's plant and concluded the Maranello Agreement for joint presentation as a peace initiative to FISA. Its major proposals formed the basis of peace concluded in Paris that March. It was called the Concorde Agreement; FOCA yielded to the sliding skirts ban, while FISA yielded on Formula 1 finances.

Regulations were drawn up which demanded a consistent 6 cm ground clearance 'at any moment when the car is in motion'. It takes a fleet-footed scrutineer to measure the ground clearance of a racing car at 180 mph, and lowering suspension devices were developed to sidestep the regulation. The poachers had fooled the gamekeepers again.

Later in the year this patently unenforceable regulation was reworded merely to specify that all cars should have a 6 cm ground clearance at the point of measurement in the pit lane. In other words, out on circuit anything goes.

This produced a generation of highly effective ground-effect skirted cars with minimal suspension movement whose jarring high-G ride quality tortured their drivers yet generated terrific cornering forces and high lap speeds.

Apart from the skirt and ground-clearance

Above, *Niki Lauda used the impressive carbon-fibre chassis of the Unipart McLaren to increase his standing in the table of Grand Prix victories.*

There's no stopping us.

The new Surefire copper core spark plug from Unipart is exactly what you are looking for. It means outstanding reliability, even in the worst conditions.

That's because the copper core greatly reduces carbon fouling and resultant misfiring.

So it fires time after time after time. So you will remain happy start after start after start.

SUREFIRE
The copper-core spark plug.

from **UNIPART**

Where else, but out in front.

question, 1981 regulations had included a weight limit of 585 kg (1289.69 lb). In a move which upset many purist engineering enthusiasts the long-lived clauses permitting use of Wankel, diesel, two-stroke and turbine engines were suppressed and these power units specifically prohibited. 'In this time of dispute', declared FISA, 'we want no further source of confusion to unsettle Formula 1'. From 1981 only four-stroke engines with reciprocating pistons were admissible, engines with more than 12 cylinders having long since been outlawed. FISA also announced a ban on cars having more than four wheels and also on four-wheel drive with effect from 1983.

When FOCA accepted the skirt ban, FISA sweetened the pill a little by dropping the minimum weight limit 5 kg to a level the 3-litre cars could comfortably attain and the turbos could not. The non-turbo teams like Williams and Brabham then took this a stage further by adopting what were claimed to be water-cooled braking systems. In these the onboard tank simply formed a legitimate ballast tank fillable prior to post-race scrutineering – as were conventional fluid reservoirs – but in this case to bring an underweight race car up to the legal limit. This ploy would ultimately be stamped out, it would not be permitted to top-up fluid reservoirs after the race, and random weighing during qualifying would also restrict the activities of ultra-light qualifying specials as exploited so notably by Brabham.

In addition, tyre company discomfort with the costs of all-out competition brought about a qualifying tyre agreement, in which only two sets of marked and scrutinized qualifying tyres would be made available for each car, and they too would be carefully policed during the qualifying sessions. Sadly, this created great pressures for the drivers to take desperate risks before their precious qualifiers 'went off', and it undoubtedly contributed to Villeneuve's fatal accident. But driver safety had also been considered.

Driver survival-cell regulations were now to apply from 1 January 1982. Two continuous box members, one either side of the driver, were to extend from behind him to a point 30 cm (11.18 in.) in front of the soles of his feet with him seated normally and 'with his feet on the pedals in the inoperative position'.

Structural material cross-section of each box member had to be 10 cm, while the overall cross-section of each box had to be 150 cm^2 to the soles of the driver's feet, then tapering forward of his feet to a 100 cm^2 section. Furthermore, the internal cross-section of the cockpit, from behind the seat to soles of feet, had nowhere to be less than 700 cm^2, minimum width 25 cm (9.84 in.) over the whole length of the cockpit, and there were further detail dimensional requirements.

Side panel regulations now demanded 20 cm (7.87 in.) high panels, 60 per cent of wheelbase in length which had to be sited between front and rear wheels at least 55 cm (21.65 in.) from the car's longitudinal axis. They had to be formed from minimum 10 mm thick composite material with a honeycomb core in metal or Nomex with expanded foam compression-resistance, and structural struts to link these panels to the tub, so absorbing lateral impact. The radiators were allowed to perform this role.

As it happened, 1982 was the last season in which underwing-section ground-effects cars were permitted, as on 3 November the FISA technical commission met in Paris and agreed radical rule changes to take effect from the next race, the opening round of the 1983 World Championship.

Any supposedly sacrosanct 'stability' regulation had been handily scrapped in the name of safety. During the season two Formula 1 cars had hurtled into the spectator enclosures at Ricard-Castellet, one in testing, one during the French GP with potentially catastrophic results, fortunately not realized. It was consi-

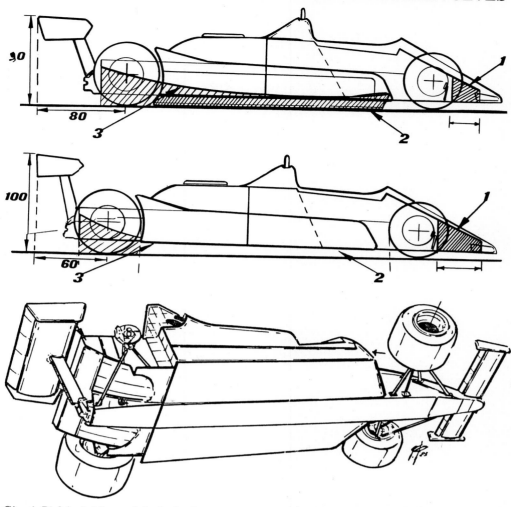

Giorgio Piola's sketches explain the flat-bottom ruling of November 1982. Top, contemporary ground-effect configuration and (centre) flat-bottom requirements showing 1, protective footbox; 2, sealing side skirts; 3, underwing venturi profiles (dimensions are tail overhang and wing height in cm). Above, a uniform flat-plane underside was demanded between trailing edge of 'the complete front wheels' and leading edge of 'the complete rear wheels'. Note venturi diffuser undersurface around gearbox.

dered that Villeneuve's fatal practice accident at Zolder had been magnified by the bouncing Ferrari's aerodynamic surfaces, while the ground-effect car form in general undoubtedly contributed to his team-mate Pironi's career-ending crash in the rain at Hockenheimring.

Under the 3 November 1982 ruling, Formula 1 cars were to be slowed down, especially in cornering, by a ban on aerodynamic skirts and shaped underbodies. Flat bottoms were now mandatory between vertical planes touching the front of the rear tyres and rear edge of the front tyres, rear wing width was cut from 110 cm (43.31 in.) to 100 cm (39.37 in.) to reduce surface area, and their leverage decreased by reducing overhang beyond the rear axle-line from 80 cm (31.49 in.) to 60 cm (23.62 in.). Wing height was permitted to increase from 90 cm to 100 cm to improve rear mirror visibility. The four-wheel drive ban was confirmed.

As yet another sop to the few surviving non-turbocharged runners, minimum weight was again cut from 580 kg (1278.67 lb) to 540 kg (1190.48 lb).

Then, with the aim of freezing engine power – some hope! – at 500-550 bhp into 1985, FISA decreed that fuel tank volume was to be reduced progressively from the 250 litres allowed in 1983 to 220 litres in 1984 and 195 litres in 1985. Refuelling during the race would itself be banned in 1984 which meant that cars would have to be sufficiently economical to survive race distance on 220 litres only. This would cause many teams problems, not merely on fuel economy, since through the brief refuelling era it had been common to fling extra

fuel through the engines purely to cool them and obtain ever-greater power.

The length of Grand Prix races was to be maintained.

Driver safety was also taken into account and was to be improved with augmented survival-cell regulations. Pedal-box length was extended from the mandatory 30 cm (11.81 in.) of 1982 to 50 cm (19.68 in.) in 1983.

For the final season within our period, the footbox regulation required that a vehicle weighing 750 kg (1654 lb) should impact an immoveable object at not less than 10 metres/second. The protective 'box was to crush in such a progressive manner that there should be no greater mean deceleration than 25G. Such an impact should not cause any deformation of the chassis itself behind the footbox, in a plane behind the pedals in their inoperative position.

Proving tests were mandatory; some teams used a fixed test section and moving 750 kg pendulum (as at Britain's Cranfield Institute), whilst others employed a moving trolley impacting a block (as at MIRA). End-on aluminium honeycomb structures worked well, but many engineers trailed home sadly from early tests with rubbish-bags full of shrapnel – all that remained of their pet footbox theories.

Rear wing regulations were also tightened to ban use of the ahead-of-the-axle-line side winglets adopted for 1984. This cut download available to all teams but by mid-1985 designers had found ways to retrieve lost values, with greater efficiency than hitherto.

So it was that the Formula evolved to the end of our period. It had been an extraordinary era.

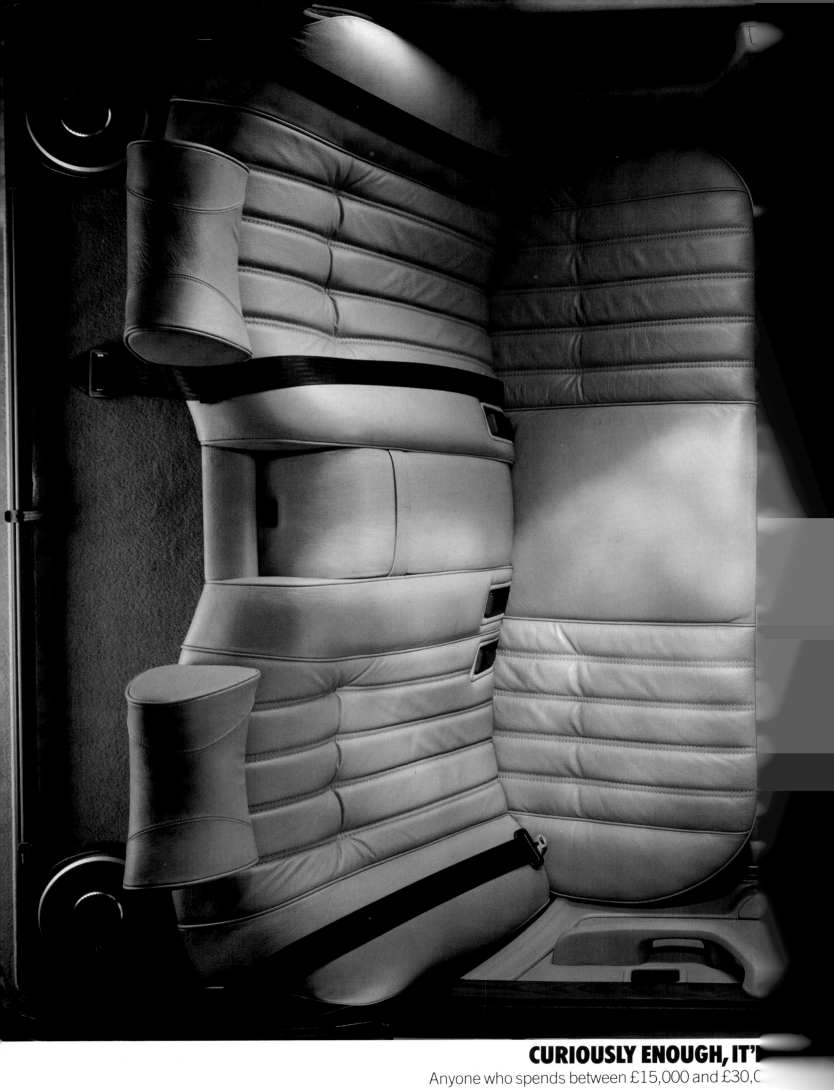

CURIOUSLY ENOUGH, IT'

Anyone who spends between £15,000 and £30,0

WCRS

THE ULTIMATE DRIVING MACHINE

OU OF YOUR TWO-SEATER DAYS.

without trying the BMW 7 Series obviously doesn't like driving.

Chapter 2

REPCO BRABHAM – THE TWO YEARS B.C.* 1966-67

*Before Cosworth

Simplify and reduce weight. Few 1966 Formula 1 cars were more simple or lighter than Ron Tauranac's Repco V8-engined BT19, seen here driven by Jack Brabham en route to victory in the Dutch GP at Zandvoort. Its simple multi-tubular spaceframe chassis was light and stiff enough to promote good handling on those Goodyear tyres, note 13 in. diameter front wheels, 15 in. rears. The combination won four consecutive mid-season GPs and the World Championship.

The so-called '3-litre Formula' saw two years racing before the Cosworth-engined cars established their Championship domination. In both these formative years, 1966 and 1967, it was the simple, lightweight spaceframe cars from Brabham which carried off the Championship titles, using Australian-made, initially American production-derived, Repco V8 engines.

Ron Tauranac's Motor Racing Developments (MRD) company, founded in partnership with twice-World Champion driver Jack Brabham, had begun manufacturing production Formula Junior cars in Victoria Road, Surbiton (to the south-west of London), during the winter of 1961/62. In their formative years of Australian racing, both Tauranac and Brabham had been regular customers of Geoffrey Russell's Replacement Parts Pty Ltd company, which had long since adopted the 'Repco' brand name.

They maintained this close triangular relationship throughout Jack Brabham's highly successful years as Cooper number one driver and it continued after Tauranac came to join him in his new British-based engineering ventures in 1960.

Tauranac and Brabham's first MRD prototype Formula Junior car emerged during the summer of 1961, and with a number of customer orders already received they laid down a production batch of a dozen improved versions for 1962. They had found the Victoria Road premises and did a deal with Repco's UK marketing people under which Repco took over warehousing space there and then sub-let production space to MRD.

In August 1962, MRD's first 'Brabham' Formula 1 car, the Climax V8-engined BT3, made its debut with Jack driving in the German GP, and a regular two-car Formula 1 team was then formed for 1963-65 as Jack's own Brabham Racing Organisation company. Tauranac had no formal share in this business, and Formula 1 design and development became something of a chore for him through those final three years of 1½-litre racing.

MRD had to design and build the Formula 1 chassis, which were supplied to BRO at an agreed price. BRO raced them, providing engines, transmissions, drivers and so on. Throughout this period MRD's prime responsibility was always to its paying customers who were buying production Formula 2, Formula Junior, Tasman Formula and even private-owner F1 cars in ever-increasing numbers.

This heavy pressure upon the factory – which was now sited alongside the Wey Navigation Canal at New Haw, within site of the huge railway embankment which flanks the old Railway Straight at Brooklands Motor Course – meant that F1 work was often delayed. Even so, it occupied much time which could be devoted more profitably to the production cars. Tauranac was as unhappy with this state of affairs as only this fiercely logical, rather short-fused man could be. He declared his unhappiness to Brabham after the production of new Brabham cars for the new Grand Prix Formula was in the balance during the autumn of 1965.

Meanwhile Coventry Climax's much-promised flat-16-cylinder 1500 cc F1 engine had been still-born. MRD had built a specially-tailored Brabham chassis ready for it – Cooper and Lotus were in the same boat – and as a new joint agreement was at last worked out between Jack Brabham and his engineering partner, so this idle frame was hurriedly pressed into service to put their green-and-gold colours on the 3-litre Formula grid. Despite the last-minute nature of their project, this Repco Brabham BT19 was actually the first of the new breed of true 3-litre Formula 1 cars to appear. It was also the first to win a race, and the first to win a 3-litre Formula 1 Constructors' World Championship title.

Here I should perhaps explain that from the

beginning of Formula Junior production, the MRD-made racing cars had been named 'Repco Brabhams' in mild recognition of the Repco group's assistance. As Formula Junior was at that time dominated by modified Ford engines, these cars became officially 'Repco Brabham-Fords'. When Climax 4-cylinder FPF-engined Tasman cars were first produced by MRD in the winter of 1962/63, they were known as 'Repco Brabham-Climaxes'.

Repco had a major interest in Tasman Formula racing which catered for 2.7-litre, then from 1964 2.5-litre, engined single-seater cars in Australia and New Zealand. The class was dominated by the 2½-litre F1-originated Climax FPF engine, for which Repco made many parts and with Climax's blessing ran a 'down-under' sales and service programme. They eventually fitted Repco Brabham name-plates to these engines and technically speaking the MRD-built cars powered by these units then became pure-bred 'Repco Brabhams'. However, we must not confuse them with the true Repco Brabham V8 Formula 1 engines and cars whose story follows.

THE REPCO V8 ENGINES

What became the World Championship-winning Australian V8 engine was conceived in February 1964, when Repco's Melbourne management had appreciated that supplies of Climax FPF parts would probably dry up within the life of the existing Tasman Formula. Chief Engineer Frank Hallam and Project Engineer Phil Irving – of Vincent motor cycle fame – were authorized to produce a new engine which would fit into existing Repco Brabham Tasman chassis.

Their answer was a V8 using an existing General Motors-made Oldsmobile F85 all-aluminium block. This represented the debris of an enormously costly and unsuccessful attempt by GM to produce a linerless alumi-nium engine for a 3-litre Buick 'compact'. The linerless idea had failed in production so a few were completed with cast-in ferrous liners, but that proved more fiddly and costly than conventional iron-block construction, and so GM understandably cut their losses and ditched the entire project. Repco picked up some of the pieces – Bruce McLaren's embryo sports-racing car team in England scooping up most of the remainder – and Repco were to turn commercial production failure into a Formula 1 World Champion.

Hallam and Irving had opted for this F85 V8 on the basis that the obvious way to extract more power than an FPF's from the same 2.5-litre capacity was to employ more cylinders, thus increasing both piston area and crank-shaft speed. The recently abandoned F85's availability made it possible to sidestep a slow and costly foundry operation by using these proprietary blocks off the shelf.

Irving found that the Olds block could accommodate a range of displacements from 2.5 to 4.4 litres so it could double as both a Tasman Formula or Group 7 sports-racing car power unit. It needed stiffening and overhead camshafts would have to replace the standard centre camshaft within the vee which GM had provided to operate ohv via long pushrods.

In their modifications, the Repco engineers applied two basic parameters: 1) frontal area should be minimized to match existing Repco Brabham body designs; 2) overall width should also fit into the existing chassis frames.

Irving's new cylinder head design produced a simple head common for each cylinder bank. It carried parallel valves angled inwards at 10 degrees from the cylinder axis in simple wedge-shaped combustion chambers. They were actuated from a single chain-driven overhead camshaft.

This modest and very 'un-racy' arrangement was preferred to a twin overhead camshaft system; firstly to keep the engine narrow

overall, secondly to reduce the length of unsupported drive chain to each shaft. The uncompromising practicality of the Repco engineers' approach is emphasized by the fact that these new heads were identical in every dimension to minimize expense and to ease the spares requirement for the private owner.

Repco took the bare GM-made aluminium blocks and filled all unwanted holes and spaces originally intended for the now redundant pushrod valvegear. A ladder-formation 3/16 in. thick steel stiffener plate was screwed to the sump flange to stiffen the engine's bottom end.

New main bearing caps were retained by long bolts which penetrated deep into the crankcase casting. The existing 3.5 in. bores were reamed and fitted with 10-thou thick Repco cast-iron liners. Bore and stroke of 85 mm x 55 mm gave the required Tasman Formula displacement of 2.5 litres. Laystall in England machined the crankshafts, which revolved in five Repco plain main bearings. Another short-cut was taken when suitably lightened and balanced Daimler 4-litre V8 production con-rods were found to fit. They were much cheaper than specially made rods – their actual price being £7 each, while a raw unmachined F85 block cost every bit of £11 . . . so who needed 16-cylinder racing engines?

By itself this must have gladdened Jack Brabham's notoriously 'careful' old heart, even though he was only now developing crucial interest in this engine.

Repco's V8 pistons were cast in aluminium-silicon alloy, with shallow valve clearance indents in the crown. Two beautiful magnesium castings completed this conversion; a Y-shaped cam-drive chain cover on the front, and a new 3-inch deep ribbed sump further improving bottom-end rigidity to accommodate the designed power increase.

Adaptors were designed to match either Weber carburettors or Lucas fuel injection, and Repco even made their own specialized oil and water pumps for the new unit. It emerged 25½ in. long overall, excluding the Climax FWB flywheel; 21 in. wide across the heads; 23 in. high, excluding induction equipment on top.

Repco's prototype V8 coughed into life for the first time on the company's Richmond, Victoria, test bed on 21 March 1965, only 51 weeks after Hallam and Irving had first set pen to paper. The run was satisfactory and testing continued while Jack Brabham and Repco made the deal to produce a 3-litre F1 version for the coming year. Phil Irving consequently spent much of that summer in England, working closely with Jack himself on detail 3-litre design.

They chose the standard 3.5-in. (88.9-mm)

Top, *make-do versus leftover; Brabham's original BT19-Repco leading Clark's 2-litre Lotus-Climax and team-mate Hulme's BT20-Repco during their terrific battle in the 1966 Dutch GP. Note different engine cowl and exhaust layouts in the spaceframe Brabhams. Centre, bottom end of the modified stock GM Repco RB600 aluminium block was stiffened by the steel ladder-plate seen here. Above, two years on, the hybrid-construction BT26-Repco 4-cam car of 1968 used riveted-on stress panel triangulation on a simplified tubular base-frame. Workmanship was beautiful, the engine unreliable.*

FOR 20 YEAR
A STRONG
THE GRAND P

Over the years 1965 to 1985, Goodyear have been involved in excess of 160 Grand Prix wins.

We have achieved this incredible record by following a simple rule. Tyre development is equally as important as car, team and driver improvement. Just look at our past

The 1968 McLaren-Ford on Goodyear.

record. We were the obvious choice to be used with the revolutionary Ford Cosworth engines back in 1968.

During the early seventies, we helped the Tyrrell team and Jackie Stewart down the road to two Formula One World Championships.

Tyrrell and Goodyear record-breaking success in the 70's.

The mid-seventies saw Goodyear totally dominate the Grand Prix circuit. Every Grand Prix during this period was won by a car using Goodyear tyres.

By 1977–78, Lotus had developed ground-effect aerodynamics. This added an extra 1½ tons download

S WE'VE HAD HOLD ON RIX CIRCUIT.

to the car, and although this meant they would go through corners quicker, immense stress was put on the tyres.

Goodyear were chosen and coped admirably with the pressure.

The Lotus 79 on Goodyear.

In 1982, the new turbo-charged Ferraris raced their way to the World Constructor's Championship. 1984 saw Goodyear introduce its new Eagle Tyres and it was these tyres

that Alain Prost and Marlboro-McLaren used to take the Drivers World Championship title in 1985.

The 1985 Marlboro-McLaren and Goodyear Eagles.

The amount of devotion we put into developing our Grand Prix tyres means you can be sure of one thing. Drivers on Goodyear will keep coming over the line first.

LEADING THE WORLD IN TYRE TECHNOLOGY

KONI

Koni shock absorbers. Out of this world.

BANKS

Koni shock absorbers are distributed exclusively throughout the U.K. by
J W E Banks & Sons Ltd., Crowland, Peterborough PE6 0JP. Tel: 0733 210316. Telex 32533.

bore and adopted a stroke of 60.3 mm to displace 2994 cc. Lucas fuel injection was chosen and in early tests this F1 unit delivered 285 bhp at 8000 rpm. Its low stroke:bore ratio of 0.68:1 suggested very high rotational speeds but, despite the short stroke, maximum power was still produced at only 8000 rpm and the engine has been described as being 'neither useful nor safe' beyond 8300 rpm due to ultimate engine breathing and mechanical restrictions.

This is perhaps to forget Irving and Brabham's true objective. Both were intensely practical and *very* experienced. Both recognized what a delusive target ultimate power can be in road racing. Mid-range torque, an engine's ability to provide real 'punch' away from low- and medium-speed corners, is what makes a potential winner on most World Championship circuits – even then when superfast courses like Spa, Reims and Monza were still in unfettered use. Their races could quite logically be surrendered to Ferrari's V12s or perhaps Maserati's similar engine tipped for Cooper, or, if the lessons of history should be overturned, to BRM's fabulous H16. That would still leave Monaco, Zandvoort, Brands Hatch, the Nürburgring, Watkins Glen, Mexico City – all slow or medium-fast circuits, forming two-thirds of the Championship trail.

And never forget that Jack Brabham and his team were professionals, racing for a living. There were potentially good earnings on offer from the non-Championship events at Silverstone (still considered merely 'medium-fast' in those days), Syracuse and Oulton Park where mid-range punch rather than flat-out power should still carry the day. In short, there was *money* to be earned.

This is what concentrates the minds of those racing purely for racing's sake. They are a different breed from those involved in intense technical research or product promotion.

The Repco engine offered a notably broad power spread, with useful torque as low as 3500 rpm, then beginning to fly at 4000 rpm and delivering peak torque – something like 192 psi bmep – at 6500 rpm. And there was still real power available up at 8000 rpm. What's more, the engine weighed only 340 lb. Fuel consumption was also most advantageous, at around 8 mpg which put the finalized cars on the starting grid with only some 35 gallons on board. Thus the light and simple Repco Brabham enjoyed a startline weight advantage over all opposition with greater power, while its relatively humble engine was still man enough to handle any competitive car of comparable weight. It could score on weight over the more powerful Ferrari, BRM Cooper-Maserati, Eagle-Weslake and Honda in their undeveloped forms, and on sheer 'grunt' over such interim stop-gap cars as the nimble 2-litre Climax and BRM V8-engined Lotus 33s and BRMs.

Once this 3-litre Repco V8 had been proven in essence, all that MRD had to do was provide BRO with a suitable chassis to carry it, but the new incentive agreement which Tauranac demanded was not finalized until that November, with the first full-scale race under the new Formula, albeit a non-Championship event, mere weeks away in South Africa on 2 January 1966. In fact the V8 engine proved adequate throughout that season when mounted in Tauranac's 'ex-flat-16' BT19 lightweight spaceframe chassis and in the new BT20s later in the year.

Repco had named this Oldsmobile F85-based V8 their Type 620, engine numbers all being prefixed 'RB' ('Repco Brabham', of course) '620'. These numerals were themselves a two-part classification, '600' applying to the modified proprietary block and '20' to the duplicated sohc cylinder head design. Individual engine numbering actually commenced at 'RB 620-E1'.

The engine was extremely reliable through

1966 and its useable power was sufficient in the lightweight, good-handling Brabhams to prove extremely competitive. At Monza for the Italian GP an engine was delivered fresh from Melbourne, with 'Monza 350 hp' stencilled boldly on its crate, thumbing its nose at the alleged '400-horsepower' opposition from Ferrari, Eagle-Weslake and BRM.

The truth of the matter is that engine 'E7' had produced a peak of 298 bhp on Repco's test bed and then, after further attention to its porting and a rise in compression ratio, BRO's ex-Climax engine specialist John Judd saw 311 bhp from it at 7250 rpm during a re-run in Climax's dyno shop at Widdrington Road, Coventry. He felt there was more to come but at this point the run ended as a piston burned out.

And the cars won four GPs in a row through that summer. It must have made BRM, Ferrari and Cooper-Maserati weep, for these green-and-gold cars with the humble pedigree were slaughtering the thoroughbreds in the Championship chase.

While the Repco engine proved itself man enough to dominate the '66 World Championship, with the combination of Tauranac's chassis and the driving skills of Jack Brabham and his team-mate Denny Hulme, the opposition largely eliminated itself, and it was obvious that far stiffer competition would emerge in 1967. For a start the intrinsic deficiencies of the production Oldsmobile block, and the time-consuming and costly operations necessary to bring it up to scratch, now made production of a tailor-made Repco replacement inevitable since the basic idea had been proved sound. A new head design was also required, for the low-level exhausts of the 620-series had given Tauranac migraines while trying to weave pipes around the chassis tubes and away through his preferred suspension system.

On the crest of their World Championship wave, Repco pressed ahead with these developments for '67; an all-new block plus new heads with their exhaust ports exiting on top within the engine vee.

General Manager Frank Hallam headed a four-man design team working at Repco Brabham Engines Pty Ltd in Maidstone, outside Melbourne, with Phil Irving's influence as their guiding light. Norm Wilson headed this team, aided by John Judd from England, Lindsay Hooper and Brian Heard.

They redesigned the crankcase to improve rigidity. It was cast in aluminium alloy. Wet liners were adopted along with cross-bolted main bearing caps, and there was also a system of main bearing studs which distributed stress right through the new crankcase. These screwed into its underside and penetrated right through it with reduced diameter, relieving stress concentrations right through to the top of the new block where they were secured by nuts which were to be tightened after the main bearing cap nuts had been torqued-down.

This purpose-built Type 700 block and crankcase saved some 30 lb weight compared to the converted Oldsmobile Type 600 which it replaced.

The redesigned cylinder heads now disposed their two valves per cylinder in line with the cylinder axis, instead of at 10 degrees to it as before, and they also emerged flush with the head-face. Camshaft centres were changed to suit, and the original 20-series combustion chamber design was replaced by a bowl-in-piston arrangement to enhance 'squish' and thus improve burning of the incoming charge. This all-new head, with its reversed porting placing the exhaust outlets in the valley of the vee on top of the engine, was the Type 40.

OK, so what became of the Type 30 head? Good question. There was a Repco Type 30 head design, but it mated the new bowl-in-piston combustion chamber arrangement with outside low-level exhausts. At that time it was felt that with parallel valves the burned gas had in any case to make quite a sharp turn as it

Jack Brabham's 1966 World Championship-winning Repco-Brabham BT19 on the pits straight at Reims during the French Grand Prix – the first Grand Prix to be won by a driver in a car bearing his own name.

left the cylinder and these pragmatic engineers felt it was surely immaterial to the gas which way they made it turn. However, test runs then indicated the fallacy of this argument, and when the chassis designer began to grumble about exhaust installation, so the 30-series design was held over and the centre-exhaust Type 40s took their place.

The 1967 season got under way, and the Repco Type 740 V8s proved themselves by giving Repco Brabham their second consecutive World Championship success. This time they took the title with perhaps a little more good fortune in face of much more potent, though crucially far less reliable, Lotus opposition. And Lotus used the brand new V8 Cosworth-Ford DFV engine.

By the end of that 1967 season, the Repco Brabham range of V8s included the now historic Olds-based 3-litre and Tasman 2.5- and 4.4-litre sports-racing RB620s, plus the new centre-exhaust purpose-built RB740s in both 3-litre F1 and 2.5-litre Tasman trim. New 4.2-litre and 2.8-litre Indianapolis track-racing variants were on the stocks, the latter employing Garrett AiResearch turbocharging.

Peak power from the World Championship-winning 740 centre-exhaust V8s had been only 330 bhp, but they had proved hugely efficient haulers in Tauranac's superb Brabham BT24 spaceframe chassis. Certainly Repco's Australian horses seemed hard workers. Cosworth claimed 408 bhp from their prototype batch of DFVs and Weslake credited their Gurney Eagle V12 with 417 bhp or so. Yet a study of the race, pole position and fastest lap record in the Appendix (page 253) shows how Repco Brabham now had to do something fairly drastic if they were to attain the unprecedented Formula 1 Constructors' Championship hat-trick beckoning them in 1968.

The Repco engineers studied two avenues of approach. One was for a short-stroke magnesium-block engine, the other for a daring new cylinder head design using a radially-disposed 4-valve-per-cylinder layout.

Test experience with the held-over 30-series head had proved conclusively that there was a power advantage offered by crossflow gas paths and the stunning debut of Cosworth's DFV in Europe served graphically to emphasize it.

ENGINEERED FOR SUCCESS

Withstanding the formidable stress and strain generated by Grand Prix racing engines is a challenge that Vandervell bearings have met, and won, race upon race, year upon year.

With vastly superior fatigue and corrosion resistance, and excellent lubricity in all conditions, they perform in a way no other bearing can match.

Quite simply, they're engineered for success.

Vandervell

At the heart of every good engine

Repco's radial-valve disposition Type 50 heads now aimed to exploit this advantage to the full. The valves resided side by side in each half of a conventional pent roof combustion chamber, the exhausts and inlets being alternately placed, diametrically opposed across the chamber. They were operated from twin overhead camshafts in each head, alternate cam lobes on each shaft acting on inlet then exhaust valves. This layout allowed very simple valve actuation compared to Dr Ludwig Apfelbeck's notorious contemporary BMW Formula 2 head design in which a radial valve disposition was housed in hemispherical combustion chambers, with valve stems protruding radially like the horns on a sea-mine.

But the Australian team added complication enough as they had to lead their exhaust stubs out within the vee as a bunch of eight small-bore pipes, while four more stubs emerged below the heads outside the vee each side of the engine. One wonderful-looking test engine was built up using these heads with the snake pit of centre exhausts in the vee up top *plus* the banana-bunch side exhausts sweeping away down below like the old 620 system.

Fortunately, after such effort, results were most encouraging, but like so many engine men's flights of fancy, it would prove to be a chassis designer's nightmare due to virtually intractable installation problems. Sheer exhaust system weight would be another handicap to be tackled elsewhere. Tests with these Type 50 heads were promising, but they were shelved.

Alternative Type 60 heads were then drawn, using twin ohc and more conventional four-valve-per-cylinder layout. The exhaust and inlet valves were paired together this time to provide conventional crossflow gas paths. There were neatly tucked-away outside exhausts, and Lucas fuel injection was housed within the vee, where the valley space was now so restricted by the extra inboard camshaft housings that in-vee exhausts really would have been sorely cramped.

In parallel with all this cylinder head development, Repco had researched an ultra-light cast magnesium block but eventually compromised, opting instead for the additional rigidity and stability of conventional cast aluminium, though the stroke was now shorter. This new block was fully 1¼ in. shallower than its predecessors from crankshaft centre-line to head-joint. The completed engine would now be considerably lighter in consequence, despite its use of a nitrided geartrain to drive the new four-cam ohc system in place of the 600/700-series' chains. While both those early blocks had carried sufficient meat to offer that wide variety of capacities, the new 860 could offer only 2.5-litre or 3-litre versions. Redesigned crankshafts were used, with fewer balance weights, saving still more weight.

Time ran out on the team during these developments, and the first 800-series block to be raced was in fact magnesium, making its debut as a 2.5 during the 1968 Tasman Championship. Later that season, in 3-litre Formula 1 form, it eventually ran out of water and pulled out of line. The block survived with John Judd in his Rugby engine development concern, long after Repco had gracefully bowed out of racing.

One short-stroke test engine was also built up using a 2½-litre Tasman crankshaft combined with a wider bore and a 5-litre sports car head, developed for the 700-series Group 7 sports car V8. This hybrid test engine showed no power advantage, and so the definitive short-block 800-series engines appeared in 3-litre form with shorter con-rods, using 5.1 in. centres in place of the original F85-standard 6.3-in. type.

The time spent on these developments bit deep into the 860 programme for 1968 and the engines appeared in new BT26 Brabham cars only as very competitive units while they were

running . . . which was rarely for very long.

By this time Repco's potential was being run ragged by the ferocity of European competition, mainly from the Cosworth-Ford DFV but also from Ferrari's latest V12s. The 12,000 mile gulf between Grand Prix battlefield in the northern hemisphere and engine development shop in Australia was just too big to bridge.

The problems which afflicted the four-cam Repco-engined Brabhams during 1968 included several dropped valve inserts, failed oil pressure, oil loss and water leaks. An honest assembly cock-up destroyed the drive gear for the right-side exhaust camshaft on Jack's car after only one lap at Brands Hatch. Then massive internal failures late season included Jack's engine running its centre-main bearing and Rindt's breaking a gudgeon pin at Monza where it did not rain (very rare in that troubled season); continuous full-bore running simply overwhelmed Repco's lubrication system. When Brabham's engine was stripped down, one gudgeon pin was found in three pieces. As his oil pressure zeroed and the centre-main bearing ran he had switched off literally a split-second before those pieces ran amok and destroyed the unit as totally as had the less sympathetic Rindt's. No prizes to guess which driver was paying the bills . . .

After that experience, John Judd had Petter diesel engine gudgeon pins machined to replace the originals. Constant and worrying wear had been found in the Alfa Romeo-made cam followers which had been used without trouble since 740 days. This now became the 860 units' latest bugbear. In the long Mexican GP excessive oil consumption dried out Jack's engine before the finish. In an effort to preserve those cam followers, which had broken behind his shoulders in the preceding US GP, some of the oil drains from the heads had been plugged to maintain more lubricant washing around the suspect followers. Unfortunately this simply caused extra leakage down the valve guides, and the BT26 oil tank just wasn't big enough to last the distance.

In between times there had been other dramas, and fleeting success which proved just how close Repco were to true competitiveness.

During practice at Spa, Jack had another valve insert detach, and Repco concluded that the material was shrinking to cause this problem. In a frantic trouble-shooting exercise, Jack Brabham flew himself home that evening while John Judd and Norm Wilson collected a fresh engine at Heathrow air-freight from Melbourne. It was stripped down overnight

The Repco-Brabhams were nothing if not forgiving. Here on his way to victory at Monaco 1967 Hulme demonstrates his BT20's full opposite lock, those fat, deep-treaded Goodyears scrabbling for grip.

with the help of BRO chief mechanic Roy Billington, while team machinist Ron Cousins came in to fit the new parts. The modified cylinder heads were then cooked in Brabham's kitchen, and his wife Betty awoke to find her house filled with acrid fumes from the oven!

The BT26-Repco 860s showed their true potential in practice for the wet Dutch GP where Rindt qualified on the front row only 0.16 sec slower than Amon's pole-position Ferrari, and Jack Brabham himself was on row two in his sister car. But they nearly hadn't made it to that race, as immediately after their transporter had left their new Guildford race shop for Dover a telex had rattled through from Melbourne warning of an assembly error. The team's fresh 860 engines had insufficient static clearance between their valves and pistons, and the twain would surely meet should the engines be started.

The ever-practical Jack Brabham promptly bought a suitable wood chisel from a Guildford hardware store and at Zandvoort his mechanics lifted the 860s' heads and chiselled down the piston crowns to provide the necessary clearance . . . and only then did they produce that fine practice performance. This is why we should not compare this type of modern racing with the *alleged* heyday of Daimler-Benz and Alfa Corse.

Yet in truth, the more we discover today of the way the giants of the past went racing, the less infallible they also seem to be. It is quite wrong to base high-flown technical judgements upon their racing records and design standards without also looking closer at the greasy-fingered background, often punctuated by similar last-minute panics and human errors. Racing cars and racing engines are made by man, and man is far from perfect, even when his efforts have been applied *en masse* by a 300-strong experimental department. Never swallow the legend whole, for legends are written by Public Relations men . . .

At Rouen for another wet race, the French GP, Rindt qualified on pole to prove conclusively there was nothing wrong in principle with the quad-cam BT26, but the car's fuel tanks split early in the race. Brabham's regular BT26 suffered a repeat fuel-feed problem which

had dogged it in previous outings. Tauranac finally concluded that when its tanks were crammed full to the brim on race day an air vent became blocked and the fuel pump lacked sufficient suction to overcome the vacuum it was attempting to form within.

The Mexican GP of 1968 was the final works outing for Repco Brabham in Formula 1, although in 1969 Jack drove a Formula 3-based Repco Brabham BT31 fitted with a 2½-litre Repco 830 engine to third place at Sandown Park and subsequently first place in the Bathurst '100' at Mount Panorama, where he set fastest lap and won handsomely in his last road race for Repco.

It was the end of a three-season relationship which had yielded back-to-back Formula 1 Constructors' Championship titles for Brabham and Tauranac and Repco, and Drivers' titles for Jack Brabham himself and for his team-mate, Denny Hulme. It had been a triumph of elegant thinking and practical expediency over high-flown sophistication, and now – albeit with real power – Cosworth's V8 would follow where Repco's had led . . .

THE WORLD CHAMPIONSHIP BRABHAM CHASSIS

The availability of the BT19 spare chassis, tailor-made for the still-born flat-16 Climax 1500 cc engine, saved the day for the Brabham Racing Organisation when the new deal was finally forged with Motor Racing Developments in November 1965.

BT19 was a one-off multi-tubular space-frame chassis. Ron Tauranac persisted in his allegiance to this form of construction despite most contemporary opposition building stressed-skin monocoque cars. Multi-tubular frames were popular with MRD's paying customers because they were simple, well-understood and easy to set up. They were also straightforward and inexpensive to repair following an accident yet rigid enough to give competitive standards of handling, traction and braking. In Formula 1, Jack Brabham's BRO team put into practice what MRD produced by racing spaceframe-chassised cars.

BT19 had a well-triangulated frame of typical Tauranac design although the use of oval-section tube around its cockpit opening was unusual. Tauranac had found some was available and had used it simply to enhance beam strength around the cockpit – 'always the weak point in a racing design'.

The suspension was typically Tauranac, with unequal-length non-parallel front wishbones formed by a transverse link with a trailing radius rod jointed to it at the top, and a one-piece wide-based tubular wishbone at the bottom. Suitably-modified Alford & Alder proprietary uprights were used (from the humble Triumph Herald saloon). Co-axial coil springs and Armstrong dampers were mounted outboard front and rear. At the rear, single top links, reversed lower wishbones and twin radius rods located specially cast uprights.

Initially, 13 in. wheels were fitted enclosing 10½ in. diameter disc brakes as had been standard on the 1½-litre cars. Later in the 1966 season 15 in. rear wheels were adopted housing new 11 in. discs and wearing the latest generation of square-shouldered flat-tread Goodyear tyres. Still later in its life BT19 was fitted with 15 in. wheels front and rear.

In original form this one-off car used a 1½-litre Formula Hewland HD five-speed transaxle, which really was not adequate for the 3-litre engine to which it was now mated. Early on, Jack Brabham always made gentle race starts, while Mike Hewland's Maidenhead-based transmission company developed a new and heavier gearbox, known as the DG, which was to become very popular in the 3-litre Formula. Both Brabham himself and his former team driver, Dan Gurney, who had now founded the Anglo-American Racers Eagle F1 team, had asked Hewland to produce

a suitable transmission and Dan was delighted to see it carry his initials, 'DG'. Mike Hewland, however, told the author years ago that in fact someone now unremembered had leaned over his shoulder while he was working at his design and asked 'What's this, a different gearbox?', and 'DG' for 'Different Gearbox' it became.

This transmission featured a ZF limited-slip differential, and it drove to the BT19's wheels via one-piece solid halfshafts with inboard rubber couplings and outboard Hooke joints.

BT19 emerged as one of the very lightest true 3-litre GP contenders, and the economical engine, as already mentioned, enabled it to survive a full GP distance on no more than 35 gallons of Esso premium grade. Even so, BT19 was some 150 lb above the minimum weight limit of 1102 lb and Tauranac was far from happy with it, regarding it as 'a lash-up', even after it had won four consecutive GP races at Reims, Brands Hatch, Zandvoort and the Nürburgring, had given Jack himself the Drivers' World Championship for the third time in his career and brought MRD the Formula 1 Constructors' Cup World title.

Once BT19 was running, work had begun at New Haw on the true 1966 3-litre F1 cars which were intended first to support and eventually to supplant the lashed-up BT19. These BT20 cars used all round-section steel tube chassis members, mostly in 18-gauge stock but some from 16- and 20-gauge. The lower chassis rails were revised compared to BT19's and the cockpit area was double-braced with twin side tubes in place of BT19's oval members. Tankage was similar to BT19's although small scuttle and behind-seat tanks were now available for the long and thirsty Italian GP, but were not required.

The BT20s employed virtually identical suspension to BT19's, but geometry was revised from new to accommodate 15 in. wheels front and rear. In its first races, Hulme's BT20 used 12 in. diameter brake discs, but these were too large and 11 in. discs soon replaced them. Mechanically, BT19 and the BT20s were identical, but the later cars had front and rear tracks wider by 1 in. and ¾ in. respectively, and their wheelbase was 1½ in. longer. Externally the two BT20s built differed from BT19 in using vestigial two-piece engine covers in place of the duck-tail one-piece cowl of BT19, and their exhaust manifolding wrapped outside the rear suspension upper radius rods while BT19's were cramped inside the rods.

Tauranac was able to tackle the Formula 1 problem far more thoroughly in 1967. That

Jack Brabham's BT24, French GP, '67. Compact F2-sized package on F1 wheels and tyres has centre-exhaust Repco RB740 V8 engine, whisker spoilers on nose, deflector ahead of front wheel to extract radiator air and engine-bay side panel.

season his new cars were based upon a highly successful Tasman Formula exercise raced in January/March that year. This had employed a production-type Brabham Formula 2 frame known as the BT23A, fitted with the prototype new centre-exhaust 2.5-litre Type 740 engine. Here, Tauranac used specially cast front uprights for the first time, replacing the Herald proprietary forgings which had done such yeoman service for so long on Brabham racing cars. The BT23's engine bay had been suitably reworked to house the V8 in place of the in-line 4-cylinder Cosworth FVA unit which would appear in these production racing cars in European Formula 2 that summer. Three largely similar new BT24 Formula 1 cars would now be built.

Tauranac regards these as his 'first real go at Formula 1, apart from the BT3 in 1962. We looked at the existing cars from end to end, slimmed and pruned everything to the minimum, used our own cast uprights all round and generally spent a lot of time designing just enough car to do the job. The amount of thought and time that went into producing a car as simple and light as that was tremendous – probably a lot more than if we had gone all complex and sophisticated . . .'

These BT24s were delightfully compact, well-packaged cars, although based on the same relatively long wheelbase as the preceding BT20. Front track had narrowed by 1½ in. while rear track was wider by ¾ in. Apart from the new cast front uprights, suspension configuration was similar to the BT20's, but the whole car was extremely neat and the BT23-type front body panel was split crosswise at the front suspension so that the nose cone could detach separately to ease freight and stowage. On the new type's debut at Zandvoort in the 1967 Dutch GP a Formula 2-type Hewland FT200 gearbox was used, saving still more weight, but it was not robust enough and so the hefty Hewland DG quickly replaced it.

These BT24s were very quick and forgiving, allowing their drivers to take liberties which the opposition could not look at. Denny Hulme narrowly beat Brabham himself for the Drivers' title while Jack had taken all new development testing upon himself, leaving the proven and reliable – and by the same token potentially slower – hardware to his rugged New Zealand team-mate.

The BT24s achieved three 1-2 victories during that season, in the French GP at the Bugatti Circuit, Le Mans, in the German GP at the Nürburgring and in the Canadian GP at Mosport Park, but in each of these races they had played second fiddle to the Lotus-Cosworth 49s until they broke, and in Germany to Gurney's Eagle V12 until it broke.

To finish first, you must first finish . . . and that was something at which the lithe little Repco Brabhams proved most adept.

The 1968 Tasman Championship saw Jack Brabham running another F1 prototype car in 2.5-litre form, this being the ultra-lightweight one-off BT23E powered by the latest Repco four-cam 830 magnesium short-block engine. Then, back home in England, Tauranac tried something new in his 1968 Formula 1 chassis design, the BT26: 'We tried to make a lighter but stronger frame by using alloy sheet panelling instead of tubular triangulation. This allowed us to use smaller-gauge, thinner section tubes for the basic frame, and the whole

Brabham and Tauranac took aerodynamic study very seriously in 1967-68. Here at Monza (below) in '67 Jack tried this bubble canopy and engine bay-side, roll-over bar and gearbox-fairing panels to reduce drag. Unfortunately parallax distorted vision and gearbox oil nearly boiled! Bottom, Tauranac with help from aerodynamicist Ray Jessop introduced a strutted wing as early as the 1968 Belgian GP. Here at the Nürburgring Brabham demonstrates the BT26-Repco 4-cam's chassis-mounted rear appendage plus balancing nose 'foils in his team's best race of the season. Above right, sheet-stiffened BT26-Repco 860.

thing was built in a different way. Instead of making the bulkheads first and then joining them together in the jig, we laid down the bottom part of the frame on a flat bed, built the top deck immediately above it, and then put the side members in between. We used similar main rails to the earlier cars, but with ⅝ in. 20-gauge square-tube carrying stressed panelling on the floor and around the cockpit deck, on the sides and behind the seat, and in the dash panel frame, around the driver's thighs. It worked OK, but it might have been cheaper to build a monocoque in the long run.'

This BT26 was a bigger car than the BT24, 1½ in. longer in the wheelbase, 5 in. wider in front track and 5½ in. wider in rear track to apply longer lever moment on the Goodyear tyres and achieve better turn-in performance. Suspension and bodywork thinking was basically similar to that of the 1967 Championship-winning cars.

Although these hybrid-construction 1968 Repco Brabhams were unsuccessful in defending their predecessors' World Championship titles, they had their day, notably in the rain and mist-afflicted German GP – typically, where the four-cam Repco engine was concerned, in face of adversity.

One and a half hours before that race began a cracked titanium valve-spring retainer was discovered in Rindt's engine, and a mad scramble ensued to replace its cylinder heads with those cannibalized from the team's spare. The race V8 was reassembled with just 10 minutes to spare before the start and Rindt splashed around in the rain to finish third while Brabham himself was fifth in the team's finest race of that troubled year.

Most significantly, Ron Tauranac was one of the first Formula 1 car designers to think deeply enough about aerodynamics to adopt add-on tabs and vanes to minimize lift. Jack Brabham was himself an enthusiastic private flyer, and he recalled the Lotus 24 which he had driven in 1962 at Reims where he found it difficult merely 'to aim between the stands' when running flat-out along the undulating straight from Thillois towards Gueux. Although it had not been realized at the time, this was almost certainly due to aerodynamic lift unloading the front tyres and reducing steering reaction to a frightening degree.

It was noticed during 1966 that the BT19 and BT20 seemed to have a distinct advantage over the otherwise more sleek 2-litre Lotus-Climax 33 in very fast corners. One self-styled technical analyst has since attributed this to the relative torsional inferiority of the Brabham chassis, stating that Tauranac believed a little

flexibility would ensure better-balanced tyre loading. Ron himself describes this theory in picturesque Australian. He has always been an advocate of chassis stiffness, 'the stiffer the better' and only remained faithful to the spaceframe as long as he did for other reasons, while being able to make his spaceframes 'stiff enough' to be consistently competitive.

In retrospect it would appear to be more the relative aerodynamic forms of the Lotus 33 and Repco Brabham nose cones which contributed to their relative high-speed behaviour. The Lotus nose-cone was notably up-turned with a lengthy exposed undersurface in the direct airstream. The Brabham cone was more bluff with less curvature on both under and upper surfaces. It seems probable that this generated less lift than the Lotus cone, and when Tauranac enlisted aid from British Aircraft Corporation aerodynamicists at nearby Brooklands in 1967-68 genuine aerodynamic progress was made, even if this only revealed a fraction of its huge and as yet untapped potential.

At Spa in 1967, old BT19 driven by Hulme carried modest strip dive-planes either side of its nose cone in an exploratory attempt to kill front-end lift, which seemed quite effective on that very fast course. At Monza that year with BAC wind tunnel advice Brabham tried a bubble canopy and gearbox-fairing cowl to reduce his BT24's high-speed drag. These devices made little tangible difference, other than to distort the driver's vision through parallax and to overheat the gearbox oil, so they were discarded for the race.

Back at Spa in 1968, Brabham tied with Ferrari – following as we shall see elsewhere in this volume, an unofficial wintertime Tasman Championship experiment by the Team Lotus mechanics – in introducing strutted rear aerofoils, mounted on the chassis, with their effect counterbalanced by broad dive-planes attached either side of the extreme nose. As the season progressed the wing era was upon us, and while the BT26s suffered the mechanical problems of their new four-cam engines it was left to others to penetrate further into the new realm of aerodynamic research.

In 1969 the BT26s were reworked to accept Cosworth-Ford DFV V8 engines, and the Repco era had passed. The Repco Brabhams in all their various versions were never the spectacularly innovative technical gems which their major opposition might claim to have been, but they had in several ways shown the way ahead – not least in proving the intense value of a rigid regard for practical simplicity . . . a lesson many others would never, ever, learn.

Chapter 3
THE COSWORTH-FORD ERA 1967-85

Theo Page's original press-release cutaway of Cosworth-Ford's brand new DFV V8 was released with the original engine in June 1967.

The story of Cosworth Engineering and of its supremely successful Ford-backed V8 Formula 1 racing engine has often been told, notably in the John Blunsden and David Phipps book *Such Sweet Thunder* (Motor Racing Publications, London, 1971) and its sequel *The Power to Win* by Blunsden (MRP, 1983).

Briefly, the 'Cos' of Cosworth is Mike Costin, while the company's 'worth' is Keith Duckworth. Sometimes known derisively in their formative years as 'Cosbodge & Duckfudge Ltd', they matured from a small-time race engineering outfit operating from somebody else's premises to become the outstanding racing engine manufacturers of their day. Their production Ford-based Formula Junior, Formula 2 and Formula 3 racing engines dominated their respective classes with rare exception from 1960 to 1965, and then a new 1600 cc Formula 2 was promulgated to replace the existing 1-litre class from 1 January 1967.

Duckworth applied his now highly experienced designer's mind to production of a new dohc 4-cylinder F2 engine, based on the Cortina 120E block. And at this point, Coventry Climax confirmed their customers' worst fears that they would indeed be withdrawing from Formula 1 racing at the end of the 1965 season, and would not be building engines to the new 3-litre Formula.

Duckworth had never designed a racing engine from scratch, but when Colin Chapman of Lotus asked him, first, if he thought he could design a new Formula 1 engine, and secondly, if he thought he should do so, the answer was affirmative. Colin asked him for a rough estimate of the cost of such a project, and the answer was 'around £100,000'.

Chapman wanted a new 3-litre racing engine for his team with an initial target output of 400 bhp. He considered this the minimum necessary to keep Ferrari, BRM, Eagle-Weslake and the rest in sight long-term. He had every confidence that Cosworth were capable of producing such an engine but now he needed someone prepared to finance it. He approached the British Society of Motor Manufacturers & Traders but, as he suspected, this proved a vain hope, the SMMT's representations to Government on his behalf drawing a blank. He also received a sympathetic hearing from Macdonald, head of the BSR (British Sound Recording) company, and from David Brown of gear industry, tractor and Aston Martin fame. Neither produced much concrete result.

Chapman had been a long-time friend of dapper executive Walter Hayes, former Editor of *The Sunday Dispatch*, for whom Colin had

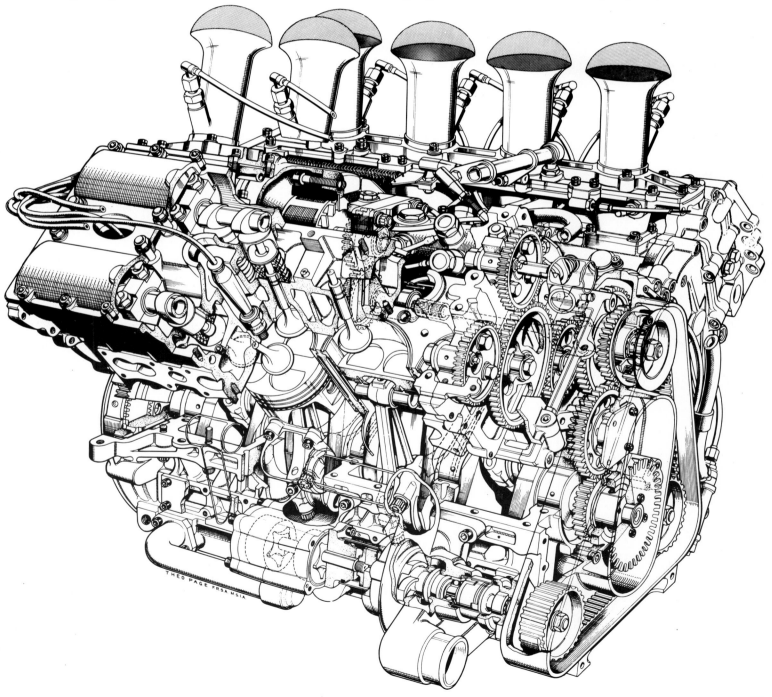

once been freelance motoring correspondent. In 1961 Sir Patrick Hennessey, Chairman of Ford of Britain, had taken on Hayes as his new Director of Public Affairs, acting on the advice of veteran press baron – and proprietor of *The Sunday Dispatch* – Lord Beaverbrook.

Largely under Hayes's direction, Ford espoused a new Total Performance image to lift them above the dull and rather tawdry 'minimum transport for the masses' image which they felt they were suffering from.

This new campaign involved them in motoring competition to an unprecedented degree. A strong Lotus-Ford link had already been forged with great success in Formula Junior and sports car racing, while the Lotus-Cortina saloon car was about to be launched and the Indianapolis 'Lotus powered by Ford' programme was also under way.

At dinner one evening in Chapman's home, Gothic Cottage, at Monken Hadley, Hayes was regaled with Chapman's thoughts and hopes for the new 3-litre Formula.

Ford of Britain's new Vice-President in Charge of Engineering was an American named Harley Copp, and Hayes found in him a racing enthusiast happy to support plans for a Ford-financed Grand Prix engine. Hayes brought Chapman and Copp together to discuss the former's concept of the perfect 3-litre racing engine. When Copp heard of Cosworth's pending intermediate plan to build a 4-cylinder F2 engine based on the Ford Cortina cylinder block he was finally converted.

As John Blunsden has described 'From Duckworth's point of view, a two-stage project in which the successful production of a 1.6-litre

Keith Duckworth, Colin Chapman (part-hidden), Jimmy Clark and Graham Hill pose at Zandvoort with the spanking-new Cosworth-Ford DFV engine bolted into one of the tailor-made new Lotus 49s.

4-cylinder Formula 2 engine could be followed by a 'doubled-up' V8 power unit, with suitable modifications to the cylinder dimensions in order to bring its displacement within the 3-litre limit, made good sense. Most important of all it would mean that the cylinder head – in Duckworth's opinion the key component of any of his competition engines – could first be tested and proven on the 4-cylinder block before it was committed to a V8 . . .'

Of course, this was also very attractive to Ford as their PR people could then highlight the direct link between their production passenger cars and the Grand Prix machinery carrying their company's name.

Another American executive named Stanley Gillen had only been in England for six days as Ford of Britain's new Managing Director when his first meeting of the Ford Policy Committee was convened. It went predictably smoothly until Gillen reached the 'Any Other Business' section of the agenda, whereupon Hayes said: 'Yes, Harley and I would like to do a Grand Prix engine . . .'

The plan was to commit £100,000 minimum to the Chapman/Cosworth project, the Policy Committee voted it through and in the spring of 1966 a tripartite agreement was drafted between the Ford Motor Company, Cosworth Engineering and Keith Duckworth. For a payment by Ford of £100,000, Cosworth and Duckworth agreed to design and develop for Ford both Formula 2 and Formula 1 power units to be known as 'Ford' engines. The interim 1600 cc F2 Cortina-block unit would be known as the FVA – Four-Valve Series 'A' – and from it would be developed, as the contract put it; '. . . a 90-degree V8 3,000 cc engine using cylinder heads basically the same as/or developed from the above FVA suitable to race in International Formula 1 races under the regulations which started in 1966 . . .'

The Formula 1 engines had to be ready for

use by May 1967, five engines to be available by 1 January 1968 and such engines would be maintained until 31 December 1968. Crucially, 'The choice of team will be at Ford's discretion, Cosworth being available in an advisory capacity if required'.

In effect, Team Lotus would have exclusive use of the engine in its first season, 1967, but rather to Chapman's dismay Ford would then offer it freely to other 'acceptable' customers from the start of 1968. This was a wise decision, and it would do more than merely give Ford blanket coverage in Formula 1 racing for the next fifteen years. It would make contemporary Formula 1 both the best-supported and the closest-fought Grand Prix class in racing history. The upshot of all this would also be to make Formula 1 irresistibly attractive to outside sponsors and their interest would change the face of racing as we knew it. The ramifications of that decision to make the DFV generally available were very significant in shaping Formula 1's future character.

This historic initial agreement became effective on 1 March 1966, but Duckworth did not first set pen to paper until 23 June that year. Although the sum of £100,000 had been arrived at more by inspiration than calculation, it proved remarkably accurate, just like the rest of Duckworth's work.

FORMULA 2 THEORY AND . . .

In his initial design for the 4-cylinder Formula 2 Type FVA engine, Duckworth had wrestled with the problem of enlarging valve area compared to his preceding 1-litre F2 SCA. The more gas one can persuade into and out of an engine, the more power it can produce from combustion of that gas – the old truism of 'the more you put in, the more you get out' which applies so widely in all our lives.

Restricted by the cylinder wall thickness in the 120E Cortina block, Duckworth could not

increase the cylinder bore very much, so to obtain adequate valve area it was necessary to resort to four valves per cylinder. Both BRM and Climax had tried 32-valve V8s during 1964, BRM's failing to come up to expectations while Climax's was quite effective but not spectacularly better than the preceding 16-valver, as it should have been.

Only Honda's 1966 1-litre F2 engine had made really successful use of four valves per cylinder, Duckworth crediting this to their being 'the only people who had managed to get their detail work right; in itself the concept has always been sound, but only if the execution is up to the same standard as . . . a good two-valve layout'. Whereas the best 1-litre Cosworth SCA eight-valver had generated 143 bhp per litre, the 16-valve Honda 'four' was obviously over 150 bhp with its four-valve head.

After careful thought, Duckworth concluded that he should now aim for 200 bhp from a 16-valve four-cylinder 1600. He planned one layout using a pent roof combustion chamber with diametrically-opposed inlet and exhaust valves, à la BMW and Repco, although the Repco RB50 head was unknown to him at that time. However, he then abandoned this scheme as it further demanded three spark plugs per cylinder for adequate ignition, while the inlet and exhaust systems on a V8 version would have been a major source of grief, as Repco would discover . . .

Consequently the FVA F2 unit emerged as a simple crossflow four-cylinder, intakes on the right, exhaust on the left, the narrow included angle between the pairs of valves being 40 degrees, the twin ohc driven by spur gears from the crankshaft nose and the standard Ford camshaft in the block retained to drive the water pump.

Talking to journalist David Phipps about his gas-flow philosophies, the always aggressively articulate Duckworth produced his classic quote: 'I have never believed there is any point in having a gas-flow rig and measuring the flow . . . A hole that looks nice and smooth and has no projections will generally flow easily . . . I would claim that I could arrive at something very close to . . . results from gas-flowing just by putting my finger down the hole and seeing what it feels like!'

He settled for the conventional pent roof combustion chamber and convinced himself that his particular design would burn most of the air he could get into it. The F2 chambers had a volume of 400 cc per cylinder; in the F1 V8 these would be reduced to 375 cc per cylinder since capacity per bank then had to be reduced to less than 1500 cc, as opposed to the F2 unit's displacement of just under 1600.

To achieve this reduction, either bore or stroke – or both – had to be decreased, and as the FVA's stroke was relatively long it was shortened for the DFV. This dictated keeping flat pistons apart from shallow valve cut-outs and decreasing the valve angle in the head. Since the F2 unit's combustion on test was clearly very good, Duckworth made this change with some trepidation. However, the valve angle reduction offered other advantages, in that it made the head rather more compact which helped minimize the danger of the V8 growing wider than might be sensible.

. . . FORMULA 1 PRACTICE

The fundamental decision in favour of a V8 had been made at a time when everybody else interested in the 3-litre Formula seemed to regard 12 cylinders as an absolute minimum. BRM had their fiendish H16-cylinder and there were even rumours of Honda building upon their multi-cylinder motor cycle expertise with a 24-cylinder! Repco, however, were demonstrating what could be achieved from the torque of even a humble sohc V8, while Cosworth had the valuable experience beneath their belts of having achieved over 140 bhp per litre from their 4-cylinder F2 engine at a time

when the 1500 cc Formula 1 V8 manufacturers were very pleased with themselves when they approached 150 bhp per litre.

Duckworth's train of thought further justified the choice of a V8 rather than V12 on grounds of greater mechanical efficiency, with fewer moving parts to foster friction loss, while in any case a V8 promised to be lighter than a V12. An advantage in mechanical efficiency also promised better fuel consumption.

However, Cosworth's four-cylinder experience had also proved that a simplified exhaust system could be achieved by adopting a flat-plane crankshaft. This crankshaft formation was a notorious vibration source in V8 engines. Duckworth admits he 'was not entirely happy about using a flat crank on such a relatively large engine', but when calculations suggested a 'maximum transverse shake . . . plus or minus 3-thou; we felt that this should not be too serious . . .and it would certainly simplify the exhaust system'. For lightness' sake an alloy block was necessary, which at that stage of metallurgical development meant using some form of cylinder liner, since attempts to develop linerless engines in which the pistons ran direct in alloy blocks had not met with great success; the Repco V8 née Oldsmobile F85 being but one.

The bore spacing necessary to fit wet liners would have meant lengthening the block, unless bore dimension was considerably reduced from that proven on the FVA. Working with his detail draughtsman Mike Hall (whose BRM experience had included their F2 and prototype H16 units), Duckworth opted to retain the FVA bore. The stroke was decreased from 2.72 to 2.55 in., while con-rod length was then increased to avoid an unacceptable rise in piston acceleration which would bring greater stress and wear in its wake. Ordinary iron cylinder liners were adopted, sealed by two 'O'-rings at the bottom and by Cooper's mechanical joints at the top.

One great problem with a 90-degree V8 is how to achieve decent chassis design when such a square-cut lump has to be installed in the rear. Because of this it seemed logical to adopt BRM's (P83 H16) and Ferrari's (1500 cc flat-12 Tipo 1512) approach and to make the engine serve as a stressed structural member, mounted rigidly on the rear of a truncated chassis forepart, with the rear suspension carried either on the engine or gearbox, or on subframes attached to them.

Duckworth worked closely with Colin Chapman and Lotus chassis designer Maurice Phillippe on this, and they decided to mount the unit rigidly via two bolts passing through an alloy bottom beam at the engine's front end, with two additional strap plates on the cam-covers bolted into the upper hips of the monocoque. The intended Lotus 49 tub's side pontoons were only 9 in. apart at the rear, traditionally being matched to Jim Clark's physique at this crucial point. So the two lower bolts in that DFV front beam were spaced at 9-in. centres. Once Duckworth had drawn the cam-box mounting plate positions, the rear face of a suitable matching monocoque could be defined by these four mounting points.

Because the engine would expand as it heated up while running, they then had to ensure that the monocoque rear bulkhead would not be stretched by this expansion. Therefore, all shear was taken on the bottom mountings, while the two thin top strap plates linking the cam covers to the monocoque pick-ups allowed 15-thou or so engine expansion without significant stress. Tyrrell designer Derek Gardner was not alone when he enthused about this mounting system as recently as April 1985, unequivocally describing it as 'a truly wonderful way of mounting a racing engine' allowing the car designer enormous freedom thereafter. Very hefty cam carriers were provided in order to transmit chassis loads into the heads from the cam-cover strap

plates and thence into the block without risking tappet seizure through carrier distortion. What's more, metal-to-metal joints were used throughout this assembly, since the loss of friction within the joints through use of paper gaskets might have allowed torsional loads to disturb the engine assembly.

From an early stage it was clear that little fuel could be carried alongside this engine due to its overall width including the low-swept exhaust system. This meant that all fuel would have to be carried within the monocoque forward chassis, and if wheelbase was not then to be exaggerated it was vital to minimize engine length.

This demanded that all ancillaries like the water and oil pumps should be fitted low down on the sides of the engine under the exhaust manifold curls, and items like the distributor should go on top within the vee. With an engine now strictly four cylinders long, a large capacity fuel tank could be sandwiched in the rear of the monocoque between cockpit and engine, ideally situated near the car's overall centre of gravity, providing constant weight distribution as the fuel load diminished.

Duckworth's detail design showed equally deep thinking. He smoothed the crankcase's internal surfaces for aerodynamic efficiency, reasoning that since the crankshaft bob-weights would be rotating at some 170 mph it was reasonable to assume they would sweep the air within the crankcase round with them, so it might as well be given as smooth a passage as possible.

The flywheel was kept as small as possible to help keep the centre of gravity low, and this meant a special tooth form for the starter ring. It was impossible to mount a starter motor capable of meshing with this tiny flywheel alongside the crankcase, so it was turned about-face and bracketed onto the gearbox casing, driving forward to the starter ring. In any case it was useful to place the starter motor weight – and believe me it was a very heavy lump on these cars – as far back as possible.

Structurally, all major castings were in 'LM 8 WP' heat-treated aluminium alloy with cover castings in magnesium.

As in all previous Cosworth engines, the crankshaft was in nitrided 'M 40B' steel. Big-end bearing diameters were identical to the FVA's, which themselves matched Ford's production 4-cylinder range although narrowed to minimize the block offset because Duckworth considered the production engine bearing areas excessive.

Main bearing diameter was enlarged to increase in-section overlap between the big-ends and mains, and to enhance crankshaft stiffness. Piston and con-rod design was along FVA lines, while the cam-drive geartrain of 14 spurs up the front of the unit incorporated a quill shaft on the crank nose, first found essential on the SCA. An injection/ignition pack slotted into the engine's vee, comprising a very heavy small-capacity alternator integrated with the distributor, injection pump and injection metering unit.

The bottom half of the engine carried the main bearing caps integral with the sump, enabling it to become a very strong beam in its own right, happy to transmit chassis loads.

In making such a short, flat-face engine, ancillary mounting was strictly confined to the sides and the vee. Only within the vee did this cause a major problem, as Duckworth had to leave more space there than he might have liked for that tubby alternator housing.

Mike Hall detailed the various pumps, metering unit and alternator assembly, Duckworth most of what remained. He worked mainly at home, often 15 hours a day, liaising with Hall and Mike Costin at the factory in St James' Mill Road, Northampton, one day a week. This went on for some nine months, manufacture then beginning of the first prototype DFV engine.

On its initial run in one of Cosworth's test cells, the DFV sounded terrific, hard and crisp as a Grand Prix engine should, but it pumped out its oil. The heads were drowning in lubricant which refused to drain down into the sump to be scavenged and pumped on around the system. A temporary fix was achieved by cutting holes in the cam-covers and tacking on collector boxes with external drain pipes to return this excess oil to the sump. The engines wore this system in the Lotus 49's first few races. It enabled the engine to breath adequately, whereupon the Cosworth dyno recorded 408 bhp – Colin Chapman's 400 horsepower target had been met.

DEVELOPMENT TRIALS AND ERRORS

During one early dyno run a tooth snapped off one of the timing gears and on strip-down the gear bearings themselves showed distress. Clearly some strange torsional vibration was upsetting the geartrain, a problem which would afflict Cosworth for some time to come. Vibration was in fact a major characteristic of the new V8. Much of the rotating and reciprocating weight had been balanced out to minimize main bearing loads, but this dropped the natural frequency vibration period, which drivers would now have to pass through primarily at 8600 rpm, then secondarily at 9600 rpm.

This effect is the engine man's equivalent of out-of-balance front wheels. Any owner-driver of a 105E Ford Anglia will remember how desperately prone those pressed-steel wheels were to going out of balance, if indeed you had bothered to have them balanced at all. At certain speeds out-of-balance vibrations would build up which could set the steering wheel juddering uncontrollably in your hands. You could accelerate through it or brake out of it. Just imagine that same effect set loose within the DFV as the crankshaft passed through those critical speeds and you have some appreciation of what its main bearings and structure had to withstand.

Where the cam-drive geartrain torsional was concerned it seemed to pose only a long-term problem. The original test engine had completed several hours of trouble-free running before that tooth failure, far more than Grand Prix distance, so it was not deemed necessary to delay the engine's public debut.

While Cosworth were completing their first 'FORD'-lettered Formula 1 V8s, Team Lotus at Hethel near Norwich were completing two prototype Type 49 monocoque cars. Initial track testing was conducted by Mike Costin at Hethel aerodrome and Snetterton, before team driver Graham Hill was trusted to take over.

As is now genuine racing legend, the DFV powered Jim Clark to win the 1967 Dutch GP first time out in the new Lotus 49, after team-mate Hill had not only started from pole position, but also led convincingly in the early stages and set fastest race lap before being sidelined by cam-gear failure.

Post-race strip-down of Clark's victorious engine revealed that it too had stripped a cam-drive gear tooth. This was serious. One cure might have been to dispense with the geartrain and adopt instead internal-toothed rubber belts, but they would have compromised the direct mounting of engine to monocoque. Therefore the geartrain itself was tackled after various expedients had been tried with vari-

These Autocar *sketches from when the DFV was unveiled in June '67, show* (top) *wide-spaced rear suspension pick-ups and, at front, engine mounts. V8 was stressed to accept chassis loads by that horizontal diaphragm linking cylinder banks and cast box sections along sides of sump. Centre, oil scavenge and pressure pump flow was designed to maintain both banks' lubricant at even temperature. Bottom, water system with pumps neatly packaged tight against crankcase.*

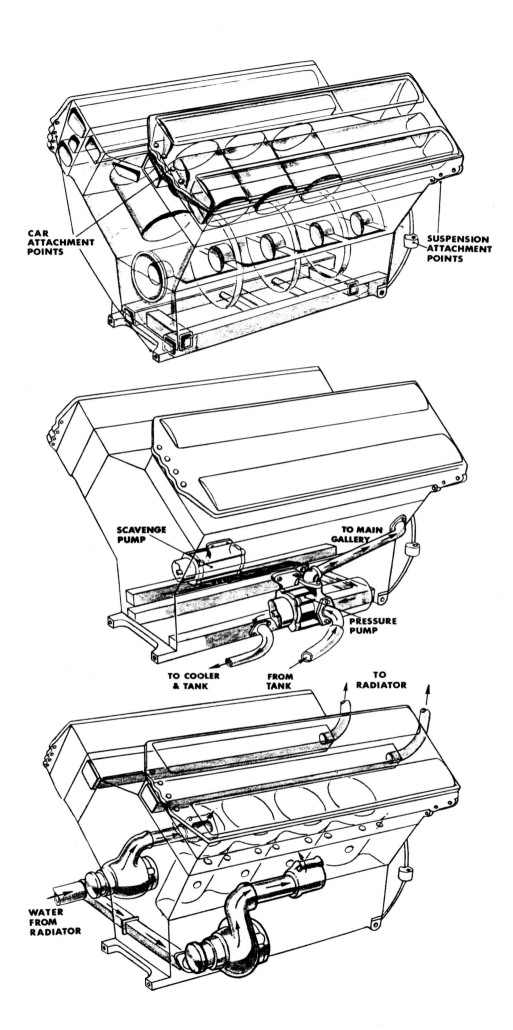

CAR ATTACHMENT POINTS

SUSPENSION ATTACHMENT POINTS

SCAVENGE PUMP

TO MAIN GALLERY

PRESSURE PUMP

TO COOLER & TANK

FROM TANK

TO RADIATOR

WATER FROM RADIATOR

able, and never complete, success. An analysis of the cam-lobe forms and their dynamic interaction across banks finally revealed very rapid torque reversals affecting the geartrain. Consequently new cam shapes were designed which minimized the torque demanded to turn the cam itself against the valve springs and to accelerate the valvegear. This modified cam form was to survive throughout the engine's competitive life although its initial purpose was purely to reduce shock loads on the cam-drive gears and so give them some chance of survival.

Still the geartrain failures occurred, despite improvements in gear design, strength, and support, until Duckworth designed a hub for the second compound gears which incorporated 12 slender quill shafts which could wind up under load to cushion gear and bearings against those still-savage torque reversals. The first of these cushioned compound gears was fitted in 1971, and despite occasional failures when run in conjunction with 'the more savage cams', or breakage of the gears below it due to crankshaft torsionals, geartrain trouble thereafter became effectively a thing of the past.

John Blunsden records that the scatter of geartrain trouble between different engines was very high. During a period when every other Cosworth runner seemed to be in constant timing gear trouble, Jochen Rindt's Lotus engine used the same set of gears and bearings in five races trouble-free! Duckworth told John they could never discover why certain engines 'would', while other engines 'wouldn't'.

The DFV undeniably had plenty of useable power throughout its life and this was particularly marked upon its introduction in 1967 for Team Lotus's use and in 1968 for other customer teams. But first-time Cosworth drivers were often caught out by the shattering way its power came in with an abrupt bang between 6000 and 6500 rpm. This made life difficult in the wet, and 1968 was a season studded with very wet races . . .

Initially, in 1967 Cosworth attempted to introduce artificially smooth throttle response by devising a cam control in which the throttle moved slowly through the first part of its opening, then very rapidly through the latter part. Tyre widths and sticky compounding progressed dramatically early in the DFV's career, and the proliferation of aerodynamic aids then added so much traction that the early embarrassment of too abrupt a power curve was minimized and the progressive throttle device was never used in anger. Duckworth in fact adopted closing springs on the injection system slides which went over-centre during their motion to provide a very high closing force, while relaxing tension as the slides were opened.

The Achilles heel of the DFV, as in so many racing engines, has been in its valvegear, particularly its valve springs. There is a natural antipathy between savage cam profiles used to gain performance and valve springs demanding adequate life. To give the valve springs a reasonable chance of survival, one trick was to use interference springs whereby the inner coil is a push-fit within the outer coil and the two rub together. Unfortunately this friction between the coils can itself cause damage and break a spring. It is better to reduce surge at source, but this solution essentially remained elusive throughout the DFV's active Formula 1 life. One problem with interference springs is that manufacturing tolerances are difficult to maintain, and different spring pairs often had differing rates of interference and therefore of reliable spring damping. Towards the end of its frontline career, the DFV was offered with specially coated interference springs designed to prevent the scuffing which can lead to weakness and ultimate breakage.

One classic hiccup in operating DFV engines has been long-term storage of ready-to-run units, in more cases than might be considered

comfortable due to F1 teams having engines rebuilt and ready but lacking the funds to pay for them upon collection as Cosworth and its licensed rebuilders normally required.

During their storage, unless they were turned regularly by hand, these engines would often damage their valve springs by keeping them trapped too long under compression. Almost inevitably, this would result in an early valve spring breakage soon after the engine had been installed and started up. If a valve dropped in, a very expensive shattering bang would ensue.

It was in 1979, after long investigation into the valve surge problems had yielded little of great value, that Duckworth initiated desmodromic, mechanically closing valvegear researches. By this time Cosworth were deeply involved in other programmes, particularly production of 2.65-litre DFV-derived DFX turbocharged V8s for American oval-track racing. When the research team encountered major problems (notably with their desmodromic valvegear test rig), the idea went onto the back burner and eventually was shelved.

From the beginning, the DFV's spark plugs had been buried deep within tubes cast into the heads, and cooling water had to divert around these tubes on its way to cool the adjacent exhaust valve areas. This obstructed coolant flow, and one day a damaged head was sectioned and Cosworth's trouble-shooters discovered that the cast-in water passage was totally blocked in places, creating local hotspots. To prevent this happening in other engines the head castings were from that time bored out and thinwall plug sleeves were inserted which both provided better coolant clearance and enabled the interior of the waterway castings to be easily inspected to ensure they were as drawn. These cylinder head plug tubes have since been a feature of all later DFVs.

Also from the beginning, Cosworth have had customer teams complaining to them that their DFV engines use/lose/overheat their oil. Cosworth have usually retorted in words of few syllables that it is the team's own silly fault, because many have consistently refused to use Cosworth's approved oil system. Engine manufacturers are much the same the world over.

Much more recently, when Porsche developed their TAG Turbo V6 engine in a *Typ 956* endurance car containing an oil tank the size of a self-respecting dustbin, they turned to McLaren on their first running of the engine in an F1 chassis and stated flatly: 'You've got a problem with your oil tank', because the engine threw out all its oil in three or four laps of

Top, *original neat Lotus 49-DFV installation impressed everyone. Note outside water rail from nose radiator, top of Lucas fuel-injection pump safe in its monocoque tunnel just ahead of lower radius rod pick-up, oil filter behind white Sperex VHT-painted exhausts. Above, era of the airbox, in this case attached to the Brabham BT34's DFV 1971.*

Silverstone. In fact any more effective tank would have been quite impossible to install in a single-seater chassis, and the TAG engine's real problem was in its internal breathing, just like the DFV 16 years earlier. Since 1961, Formula 1 regulations have banned addition of oil during the race, so oil consumption problems are of crucial significance.

The first DFVs' steel liners had an unacceptably high rate of wear. Experiments with Tuftrided steel liners were unsuccessful. The problem was then exacerbated in 1970-71 by the adoption of induction airboxes which inevitably scooped in all manner of debris along with nice fresh air, and promptly dumped it into the rearmost cylinders, scoring the liners and causing rapid failure thereafter.

Special molybdenum-sprayed spheroidal graphite iron liners were tried, but they cost power and regretfully Duckworth reverted to cast-iron liners, which were tough as the proverbial old boot but which would shatter rather than merely dent or distort in the event of major mechanical failure from within, or from above, as when that perennial valve-surge problem might set a valve free.

Eventually Mahle Nikasil aluminium liners appeared, which at a stroke not only cured the oil consumption problems, but also saved 8 lb weight overall, reduced the number of expensive full engine rebuilds and obviated the need for lapping-in and fine-finishing rebuild time using less advanced liners.

Through the '70s Cosworth became the biggest supplier of forged pistons in the UK, having initially installed their own drop-forge to protect and supply their own requirements since the major piston manufacturer Hepworth & Grandage had opted out of the forged piston business as the British motor cycle engine industry finally laid down and died.

The DFV piston was changed in detail early on, but persistent oil control problems led Cosworth to study ring performance and occasionally question their supplier's consistency of manufacture. Formula 1 engine life is such that they are never adequately run-in, and original manufacturing accuracy and tolerance is all-important if they are to give of their best. In 1983 Duckworth told John Blunsden 'the reason that we are not in ring trouble with the Nikasil liners is probably that the abrasiveness of the liner from new is such that it rapidly corrects any ring geometry imperfections!'

In its earliest days the DFV crankshaft caused much heartache. The original shafts were machined from bar, later they were forged, then forged from better material, with close scrutiny maintained of material cleanliness. This has always been a bugbear for serious Formula 1 constructors who too often find that their suppliers neither understand nor appreciate how vital material quality must be . . . not only to race success, but more vitally to driver safety.

Early on, Cosworth had a failure connected with the way in which the core plugs had been inserted to block the crank's internal drillings, and so an alternative plugging method was adopted. Then in 1970 came the celebrated 'bad batch' of Cosworth DFV crankshafts which had such a literally shattering effect upon many teams' hopes.

The shafts were toughened by the nitriding process and then finish ground, and it was

The ultimate 3-litre F1 'Cossy' was the Cosworth-Ford (Ford preferred Ford-Cosworth) DFY V8, drawn by Diana Stevens when first announced in 1983. This shows revised heads, modified valvegear, block, drive-geartrain etc, and pound-for-pound still arguably the world's most powerful 3-litre atmospheric-induction engine.

during this finish grinding process that somebody enthusiastically ground clean through the nitride-toughened upper surface of the crank in the corner of a radius. An entire batch of shafts was utterly ruined in this way, all breaking or cracking while on the dyno. The batch should have carried Cosworth through 1970 but they had to be scrapped, a replacement batch took several months to come through so Cosworth had to make do and mend wherever possible with old engines and salvaged cranks.

In 1977 Duckworth experimented with magnesium engines, having dabbled earlier with magnesium blocks in his company's experimental four-wheel drive Formula 1 car of 1969. Unfortunately, the main bearing housings were found to expand considerably in these units.

Duckworth wanted to restrict oil flow through the engine since it threatened to overwhelm the scavenge capacity of the pumps and lead to churning as the crankshaft dipped into excess oil accumulating within the sump. Consequently the crankshafts were redrilled to offer lower main bearing pressure. Whereas earlier engines had run never less than 85 psi oil pressure, the redrilled 'low-pressure crank-shafts' now ran around 52 psi, and nearly all existing DFVs in serious use were converted at their subsequent rebuilds. After this, bottom-end bearing failures in the DFV became virtually a thing of the past except where other lubrication system failures or major leaks had occurred.

Meanwhile, Cosworth had sidestepped that original 1967 cam-box oil drainage problem and its stop-gap cure with those ugly external boxes and pipes by fitting an air pump. It lifted air and combustion 'blow-by' products – gas forced down the cylinder past the rings – from the bottom of the engine up into the heads, but this also transferred a lot of oil in the same direction.

The air pump was then employed as an additional oil pump, and now the total output of both scavenge pumps and the air pump was piped back to the oil tank. This ran the entire engine at an atmospheric depression, and what

had formerly been a conventional breather pipe now served to draw air *in* from outside. Unfortunately this system then fed so much air mixed with the oil back to the oil tank that the tank's oil/air separation systems were overwhelmed, and some cars now blew up their engines soon after blowing all their oil overboard through the oil tank breathers!

The cure this time was to design enlarged-capacity Roots-type scavenge pumps complete with air separators, which drew air through the heads and pressured it to force-drain oil into the sump. The separation systems then split air from oil, blowing air from the top of the tank to atmosphere, while the oil was circulated to the cooler matrices and on round the system for another exciting ride through the pumps.

Ever-increasing cornering speeds and rising lateral G-forces posed increasing problems in the DFV's later life as the wing-car era developed from 1978, and ever-larger scavenge pumps were adopted to slurp away oil before it could accumulate on one side of the sump or the other under lateral G. The air separator itself also came in for considerable development. The in-drawn mixture of oil and air was separated by being centrifuged, the heavy oil being hurled outwards leaving the air in the centre. Initially the oil was thrown against a stationary canister wall, from which it tended to splash back and would froth. It was redesigned with a rotating outer wall travelling at much the same speed as the centrifuging oil, greatly diminishing the splash-back effect, separating the oil and air more effectively and also weighing less and being more compact than its predecessor.

Ignition systems originally used the dreaded Lucas-OPUS contact-breaker system to which this author had a great deal of less than happy exposure when involved in rebuilding Lotus 49 'R3' during 1982-83. One DFV specialist contacted for help at that time asked, 'What system is it you're having trouble with?' 'Lucas-OPUS', I replied. 'Aah well, you'd better make yourself comfortable then, because you're in for a looong, haaard, frustrating night . . .', he said, and he was absolutely right.

The OPUS pick-up was replaced early on by a magnetic trigger but heat build-up around the trigger site within the vee affected the pick-up magnet and it would all go awry.

The DFV originally required a rev limiter to defend its conservative 9000 rpm safe limit. This was an electro-mechanical system, the mechanicals suffering terribly under the DFV's characteristic fierce vibration.

Capacitor ignition provided a great leap forward, led by Walter Scherag of Germany with their Contactless system first adopted by Tyrrell. It enabled use of surface discharge plugs with their greater heat range. The immense energy of the capacitor ignition's short-duration spark prompted drivers to comment on improved pick-up from corners although this improvement was quite impossible to quantify on the dyno. Monaco was tailor-made to show this ignition at its best.

Magnetti Marelli from Italy had been anxious to break-in on the DFV market and they produced a capacitor discharge system suitable for the DFV, as did Lucas of Britain, abandoning their now obstructive policy of only providing the racing world with adaptations of equipment already in commercial passenger car production. The amplifier box necessary for 'my' Lotus 49, for example, was identical to that used in the Jaguar XJS V12, right down to the same part number.

Where fuel systems are concerned, early 1967 problems were caused by dirt blocking the filters and slashing fuel pressure. Initial suspicion that the fuel bag material was breaking up saw larger filters inserted, and then a mod was made to the in-line filter 'O'-ring which was found not to seat satisfactorily and therefore allowed debris to pass through.

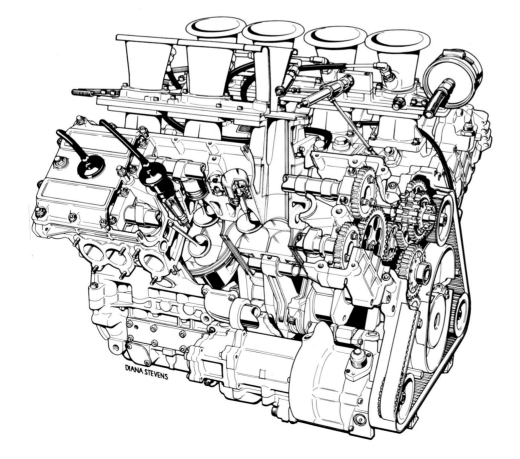

DIANA STEVENS

Initially the Lotus 49 and its imitators used an electric high-pressure pump to start the engine. A mechanical pump took over once the engine was running to build up to full power. These were subsequently replaced by a combined electro-mechanical pump incorporating a tiny electric motor and a one-way clutch assembly enabling the motor to drive the pump as long as the engine was running at lower rpm than the motor in question. Once engine speed exceeded motor speed, mechanical drive took over.

In response to demand from ground-effects car designers in 1980, Cosworth introduced a new range of so-called 'slimline auxiliaries', moving everything as far forward as possible into the shadow of the car's monocoque out of the path of underbody air.

During the 1967 season Team Lotus's drivers began using 9500 rpm with relative impunity on their first DFVs, and only in face of Ferrari's new flat-12 cars in 1970 did serious DFV power development commence. Until that time it had offered the best all-round power/reliability/consumption/installation package since its inception in Formula 1; only now – in relative terms – did it have to begin to work hard for its living.

Ports were enlarged, trumpets shortened, revs and power rose. Subsequent developments included detail mods to pistons and connecting rods, one major machining change on the bolt-seat area of the con-rod caps alone greatly reducing stress at that point and dramatically improving component life. The original forged steel con-rods were themselves superseded by a vacuum remelted fat forging. The requirement for high revs led to detail investigation of big-end bolts and adoption of modified thread forms therein, spreading the loads over more thread surface.

As the DFV's power output was forced ever higher through the late-Seventies by the attentions of Ferrari, and then the emergent turbo engines, ever-increasing attention had to be paid to relieve stress concentrations in every component of the faithful old DFV. Nevertheless, Cosworth kept abreast of the problem and, with the chassis designers' help, abreast of all competition until 1982 when the magnificent 15-year winning run of the DFV V8 engine finally reached the end of the road. For Cosworth Engineering, the greatest compliment that can be paid them is that they put a Grand Prix racing engine into quantity production and kept it at the top of the class for much more than a decade. The engine spun off variants which won the 24-Hour race at Le Mans in addition to other, lesser sports car endurance events, and also came to dominate high-speed oval-track racing in the USA.

Emerson Fittipaldi's works Lotus 72 notched the DFV's 50th Grand Prix victory in Spain in 1973, while Jody Scheckter's Wolf took the engine past the 100 mark at Monaco in 1977. It was fitting that Elio de Angelis's works Lotus should just scrape home by mere inches to win the 1982 Austrian GP from Keke Rosberg's hard-charging Williams-DFV, to achieve the engine's 150th *Grande Epreuve* victory, the last one that project catalyst Colin Chapman would see.

With that victory the faith which he had shown in Keith Duckworth and his fine company way back in 1965-66 had been more than merely repaid.

At the end of that season, despite the failure of fairly concentrated efforts to have the 2.0 equivalency factor changed between atmospherically aspirated and turbocharged F1 engines, there was still sufficient demand for Cosworth to embark upon a major modification of the V8 engine.

Throughout the major part of the DFV's life, Cosworth's licensed outside engine rebuilders, like John Judd's Engine Developments concern in Rugby, Nicholson-McLaren at Hounslow and Hesketh at Towcester, had built their own

preferred tweaks into their engines, often aiming to improve cam profiles compared to Cosworth's age-old standard 'DA1' design.

Now, going into 1983, Cosworth offered an experimental design known as the 'DA12', offering 0.460-in. lift compared to the DA1's standard 0.410-in., with slightly steeper slope angle to make the valves open more rapidly. This DA12 went into production and some of the outside specialists then switched from their own designs back to the Cosworth product.

In Northampton, Keith Duckworth now re-examined the aerodynamic performance or 'windage' within the DFV crankcase in order to improve oil scavenging still further and reduce power loss. He found that oil was not being collected as intended and when redesigned collection slots were provided oil collection improved markedly, releasing several extra horsepower.

In parallel with this development, a new short-stroke version of the V8 engine to be known as the DFY was being designed. Two DFY programmes were in hand. To accommodate the largest possible valve area the 90 mm bore of the derivative 3.95-litre DFL long-distance sports car engine was adopted, and this was combined with a piston stroke of 58.8 mm for 2994 cc.

The initial DFYs emerged using cylinder heads broadly similar to DFV practice although recast to a new and distinctive design. Inlet and exhaust ports were enlarged and the head design enabled use of the 1.25-in. exhaust valves as fitted in later DFVs, but now the inlet valve size was also increased to 1.42 in.

These early DFYs used 0.432-in. lift 'BD4' inlet camshafts and 'DA10', 0.410-in. lift exhausts, valve angle being 16 degrees. With the latest head and crankcase mods the ultimate DFV version matched this initial DFY. The DFY added a shorter exhaust system and intake trumpets, and new magnesium inlet manifold and water pump plus various head modifications reduced overall weight from the 351 lb of the definitive DFV to only 307 lb, which wasn't bad with some 520 bhp available.

The first four DFYs were delivered to McLaren and the Williams team just in time for the 1983 French GP. The second DFY head design should have been available in time for Monaco that year. This was a completely new and entirely different design saving even more weight while offering greater long-term development potential. Cosworth's newly enlarged development team concluded that certain advantages were available from a more compact combustion chamber shape than was

End of the line – for the 155th time a Cosworth-Ford V8 engine wins a World Championship Grand Prix as Alboreto acknowledges the chequered flag ending the 1983 Detroit GP, appropriately enough on Ford Motor Company's home ground. Tyrrell 012-DFY was just enough machine to do the job that day.

possible with the basic DFY's short-stroke dimensions and the 16-degree valve angle.

Consequently this second DFY head disposed its inlet valves at 10 degrees and its exhausts at 12.5 degrees. This narrow-angle DFY head also featured an integral instead of separate cam carrier, contributing to a further 15 lb saving in weight, penetrating the 300 lb barrier for the first time and achieving a record low of 292 lb.

Valve diameters became 36.5 mm inlets and 32 mm exhausts, seating on bronze inserts and using inverted bucket tappets. A new forged-steel flat-plane crankshaft was employed; its shorter throw and the use of four instead of eight counter-weights saved much weight. New enlarged-bore aluminium pistons were carried on 3 mm longer H-section machined forged-steel con-rods. Each new head assembly saved some 3.5 kg (7.6 lb) over the DFV's. Ports were enlarged and revised and, still using Lucas injection and ignition, the power curve was improved virtually throughout the range, as was torque. The old torque surge around 6500 rpm was no more and now the DFY offered useable power right from 6000 rpm to the unchanged limit of 11,300 rpm. The reduced stroke cut piston speed and acceleration, minimized valve-gear inertia and promoted quicker valve opening. Greater efficiency reduced the DFY's fuel consumption increase relative to gains in power and torque.

Although the short-stroke DFV and the definitive narrow-angle valved DFY both became known as 'DFYs', only seven of these true engines were built (for Tyrrell). This number was reduced to six as late as the 1985 German GP (the British V8's last World Championship race) when one blew up and was deemed to be beyond salvage.

During the DFV/DFY engines' long reign in Formula 1, some 382 of the V8s had been built.

Tyrrell's win at Detroit that year was Cosworth's 155th at World Championship level. The engine which had revolutionized Formula 1 by opening it up to so many specialist constructors and teams had finally reached the end of the road.

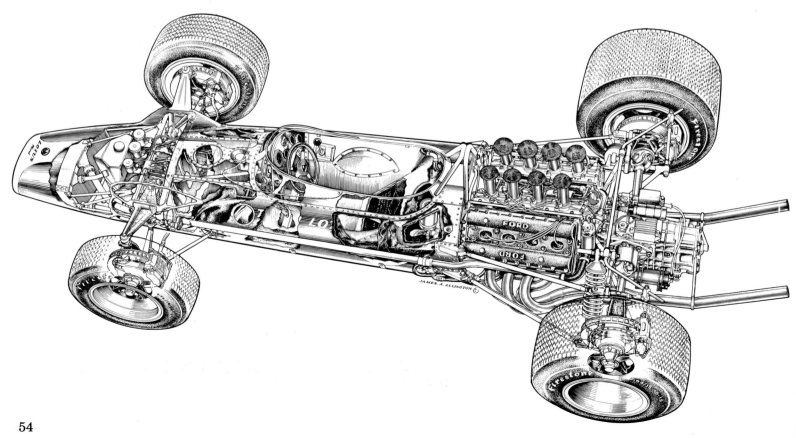

Chapter 4

THE LOTUS-COSWORTH FORD DFV TYPE 49 1967-70

James Allington's artistry X-rays the first pair of Lotus 49s built in 1967, later cars from chassis 'R3 replacing the round scuttle-top hatch shown here with a rectangular type. Note also original heavily vented brake discs, shortly to be replaced by solids, and ignition units on tray above gearbox, also soon re-sited within engine vee. The ZF transaxle-cheek stiffening plates shown were fitted from the British GP. The bumper bars protruding from the gearbox tail-plate which were necessary only to make the tuned-length exhaust overhang legal have been omitted, so this is actually an illegal F1 Lotus. However, in 1967 serious protests were unheard of, a 'quiet word' being order of the day.

While Keith Duckworth, Mike Costin, Mike Hall and the Cosworth Engineering men were working on Ford's new Grand Prix engine, Team Lotus at Potash Lane, Hethel, in darkest Norfolk were finalizing detail design of their beautifully integrated Type 49 car intended to carry the new engine.

Lotus had made do through 1966 first with nimble little 2-litre V8 cars using specially modified Climax and BRM engines left over from the 1500 cc Formula. They had 3-litre BRM H16 engines on order which BRM's Chief Engineer Tony Rudd had designed to be attached to the rear closing bulkhead of a truncated monocoque forward nacelle in similar manner to the forthcoming DFV. Even earlier, the Type 39 Lotus designed by Maurice Phillippe to carry the still-born flat-16 Climax engine in 1965 would have used something close to this system, although that engine would have been steadied by aviation-style perforated angle-beams on either side.

There were two distinct Lotus monocoque chassis made for BRM's H16 engines. One was the Type 42 intended for the still-born 4.2-litre Indianapolis engine, and the other 'our' Type 43 for 3-litre Formula 1. Both used what was known at that time as 'full monocoque' construction, in that the stressed-skin scuttle sections completely encircled the driver's legs, while there was also a complete 360-degree stressed-skin fuel tank section behind his shoulders. The Formula 1 car was handicapped by the unreliability and gearchange difficulties which afflicted the BRM engine, until the US GP at Watkins Glen in October 1966, where Jim Clark's mechanical sensitivity actually managed to nurse the thing to the finish in first place using the BRM works team's spare H16 engine after Lotus's own had broken conclusively in practice.

The 43s were last driven in anger by Clark and his new team-mate Graham Hill in the 1967 South African GP. Two-litre V8s were used at Monaco and then came the Dutch GP at Zandvoort on 4 June 1967 and the stunning debut of the new DFV-powered Lotus 49s.

Colin Chapman had specified 'a simple car which wouldn't give us any problems, so we could sort out the engine' and it emerged as a very simple, essentially twin-boom, monocoque fuselage in general Type 42/43 style. There were full 360-degree stressed sections in the

scuttle and behind the cockpit. At the front there was a rectangular footbox built around suspension-supporting square-tube frames. The centre tank's sloping forward-bulkhead formed the driver's seat back, while the tub terminated in that tank's rear closing plate, against which the fully-stressed new engine snuggled up close.

This tub was skinned in 18-gauge L72 Alclad aluminium-alloy sheet shaped over internal mild-steel bulkheads to which the skins were riveted. The side booms carried circular access hatches on the outer scuttle sides, while large indented hatches in the cockpit inner skins gave the drivers elbow room and opened onto the internal tank space into which 15-gallon FPT rubber fuel bags could be inserted, then 'poppered' into position and piped up.

These two side tanks drained through non-return valves into a 10-gallon capacity centre tank behind the driver. Fuel pick-up was from a pot in this tank's base, which topped up with fuel from the side cells as the car accelerated, fuel surge in the side bags washing through one-way valves into the centre tank.

A tiny circular access plate on top of the scuttle opened onto the pedal assembly for service and adjustment, while ahead of the footbox – which contained the steering rack – there was a vee-planform oil tank attached by rubber bungees, and a light tubular subframe supporting what by modern standards was an immensely heavy brass radiator with twin cores, one for water, one for oil.

A detachable glass-fibre nose cone, swept well down hopefully to minimize lift, clothed this area and was the only detachable body panel in the piece, the rear-mounted engine being left entirely naked and unashamed. Hot air exiting the radiator was deflected by the shape of the oil tank out through the front suspension cut-outs. The underside of the tub was stepped to form pipeways on both sides for oil and water feed to the engine, although the large-diameter water return pipe was completely external, slung high on the left-side of the tub.

Suspension accorded with familiar Lotus practice, using robust fabricated top rocker arms to actuate inboard coil-spring/damper units tucked well out of the airstream each side of the footbox. A fabricated lower link was jointed to a radius rod leading from an inboard pick-up buried well back on the hull. New cast uprights supported thick ventilated brake discs mounted well inboard of the Lotus cast-magnesium wheels and thus exposed to direct airflow. Anti-dive geometry was built into this suspension system.

At the rear, triangulated tubular frames provided inboard pick-ups on the cylinder heads, with a cross-beam offering lower mounts bolted beneath a tailor-made, very light but uprated ZF 5DS12 five-speed and reverse transmission. This incorporated elegant sliding-spline joints within its output shafts on each side. Colin enthused about how 'ZF did us a beautiful job on those'. Others connected with Team Lotus were less sure . . .

Suspension location featured the usual top links, reversed lower wishbones, twin radius rods feeding drive and braking torques into the monocoque's rear corners, and an anti-roll bar. The inclined outboard-mounting coil/damper units were ahead of the axle, and the massive brake callipers were behind it, front and rear, clasping those thick ventilated discs.

As always, Chapman's touch was evident in the detail. Everywhere there was only just enough car to do the job – there was nothing staggeringly innovative about any part of it. The 49 was never another 25, nor 72, nor 78/79, but Chapman had wanted a simple car sufficient to allow Team to race a brand new untried engine, and this was it.

Ford had sensibly been wary of bad publicity from making too much promotional fuss too soon before the engine had proved itself, so the DFV's introduction was muted, without any great razzmatazz.

The first of the five V8s planned for Team that season was handed over on 25 April 1967, two days after completion and five months after commencement of manufacture. The original target debut date of 7 May, for the Monaco GP, was postponed, and much more sensibly the two extant Lotus 49s made their classical debut at Zandvoort, as had the Type 25 before them and as would the four-wheel drive Type 63 two years later.

Of course that was a fairytale debut. Hill's pole position practice time was fully 4.2 per cent faster than the existing Zandvoort record, an astonishing margin. By the end of the first race lap Hill's prototype car 'R1' led Brabham's Repco BT24 by some 200 yards, with Clark – who had done little testing since tax considerations kept him out of the UK – finding his feet in 'R2' in sixth place. After 11 laps Hill's engine suffered its cam-gear failure, and Clark took utter command to win as he pleased.

In some ways this initial brilliant success flattered only to deceive, for Lotus reliability was dreadful through that mid-season. In performance terms, however, the 49-DFVs simply set new standards.

They were to take pole position for the next 11 consecutive Grands Prix, and while Hill often led races in his car it was always team-mate Clark's which would survive to win three more GPs; the British that July, and then after a long hiatus, the end-of-season US and Mexican events.

While Chapman himself professed delight with ZF's specially tailored gearbox, Duckworth and Costin were unconvinced, judging it to be under-engineered for the job in hand. The French GP on the little Circuit Bugatti at Le Mans saw savage transmission torque reversals engendered by the stop-go racing there, causing casing flexure and crown-wheel and pinion failures which lost the Lotuses a dominant 1-2 lead, Hill's final-drive shattering after 14 laps and Clark's after 23.

The perceived advantage of the ZF transmission had been that it was considerably lighter than the alternative Hewland 'bunch of old mangle-gears', as Colin would affectionately dismiss them, then being used by most of the opposition. The Circuit Bugatti disaster, however, brought immediate ZF modification,

with massive cross-bolted side plates being fitted as a temporary (British GP-winning) expedient before ZF came up with entirely redesigned – and inevitably heavier – casings. Thus one advantage over the bunch of old mangle gears was immediately forfeit.

More seriously, the ZF gearboxes had always featured fixed intermediate ratios and final-drives, so ratios could only be changed by near-total strip-down which was both time consuming and ill-advised in the often spartan and dusty race paddocks of those days. Ever since Team had first adopted ZF transmissions with their Type 21 car of 1961, they had taken a selection of ready-assembled 'boxes to each race to have a choice of final-drive and intermediate ratios. With the DFV's abrupt torque characteristics, Team was learning its circuits anew. The disadvantages of the ZF gearboxes could no longer be borne. Early in 1968 Hewland's easily gutted, omni-adjustable quick-ratio-change gearbox was adopted.

The original heavily ventilated brake discs were quickly abandoned since they over-cooled and glazed their brake pads, the pad losing its bite thereafter. Softer pad materials had been tried before thin solid discs offering more consistent temperatures were adopted.

The strength of those tapered front suspen-

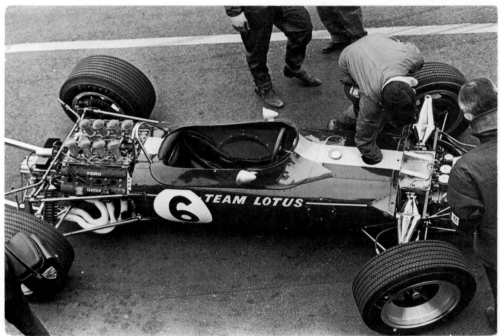

Top, *Colin Chapman and Jimmy Clark discuss their new toy at Zandvoort '67. Above, the object of their conversation, the Lotus 49, was merely a simple trouble-free 'bracket' to carry engine and suspension, fuel and driver. The external oil-drain boxes necessary on the earliest DFVs are visible on that right-side exhaust cambox. Engine comprises rear of chassis structure, supporting gearbox and rear suspension.*

sion top rocker arms proved suspect and they were strengthened twice, after the British GP and – surprise, surprise! – after the German race over the humps and bumps at the Nürburgring. Hill had led the British race at Silverstone until a rear suspension Allen screw worked loose and fell out, allowing one rear wheel to flop against the top rocker arm. Graham limped into the pits where the suspension link was put back in place and a fresh bolt wound home. After rejoining the race and tearing back through the field, his DFV engine blew up.

He was using a brand new 49, chassis 'R3', which had been frantically built up in an overnight panic after regular car 'R2' had damaged itself severely in practice due to another suspension failure. In the overnight construction panic at Hethel that vital Allen screw could not have been tightened adequately. The driver's comment in the paddock afterwards, 'Yeah – bugger innit', spoke volumes for the patience a World class driver can show when he knows that despite tribulation his is the dominant car of its time.

This third 49, 'R3', differed from its predecessors in that the tightly confined circular scuttle hatch opening onto the pedals in the first two cars had now been replaced by a much larger and more practical rectangular hatch, the side torsion boxes in this area being strengthened to compensate for the larger cut-out by inclusion of two extra internal bulkheads. Their inclusion meant shortening the main pontoon bag tanks, then adding two additional small-capacity bags ahead of these new scuttle bulkheads. All subsequent 49 tubs were built – or rebuilt – to this general structural form, though further modifications were made.

The top-link mount which had given trouble in the Silverstone incident was twice modified to prevent any recurrence of the fixing loss, and rear radius rod pick-ups on the monocoques were also reinforced – I have to say, from personal experience of having overseen restoration of 'R3', very crudely.

At the end of that first season stronger rear suspension subframes were adopted, bolting as they did onto the rear of the DFV engine heads and block.

Money availability has always dictated much of Formula 1 racing's technical development. At the 1967 London Motor Show the Esso oil company confirmed rumours that they were ending their motor racing sponsorship. Esso had been Team Lotus's financial mainstay for many years. Now Chapman's men beat the bushes for a replacement sponsor, and they came up with the Nottingham-based John Player tobacco company. Gold Leaf Team Lotus was born and, following their lead,

Fairytale debut – Clark catches an incipient power slide out of the Hunzerug *on his way to winning the 1967 Dutch GP in Lotus 49 'R2, learning all about the new DFV's wicked power characteristics. Note neat cast front uprights and hefty top rocker arms.*

national-colour Formula 1 racing teams would, apart from Ferrari, become a matter of history.

The fourth Lotus 49, 'R4', appeared for the South African GP opening the 1968 season and Clark promptly won in it to surpass Fangio's career record of 24 *Grande Epreuve* victories, setting the new record at 25. This race saw the first DFV engine appearance in another customer's hands as Ken Tyrrell's Equipe Matra International fielded its driver Jackie Stewart in a hybrid Matra-DFV special, and it initially led the race before Clark went ahead.

Special 2.5-litre versions of the DFV engine, known as the Cosworth-Ford DFW, were made for the Tasman Championship races in New Zealand and Australia from January to March that season, and 49s 'R1' and 'R2' were fitted with these units as 'Type 49T' cars, Clark contesting the entire series while Hill joined him in the Australian events. During their New Zealand tour, the Team mechanics experimented with a silly idea – taking a scrap section of helicopter rotor blade, and mounting it on the tail of Clark's car to add aerodynamic download . . . Young Gianni Marelli, the Ferrari engineer caring for Chris Amon's Ferrari 246T V6 during that race-series, was fascinated by what most regarded as a Lotus 'try-on' and he photographed the device assiduously from every angle.

On 7 April 1968, Clark was killed in a piddling little Formula 2 race at Hockenheim. His passing marked for many the end of the sporting era of Grand Prix racing. This may well be true by pure coincidence, but from here on it became the highly commercialized big-business promotional 'front' which we know and perhaps simply try to ignore today. Irrespective of anyone's personal prejudice, commercial sponsorship could now support more teams interested in Formula 1 than ever before. The best-funded teams could also indulge in experimentation of a type only previously accessible to major industry.

During the early months of 1968 Team's experience with new-generation, ever wider tread Firestone tyres indicated that a more rearward weight bias would be advantageous.

As tyre contact patches increased in size so loadings had decreased. Instead of finding greater traction with wider tyres, drivers found that in other than the most ideal track conditions these lighter-loaded tyres were more prone to slip and slide. The answer was obviously to load them more heavily to compensate. An analogy is to think of the girl wearing stiletto heels whose weight thus concentrated can pierce flooring, whereas the same girl, same weight, in carpet slippers can glide effortlessly across that same surface.

Initially this extra rearward loading was achieved by running the brand new so-called 'B-spec' car 'R5' at the Race of Champions with a huge oil tank wrapped saddle-fashion over its gearbox, carrying a small oil cooler perched on top, thus relieving the nose radiator of oil-cooling duty. Wider deep-cone wheels were fitted to carry the latest generation Firestone tyres, suspension geometry being altered to suit by the adoption of new rear uprights with less projection above hub level, and lower top radius rod mountings. After this outing the new car was torn down to be comprehensively reworked as the true prototype Lotus 49B.

Here Chapman and Phillippe lengthened the wheelbase by raking the front suspension arms 3 in. forward to put more load on the car's rear end. To limit rear-wheel toe-steer, tunnels were sunk into the lower rear quarters of the monocoque tub, and the lower rear radius rod pick-ups were resited well forward in them, closer to the car's centreline axis. At the rear the engine still mounted in its classically simple fashion, while more substantial subframes on the back of it carried the rear suspension, oil tank and Hewland's latest 'bunch of old mangle-gears', the FG400. Now the DFV cylinder heads were relieved of carrying suspension loads direct.

The deep-cone cast-magnesium road wheels had grown from 8 in. to 10 in. wide front rims in the final two races of 1967, and now 12 in. wide fronts became standard with 15 in. diameters. The rear tyres were 15 in. wide across the shoulders and now presented such a major element in the car's overall frontal area that

Lotus's traditional frontal area parsimony now seemed futile. Ron Tauranac of Brabham had experimented with vestigial trim tabs and spoilers to improve the handling of his Repco-engined cars at Spa the previous year, and now Chapman and Phillippe had evolved their wedge-elevation Type 56B turbine cars for the continuous high-speed regime of Indianapolis. From this exercise the new Formula 1 Type 49B inherited as near a wedge profile as was possible with a nose-mounted radiator.

The nose cone itself was largely unchanged, but a cuneiform glass-fibre engine and gearbox cowl was now adopted, incorporating a deck-top NACA duct feeding an oil cooler matrix buried beneath. Its expended air then exited through a vent in the cowl's rear transom. Whatever download this tail cowl hopefully imparted was trimmed-out by a pair of airfoil-section fins or dive-planes projecting either side of the nose cone, so that the total download now acted about the car's centre of gravity.

Hill had won the Spanish GP at Jarama in face of mechanical mayhem amongst meagre opposition to notch the final success of the definitive original Lotus 49 (actually using prototype/ex-Tasman chassis 'R1') and now at Monaco in the rebuilt 49B 'R5' he won another race most notable for a staggeringly high rate of attrition. His new team-mate Jack Oliver made an inauspicious debut by destroying 'R1' early in the race. Back home the wreck was stripped and rebuilt as a new 49B which would be numbered, in sequence at that time, 'R9'.

This 'salvage and restore' policy became standard practice at Potash Lane, accounting for the nine Type 49 'entities' using 12 individual chassis numbers in their time.

The semi-wedge 49Bs ran two more races only, as more ambitious aerofoil aids were on the way. At Spa, where Oliver appeared in brand new 49B 'R6', strutted chassis-mounted rear aerofoil aids had appeared on Ferrari and Brabham cars, their effect balanced by trim vanes on the nose cones. Chapman was to take this new ploy further than most, his Lotus 49Bs progressively developing wings which were taller, wider and more powerful than the opposition's and his drivers became test pilots penetrating the unknown as surely as had the Dukes, Yeagers and Lippitsches of aviation history.

For the 1968 French GP at Rouen-les-Essarts, Team emerged with its 49Bs carrying strutted aerofoils acting direct upon the rear suspension uprights to convert maximum download into pure traction. Colin estimated 400 lb download at 150 mph, but in practice Jack Oliver edged his new 49B 'R6' into another car's slipstream on the rush towards the pits and the winged Lotus simply slithered away from under him and smashed into a brick gate-post alongside the track at around 140 mph. The left-hand side of the tub deformed grotesquely under impact, absorbing the shock and enabling Oliver to emerge understandably shaken but unscathed, while the gearbox and both rear suspensions were torn bodily off the engine.

This incident simultaneously demonstrated the dangers of toying with aerodynamic forces which were not yet properly understood, and the remarkable strength of the modern monocoque single-seat chassis. We should also remember that these were pre-seat belt days. Retention harnesses would not become mandatory until the following season, 1969.

These new wings were increasing drive-line loadings quite dramatically. The introduction of Firestone's sticky Y-construction, B11-compound tyres aggravated the problem, removing a vital element of slippage or drive-line cushioning which condemned many a halfshaft UJ, and occasionally the shafts themselves, to traumatic failure.

Heavier shafts were fitted, Mercedes-splined on the first 49Bs, and a succession of ever-stronger BRD and Hardy-Spicer joints followed

Graham Hill in the German GPs of 1967 and '68. Top, 'R3 in the Karussel, *suspension thoroughly loaded. Above, 49B 'R5 in GLTL livery '68, also in the* Karussel, *showing off upright-mounted rear wing and nose 'foils, swept-forward front suspension, longer lower-rear radius rods tunnelled into tub side, and tail-mounted oil tank. Right, Hill won the '68 Monaco GP in 'R5.*

until finally, for the 1968 US and Mexican GPs, the first Lohr & Bromkamp 'Lobro' plunging CV joints were adopted. They proved capable both of accepting the DFV engine's savage torque and the extremes of suspension movement which the Lotuses required.

Lotus 49B 'R7' appeared new for Rob Walker's private team at the British GP in July 1968, where Jo Siffert promptly won with it. The team had begun the season with ex-49T 'R2' on loan. Siffert crashed it at Brands Hatch in practice for the Race of Champions upon its Walker debut. It was destroyed by fire while being stripped prior to repair.

In March 1969, strutted airfoil aids doubled-up, fore and aft, acting on both front and rear suspension uprights. Some called this a biplane arrangement, but 'biplane' to me suggests Sopwith Camels and De Havilland Tiger Moth-style arrangements with one wing above the other. Hence my use of the term 'bi-wing' elsewhere in this volume to describe cars with full-width aerofoils at both front and rear.

Passive mounts, with the wing incidence pre-set on assembly, or by adjustment when stationary, were normal; however, in Mexico City in the Championship decider of 1968 – which Hill and Lotus won – a feathering rear wing was employed. This was actuated by a fourth foot pedal to the left of the clutch, on which the driver would park his foot along the straight, a Bowden cable feathering the rear aerofoil into a neutral position to minimize drag. Entering corners the driver would move his foot onto the clutch, releasing the wing pedal; bungee cords in tension yanked the aerofoil down into its maximum attack angle, adding drag to help slow the car and download to assist traction away from the turn.

At Barcelona, for the Spanish GP on 4 May 1969, the two works 49Bs for Hill and Rindt wore the largest, tallest, widest wings yet. They were skinned in aluminium over too few section formers and their mid-span surfaces were unbraced. The struts themselves had been adequately stressed to accept compression loads but could not handle negative loading as the cars 'fell away' from beneath them over the Montjuich Park circuit's notorious hump beyond the pits. Both Hill's and Rindt's cars suffered horrendous accidents due to wing collapses at this point. Graham's already once-rebuilt 'R6' would be rebuilt again but Jochen's horribly mangled 'R9' from which he emerged without serious harm, was fit only for the scrapman's skip.

This spectacular incident demanded action from the CSI and in the middle of practice for the very next GP, at Monaco, they announced a peremptory wing ban pending adequate definition of permissible aerodynamic aids. The teams fudged temporary expedient devices to see them through that street race, such as semi-wedge gearbox covers fashioned from the interior panelling of the Team Lotus transporter on the 49Bs, while the nose vanes remained

unaffected.

There was a new B-spec car 'R10' there for Hill, Rindt's destroyed 'R9' having made its debut in the South African GP right at the start of the season, where it had been accompanied by another new 49B, 'R11', driven by guest driver Mario Andretti. This car 'R11' would be sold immediately thereafter to American privateer Pete Lovely, who still owns it at the time of writing today.

At Monaco, Hill's stand-in team-mate Richard Attwood – deputizing for the injured Rindt – drove an old-style car. After the grievous damage to 'R6' and the loss of 'R9' this was actually a 49T with right-angle front suspension, being chassis 'R8' built specifically for Hill's use in the Tasman Championship the preceding winter. It had just returned from Australia buried under tons of rotting fruit in a delayed freighter, and the Lotus mechanics had hastily burrowed down to it upon their return from Barcelona and prepared it just in time to leave for Monte Carlo!

After the Barcelona upset and the sudden wing regulation change, Hill emerged to win his fifth Monaco GP, his second in a row in a Lotus 49B, the Swiss driver Jo Siffert was third in Rob Walker's private 49B 'R7' and Attwood was fourth in his old nail, having set fastest race lap.

Now at Monaco, relieved of those wing loadings the 49s had emerged as case-hardened warhorses, strong and robust. For those who would still rubbish Lotus as manufacturers of fragile Grand Prix cars, Monaco 1969 proved a salutary lesson.

As already described, the CSI's new wing regulations were applied in time for the next Grand Prix race, at Zandvoort, imposing limits of 80 cm (31.50 in.) height above the underside of the car and 110 cm (43.31 in.) width overall behind the rear axle line. That Dutch GP witnessed internecine Lotus warfare between

Below, the truncated Lotus 49 monocoque was an essentially simple riveted sheet aluminium affair with a square-tube framed sheet footbox, stepped underside to provide pipeways and front suspension bottom pick-up braced by that tube-stay up front.

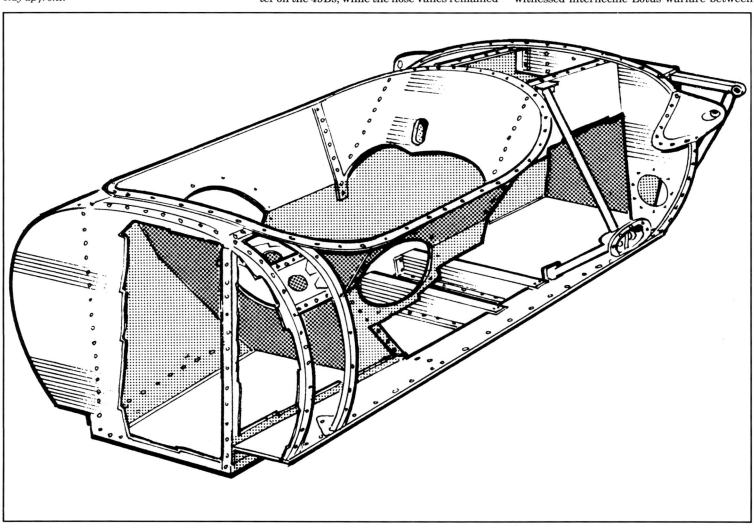

Hill and the recovered Rindt, and through the rest of that season the abrasive and outspoken Austrian established himself as much the faster of the two. The season saw some terrific battles between his Lotus 49B and the dominant World Championship-winning Matra MS80 of Jackie Stewart which we shall study shortly (see Chapter 5).

Team Lotus effort was split that season by the debut of their Type 63 four-wheel drive cars, and Chapman tried desperately hard to persuade his drivers to take the new model seriously, rather than concentrate upon their proven but now ageing 49Bs in their hunger to accumulate World Championship points. To force the issue he sold 49Bs 'R8' and 'R9' respectively to Jo Bonnier and to John Love in South Africa (who already had old 'R3'), leaving Team with only 'R6' in its umpteenth incarnation and the two 4WD Type 63s. For the British GP meeting at Silverstone Team's joint number one drivers complained bitterly about this move and Chapman was forced to relent, Bonnier's car being retrieved for Hill while Rindt took 'R6'. Bonnier was put into one Type 63 'on loan' to keep him sweet as possible – which was not a lot – and cadet works driver John Miles took over the other 4WD car.

The John Love sale was rescinded as the 4WDs failed to show any form, and Rindt eventually notched his long-awaited first Grand Prix victory at Watkins Glen that season, driving 'R6' while Hill crashed 'R10' heavily and did himself serious injury when a tyre deflated. He had spun and stalled, push-started the car and drove on without being able to refasten his now compulsory seat belts.

So Team Lotus's third season with the 49s ended with two more GP victories to their credit, but their World titles had gone to Matra-DFV and to Jackie Stewart.

Now the Type 49s had run far beyond their expected life due to the failure of the intended replacement Type 63s. They had only ever been

intended as short-term expedient cars in which the new Cosworth-Ford DFV engine could be proven, but learning first about the new age of aerodynamic aids and then the complex demands of the 4WD programme had prevented early development of an adequate replacement.

The cars were notorious for their fuel-system problems – repeatedly failing to scavenge the last few gallons from their now multiple bag tanks – and also for roasting their drivers with hot air from that nose-mounted radiator filling footbox and cockpit and heating the foot pedals.

In a determined effort to improve cooling and aerodynamic performance, top-ducted radiators had been adopted in time for the Italian GP, lipped and ramped vents in the top of the nose cone funnelling expended radiator air upwards along each side of the screen enclosure instead of 'hopefully' outwards low down on either side as before. The cars were improved but it was not a complete answer to the cockpit cooling question.

Add to these troubles the fierce, often instrument-wrecking natural vibration of the DFV engine and you have some idea of the conditions which those drivers endured.

The 49s were prone to marked pitch-down and tail-light wandering under braking – this being a trait which Siffert in particular enjoyed exploiting to the full when running in close company. He won himself the title 'Last of the Late-Brakers' and few friends amongst his fellow drivers by demonstrating the art at too close quarters.

Certainly the 49 was far from perfect, but it still had another season left in it . . .

Early in 1970, development of the latest Chapman-Phillippe two-wheel drive replacement car was lagging behind, and the old 49Bs were reworked yet again. Firestone developed a new 13 in. front tyre and four 49Bs – works team chassis 'R6', 'R8' and the freshly reincarnated 'R10', plus Walker's veteran 'R7' – were

Roll, bowl or pitch? The 49s were prone to pitch and squat and Rindt's 49B is in characteristic pose during the 1969 British GP. Those GRP nose cones rapidly wore through underneath. Here 'R6' displays state-of-the-art Firestone tyre sizes, top-ducted finned nose and end-plated rear wing.

modified accordingly with new front uprights and front suspension geometry to accept 13 in. front wheels. These four cars were redesignated Lotus 49Cs. Meanwhile one final 49B had been built up as a display car for Ford of Britain, finished in GLTL livery and numbered 'R12'. It would not be used in anger.

Rindt was joined by Miles in the works team, while the barely-recovered Graham Hill entered the twilight of his honoured career in Siffert's place with Walker. The old cars proved remarkably competitive until the startling new Type 72 made its debut, and when the new wedge-shaped car required an early partial redesign the works 49Cs were dusted down for a final frontline World Championship outing at Monaco. There Rindt triumphed over his own disinterest after stroking sulkily around until half-distance. Realizing he was in with a chance he took victory on the final corner of the final lap as race leader Jack Brabham made a rare mistake and slid off the road.

In the end, as late as April 1971, Tony Trimmer drove Rindt's Monaco-winning car – faithful old 'R6', which had had such a long racing history – in the Good Friday Oulton Park International. He damaged the car in a practice crash, and it was hurriedly repaired with parts cannibalized from 'R10' which fortunately happened to be on display in a garage not far away at Bradford. Yes, it was just like old times . . . Team Lotus in a last-minute panic.

Trimmer survived a pit stop and finished a distant sixth, four laps behind Rodriguez's winning BRM V12. It was the end of a classic Grand Prix design's International career.

Monocoque Chassis

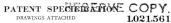
When Colin Chapman and Team Lotus successfully introduced 'monocoque' chassis to Formula 1 with their 1962 Type 25 they set new standards of weight:stiffness and set a new trend.

For 50 years monocoque construction had been standard practice in aviation. Credit for its introduction may go to Frederick Handley-Page for his aircraft shown at London's Olympia exhibition hall in 1911, or to Ruchonnet in France, but it was another French designer, Louis Béchereau, who produced the first streamlined fuselage deriving its stiffness and strength from its load-bearing stressed skin. Béchereau's Deperdussin racer of 1912 featured a skin formed from three 1.5 mm laminations of tulip-wood veneer glued together around a former. When cured, the structure was inherently rigid without internal framing. It was like an eggshell. Hence the nickname 'monocoque' was coined, mongrelized from the Greek *monos* and Latin *coccum* — 'single-shell'.

As early as 1915 a monocoque Cornelian light car raced at Indianapolis. In 1923 Gabriel Voisin built near-monocoques for the French GP, and in the UK around World War 2 Alec Issigonis and Laurie Bond both built monocoque sprint cars. Tom Killeen produced his monocoque-fuselage sports car for the early-1950s, Jaguar's famous D-Type used a stressed-skin monocoque centre-section with tube-frame engine bay, and the 1955-57 BRM P25s were part monocoque, using structural body-panelling around the cockpit opening. The lads at Bourne christened them the 'over-stressed skin specials'. They were light, stiff and very fast, but accessibility was 'barstorial'.

Six years later, Lotus tests with the prototype backbone-chassis Elan proved this structure immensely rigid for its weight. In planning lunches at a local Cheshunt restaurant Colin Chapman literally sketched on a table napkin his original scheme to apply a backbone chassis to a single-seater.

'I thought "Why not space the sides of the backbone far enough apart for a driver to sit between?" If we made the sides of the backbone as box-sections we could carry fuel inside them in rubber bags . . .'

So the Lotus 25 evolved, not a single-shell at all but instead two parallel D-section stressed-skin torsion boxes linked by bulkheads and a stressed-sheet floor panel, the open top being closed by clip-on glassfibre body panelling. The 25/33 series tubs weighed around 70 lb, and with engine installed offered torsional stiffness around 2400 lb/ft per degree deflection along their length. This should be compared to around 1000 lb/ft per degree for a contemporary spaceframe chassis.

Tony Rudd and BRM then improved this open 'bath-tub monocoque' with fully-enclosing 360-degree panelling fore and aft of the cockpit in their 1963 P61 and 1964 P261 designs, while Forghieri of Ferrari developed their 'Aero' hybrid monocoque with stressed panels stiffening a sketchy internal tube-frame in 1963.

Chapman associate Len Terry produced a definitive full monocoque design in his superb Indianapolis-winning Lotus 38 and its Gurney-Eagle descendants. For 1966, it was Rudd and BRM again who developed the truncated three-quarter-length monocoque chassis which terminated just behind the cockpit in a bulkhead to which a fully-stressed structural engine could be attached to support major rear suspension loads. Ferrari had supported their 1965 flat-12 engine in broadly similar manner on a 1965 truncated 'Aero' tub.

Robin Herd's 'Mallite' McLaren aluminium-balsa sandwich tub of 1966 attained unheard-of rigidity, around 11,000 lb/ft per degree, approximately three times stiffer than any preceding single-seater and better than some unitary-shelled production saloons.

Another Chapman designer/disciple Maurice Phillippe followed suit with the Lotus 49 of 1967, Maurice being an ex-de Havilland aviation engineer who had built his own monocoque-chassis MPS sports-racing car as early as 1955.

1968 saw Bernard Boyer of Matra introduce a more rigid highly subdivided monocoque carrying its fuel direct in spray-sealed side boxes, without bag tanks. Regulation changes for 1970 effectively made rubber-bagged monocoques *de rigueur* in Formula 1, Brabham being the last refuge of the multi-tubular spaceframe.

In 1968, Honda had suspended their air-cooled V8 from a high-level projecting rear monocoque horn and two years later Ferrari adopted this idea in their supreme flat-12 312B package.

From 1973, deformable structure tank protection measures saw McLaren's adoption of integral foam-packed moulded GRP hip radiator ducts to form the most complex monocoques yet. From 1976 Gordon Coppuck made extensive use of aerospace honeycomb

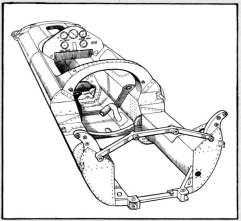

Below, *sketch showing Colin Chapman's Lotus 25-style twin-pontoon monocoque, drawn to accompany his original Patent Specification*

lightweight panelling in his McLaren M26 design, and from 1978 Gordon Murray of Brabham began to use carbon-composite structural top panels in his otherwise sheet aluminium BT48-Alfa Romeo cars.

Ground-effect aerodynamics demanded ever-slimmer monocoques. The problem then was to achieve adequate stiffness despite the reduction in beam cross-section.

The 1977 Lotus 78s co-devised by Ralph Bellamy, Martin Ogilvie, Peter Wright and Tony Rudd under the Chapman umbrella used aerospace aluminium honeycomb. Harvey Postlethwaite then popularized folded aluminium honeycomb sheet tub construction in his 1978 Wolf which begat the standard-setting Patrick Head-designed Williams FW07 of 1979-81.

Stiffness to resist ground-effect aerodynamic and suspension loads was still desperately needed. By 1979-80 torsional tests of new honeycomb and aluminium tubs commonly returned figures around 4500-5000 lb/ft per degree. With use this could fall to 3500 lb/ft, or less. Carbon fibre and composite moulding held the answer.

Peter Wright, the Lotus boffin so often mentioned in these pages, led Team this way, their Type 88 of 1981 being beaten to its public introduction by John Barnard's McLaren MP4/1. The essential difference was that the Lotus tub was built-up from numerous flat pre-cut composite panels, using the new material virtually as 'black aluminium', while McLaren tubs were true aerospace integral mouldings. Moulded-composite tubs into 1984 commonly returned 12,000-15,000 lb/ft per degree in torsional testing, and maintained it.

Yet into the mid-Eighties Brabham again became the last frontline refuge of an 'outdated' technology for their own excellent reasons, and still achieved Mallite McLaren-standard rigidity, I assume from Gordon's tacit nod, despite retaining sheet aluminium outer tubs. Meanwhile, his rivals adopted moulded carbon-composites, albeit tentatively in that until they gained experience they did not fully exploit their full weight-saving potential.

With the flat-bottom regulations of 1983, Gordon Murray and David North introduced a new form of 'modular' construction in their BT52, mounting the entire front suspension, steering etc. as a sub-assembly on a one-piece aluminium front bulkhead machined from the solid, which in turn was inserted into the nose of a folded aluminium sheet – not honeycomb – outer tub. A complex moulded carbon-composite insert then stiffened the tub, forming scuttle top, cockpit accommodation, seat back and fuel tank top, a tall fully-machined aluminium bulkhead closing the tub at the rear where the BMW engine attached with its tube stays. The tailor-made Brabham gearbox casing then provided basis of the rearmost module, carrying major rear suspension elements. By juggling these ready-assembled modules the team could make rapid alterations or repairs in the field.

By the end of 1985, the Formula 1 car monocoque chassis had come a long way from Colin Chapman's original British patent application No. 21977/62, dated 6 June 1962.

filed 6 September 1963 (top). Above left, *Cooper's catamaran-style tub, 1968.*

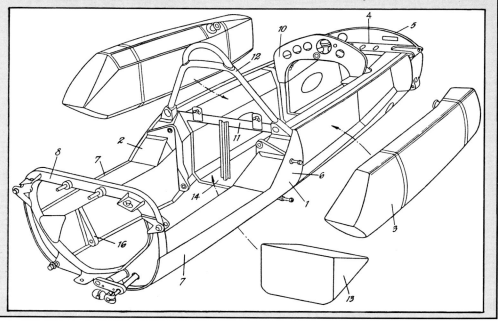

Chapter 5

MATRA'S MAGNIFICENT HYBRIDS 1968-69

In 1969 Jackie Stewart proved virtually invincible behind the wheel of his Ken Tyrrell-managed, DFV-powered Matra cars carrying the 'Equipe Matra International' banner.

The French company Engins Matra is essentially a major aerospace, missiles and arms manufacturer. It was founded prewar by Marcel Chassagny, under the name CAPRA, as an aeronautical engineering sub-contractor. In Vichy France in 1942, Chassagny changed the name to *Mécanique-Aviation-Traction,* which was soon abbreviated to 'Matra'.

Postwar, the French Government was desperate to keep in touch with American and British missile development. Chassagny tendered for and won numerous contracts and Engins Matra's fortune was founded.

Chassagny had a friend named René Bonnet who built minor-Formula racing cars in conjunction with an aerodynamicist named Charles Deutsch. Their Deutsch-Bonnet ('DB') range of single-seater and sports cars often featured in the teeny classes at Le Mans using Panhard engines, and Chassagny put some capital into their company to help his friend. Financier Sylvain Floirat acquired a major shareholding in Chassagny's Matra concern and contributed greatly to its development.

In 1961 Deutsch and Bonnet split, and Bonnet decided to continue alone building Renault-powered competition cars, followed by a sleek little road-going Coupé named the Djet. He had a tough time, however, and with Floirat now controlling Matra's purse-strings Chassagny's backing could not be guaranteed. Soon afterwards, *Automobiles René Bonnet* went to the wall.

Chassagny, however, was able to buy Bonnet's assets and so Matra found itself in the motor manufacturing business. An engaging and dynamic young executive named Jean-Luc Lagardère became general manager of this new division, which they named Matra Sports. He recognized immediately the importance of promoting an image which would make the newly rechristened Matra Djet cars appeal to the moneyed youth market then emerging as much in France as elsewhere in the West. He concluded that Matra should pursue an energetic sports policy, and in 1965 the first Formula 3 Matra *monoplace* appeared, based on Bonnet's exploratory monocoque experience.

Lagardère would brook no half measures. The René Bonnets with Renault engines had lacked the power to be competitive. Ford engines were dominant in the class, so Lagardère's F3 Matra used a British-made Ford engine . . . no compromise.

Matra historian Jabby Crombac has highlighted the pragmatic approach of the former René Bonnet design team responsible for this F3 car. They arrived at its wheelbase and track dimensions simply by averaging those of every British F3 car at the 1965 London Racing Car Show: we all have to start somewhere.

What was unusual about the new car was the uncompromising aerospace construction of its monocoque chassis, for whereas Lotus and Lola

in the UK were building stressed-skin punt-type tubs carrying their fuel within rubber bag tanks inserted into the box-section pontoons on either side of the cockpit, Matra's new F3 carried its fuel direct in sealed pontoons, without the bag tanks.

This technique offered a major advantage in that the interior of each pontoon could be punctuated by numerous lateral bulkheads, greatly enhancing its torsional rigidity. If bag tanks were to be used this would have involved as many as eight or ten individual bags per side. That would have involved nightmares of plumbing and the strength-robbing necessity of providing a separate access hatch for each bag to be inserted, serviced and removed. To ensure fuel tightness within this 'bagless' sheet aluminium structure, its inner surfaces were treated with polymer resin. Construction was time-consuming and fiddly, but Engins Matra as an aerospace concern already employed similar techniques and had a labour force skilled in this technology.

The result was one of the most torsionally rigid F3 chassis, which, when properly set up, offered its drivers a narrow handling advantage which could make all the difference in such a tightly regulated and competitive class.

But in 1965 the cars were not very impressive in their first few outings, until at Reims-Gueux during the July speed weekend works driver Jean-Pierre Beltoise scrambled across

Stewart's Dunlop-tyred Matra MS80-01 during the team's 1969 French GP 1-2 features all-outboard spring suspensions, top-ducted nose radiator, podgy centre-section tankage and neat rear wing/oil-cooler duct/engine cowl moulding.

the line first to win France's most charismatic F3 race of the season. The French enthusiast public was quite rightly elated. A race-winning new French-blue racing car had emerged after more than a decade in the doldrums.

Meanwhile during that season in Formula 2, the British quasi-works Cooper team had been run by Ken Tyrrell with little success. Their spaceframe chassis were by that time relatively uncompetitive while their 1-litre BRM P80 4-cylinder engines proved highly unreliable. Tyrrell's 1-litre Formula 3 Cooper-BMCs had dominated both French and British Championship racing the previous year when lead driver Jackie Stewart had shot to stardom.

By the end of that season Stewart had signed a works BRM Formula 1 contract for 1965, and this brought Tyrrell the Formula 2 BRM engines for the Coopers which Stewart drove between Grand Prix commitments to BRM.

It was at the end of this season that Tyrrell made the trip to Paris for the *Trophées de France* F2 series prize-giving function at BP France's headquarters. There, journalist Crombac introduced him to Lagardère of

Matra. He wanted his company to progress into F2 racing in 1966 but lacked the star name driver to make such an expensive step worthwhile. Now here was Tyrrell who had that driver. Stewart was to stay with BRM for Formula 1 through 1966-67, and their Formula 2 engine was being improved that winter, so Tyrrell would continue to use it in the coming year. Having now abandoned hope of Cooper producing a decent chassis Tyrrell was looking for a competitive replacement.

Over dinner at Orly, Lagardère agreed with Tyrrell to supply an F3 monocoque Matra chassis fitted with an F2 engine for Stewart's evaluation at Goodwood circuit in Sussex.

Sylvain Floirat ran a string of race horses and owned a Bristol Freighter aircraft specially equipped to zoom them around Europe. Now it was used to deliver the Matra test car to Gatwick Airport not too far from Goodwood. Stewart had his doubts about this rather ugly little 'Frogmobile' before driving it hard, yet he emerged fascinated and very impressed by its sheer traction. It really did work well, so Tyrrell ran Matra-BRM Formula 2 cars through that 1966 season.

As it happened, the Brabham team had a better solution to that last season of 1-litre Formula 2 racing, for they had exclusive use of the 16-valve Honda 4-cylinder power unit which left Cosworth's SCA and BRM's P80 gasping in its wake. The Brabhams used 'old-fashioned' spaceframes, but there was nothing that Stewart and the Matra's chassis could do about their horsepower.

A new 1600 cc Formula 2 took effect in 1967, and that season saw everybody of any significance using the new Cosworth FVA 4-cylinder engine. Stewart now achieved considerable success in his Tyrrell-run Matra-Cosworth MS7 cars, as did the French works team itself, with drivers like Henri Pescarolo, Jean-Pierre Beltoise and 'Johnny' Servoz-Gavin.

Meanwhile in France the Government had become interested in the prospect of retrieving lost national prestige in Grand Prix racing. The publicity surrounding Matra's exploits in Formula 3 and Formula 2 had attracted influential attention, and the time was right. A new state oil company had just been created, under the 'Elf' name – some attributing this title to 'Essence et Lubrificants Française', while the company merely credits it to a marketing man's invention.

Another analyst found that sponsorship of motor racing at all levels would promote Elf more effectively than any mere advertizing campaign employing less tangible devices. Elf therefore decided to back Matra in production of a Grand Prix car. These plans were finalized on 19 January 1967 at a meeting in Monte Carlo during the annual rally. Elf MD Jean Prada and Lagardère of Matra announced they would be co-operating technically and financially in design and development of an all-French GP car to be powered by a new V12 engine. Chief engine designer for Matra Sports was to be former Simca technician Georges Martin. Crombac tells how Martin saw a racing car for the first time in his life at that year's London Racing Car Show. They really were starting from scratch, but they had a lot of help.

In April that year the Government under Georges Pompidou announced a state grant of six million Francs – about £800,000 at that time – to assist the Matra Sports' Formula 1 programme. That June saw Ken Tyrrell present at the Dutch GP. He flew home determined to run Jackie Stewart in a Formula 1 car powered by one of these new engines in the coming season, 1968. The Scots star was very unhappy with his BRM Formula 1 equipment by that time and was not going to renew his contract with them. He had spent some very happy years with Tyrrell whose judgement and team he trusted implicitly, and he was willing to drive whatever halfway decent car Tyrrell could put under him in Formula 1. The only real opposition to Tyrrell's offer came from Ferrari, but that drive eventually went to a younger Tyrrell discovery – named Jacky Ickx . . .

Through that summer the ambitious Ken Tyrrell extracted a promise from Ford that he would indeed be able to purchase DFV engines for the coming season. Stewart agreed to join him for both Formula 1 and Formula 2, with the British Dunlop tyre company paying the bill. All Tyrrell lacked now was a suitable chassis. He approached Lagardère and Matra, and again the timing was perfect.

With taxpayer's money involved, and a lot of premature publicity promising great things for it, the Matra V12 engine was in danger of causing more trouble than it was worth unless it achieved early success. Nobody but an opposition politician has any use for a state-backed loser.

Now here was Ken Tyrrell with potentially the world's finest driver under contract, asking if a Matra chassis might be available to use what was obviously the outstanding proven engine in Formula 1. If Matra would build a car to carry it, any success this hybrid might achieve could certainly offset bad publicity should Matra's own engine develop problems.

So Tyrrell got his cars. A specially-modified version of the proposed V12 chassis would be produced to accommodate the British V8 engine, and Elf agreed to co-sponsor Tyrrell's new Formula 1 team which would operate under the name Equipe Matra International.

THE MATRA-COSWORTH F1 CARS
Tyrrell's first Formula 1 Matra was the MS9 test hack prototype. It used a Formula 2-type MS7 monocoque set up experimentally with fully adjustable suspension pick-up points to research systems proposed for the new V12 car.

At that time, in December 1967, Matra Sports' subsidiary long-distance team had already been campaigning 2-litre BRM V8-engined Coupés at Le Mans and other suitable events. The MS9 prototype was to have been tested with one of these V8s installed, but the Tyrrell deal was struck before the car had been completed and it was therefore modified to accept the fully-stressed DFV engine hung Lotus 49-style on the rear of its truncated forward monocoque nacelle. This tub naturally used Matra's successful multiple-bulkhead so-called 'structural' fuel tank design.

The F2 MS7s had carried their unstressed Cosworth FVA engines on two pontoon horns extending either side of the engine bay from the rear cockpit bulkhead. The forthcoming V12 car was to use this engine mounting, which helped dictate its eventual 60-degree vee angle which was chosen to keep it narrow overall.

The stressed-block Cosworth DFV engine needed no rear chassis horns to sit upon. But its use fully-stressed in Lotus 49-style meant that an engine-change in the field would necessitate removal and replacement of the suspension-supporting subframes on the rear of the engine. Matra's chassis designer Bernard Boyer felt he could save valuable resetting and brake bleeding time by including a lightweight tube frame extending from the monocoque's rear panel to a fabricated suspension pick-up diaphragm fitting round the gearbox. This device was not intended to accept suspension loads with the

*Opposite, the F2-derived Matra MS10-02 at
Nouveau Monde hairpin during the wet 1968
French GP, Rouen-les-Essarts. Matra were
surprisingly slow in developing aerodynamic aids.*

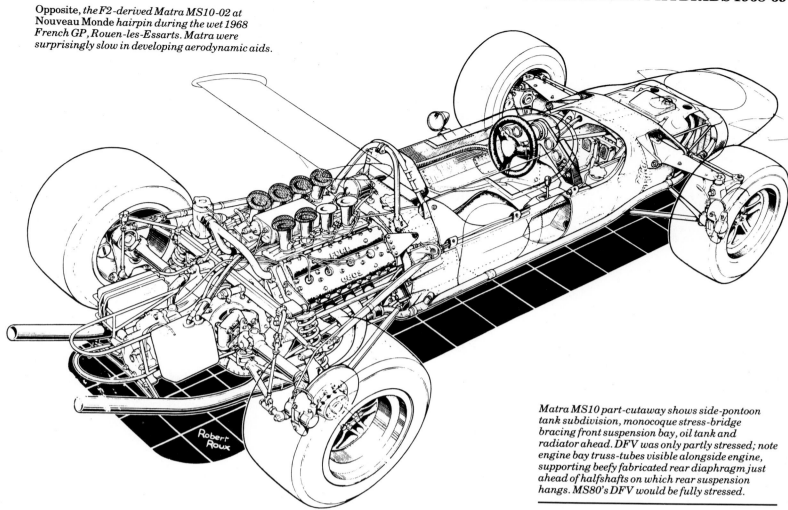

*Matra MS10 part-cutaway shows side-pontoon
tank subdivision, monocoque stress-bridge
bracing front suspension bay, oil tank and
radiator ahead. DFV was only partly stressed; note
engine bay truss-tubes visible alongside engine,
supporting beefy fabricated rear diaphragm just
ahead of halfshafts on which rear suspension
hangs. MS80's DFV would be fully stressed.*

car in action, merely to keep the suspension
undisturbed while the engine could be removed
and replaced with relative impunity.

Otherwise this MS9 monocoque was very
similar to its little-sister MS7s, even to the
extent of sharing their short-race fuel capacity,
for it was a test car and no more.

Either side of the cockpit, its two tank
pontoons extended full length, linked at the
front by a footbox housing pedals and inboard
suspension elements, amidships by a box-
fabrication dash-panel bulkhead in which the
lightening holes doubled as instrument
mounts, and behind the driver's seat by a
robust third bulkhead section.

Rocker arm front suspension was broadly
similar to Lotus 49 practice, as was the single
top link, reversed lower wishbone and twin
radius rod arrangement at the rear. Major
suspension components, like the uprights and
hubs, were borrowed from the company's
MS630 sports-prototype cars. Cast-magnesium
15 in. diameter road wheels replaced the
otherwise similar 13 in. wheels of the F2 cars,
accommodating enlarged Girling disc brakes.
Like the 49s, the Matra MS9 employed a
combination water/oil radiator core in the nose,
slung ahead of a delta-form oil tank designed to
cleave hot airflow exhausting from the radiator
and fend it away through the suspension
cut-outs on each side. The DFV engine, bolted
on in its classical manner at the rear, drove via
a Hewland DG300 five-speed and reverse
gearbox. Rubber doughnuts and Hooke joints
catered for halfshaft angularity and length
variation as the road wheels rose and fell on
bump and droop.

With Dunlop's backing, Tyrrell decided that
an extended series of fine-weather tyre tests
would form a valuable curtain raiser to his
team's maiden Formula 1 season, and so a
prolonged programme was undertaken at
Kyalami in South Africa, following the South
African GP there on 2 January 1968, which

Tyrrell and Stewart had decided to enter
despite Matra misgivings.

Matra had also sent a Formula 2 MS7 car
with 1600 Cosworth FVA engine, ballasted up
to Formula 1 minimum weight, for Jean-Pierre
Beltoise to gain Grand Prix experience.

Matra themselves were so dubious about
Tyrrell's ideas of actually racing MS9 that, as
Crombac had recorded, Tyrrell was '... far
from impressed when (his) car turned up – after
a very short test at the Montlhéry track near
Paris – painted in a coat of ugly green primer,
just to make him feel this was not a proper
racing car!'

At Kyalami the altitude rendered the cars'
restricted fuel tankage slightly less of a
problem although they would definitely have to
make one refuelling stop if they lasted the
distance. The MS9 hack's nose cone proved too
restricted for adequate cooling and had to be
cut back making this fungus-green ugly duckling even uglier, and an extra water tank and
cooler were added under the roll-over bar.
Stewart promptly qualified on the front row of
the grid, led Clark's Lotus on the opening lap
but fell back before his DFV engine dropped a
valve. Beltoise survived race distance in the
ballasted F2 car to finish sixth and add to this
worthwhile Matra Formula 1 debut.

After its Kyalami race and test programme,
MS9 would only run once more, in Albi testing.
The definitive Matra-Cosworth F1 car which
followed was the MS10 in which Boyer introduced an extra tank cell à la Lotus 49 in the
rear of the tub, between driver and engine
bulkhead, raising the fuel capacity to a full 190
litres (41.8 Imperial gallons). Meanwhile, the
MS11 chassis intended for the new V12 engine
was to offer extra fuel capacity within its
engine bearer horns. These extra tanks were
obviously items which the DFV-powered MS10
neither required nor possessed. The hybrid
MS10 weighed in at 560 kg (1234.5 lb), 20 kg
(44 lb) heavier than the MS9 hack and 60 kg

(132 lb) over the minimum weight limit.

Through 1968 the functional-looking pale-
blue Matra MS10 brought Matra Sports the
tangible success they required while their own
MS11 V12 suffered, as predicted, its share of
teething troubles while generating one of the
most spine-tingling exhaust notes on the
Formula 1 scene.

'MS10/01's debut came in the minor Race of
Champions at Brands Hatch that March. And
Stewart was appalled. It wandered frighteningly along the straights and understeered
savagely in corners. As on MS9, Boyer had
again adopted modestly-lightened wheels and
suspension uprights from his MS630 long-
distance sports cars and they were still too
heavy, seriously affecting the F1 car's sprung/
unsprung weight ratio.

The offending components were further
lightened. Titanium stub axles were used, but
flexed, promoting brake pad knock-off as they
tremored under brake reaction, giving the
driver a dauntingly spongy pedal. Stewart hurt
a wrist in an F2 Matra shunt at Jarama, Spain,
and missed the subsequent Spanish GP held
there. Beltoise took his place, crashing '10/01
mildly in practice due to this very brake
problem, then leading the GP convincingly
until an oil filter leak sent him into the pits. He
rejoined, set fastest lap and was back in fifth
place at the finish.

Beltoise drove the MS11 V12 for its ear-
splitting debut at Monaco and, with Stewart
still on the sick-list, Servoz-Gavin drove MS10,
qualifying on the front row and leading from
the start only to brush a barrier in his
excitement and break the car's transmission.

Steel stub axles and aerodynamic nose
planes featured at Spa where Stewart returned
and inherited the lead only for the high
G-forces on this super-fast course to wash the
car's final four gallons of fuel away from the
pump pick-up and send him into the pits at the
last moment, robbing Matra of a certain

maiden victory.

A new, lighter 'MS10/02' with 2 in. wider front track was available for Zandvoort where Dunlop's wet weather tyre superiority assisted Stewart's maiden Matra-DFV victory and Beltoise's MS11 V12 second place. A lighter Hewland FG400 transaxle was fitted for the French GP at Rouen, where despite their aerospace pedigree Matra lagged behind in aerodynamic development, using only small and crude sheet foils fitted to the front suspension rocker arms. Poor tyre choice made this the first 1968 GP which a Matra-DFV did *not* lead . . .

A chassis-mounted midship wing was then tried at Brands Hatch but removed for the race in which Stewart's still-damaged wrist suffered terribly. Then at the Nürburgring the wing was used, Dunlop's wet tyres did their stuff and the streaming surface helped lighten the steering sufficiently for Stewart's wrist to hold up and he scored the most heroic victory of his entire career – simply leaving mere mortals as if for dead in appalling weather on the most demanding of all Grand Prix circuits.

Stewart's '10/02' then won the minor Oulton Park race; for Monza Servoz-Gavin took over the later MS10 with its midship wing to place second and Stewart used his older car now updated with a less buffet-prone cockpit and a rear wing mounted directly on the suspension uprights, but his engine broke its timing gears during the race itself.

At Watkins Glen, Stewart won in the spare car after his preferred mount had been set on fire by Mr Tyrrell (while fuelling it in the garage) and the World Championship title was then open going into the last race in Mexico City, between Stewart, Hulme and Hill – Matra, McLaren and Lotus – and all of them using DFV engines.

Stewart's chance was lost, ironically by Matra's unique constructional method, as tank sealing polymer broke loose and partially blocked his car's fuel pump.

Winter development saw bi-wing airfoil aids developed in time for the 1969 South African GP, in which the two MS10s appeared with a front 'foil mounted on the chassis and a very tall rear 'foil on the suspension uprights. Stewart won both this race and the minor BRDC Silverstone event which followed with

Stewart's MS80, Silverstone, 1969 British GP. Now Matras were adequately be-winged with fences controlling airflow on nose and tail 'foils and nose-top. See how aerodynamically obstructive outboard suspensions could be.

his 'MS10/02' in this form.

Matra had been extraordinarily slow to react in the aerodynamic war, considering the massive group expertise which should have been on call, and although they introduced a moveable 'foil actuated by a small aerospace electric motor, this was only available on Beltoise's factory V12 car, while the DFV-powered Tyrrell entries were demonstrably more competitive. Matra were in fact handicapped by the convulsion of social unrest which France suffered in May-June 1968, and developing their V12 had demanded close attention and massive effort. Dunlop tyre development, however, was extremely rapid. Matra wheel rims had grown through 1968 from 9 in. front/13 in. wide rear to 10 in./15 in. dimensions . . .

The Matra programmes were revised for 1969, the V12 engine now being reserved totally for sports-racing while Formula 1 effort was concentrated solely upon Equipe Matra International and their DFV-engined hybrids. Beltoise joined Stewart in this team and an all-new chassis design programme was initiated for them. There was also a plan for Jochen Rindt to be provided with a similar DFV-engined chassis which his Winkelman Racing F2 team manager Alan Rees would operate for him. This deal did not materialize and Rindt signed for Team Lotus instead.

During that winter of 1968/69 there was much talk of the potential of 4-wheel drive in putting DFV power through to the road more efficiently than could existing rear-drive chassis and the tyres of the time, with or without aerodynamic aids. Stewart wanted a 4WD car available for wet races, of which there had been many in the '68 season. Matra could not afford to tackle endurance sports car racing as well as conventional F1 plus 4WD F1, so they arranged their budget to run to two new F1 chassis – the MS80s – for Tyrrell's team, plus an experimental 4WD car, the MS84. Tyrrell would supply both the DFV engines and the Ferguson 4WD transmission while Matra would be responsible for the chassis.

Meanwhile, Martin and his team revised their V12 engine design for a possible Formula 1 reappearance in 1970. At the end of the 1968 season the V12-engined MS11 car became purely an experimental hack, being fitted with engineer Caussin's hydraulic transmission system in a hasty conversion between 15 April and 18 May 1969. The original V12 engine, known as the MS9, had suffered from chronic overheating and Martin concluded that a complete redesign, with new block and head castings,

was the only sensible remedy. MS11 was hill-climbed once during that season, refitted with conventional transmission and driven by Beltoise. For this outing it used a pre-production MS12 V12 engine destined for the forthcoming MS120 Formula 1 chassis.

Meanwhile, Boyer's 1969 MS80 design for the DFV engine was set out during the autumn of 1968, aiming to compensate for the known deficiencies of the MS10. Its afterthought midship fuel tank had been inadequately stressed, which compromised the monocoque's torsional rigidity. Front suspension offered more camber change than was comfortable on Dunlop's latest wide-tread tyres, tending to up-edge them on bump and droop with consequent sudden loss of contact area and hence ultimate grip. This manifested itself in too much inherent understeer and instability under heavy braking. The rear suspension was imperfect, allowing too much toe-steer for the rear wheels as the suspension moved through its arc. The inboard front coil-spring/damper mounting had also caused problems as the dampers overheated and extra cooling intakes had to be provided for their survival.

To improve rigidity, Boyer used his successful structural fuel tank system, Lagardère authorizing this feature even though it was already known that the CSI would be demanding rubber bag fuel tanks from 1 January 1970. As described earlier, this form of chassis structure prohibited use of bag tanks, so the new MS80 would be purely a one-season, one-shot car, ineligible for Formula 1 use into the '70 season. Consider the implications of this decision, and you will appreciate just how much faith Matra placed in their unique form of monocoque chassis construction.

Boyer concentrated his new car's tankage within its wheelbase in so-called 'Coke bottle' planform pannier tanks, concentrating the fuel load around the car's centre of gravity. To comply with latest regulations, these tanks were baffled by addition of polyurethane foam, fed in through a row of small detachable access plates – far smaller than would be demanded if bag tanks had been used, even if the internal bulkhead layout had permitted. Boyer again used a fully stressed 360-degree scuttle section to stiffen the front end of his monocoque tub while the oil tank was moved from its MS9/10 forward mounting to a site between driver's shoulders and engine.

After the damper overheating problems of the MS10, outboard coil-spring/damper units appeared in the new MS80 front suspension, obviating the need for those strong but heavy and no less aerodynamically obstructive top rocker arms. At the rear Boyer took up the Len Terry/BRM-originated parallel link lower location. This offered much better toe-steer control than the preceding reversed lower wishbone with its single-point mounting on the chassis. It also eased provision of anti-squat geometry, to limit weight transference under acceleration.

Suspension geometry was dictated by needs of the latest generation Dunlop tyres. Front wheels were now 13 in. diameter, rears 15 in., and Teflon-lined self-lubricating suspension ball joints were used since problems had been experienced with greased joints drying out on the MS10s. Unsprung weight at the rear was reduced by mounting the disc brakes inboard on the cheeks of the Hewland transaxle. Broad nose 'planes were fitted, trimming the effect of a tall strutted upright-mounted rear wing.

When it emerged, this podgily pregnant-looking MS80 scaled 535 kg (1179 lb) – 15 kg (33 lb) less than MS10. Its fuel capacity was enlarged to 210 litres (46.2 Imp. gallons) to cater for the greater thirst of the latest-tune so-called 9-series DFV engines, which were guaranteed to deliver 430 bhp at 9500 rpm.

The prototype MS80 tested briefly at Montlhéry before being flown out to Kyalami where it was used briefly in practice for the South African GP but not raced there, because Ken

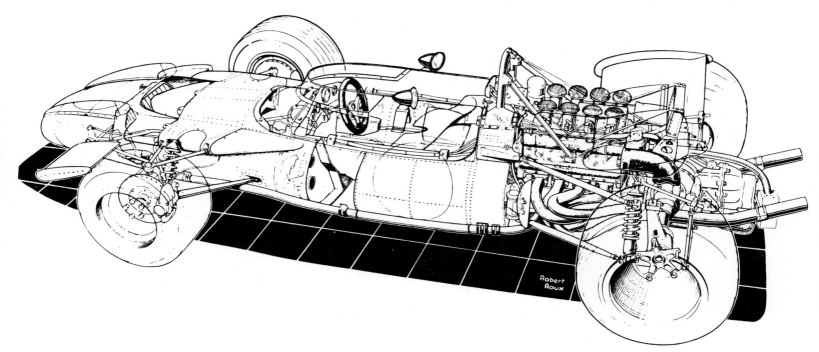

Tyrrell considered it as yet unproven. The old MS10 was indeed man enough to do the job, and driven by Stewart it won that race.

Stewart then gave 'MS80/01' its race debut in the minor Brands Hatch International, which it won. A flatter nose appeared for the Spanish GP where Dunlop's tyres proved inferior to those offered by Firestone and Goodyear, but when their runners struck trouble Stewart won by default and team-mate Beltoise in the number two MS80 – a brand new car at that meeting – finished third despite a delay when its gear linkage worked loose.

The celebrated Lotus wing-collapse accidents occurred in this race, and in mid-practice at Monaco two weeks later the CSI wing ban was applied, until new wing limitations could be introduced for the following Dutch race at Zandvoort.

Monaco was a catastrophe for the MS80s as both cars were found to have cracked transmission UJs on race morning and both broke these components on the same lap in the race itself. At Zandvoort, wingform engine covers and wider rear tyres appeared, Stewart winning comfortably; at Clermont-Ferrand Stewart, Beltoise and the MS80s placed triumphantly 1-2 before a French crowd – this splendid home performance doing promotional wonders for Matra Sports and Elf.

After a practice crash caused when a thrown-up piece of loose kerbing burst one of his MS80's front tyres, Stewart won the British GP – his fifth *Grande Epreuve* of the season – in Beltoise's usual car. The German GP was lost narrowly to Ickx's Brabham-DFV using the latest and now superior G20 tyre from Goodyear, while at Monza the wily Tyrrell counselled use of an extra-high second gear to enable Stewart to make the final dash from the *Parabolica* corner to the finish line without having to change-up. The last lap race situation was tailor-made for Stewart to exploit this advantage, and as main rival Rindt's DFV engine was bounced frantically on its rev-limiter, the wee Scot's Matra MS80 crossed the line first by inches, both to win the Italian GP and to clinch the World Championship titles for driver and constructor.

Team-mate Beltoise was also in that leading bunch, though without that specially cut long gear. His MS80 wore its rear wing, Stewart's ran low-drag configuration shorn of both nose planes and rear wing. Beltoise was able to enter that final corner first using the extra braking grip generated by his car's aerodynamic aids,

but he was simply unable to exit as quickly with his standard gearing and finished third, merely 0.19 secs behind his team leader and 0.09 behind Rindt's Lotus.

Sure as eggs is eggs, the result of that thrilling Grand Prix had been decided pre-race, by Equipe Matra International's technical forethought and tactical vision. Most emphatically, Grand Prix racing is *not* all about drivers.

The 1969 season, and the Matra MS80s' racing career, ended with the Canadian, US and Mexican GPs in which team and drivers were largely out of luck, but the operation had in any case lost a little incentive with the World titles already in the bag. And now the storm clouds had gathered . . .

Matra raced largely to promote its road-going Type 530 production car, successor to the Djet. Commercial success with this model had been hamstrung by Matra's lack of a proper dealer network. Although the car used the Ford V4 engine Ford refused to market it. Consequently Matra had begun planning a new production car powered by a proprietary engine from a more amenable source. Chrysler-France, building the Simca range, was now headed by Bill Reiber who, as former head of Ford-France, had made the original V4 deal with Matra! Now he was happy for them to use Chrysler engines but they would have to sever all links with Ford which meant the end of the Formula 1 Matra-DFVs. It made commercial sense, so for 1970 Matra refused even to consider modifying their World Championship-

Compare this shot with that on page 59 of Rindt, trying equally hard, same place, same race, in the Lotus 49. The Matra MS80's anti-squat front suspension is working well, restricting forward weight transfer and reducing tendency of rear brakes to lock as the wheels 'go light'.

winning MS80s to suit the new bag-tank regulations, nor would they build chassis for any engine other than their own V12. They would race under the Matra-Simca name.

At Lagardère's request Tyrrell organized back-to-back tests for Stewart between V12 and DFV-engined cars at Albi, and the Scot was insistent that the DFV was a better proposition. Matra Sports would not compromise their Chrysler agreement by building new bag-tank chassis for the Ford-backed Formula 1 engine, so Tyrrell had to look elsewhere, turning initially to the upstart new March company while secretly having an MS80-like car of his own designed and built.

After a season's hiatus, Matra's reworked V12 engine reappeared in a rather weird looking new MS120 works team chassis for 1970, but Matra Sports' cars would never win another Championship-qualifying F1 race. More years and more work would eventually see Ligier do the trick with the V12 engine, but it would never aspire to the heights of those Tyrrell-entered Matra-DFV hybrids of 1969.

Four-Wheel Drive

In search of improved traction to handle the new-found power and sudden torque of the Cosworth DFV engine in 1968-69, Cosworth themselves, Lotus, Matra and McLaren all experimented with four-wheel drive Formula 1 cars.

Much was made of these experiments both at the time and since but, after the final withdrawal of the 4WD Lotus 56B turbine car at the end of 1971, nothing came of these costly experiments in Formula 1 terms. Drivers could not adapt to the demands which the rather crude transmission systems employed placed upon their nervous systems and there was always a weight penalty.

Advances in aerodynamics and tyre development helped find solutions to the original traction problem which obviated the necessity for four-wheel drive. In retrospect, however, it is now apparent that devices such as the modern Ferguson Research viscous coupling, front-end limited-slip differentials plus modern racing tyre technology could have made the story's outcome completely different.

Essentially, four-wheel drive was a brief aberration in the story of Formula 1 development and was of *no* significance to the mainstream which followed, other than having indicated what not to do. For other reasons the March 0-2-4 and Williams FW07D six-wheeler projects employed four-wheel drive divorced from the steerable front wheels, which could have been successful had circumstances – and the regulations – been different. It was not until the Audi Quattro and Peugeot 4WD rally cars of the 1980s began re-writing the rough-road rallying record book that all-wheel drive was able to find its successful niche in ultra high-performance motoring, most notably with Tony and Stuart Rolt's Ferguson concern in the van of development. It is in modern rallying and road-vehicle use that four-wheel drive has now proved its real value. The story of the 1969-71 4WD Grand Prix cars has been told most adequately elsewhere and in any case was, I believe, little more than an historic curiosity.

The story might have been different if 4WD had not finally been banned from Formula 1 in 1982, at a time when Williams had considered adopting a six-wheel design with the rear four driven, mainly for aerodynamic reasons. By 1985 so much power was available that had 4WD still been an option, the leading designers would certainly have tried again.

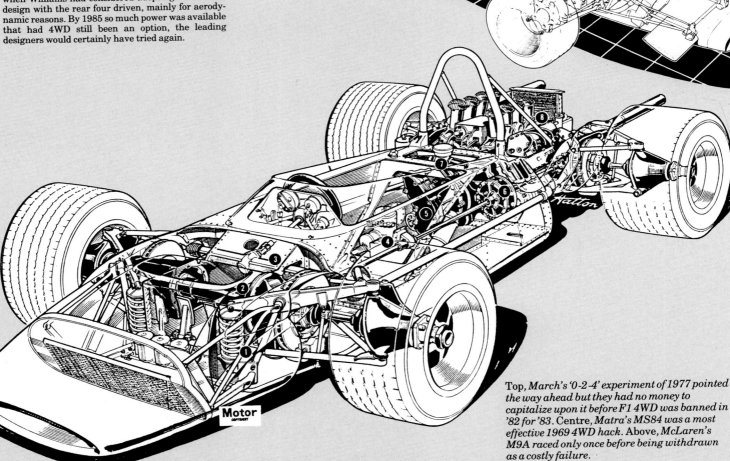

Top, *March's '0-2-4' experiment of 1977 pointed the way ahead but they had no money to capitalize upon it before F1 4WD was banned in '82 for '83. Centre, Matra's MS84 was a most effective 1969 4WD hack. Above, McLaren's M9A raced only once before being withdrawn as a costly failure.*

Chapter 6

LOTUS 72 – INTRODUCING NEW STANDARDS 1970-75

During the Lotus 49's three-season life, Colin Chapman was increasingly irritated by this essentially simple design's inevitable deficiencies. He was particularly niggled by Graham Hill's habit of covering countless miles in race practice trying to find what he considered to be proper bump-stop settings.

Colin once told me, between laughter at the memories, 'My big dream for a car for Graham was one with rising-rate suspension so he could *never* get on a bump stop! Then he couldn't play around with it, and that alone would have made my season . . .'

Planning for the 1970 Lotus 49 replacement began as soon as the four-wheel drive Type 63 proved that approach to be a complete blind alley. Chapman and Maurice Phillippe discussed their new concept interminably and a specification was eventually drawn up. While the 49 concept hinged totally upon requirements of the new Cosworth-Ford engine, that for the new 72 hinged crucially upon two things – integration with a new Firestone racing tyre and optimisation of aerodynamic form to generate maximum possible download under the new wing regulations.

Basic tenets of the design included very low unsprung weight. Brake layout would reject the minimum possible heat into the hub/wheel/ tyre assemblies. Combined with minimum overall weight and smooth, pitch-free riding characteristics, this would allow the new car to exploit softer – for which read 'faster' – tyre compounds than the opposition, without overheating and destroying them. This was the usual outcome when attempts had been made to race such tyres on vehicles not specifically designed for them. Now the forthcoming Lotus 72 was to give these virtual 'qualifying tyres' race-distance life.

The Lotus designers decided to achieve this aim by using rising-rate suspension, which would provide very soft springing free from the lack of control inherent in soft springs as such, and which normally allowed dangerous bottoming when the fuel tanks were full. Torsion bar springs were chosen as offering the neatest progressive-rate system, and 'compound' torsion bars – explained shortly – would place the least demand on space.

Indianapolis track-racing experience with the Type 56 turbine cars in 1968 had proved that the wedge-shaped aerodynamic profile was very effective in generating negative lift – download – and to employ that shape on the 72 the nose radiator siting was dropped in favour of two radiators slung amidships on either hip. This in turn removed one heat source which had roasted drivers so often in the 49s. Resiting the oil tank in the tail also helped control cockpit temperatures and contributed to the 72's greater rearward weight bias, which extended the 49B philosophy of adding load on the rear tyres.

Mounting the disc brakes inboard on the footbox and transmission cheeks slashed unsprung weight and isolated a major source of heat from the wheels where experience had shown how much it could distress an already hard-worked racing tyre. Overall plumbing weight was reduced and mass concentrated around the centre of gravity.

The whole design was centred upon an all-new wedge-section monocoque chassis, whose aerodynamic effect was to be enhanced and trimmed by a new design of three-tier tail wing and large nose planes.

The compound torsion bar springs used an outer tubular sleeve which was internally splined at one end to mate with an internal solid bar passing back through the outer sleeve. This outer was then mounted rigidly upon the chassis structure at its open end, from which the inner bar element protruded to pick up a

Over the dune and far away – Rindt's Lotus '72/2' hammering on towards its first Championship round win in the 1970 Dutch GP. Just rebuilt sans anti-dive and anti-squat the hip-radiatored 'doorstop' was possibly the only F1 car of that season to enjoy net aerodynamic download over its front wheels.

linkage attached to the wheel upright and actuated by vertical movement of the suspension. The geometry of this linkage was such that the more the suspension deflected, the rate of twist on the torsion bar spring became proportionally greater still. This provided self-adjusting suspension to maintain virtually constant ride height and handling characteristics irrespective of changes in the car's fuel load as it was consumed during the race.

These compound torsion bars were so convenient because they were only half the length of conventional bars of similar rate, and they occupied far less inboard volume than conventional coil-springs. They were machined to very fine tolerances on equipment normally used for making gun barrels, and the bar's business end used crowded roller-race bearings to maintain minimum-friction clearance between outer sleeve and inner bar.

Suspension location was by conventional upper and lower wishbones, fabricated from nickel chrome-molybdenum sheet at the front and steel tube at the rear. The front wishbones were mounted on a front subframe, with their forward pick-up points lower than the rears to provide anti-dive characteristics. At the rear, forward pick-ups were higher than rearward ones to give pronounced anti-squat, preventing the car burying its tail under power.

This arrangement was intended to provide the required smooth-riding, low-pitch characteristics of the Type 56s upon which the Indy car drivers had commented so favourably, and to improve upon the 49s' notoriously acute nose-down-under-braking, tail-down-under-power pitching.

The new Type 72's inboard-mounted front brakes reacted on the wheels through specially made brakeshafts using Hardy-Spicer and Lobro driveshaft joints. The discs were solid, cooled by airflow entering via flush NACA ducts formed in the nose cowl, while expended air exited through moulded chimneys on the same cowl's upper surface.

The monocoque chassis itself was formed over steel internal bulkheads. Inner panels were in 20-gauge L72 Alclad sheet, while the outer skins were in softer, more malleable 18-gauge NS4 alloy to follow the necessary compound curves where the tub waisted-in towards the hip-mounted radiator ducts.

The whole tub tapered forward in wedge form, and much was made of its external flush-riveting – aerospace style – to slash aerodynamic surface drag to an absolute minimum. Its inner panels sloped sharply towards the floor to provide necessary volume within the side pontoons for the FPT rubber fuel bags which fed a collector tank behind the sloping seat back panel.

A footbox structure projected at the front of the tub, fabricated upon a $\frac{5}{8}$ in. square-section tubular steel frame which carried pedals, master cylinders, front suspension and a fragile-looking forward frame to support the battery and body mounts.

At the rear the DFV engine bolted against the monocoque rear bulkhead, and suspension loads were carried on sandwich plates assembled into the Hewland FG transaxle casing. Since the suspension was relieved of major braking loads by the inboard disc mounting, only upper radius rods were fitted at the rear.

The Lotus 72's wing package was also a new development, in that its three-tier rear aerofoil enabled the wing assembly overall to run at a greater combined incidence than would have been feasible with a one-piece wing, which would have stalled at such a sharp angle of attack. This wing mounted above a three-gallon oil tank wrapped over the gearbox. Balance was provided by broad adjustable planes either side of the nose cone.

Upon the type's debut in the 1970 Spanish GP at Jarama, there were immediate problems. Rindt had an insulating spacer (which clamped between the front brakeshaft and disc to prevent heat-soak melting the drive-joint lubricant) overheat and disintegrate. This

allowed the fixing bolts to fidget and stretch until they snapped, which left the driver with braking on only three wheels. Ventilated brake discs promptly replaced the solid originals on his car, chassis '72/2'.

Ambient temperatures in Spain were also too high for the new cars to cool adequately, so the radiator draught-includer ducts were enlarged by the simple expedient of outrigging them on spacers between pod and hull.

Type 49C wheel sizes were being used, 13 in. diameter fronts and 15 in. rears while rim widths were 10 and 15 in. respectively. Some 17 in. wide rears were tried by Rindt, but this set-up generated so much rear-end grip that the front end was utterly overwhelmed and understeer became excessive.

In fact, irrespective of wheel and tyre sizes, there were severe handling deficiencies. The 72s seemed to roll excessively and lift their inside rear wheels in cornering. Wet practice for the minor Silverstone race, however, showed them to be finding adhesion in conditions which essentially offered none. This would become characteristic of the 72s throughout their long frontline life.

After another poor showing in the race at Silverstone there was a major rethink. Only '72/1' was taken to Monaco, but as spare car, and Rindt astonishingly won there in his elderly 49C.

Meanwhile at Hethel, Colin Knight's fabricators tore down '72/2' to remove both anti-dive and anti-squat from its suspension systems. Removal of anti-squat was no great problem, merely requiring new rear subframes to be designed and made, but removing anti-dive was far more fundamental. Alteration of the front subframe and pick-ups meant that the original side skins would no longer fit so they had to be unstitched and scrapped and the monocoque completely reskinned around revised bulkheads to match the new front end requirements. In effect '72/2' was so extensively rebuilt that only the original rear cockpit

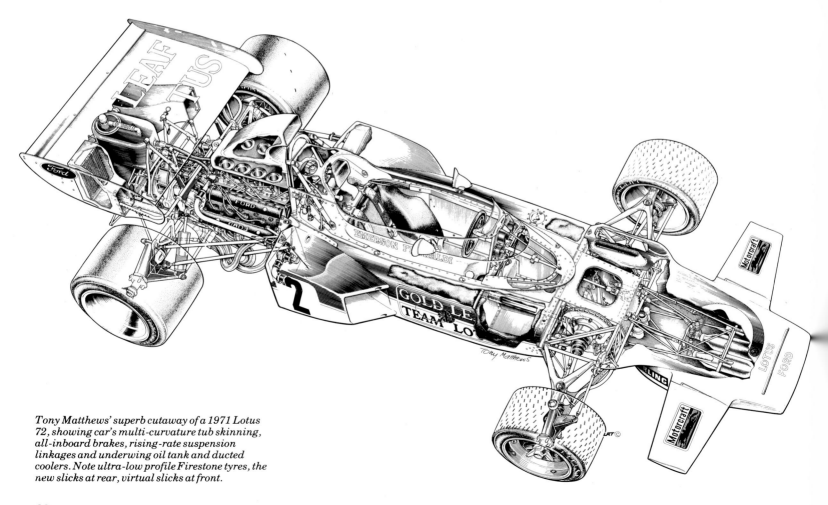

Tony Matthews' superb cutaway of a 1971 Lotus 72, showing car's multi-curvature tub skinning, all-inboard brakes, rising-rate suspension linkages and underwing oil tank and ducted coolers. Note ultra-low profile Firestone tyres, the new slicks at rear, virtual slicks at front.

bulkhead and engine mounts survived.

It had been considered necessary to remove both anti-dive and anti-squat because the former characteristic rendered the already light steering eerily feelingless as the suspension stiffened under braking. Anti-squat was suspected of inducing a diagonal jacking moment across the car, causing that inside rear wheel to lift in corners.

The other extant Type 72, chassis '1', was less comprehensively rebuilt, the tub being unchanged and thus retaining anti-dive while the simpler rear end conversion was made to in-line pick-up frames removing anti-squat. This car was entrusted to Rindt's new team-mate John Miles, who was still finding his feet in Formula 1. A new parallel-suspension car, '72/3', became available for him at the German GP at Hockenheim in August. The old proto-type '72/1' was then reduced and rebuilt as new with parallel suspension and it became Rob Walker's late-delivered replacement for his wonderful old Lotus 49C 'R7', driven by Graham Hill. This rebuilt car took the serial '72/4' and would have a very short active life.

Meanwhile the 72 had come of age after these extensive modifications. Rindt won on merit in his newly rebuilt '72/2' at Zandvoort and with luck at Clermont-Ferrand where the chassis had been further stiffened with cross-bracing in the rear of the tub and stronger suspension pick-ups. The rear dampers had also been resited as hot air exhausting from the hip radiators had caused them distress.

For the British GP at Brands Hatch, Rindt's 72 introduced the engine airbox to modern Formula 1, gulping air into its injection trumpets from ducts situated either side of the roll-over bar. This at least would set new trends. Rindt was in luck once more and after Brabham's BT33 had left the Lotus for dead in second place, it ran out of fuel on the last lap and Rindt won again. At Hockenheim, Lotus could match Ickx's speed in the ever-improving flat-12 Ferrari and Rindt won on merit, by 0.7 second. Then the 72s hit trouble in Austria . . .

There the scrutineers spotted that the early-season Jarama radiator pod extension had taken the 72s' fuselage width beyond the 110 cm maximum. The pods had to be drawn in accordingly and the drivers promptly pulled 200 extra rpm along the straight! The lower ambient temperatures in the Styrian hills compared to the Jarama flood-plain enabled the cars still to cool adequately.

Rindt lost fourth place after a spin when his car's engine tightened, while Miles brought his car to a safe halt after suffering a front brake-shaft fracture. This was caused by an imperfection in the shaft's centre-drilling. John described the failure symptoms in the following way. '[It was] as though the moment I touched the brake pedal some enormous extra-terrestrial force had grabbed the steering and slammed it onto full lock. Fortunately I had room to sort it all out and go into the pits – very pale and utterly demoralized . . .'

The shafts were hollow to give some 'spring' to the brake-driveline, cushioning shock, and to save a little more weight. In this case the drill had been run in from either end as usual, but the two drillings had not met perfectly in the middle, so leaving a stress-raiser ridge from which the shaft had fatigued. For the next race, the minor Gold Cup at Oulton Park, stop-gap solid brakeshafts were fitted to Rindt's '72/2'. The dark-blue Walker '72/4' made its muted debut there with Graham Hill driving. Rindt won the second heat; then came the Italian GP at Monza . . .

Rindt and Miles drove their usual cars while new team member Emerson Fittipaldi had a fresh works car '72/5'. In practice on the Saturday morning Rindt took out '72/2' running experimentally without wings, with standard brake ratios and on unscrubbed new tyres. Under braking from maximum speed into the right-handed *Curva Parabolica* his

right front brakeshaft almost certainly snapped, sending Rindt crashing into the left-side Armco barriers and stanchions. A barrier joint parted and the car's front end was demolished as the left-front suspension burrowed underneath and then hit an unyielding stanchion virtually head-on. The tub's forepart was first crushed, then ripped apart and Rindt was killed. Seven long years later an Italian court ruled that the initial loss of control was indeed caused by brakeshaft failure, but that poorly installed safety barriers were the crucial cause of the World Champion elect's tragic death.

At Watkins Glen new drivers Fittipaldi and Reine Wisell finished 1-3 in '72/5' and '72/3' to clinch the Drivers' title posthumously for Rindt and their fourth Formula 1 Constructors' Championship for Lotus.

THE LOW YEAR

Winter changes for the 1971 season included a new lubrication system and a return to drilled torsional front brakeshafts in place of the hefty solid components employed in the final North American races of 1970. Firestone were to introduce a new low-profile tyre in quest of more consistent contact area control due to the stiffer sidewalls which low-profile construction could offer. This involved suspension modifications to accommodate the new lower wheel/tyre centrelines. The original magnesium uprights had been suspected of twisting. As cast-magnesium uprights robust enough to resist deflection would have been heavier than fabricated steel, the change was made to fabricated steel.

Top, Rindt's '72/2', Österreichring, 1970. Note wedge profile, wings, radiator ducts, rear torsion bars protruding at tail and new lop-eared engine airbox from which idea the tall 'snorkels' would quickly grow. Above, a 72's rear-end reveals anti-roll bar, vented inboard brake discs, and naked damper barrels with rising-rate geometry torsion bar linkages passing just behind.

For the Good Friday Oulton Park meeting '72/5' used a new one-piece rear wing, and an in-line oil tank replaced the old saddle type to clean up airflow under it.

For the chassis number pedant, the Lotus 72 progression had been first to '72B' with the removal of anti-squat, followed by '72C' with the removal of anti-dive and its associated tub rebuild, and at Monaco in 1971 the '72D' emerged in Fittipaldi's regular '72/5' which now incorporated rear suspension geometry revised to match the new low-profile Firestones more efficiently. This new system featured twin radius rods, instead of single, on either side, while parallel lower links replaced the original bottom wishbone better to control toe-steer – a feature which BRM had espoused in 1967-68, and Matra in 1969. These changes helped tame a sudden changeover from under-steer to oversteer which had troubled Team's drivers earlier in the season.

At Silverstone for the British GP, the original lop-eared style airbox was replaced by a tall single-scoop design. Maurice Phillippe left Lotus that autumn to design USAC and eventually Formula 1 cars – 72 derivatives in effect – for the Vel's Parnelli Jones Racing Team in the USA.

Prior to the 1971 US GP the 72s were further modified because rising-rate geometry no longer seemed advantageous. It was suspected of exacerbating the new low-profile tyres' chronic vibration problem, and was therefore removed from the rear suspension. Higher-profile tyres carried on smaller 13 in. diameter rear wheels were used brilliantly there by Fittipaldi to qualify only 0.017-second slower than Stewart's Tyrrell pole position time, but a multitude of problems then dropped him to 17th in the race.

This was in fact Team Lotus's worst Formula 1 season since 1959, for in every other season from 1960 to 1970 they had won Formula 1 races, yet in 1971 they won none. They had been handicapped by the morale after-echoes of Rindt's death, but more so by the relative inexperience of their two new drivers. Addi-

The Lotus 72s won their second Constructors' Championship in 1973. Here Fittipaldi leads Peterson at the Österreichring while, bottom, Emerson slams 72/5 round Barcelona on his way to scoring Lotus's 50th Championship GP victory, undeterred by a deflating rear tyre.

tionally, the faster of the two, Fittipaldi, had been injured in a mid-season road accident and although he continued racing, team manager Peter Warr believed he had been more seriously affected than he was prepared to admit – a factor affecting car performance as surely as anything an engineer can do.

THE 72s' SECOND TITLE

New 1972 regulations demanded fuel tank protection in 16-gauge sheet, so the existing active 72s were reskinned in suitable material, while a sponsorship policy decision introduced the black-and-gold 'John Player Special' livery in place of the garish old red-gold-white Gold Leaf graphics.

Winter testing prior to the new 1972 season-opening Argentine GP proved a third-generation rear wing design, but this season witnessed a long succession of alternative oil tank, wing-mount and wing revisions made by Phillippe's successors, Martin Waide and Ralph Bellamy. Wheel diameters stabilized at 15 in. at the rear and 13 in. at the front, exhaust systems wove differing paths through ever-revised rear suspensions and Fittipaldi fulfilled all his huge promise.

The cars won World Championship GPs in Spain, Belgium, Britain, Austria and Italy plus minor F1 events at Brands Hatch, Silverstone and Vallelunga and the one-off major 312-mile Libre race back at Brands Hatch later in the season. By the time of the Italian GP that September, either Hulme of McLaren or Stewart of Tyrrell had to win all three remaining GPs without him improving on fourth place in any of those events to deny Fittipaldi and Lotus the World Championship titles. But he won at Monza, and so he became the youngest-ever World Champion Driver and Team Lotus took their fifth Formula 1 Constructors' Championship.

FOURTH SEASON – THIRD TITLE

Now the so-called 'super-team' syndrome prevailed for 1973, with Player hiring Ronnie Peterson to join the reigning World Champion

in Lotus's still-further developed Type 72s. Firestone's top management had dithered about whether or not to stay in racing, and consequently Colin Chapman – who never liked anyone messing him about – forged a replacement deal with the rival Goodyear concern. This necessitated considerable suspension retuning to match the different tyres, but Fittipaldi still won the first two GPs of the season untroubled in South America. In practice at Interlagos, Brazil, the elderly Lotuses were over a second faster than their opposition, and their advantage was so great that they were faster even on full tanks to demonstrate an awesome combination of chassis, tyre and driver power.

Chapman returned to Hethel after that race and briefed Ralph Bellamy to design – at last – a 72 replacement. 'All we need', he said, 'is a 72 100 lb lighter'.

From the European season-opening Spanish GP that year, new deformable structure tank protection regulations were to take effect, and Martin Waide drew the 72s' conversion. The ageing tubs were unstitched, rejigged and reappeared, initially at the Race of Champions, with double-skinned crush pads formed into integral radiator pods which replaced the earlier separate pod mouldings. New undertrays projected beyond the original tub sides to accept these additional structures.

Meanwhile, progressive development of the fabricated steel uprights had made them heavier now than comparably strong magnesium castings. Just as new castings were being made, Goodyear abruptly changed their tyre sizes, and consequently a stop-gap upright appeared which was very large and very ugly and in fact worked rather well.

During that 1973 season a series of alternative airboxes and far-overhung wing-mounts extending rearwards appeared, while Peterson's cars were progressively reinforced until they became strong enough to endure his driving style. He set the performance standards of the season but lost several races through car failure, until in July at the French

GP he at last survived to the finish and won as we all knew he eventually would.

There was inevitably internecine rivalry between Peterson and his essentially senior partner Fittipaldi, but the reigning Champion's cause suffered at Zandvoort when a wheel collapse during practice effectively destroyed his faithful '72/5' and a virtually new car had to be built up – slowly – to replace it.

The 72s' fiercest opposition that season came from the new ultra short-wheelbase Tyrrells and the hip-radiatored McLaren M23s. Both these designs had more even weight distributions than the Lotuses, placing greater load on their front tyres, which were also produced by Goodyear. In an effort to load their front tyres more adequately, Lotus now experimented with wide-track suspensions necessitating stiffer torsion bar springs. These alone took ages to be made and delivered by Lotus's supplier. Magnesium rear uprights now proved overweight yet again, and another attempt was made with fabricated steel. The great expense in Formula 1 lies in the parts thrown away . . .

Although the Lotus 72 brought its manufacturer the coveted Constructors' title, neither of its drivers would take their competition's crown. Fittipaldi won three GPs, all early in the season, while Peterson won four, all later in the year. Meantime, Stewart won five in his Tyrrell to beat them both.

FINAL SEASONS AND SUCCESSES

Into 1974 the intended Lotus 72 replacement, the Type 76, was at last on the way. Goodyear reverted to 28 in. overall diameter rear tyres. Fittipaldi had joined McLaren, and Peterson was joined by Jacky Ickx in Team Lotus. In Brazil the 72s were fitted with year-old uprights to match the new 'tall' Goodyear tyres. Ickx won the minor Brands Hatch race against the odds in pouring rain, and as the new Type 76 cars failed dismally, the faithful if now positively geriatric 72s raced on.

Yet Peterson's prowess reaped victories in them at Monaco, Dijon-Prenois and Monza on three of the calendar's most widely divergent circuits. So effective did his car, '72/8', prove that a final all-new machine was built up at Hethel, chassis '72/9', but while it was still incomplete parts were cannibalized from it to repair '72/8' after a heavy practice accident at the Nürburgring. Wider front track – by just over 1 in. either side – appeared at Dijon. Drilled brake discs were adopted for the British GP at Brands Hatch. In favour of reduced frontal area promoting higher straightline speed, a reversion was made to narrow-track form for Monza and it continued into the US GP at Watkins Glen.

There, however, the 72s ran into a massive understeer problem on the latest generation Goodyear tyres, which were better tailored to the front-end demands of the rival Ferrari, McLaren and Tyrrell cars which were in direct confrontation for those highly-significant (discounting personal prejudices) Championship titles.

Now the Lotus 72 was in a minority of one. Goodyear could only afford to tailor tyres to the competitive majority and once the Lotus 72 slipped off that tightrope of success, it was all downhill. Major changes had to be made to match the old cars to the available tyres, for the tyres were no longer being tailored to these highly individual cars.

Lotus's 1975 season was thus catastrophically bad. Group Lotus was in trouble, Chapman's personal attention was often distracted. Money seems to have been short, there was insufficient to invest in serious development of that long-overdue Formula 1 replacement.

The so-called 'lightweight' chassis, '72/9', was still not ready for Peterson's use as the season began in Argentina. In Brazil his '72/8' and Ickx's long-faithful '72/5' ran with new rear uprights offering further revised geometry. Both cars used large front brake discs. Peter-

son's new car emerged in time for the minor Brands Hatch race where he finished third, but by this time he was very restless with the team.

A driver named Jim Crawford was brought in to handle Ickx's car at Silverstone but he suffered two major accidents, one in testing, the other in practice. Steel cable torsion bar actuation was being tried, operating only on bump when the cables came under tension. The new Goodyear tyres' radial rates demanded the heavier loadings imparted by cars like the contemporary Ferraris, McLarens, Tyrrells and Brabhams to achieve adequate working temperatures and Team Lotus suffered badly as the 72s simply would not heat these tyres adequately.

At Ricard-Castellet, Peterson's spare '72/8' featured helper coil-springs wrapped round the front damper barrels to assist the torsion bars because weight distribution had been radically altered by outrigging the engine some 5 in. aft of the tub on a tubular framework. A new oil tank was inserted 'twixt tub and engine to replace that over the gearbox, throwing more weight further forward. Ickx's '72/5' was rigged in a similar long-wheelbase form but without the helper coils. Peterson raced his regular short-wheelbase '72/9' and finished tenth while

By 1975 Goodyear had to tailor its tyres to more advanced cars than Team's old warhorse. Peterson's '72E/9', fourth at Monaco, sports deformable-structure tub shape, new wings and airbox.

Ickx retired. It was his last race for Lotus, while Peterson was persuaded to persevere.

In the British GP he was joined by both Brian Henton and Jim Crawford, handling 72s '5' and '8' with pure coil-spring rear suspension in place of torsion bars. Conversely Peterson ran '72/9' in 1973 form – and that didn't work either.

John Watson had a one-off Lotus drive at the Nürburgring, and in the US GP at Watkins Glen Peterson drove '72/9' and Henton '72/5'. They started the race 14-19 on the grid and finished it 5-12 in the results, Peterson stealing two final World Championship points in what was the Lotus 72's long-overdue swansong six seasons after its introduction.

During that period the classic Lotus 'wedge' had won no less than 20 Grand Prix races and had brought Team Lotus three Formula 1 Constructors' World Championship titles. By any standards the Lotus 72 was a truly great racing car.

Wings and things

Considered over our whole period, aerodynamic behaviour and effect is the biggest single factor affecting the performance of the Grand Prix car from 1966 to 1984, with design and performance of the racing tyre perhaps close behind.

As early as 1928 Fritz von Opel employed 50 in. span negative-incidence wings projecting either side of his Eugen Sander-built Opel RAK 2 rocket car, hopefully to keep him in contact with Berlin's AVUS speedway as, wreathed in smoke and trailing flame, he demonstrated its 120 mph performance.

In the 1950s, Mercedes-Benz briefly adopted strutted wings on their racing 300SL Coupés, and at the Nürburgring Swiss engineer Michael May arrived with his Porsche sports car sporting an enormous strutted wing high above its centre of gravity just rear of midships. The scrutineers patted him on the head, expressed a hope that the headaches would go away, and he was compelled to remove it.

At Daytona Beach in Florida an Indy car named 'Mad Dog' hurtled round the then-new banked superspeedway with Opel-like negative-incidence wings each side.

Then it became serious: by 1966-67 Texan Jim Hall's GM R&D-backed Chaparral sports-racing cars emerged with enormous strutted rear aerofoils acting directly upon their rear suspension uprights and thence directly loading the tyre contact patch against the road.

An early GM-Chaparral inverted aerofoil-form body had pointed the way towards ground-effects aerodynamics as described elsewhere but flopped due to 'lack of correlation between actual high speed ground vehicles and simulation in a wind tunnel'. This failing would be repeated countless times by many other R&D teams.

GM-Chaparral further found that giant nose spoilers decreased drag while tail spoilers increased it. Restricting airflow beneath the car cut drag. At the tail there was a tricky choice between either download or low drag. An experienced pilot, Hall promptly developed a deck-hinged feathering rear wing which gave download into corners and low drag along the straights.

However, download on the body overwhelmed suspension travel in springs soft enough for good low-speed handling. So the ideal would be to react spoiler or wing loads direct into the top of the wheel uprights, acting directly through them to the wheel and tyre, leaving the car's sprung mass unaffected.

Thoughts turned progressively to fitting aerodynamic flaps on the suspension, then the possibility of a strutted flap above the body and, logically enough, why not a wing on tall struts running in clean undisturbed air?

In April 1966 the first wing was carved from solid pine and tested two feet above the rear of a Chevrolet Stingray, followed by a foam-filled monocoque lightweight wing for the Chaparral 2E CanAm sports-racing cars. Once structural problems in the support struts had been corrected they were effective. They were still driver-switched, giving high-drag/low-drag, high-download/low-download as required.

By the end of 1969 the ultimate strutted-wing Chaparral 2H ran in California with the biggest midship wing ever seen. In Formula 1, meanwhile, high strutted wings had run their course.

Following the Chaparral lead, Lotus World Champion driver Jim Clark had been interested enough to suggest a similar device to his mechanic Leo Wybrott and brothers Dale and Roger Porteous during their 1968 Tasman Championship tour of New Zealand.

Jimmy was driving a Lotus 49T in the South Island race meeting at Teretonga, Invercargill, and, using the Porteous boys' knowledge of aircraft, the car was rigged with a small airfoil standing on struts above its gearbox. The aerofoil itself was in fact a sawn-off section of scrap helicopter rotor blade acquired from a nearby airfield dump.

Leo, in recent years Works Manager for McLaren International, described how Jimmy thought it unwise to race the device after practising with it as Colin Chapman back home in the UK did not know what they were up to, and if anything went wrong there would be 'hell to pay'.

But young Ferrari engineer Gianni Marelli, who was there with Amon's Tasman 246T car, was fascinated by the thing and painstakingly photographed it from every angle.

The Belgian GP at Spa that June was the fastest race in the calendar. Brabham and Lotus had run small whisker nose spoilers there in 1967 to minimize lift at speed, and this year Ron Tauranac and Ray Jessop arrived with strutted rear airfoils ready to fit on their Brabham, only to find Ferrari and Forghieri had thought along similar lines and their 312 V12 cars already had similar wings fitted.

Forghieri insists this development was sparked by conversation with fuel-injection and combustion expert Michael May, of bewinged Nürburgring Porsche fame, who since 1962-63 had acted as a consultant to Ferrari. Nevertheless the coincidence of Marelli's interest in that far-distant Lotus experiment at Teretonga is too great to be ignored.

Through 1968 and into 1969 strutted wings went forth and multiplied. They grew higher, wider, shifted their feet from chassis to suspension uprights, appeared on both front and rear while the Winkelmann Formula 2 Brabham team even ran in practice at Albi a truly biplane device which would not have been out of place above the Western Front, 1914-18.

Fixed and feathering wings were developed until the Spanish GP of 1969. Lotus accidents there caused by wing failure persuaded the CSI to act and apply height, width and fixing rules to such devices.

For engineers in search of enhanced download to improve traction and cornering and braking grip, the strutted wing was a godsend. It weighed merely a few pounds, so unlike four-wheel drive represented very little additional mass to be accelerated, braked and cornered, yet in dynamic download it could generate a force of several hundred pounds which greatly improved lap speeds around a circuit.

Nose aerofoils were used to balance out the loads of tail wings around the car's centre of gravity, and all manner of minor improvements and ploys would be used to gain ever more advantage . . . but that's another story.

The 1967 Belgian GP saw very high speeds as the new 3-litre cars came on song. Below, Clark's Lotus 49 leads Brabham's BT24-Repco, its bib spoiler minimizing front-end lift while Brabham ran separate cheek vanes in the race. Bottom, just before the ban on strutted wings, Brabham's 1969 BT26-DFV won at Silverstone under this bi-wing arrangement.

Chapter 7

UNCOMPLICATED CRAFTSMANSHIP – THE CHAMPION TYRRELLS 1970-73

Geoff Goddard's unusual Monaco shot shows wet practice for the 1971 GP, with Stewart's hammerhead-nosed Tyrrell 001 T-car lining up for the quayside chicane. It emphasizes the large proportions of frontal area occupied by tyres and by wings when set to high incidence for the wet on this low-speed circuit.

When it became clear that Matra were not prepared to build a DFV-powered Formula 1 chassis for the Tyrrell team's use in 1970, and both Ken Tyrrell and his World Champion driver Jackie Stewart were disinclined to accept Matra's offered V12 engine, Tyrrell had to find a viable alternative.

For the short term he ordered three Type 701 cars from the new March Engineering company . . . and while working hard to ensure the best possible back-up from them, he knew they could only ever be a stop-gap expedient. The only way ahead was to invest at long last in the design, development and construction of his own chassis. To do that he had to find a designer capable of creating a competitive car fit for Stewart's proven class.

His choice fell upon Derek Gardner, formerly with Ferguson, who had been responsible for the four-wheel drive transmission system used in Tyrrell's Matra MS84 experimental car during 1969. This quiet, precise Midlander with his gentle sense of humour had impressed Tyrrell as a very capable and well-qualified deep-thinker; perhaps just as important, he was not widely known in the racing world, and even if people did start asking him questions he was clearly very capable of keeping his mouth shut. This was most important, as nothing must be allowed to compromise the working relationship between Team Tyrrell and March Engineering.

Coincidentally, Gardner had just decided to leave Ferguson and to go freelance when Tyrrell telephoned with a proposition. They met in a pub at Henley-on-Thames, roughly halfway between Tyrrell's base at Ockham, Surrey, and Gardner's home in Leamington Spa, Warwickshire. Tyrrell asked Gardner if he felt capable of designing a Formula 1 car. After due – and typical – deliberation, Gardner jumped at the chance.

The new car had to be simple, it must need only minimal development before proving competitive. Tyrrell stressed the vital requirement for total secrecy then emphasized that the machinery of racing sponsorship demanded it be ready for the Oulton Park Gold Cup race on 22 August. If it was any later 'you might as well chuck it in the Thames . . .'

In February 1970, at about the time that March were proudly unveiling their new Type 701s to the press, Gardner began work on what would be his first complete car design. He converted a bedroom at his home in Parklands Avenue, Leamington, into a drawing office and began his design study from a blank sheet.

He analyzed all contemporary designs and decided his own parameters for the best all-round aerodynamic form, minimum legal weight, and a low polar moment central mass concentration to promote the most favourable front/rear weight distribution. Acting ostensibly as a private individual, he began ordering forgings and castings for the new car and was amazed at the fine cooperation he received from the specialist suppliers concerned.

The first sacrifice of his racing career followed. He had to build a mock-up of the chassis and to make space for it he had to sell his beloved Mark VII Bentley, which he 'simply couldn't bear to leave outside in the weather'.

A local joinery firm built the wooden mock-up for him, which Derek completed with aluminium sheet, cardboard and a lick of blue paint. Now there was something tangible in existence, and Tyrrell's mechanics – who learned of the SP ('Secret Project') late in the day – offered comments and suggestions on its detail design. A DFV engine and Hewland gearbox were delivered to Derek's home and Stewart broke a Formula 2 test day at Goodwood to fly to Coventry to try the mock-up for size.

Derek's young daughter was a great Jackie Stewart fan, yet secrecy was such that she had

no idea that the great man had been in her home until many weeks later . . .

By mid-summer the design finally seemed as painstakingly detailed as it could be. Only then was the first metal cut, but despite growing pressure upon time nothing was accepted without rigorous inspection and several made parts were rejected and had to be made again, acceptably.

THE PROTOTYPE EMERGES

Gomm Metal Developments of Old Woking, Surrey, only five miles from Tyrrell's Ockham workshops, made the prototype monocoque, which was an open-topped 'bath-tub' type for accessibility's sake, unlike the stressed scuttle design of the team's previous Matras. The tub was formed over fabricated steel bulkheads, with 18-gauge NS4 malleable aluminium alloy skins. The forepart of the tub enclosed the driver's foot pedals, and a tubular subframe extended in front to carry the radiator and forward pick-ups for the lower front suspension members.

A massive front bulkhead structure extended into Matra-like 'wings' on each side, supporting tiny split upper wishbones and top mounts for the outboard coil-spring/damper units. Very wide-based fabricated lower wishbones were used and, despite Ken Tyrrell's desire to have unsprung weight reduced to the minimum, outboard front brakes were retained to keep the car simple.

The rear suspension hung on the DFV engine and Hewland FG400 transaxle via tubular subframes. Parallel lower links were used for toe-steer control, there was a single top link, twin radius rods and outboard coil/damper units. The rear brakes were mounted inboard on the transaxle cheeks, using 10½ in. ventilated discs similar to those in the front wheels, which were special centre-lock magnesium-alloy castings made by Aeroplane & Motor, as were the unusual and very lightweight suspension uprights and other castings. The stub axles were by Laystall, and most machining was performed by Jack Knight Engineering who were based not far from Gomm's sheet metal shop.

Gardner had tested a tenth-scale model of the car in the mechanical engineering department wind tunnel of the University of Surrey at Guildford. The result was an unusual-looking nose cowl with a wide blade-like airfoil span formed above an underslung 'shark-mouth' radiator air intake.

Hot radiator air exited through vents formed into the cockpit surround-cum-scuttle panel which was shaped in aluminium, and a broad central spine then diverted airflow around the cockpit sides and screen. Gardner intended this feature to feed relatively clean air back onto a two-tier tail wing which would be strut-mounted above the gearbox.

Fuel load was carried in four bags concentrated well within the wheelbase around the centre of gravity within a podgy Matra MS80-like 'Coke bottle' tub. When the prototype car was first assembled and weighed it scaled some 100 lb less than the team's proprietary March 701s, and was only 32 lb above the minimum weight limit. It had cost Ken Tyrrell £22,500, less engine and gearbox, compared to the purchase price of £9000 each for his March 701s. Now the new Tyrrell '001' had to prove its worth.

Its race debut at Oulton Park was indifferent during practice as the fuel metering unit drive failed, then the injection system blocked. Stewart elected to start from the back of the grid in this possibly recalcitrant new mount. On lap 2 of the first heat '001's throttles jammed and Stewart screamed into the pits to have the linkage freed off and loose bodywork re-attached. He then stormed out again and broke the lap record twice before an oil pick-up problem caused the engine to fail. Tyrrell then gave Stewart choice of either his familiar March 701 or the new Tyrrell '001' for the remaining World Championship GPs.

At Monza in practice for the Italian GP the new car's main tanks refused to feed the collector quickly enough to keep the engine running cleanly at sustained high rpm. There, Stewart was shattered by his friend Jochen Rindt's fatal accident in the Lotus 72, but he raced his March 701 hard and fast.

The Tyrrell's fuel system was improved for the trans-Atlantic trip to Canada, the USA and Mexico and '001' ran in each race driven by Stewart. They started on pole in Canada and on the front row at Watkins Glen and Mexico City. Stewart led both the Canadian and US GPs, and ran second before a minor delay, then hit a stray dog, in Mexico.

Thus in Stewart's hands the new car had shown terrific potential and had achieved more than enough to secure Tyrrell's sponsorship for 1971. There had been further teething troubles. Its wheels repeatedly worked loose during practice in Canada, then a much more serious left-front stub axle failure occurred when leading the race there. Gardner designed far more beefy replacement components which were machined from solid magnesium block by Jack Knight's craftsmen in time for the American race, which Stewart only lost when an oil-line retaining clip parted, causing the plastic line to fall against a hot exhaust manifold and burn through, which allowed the lubricant to haemorrhage away.

THE FIRST CHAMPIONSHIP TITLE

For 1971, Elf-Team Tyrrell was formed and Derek Gardner joined the Ockham team full time. Dunlop had withdrawn from Formula 1 tyre manufacture and Goodyear took their place supplying Tyrrell.

One most significant reason behind the team's success thus far had been that both Tyrrell and Stewart understood the immense value of prolonged tyre testing. January 1971 found them running '001' at Kyalami using 400 Goodyears specially flown out for the test programme. Cosworth had decided to build

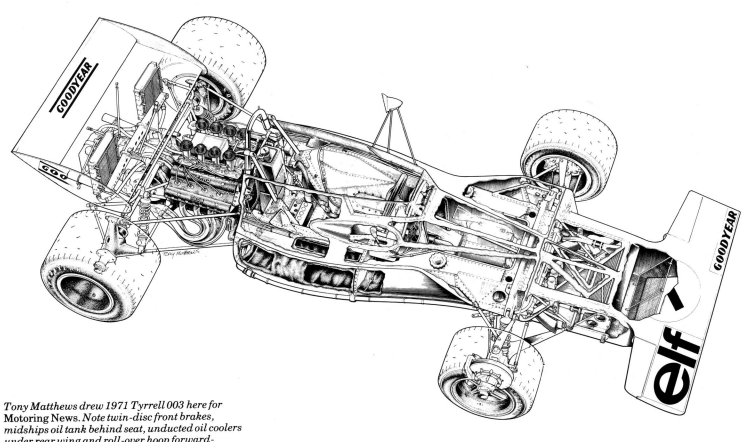

Tony Matthews drew 1971 Tyrrell 003 here for Motoring News. *Note twin-disc front brakes, midships oil tank behind seat, unducted oil coolers under rear wing and roll-over hoop forward-braced in case engine should break away from tub in an accident.*

only 15 new '11-series' DFV engines for that season, all of which they would maintain themselves while licensing approved outside concerns to service and rebuild the older units. Tyrrell were to have two of the latest engines, while JW Automotive – of Gulf-Porsche endurance racing fame – were to service their others.

Stewart ran one engine for no less than 986 miles at Kyalami before deciding it was due for a change. Tyrrell was confident that his new car's unreliability was now a thing of the past.

Certainly during the Stewart period, the Tyrrell team was in the box seat so far as supply of the finest Cosworth-Ford engines was concerned. But in appraising their success it would be asinine to ignore the superb workmanship and top-quality preparation which went into the cars which those engines powered, and which that driver drove. It was certainly a major factor in the success of cars which technically were perhaps regarded as more competent than sensational. Even so, few teams were as active in research and experimentation as Elf-Team Tyrrell under Derek Gardner's technical direction.

Continuing the Kyalami tests with a new engine, '001' went on through the 1400 mile mark until a pebble jammed between throttle pedal and bracket, and the dark-blue Tyrrell crashed quite heavily. Stewart jarred his wrist, while the monocoque's left-front corner was crushed back some four to five inches. The wreck was rushed back home where the damaged tub was unstitched, the skins beaten true and then reassembled.

Meanwhile, the new second car '002' – the first entirely Tyrrell-built vehicle – was progressing alongside this repair work in the Ockham workshop. The new car's tub was four inches longer than the prototype's largely to accommodate number two driver François Cevert's lanky frame. The new car's wheelbase was only 1½ in. longer than '001's but there were several other detail differences.

The cockpit offered more elbow room. Thicker 16-gauge NS4 alloy outer skins were now used instead of 18-gauge. The front bulkhead no longer used steel tubing within the tub. Now a more simple suspension-carrying frame was first made up on a jig, then slipped over the stressed-skin monocoque to which it was then riveted from outside.

A hefty 360-degree roll-over hoop encircled the rear bulkhead, being both spigoted and bolted through into the tub. The stressed DFV engine was also then bolted through this hoop, while forward radius rod pick-ups were carried on it. Other changes included new one-piece lower front wishbones, made from S514 aviation-spec material and chromed for protection from flying grit and debris; side fuel fillers replacing '001's central pot; and twin gearbox-mounted oil-coolers in place of the single matrix which had been found deficient at Kyalami.

A new large-capacity Graviner fire extinguisher bottle lived in the stiffening panel under the driver's knees while the fuel collector, battery and oil tanks still tucked away behind his back. Solid brake discs appeared at the rear instead of ventilated and a stronger pedal assembly was fitted, all to improve 'feel'. Gardner was examining alternative body designs, but for the moment bodywork was unchanged, although glass-fibre cockpit surrounds were on the way, to replace the original aluminium type.

Returning to Kyalami for the season-opening South African GP on 6 March, Cevert mangled both ends of his brand new '002' while Stewart qualified '001' unchallenged on pole position at record pace – faster even than in tyre testing there. But he was then handicapped by indifferent performance from both engine and tyres during the race and finished a poor second. Three minor races followed with Stewart driving '001' as a lone Tyrrell entry while '002' was being repaired, and being

1971 Race of Champions: Jackie Stewart heats up short-wheelbase Tyrrell 001's tyres. Scuttle-top spine deflected hot radiator air along each side away from driver's face, the cockpit surround bulge gave gearchange space.

beaten each time. The team was beginning to wonder just what kind of car it had, when '003' was completed in time for the Spanish GP at Barcelona. This was a new car specifically for Stewart's use, and with luck he was able to win with it in Spain, and then at Monaco, and in the French, British, German, and Canadian GPs by season's end, while Cevert won the US GP in his regular car '002' and was second behind his team leader in France and Germany, and third in Italy.

Stewart won the Drivers' World Championship going away and Tyrrell became Formula 1 Constructors' Champion at their first attempt.

The only tangible difference between cars '002' and '003' was that Stewart's had adjustable foot pedals installed to compensate for his height deficiency compared to Cevert.

After the Spanish victory a new wedge-shaped nose cowl, rather like the contemporary Matra MS120's, was tested at Ricard-Castellet. It cancelled more lift with less drag than the blade nose but its effect was more than the existing rear wing could balance adequately, so Gardner returned to the University of Surrey for further wind tunnel model research.

Cars '001' and '003' were then taken to the minor Silverstone race for Stewart to choose between, '001', wearing experimental Girling twin-disc front brakes. There were two solid discs on each hub, spaced by a double thickness of pad material, and with pistons on only one side of the calliper. The discs were given a degree of side-float which allowed them to move sideways, cramped by the pads, when the brakes were applied. The idea was to double pad and disc area and provide better heat dissipation plus the opportunity to reduce line pressures which permitted the use of smaller pistons and less deflection on pad wear. The problem had been that conventional discs were wearing the brake pads into a taper form. This in turn promoted 'knock-off' when the drivers braked hard, giving a spongy pedal feel and slashing driver confidence.

Stewart raced '003' at Silverstone, winning the first heat, but then he crashed heavily on the first corner of heat two. This appeared to have been caused by yet another jammed throttle, since the car powered straight on into the outside bank with its front wheels locked solid under heavy braking, but no cause could be found as the wreck was dismantled.

The whole front end of the monocoque had been wrenched to one side, grievously damaged

with less than two weeks' grace before the Monaco GP. Yet flat-out work got the car to Monaco, where the Matra-like nose was tried in practice. The standard blade type was used in the race after Stewart had qualified on pole with it, fully 1.2 secs faster than Ickx's Ferrari, his closest rival.

Completing the warm-up lap, Stewart complained of locking front brakes. A Rose joint on the brake balance bar had come unwound and there was no time for it to be readjusted before the race began with the Tyrrell virtually brakeless at the rear.

The driver's personal genius shone as he came home regardless to a perfect win, having led all the way from pole and set fastest lap. He was violently sick as he climbed from the car, and the mechanics found its engine had consumed nearly two gallons of oil. That brilliant race had taken a lot out of both man and machine.

After Monaco, Gardner made his first real bodywork changes in time for the Dutch GP at Zandvoort where both regular cars appeared with double-disc front brakes and squat glass-fibre ram airboxes above the engine inductions. Lotus's 72s had been using small intakes to feed clean air since the previous year's British GP, while Matra used a rough snorkel-type intake which was really a mere airstream guide as it was not properly sealed. The idea intrigued Gardner, and now his properly sealed version really set the fashion. They worked well if kept clear of hot air from the radiators.

Also new in Holland, although only shown on '003' in scrutineering, was a bluff nose cone, reminiscent of a Porsche 908/3 sports-racing car's which extended to the legal maximum width ahead of the front wheels and served to fare airflow over their tyres. This fairing killed a proportion of the aerodynamic lift which they – as, in effect, rotating cylinders interposed in a moving airstream – inevitably generated. Reducing that lift also reduced its inevitable companion, drag, and would yield great dividends.

The bluff nose made its racing debut in the French GP at Ricard-Castellet where its improved download and reduced drag helped make '003' quick through the corners and simply uncatchable on the long Mistral straight. The twin-disc brakes were removed there from both Tyrrells, after Stewart had a harmless practice spin into the catch-fencing, for Girling seemed happy with the lessons learned thus far. In the race, which Stewart won handsomely with Cevert second, the Frenchman's car lost an exhaust tailpipe. Safety keeps were fitted thereafter. At Silverstone for the British GP, both Tyrrells wore bluff noses and Stewart won so convincingly that '003's engine was sealed and its capacity checked and verified by the scrutineers post-race. In France fuel samples had been taken away for analysis. Neither check revealed anything illegal. The Tyrrell-DFVs driven by Stewart and Cevert simply had the measure of their opposition. The spare car, '001' received a bluff nose in time for the German GP, which yielded another Tyrrell 1-2 victory, and now Gardner had begun experimenting with an eye on 1972.

The later two cars' longer wheelbase seemed to make them more forgiving to drive than the original short-wheelbase prototype. Therefore '003' was rigged with a 4.3 in. long distance piece inserted between engine and gearbox, and incorporating a lengthened gearbox mainshaft, extended clutch release mechanism and lengthened rear subframes and radius rods. The whole rear suspension and gearbox assembly moved rearwards, altering weight distribution and raising polar moment.

The car was run in this form during first practice at the Österreichring, then returned to standard spec for second practice and the race, but lapped no faster. Gardner was interested in placing more weight on the rear wheels and cutting drag still further.

For Monza, '003' was set up with the long wheelbase kit plus a tray-type rear wing carrying the water radiators and oil coolers. The standard nose radiator remained in place, with a simple blanking plate to mask it off when running experimentally on the wing radiator system.

This worked well enough but temperatures were borderline by the standards of that time. Four years later similar temperatures wouldn't

Stewart's Tyrrell 003 dominated mid-1971 GPs, thanks to new Cosworth exhausts, bluff nose to minimize drag-inducing front-wheel lift, and well-sealed engine airbox. Fenced rear wing showed further sophistication. Top right, Girling's experimental twin-disc Tyrrell brake.

raise an eyebrow. Stewart raced '003' with the nose radiator in commission, though the tray-type rear wing and oil coolers were retained.

Both race cars reverted to standard trim with airboxes, bluff noses, front radiators and normal wheelbase for the money-making trip to Canada and the USA, winning both times. A third standard-wheelbase car '004' was completed right at the end of the season as a spare for Stewart.

BUILDING FOR THE FUTURE

Now Gardner had digested the results of his long-wheelbase experiments he believed that a driver of Stewart's perception and touch, or of Cevert's – for he had developed into a most capable *pilote* – could probably extract more from a skittish shorter-wheelbase car like '001'.

He had completed preliminary design sketches for a new Tyrrell to replace the relatively simple, short-life cars of the original series, '001-004'. While his team were racing in North America, Derek stayed at home, testing a full-scale mock-up of the new design in the MIRA wind tunnel at Nuneaton.

The new tub was low, broad and with a wedge profile, a chisel nose, midship water and oil coolers *à la* Lotus 72, and with a conning tower cockpit surround to compensate for the low tub height in defending the driver from the airstream. Steeply dihedral fins protruded either side of the nose cone and there were vertical fins on each radiator pod. The tall arching airbox had a radiused triangular air intake orifice derived from the tailfin engine pod of a BAC Trident airliner – which one of Ken Tyrrell's sons flew. Outboard coil-springs were retained on conventional rear suspension and with a new very wide-based wishbone system up front.

Derek Gardner had been intrigued by a finned Matra prototype. Fins, he felt, could be effective in cleaning up airflow to the rear wing with the car in yaw – sliding at a slight angle to its true direction of travel. Unfortunately, tunnel results indicated that the car would indeed be stable in a straight line but would be difficult to control in a slide. It wasn't worth the complication.

Stewart and Cevert concentrated upon their familiar '003' and '002' cars at the start of the 1972 season. Stewart would win the Argentine and French GPs in the ever-faithful '003', adding to his 1971 successes with the old car to make it arguably the most successful individual chassis in Grand Prix history, with no

less than eight Championship-qualifying victories to its credit. François' car ran new front suspension uprights integral with brake callipers in South Africa. These were subsequently adopted as standard. Derek's substantial makeshift uprights had been used throughout 1971, making him shudder whenever he saw them.

Stewart blooded the spare '004' at Monaco, but he was off form, and an ulcer was diagnosed soon after which meant he missed the Belgian GP at Nivelles. Immediately after that race the prototype 'series two' Tyrrell, chassis '005', was completed.

Gardner explained how he 'wanted to build a small car, a light, manoeuvrable, well-handling car. The type of car Jackie could make the most of . . .'

The new vehicle was as wide as its predecessors, but was lower and shorter, aiming at a more central mass concentration to reduce its polar moment of inertia, thus making it more swerveable and quicker to respond to steering and attitude inputs than its predecessors.

Its monocoque was a flat-topped, slab-sided bath-tub holding 41 gallons of Elf fuel in its pontoon bag tanks and raking down wedge-profile towards the nose. Deep cut-outs in the cockpit inner panels gave the driver elbow room, making this a difficult tub to build. Suspension followed Tyrrell practice though the top front wishbones were new one-piece fabrications. At that time only Lotus had adopted and remained faithful to all-inboard brakes, front and rear. This reduced unsprung weight, allowed the wheels to change direction more rapidly from bump to rebound – and thus reduced the chance of their bouncing uncontrolled clear of the road surface. No matter how sticky the tyres might be, they need to be in contact with something in order to stick to it.

In face of Stewart's misgivings, remembering his friend Rindt's death, Gardner considered that the bugbear of brakeshaft fragility had now been laid to rest and he adopted ventilated discs and callipers mounted each side of a narrow pedal-box projecting from the tub's front end. They reacted on the wheels through solid GKN shafts equipped with double CV joints to cater for suspension and steering angularity.

Little '005' was very clean aerodynamically. Its nose was fully two inches lower than the 'series one' cars', its wheelbase two inches shorter. A nose radiator was retained, but the oil coolers were now in neat midships ducts which faired back into a flat rear deck combining with the airbox to encase the engine and feed clean air onto the tail wing. The conning tower idea emerged here in the plastic, with moulded horizontal strakes on each side to deflect hot radiator air away from the driver's face after exhausting through top ducts on the nose.

The new car was driven by Cevert in Silverstone tests, then more seriously in practice for his home GP at Clermont-Ferrand. After setting fastest time there he lost control and clanged into the Armco head-on. Because of the deep elbow cutaways in the cockpit, the whole tub was found to have bent its back. It was not strong enough to endure that kind of

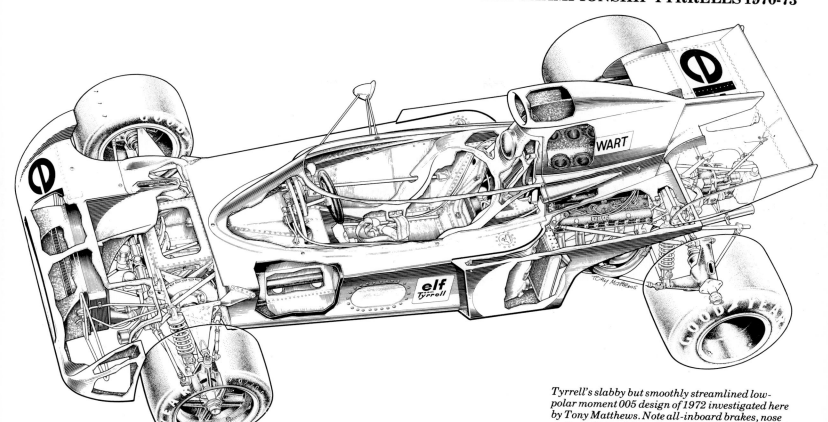

Tyrrell's slabby but smoothly streamlined low-polar moment 005 design of 1972 investigated here by Tony Matthews. Note all-inboard brakes, nose water radiator, hip coolers and tall airbox flowing into rear wing.

mistreatment. Team Tyrrell was short of spares for its new baby, so the car was set aside to be repaired and strengthened with steel plates beneath its top skins.

Stewart won the Clermont race in '003' while Cevert finished fourth in '002' and cadet driver Patrick Depailler made an appearance in the spare '004'. He would drive it again in the US GP and would find a permanent place in the team 18 months hence.

New car '005' reappeared at Brands Hatch for the British GP, where Stewart set third fastest time in first practice and second quickest in the second session before a rear suspension Rose joint parted, releasing a radius rod which sent '005' into the bank again. This time the damage was minor. Chief Mechanic Roger Hill actually drove the car back to the pits but once again it would not be raced. During the GP Cevert crashed '002' heavily, ripping off its left-front wheel, and another car subsequently crashed into the wreckage, amputating both the Tyrrell's surviving suspensions. It was still repaired in time for the German GP, two weeks later at the Nürburgring, and Cevert promptly crashed again in practice, doing it further major injury. Despite such treatment of '002', he disliked the spare car '004' so it was cannibalized and its entire rear end bolted to '002's hastily beaten-out monocoque in time for the race.

While these dramas afflicted '002', aspiring club driver Vern Schuppan was testing '005' at Silverstone, hacking up and down Hangar Straight with a mass of recording apparatus attached to investigate front-end vibrations as the inboard brakes were applied. Unfortunately vibration proved so severe it upset the test equipment so Gardner took the car to MIRA where its tremors were investigated on a rolling road. Inboard brakes clearly required further research, so '005' appeared in Austria with outboard front brakes and the Trident-type airbox. The original lower type had been gulping hot radiator air, and now he was climbing higher in search of a fresher draught.

Stewart raced the car at the Österreichring and built a spectacular lead until it began to vibrate and oversteer. He felt sure something

had broken, but he persevered to finish seventh, after which nothing seemed to be amiss. In subsequent investigative testing at Silverstone '005' continued to misbehave, until the left-front tyre from the Austrian race was changed. Magically, it all came good. That tyre's inner shoulder had worn unevenly, possibly due to excessive suspension camber, and no other fault could be traced.

Monza followed, and either Stewart or Hulme of McLaren had to win there and in the final two GPs of the season to deny Fittipaldi and Lotus of the World Championship titles. Stewart drove '005' again while Cevert's '002' appeared with a large diameter sleeve over each exhaust tailpipe, cowled from the oil coolers ahead of them. The intention was to harness exhaust gas energy to entrain air through the sleeve and so enhance cooling flow through the oil coolers. Sadly the whole panjandrum disintegrated after very few laps, the pieces bouncing and cartwheeling into history in the Tyrrell's wake. Gardner filed the idea for future reference . . .

For the North American trip, another 'series two' car, '006', was completed and it too used outboard front brakes although mounts were incorporated for the inboard type. Cevert took it over happily and while Stewart won both races in Canada and the USA, Cevert followed him home for a Tyrrell 1-2 at Watkins Glen.

In late-season tunnel testing Gardner had tried another mock-up to investigate what he called a 'rectilinear structure' car, very short with a 91 in. wheelbase, and square cut with a long extended bluff nose. He toyed with eccentric looking wing sections and also had a dry-sump gearbox lubrication system made which was used for the first time in the Canadian GP.

1973 – WINNING AND LOSING

Those dominant performances at the end of 1972 determined Elf-Team Tyrrell to retrieve Champion status in 1973. In Argentina to start the new season, both '005' and '006' appeared with inboard front brakes installed, coupled to the hubs via new large-diameter drive tubes in

place of the original solid shafts. These provided instant indication of undue stress and impending failure.

The Brazilian GP was run at the long and bumpy Interlagos circuit. Tyrrell had tested there in December and found their short-wheelbase cars pitching and skipping in an unnerving fashion. Consequently the 1971 long-wheelbase conversion kit was reused. '005' ran first Brazilian practice in this form but was slower than Cevert's standard '006'.

A torsion-bar sprung rear suspension had been designed between these two South American races and a new wedge-shaped car with midship water radiators and a very stubby monocoque skinned in Mallite sandwich material was under study. This aerospace composite, sandwiching end-grain balsa wood in thin aluminium sheet, had been used by Robin Herd of McLaren back in 1966 but its manufacturers were astonished when Gardner visited them to order special sheets using Formula 1 regulation 16-gauge thick sheathing. The new car was initially to use coil-springs, because torsion bar delivery would take almost a year.

As late as the 1973 Italian GP, the new '74 Tyrrell was intended to be this very short car, narrow at the rear where the torsion bars would be fitted, with inboard-mounted rising-rate front suspension and hip radiators gulping air through a large NACA duct sunk into the top of the nose. But it was not to be.

Meanwhile, in Kyalami practice Stewart had a rear brake-line chafe through, losing one brake circuit and crashing heavily, mangling '005's left side. Tyrrell had no spare car. The wreck had to be repaired with a set of outboard front brakes installed. Stewart took over Cevert's '006', set it up to his liking on race morning, and salvaged victory from that practice disaster.

On the Monday after the race, Cevert ran some Goodyear tyre test laps in the victorious '006'. A tyre overheated, so he stopped to have it changed. Unfortunately, wheels were stacked in the pits for both inboard and outboard brakes, and in error an outboard-brake wheel lacking the drive pegs necessary to lock it onto the inboard-brake drive tube was fitted. As Cevert entered Crowthorne Corner where Stewart had crashed, he braked hard, the brake tubes were retarded, but that unpegged front wheel revolved unhindered. Consequently, '006' spun viciously and smacked into the same wall which had mauled its sister. Fortunately damage was relatively minor.

Back home, a brand new 'series three' car was being completed for Stewart's use in Europe where the new deformable structure tank protection regulations would take effect in Spain. This new regulation had been published so late the previous year that '005' had been designed without foreknowledge. Had Gardner known beforehand, '005' would not have been built the way it was. However, it had more than proved itself, and since nobody wanted to change the basic design, separate crush pads were now added to these three Tyrrells as 38 lb afterthoughts.

The latest '006/2' had larger oil-cooler side pods to allow the water radiators to be moved there subsequently from the nose. Its older sister '006' was tested with a longer bluff nose to balance a rear wing outrigged further aft.

Using '006/2' Stewart won at Silverstone upon its debut, and then rewrote the World Championship record books. He won the Belgian and Monaco GPs to equal Jim Clark's career record of 25 Championship-round wins, then surpassed his late compatriot's total with further victories in the Dutch and German races. Cevert was second to his team leader at Zolder, Zandvoort and the Nürburgring to underline Tyrrell's strength, but Lotus were able to accumulate more Constructors' Championship points with their Type 72 cars, both their drivers – Peterson and Fittipaldi – winning GPs during that year to foil Tyrrell's chances of a second Constructors' Cham-

pionship title.

During that 1973 season, Tyrrell had encountered terrible trouble with overheating brakes at Barcelona and Zolder in Belgium, and new heavier, thicker Lockheed callipers and discs were fitted to '006' and '006/2' while '005' carried heftier Girlings for comparison.

This car had now become an experimental hack, and it practised at Zolder with hip water radiators, and a very sharp chisel nose with a NACA duct sunk into its upper surface feeding a front-mounted oil cooler. It then returned to bluff nose form for Monaco, chisel for Sweden, bluff for Ricard-Castellet and back to chisel nose thereafter, though it was bobbed slightly for the Dutch GP. In Canada and the USA '005' was entered for third driver Chris Amon.

Stewart's '006/2' was converted briefly to chisel nose form in Canada, and after Cevert's regular '006' was written off in that race a brand new car, '006/3', was completed for his use at Watkins Glen.

In practice there he crashed horribly and was

killed, and the brand new car was demolished.

After the accident, towards the end of the afternoon practice session, Stewart and guest driver Chris Amon circulated briefly in their cars, and then Ken Tyrrell withdrew his entries that evening and the team sadly packed and returned disconsolately home.

Jackie Stewart had driven his last Grand Prix race, his 99th, in Canada and would not now reach his century. For Elf-Team Tyrrell it was the end of an era built around the greatest driver of that period. After Cevert's death they now had to plan and build anew for 1974, and Derek Gardner's plans for a highly-strung thoroughbred car from which only the masters could extract an elusive potential now had to be set aside. With Stewart retired and Cevert dead, the new team drivers would be comparative schoolboys, and it was considered prudent to design completely different cars in keeping with their inexperience. Never again, within our period, would Tyrrell win the World Championship.

Above, Cevert testing stubby new Tyrrell 005 at Silverstone in 1972, see-through front wheels betraying inboard brakes in Gardner's well-faired prototype low-polar moment design. Below, Stewart equalling Clark's record 25 GP wins, Monaco '73 in deformable-structure '006/2'. Note tall 'Trident' airbox and brake cooling chimneys.

The Tyrrell Six-Wheeler

In 1975 the Tyrrell Racing Organisation sought an unusual advantage over their fellow Cosworth DFV and Goodyear tyre users as engineer Derek Gardner evolved his remarkable six-wheeled Project 34 design.

The idea, as he tells the story, '. . . was to minimize induced drag by reducing lift at the front and to turn that small gain into the ability to enter and leave corners faster. It was a matter of trading downforce for cornering power and it seemed to work.

'Tyres stuck out in the airstream generate lift so one has to counteract that by adding downforce. If everyone else does more or less the same you all end up with very similar performance given that we all used the same engine and effectively the same tyres.

'If one can reduce lift it gives you extra effective downforce to play with and more downforce translates into more cornering speed.'

To achieve this aim he adopted a very broad bluff nose section masking two small-wheeled front suspension sets running 10 in. diameter front wheels and tyres. There was no advantage in car frontal area, since its value was still dictated by the huge standard-sized rear tyres, but this was not at all what Derek was seeking.

A rotating cylinder – such as that presented by a racing car wheel and tyre – introduced into a moving airstream will generate a force at right angles to its cylindrical axis, the magnitude of that force being related to the cylinder's radius. In the case of a rotating racing car wheel and tyre this force is exerted in an upward direction as lift. Appreciation of this effect is what led Tecno and BMW in Formula 2 and Gardner in Formula 1 – after Matra had introduced their full-width chisel affair at Kyalami '71 – to adopt the broad bluff wheel-fairing noses of 1970-71.

However, by reducing the front-wheel size in the P34 this lift was instantly reduced, enhancing cornering and braking forces, the actual reduction in overall diameter being from 21 to 16 inches.

Naturally, all four steerable front wheels were braked, and a further considerable advantage was found in using four front discs, offering increased mass of cast-iron in the discs themselves which short-term reduced working temperatures; furthermore, an enlargement of the disc swept-area improved brake cooling by radiation. Increased rotational speed enhanced cooling airflow through

the ventilated disc drillings and passages. Total pad area was also increased, which reduced working temperatures, and a gain of nearly 40 per cent in useable pad volume greatly extended pad life on certain demanding circuits.

Brake balance had to be achieved between the front two axles and the rear, and Gardner developed a triple master-cylinder system, each feeding the brakes on one axle. The driver's brake pedal was attached to a balance bar acting at one end on the rear-brake master cylinder and at the other end onto a secondary balance bar which could be adjusted similarly to divide effort between the two front-axle master cylinders.

The team would set the balance first between the two pairs of front brakes, bearing in mind that if the first-axle brakes locked first then the effective wheelbase would be shortened, if the second-axle brakes locked first it would be lengthened, with consequent queasy changes in handling and driver 'feel'.

Disadvantages in the braking sense included the

Left, Motor Sport's *Denis Jenkinson inspects 'P34/1' in 1975. Right, Scheckter demonstrates the car's front-end grip into Monza's* Curva Parabolica *in that year's Italian GP. Below, Piola's exploded sketch amply illustrates the Tyrrell P34's complexity.*

higher rotational speed of the small front wheels and discs for a given road speed, but since the discs themselves were smaller the critical rubbing speed at the pad surface was about the same as normal.

Once they had learned how to operate – and to drive – these unusual cars early in 1976, the Tyrrell team achieved significant success, as described in the Team Directory.

Taking contemporary tyre technology early that year, they had a distinct advantage in suitable conditions, but as the season progressed they encountered problems which outstripped Goodyear's development capabilities.

That was the season of Ferrari versus McLaren and quite rightly Goodyear concentrated development upon the needs of those cars, the 312T2s and M23s. When newly developed conventional front and rear tyres were introduced, the P34s could use the rears but there was no compatible new 10 in. front tyre for them. Consequently they had either to run unbalanced or to retain outdated rears.

To combat this small-diameter front tyre stagnation Gardner had only one option for 1977: progressively to increase the front track to load up available fronts to match latest compounds and construction. The small wheels' high rotational speeds in any case played havoc with the profiles of contemporary cross-ply racing tyres, the crown centre 'throwing out' to diminish contact area against the road surface.

The wider front track for 1977 necessitated bodywork changes in an attempt to retrieve aerodynamic advantage and the already overweight cars grew less and less competitive and became even heavier.

In retrospect, Gardner believes that radial-ply front tyres would have been the answer. 'If Tyrrell had been on Michelins the story might have been different' – and indeed Michelin were interested in assisting. However, by the time they had developed a new 10 in. size from scratch, Goodyear's conventional tyres for conventional cars would have leapt three or four stages further ahead.

Gardner had received an attractive offer to return to his first love of transmission engineering with Borg Warner and while an Elf-backed potential engine supply deal was being set up with Renault he had already taken on Maurice Phillippe to develop a Tyrrell chassis for a Renault engine.

After he had handed total responsibility to Phillippe and left the team, the Renault plan – which had included both a broad-arrow 3-litre nine-cylinder and a 1500 cc turbocharged V6 – evaporated. Maurice introduced a four-wheeled P34 replacement for 1978 and this was destined to win on conventional, competitive and untroublesome Goodyear tyres . . . only four per car.

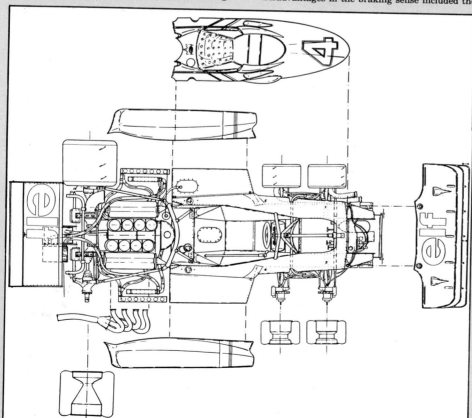

Chapter 8

THE McLAREN M23, 1973-77

During the summer of 1972 all Formula 1 teams were thinking towards the deformable structure regulations which would become effective early in the new season. At Colnbrook, under the Heathrow flight paths west of London, Team McLaren thought more deeply than any other.

Not for them any afterthought tack-on crush pads in their new car. They determined to build a properly integrated tailor-made monocoque which would optimize their long-held tenets of strength, practicality and simplicity combined with sheer product quality.

Engineer Gordon Coppuck had been mainly responsible for McLaren's highly successful and innovative CanAm and Indianapolis cars during this period, but when ex-Brabham designer Ralph Bellamy – who had designed the M19s – left to return to Brabham at the end of 1971, Coppuck remained alone in charge of the drawing office.

He began work on the new 1973 Formula 1 car, drawing deeply upon his Indianapolis M16 experience with a wedge-form monocoque and hip-mounted radiators. McLaren's method of design had always pivoted around a workshop discussion which would include the team principals, drivers and mechanics in addition to the nominal designer himself. This system worked very well for the team for many years.

The basic M16 shape had followed the lead of the Lotus 56 and 72 wedges of 1968-70, to take full advantage of the constant high-speed regime prevailing at Indy. Now, during 1972, Coppuck recalls how 'we had taken an M16 tub and a Cosworth rear end from the M19, sat them down on the workshop floor, looked at them; thought about them, and weighed them, and all the answers told us the right thing. Do it. So we did, and the M23 came into being.'

The M19 in its final C-specification form had handled very well but was slow on the straight and overweight. The long and arduous develop-

ment of its rising-rate suspension system had achieved a very efficient front end, but at the rear the team had admitted defeat and reverted to a constant-rate layout.

Eventually they could attribute the M19C's good handling to its big wings and rising-rate front end. Its poor straightline speed could be blamed on induced drag from those big wings and high profile drag from the bulbous, heavily-riveted tub.

The new M23 was Gordon Coppuck's first Formula 1 design. Its tub was formed in 16-gauge aluminium sheet, shaped over a massive fabricated steel bulkhead at the front and a capacious tank section at the back, between the driver's seatback and engine bulkhead, which was itself a three-quarter affair, with separate steel fabrications for the top engine mounts. The dash frame consisted of steel bracketry rather than a conventional intermediate bulkhead, while steel pick-ups were built in for the rearward legs of the lower front wishbones, the front bulkhead itself extending back into the monocoque for eight to ten inches.

In the usual McLaren manner, which was unusual when originated by Robin Herd in 1968, all panel joints in these tubs were bonded with epoxy adhesive as well as being riveted – the riveting in effect securing the joint while the adhesive cured.

This new tub tapered in planform and also – at the front – in section where the front bulkhead was wider at top than bottom. Unlike the detachable radiator side pods of the Lotus 72 and the McLaren M16 Indy cars, those of the new M23 were formed as an integral delta-form extension of the monocoque structure, the intention being to provide two-stage deformable protection under impact.

The tub's horizontal 16-gauge aluminium skins extended over and under these pods, shaping into their outer vertical panel while a

Denny Hulme winning the 1973 Swedish GP at Anderstorp in McLaren 'M23/1' – a lucky win at the expense of Peterson's Lotus 72 though the McLaren also set fastest lap. This was the first of the long M23 series' 21 frontline race wins.

glass-fibre insert section then slid into the pod intake, mating neatly with the aluminium skins and extending into the midship monocoque flank itself. Once the assembly had been drilled, countersunk and flush-riveted this left a gap of about ¾ in. between GRP insert and aluminium skin, which McLaren's build crew under Don Beresford then filled with twin-pack aerosol foam. The foaming reaction began as soon as the two chemicals mixed at the injector nozzle, and precautions had to be taken to prevent the pressure created by the expanding form then blowing out the GRP insert and distorting the aluminium. A shaped block was made up from the GRP mould to support the plastic against foam pressure, while the rest of the tub structure had similarly to be strapped and supported during this cavity-filling operation. A row of half-inch drain holes allowed excess foam to escape, and once the foam had set then the residue could be trimmed back, the holes capped and sanded smooth. The end result was a very good deformable crush pad built integrally into the hull and contributing towards its torsional rigidity without undue weight penalty.

Learning the intricacies of this new technique caused some heartache but, once the McLaren crew became accustomed to it, it worked well. One major drawback, however, was that it complicated damage repair.

Fuel tankage was concentrated amidships with relatively little capacity extending toward the dash panel on each side to promote Matra/Tyrrell/March-like low polar moment. All previous McLaren F1 tubs had carried their fuel right from front bulkhead to rear.

The M23's cockpit was as confined as possible to narrow the tub and ease airflow into the hip radiator ducts, which housed both the water radiators and oil cooler cores. Deletion of the nose radiator instantly reduced cockpit temperatures, further helped by the insulating effect of the large fuel tank between driver and hot engine bay. This set the driver further forward than ever before, with his feet ahead of the front axle line.

In the cockpit the Graviner fire extinguisher bottle sat crosswise beneath the driver's knees. For his protection the steering box was now inboard of the front bulkhead, just ahead of the dash panel and less than 12 inches from the steering wheel. All steering links and arms were behind the front uprights, leaving the front monocoque bulkhead extremely tidy with only the brake master cylinders and slender front anti-roll bar protruding.

A neat tray arrangement carried the lightweight Varley battery while a spidery tubular subframe extended further forward to accept the wedge-shaped detachable nose cone and its front aerofoil aerodynamic loadings. NACA ducts moulded into each side of this cone fed slots through the front bulkhead which played cooling air onto the inboard coil-spring/damper units buried just behind.

The rising-rate front suspension comprised wide-based lower wishbones and triangulated tubular top rocker arms whose inboard extremities compressed the spring/damper units via linkages with rising-rate geometry. With the new midship fuel tankage, variation in fuel load made much greater percentage difference to the load carried by the front wheels than by the rears. M19 experience showed that this allowed a much simpler system to be used there, with progressively wound coil-springs of the type which become coil-bound from the lower end as load increased.

Rear suspension location was by reversed lower wishbones, adjustable top links and twin radius rods. Some vital unsprung weight had been saved by dispensing with conventional sliding-spline driveshaft joints. These normally allow the driveshafts to telescope, so accommodating changes in length between their inboard anchorage on the final-drive outputs and their outboard anchorage on the wheel flange as the

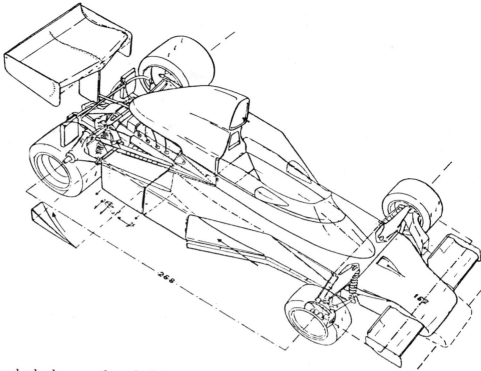

road wheels move through their suspension arc. Now Coppuck had adopted a floating axle system tried successfully on the M19s. It used two needle roller bearings in the upright instead of the conventional single needle roller and one fixed bearing. Two diameters were machined to suit on the fixed-length shaft, and it was allowed to float sideways in and out of the upright as the suspension rose and fell. The wheel face prevented the shaft pulling through one way, the fixed universal-joint yoke the other way. Shims fitted in assembly ensured the upright centred statically in the middle of the driveshaft bearing track provided.

This system worked very well, saving the considerable weight of a conventional sliding-spline joint, and a further saving followed when Titanium driveshafts were adopted with steel yokes pushed onto them.

Lockheed CanAm-developed four-pot brake callipers were used, clasping 10.5 in. ventilated discs all round. At the front, where live stub axles were used, rotating within the cast magnesium uprights, the discs were mounted outboard but not fully buried within the 13 in. diameter/11 in. wide wheels. At the rear, where road wheel sizes were 13 in. x 16-18 in. wide, the brake discs were inboard, further reducing unsprung weight. While the oil coolers sat right behind the water radiator cores within those integral side pods, the oil tank itself was buried in the left-rear corner of the monocoque, while the system catch tank formed a saddle over the bell-housing for the Hewland FG400 five-speed transaxle.

The oil cooler mounting tidied up rear-end plumbing to clear airflow beneath the working undersurface of the tubular-strutted rear wing.

At the time of its release in February 1973, the M23 was unusual in being so fully bodied, following Gardner's lead with Tyrrell 005 the preceding summer. The untidy engine induction was concealed within a shapely airbox cowl merging into the rear tub-cum-side pod form.

The M23 was an inch longer in wheelbase than the M19, at 101 in., and the tub was lower than its predecessor but the airbox extended taller than before in search of cleaner air, making the car noticeably higher. Front track was 65 in., rear track 62.5 in. overall length 170 in. and claimed weight 1270 lb distributed 34 front/66 rear.

In the next four seasons, thirteen McLaren M23s would be built – chassis number '13' being skipped for superstitious reasons so the

Piola again, showing dimensional data of McLaren's multi-wedge M23 as modified for the 1975 season.

final car took the number M23/14. The cars would bring their drivers two World Championship titles and their manufacturer one Formula 1 Constructors' Cup victory, and they would win no fewer than 20 Championship-qualifying Grands Prix, and arguably 21 if another on-the-road victory is counted from which car and driver were subsequently disqualified. The series was incredibly long-lived, like the Lotus 72, being in frontline use through four seasons.

In the first of those, 1973, four M23s were built, followed by four more in 1974 and two in 1975. No new M23s were produced in their second Drivers' Championship season of 1976, but two new works cars and the final private-entry car for American Brett Lunger followed in 1977 before the type was finally replaced by the slow-to-develop M26.

Of all these cars, chassis M23/4, M23/7, M23/8 and M23/9 were effectively written off in racing accidents. Only M23/7 would not be rebuilt at all, while number 4 was resurrected as a non-running promotional show car for Marlboro who were the team's sponsors from 1974 onwards, and number 8 was rebuilt as another show car, taking the chassis tag number '10'. Chassis 9 was rebuilt as a running museum piece in later years.

Meanwhile, the M23s had developed through B, C, D, E and F-specifications. The modifications involved can be listed as follows:

M23B – 1974, chassis change around the front bulkhead to accept alternative progressive-rate or rocker arm front suspension – longer wheelbase – parallel-link rear suspension.
M23C – 1975, further revised suspensions – different airbox – driver-adjustable front anti-roll bar – short nose and side panel extension aerodynamics.
M23D – 1976, from 1 May, low regulation airbox – short-lived driver-adjustable rear anti-roll bar – air starter introduced – six-speed McLaren-Hewland gearbox – longer cockpit surround extending onto nose cone to accommodate James Hunt.
M23E – 1977, detail changes headed by redesigned front uprights to cater for new-diameter Goodyear tyres.
M23F – Category for McLaren-made parts intended for private-customer sale

All of which sounds simple, but as we shall see the story was far more involved and the progression of development changes far more complicated and chronologically jumbled than this list records. In the real world, Formula 1 racing can be a confused and confusing business.

Back at the start, in 1973, the prototype chassis M23/1 was tested for some 65 laps at Goodwood before being flown to Kyalami ready for the South African GP there on 3 March. Even on its very first day at Goodwood it was faster than the extensively tested, two-year old M19. Hulme commented on how unusual its far-forward driving position felt: 'you can almost lean out and touch the front wheels . . .'

For the first 10 laps or so he found it very difficult to judge rear wheel placing and to sense incipient oversteer. But with more practice he was able to induce oversteer at will and control it far better than was possible on the M19. The M23 would enter a stable and sustainable oversteer which the M19 had never offered. The cooler cockpit was also welcome, obviating a major cause of driver fatigue.

In the heat and altitude of Kyalami the twinned mounting of water radiators and oil coolers within the same pods proved to be a mistake, the coolers being resited either side of the gearbox, which also put more weight on the rear wheels.

The car was very quick, and Hulme took his first-ever GP pole position in it. He led the race, but an early-lap collision had sprayed the roadway with debris and he suffered a puncture. Rejoining with a fresh tyre fitted, Hulme was astounded to see a plume of smoke stream from the M23's left-front tyre on every right-hand corner. Presuming this tyre too was punctured, he stopped again to change it, but it was in fact intact. He finished only fifth after these delays but the M23 had shown terrific promise.

Through the rest of that season the works M23s would qualify regularly within the first three or four on the GP grids. A second car, M23/2 of course, was ready in time for Peter Revson to drive it in the minor Silverstone race on 8 April, in which he finished fourth while Hulme retired the prototype.

Three M23s were available in time for the first 'deformable structure' GP in Spain on 29 April, and at Zolder on 20 May Hulme's car

carried a Graviner life-support system for the first time. This offered a breathable air supply piped into the driver's helmet and triggered in case of fire.

Revson crashed his car M23/2 in this event and the wreck was subsequently savaged as Jarier's March flew off on the same patch of disintegrating asphalt and crashed into the stricken McLaren.

Hulme won the Swedish GP with fortune on his side, though he also set fastest race lap, and when Revson was committed to a USAC race on French GP weekend, cadet driver Jody Scheckter made his European GP debut for the team by driving the latest chassis, M23/3. He qualified faster than Hulme, started from the front row and led the race until just 12 laps from the end when he and Fittipaldi of Lotus fell over each other in a corner.

All three M23s ran for the first time in the British GP on 14 July which has passed into history for 'Scheckter's shunt'. He lost control ending lap one between the pits and main grandstand and spun in front of the pack, causing a multiple accident which eliminated nine cars and stopped the race while the mess was cleared up. Revson won the restarted race in M23/2 while Hulme finished third.

Scheckter's M23/3 was still under repair one week later when the new M23/4 emerged as team spare at Zandvoort for the Dutch GP. This car was then driven by guest driver Jacky Ickx – a fugitive from Ferrari at this time – in the German GP at the Nürburgring, where his specialist circuit knowledge helped him finish third behind the dominant Tyrrells.

Coppuck meanwhile was developing a revised geometry suspension package for the cars but Silverstone testing was inconclusive so the M23s ran on unchanged.

The Canadian GP was another shambles, this time due to bad weather, but Revson won again, using M23/4 while Scheckter collided with Cevert's Tyrrell and mangled M23/2's left-front corner and side pod. The damage was repaired in McLaren Engines' facility at Livonia, Detroit, in time for the US GP at Watkins Glen, where Hulme and Revson finished 4-5 and Scheckter retired when a rear wishbone broke . . . fortunately this time without hitting anything hard.

1974 – FIRST CHAMPIONSHIP SEASON
For 1974, the Texaco-Marlboro McLaren team was born, with Hulme being joined by Emerson Fittipaldi since Revson had moved to Shadow and Scheckter to lead the Tyrrell team. McLaren's previous Yardley sponsorship continued into the new year with a one-car operation running an allegedly identical M23

for Mike Hailwood.

During the winter at Colnbrook, two brand new M23s had been built up, chassis M23/5 and M23/6. Lengthy winter testing at Ricard-Castellet had persuaded Coppuck and the McLaren team to modify their promising original design to compensate for the effects of the new rear wing overhang restrictions. The rear wing had to come forward some 10 in. from its 1973 position, but since this was measured relative to the rear wheels the answer was obviously to move the rear wheels further back. This would leave the wing in relatively clean air, well aft of the airbox. Airflow would also be improved by widening the rear track to minimize interference from tyre turbulence.

Consequently, wheelbase was lengthened by three inches with a bell-housing spacer extension between engine and gearbox setting the rear wheels further back. The front bulkhead structure was modified to accept either fixed-rate geometry rocker arm front suspension or the old progressive system. Rear track was widened by two inches and geometry changes were made to enhance traction away from slow corners.

New driver Fittipaldi did the lion's share of winter testing, Hulme as always being content to sit back and let someone else do the work.

Hailwood's Yardley-liveried prototype M23/1 was modified to similar specification and M23/4 in Marlboro livery became team spare when the 1974 season began in Argentina.

Fittipaldi took to team and car like a duck to water and did 97 practice laps in celebration at Buenos Aires! He was delayed there in the race by a stray plug lead, then inadvertently knocked off the electrical 'kill-switch' on his steering wheel. By the time he realized his mistake he had lost much ground. Meanwhile Hulme found his LWB M23 the fastest car present through the long fifth-gear loop at the end of the main straight and he closed on the leaders until Reutemann's dominant Brabham fell sick and Hulme took the lead on the penultimate lap and won. Hailwood finished fourth despite having a stone puncture in one radiator.

Optional higher radius rod pick-ups were provided on the chassis in Brazil where the bumpy Interlagos bankings demanded more suspension movement. Fittipaldi started from pole and led from lap 16 to lap 32, whereupon the race was flagged to a finish due to heavy rain, and Marlboro-McLaren's M23s had won two in a row. When Fittipaldi won the minor Brasilia race after Reutemann's leading Brabham blew up, the new M23 team had won the first three Formula 1 races of the season. The Brabham BT44 seemed clearly quicker, but McLaren preparation and reliable competitiveness had paid off handsomely.

Now the team began experimenting in earnest, just as had Derek Gardner with the Tyrrells in 1971.

Back in Europe for the minor Brands Hatch event, an ingenious new rear wing mounting appeared, copiously drilled on various arcs to enable a vast range of alternative wing incidences to be used at will. Another experiment involved a slender 'winkle-picker' wedge nose carrying longer-span, high-aspect ratio front foils, using a similar very exaggerated banana section to the tail wing.

At Kyalami, scene of the M23 prototype's very promising debut 12 months previously, Goodyear offered their new 28 in. outside diameter tyres.

For baseline purposes, Hulme's M23/6 was rigged initially in 1973 trim, complete down to the original wheelbase, rear track width, older-style wing sections and 26 in. outside diameter rear tyres. It simply ate the latest-compound Goodyears and Hulme reported it felt awful.

In the second day's practice, M23s 1, 5 and 6 all ran in Brands Hatch form, finding better stability and much improved traction on the

Hailwood's ill-fated Yardley M23 leaves Karussel *at the Nürburgring prior to his career-ending 1974 German GP crash. Note centre-pillar rear 'banana' wing, deep-cambered nose 'foils and slender large-profile tall airbox.*

McLaren experimented extensively: Hulme's 'M23/ 6' runs shortlived winkle-picker nose for 1974 Race of Champions. Whole car is neat, simple and exquisitely prepared. Clean airflow beneath rear wing was vital.

new 28 in. tyres, as well as better download with the older-style broad nose cones which replaced the experimental winkle-pickers. Hailwood subsequently recorded the twin team's best finish, in third place.

The seventh M23 to be completed was ready for him to use in Yardley colours at the minor Silverstone race on 7 April, in which he lay briefly second before early retirement with clutch failure.

Five M23s were taken to Jarama for the Spanish GP, and Coppuck had them all set up in short-wheelbase form for more nimble response on the tight Autodrome circuit. Hulme's M23/6 had five alternative lower and three alternative upper pick-ups fitted for the rear radius rods to research optimum anti-squat characteristics, while Hailwood's spare M23/1 was in standard form as a comparative baseline.

There was considerable head-scratching about lessons learned from this exercise and at the faster Nivelles Autodrome for the Belgian GP all the M23s were delivered in long-wheelbase form, and Fittipaldi became the first driver of the season to win two GPs, staving off a strong Ferrari challenge to do so. Hulme was only sixth but set fastest lap, while Hailwood had run fifth before fuel pick-up problems slowed his car.

Short-wheelbase form might be considered most suitable for the tight street circuit at Monaco, but there Fittipaldi's regular M23/5 used a short spacer between engine and gearbox, while Hulme's M23/6 had a long spacer and Hailwood's a medium-length one! Each carried a winkle-picker nose with long-span front foils, while Fittipaldi's had the extra feature of tall vertical sighting masts on the foil tips to judge car placing better.

An unwell Fittipaldi inherited fifth place after a careful drive, to lead the World Championship standings.

New slimline airboxes with a much larger

side profile appeared at Dijon-Prenois, extending further back towards the rear wing to improve airflow onto it. Vestigial plastic skirts around the under-periphery of the car were tried briefly at this meeting, in an attempt to exclude air from underneath and so minimize aerodynamic lift, thus allowing the wings to apply their download more effectively against diminished resistance. But the plastic skirting had only to touch the track surface to wear away. Any advantage seemed uncertain and slight.

Meanwhile a further modified brand new M23, chassis 8 in the series, was nearing completion at Colnbrook. It emerged at Brands Hatch, featuring low-offset front suspension with revised steering geometry, and parallel-link rear suspension which replaced the original reversed lower wishbone system. Fittipaldi liked the new car's reduced steering effort and used it in the race, inheriting second place.

Two weeks later, at the Nürburgring, the spare M23/5 appeared with parallel-link rear suspension and low-offset front end, while Hulme's regular car and the two Yardley chassis retained the earlier set-up.

During practice Hailwood crashed M23/1 heavily when it unaccountably turned sharp right out of the corner before the pits and smeared itself into the Armco. He continued practising in M23/7, convinced something had broken on the older car. In the race he then crashed chassis 7 very heavily after landing askew after a yump and hitting the barriers almost head-on. The steel feet carrying the bottom-front wishbone pick-up punched back into the monocoque and smashed the unfortunate driver's ankle and shin, ending his career and sparking a major reinforcement subsequently built into all M23s to prevent a recurrence. Chassis M23/7 was totally destroyed and uniquely amongst its family would never be rebuilt.

Fittipaldi had been stranded at the start,

unable to find a gear, and he was rammed from behind by Hulme's sister car, so it was a bad weekend all round for the Colnbrook teams.

Since Phil Kerr's Yardley operation had lost both its chassis, M23/1 and M23/7, at the Nürburgring, the Marlboro team's spare M23/4 was resprayed to suit in time for the Österreichring, where David Hobbs was invited to drive it. This old car had last appeared in Hulme's hands at Jarama. Fittipaldi raced the latest-spec M23/8 while Hulme's older M23/6 still retained the reversed-wishbone rear suspension, though spare car M23/5 was to the latest spec. Fittipaldi's engine failed when running third. Hulme drove steadily to inherit second behind the winning Brabham BT44.

At Monza, Fittipaldi was second to Peterson's Lotus 72 by just 0.8 second, but McLaren displaced Ferrari at the head of the Constructors' Championship table. Only two Championship rounds remained: the Canadian and US GPs in North America.

Yardley took Jochen Mass there to drive their entry in these events where the cars ran in unchanged form other than the fitting of USAC team two-way radio sets for Watkins Glen, where Fittipaldi secured the Drivers' title, McLaren confirmed victory in the Constructors' Championship, and Denny Hulme retired from the race, and from racing, when his engine blew on the fourth lap.

1975 – UNSUCCESSFUL TITLE DEFENCE

The M23 entered its third season's racing in 1975, substantially unaltered from 1974 form although early in the season there were various suspension revisions tried to improve front-end adhesion and 'turn-in' performance. Four cars were used, two being written off during the season by Fittipaldi's new regular number two, Mass, both ironically on his home soil at the Nürburgring.

Ferrari had the most powerful and reliable cars of the season in their latest 312Ts, but McLaren's preparation managed by Alastair Caldwell gave the team a 74 per cent finishing record – 20 finishes from 27 starts – which Ferrari could shade only marginally with 75 per cent.

Another brand new car had been built for Fittipaldi's use, chassis M23/9, which made its debut in Buenos Aires. It carried Brabham-like front suspension in which the original tubular frame rocker arms had been replaced by substantial swept-back fabricated top arms with pullrods attached under their outboard extremities, pulling up a shaped actuating arm at the foot of gently inclined semi-inboard coil-spring/damper units. Mass's M23/8 retained the old fully-inboard front suspension system, while Emerson's new car also used appreciably narrower rear track and both cars were fitted with abbreviated nose cones.

Fittipaldi promptly blooded M23/9 with first-time victory, the eighth World Championship round win for the M23 series, while in Brazil the team cars finished 2-3 behind Pace's victorious Brabham BT44B.

Chassis M23/9's Brabham-crib front suspension was modified in time for the South African trip with right-angle instead of swept-back arms, which served to lengthen the wheelbase and throw more load onto the front wheels. M23/8, meanwhile, had been brought up to South American specification, with swept-back pullrod front suspension and the shorter or standard wheelbase. When Fittipaldi's engine blew in practice, his spare car, M23/6, was prepared with the latest-style suspension and he raced it – unsuccessfully – in this form.

Back home for Brands Hatch, the old chassis M23/4 was prepared and offered a third variant front suspension layout, this time with the coil/dampers mounted totally inboard again, but this time vertically and actuated by conventional fabricated steel top rocker arms, the team being unconvinced by their pullrod experiments. After Silverstone's non-Championship race, non rising-rate fully-

inboard front suspension was adopted as standard. The two regular cars at Barcelona – chassis 8 for Mass and 9 for Fittipaldi – used it, while chassis 5 last used at Kyalami retained the South American style rising-rate layout.

There at Montjuich Park, Fittipaldi was deeply unhappy with circuit safety and boycotted the race, while Mass competed and was declared the winner when a bad accident caused the race to be stopped.

The regular cars reappeared at Monaco, in 1974 medium-wheelbase form for agility, and Fittipaldi's carried a new cockpit-adjustable front anti-roll bar, enabling him to soften roll-stiffness as the fuel load diminished during the race. He finished second to Lauda's dominant Ferrari.

All these interminable changes and modifications owed more to practice than theory. You had a hunch, and you tried it, and if the car lapped faster you used it. This is race development in the real world, nothing like the academic engineering journalist's theorizing.

For Zolder, the long-wheelbase form returned and in mid-practice a rapid narrow-track mod was made to Fittipaldi's car and it promptly lapped faster, though the rival Brabhams and Ferraris were faster still. In time for the Swedish trip Coppuck developed further suspension mods but Fittipaldi was unimpressed. At Zandvoort the big articulated McLaren transporter disgorged its fleet of M23s with Coppuck smilingly claiming 'the Mark 197 arrangement' for M23/9, with its rear suspension modified this time, and with rearward side pod extension panels to improve airflow further beneath that vital rear wing.

Mass crashed M23/8 heavily in this race, mauling its front end, so for the subsequent French GP at Ricard-Castellet, he raced M23/6 while Fittipaldi persevered with M23/9 in its Zandvoort form. As it happened Mass drove one of the best races of his life to finish third, close behind the second-placed Hesketh 308, while Fittipaldi was handicapped by poor-handling and finished a distant – and fortunate – fourth.

At Silverstone for the British GP a new swallow-tailed rear wing was featured on Fittipaldi's car, and when the race was beset by heavy rain showers which sent cars spinning in all directions he emerged as lucky winner. McLaren always seemed to win the funny races – British and Canadian GPs '73, and now Spain and the British GP '75 . . . But Fittipaldi had kept his head while all around were losing their cool; it was a touch of class which made the most of his ageing car.

Mass's M23/8, damaged at Zandvoort, was

M23 details: top, *rigid plastic draught-excluder on the periphery of Mass's 'M23/9', 1976 British GP; that year's extended radiator ducts with oil cooler behind water cores; rear monocoque fillet, designed to coincide with DFV top mounting plate angle.* Centre and above, *Scheckter tested the M23's integral deformable radiator ducting in his 1973 British GP accident.*

rebuilt in time for the Nürburgring where the McLarens wore new contoured flairs on the trailing edges of the radiator pods and plastic vestigial skirt draught-excluders reappeared underneath. Fittipaldi's M23/9 had lost its driver-adjustable front anti-roll bar for this meeting.

Mass tried too hard in practice and wrote off his freshly-rebuilt M23/8, then had a front tyre collapse on his spare car M23/4 in the race and destroyed this chassis as well.

Back at Colnbrook the intended M23-replacement M26 car was now being finalized but frantic work began to restore a full complement of M23s meantime. No spare car was available for the Austrian GP in which Mass took over the ex-Hulme M23/6, while a brand new car was built from the ground up in two weeks for Fittipaldi to blood in the so-called 'Swiss GP', a minor Marlboro-sponsored race at Dijon. This car was really number 10 in the M23 series, but there was no time to arrange new customs paperwork for it, so its chassis-plate carried the number M23/8-2 to inherit the Nürburgring write-off's carnets. When McLaren works manager Leo Wybrott later rebuilt the original M23/8 as a collector's car, it took the plate M23/10, which it retains in private hands to this day.

In the final race of 1975 at Watkins Glen, Fittipaldi again showed real fire. He was only narrowly bumped off pole by Lauda's Ferrari, and he finished an honourable second after being very badly baulked by the second-string Ferrari. McLaren ended the season third in the Constructors' Championship, behind Ferrari and Brabham.

Reigning Champion Fittipaldi at Monaco 1975 in 'M23/9' showing its fabricated top rocker-arms and exceptionally wide track rear suspension.

Testing at Ricard-Castellet in November, Fittipaldi crashed and broke a finger. Amid some acrimony he left McLaren at short notice later that month, but was replaced admirably by James Hunt whose former Hesketh team had just effectively closed down.

Hunt drove his first McLaren laps at a mist-shrouded Silverstone that December using the ex-Fittipaldi M23/8-2 with its pedals suitably moved forward to accommodate the Englishman's taller frame.

That winter saw the new Coppuck-designed M26 honeycomb car continuing its delayed development, while Alastair Caldwell had translated a personal pet theory into reality through the previous season. He felt there was room for a sixth speed within the existing Hewland FGA transaxle, and the team's Nicholson-McLaren tuned DFV engines could be tailored to a more peaky power curve which could be used to advantage with a six-speed gearbox. Caldwell was an abrasive character but he had played a major part in McLaren racing, insisting on quality in everything, and his pet six-speed gearbox project would now pay real dividends.

1976 – CHAMPION SENSATION

By the time the Brazilian GP opened the new season on 25 January 1976 some 30 lb weight had been trimmed off the existing M23s, in part by use of lighter body panels, stiffened with carbon-fibre filament. The parallel-link rear suspension had proved effective but heavy, and so reversed lower wishbones now reappeared, with toe-steer being adequately controlled by very accurate setting up of the radius rod lengths upon assembly – the joints at each end of the radius rod of course being screw-adjustable for length.

From the sponsor's viewpoint, this race also introduced the now familiar Marlboro dayglo red livery, to improve the cars' 'TV identity'. It was expensive but very effective.

The M23s were not ideal for Interlagos but the new six-speed gearbox, which the team kept quiet, served to plug some gaps around the course and Hunt promptly qualified on pole ahead of Lauda's Ferrari. He then ran second until a freak failure saw one of the fuel injection trumpets rattle adrift, taking the screwed-in injector nozzle with it. Hunt continued on only seven cylinders until the errant trumpet jammed the throttle slides open and M23/8-2 spun off into the catch-fences, damaging its rear wing and oil coolers.

Another Caldwell development then appeared on the cars at Kyalami. The normal electrical starter motor was a heavy affair ill-suited to any racing car. Now he had developed a compressed-air starter system which appeared on the M23s, using an onboard reservoir chargeable from any air-line and activated by a small solenoid. An onboard battery powerful enough to turn over the normal electric starter was no longer necessary, saving another few pounds weight and unnecessary complication. This invention would be taken up by every other team in Formula 1.

Both cars practised at Kyalami wearing plastic aerodynamic underskirts, but they were removed after protest during a dispute over legal wing heights and what now constituted the 'underside' of the car.

Again Hunt started on pole and he was beaten by Lauda's Ferrari by only 1.3 secs after a hard race. The Hunt/M23 combination then scored its first victory at Brands Hatch one week later.

For Long Beach, California, the M23s wore CanAm brakes with 35 per cent greater pad area than normal. Hunt was barged out of the race by a Tyrrell but Mass placed fifth. Then at Silverstone Hunt won again, in a class of his own, the only driver in the 1;17 bracket in practice, starting his regular M23/8-2 from pole, leading all the way and setting fastest lap.

Fittipaldi demonstrates 'M23/10's' flat-topped deltaform at Monza 1975, top rocker-arm front suspension, steering behind the hubs, moulded front brake cooling ducts wrapping close inside the front tyres, low-slung tail oil coolers visible.

In Spain, where the new airbox regulations took effect, McLaren adopted an eared affair low behind the roll-over bar, forming the M23D variant. Mass took over the team's former spare M23/9 for this race, setting aside his usual M23/6 which he felt must be deficient in some inexplicable manner, having been quite unable to match his new team-mate's pace in the sister car. Unfortunately for him, Hunt promptly took out M23/6 and lapped just as fast as in his regular car, '8-2.

The two McLarens looked set for a 1-2 victory in this race until the luckless Mass's engine blew, leaving Hunt a winning margin of nearly 31 seconds over Lauda's Ferrari. But at post-race scrutineering the M23 was found to be 1.8 cm too wide across the rear wheel rims and the car was disqualified. McLaren protested and had the penalty reduced to a $3000 fine. This took time, and in the interim second place man Lauda's Ferrari had been declared winner, then demoted again as the original result was confirmed. This created an atmosphere of dissension which intensified as the season progressed.

Meanwhile, for the Belgian GP at Zolder the M23s' rear track was pulled back well within the new 215 cm limit – which itself had been

based on the M23 dimension as it was the widest car in contemporary Formula 1 – by machining the inside wheel faces and adjusting the wishbone mounting points to match. Oil coolers had returned from the tail to the side pods, but early in practice Mass's M23/9 lost oil pressure so the coolers migrated back to the tail next day to reduce lubricant temperatures. Hunt led the Ferraris off the line, but his M23's handling was 'positively evil', the car began to smoke: he retired with dry transmission.

That hasty oil cooler move in the Zolder paddock had returned them almost, but not quite, to their South American siting. That 'not quite' proved vital. Suddenly the M23s seemed impossible to balance. The problem cost a month's competitiveness before being pinpointed. The resited coolers were robbing the wing underside of clean air and upsetting its performance.

Monaco gave little clue. Mass ran there with an additional new low-level rear wing in practice. In race morning warm-up they ran without the airbox, which improved airflow to the rear wing and enhanced download. But Hunt spun, and in Sweden he spun again, many times, before salvaging fifth place and another points-scoring finish at last.

Brainstorming the cause of their lost form, McLaren then resited the oil coolers precisely in their Spanish GP mounts. Testing commenced at Ricard, prior to the French GP, and as if by magic the old balance had returned. At that point in the season, halfway through the Championship, Hunt was a massive 47 points behind his main rival, Lauda of Ferrari.

How Hunt and McLaren fought back to win the French, British, German, Dutch, Canadian and US GPs – and were then disqualified from the British victory in Lauda's favour – and how Lauda then crashed near-fatally at the Nürburgring, is all part of recent racing history.

In Austria the prototype M23 replacement M26 emerged at last although it was not raced as Hunt again set M23/8-2 on pole position and led initially before running into mud and debris scattered onto the track by a Tyrrell accident. The car's handling deteriorated and he finished fourth. When his crew examined the car afterwards they found the left-front foil had been thumped from underneath and its angle of attack flattened slightly. Something had punctured its undersurface and the hole was stuffed with mud.

In the Dutch GP a flapping front brake cooling hose interrupted airflow over one of these sensitive nose foils, possibly causing excessive understeer which hampered Hunt until his opposition retired. Mass raced the M26 in this event, unhappily.

Spot fuel checks at Monza during Italian GP practice saw McLaren judged guilty of using illegally high octane Texaco mix, though this interpretation was subsequently overthrown. Short-term it still destroyed the team's

chances as Hunt was forced to start from the back of the grid and went off the road trying to make up the deficit.

This dramatic season then reached its climax in the last three rounds – Canada, the USA (East) and Japan – and Hunt won the first two events in ever-faithful M23/8-2 and was third at Mt Fuji after a dramatic tyre change to steal the Drivers' Championship by one point from Lauda, though McLaren could not catch Ferrari in the Constructors' Championship. On the road Hunt had matched Jim Clark's record of seven GP wins in a season, only to be disqualified from two first places, then reinstated in only one of them. But there was to be no second Constructors' Championship victory for the Colnbrook cars . . .

1977 – TWILIGHT
In 1977, the team played safe for the South American season-openers by fielding their trusty M23s although intensive winter development had seen the replacement M26 improving rapidly. Hunt drove his faithful M23/8-2, Mass M23/9 and M23/6 was team spare. Hunt crashed in Buenos Aires when a right-rear suspension bolt broke, while in Brazil Mass crashed heavily when under pressure from Andretti's new Lotus 78 'wing-car' and a spinning Tyrrell later did further injury to poor chassis 9. No M23 had suffered serious frontal damage since Hailwood's Nürburgring crash in 1974 and examination of Mass' wreck prompted detail monocoque reinforcement to the surviving cars prior to departure for Kyalami.

The remains of M23/9 were rebuilt years later by Leo Wybrott, using much of the original tub with new panels inserted. The M23 monocoques were so complex that no damaged ones were ever torn right down and reconstructed merely around the original bulkheads. Only one 'write-off' had proved total, and that was Hailwood's M23/7 whose mortal remains were indeed scrapped.

Due to slow development of the troublesome M26 replacement car, two brand new M23s were built for the first time since 1975 – chassis 11 for Hunt and 12 for Mass. Hunt put his new

car on pole in South Africa, then won in old '8-2 with driver-adjustable rear anti-roll bar at Brands Hatch. This was the 21st and last race win for a works-entered McLaren M23 (including the 1976 British GP).

Mass's new mount made its debut at Long Beach but from the next race, the Spanish GP at Jarama, Hunt ran the latest M26 and it was left to Mass to tail off the M23s' frontline career up to the British GP at Silverstone when his own new M26 became available.

The Spanish private entrant Emilio de Villota campaigned old M23/6 during this period, attempting to qualify for World Championship GPs while also running in a British club-racing series. Bob Sparshott's BS Fabrications team ran the brand new customer M23F chassis 14 for their American customer Brett Lunger, replacing an old March which he had campaigned formerly. This little team later added ex-works car M23/11 as a second choice for Lunger.

Hunt's 1976 World Championship-winning car M23/8-2 was also dusted off and wheeled out again during the year, giving a little-known French-Canadian driver named Gilles Villeneuve his Formula 1 debut at Silverstone in the British GP, and then being handled by Italian Formula 2 star Bruno Giacomelli at Monza on 11 September 1977. This was the last M23 works entry, almost exactly 4½ years after the type's debut in March 1973.

Lunger subsequently ran chassis 14 privately on into 1978, competing in the Argentinian, Brazilian and South African GPs. This car was then sold to the British Melchester racing team for club driver Tony Trimmer's use, while Lunger failed to qualify his older chassis 11 in Long Beach before taking delayed delivery of a new M26. Trimmer failed to qualify M23/14 for the British GP while in the Austrian race a youthful Brazilian Formula 3 Champion named Nelson Piquet raced M23/11 and crashed it. He used the old car again in the Dutch and Italian GPs, finishing ninth in that latter event, on 10 September 1978, to mark the end of this remarkable McLaren model's World Championship career, 5½ years after it had begun.

Hunt's disqualification from the 1976 British GP caused much dispute. See the M23D-spec's new regulation airbox, forward roll-over bar within screen and undertray chevron air dam – the ground-effects era unwittingly dawns.

Racing Tyres

Make no mistake, along with aerodynamic development racing tyre technology has been the ultimate arbiter of Grand Prix car performance throughout our period. Duff tyres equal duff results – it has been as crude and as simple as that.

Through much of the 1500 cc Formula of 1961-65 Dunlop held a tyre supply monopoly. They developed their racing tyres essentially to carry a 2000 lb car round Le Mans for 24 hours at about 180 mph, and that's what the Formula 1 people had to use on their 1200 lb cars screaming round Reims for two hours at a maximum 165 mph. During the 1963 season, Jimmy Clark's Lotus 25 completed – according to Colin Chapman who told me so himself – four consecutive GPs on the self-same set of tyres.

Times changed. In 1964, Firestone entered the road-racing fray and Goodyear followed earnestly in 1965. A three-way tyre war broke out on the Grand Prix circuits of the world.

In this history of the Grand Prix car I feel there can be no place for an adequate story of Formula 1 tyre development for it would fill a sister volume by itself. Nevertheless, some significant points must be made.

The contact patches of the tyres are the *only* points of contact (if one disregards the era of sliding skirts) between a car and the road. These small and ever-changing elliptical patches must transmit drive and cornering and braking reactions. Each supplier has developed tyre technology to produce carcass constructions and tread compound characteristics which enable the car using those tyres to transmit dynamic forces more effectively than its rivals.

At the start of our period tyres were relatively tall and narrow. Conventionally, they were all of cross-ply construction, the casing plies being woven from variations of man-made textile cord and laminated one above the other, each ply carrying perhaps 30 cords per inch arranged four-ply deep.

Each cord layer would be moulded into the rubber compound devised by the manufacturers' chemists, the compound insulating each layer from the next to minimize internal friction which would overheat the tyre.

Wire cord controlled the tyre bead to keep it on the wheel rim, safety bolsters and bolts being adopted after instances – including Jimmy Clark's death – of a deflating tyre collapsing explosively as pressure loss allowed the beads to pop inwards off the rim ledges.

The tread compound was applied some 0.2 in. to 0.4 in. thick across the tread, as the period progressed, thickening to perhaps 0.32 in. to 0.6 in. in the shoulder. The chemists based their compound brews on synthetic styrene-butadiene-rubber, polymer science flexing its muscles to offer compound mixes resisting abrasion and controlling internal heating because an under-heated tyre will not generate its full grip, and an overheating tyre will lose grip, blister, break up and fail.

The tyre compounder would add carbon black (for good tensile strength and wear), oils, waxes, vulcanizers, accelerators, decelerators, zinc oxide, sulphur . . . all with much the same enthusiasm as the three Witches.

Ever-softer compounds were tried by Goodyear, the giant, by Firestone and Dunlop as they sought ever-greater performance in all conditions. Some compounds proved too soft and sticky to endure race distance, but they produced prodigious lap times during their brief life. These race-distance failures became the great successes of qualifying, and 'qualifying tyres' had been born.

The compounds in these tyres were very oily, heating up rapidly to pass through a level of optimum grip then losing performance with equal rapidity. For 1981 only two sets of four qualifying tyres were permitted for each car, each set being marked with the car's number and scrutineered during official timed qualifying sessions to ensure that nobody could literally 'pull a fast one'.

Although this move was intended to control tyre company costs and logistical pressures following a period when the top few teams had access to a mountain of alternative tyres but the also-rans had virtually nothing at all worthwhile, it also created some suicidal qualifying performances by drivers anxious to put in a quick lap before their precious and exhaustible supply of tyres 'went off', and contributed to Gilles Villeneuve's death.

Tyre widths and heights and profiles altered greatly through our 20-season period, slick tyres coming into use in 1970-71 to offer greater contact area uninterrupted by tread pattern channels. They also helped to stabilize the ever-softer tyre tread compounds which, with the introduction of separate

tread blocks, had begun to overheat due to 'squirm' when in use.

Slick tyres were introduced by Goodyear in the South African Grand Prix at Kyalami in 1971. Firestone rapidly followed suit at the Spanish Grand Prix. These immediately put more rubber on the road to enhance grip under all loads, simultaneously enabling the use of softer compounds than ever before without serious danger of overheating and tread destruction since heat-inducing squirm was now under control. Slots or drillings were the only blemishes remaining in the tread surface, being designed purely to enable tread wear and remaining depth to be measured by the tyre engineers. The slots were also handy places to prod with their thermometer probes.

Tyre and rim widths grew progressively until regulations limited further development, while tyre height and sidewall height (profile) altered from one extreme to another during our period.

To limit movement within the tyre, very low profiles were adopted by Firestone in 1971-72, but this led to severe vibration problems and Goodyear then knocked Firestone out of competition at the end of 1974. Dunlop had long since thrown in the towel. Progressive development of tall new 'wrinkle-wall' dragster-technology tyres had produced a taller sidewall tyre which engendered a wind-up effect which heated the tyre very effectively and gave terrific traction away from the corners.

These taller profile tyres had problems of lateral stability, however, as the car would roll and take-up sidewall 'squidge'. The greater a tyre's overall outside diameter the softer the compound it could preserve because its rotational speed was less than a smaller outside diameter tyre and therefore it asked less from its tread in terms of work.

Variation in manufactured size was always a major problem with cross-ply racing tyres. Racing cars, and perhaps even more so racing drivers, can be sensitive animals, and unequal overall dimensions between tyres on either end of a common driven axle could have both literally climbing the walls.

This difference was known as 'stagger' and the effect would be for the car consistently to dive to one side or another under acceleration, as the greater circumference tyre on one side covered a greater distance during one revolution than did its partner, save for differential effect. Each team developed a 'tyre man' whose main task was solely to measure and carefully match sets of equal-sized, stagger-free tyres.

In certain cases, stagger could be advantageous on particular circuits for which equally carefully *mis*-matched tyres could be fitted, and very often painstaking tyre choices have been made which have won or lost races by running tyres of differing compound and construction on each corner of a car to match or combat given conditions.

In particular, the left-front tyre of any racing car is especially hard-pressed on a conventional clockwise racing circuit in which the majority of turns are right-handers, and often harder more durable compounds would be fitted there which would heat in sympathy with their three softer partners – four-wheeled cars these! – purely through the greater work they were asked to do.

Wet-weather tyres employed very soft compounds which would heat adequately even when douched continuously by standing and falling water. They

were cut with continuous and interconnecting drainage channels and sipes to funnel water away, prevent aquaplaning, to squeegee the track surface near-dry and enable clean tread contact to be maintained.

In 1977, the French Michelin company entered the fray, first on Renault, later Ferrari. Michelin had made their name on the 'X' range of radial-ply road tyres and extended this technology into Formula 1.

Radial-ply tyre casings, as the name suggests, had their ply cords arranged (in theory) at 90 degrees to the direction of travel; that is, on a line following the wheel and tyre radius and passing through its hub centre.

In practice this was not quite true, for the bracing cords were more 'bias-belted' than truly radial, running for example at some 23 degrees across the tread although Michelin security was so tight and change so rapid one cannot be adamant.

The tyre tread section was then further braced by a steel or textile band moulded integrally into the rubber capping with the tread on top of that. The radial-ply tyre offered less tread distortion under load than a cross-ply, while its sidewalls were far more flexible, generating higher cornering force, better traction under power and braking, and better straightline stability.

In practical terms the radial racing tyre, like the radial road tyre, offered higher ultimate grip than its cross-ply predecessor but was liable to give less warning of incipient breakaway. To run radial tyres suspension settings with more camber change became necessary as the suspension rose and fell through its arc. Radial-ply tyres also ran inherently cooler and had better squirm characteristics than cross-ply tyres so again were capable of using softer, stickier and faster tread compounds.

The Italian Pirelli concern joined the fray in 1981, also with radial-ply tyres, although they had little success and development seemed very half-hearted compared to the multi-million spending giants, Goodyear and Michelin.

Goodyear fought a terrific rearguard action for the cross-ply racing tyre, enduring the height of the ground-effects era in which aerodynamic downloads of 3000 lb or more had to be endured and sustained.

A brief Goodyear withdrawal from racing in early 1981 set many teams screaming and Avon tyres were brought in fleetingly just to keep the cannon-fodder teams mobile. The giant Goodyear company which had supported and often dominated Formula 1 for so many years subsequently returned in mid-season and progressively developed very effective radial-ply Formula 1 tyres of its own.

Racing tyre design and construction is an awesomely expensive business in which the technological development pace and staff learning curve is quite extraordinary.

Lessons learned in the crucible of Grand Prix racing have spun off into many other more mundane areas, worlds away from everyday road vehicle tyre design and production, although this has also benefited of course. In this area at least, Grand Prix racing really has, quite demonstrably, improved the breed.

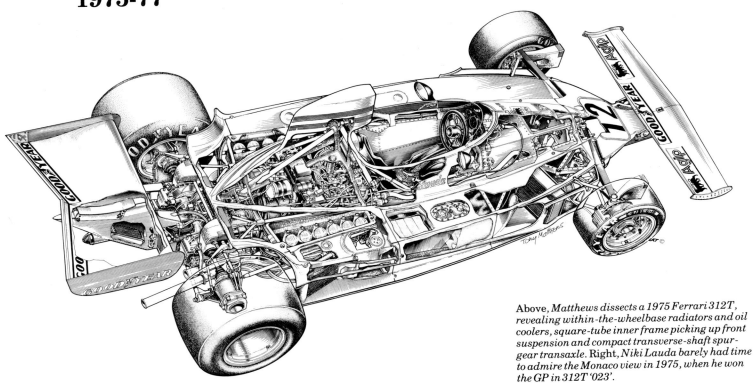

Above, *Matthews dissects a 1975 Ferrari 312T,
revealing within-the-wheelbase radiators and oil
coolers, square-tube inner frame picking up front
suspension and compact transverse-shaft spur-
gear transaxle. Right, Niki Lauda barely had time
to admire the Monaco view in 1975, when he won
the GP in 312T '023'.*

Throughout the 1974 season Ferrari re-established itself as a serious force in Formula 1 following two indifferent Grand Prix seasons. Their time and money-consuming sports-racing car programme had now been shelved and Maranello's racing department concentrated its efforts totally upon Formula 1.

As we shall see later, during 1974 their *Tipo 312B3* flat-12 was developed into a very successful design which failed to bring Ferrari their first Formula 1 Constructors' Championship title in 12 years partly through the relative inexperience of its lead driver through most of the season, until the team failed him in the crucial deciding races at the end of the year.

The driver was Niki Lauda who was accompanied by the hugely experienced and capable – if not quite as quick – Clay Regazzoni. Ferrari's concentration upon Formula 1 and the completion of their own private test track just across the main Formigine Road from the factory, at Fiorano, enabled them to test interminably, and Lauda always made himself available for testing. He realized that his future and that of the team depended upon their exploiting every advantage they had, and having once created a new Formula 1 car they could literally 'throw everything at it' in their extensive tyre testing work for Goodyear.

If five alternative wing sets were available, then Ferrari would test each pair individually, then rear wing A would be tried with nose wings B, C, D and E, rear wing B with nose wings A, C, D, E – and so on, until every possible combination had been studied and extended to its potential in painstaking detail. Every conceivable minor alteration and change would simply be tested fit to bust, until the sun went down and the brief Emilian dusk settled over Fiorano.

Since they had this luxury of their own private and comprehensively-instrumented test track, there was never a problem with

booking public circuit time, while transporting the cars from factory to test venue took a matter merely of minutes. Once Ferrari had won their labour unions' support and they had got their own management act together, they were able to tackle Formula 1 racing more seriously than any other team.

In this way they could compensate for some distinct shortcomings particularly in chassis engineering, which would occasionally leap out of the bushes and beset them in coming years, notably once the aerodynamic area became increasingly sophisticated.

But for three halcyon years, 1975 to 1977, Ferrari were really on top of their game, and they became the first Formula 1 team in history to put together a hat-trick of three consecutive Formula 1 Constructors' Championship titles.

ENTER 'MODELLO 312T'

At the end of their 'so near yet so far' 1974 season, the racing department took stock. *Capo Ingegnere* Mauro Forghieri was able to reflect upon a year of adequate flat-12 engine reliability, although major failures at Österreichring and Monza had damaged their cause. The 312B3-74 chassis had survived without major modification other than detail aerodynamic changes but Forghieri felt that the basic concept still offered as yet unrealized potential. It was actually on 27 September 1974, before the team left home for the Championship-deciding US GP at Watkins Glen, that the new year's prototype 312T model was unveiled to the press at Fiorano.

Forghieri in effect was following the path which Derek Gardner of Tyrrell and Robin Herd of March had trodden in 1972, seeking further concentration of mass within the wheelbase to minimize polar moment of inertia and so produce a highly manoeuvrable, nimble car which might seem too nervous to the

average Formula 1 driver but which with a Ronnie Peterson or Niki Lauda ensconced would prove to be a formidable weapon.

Whereas the preceding 312B3's front suspension coil-spring/dampers had nestled each side of the footbox, and used a spidery forward tube subframe to pick up the leading elements of the lower wishbones, now the redesigned 312T tub carried all its major front suspension components on the forward face of its monocoque's front bulkhead.

Very long fabricated top rocker arms actuated steeply inclined Koni dampers with co-axial tapered wire rising-rate coil springs whose feet were firmly anchored in a cast magnesium tray affair fitted to the bulkhead. The front end of the new monocoque was itself considerably narrower than that of the 'B3 which it superseded. Disc brakes were outboard at the front, inboard on the cheeks of the new lateral gearbox at the rear.

A system of links and levers actuated an exquisite little anti-roll bar which was bracketed to the centre of this assembly, and a trailing top link from the upper arm fed back into the meat of the tub, passing through an air duct section designed to feed water radiators slung either side just behind the front wheels.

Further aft, long side ducts fed air through oil coolers each side just ahead of the rear wheels, while beautifully moulded GRP body sections included a sharp-pointed shovel nose, with a strutted full-width airfoil wing perched on top. Side pods accommodated the regulation deformable structures, which overlapped the monocoque sides, the tub itself using Ferrari's familiar hybrid construction in which the stressed-skin structure was reinforced internally with steel strip and angle framing. The cockpit surround and engine cover-cum-tall airbox were in integral mouldings, smoothing airflow onto the centre-strutted rear wing while curled flip-ups moulded ahead of the rear

wheels faired airflow around the broad Goodyear tyres.

Rear suspension was by reversed lower wishbones, replacing the original toe-steer restricting parallel link system in an apparently retrograde move, although it saved some weight. Like McLaren, Ferrari felt confident they could control toe-steer adequately by careful setting-up adjustment in assembly.

Wheelbase was increased to 2518 mm (99.1 in.) while front track was reduced to 1510 mm (59.4 in.) and rear track to 1530 mm (60.2 in.)

The most significant technical innovation however was the brand new *trasversale* – transverse – gearbox, which mounted on the rear of the flat-12 engine but with most of its mass now ahead of the axle line, within the wheelbase, to enhance that central mass concentration. The gearbox input was turned through 90-degrees by bevel gears to enable the gearbox shafts to be arranged laterally, final drive being via spur gears.

Franco Rocchi's engine development team had worked hard on the flat-12 engine and in its latest form 500 bhp at 12,200 rpm was being claimed. In Fiorano testing, Lauda immediately found the new car far more demanding to drive than the 'B3, as predicted, but equally its ultimate limits seemed much higher and with practice he was able to drive closer to those higher limits for longer than hitherto . . . he was maturing too. He was soon lapping Fiorano at 1 min 13 secs, compared to Merzario's best of 1;14.2 set in the original 'Forghieri 'B3' (see page 184) 15 months previously. At Vallelunga further testing saw Lauda down there to 1;07.5, a second inside the best 'B3 time of 1974; back-to-back tests between the 'B3 and the new 312T at Ricard-Castellet proved the new model's superiority.

When the team returned from racing the old 'B3s in South America at the start of the 1975 season, Lauda got down to 1;11.9 at Fiorano and two new 312Ts were then completed and available for the trip to Kyalami for the South African GP in March. Lauda drove the prototype car chassis '018' while '021' was available for Regazzoni. The intervening two chassis numbers '019' and '020' were, according to Ferrari, allocated to the last two 'B3 models. Neither of these was raced, '019' being heavily damaged in a testing accident and being broken up, while '020' simply went into store for potential future display duties before sale to a collector. Thus '018' remains rather isolated as the 312T prototype, and '021' then commences the transverse-gearbox flat-12 series proper, which would encompass the future types 'T2 to 'T5 and would include no less than 26 further individual Formula 1 chassis in the six seasons from 1975 to 1980 . . .

1975 – THE FIRST CHAMPIONSHIP

This is not the place in which to relate the racing exploits of these cars and their drivers in any detail, but initially where the 312T is concerned, suffice to record that Lauda won the minor Silverstone International to open the type's winning account early in the 1975 season. He then added victories at Monaco, Zolder, Anderstorp, Ricard-Castellet and Watkins Glen, while team-mate Regazzoni won the minor 'Swiss GP' at Dijon-Prenois and the major German GP at the Nürburgring, to bring Ferrari their first Formula 1 Constructors' World Championship title since 1964 and Lauda his first Drivers' title. The team made 30 starts that season, including the 'B3 outings in South America and South Africa – where Regazzoni raced one of the older cars – and they recorded 24 finishes, eight of which were in first place. They added one second place, four thirds, two fourths, three fifths, two sixths, a seventh, eighth and ninth and one lowly 13th. Between them, Lauda and Regazzoni also amassed no

less than nine pole positions and six fastest laps during that memorable Ferrari season, and they proved that the combination of their skills and the Ferrari's power, reliability and now handling, was by far the fastest in contemporary Formula 1. Lauda in fact only failed to finish one race – the Spanish GP at Barcelona, in which he and his team-mate collided on the opening lap! Ferrari's first *trasversale* season was very much the more competitive Seventies equivalent of Mercedes-Benz domination in the Fifties.

Initially, however, the new car's debut at Kyalami had been indifferent, Lauda crashing '021' during practice when another car's engine blew up ahead of him and he slithered off on its spilled oil. Lauda's engine then lacked power during the race, and it was subsequently found that its fuel metering unit drive belt had stripped some teeth and slipped because of that, restricting output to some 440 bhp, which was less than the rival Cosworth DFVs.

Lauda's Silverstone victory marked the debut of the third 312T to be built, chassis '022'. Another new chassis, '023', was ready for Lauda's use at Monaco and he won in it, despite falling oil pressure towards the finish caused by leakage through a defective pump seal. The engine was dangerously close to seizure in the final laps, with Lauda sensibly declutching and coasting through the corners, while Fittipaldi's McLaren closed rapidly just before the finish . . . one more lap and he might have got past.

Regazzoni crashed '018' heavily in this race, at the chicane, and both drivers had already crashed their cars in practice so the team mechanics were kept very busy indeed that weekend.

For Zolder new exhaust systems were fitted in search of improved low-speed pick-up. Normally the three front and three rear cylinders on each bank fed individual tailpipes.

Now a balance pipe linked the front and rear set of manifolds each side, before they merged into twin exhaust megaphones, rolled from titanium sheet. One of these pipes split during practice, so the older system was refitted. Lauda had another manifold split on lap 58 of the race and he lost 300 rpm on the straights for the remaining dozen but he still won by a margin of fully 19 seconds from his closest pursuer.

Anderstorp saw a very lucky Ferrari win, for the strange Swedish circuit with its geometric semi-banked curves posed peculiar setting-up demands which few teams ever mastered, Derek Gardner of Tyrrell perhaps doing better than most. In this case Lauda had inherited second place when one Brabham faltered and he then took the lead in the last 10 laps when the other slowed due to track debris accumulating on its rear tyres, while the Ferrari's harder-compound rears were not so badly affected. Any good team makes its own luck – Ferrari could claim a 'brilliant' tyre choice.

The fifth 312T, '024' made its debut at Ricard-Castellet for the French GP but its engine failed on the seventh lap, sidelining Regazzoni. In contrast Lauda drove '022' from the start right away into the Mediterranean heat haze and his rivals never had sight of him again as he led by two seconds ending lap one and despite late understeer as his tyres wore he won as he pleased, quite uncatchable.

The rain-swept British GP at Silverstone degenerated into a lottery but the Ferraris were never in genuine contention there once Regazzoni spun from the lead and Lauda suffered a bungled stop for rain tyres, being despatched with one wheel unsecured and falling off in the pit lane . . . aah miseria!

While Lauda had luckily won in Sweden at Brabham driver Reutemann's expense, Reutemann won at the Nürburgring at Lauda's expense as the Ferrari number one was leading handsomely until a tyre punctured. The Austrian GP was another rain-stopped farce, then for the major Italian GP at Monza Ferrari introduced new cylinder heads improving mid-range torque for the slow-speed chicanes which now despoiled this once super-fast speedway. Yet one of these new engines had failed in pre-race testing on Regazzoni's '024' so Lauda's '023' was fitted with a standard unit for the race. Regazzoni – the Italian-speaking member of the team – was given the 'high-

torque' race engine. They started 1-2 on the front row of the grid and finished 1-3, Regazzoni victorious to a delirious reception from the *tifosi* while Lauda, handicapped by a minor damper problem, fell behind Fittipaldi's second-placed McLaren after holding the lead for 45 of the 52 laps. This success clinched the World titles for Ferrari and Lauda. Monza-headed engines were then used for the final race of the season at Watkins Glen.

Eleven days after that event, on 26 October 1975, Ferrari's new 1976 contender, the 312T2, was unveiled at Fiorano, but while its development progressed in similar fashion to that of the 312T the previous year's cars would run on into the first races of the new season.

In the 312T's case this involved the 1976 Brazilian, South African and US GP West at Long Beach and two minor British races before the new 'T2s took over, though their actual race debut came at Brands Hatch on 14 March in the Race of Champions. The Brazilian GP opened the new season at Interlagos on 25 January, with Ferrari fielding 312Ts '023' for Lauda and '024' for Regazzoni, the Austrian winning from pole position while Regazzoni led before a stop to change a damaged tyre.

At Kyalami, Regazzoni's '022' broke its engine while Lauda's '023' was hampered in the vital final qualifying session when one of its tyres proved to be oversize causing queasy handling and leaving McLaren to steal pole position. Lauda led but from lap 20 his car's left-rear tyre began to deflate. His chosen brake balance reversed during the course of the race yet by judicious use of lapping backmarkers he managed to hold off Hunt's McLaren long enough to win again, this time by 1.3 seconds. He also set fastest race lap but it was now evident that the Ferrari's 1976 advantage over the opposition was nowhere near so marked as it had been in 1975.

Consequently a new 'T2 made its debut at Brands Hatch while old '021' – the second 312T built – appeared there on loan to Scuderia Everest for Giancarlo Martini in a Fiat-Ferrari approved effort to bring on young Italian drivers. The unfortunate Martini qualified second slowest and then crashed on the warm-up lap when a brake snatched. He non-started.

The proven 312Ts '023' and '024' were used by Lauda and Regazzoni at Long Beach. It was the Ticinese's weekend as he qualified on pole, led all the way and won handsomely while Lauda settled for second place after flat-spotting a tyre early in the race then encountering gear selection difficulties – accompanied by horrible noises – in the closing stages.

This was the final appearance of the factory team 312Ts as the next race was the Spanish GP introducing the new regulations to which the 'T2 had been tailored. Before the Spanish race the Everest 312T again emerged in Martini's hands, at Silverstone. He both qualified and finished in tenth place, marking the end of the original *trasversale* series' racing career.

'MODELLO 312T2'

The 1976 model Ferrari was based upon a longer wheelbase than the perhaps over-sensitive 312T, nominally up some 1.7 in. to 2560 mm (100.8 in.) while track was cut to 1400 mm (55.1 in.) front and 1430 mm (56.3 in.) rear. These are works dimensions; actually both track and wheelbase were adjustable, the latter by fitting different top front rocker arms and lower front wishbones with alternative angles of sweep from chassis to wheel hub. Normally they swept rearwards for the standard wheelbase, but it was lengthened by right-angle items.

The new regulations due to take effect from the Spanish GP limited airbox height and rear wing overhang, and introduced roll-over protection at both ends of the cockpit. Overall width was now restricted to 215 cm (84.65 in.)

The 'T2 had been designed in detail to meet these requirements, while the loss of the tall engine airbox was compensated for by provision of shapely intake nostrils moulded into the forward end of the cockpit surround, feeding air into trunkings formed integrally with the body panel and feeding plenum chambers low down on either side around the flat-12 engine's inductions.

The prototype car was first shown fitted with an experimental tube-frame de Dion rear axle system, sprung on coils and attached to the chassis structure beneath the *trasversale* gearbox by a Watt link. This parallel wheel movement system had been developed at Fiorano in conjunction with Goodyear as part of their 'vehicle dynamics' research programme, and it was intended to make optimum use of the American-financed, British-made racing tyres on very smooth circuits. It was easily interchangeable with the conventional 312T-derived, fully independent rear suspension system and in fact, save for a brief practice outing during the French GP meeting at Ricard-Castellet, the conventional system would always be preferred. At one stage, de Dion-framed front suspension was also tested, but this was not even practised in public.

As first shown, the 'T2 also wore streamlined front wheel spats which doubled as brake cooling ducts. They were designed to improve the flow of air off the nose wing and to act as fairings for the front wheels to minimize lift. But since they steered with the front wheels they would be deemed 'moveable aerodynamic devices' when Ferrari attempted to race them and would be rejected. Water and oil radiators remained in their 312T positions with suitable ducts moulded into each side panel as before.

The 'T2 monocoque was considerably lighter than the preceding designs, with aluminium internal framing replacing the previous steel infrastructure, while a true monocoque version was now also on the way. Apart from small triangular planform sections of the side cells, the whole fuel load was carried in three bags virtually line abreast across the tub behind the driver's shoulders.

Whereas the 312T had scaled 598 kg (1318 lb) dry, the new 'T2 weighed in at 575 kg (1268 lb) – right on the minimum weight limit, if Ferrari's public claims were to be believed.

Despite extensive testing, notably at Mugello in November 1975 and subsequently at Vallelunga and Kyalami in February 1976 in addition to the normal 'home' programme at Fiorano, the new 'T2 failed to show the kind of advance over its predecessor that the 312T had demonstrated over the definitive 312B3.

The name of the game – Lauda's 312T2 '026' wins the 1976 Belgian GP at Zolder, the tall '75-style airbox now replaced by those moulded cockpit-surround integral ducts, the full-width blade wing still working well.

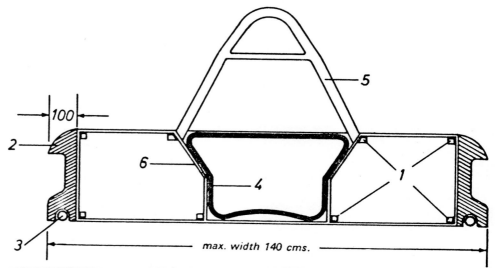

1976 – THE SECOND CHAMPIONSHIP

Lauda drove the prototype car '025' in the minor Brands Hatch race between the South African and Long Beach GPs. Conventional rear suspension was fitted, and after possibly setting fastest practice time (Scheckter's pole time for Tyrrell being considered suspect) Lauda ran an unspectacular fourth until a brake pipe parted after 17 laps.

The revised regulations then came into force at Jarama for the Spanish GP, so that race witnessed the 'T2s' serious debut. Lauda had injured his ribs in a domestic tractor accident yet he qualified on the front row in the new 'T2 '026' and led before running over a kerb and jarring his rib-cage; the understandable pause to wince and catch his breath allowed Hunt's attendant McLaren to go by and win, until the M23 was disqualified for being over-width in post-race scrutineering.

This latest 'T2 used a true monocoque chassis – in the Formula 1 sense – in that its hull was formed purely in stressed sheet shaped over internal bulkheads without the aluminium U-piece internal framing of the prototype '025'. Old 312T '018' was used as team spare, updated in line with the new regulations.

The two new 'T2s dominated in Belgium, Lauda-Regazzoni 1-2, and at Monaco the third new car was ready, its completion having been delayed by one of Italy's perennial metal-workers' strikes. This car, 027', was allotted to Regazzoni, while Lauda kept the structurally similar '026'.

During first practice there an interesting experiment involved use of a thin plastic-coated wire stretched across the leading edge of the rear wing to split the airflow and lower skin friction – or so they said. The 'T2s qualified 1-2 and Lauda scored Ferrari's sixth victory of the season, his third in a row counting the Spanish fracas, and eighth of the technically unbroken series which had begun at Monza the previous September.

Regazzoni's new '027' had lost third place when Hunt's McLaren blew up right in front of it at the harbour chicane, and Regazzoni slithered up the escape road on spilled oil. He rejoined fourth, fuming, stole third place and tackled Scheckter's six-wheeled Tyrrell for second. Just four laps from the end he pressed too hard and clanged into the guardrails, bending '027' quite extensively and ending Ferrari hopes of another spectacular 1-2.

Ferrari had never come to grips with Anderstorp, home of the Swedish GP. There they fielded the Monaco cars and experimented with cylindrical end 'plates' for the rear wings in place of the conventional flat aluminium sheet fences. The novel Tyrrells were uncatchable in the race, Lauda third, Regazzoni tenth, embarrassingly behind a flat-12 engined Brabham-Alfa Romeo . . .

The de Dion rear suspension was tried only briefly at Ricard, as were the quasi brake-scoop front wheel fairings, which the scrutineers rejected out of hand. The cars ran faster with standard scoops. The de Dion system had at one stage proved faster than the conventional kind at Fiorano, but Goodyear altered their tyres so often Ferrari were always having to catch up with what Goodyear did, rather than setting the pace and specifying the tyres which they required.

Now, at the end of Ricard practice, traces of oil were noticed issuing from the flat-12 engines.

Lauda built a three-second lead in the first three race laps, set fastest lap next time round

Top, 312T2 cross-section showing 1, internal stressed-skin stiffened square-tube base frame; 2, deformable structure crush pads; 3, water rails between radiators and engine; 4, seat moulding; 5, roll-over bar; 6, fuel tank bay inner skin. Right, Regazzoni's 312T2 '027' displays its podgy planform, Monaco '76. Flat-12 engine optimized overbody airflow towards banana rear wing.

and on lap nine '026' was shrilling down the long main straight flat-out at around 12,000 rpm when its engine cut with an abrupt crunch of shattering metal. The rear wheels locked momentarily and Lauda was lucky not to come to further grief.

The auxiliary drive flange pressed onto the crankshaft nose had been badly machined and fitted poorly. This initiated cracking, and the crank had broken, an identical failure later eliminating Regazzoni's '027' when in second place.

The third true-monocoque 'T2, chassis '028', was available for Lauda's use in the British GP. Regazzoni used '027' again and '026' became spare car. Lauda cut across his team-mate on the charge into the first corner and the Ferraris collided, sparking a multiple accident and a restart in which Hunt took part again. Ferrari consequently protested when he beat Lauda, who was handicapped by a badly-fitted gear-change bush which tightened up during the restarted race.

Regazzoni had taken a spare car since '027's left-side water radiator and pipework had been torn up in the collision. He saved Ferrari further embarrassment when he switched off in face of plummeting oil pressure. The management blamed him for the collision – which seemed harsh. Hunt was disqualified by appeal to the FIA in Paris on 24 September, some two months after the event, and Lauda was declared winner.

His car '028' had by that time been destroyed in his ghastly Nürburgring accident, which seems to have been triggered by a rear suspension failure. Regazzoni's car led until an almighty high-speed spin on that opening lap dropped him way back, and perhaps he was willing to sit back and finish ninth after two pit stops following his team-mate's crash. Mr Ferrari obliquely blamed Goodyear for the team's set-backs at season's end.

How Lauda came back to race again in less than six weeks is all part of sporting legend. Ferrari reacted stupidly by cancelling their Austrian GP entries, rather then racing on to deny further Championship points to McLaren and their driver Hunt. They then saw sense in time to send Regazzoni to Zandvoort as a lone entry in '027' but he was unaccountably slow in

practice. He then mounted a late charge in the race and finished a very close second to the McLaren. He was then in the dog-house again with Ferrari for having started his charge too late . . . Some people can't do anything right.

Ferrari proved as much by hiring former Brabham-Alfa Romeo driver Reutemann to take Lauda's place at Monza, but the spring-steel Austrian bounced back and returned to the fray, still with a chance of retaining his drivers' title and assisting Ferrari to their second consecutive Constructors' Championship. Consequently the factory prepared three 'T2s for Monza: the heavyweight prototype '025' for new-boy Reutemann, '026' for Lauda and '027' for Regazzoni.

Ferrari reliability plus Regazzoni showing more fire than at any other time since Zolder yielded second for him, fourth for the singed Lauda and ninth for Reutemann, whose lofty frame was badly cramped in the prototype 'T2's cockpit.

Rest rather than test between Monza and Mosport Park then did nothing for Ferrari's chances as their end-of-season performances fell apart. In bitter Canadian cold the 'T2 lacked traction and oversteered badly, refusing to heat its tyres adequately. The oil cooler had been moved from its neat wing strut housing to sit on the gearbox casing itself, apparently at the CSI's insistence as it had been too outboard and vulnerable. This was only a tiny mass movement, but it could still transform the balance of such a delicate instrument as a modern Formula 1 car.

New rear top link suspension mounts were being used and they broke on both the Lauda and Regazzoni cars in the race, only Regazzoni salvaging one point for sixth place after barging Pace's Brabham-Alfa Romeo into the pit barrier . . .

Ferrari's continuous tyre test programme with Goodyear had been badly disrupted by their mid-season dramas, while McLaren's had progressed apace. Now each team reaped the inevitable result. At Watkins Glen the gulf between Ferrari and McLaren was wider than ever before. Only Lauda was at all in contention and his '026' again oversteered as its fuel load burned down and the rear tyres in particular proved too lightly loaded to heat adequately. He placed third, and the Championship outcome depended on the inaugural Japanese GP.

At Fuji, Lauda's '026' was fitted with revised geometry front suspension supposedly promoting increased camber change but he muffed his

start in heavy rain and after two laps retired in the pits, unwilling to race in such conditions. Hunt stole the World Drivers' Championship but Ferrari retained the Constructor's title for a second successive year as Regazzoni finished fifth for two points and the second McLaren failed to score, so Ferrari beat McLaren by nine clear points.

To Mr. Ferrari this was everything but his backers might still have preferred Lauda to have taken the charismatic and more promotable Drivers' title.

During this fraught season, Ferrari's Formula 1 team cars started 31 times, achieving 23 finishes with 'six' firsts including those disputed results in Spain and Britain, four seconds, two thirds, a fourth and fifth, two sixths, three sevenths, an eighth, ninth and Martini's private-entry tenth at Silverstone in early season.

1977 – THE HAT-TRICK SEASON

The 'T2s ran on into the 1977 season but Ferrari developments were affected by the heart trouble which afflicted both engineer Rocchi and his colleague Salvarani that winter, and this following on the hiatus of the preceding autumn caused by the aftermath of Lauda's German accident.

A new 'T2 chassis '029' made its debut with Regazzoni's replacement Reutemann driving on home soil in Argentina to open the new season, while Lauda used '026' there with '027' in reserve. All three cars had been modified to feature the Fuji front suspension mod, while rear track had been increased marginally from the '76 spec. The engineers claimed 'twelve more horsepower' from the flat-12 engine but Lauda had been pointedly excluded from the winter test programme. Various body changes had been tested at Ricard-Castellet without his involvement and he had found it harder generally to arrange test miles. It was going to be a problem year for Maranello . . . again.

In Buenos Aires the little-changed 'T2s were uncompetitive on race day. Reutemann's car handled poorly, skittering from understeer to oversteer, while Lauda retired with his engine misfiring and a furious vibration within the car. At Interlagos, Brazil, a new-section rear wing was available which Reutemann used and which Lauda claims was, significantly, not offered to him.

One might be forgiven for thinking we are discussing a team run by twelve-year olds. This reversion to setting one driver against another was a grotesque throwback to less competitive times in the '50s and '60s when less than total team effort could still achieve results, and internecine rivalry paid Ferrari dividends. In the combative late-1970s they needed real luck on their side to get away with it.

On the long and difficult Interlagos track, Lauda's '026' was set up with too much castor, making its steering intolerably heavy. The inboard ends of the top rockers were binding against the fluid reservoirs on the front bulkhead. Consequently the car ducked and weaved dangerously on the bumpy bankings. That day saw Regazzoni, now driving in the tiny British Ensign team, lapping faster than both Ferraris!

Yet Reutemann was able to win a race

dictated by broiling heat and a disintegrating track surface, while Lauda inherited third for the team on reliability alone, amongst just seven finishers.

Thereafter Lauda read the riot act to the powers at Maranello. He galvanized the team, jerking them back into gear. By force of personality – and an overdue dose of logic – he evidently made Forghieri drag out every extant 'T2 for comparative testing at Fiorano.

This programme then continued at Kyalami prior to the South African GP, which Lauda won in '030', brand new with revised rear suspension pick-ups, the top mounts being fabricated structures with integral brake ducts to cool the inboard brakes. Battery, oil tank, catch tank and gearbox oil cooler had been moved forward from their old mounting around the magnesium rear wing strut and they had lost their plastic fairing there, leaving the strut naked. A slimmer nose cowl was adopted, though retaining the now distinctive full-width front wing. 'The Old Lauda' re-emergence was confirmed as he took the lead from Hunt's McLaren on lap seven and won comfortably despite his car collecting some debris from the tragic accident which killed Shadow driver Pryce and a track marshal. The Shadow's detached roll-over bar wedged beneath the Ferrari's left side, puncturing its water system, and both Ferrari lower front wishbones were damaged. As coolant dribbled away so temperatures rose and oil pressure fell. Although the orange oil pressure warning light on the dash glowed brightly throughout the final laps Lauda was able to nurse it across the line to win by 5.2 secs before switching off immediately after the flag.

Lauda's 'T2 was then second and set fastest lap in the sensationally close US GP West at Long Beach which Andretti won in the new Lotus 78 'wing-car'. Jarama saw the Austrian break a rib during practice and he was unable to start, while a Ligier wheel coming loose rewarded Reutemann consistency with second place in Andretti's victorious slipstream.

The Ferraris achieved a reliable 2-3 finish at Monaco, but only after both flat-12 Brabham-Alfa Romeos had led them consistently before retiring. At Zolder the Lotus 78 was making the standards of the time, Lauda was second to one. By the time of the Swedish GP the Ferrari team was again pulling apart, Lauda insisting the engineers should introduce a new car while Reutemann felt what they had was good enough. Ferrari disarray was perhaps exacerbated by Goodyear concentration upon the tyre requirements of the dominantly fast if fragile Lotus 78. With its underwing aerodynamic loadings it demanded more rigid tyre sidewall construction than hitherto. When Goodyear reacted accordingly, the Ferraris proved unable to heat these tyres adequately. It was the late-1976 syndrome all over again, only more so.

New chassis '031' – still a 'T2 – appeared at Dijon for the French GP, offering little new beyond restyled radiator air exits. The Ferraris finished 5-6. At Silverstone, Lauda patience inherited second place and another six points for himself and his team, then at Hockenheim for the German GP Ferrari's reliable power at last asserted itself and Lauda won after a Brabham-Alfa had retired and the leading Wolf slowed. This victory with six rounds still to run made the Drivers' Championship look like Lauda's, despite the team's problems.

Fairings were tried behind the 'T2s' rear wheels to reduce drag on this high-speed circuit but neither driver could detect any difference, so they were removed and quietly forgotten.

In Austria, Lauda was second and Reutemann fourth thanks to other competitors' failures and both Championship crowns were now clearly within reach. An F1 Constructors' Championship hat-trick had never before been achieved. It would be a Ferrari first.

At Zandvoort, '031' was fitted with a revised

exhaust system to add mid-range torque but Lauda was convinced the advantage was as illusory as had been the after-wheel fairings at Hockenheim, and a standard system was refitted. Lauda won, again profiting from faster cars' failures. Reutemann was sixth after a wing damaging incident during the race.

By this time Lauda had arranged to leave Ferrari to join Brabham in 1978. It was an open secret by the time of the Italian GP at Monza, where Lauda paced home second behind Andretti's at last reliable Lotus 78. Now he needed just one more point to deny Scheckter's Championship ambitions with Wolf.

It came at Watkins Glen where Lauda placed fourth, for three points in fact, but the summary dismissal there of Lauda's Chief Mechanic, Cuoghi, in practice had decided him to withdraw from the team on the morning of first practice in Canada. He had driven his last race for Ferrari, and had left them as Formula 1 Constructors' Champions for the third consecutive season, and with a second Drivers' title under his own belt.

There was minimal 'T2 development for the last two races of that season in Canada and Japan, where Gilles Villeneuve joined Reutemann as team driver.

This turbulent but again undeniably successful season had seen Ferrari make 33 starts in the 17 World Championship rounds, Lauda scoring in every one of the 12 races which he finished – out of only 14 started. He won three times, took six second places on reliability and added a third, fourth and fifth. Reutemann's fourth place in the Drivers' Championship was achieved from 11 scoring finishes in the 13

Top, all-round visibility is not an F1 car requirement – here's Regazzoni submerged in 312T2 '027', Zandvoort '76. Also noticeable are the mandatory electrical system cut-out switch, clearly marked as required since 1969, hex-nut, centre-lock wheel and purely functional Ferrari sponsors. Above, Lauda's '030 flashing its flat bottom at Long Beach '77, underbody airflow had yet to be harnessed.

events he finished from 17 started, including one win, two seconds, three thirds, two fourths and three sixths.

Since the birth of the *trasversale* series in 1975, Ferrari had raced cars built under 12 individual chassis numbers, five 312Ts built in 1974-75, and seven 'T2s built 1975-77. Chassis '023' started life as a '75 312T and raced on into the start of '76. It became the most successful individual chassis within the series, winning the Monaco, Belgian, Swedish and US GPs of 1975 and the Brazilian and South African races of 1976.

Now, at the end of 1977, Ferrari had taken their third Constructors' title with a design which was neither the fastest nor the most competitive, but crucially it was the most consistently reliable so their winning margin was a vast 33 points, with a total of 95 compared to Lotus's 62, McLaren's 60 and Wolf's 54. The team was to abandon Goodyear racing tyres in favour of Michelin in 1978, but they would not retrieve the World Championship mantle until the following year, 1979, with the model 312T4 whose story we shall trace shortly.

Ground Effects

Many years ago, a physicist named Bernoulli described the principle of velocity and pressure changes in a flowing fluid. Accelerate flow and pressure falls within the fluid. Now air is a fluid and if an airstream is introduced into a narrowing but otherwise open-ended tube or tunnel (a venturi) it is accelerated and its pressure falls.

This principle is harnessed in the venturi throat of a carburettor to suck in fuel, and having ventured into the area of wing form aerodynamics from 1967, Formula 1 engineering came to appreciate Mr Bernoulli very much some years later, in 1977-79.

As early as 1961 Texan oil-man, private flyer and intuitive race-engineering genius, Jim Hall, had beaten the hot British-built Cooper Monacos in an SCCA event at Elkhart Lake, driving his Troutman-Barnes built front-engined Chaparral 1 sports car with a Chevrolet V8 engine.

Chevrolet R&D sat up and paid attention. Some of their aerodynamicists then worked with Hall to produce an 'inverted airfoil' Chaparral body, with upswept undersides at nose and tail to form what was in elevation half a venturi tunnel between car underside and road surface. The car's passage through the air would then cause airflow to accelerate beneath the car, thus losing pressure and thereby sucking the car down against the road.

At least, they thought Mr Bernoulli had said it would . . . but it didn't.

When Hall tested the inverted airfoil car at GM's Proving Grounds the front suspension reached full rebound at 120 mph as the nose rose, attempting to lift the front wheels clear of the ground. A massive snowplough air dam was then fitted to *exclude* airflow running beneath the upturned under-nose section and this created so much downforce that Hall stopped half-way round his first lap with the front tyres grinding their way out through the front fender tops.

Had some form of skirting been suspended to seal that 'inverted airfoil' underbody against the road surface on each side, racing history could have been very different.

The modified Chaparral's problem stemmed from too much aerodynamic infill rushing in from ambient pressure between the wheels on each side, plus so much lift from the under-nose surface that enormous aerodynamic pressure under the nose attempted to flip the car over on its back. Perhaps only the weight of its hefty front engine saved the day until that air-dam was added with its consequent effect.

There followed a period when designers sought actively to exclude airflow from beneath their cars, to obtain downforce by harnessing airflow over the top of the bodywork and beneath their add-on airfoil wings.

Chaparral-Chevrolet continued to toy with wings and things, until in 1968-69 an anonymous race fan sent Jim Hall a sketch of a sports-racing car sucked down against the roadway by horizontal fans extracting the air from beneath it.

GM R&D engineer Paul van Valkenburgh, Chaparral's Don Gates and GM department head Charlie Simmons pursued the idea with test models which showed promise.

Gates worked out a fan and a skirt infill defence system while Don Cox, Ernie DeFusco and Joe Marasco engineered a chassis to match. The resultant Chaparral 2J 'sucker car' first ran in November 1969 and after considerable development was raced in the 1970 CanAm series where it created a sensation before being banned!

A 55 hp JLO snowmobile auxiliary engine had been adapted to run two extractor fans, reducing air pressure in a massive Lexan-skirted compartment around the car's centre of gravity and engine bay. The car proved blindingly fast, sucking itself to the road and exhibiting immense cornering power and traction – hence the ban, from which the restriction on 'moveable devices with a primary aerodynamic function' became entrenched.

Meanwhile, in England, BRM boffin Peter Wright had tackled the problem of cleaning up aerodynamic turbulence and obtaining some extra airfoil download area on the 1968-69 V12 cars. He conceived a bolt-on very high-aspect ratio wing-shaped pannier to mount each side of the slender monocoque hull of that period, projecting into the space between front and rear wheels. One BRM V12 was rigged in this manner with moulded glass-fibre wing panniers and was

tested at Snetterton in 1968. Results were inconclusive, but promised enough for Peter and his boss Tony Rudd to produce a wind tunnel test model of a full-bodied 'wing-car'. It was tested briefly by them in early-1969 before the palace revolution which saw Rudd's resignation in mid-summer.

BRM's wing-car ideas were set aside. Rudd became Group Lotus Engineering Director for Colin Chapman; Peter Wright joined Specialised Mouldings, the racing car plastic body manufacturers, and set up their wind tunnel R&D facility. Wearing an SM hat he suggested the BRM-clone March 701 pannier wing tanks to Robin Herd. These were raced in 1970, their shaped undersurfaces forming a half-venturi section with the road surface, but still high above it and lacking skirt sealing to prevent infill.

Then in 1973 Gordon Murray's pyramid-section Brabham BT42 punched a very small hole in the air, maintained good downforce from its upper surfaces and excluded most of the airstream from underneath. In his improved BT44s of 1974, Gordon ran a horizontal thrust-forward splitter or nose tray to exclude airflow. As the car pitched, however, so some of this sacrificial tray would wear away, some would survive.

That prompted him to consider fitting a dam amidships beneath the car's belly, near its pitch centre where the dam could never hit the road. He used a very thin, slightly flexible glass-fibre dam, divided to form a vee or chevron section beneath the car. Testing dictated 1.5 in. skirts for fast circuits, 7/8 in. for bumpy courses.

Brabham's former BAC aerodynamicist and co-adoptor of the 1968 Belgian GP strutted wings, Ray Jessop, had taught Gordon how to use a manometer for air-pressure tests. Now Gordon fitted a liquid manometer clear U-tube on the car's side, with one end tapped to the site to be tested, behind the dam under the car for example, and using a coloured fluid and graduated pressure scale within the driver's vision.

Below, *Peter Wright and Colin Chapman;* centre, *Wright tested wing tanks on this V12 BRM, Snetterton 1968.* Bottom, *Wright's BRM wing-car test model in the wind tunnel. Only the vital skirts were missing.*

Initially the driver would observe what level the liquid reached as he drove the car, and he would then report back. Subsequently they fitted an over-centre lever to clasp the plastic tube and hold the pressure difference for examination in the pit. This way they measured pressures on top of the nose, on the high airbox and beneath the car and when they found a pressure difference of perhaps 0.5 lb per square inch and multiplied that by the area of the car's underside over which that differential had been detected they were on their way to finding *several hundred pounds* useful download.

The under-belly air dam promoted an atmospheric depression which extended back for perhaps three or four feet. It was a practical expression of ground effect although the Brabham people did not really grasp its significance.

Fitting the skirts ahead of the centre of gravity enabled them to reduce wing incidence and that coincided with, as Gordon recalls 'an idea I pinched from Indy. We saw some photos from David Phipps at the end of '73 showing the Liebeck lip on the back of a wing, a little curl now universal. It developed into the banana wing with its leading edge as high as the trailing edge, a wing with great camber but minimal frontal area. We had about 300 lb downforce from a wing like that plus, say, 150 lb from under the car – proved by the numbers we were seeing on the manometer . . .'

They attempted to keep it all secret through 1974 – though the belly dams were mentioned in the press – but McLaren had a good look and appreciated what was happening, and the McLaren M23s soon emerged with plastic appendages beneath their monocoques.

By 1976-77 Peter Wright headed Team Lotus aerodynamic research using Charlie Prior-made models in the Imperial College wind tunnel in Kensington, London. There he realized that the trick was to exclude airflow on either side of the car from infilling airstream-acceleration sections which could be formed by shaped underwing side pods on each side of the central chassis tub. The ground-contact aerodynamic skirt, *à la* Chaparral 2J of 1970, was adopted and rapidly perfected for Formula 1, and the ground-effects revolution was upon us.

The reduction of air pressure achieved in Wright's underwing venturi tunnels of course exerted its force in all directions, so not only did it suck down the car from below, it also sucked in the skirts on each side while accelerating air throughflow initiated by the car's passage.

In the sliding-skirt era from 1978 to 1980, it became vital to provide smooth, friction-free skirt travel to prevent these skirts from skewing or binding in their guides. Consistent contact with the ground had to be maintained to achieve consistent download as the awful bouncing or pitching effect known as 'porpoising' reared its ugly head. Intermittent skirt contact made and broke suction and, exacerbated by centre of pressure instability, in which the c.o.p. itself raced to and fro, the car self-excited and simply passed beyond suspension control.

The good cars did it well, most notably the Williams FW07 and Brabham BT49s, some others did it badly, particularly the Lotus 80, Arrows A2 and the dreadful Ferrari 312T5s.

Ground-effect aerodynamics, however, were here to stay, even after sliding skirts were banned, and despite the flat-bottom rule of 1983 banning venturi sections within the wheelbase. Useful ground effect was still to be obtained from low-set nose wings and end-plated diffuser surfaces slung beneath the gearbox.

Progress can never be un-invented . . .

Chapter 10

USING THE BREEZE – LOTUS 78 AND 79 1977-79

Ferrari were just hitting new heights with their model 312T and McLaren were defending their World Championship titles with the M23s through the summer of 1975, when Team Lotus found themselves in really deep trouble. Their Type 72 cars were at last at the end of their long development, and their front suspension characteristics did not permit them to adapt adequately to the latest generation of Goodyear tyres.

Colin Chapman pondered the future. Sitting in his vast office at Ketteringham Hall three years later he told me how he had 'sat down and thought seriously about what we wanted, and decided the answer was a wing car.'

This new concept in racing car design found its pioneering expression in the Lotus 78 of 1977 followed by World Championship domination in the Lotus 79 of 1978. The story of these two cars is virtually indivisible and so both will now be described in some detail, although only the latter achieved Constructors' Champion status.

Initially, Colin Chapman compiled a detailed concept document setting out his requirements and presented it to his engineering director, Tony Rudd, the former Chief Engineer of BRM. He was to establish a new research and development unit within the Lotus group.

As Rudd tells the story, that brief was far more than just an outline for a new car design – indeed a whole new car concept – it was a measure of Chapman's greatness.

'He realised that in racing we were down and out, and that we'd got it all wrong by the latest standards. And he made the right long-range strategic decisions while still involved in racing day-to-day. In his famous 27-page brief not only did he suggest the way to go, but he also listed all the things he didn't know, and then he left it to an old has-been like me and to a bunch of new boys to tell him all the answers . . .'

Rudd was anything but a has-been – he could not have held down his post with Lotus if that had been true – but he had not been closely involved with the racing cars until 1975, when research and development work began under

his direction at Ketteringham Hall.

This was a rambling old country house folded within the woodlands close by the main Lotus plant at Hethel. During the Second World War it had been a Bombardment Group HQ for the US 8th Air Force, which flew Liberators from Hethel and the similar airfields dotted across the Norfolk plain nearby. The Hall later became a private boarding school before falling virtually derelict. Lotus acquired it, and former Brabham and McLaren designer Ralph Bellamy became one of its first inmates with a project to develop a new lightweight Lotus racing gearbox.

Rudd's Esprit production car design group arrived soon after, and with that project's conclusion Chapman put Rudd in charge of long-range Formula 1 research for Team Lotus. This new unit was to operate quite independently of Team and its everyday race commitments and pressures. It was to give Chapman the answers he wanted and to test the feasibility of the type of car which he had outlined.

His concept document was dated August 1975, one month before the release of the highly-adjustable new Lotus 77 Formula 1 car (see page 195), Team's second serious attempt to produce a Type 72 replacement.

Ralph Bellamy became one early member of the Formula 1 R&D group, and a boffin named Peter Wright was another. He had been with Tony Rudd at BRM in 1969, and there they had laid down advance plans for a wing-car.

Chronic lack of success and eccentric management there had led to Rudd's summary dismissal in mid-season 1969. Tony Southgate had been appointed chassis designer in Rudd's place, Chapman had snapped up Rudd's services for Group Lotus and Wright had followed him there after a spell in charge of Specialised Mouldings' wind tunnel, for he was an aerodynamicist. After Rudd and Wright had left BRM, their wing-car programme was junked by the new regime. Wright had eventually joined Lotus to run their plastics research, and when that programme had been completed success-

Giorgio Piola's explanatory ground-effects sketch is based on the Lotus 79 and shows below 1, nose fins; 2, venturi underwings; 3, expanding diffuser section; 4, suspension uprights well outboard to clear underbody airstream; 5, inboard spring/damper mounting for same reason; 6, inboard brakes (bad move); 7, end-plate mounted rear wing. Bottom, 1, cambered nose fins; 2, improved 'Mosquito' leading-edge top-ducted radiator mount; 3, sliding skirt seal; 4, upswept exhaust efflux; 5, rear deck/engine cowl; 6, cambered rear wing.

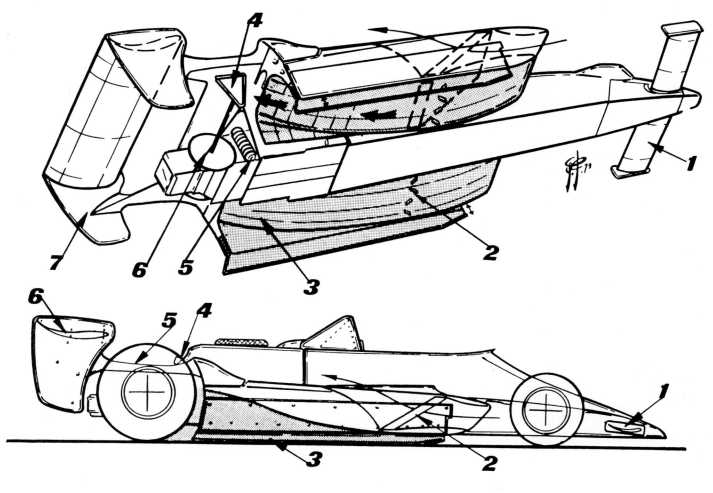

fully his brilliant mind was applied to the new Formula 1 project.

The first BRM wing-car concept used stub wings sprouting either side of the central monocoque to clean up the aerodynamic turbulence between front and rear wheels and find some extra download. Robin Herd used a similar layout in his March 701 design of 1970, but the idea was not then pursued to its ultimate conclusion since airflow management was not applied which would close off the underwing airstream from the general diffuse airflow around the outside of the car.

Wright joined Rudd and Bellamy at Ketteringham Hall – or 'Fawlty Towers' as it was known within Group Lotus – and through the autumn of 1975 this trio discussed Chapman's myriad questions of principle.

The philosophy was simple in essence: harness the car's entire form to generate advantageous aerodynamic effect, instead of merely using relatively tiny bolt-on wings at front and rear to load an aerodynamically redundant hull.

At that time every Formula 1 designer had studied in varying depth the effect of airflow around the sides and over the top of his car. Few, apart from Gordon Murray of Brabham and the McLaren boys, had tackled the potential embodied in the air flowing underneath it. Indeed, even then most had been trying various ploys to prevent too much air flowing under their cars at all.

Now the Lotus R&D group retained Charlie Prior, a first-class model and pattern maker from the Esprit team, to build quarter-scale model cars and aerodynamic devices for assiduous wind tunnel testing conducted by Wright at Imperial College, London.

A wind tunnel there was provided with a moving belt floor in the test section which mimicked the roadway passing at speed beneath a car. Little previous research had been conducted in this way. Normally test models sat on a stationary surface, or even less satisfactorily were suspended in space. This was fine for aviation testing but bore little resemblance to reality where land vehicles were concerned.

Questions were pursued in depth. If either bluff or chisel noses could be used, then both would be tested. If the chisel for example promised better, they would consider why; if it worked so well, should not other chisel sections

then be used to gain more download somewhere else on the car?

Radiator siting is a vital cornerstone of any racing design. Rudd had been in charge of Rolls-Royce Merlin aero engine fault investigation during the war, and the inner-wing section radiator mounting of the De Havilland Mosquito aircraft came to mind. Its radiators were buried within ducts sunk into the inner wings' leading edges, air passing through the core and then exiting through conveniently sited ducts further back on the wing chord. Would side pods based upon this inner-wing section generate download when slung either side of a single-seat racing chassis?

A model mimic section was made and tested upside down in the wind tunnel to provide negative lift. Lift:drag ratio was the vital criterion – the best possible lift for the least possible drag being the target. Tony Rudd still recalls the message he received from Imperial College that Christmas. It read simply 'The Mosquito flies'.

Ducted radiators and pod sections of this type would be used to harness airflow beneath the pod underfloors – or underwings – to generate download. The low-pressure areas created by the acceleration of this airflow (see page 94) would be protected from infilling on each side by a skirt system which would extend from the pod side panels down to the road surface.

Now that overall concept, shape and principles for what would become the Lotus Type 78 had been decided, Bellamy settled down to draw the car while Wright delved further into its aerodynamics.

Mike Cooke set up and ran a test rig, simulating racing loads on every component as it was made. Unacceptable deflection brought immediate redesign until stiffness became adequate. The rig itself was rather crude, loading parts via cables passing over pulleys and attached to concrete-filled oil drums, but it was invaluable in building structural reliability into the new car. It also served to pinpoint some of the contemporary Type 77's deficiencies and helped bring that car to competitiveness by season's end, when Andretti drove it to win the Japanese GP.

Once Bellamy had finalized his layouts, Martin Ogilvie moved up from Team's base at Potash Lane to detail the new car's suspensions and other 'bits that moved', while Bellamy completed the chassis and they then combined on body design.

The prototype Lotus 78 – known in the curious sponsor-pleasing 'John Player Special' series then in use as chassis 'JPS/15' – was driven first time out at Hethel by Ketteringham's shop foreman, Eddie Dennis. Although a

new Lotus racing gearbox was under development, it was not used on this prototype car 'to limit the unknowns' as Chapman put it.

Nigel Bennett, a former Firestone racing tyre engineer who had joined Team when the American company withdrew from racing at the end of 1974, conducted onboard instrumentation tests using borrowed Goodyear equipment while Andretti and his team-mate Gunnar Nilsson drove in extended circuit testing.

By the time Chapman decided to race the new car his R&D group had accumulated 2.2 miles of test-recording tape, had completed over 150 individual investigations, 54 rig tests and 400 hours of wind tunnel time at Imperial College. The statistics were impressive, but did the car work?

Tests indicated that it did, although aerodynamic values realised full-size were easily 25-30 per cent less than those predicted by wind tunnel model tests.

The new 'John Player Special Mark III' – alias Lotus 78 – made its public bow at a reception held in London's Royal Garden Hotel on 21 December 1976. Andretti was there, enthusing about its 'boulevard ride', and it certainly looked different . . .

The centre monocoque nacelle was slim, like the preceding Type 77's, but it had broad panniers slung either side between front and rear wheels. The tub was formed into a fully-stressed tank section behind the driver's shoulders, while a structural scuttle panel passed above his legs up front. The new tub was light and very stiff through liberal use of Cellite sandwich material in its front bulkhead and side skins.

This material consisted of two thin dural sheets sandwiching aluminium honeycomb. It was very strong and stiff yet light and was borrowed direct from aerospace where the actual section employed by Lotus was used in Trident airliner flooring. Lotus's panels were actually made up for them by Technical Resin Bonders. The material had also featured in one panel on the Cosworth 4WD car of 1969 and had been studied closely by Derek Gardner during his Tyrrell researches of 1971-73.

Front suspension comprised swept-back front rocker arms and wide-based fabricated lower wishbones, carrying neat cast uprights with Lotus 77-style Lockheed twin-calliper disc brakes. These were a cooperative development between the two companies offering duplicated callipers clasping both leading and trailing edges of the ventilated discs. Originally they had doubled as structural members in the Type 77s, bolting on inboard, with the suspension elements in turn bolted onto integral lugs cast in the calliper bodies. An early modification to the Type 77 had seen the front brakes go outboard into the wheels, which is where the 78 now carried these 'balanced calliper' brakes.

Inboard coil-spring/damper units resided in neat niches recessed into the tub flanks. Massive fairings streamlined the tubular top rocker arm pivot supports which had been exposed on the Type 77s.

At the rear, the Cosworth DFV/Hewland gearbox assembly matched the 77's in all save two major details. Where the 77 had used a single bottom link, the new 78 used a massive fabricated wishbone, though the geometry was initially identical. On the 77 the inboard structural balanced brake callipers had been carried on special transaxle side plates which could be rotated to adjust anti-squat. Parallel top link suspension picked up on these inboard callipers. A neat innovation on the 78 on show (actually the second chassis JPS/16) was the oil tank which was now integrated into the bell-housing spacer between engine and gearbox. This feature was to be widely copied, along with so many other features of the Type 78.

On JPS/15 oil had been carried in a tank accommodated within a four inch longer rear section of the tub. All subsequent 78s were

Andretti in the Lotus 78 at Monaco, showing off its broad flat side pods incorporating underwings within, top-ducted leading-edge radiators and nose-top oil cooler.

built along JPS/16 lines, using the shorter tub and bell-housing tank. This gave them a 107 in. wheelbase against the prototype's original 110 in. type.

However, the new Lotus's magic ingredient lay within its side panniers. Essentially they housed wing fuel tanks towards the rear – around the car's notional centre of gravity – with the water radiators ahead of them in their 'Mosquito' mounts, exhausting expended air upward through shaped pannier-top vents. The ramp surface guiding this air out through the top vents was actually the upper face of the wing fuel tank panelling.

The tank undersides then curved upwards towards their trailing edges, terminating in line with the engine mounts to present what could be called an inverted wing section to the airstream. In fact it exerted its influence on the venturi principle described elsewhere (p. 94).

Having generated an area of low pressure beneath these underwing sections, capable literally of sucking the car down onto the road surface, measures then had to be taken to prevent air infilling this depression from either side. This was the crucial step which had not been taken in the BRM experiment nor in the March 701.

Now Wright recommended that the 'tips' of these very long-chord, short-span pannier wings be closed off by Cellite end plates which extended virtually the full distance from front to rear wheel on either side. Furthermore, extending beneath the Cellite end plate, which might be better described as a 'side plate' in this instance, a bristle skirt extended down to road level. The hunt was on to discover an air-impervious material which could survive high-speed rubbing contact with the road surface, and a brush just seemed a reasonable expedient with which to start.

The panniers' upper decks, meanwhile, extended alongside the engine to terminate in flick-ups above the exhaust manifolding ahead of each rear wheel.

Conventional wings and fins provided trim and balance, but still there was more. Mounting the side radiators just aft of the front suspension gave more forward weight bias than hitherto, and this was further enhanced by the oil cooler being buried in a nose duct well ahead of the front axle line and by the far-forward driving position, forced there by the three fuel cells in line abreast behind the seatback. This concentrated fuel load around the car's notional centre of gravity and achieved Chapman's requirement for 'minimum change in handling and response as the fuel load lightens'.

After testing permutations with his highly-adjustable type 77 – which was as much a research vehicle as a serious racing car – he decided that only three things really mattered: 'how long it is, how wide it is, and where the weight is! We'd tried seven different rear-suspension geometries on one occasion and the drivers were hard pressed to notice any difference. But when we increased the front track by an inch they raved.'

Consequently the 78's front track was extended close to the maximum limit, wider than the 77, so the new car could literally stick out a paw as its driver applied steering lock and the longer lever arm would give extra 'bite'.

Now Goodyear's contemporary front tyres were loaded as never before by a Lotus, and there was no problem in working them up to adequate temperature. Front-end grip was the greatest the drivers had ever known, and in turn it then allowed use of near zero-slip differentials to limit wheelspin, which in a design with less front-end bite would merely induce uncontrollable understeer.

This was partly at Andretti's request. He then prompted addition of a USAC-style driver-adjustable rear anti-roll bar, similar to that being introduced by McLaren from their Indy experience. He also recommended a

Andretti and Nilsson in Team Lotus's two new Type 78s, chassis '3 and '2 respectively, Jarama, 1977 Spanish GP. Mario won, with Gunnar fifth. See the Tony Southgate-inspired Shadow-like nose oil coolers.

preferential fuel drainage system, which would enable him to choose the order and degree in which his three available fuel cells drained down – thus further adjusting weight bias within the car during a race as its total fuel load burned away.

Andretti had forged a rare empathy with Chapman, rather similar to the relationship which this gifted engineer had once shared so successfully with Jim Clark. Andretti had the experience and innate sensitivity to trim his car into optimum balance on the fuel changeover tap and anti-roll adjuster. He worked unceasingly during that 1977 season to set up his Lotus 78s to an unprecedented pitch.

In USAC left-turn only track racing, 'stagger' – the use of unequal circumference tyres giving the car a directional bias under power and braking – had become a highly-developed practice, though still perhaps more art than science. Similarly, 'cross-weighting' – diagonal stiffness in the car adjusted on its spring platforms – was a familiar track-racing tweak to find optimum traction in the important corners on a circuit, and Andretti had the ability to appreciate when, where and how these finer points could be applied.

For Formula 1 he and Team Lotus took great pains to match sets of tyres. Manufacturing processes for cross-ply racing tyres inevitably produced variations within finished cover sizes and characteristics. Working with Chapman, Bennett and, briefly, Tony Southgate, another BRM refugee to come to Lotus (in his case via Shadow), even lateral tyre stabilities were explored. This was done by altering wheel-offsets with the Speedline bolt-together sectional road wheels used.

The end result of this deep-thinking programme was that Andretti led more World Championship race laps than any other driver that 1977 season. He won four Grands Prix and his team-mate Nilsson won a fifth for the team in Belgium, in the rain.

But a string of five engine failures and three other mechanical faults kept Andretti, Lotus and the World Championship titles apart. Three new Cosworth development engines, using more radical cams and porting than the standard production units, failed behind Andretti's shoulders. Alternative Nicholson-McLaren rebuilt DFVs failed him twice more.

But Andretti won with luck and Nicholson power on his side at Long Beach and then from genuine merit, still Nicholson-powered, in the Spanish GP at Jarama. Luck gave him a third victory at Dijon when Watson's Brabham-Alfa Romeo faltered on the very last lap with

Andretti and the Lotus 78 well beaten. Sweetest victory for this Italian-born American driver came at Monza in his 'home' GP where a revised Cosworth development engine with less radical valve timing survived to the finish, and the 78 was simply uncatchable.

The repeated engine failures were blamed by Cosworth upon a suspect oil tank in the car, causing aeration difficulties, but though Lotus changed the system as advised the precise nature of the problem was neither traced nor proved.

On the 78's debut in the heat of Buenos Aires, Andretti's 78/2 had had its front-end blown apart by an exploding onboard extinguisher bottle. Dangerous stuff, this safety equipment . . . In Brazil the same unfortunate car had then caught fire. Race retirements in both these events were mechanical, caused respectively by RHP/Lobro joint failure and then by a battery solenoid malfunction. In Sweden, having led 68 of the GP's 72 laps, Andretti's car ran low on fuel due to its Nicholson engine's metering unit having vibrated itself onto a full-rich setting, increasing its consumption.

These failures frustrated the unfortunate driver, while lapses on his part agonized the team. Despite his vast experience he would too often try to win his races on the opening lap, sparking first-lap accidents at Zolder and Fuji which put him out.

During the season four Type 78 chassis were built, plated as 'JPS-15-16-17-18', all of which survived the year. Chassis '78/1' (i.e. 'JPS-15') would be sold to Mexican privateer Hector Rebaque for 1978 and he would also purchase '78/4' ('JPS-18') during that season. Team retained 78s '2 and '3.

The Lotus 78s' season was characterized as win or bust. By the end of it, the lack of minor place scorings left Lotus-JPS second to Ferrari in the Constructors' Championship, and Andretti third and Nilsson eighth in the Drivers' competition. Yet Andretti had still won those four GPs, while World Champion Lauda and runner-up Scheckter had won only three each, more reliable minor placings producing their greater points total.

The World Championship scoring systems rewarded consistency more than winning, and

Chapman considered wryly 'merely driving for points just isn't the name of the game as far as I'm concerned'.

His Lotus 78 was undoubtedly the star of that 1977 season, but its performances had not been so clear cut as to convince the opposition – yet – that Lotus really had something in this ground-effects underwing business. Reliability had been poor, and while the car undoubtedly developed much download it also added much drag and was slow on the straights.

At that time several leading drivers would say 'Gimme a car that's fast on the straight, and I'll block 'em all off in the corners . . .'

Team Lotus was not unduly worried by the 78s' perceived straightline speed deficiency. They felt that other factors had intruded on the faster circuits, and in any case the car offered so much download that its drivers always wanted to use it *all*, not trim some out to diminish drag and so gain straightline speed. They loved its secure feel in corners, blinding round their opposition often on the outside line, with some adhesion still in hand.

Above all, the 78 excelled on turn-in bite into corners and on traction away from them. Its 'wing-car' aerodynamics worked and now for 1978 Team prepared a new design which would make the most of the 78's new technology.

1978 – THE BLACK BEAUTY
The existing Type 78s raced on into the new year with Ronnie Peterson joining Andretti to constitute perhaps the strongest driver pairing in Formula 1.

Andretti began the year by winning at Buenos Aires, while in South Africa Peterson won an extraordinary wheel-banging going-slow race from a Tyrrell on the last lap after Andretti's 78 had run low on fuel (again) and lost the lead.

Meanwhile, a much-refined Lotus 79, or JPS Mark IV, was on the way to capitalize upon experience with the 78, alias JPS Mark III. While the 78 had used relatively simple inverted side wings to generate its download, the new 79 went much further towards being a true ground-effects vehicle, in that its pannier underwings formed a far more sophisticated venturi section against the road surface and thus accelerated air passing beneath to reduce its pressure and so download the whole vehicle.

It was now hoped to find the missing 25 per cent of aerodynamic download which had been somehow misplaced between tunnel-testing the models for the Type 78 and running the real car full-size.

Lotus had claimed that the Type 78s had started out as heavy cars, and had shed weight during their racing career – the reverse of normality – but even so they were still too heavy for choice. One interesting suggestion in the Chapman concept document had been provision of onboard jacks to save time in testing and pre-race qualifying. The original cars had turned out too heavy to dare install them, but the 79 was to come that much closer.

Meanwhile, the Ketteringham R&D group had become diluted. Southgate returned whence he came to Shadow in mid-1977, and now Bellamy moved to Copersucar. Both embarked on new wing-car designs, the former more successfully than the latter. It appears that Bellamy had been the great advocate of using honeycomb in the 78 but towards the end of his time there his relationship with Chapman had deteriorated. Now 'The Old Man' took charge of the 79 project and, according to one member of his design team, 'decided perhaps to do it his own way, using sheet aluminium which he understood from the old days'.

There would be minimum use of honeycomb in the new chassis. This was arguably a retrograde step, and structurally the 78 would remain more advanced than its replacement.

But there were disadvantages with using honeycomb panels. Skin damage transmitted to the core was virtually impossible to repair short of total replacement and Team found major headaches achieving adequate strong-point mountings in the very thin aluminium skins. Consequently the 79 grew as a conventional sheet aluminium tub, with a high-set beam arrangement within its cockpit sides from which to hang the side pods and attendant structures.

Under the usual beady-eyed direction of 'The Old Man', the new Type 79 was drawn and detailed by Geoff Aldridge and Martin Ogilvie. One major objective was to improve airflow through the side panniers, and to achieve this the outboard fuel tanks and rear suspension spring/dampers of the Type 78 were deleted.

Formula 1 regulations had set an 80-litre maximum capacity for individual fuel cells, but now Chapman wanted to concentrate his entire fuel load in a single cell buried far from threat, deep in the rear of the tub. Application was made for the 80-litre limit to be waived, and the new 79 accommodated all its fuel in one single rear-tub cell between engine and driver. In an early design scheme, however, two tanks were drawn here.

The tub itself was made as slender as

possible, to devote maximum width to those vital underwing panniers. The structural sections along either side of the cockpit were minimal. The forepart of the tub was strengthened by a perforated stress-panel bulkhead around the dash panel area, like the 77/78 series and very reminiscent of much earlier Lotus products from 1958 to 1962. An arched scuttle panel enclosed the driver's shins, tapering down into the shallow and slender nose. All structural panels were in aluminium sheet, apart from the tub floor which was honeycomb sandwich.

Front suspension was now squared up rather than raked back as in the 78, and the inboard coil/damper units were buried well out of the airstream within the tub sides. Top rocker arms and wide-based lower wishbones were spaced as far apart as possible to free air entry into the side pod radiator and underwing ducts. There was no sense in forcing a massive volume of air into these pods only for its free exit to be obstructed at the other end. For this reason the 78's outboard rear coil/damper mounting was replaced by an inboard variety, nestling the springs tight against the gearbox cheeks. New up-and-over high-level exhaust manifolds were introduced to remove another obstruction.

The now familiar double-calliper brake discs reappeared, outboard front and inboard rear. A single large water radiator hung raked steeply forward on the right-side of the tub, within its side pod, while a smaller oil cooler was in the left-hand pod.

Without its bodywork the new Type 79 looked extremely gawky and spare, but with the large and voluptuous new body panels fitted it was transformed into by far the best-looking Formula 1 car of its time – Black Beauty indeed.

Peter Wright described the Lotus 78 as a car which tried out new ideas, while the Lotus 79 was the car designed around those ideas. Chapman had also long cherished plans for a lighter, longer-lived gearbox than the Hewland which would also allow two-pedal clutchless driving which for many years had been one of 'Chunky's' hobby-horses.

The prototype Lotus 79 (chassis 'JPS/19') was tested at Ricard-Castellet in December 1977. Wright reflects 'nobody fully appreciated what ground effect was going to do to loads and what those loads would do to a ground-effect car . . . *all* structures began to fatigue at an incredible rate!'

After some 150 miles of Ricard testing 'JPS/19's monocoque was shown to be woefully inadequate in torsional stiffness. There was also room for aerodynamic improvement, because the 79 had been intended as a 78 that was also quick in a straight line, and in this original form it just wasn't. Its original low-arch scuttle structure was also too confined for tall new Team driver Ronnie Peterson's comfort. The new Lotus-Getrag gearbox also showed room for improvement in these initial tests. At first it felt like a real advance over the Hewland, being much lighter in weight, lighter to use and quicker-changing, but after a few laps running its selection mechanism would wilt under Formula 1 torques, having been far under-stressed in design. Chassis '19 was returned to Ketteringham's race workshop and dismantled. It would subsequently be rebuilt as a gearbox development hack – replacing an old Lotus 77 in that role – then later in the season would be rebuilt again to latest specification and pressed into service as a Team spare.

Meanwhile, the second Lotus 79, chassis 'JPS/20' (or, more logically, '79/2'), was completed in effect as a Mark 2 car with a stiffened monocoque featuring stronger cockpit sides, and a raised dash hoop and front scuttle panel to give the lanky Peterson some knee room. Rear suspension was also modified with a deeper upright and longer lower wishbones picking up beneath the gearbox on the car's centreline. The bolt-on moulded side pods

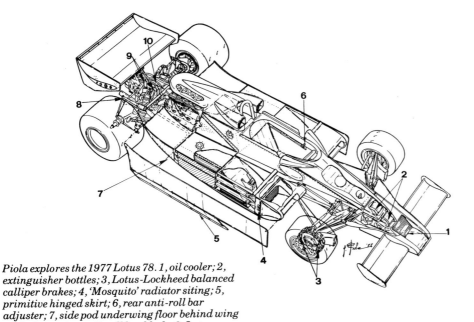

Piola explores the 1977 Lotus 78. 1, oil cooler; 2, extinguisher bottles; 3, Lotus-Lockheed balanced calliper brakes; 4, 'Mosquito' radiator siting; 5, primitive hinged skirt; 6, rear anti-roll bar adjuster; 7, side pod underwing floor behind wing tank; 8, rotating anti-roll bar blade; 9, Lotus-Lockheed balanced rear callipers; 10, Hewland FG400 transaxle.

retained carefully shaped top-exit cooler ducts and carried underwing floors below to offer higher download values than the interim style of the Type 78.

On the Ricard car these underwing sections had terminated at the front engine mounts, but in '79/2' they extended rearwards alongside the engine. The top body deck around the engine induction system was lowered and flick-ups were added to fair-in the rear wheels and improve airflow under the end plate mounted rear wing.

Andretti drove the car in this form in the Silverstone International, but after 58 practice laps – which was a long way – the new Lotus gearbox failed. A sister transmission fitted to Peterson's old 78 failed at precisely the same distance. Still the Swede qualified on pole with Andretti third fastest and loving every yard in his new car.

Team draughtsman Martin Ogilvie recalls Peterson going round lap after lap, proving the Lotus-Getrag gearbox, then suddenly going faster . . . 'And when he came in we said, "Ah, you've sorted out the selection problem", and he just smiled that slow smile and said, "No. I yust stopped you-sing the clutch."'

On race day it rained furiously. Peterson crashed during the warm-up while Andretti led briefly before aquaplaning off-course into an earlier victim of deep puddles at Abbey Curve and damaging '79/2' quite extensively.

Nevertheless, he commented: 'All in all, the 79 really gave us a message at Silverstone. Boy, that thing was good in the wet, really exceptionally good . . . but we had to have a Hewland gearbox in the car . . . with the Getrag I was having trouble hooking fifth even on the first lap . . .'

The car was rebuilt while 'JPS/21' ('79/3') was being completed and both emerged in a further-revised 'Mark 3' form. Chapman now reluctantly dropped the Lotus-Getrag transmission for further development – it would ultimately be shelved entirely – while Hewland 'mangle-gears' reappeared and over-the-gearbox exhaust systems were adopted to pull their profile closer to the rear cross-section of the tub. 'Clapper board' aerodynamic skirts were adopted, made from rigid Cellite sheet with an abrade-resistant lower edge, running in channels beneath the panniers. This would prove to be the rigid sliding skirt's definitive form, as only material and guide/control mechanisms improved further.

Lotus's lads rebuilt '79/2' so rapidly it appeared at Monaco as Team's spare car, and in practice there Andretti was stunned by its potential: 'It turned in as good as the 78, but the back end was at least as good as the front where on the 78 the front had always tended to overwhelm the back. It seemed like here was the perfect race car, with grip at the front, grip at the back, *incredible* traction . . .'

It was still considered unraceworthy, especially for the hurly-burly of Monaco, but then followed a Goodyear test session at Anderstorp in Sweden where Peterson drove the 79 and set times the opposition could not contemplate. He ran some 700 miles, then the car was taken direct to Zolder where it was intended to be Andretti's spare for the Belgian GP. Team engineer Nigel Bennett told Andretti he thought they could 'make a race car out of it'. Andretti talked to Chapman and they put $500 each into an encouragement kitty for the mechanics if the 79 survived race distance without a failure.

The rebuilt 'JPS/20' thus started its first Grand Prix . . .

By that time the old Lotus 78s had already proved themselves to be the cars to beat. Andretti had raced '78/3' and Peterson '78/2' in each of the five races from Argentina in January to Monaco in May. Their ten starts in these races yielded two first places – in Argentina and South Africa – one second place, two fourths, one fifth, a seventh (after leading),

eleventh and two retirements – one mechanical, the other due to a collision in Brazil which broke the Peterson car's suspension.

At Zolder, in the sparkling rebuilt '79/2', Andretti qualified as he had done the previous year in the early Type 78, over a second faster than the rest of the field. He led from start to finish with little apparent effort and Peterson's sister 78 was delayed by a pit stop to change tyres but soared back through the field to finish second and so bring Team Lotus – two days after Chapman's 50th birthday – their fourth 1-2 result in a *Grande Epreuve*.

In the Spanish GP at Jarama, Peterson was out in the brand new '79/3' and the Lotus pair not only qualified 1-2 on the grid but again finished 1-2 in the race, while Andretti set fastest lap. Mexican privateer Hector Rebaque had bought old '78/1' and drove it sensibly before retiring. In the Swedish GP at Anderstorp the hastily-completed Brabham answer to Lotus ground-effects emerged as the controversial fan-car. Lauda won with it after Andretti had started from pole and retired, and Peterson was third, after being blatantly baulked by the Arrows in second place. Andretti's failure was put down to titanium valve spring caps dishing under load, allowing the retainers to fall out in three cylinders, whereupon a valve had broken.

The fan-car was ruled out of competition thereafter and the Lotus 79 was reinstated as the only ground-effects car of the season, although other teams like Wolf made valiant attempts to close the gap. Another Type 79 1-2 was scored in the French GP, while at Brands Hatch Peterson qualified his car on pole but both 79s failed after leading in the early stages. Andretti won the German race from pole. Peterson started alongside him on the front row, led and set fastest lap before retiring with gearbox failure. Rebaque was sixth in chassis '78/4', one of the two type 78s he had bought, and scored a Championship point.

Ever since whumping '79/3' over a kerb during qualifying at Ricard and losing pole there to Watson's Brabham-Alfa Romeo because of this error, Andretti had felt sure his chassis was somehow out of true, despite having been back on the jig at Ketteringham; but Hockenheim dispelled his fears. Until then he had doubted the 79's straightline speed on such a fast circuit; 'Any doubts I had about the car were gone now. Really fast tracks I'd got to dread with the 78 but the 79 could run with anybody.'

The prototype '79/1' had been extensively rebuilt to the latest standard as a spare car for the late-season races, while Andretti regularly used chassis '3 and Peterson chassis '2. In Austria the 79s qualified 1-2 on the grid for the third consecutive time and set new perform-

Birth of the John Player 'superteam': winter testing at Ricard 1977/78. Andretti and Peterson pose with '79/1' as Black Beauty belies its numerous teething troubles.

ance standards, though not without problems.

Andretti's car ran new aerodynamic-section wishbones there in practice and with rear wing eased off to two degrees incidence for high speed the car felt 'really spooky through the quick turns'. The wishbones were the only new thing on the car, so they were replaced by the normal type, and it all came back as good as ever, indicating just how sensitive were these new-era cars.

Torrential rain then washed out the first attempt at running the GP after only seven laps had already seen Andretti – too anxious to clinch his World Championship – and Rebaque both crash. Peterson then won the restarted 47-lap second section of the Grand Prix from pole position in '79/2' and set fastest lap along the way.

In the Dutch GP at Zandvoort the 79s again qualified fastest in team order and finished 1-2 yet again, Andretti winning from pole in new car 'JPS/22' ('79/4') using parts salvaged from his wrecked Austrian '79/3' hung on a replacement tub.

The Italian GP followed at Monza. In race morning warm-up Peterson crashed his regular '79/2' following brake problems. No spare 79 was available so he fell back on his veteran '78/3' spare car for the race.

Andretti started from pole in his latest car '79/4' but a starting procedure muddle sparked a horrifying multiple collision on the charge into the first corner, and Peterson's Lotus 78 was barged head-on into a guardrail at high speed and its single-skin forward monocoque section collapsed upon impact, breaking both his legs. The chassis was demolished, its fuel system ruptured and the wreck caught fire, although Peterson was quickly pulled clear by fellow drivers. He was seriously injured but alive and in no apparent danger, only to die that night in hospital due to complications following fracture surgery.

Meanwhile the race had been restarted, Andretti won on the road but was docked a minute for jumping the restart and classified sixth. He still set fastest lap and clinched his World title, but any joy Team might have felt was nothing compared to their loss.

They were committed to run two cars in the US and Canadian GPs ending the season and the French driver Jarier was taken on to accompany Andretti. At Watkins Glen the Italian-American qualified '79/4' on pole while Jarier drove '79/3', rebuilt since its Austrian crash. In race morning warm-up Andretti's car broke its right-rear stub axle and threw a wheel. He took over '79/3' for the race, guessing at correct adjustments to suit his needs while Jarier was strapped into old '79/1' – which had arrived from the UK only that morning – for its race debut.

Andretti led the Ferraris initially in the viciously oversteering spare 79 which also suffered spongy brakes and, after the Ferraris got by, his race ended with engine failure. Jarier meanwhile was plagued by tyre and fuel problems but after an early stop to replace a left-front tyre burned out by his inducing too much understeer on full tanks, he tore back through the field and challenged for second place until his tank ran dry with three laps to go. He set fastest lap, emphasizing the 79's superiority.

In Montreal for the Canadian GP, the Frenchman then took pole position in '79/3' and pulled out a huge 30 second lead by half-distance, only to drop back on lap 49 as brake fluid leaked from a defective line and he was forced to retire.

Andretti's '79/4' handled poorly throughout this meeting and its monocoque was found subsequently to have been twisted by the Watkins Glen incident. He could not use his spare car in this long race because its fuel capacity was too restricted. After a minor collision early in the race he could only finish a distant and disappointing tenth to end Lotus's trend-setting but bitter-sweet season.

The Type 79s had made 20 starts in eleven Grand Prix races, taking six first places, four seconds, a third, a sixth, one tenth, and a 15th (Jarier's final classification at Watkins Glen); there were six retirements. During that high summer of their success they accumulated 10 pole positions, the last seven in consecutive races – eight to Andretti, one to Peterson and one to Jarier. Only the French GP at Ricard broke their run, where Watson's Brabham-Alfa Romeo bettered Andretti's front-row time by a quarter of a second while the kerb-damaged Lotus 79 was being checked over.

The cars also set five fastest race laps – two each to Andretti and Peterson, one to Jarier. When they were beaten for fastest lap they still set second and third fastest times, behind the Brabham fan-car, in Sweden; third and fourth at Ricard; second and third at Zandvoort, by 0.01 second behind Lauda's Brabham-Alfa Romeo; and fourth fastest (by Jarier) in

The gawky monocoque '79/2' being set up on travel wheels in Team Lotus workshops, early-1978. Note raised scuttle, shallow slender tub alongside cockpit, and water radiator laid bare without the side pod in place.

Canada at the season's end.

After the 79's introduction into Championship racing at Zolder, the works 78s made only two more starts. Belgium yielded second place and fastest lap for Peterson in '78/2', while the Type's tragic swansong was at Monza where Ronnie was injured in '78/3', which of course was utterly destroyed.

So this remarkable if marred season saw Team Lotus take the Formula 1 Constructors' title by 86 points to Ferrari's 58, while Andretti took the Drivers' title from Peterson's tragically posthumous second place.

The 79s would run on into 1979 while the intended replacement Type 80 was being developed. Today this Lotus season tends to be recalled glibly as a total disaster. In truth it started quite well, although it was immediately clear that the opposition were not only following where Lotus had led into ground-effects aerodynamics but were immediately threatening to do a better job . . .

Team had new sponsorship from Martini in 1979 and appeared in British Racing Green livery with the red-and-blue Martini stripes made famous on so many long-distance racing Porsches. The prototype Lotus 80 would carry the chassis number 'ML23' following on from the John Player Special 'JPS' number system, but it was old 79s chassis '2-3-4' which began the season, with a brand new 79, chassis '5', out for Andretti at the third race, in South Africa.

Right at the start of the season it was obvious that Gérard Ducarouge's Ligier-Cosworth JS11 design was far more effective. These cars dominated the Argentinian and Brazilian GPs but Team's new joint number one driver Reutemann finished second behind the winning JS11 in Buenos Aires and Andretti fifth, so the 79s were still in contention. The Lotus drivers then qualified 3-4 behind the Ligier pair in Brazil, and Reutemann finished third behind them in the race. The Lotus 79 was still 'the best of the rest'.

At Kyalami the 79s finished 4-5 with Andretti capable of setting third fastest race lap in his new '79/5'. Reutemann qualified on the front row at Long Beach, while Andretti finished fourth and set fastest lap.

The new Lotus 80 made the first of its only three race appearances in Spain where it placed third, with Reutemann inheriting a distant second in old '79/2' but suddenly was unable to match the race pace.

Thus far, Andretti had raced '79/4' in South America before taking on '5', then the 80, while Reutemann had used '79/2' everywhere but Brazil where he drove chassis '3'. In Belgium the 80 was set aside and Andretti returned to

'79/5' for the race. But he retired with brake trouble while Reutemann finished fourth, and in Monaco Reutemann drove '79/4' into a reliable third place after Andretti qualified slowly in the 80 and left the race with rear suspension failure.

At this point in the season, with seven races run and eight to go, the Williams FW07 came on song, the Ferraris were showing their sheer power and reliability, and the Ligiers were still very quick though they had lost their South American edge. Team Lotus toppled off the tightrope of competitiveness as surely as they had in 1975 with the old Type 72s.

In those first seven races of the '79 season, Team's entries had started 14 times and had finished in the Championship points 11 times. In contrast, the final eight races would see them start 16 times and achieve only four finishes, only one of which was in the points – Andretti's fifth at Monza, where he also set sixth fastest race lap and Reutemann finished seventh.

Two non-Championship race starts had also been made. Early in the year at Brands Hatch Andretti actually qualified '79/3' on pole and finished third, while at Imola in September, Reutemann qualified '79/2' third fastest and inherited second place in a sparse field. But that was a rare late-season highlight.

The 80 made its last race appearance in the French GP where its brakes, suspension and general aerodynamic misbehaviour caused Andretti despair, and thereafter Team had to campaign the 79s which were being run ragged by the opposition.

Team's nadir came in Austria, where Andretti's clutch failed at the start and Reutemann stopped to change tyre compounds and eventually gave up with 'handling problems'. After that third place in Monaco he seemed to have given up completely and was not in contention for the rest of the year. Some of Team's people nicknamed him 'Doris' . . . yes, it had got that bad.

Andretti did his determined best, but it was clear that whereas the Lotus 79 had been in a class of its own the previous year, times had changed since then and it could not withstand the pressure.

Peter Wright: 'In its day the 79 had been very effective, but then it had been the only proper ground-effect car around, and a lot had been compromised to make it effective . . . Now in 1979 it was up against second generation ground-effect cars which showed up its deficiencies in cooling, brakes and also in structural stiffness I am afraid. The 80 had been our second generation car which had all the right capabilities in braking, cooling and structural rigidity but while we tried to find out what was wrong with its aerodynamic behaviour we had to go back to the 79 and with the pressures of the calendar preventing proper test and development it was no longer adequate into the second half of the season . . .'

The one-time pace-setting Lotus 79s' front-line racing career ended at Watkins Glen on 7 October 1979. Reutemann qualified remarkably well; sixth fastest in '79/3' and ran third in the rain-swept opening laps before being distracted by the fire extinguisher sensing unit which had come adrift and was bouncing around inside the cockpit. He lost control and spun off. Andretti meanwhile had '79/5's gearbox progressively strip teeth before jamming in fourth and causing retirement on the 16th lap.

The Lotus 79 was a classic beauty whose career shared enormous early success with subsequent mediocre failure. It represented both the pinnacle of Lotus's middle period at the top of the pile and the beginning of their dismal slump in the early-1980s. However, it is properly best remembered as the last of Colin Chapman's team's blinding flashes of brilliance – and one more which simply revolutionized all racing car design . . .

Hewland Gearboxes

Of all racing gearbox manufacturers – and there are few – Hewland Engineering of Maidenhead, in the Thames Valley, is the best known and its range of transaxles used in Formula 1 has progressed throughout our period.

A beginner's guide to Hewland gearboxes shows that they offer very easy quick-change final-drive ratios and a range of good quality, proven components which every Formula 1 team save Ferrari and Alfa Romeo has used at some time, if not throughout.

Their '3-Litre Formula' involvement began with the DG300 ('Different Gearbox') five-speed of 1966, which soon became 'too heavy'. The Formula 2 FT200 developed for the 1600 cc Formula was, in comparison, 'too light' for Formula 1 power and torque, so the two were married together in a slightly different casing for 1968 and Mike Hewland named it the 'FG'.

In 1973 the FGA400 emerged, 'using a posher diff, Salisbury or cam and pawl' and its heavier casing provided mounts for inboard rear brakes.

The 'TL', introduced that same year, was essentially a 24-Hour sports car box which Shadow adopted but it won itself a bad name because in its debut a bad batch of pinion shafts broke 'and the muck stuck and nobody liked them'. In fact only two TLs had bad shafts, and unfortunately Shadow had them both!

The 'FGB' emerged as 'a posh FGA' with integral oilways in its casing whereas the others had external piping.

Teams would adapt Hewland internals to their own requirements, having their own casings cast and adding many tweaks and modifications, using separate dry-sump oil systems, extensively filtering the oil, passing it over magnets to remove ferrous debris – anything to make what Colin Chapman described rather affectionately as 'Mike Hewland's bunch of old mangle gears' survive race distance.

Towards the end of our period most Formula 1 teams held a bigger Hewland part inventory than the Maidenhead company itself. McLaren began the six-speed Hewland conversion fashion in 1976, Hewland subsequently making their own six-speed FGAs which remained current into 1985 with some teams.

Regarding their price, Jimmy Buss, who runs Hewland's commercial side and is a familiar figure to all racing people, recalls that the 1967 'FT' 'was the price of a Mini, £420, and today [1985] a Mini is over £3000 and our FT is only £2078. The DG in 1966-67 was around £480, an equivalent DG is now £2,420 and a DGB £4725 . . . we offer good value, don't we?'

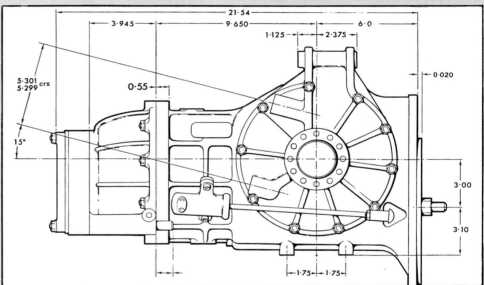

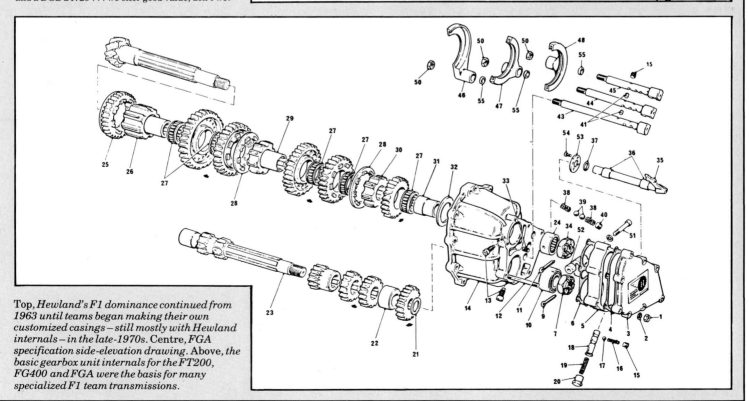

Top, Hewland's F1 dominance continued from 1963 until teams began making their own customized casings – still mostly with Hewland internals – in the late-1970s. Centre, FGA specification side-elevation drawing. Above, the basic gearbox unit internals for the FT200, FG400 and FGA were the basis for many specialized F1 team transmissions.

Chapter 11

THE FERRARI 312T4 – FLAT-12'S FAREWELL 1979

During 1978 the Ferrari 312T3 design, tailored to the team's new Michelin radial-ply tyres, had proved itself a deceptive beauty. The Italian team lost its coveted Constructors' Cup Championship title to Lotus's new breed of ground-effect Type 78/79 cars . . . and it hurt.

The Maranello engineers appreciated that Lotus had unlocked a new box of delights in using the underside of the car to generate so much aerodynamic download. But what was fine for Lotus and the other Cosworth V8 engine users was really bad news for Ferrari. Their otherwise superb flat-12 engine – with its remarkably low centre of gravity, excellent power and reliability – was too wide at a disastrously inconvenient low level to clear airflow adequately through underwing tunnels which would have to be crafted somehow on each side of the central monocoque spine.

Brabham had been in a similar bind with their Alfa Romeo flat-12 engine, but at Gordon Murray's request in August 1978 Alfa's Autodelta racing division under Carlo Chiti had buckled down and redrew their 12-cylinder as a narrow-based 60-degree vee, and the prototype such unit was out and running that December.

Although there may have been much to criticize in the Alfa Romeo engines, none could carp at such reaction time, for they had just designed and made an effectively new Formula 1 engine from scratch in only 15 weeks!

Just for once, Ferrari could not match their Milanese rivals. *Ing.* Forghieri's team had to devise their first real ground-effects chassis as best they could around their existing engine, as the decision had been taken not to ape Alfa and build one with a narrower base using flat-12 components. This was not penny-pinching; it

was instead Mr Ferrari again proving his extraordinarily far-sighted ability to make the right long-term strategic decisions.

It seems he had listened to his engineers' thoughts on the potential of 1500 cc turbocharged engines for Formula 1, and had decided that future investment should lie there rather than in the short-term but costly expedient of building a new 3-litre which might be outclassed in 18 months.

The prototype Ferrari 312T4, chassis '037, was unveiled to the usual excited scrum of Italian pressmen on 15 January 1979. It was an ugly duckling of a car, one commentator derisively describing it as 'a motor mower', but it would prove itself every bit as practical . . . and decidedly faster.

It used the normal aluminium-sheet monocoque nacelle stiffened by internal aluminium angle-section fabrications bonded and riveted to the outer skins and the inner cockpit flanks. This was a reversion to pre-'T2 true monocoque practice, but stronger and far narrower than previous Ferrari tubs following Lotus 79 style to offer a wide underwing area either side.

The large midships single fuel cell of the Lotus 79 looked to have been adopted, but in this case the tank section standing tall behind the seatback bulkhead actually accommodated three separate fuel bags. Due to the flat-12 engine's thirst the midship cell alone was insufficient so an extra cell was added in ugly 'step-outs' on each side. As so often in Ferrari chassis design, they looked like an afterthought, but to Ferrari the engine was all-important, the thing holding the wheels on always came second. In this case these stepouts intruded on available underwing tunnel area, but if they had not, there was always the

flat-12 engine head and induction right behind them to form that obstruction. There, however, the effect would not have been so problematic, as the side-step tanks affected what should have been the shallow part of the underwing venturi.

A massive but light titanium roll-over bar stood on top of the main tank section, its rearward braces panelled-in for rigidity and to provide convenient housings for the communications box, and emergency switchgear and triggers.

The front of the tub was tied together by a magnesium bulkhead casting, carrying the master cylinders, anti-roll bar and front leg pick-ups for the very wide-based lower wishbones. The dash panel was mounted within a front-braced titanium forward roll-over bar, its front braces panelled in aluminium, with the familiar chassis plate riveted high. Cast magnesium brackets fitted to the tub floor provided pedal pivots. Steel or magnesium insert strongpoints provided pick-ups for other items hung on this rather untidy-looking tub.

It carried inboard front suspension along 'T3 lines, but the 'T4's nose box was narrower and the Koni dampers and co-axial coil-spring units nuzzled tight against the tub skins to clear airflow into the radiators and underwing tunnels. The lower wishbones were crossbraced to add rigidity. The inboard coil-damper units were actuated by fabricated tube-frame top rocker arms, pivoting on pins suppported by triangulated tube braces projecting from the heavily riveted front tub bulkhead. These

Ferrari's 312T4 with its extensive overbody surfaces was not the prettiest thing around in 1979, but it worked well enough to win the Championship. 1, wing; 2, nose cone; 3, body top; 4, brake duct; 5, coil/damper; 6, steering rack on floor; 7, roll-over stiffening; 8, radiator; 9, engine-air intake; 10, rear anti-roll adjuster; 11, vents; 12, tub fillets; 13, oil tank; 14, sliding skirt; 15, intercom; 16, stepout tank; 17, main tank; 18, engine stay; 19, tailpipe; 20, battery; 21, tyre fairing; 22, upright; 23, brake duct; 24, top rocker; 25, tailpipes; 26, anti-roll bar; 27, gearbox; 28, wing pillar; 29, wing.

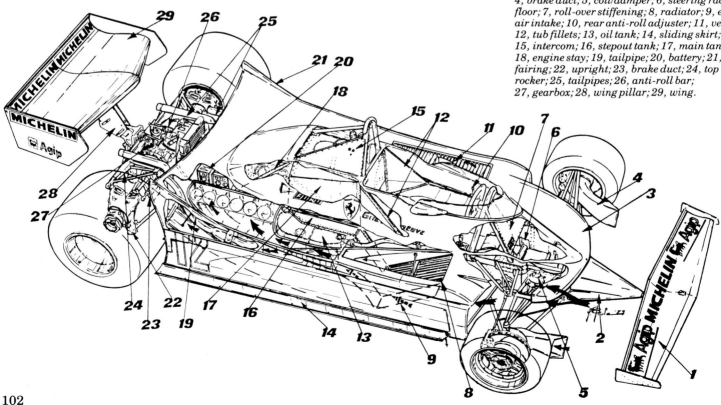

braces were further supported fore and aft by long tubular members linking the pivot position to the meat of the tub at dash bulkhead level.

The rear coil/damper units were also inboard mounted, standing in channel sections against the transmission case casting behind the axle line. Tubular steel bottom wishbones located the typically Ferrari cast magnesium wheel uprights. Fabricated-sheet top rocker arms actuated the coil/damper units, pivoting on cast magnesium horns which projected each side of the familiar *trasversale* transmission housing.

The radiators were slung just behind the front suspension on each side of the tub, raked steeply forward to mate with ducting provided in the vast moulded upper body panels. Water radiator was on the left, oil cooler on the right, both fed from the engine pumps. Hot coolant was channelled through galleries in the bottom of the cam covers into the water radiator piping, and cooled water then returned from the radiator through galleries in the tops of the same covers before being led away around the engine via the head waterways. The large oil tank further intruded into the right-side underwing tunnel, being slung outside the 'step-out' fuel tank structure there. A small gearbox oil cooler sat on top of the final-drive, exposed to the airstream above the rear bodyshell lip.

The body itself comprised a substantial one-piece removable top cover designed to generate as much download from above as from those improvised underwing tunnels down below. Its upper surface extended far forward into a projecting tray above the slender winkle-picker nose cone which faired-in the front of the tub and supported a full-width Ferrari wing of the type familiar since 1973-74.

The cockpit surround was moulded as narrow and short as possible, ending in an abbreviated dorsal fin behind the roll-over bar to leave the smooth rear deck offering maximum airflow onto the underside of the centre-pillar mounted rear wing. Pronounced moulded flip-ups faired the broad rear Michelin radial-ply tyres.

The radiator slings projecting each side of the monocoque doubled as body supports. Moulded into the body, behind the radiator ducting with its top exit louvres, the underwing floors of the side pod flared upwards to clear the low-level step tanks, oil tank and the flat-12 engine heads and exhaust manifolding. Integrally moulded intake trunks picked up cool air outboard of the radiator cores and directed it into plenum chambers sealed against the engine induction trumpets each side.

The outer flank of each side pod formed a box housing the sliding skirts, the skirts themselves riding on the track surface on singlelength resistant strips which according to some reports were actually hard-wearing rubber, to other reports were ceramic, which seems more likely.

Brakes were by AP Lockheed, ventilated front and rear with single four-pot callipers. Steering was via a two-piece adjustable column passing down between the driver's shins to a Ferrari-made rack mounted on the monocoque floor.

Dimensions included a wheelbase of 2700 mm (106.3 in.); front track 1700 mm (66.9 in.); rear track, 1600 mm (62.9 in.); length, 4460 mm (175.5 in.); width, 2120 mm (83.4 in.). The new 'lawn mower' weighed in, less fuel and driver, at around 590 kg (1301 lb), while Ferrari claimed that the further uprated 312B engines that year delivered a minimum 515 bhp at 12,300 rpm. The finished car was fully 10 in. longer than the preceding 312T3 to give sufficient aerodynamic surface for Forghieri's requirements, while the wheelbase was 6 in. longer than the 'T3 to provide adequate space for worthwhile venturi underwings before the various intrusive tanks, engine heads and manifolds were encountered.

In aerodynamic terms the car was a groundeffects start for Ferrari – though they had previously lashed up their 'T3s as quasiunderwing cars – but it was a poor compromise compared to the contemporary Williams FW07. We were all about to discover how aerodynamics wasn't everything . . .

The South African driver Jody Scheckter had joined the mercurial French-Canadian Gilles Villeneuve in the Ferrari team for that season, and they began their year in the old 312T3 cars uprated with makeshift underwings and sliding skirts which were notoriously ineffective and unreliable. The team was very conscious of these problems and 'T4 development included painstaking real-car test sessions in the huge Pininfarina wind tunnel near Turin.

In Argentina a multiple pile-up and a restarted race, in which the mildly injured Scheckter was not permitted to compete, fuelled vociferous condemnation of groundeffect skirted cars from this driver. Had all such Formula 1 cars felt as awful as his interim 'T3 he would have received more support from his fellow drivers.

The new Ligiers won in both Argentina and Brazil, before the new Ferraris were introduced to racing at Kyalami for the South African GP on 8 March 1979. Two new 'T4s were present, chassis '037 for Villeneuve and '038 for Scheckter on his native soil. Experiments were conducted in running without the front wing, but both cars not only felt less stable but were also slower on the straight.

The race was spoiled by a heavy rainstorm, which brought out the red flag. Villeneuve led the restart, still on a wet track, while Scheckter gambled by starting on dry tyres, believing the surface would dry out. He was right but he blistered his tyres after inheriting the lead as Villeneuve stopped to change from wet tyres to dry. Scheckter clung to his lead until a locking front brake flat-spotted a tyre and forced him into the pits for a change on lap 53. His delay handed the race back to Villeneuve who held off his team-mate to the finish for a notable Ferrari 'T4 1-2 victory on the type's debut.

Equally good results would follow, for Villeneuve won in another Ferrari 'T4 1-2 finish at Long Beach, starting from the first Grand Prix pole position of his career and setting fastest lap along the way. In the minor Brands Hatch race he then completed Ferrari's hat-trick for the season by winning again in the old 'T3 chassis '033'.

In Spain the Ligiers were dominant, while Villeneuve's hopes of a Championship round hat-trick evaporated in a spin soon after the start when trying to pass Reutemann. Next time round he spun again. Scheckter's race deteriorated with his Michelin tyres and engine losing power, finally finishing fourth while Villeneuve was seventh.

Scheckter won at Zolder after the superior Ligier and Williams FW07 ran out of luck, driving the new 'T4 chassis '040 which would become his regular mount. Villeneuve set fastest lap in '039 after smashing his nose in a minor collision, rejoining the race 23rd and last and soaring back up the field like a homesick angel. He was challenging for third place in the closing stages when the hard-pressed 'T4 ran out of fuel.

At Long Beach the 'T4s had dominated with forward-mounted rear wings and brilliant traction on a circuit where ultimate download was not of prime importance. The forwardmounted rear wings were used again at Monaco, where Scheckter took pole from Villeneuve, the 'T4s again setting the standard. The South African led from start to finish for his second consecutive Grand Prix victory – this time on real merit – while Villeneuve lay second until his car's transmission failed around half-distance, probably due to a hurried engine change after the morning warm-up in which the unit had blown off an oil pipe.

Late in the race Scheckter had come under fierce attack from Regazzoni's Williams FW07, finally winning by less than a second. The 'T4 was not the class car of the season, in that others like the FW07 and the Ligiers could be quicker, but it had the strength and reliability to win consistently, which they lacked.

At Dijon-Prenois the turbocharged Renaults won their first Grand Prix and Ferrari were overshadowed after their terrific early season with the 'T4. In the four races from the French to the Austrian GPs, Ferrari's best performances were Villeneuve's second at Dijon – wheel-banging with Arnoux's Renault – and second again in Austria, both times driving '041, which had made its race debut in France. Scheckter had scored points consistently, with fifth at Silverstone, fourth at Hockenheim and the Österreichring, and after taking second place at Zandvoort he was set to clinch the World Championship for himself in the Italian GP at Monza.

Both team drivers had a choice of two cars each for this event, a pair of conventional 'T4s plus alternative revised 'T4Bs, which featured outboard rear brakes, revised suspension geometry to suit and balanced callipers, one ahead and one behind the axle line to improve braking performance. The exhaust system was revised to tuck closer against the gearbox sides, the upper tailpipes flicking higher over the suspension arms to clear more underwing tunnel space down below. Villeneuve preferred his 'T4B configured chassis '038 and raced it while Scheckter raced his faithful '040 'T4. Once the leading turbo Renault had been halted by electrical failure the two Ferraris ran 1-2 from laps 13 to 50 for another outstanding 1-2 win on home soil, the Ferrari 'T4s' third double of the season.

In celebration, 'T4Bs '038 and '041 were taken to Imola for the Dino Ferrari nonChampionship GP, Scheckter finishing third and Villeneuve seventh after a collision with the Brabham-Alfa Romeo which eventually won. It was an Alfa Romeo victory over Ferrari in a Ferrari Champion year – a unique occurrence.

Villeneuve was hell-bent upon winning the Canadian GP at Montreal and nearly did so, before being shouldered out of the way by a more nimble Williams FW07, which beat him into second place and lapped faster. Scheckter drove a subdued race and finished lapped in fourth place after a tyre-change stop. The season ended at Watkins Glen in the rain where Scheckter drove '040 and Villeneuve '041, the latter scoring the 'T4's sixth victory of the season, with luck on his side. Scheckter suffered a Michelin tyre disintegration after changing from wets to dries early on in a race dictated by rain.

Ferrari won the Constructor's Championship with 113 points to Williams's 75, while Scheckter was Drivers' Champion and Villeneuve runner-up.

Five Ferrari 'T4s had been built for the season, chassis numbers '037, '038, '039, '040 and '041, amongst which all but '039 had appeared in 'T4B configuration at the end of the year. They started 26 times in Championship Grand Prix races, returning six wins, seven second places, four fourths, one fifth, three sevenths, one eighth, and four retirements – although one of them yielded a 14th place classification. In addition the cars had run in the non-Championship event at Imola, finishing third and seventh.

This was the last Formula 1 season in which a compromise car could run strongly enough to take the World Championship titles and the Ferrari 'T4 had emphasized the wisdom of its manufacturer's long-term strategy. The following season's flat-12 'T5 would be an uncompetitive disaster, as the sliding-skirt ground-effects car era reached maturity. Ferrari meanwhile concentrated upon the next step forward, with their turbocharged V6 *modello* 126.

Chapter 12

THE WILLIAMS FW07-SERIES CARS 1979-82

After the Lotus 78s and 79s had so successfully introduced 'ground-effect' aerodynamics in 1977-78, the replacement Lotus 80 flopped and it was left to others to hone the ground-effects principle to its keenest edge. The most successful of these successors to the Lotus 79 was the long line of Patrick Head-designed Saudia-Williams FW07s.

He had become Chief Engineer of Williams Grand Prix Engineering upon its formation in 1977. They had campaigned a March-Cosworth that year to find their feet, while Head watched the exploits of the fast-cornering Lotus 78 with interest, noting its weaknesses, its slow straightline speed and the unreliability of its special Cosworth 'development' engines.

He did not fully understand its aerodynamic approach and his fledgling team lacked the funds to invest in the wind tunnel test time which could have taught him what he did not know. Consequently, his first Williams Formula 1 design for 1978, type number FW06 in the Williams series, did not attempt to emulate the Lotus wing-car principles.

It was instead a conventional machine, elegant and simple as all Head's cars would be, arrowhead-shaped in planform. It proved itself amongst the best of the rest when driven so hard by Alan Jones during the Lotus-dominated season of '78.

That season over, Head then concentrated upon attempting first to match and then to improve upon Lotus's achievement. He appreciated that aerodynamics are the biggest single factor affecting the performance of a Grand Prix car.

'I was aware that Lotus did much of their wind tunnel testing at Imperial College in London, using quarter-scale models. Their tunnel incorporated a moving ground surface beneath the model being tested and I appreciated why that was important because racing cars do not fly through the air but roll along a road surface on their wheels.

'So I found the phone number of Imperial College, called them and asked for the head of the department of aeronautics who turned out to be Dr John Harvey. We met, and he explained that Lotus did their work in the tunnel, he did some consultancy work for Arrows, and there was room for one other team. We wanted to be that other team . . .

'Having seen the Lotus 79 dominate that season we had a clear idea what we wanted to do. We didn't copy the 79 line-for-line, but it was undeniably the major influence upon the design of our new FW07, as it was on most other Formula 1 cars being built for 1979.

'We made a crude wooden model of what we wanted to test, put it in the wind tunnel, and found it was unbelievably bad!

'We ran several more tests with models of differing types – including one with very long ground-effect underwing surfaces which indicated the most prodigious downforces, but I shied away from using it because we were very new in this area, it would have been a very complex car and I wanted to set out with something fairly straightforward . . .'

He in fact designed something rather like the Lotus 79 in superficial appearance 'but I tried to optimise that layout'. When the new Lotus 80 flopped, however, Lotus developed their Type 79s further only to find them deficient in that year's company, while Head's optimization proved to be virtually everything he might have hoped.

In achieving this aim it was first important for Williams to have more engineering experience on hand. Head's first assistant, Neil Oatley, joined the team at this time, followed soon after by ex-Hesketh engineer Frank Dernie. He started at the tiny Didcot works in January 1979, by which time Head and Oatley were already halfway through the '07 design.

At Watkins Glen at the close of the previous

Williams Grand Prix Engineering certainly flew the flag in 1980, as here at Ricard-Castellet after Alan Jones won the French GP. In their FW07B cars WGPE paid as much attention to overbody airflow as ground-effects efficiency, exemplified by the low rear body clearing the deck ahead of the rear wing. The sliding skirt with its abrade-resistant edge rides on the road surface.

season, Jones's FW06 had suffered a structural failure when a hub broke, throwing a wheel. It was not a design failure, but a material deficiency for the steel from which the hub had been made was found to be full of 'inclusions' – impurities which compromised its integrity.

This failure both mortified and alarmed Head. It was a salutary reminder of the forces he was playing with in Formula 1.

'As Chief Engineer I felt it was my prime responsibility to see that things didn't fall off or come apart, and I took that very heavily . . . It was one of the major factors which made me rather slow in completing FW07. I purposely wanted to take a long time over it to ensure that every calculation was double-checked and confirmed, to be certain everything was sound and strong enough. What also delayed '07 was that we set out with a staff which was still tiny. Our manpower shortage definitely conditioned the rate at which we could make things . . .'

He and Frank Williams also considered, after finishing second and then running second in their last two races of 1978, that their existing FW06 cars could remain competitive in the early races of the new season. They were mistaken. Head had underestimated the development pace of most other teams, and his non ground-effects '06s were completely outpaced by the new-generation cars as the season got under way in Argentina.

For the first time WGPE was fielding a full two-car team with drivers Alan Jones and Clay Regazzoni. They finished only ninth and tenth in Buenos Aires, 15th and a retirement in Brazil, ninth and another retirement in South Africa. Late sponsorship payment further delayed the FW07 project.

Eventually the first prototype Williams FW07/1 was ready in time to go to Long Beach, California, for the fourth Grand Prix of the season, but it lay in the Tech Center there, unused, covered by a dust sheet . . . except when an over-inquisitive rival team chief was caught under that dust sheet studying the goods!

By the end of April sponsorship money had been freed at last and two '07s emerged for the Spanish GP at Jarama. Both retired, though for those with the eyes to see it had been significant that in race morning warm-up Jones's '07 had left Andretti's Lotus 80 for dead, despite carrying a full fuel load. Andretti simply refused to believe that Jones's car was not running light; 'I couldn't stay with him,' he gasped.

In the race, Jones set the second fastest lap, bettered only by a Ferrari which was using sticky qualifying tyres to regain lost ground after a pit stop. The Williams men now began to appreciate FW07's enormous potential.

The type would evolve as the most successful of the ground-effects era Formula 1 chassis, winning two consecutive Constructors' Championship titles in 1980-81. It used an aluminium honeycomb sheet chassis structure, and since it was so typical of this type of late-Seventies/early-Eighties construction we will take a detailed look at its anatomy and manufacture.

A new FW07-series chassis began life as a flat sheet of aluminium honeycomb sandwich. The sheet itself was about 82 in. long, tapering towards what would become the tub's nose, and it was specially bonded to Williams's requirements with 22-gauge skins sandwiching 0.45 in. thick aviation specification honeycomb-cell filling.

Various aluminium inserts and dowels were fitted into drillings within the sheet to act as mounting strong-points, then two longitudinal slots were routed-out by removing a sliver of inner skin while leaving the interior honeycomb intact. This then allowed the sheet to be folded along the slots like a child's cut-out card model to form the basic U-section tub. The various necessary brackets were then bonded and riveted into place.

The tub's general layout matched that of the Lotus 79; slender, with a large single-cell tank section behind the cockpit and a tall arched scuttle up front.

The basic channel structure was stiffened by added tank-top and seatback panels, plus 20-gauge aluminium inner skins which were shaped over internal bulkheads either side of the confined cockpit. In original 1979 form this cockpit area flexed too much and in the 1980 FW07B development folded fillets were inserted around the driver's shoulder area where the original design had left a sharp angle between seatback and cockpit side.

The front end of the tub supported a very robust suspension pivot bridge. Pedal mounts were bonded and riveted to the tub floor with inserts passing through the front bulkhead to the master cylinders which protruded above an open topped sheet tray supporting the front wings and nose body.

The whole footbox/suspension bridge/driver's leg area was then enclosed by the tall arched scuttle panel, bonded and riveted to the dash hoop, the hoop in turn incorporating the regulation forward roll-over bar.

The tub structure was completed by addition of a closing plate at the rear, where the DFV engine would hang. Great care was then taken to grind off all intruding rivets to protect the American-made ATL 40-gallon fuel bag which was inserted through a bolt-on oval hatch in the top of the tank section, carrying an

Patrick Head (left) and Frank Williams (right) built a remarkably successful team around Alan Jones from 1978 to 1981. In their second consecutive Constructors' Championship-winning season, they are at Hockenheim with 'FW07D/16'.

Avery-Hardoll aircraft-type non-spill filler.

As can be seen, the Williams FW07 'Lotus 79 clone' was in fact very different structurally. Its nearest similarity was in the tall arched scuttle panel, but just like the Lotus 79 this area proved far from satisfactory in torsional strength.

On the back of the tub, the familiar DFV engine hung on $\frac{3}{8}$ in. UNF bolts at four points; feeding in loads via multi-angular aluminium blocks under the conventional engine strap-plates at the top, and ready-inserted into the honeycomb underneath.

A complex cast magnesium adaptor bolted between the engine and transmission, incorporating the oil tank as well as encasing a lightweight Desoutter air-starter motor and the clutch slave unit, thus performing four functions simultaneously. Furthermore, the adaptor to final-drive and final-drive to gearbox joint faces sandwiched two transverse plates which extended each side to carry the rear suspension pivots.

The Hewland FGB five-speed and reverse gearbox was bought from the Maidenhead manufacturer in virtual kit form and modified by all the customer Formula 1 teams to their own requirements.

As standard, the FGB gearchange entered the box at bottom right. Williams, however, converted it to enter top right, thus lifting the linkage rod clear of the airstream through the side pod and coincidentally shortening and stiffening it to improve the change.

Williams fed oil up the gearshafts and the gearbox oil cooler itself was fed with air from a duct sunk into the rear body deck. The engine oil catch tank was mounted above the gearbox. The rear wing pillar carried the regulation red rear light. On its left side there was an air-starter bayonet socket to connect with an external air-line. On the right was a jackplug socket which automatically retarded the ignition when connected for easy starting. Removing the plug returned the ignition to nominal setting.

The downloads achieved from the FW07-series' very effective underwing sections could be as much as 4-5000 lb. So the suspension had to be very stiff. Spring rates in fact varied between 600 and 1000 lb per cent per inch of deflection stiffness at the front, and between 800 and 1500 lb at the rear dependent upon the type of circuit and the downloads being generated. If the suspension was not rigidly controlled in places in which its designers did not want it to move, then flexure would compromise grip and traction and could also simply give the driver 'the willies'.

To help provide very rigid and well-controlled front rocker arm pivots, Williams's

Below, the FW07 was prompted by Lotus 79 practice, but only the tall arched scuttle drew direct from Lotus design and was one of the least successful features of the Williams. Bottom, Regazzoni demonstrates 'FW07/2's clean lines, 1979. The wider-chord rear wing centre section compensated for reduced airflow there due to the bodywork obstruction ahead.

suspension bridge there consisted of two substantial but still elegant ³⁄₁₆ in. thick HE30 TF heat-treated aluminium plates up-edged above the driver's shins. Because both mounts fore and aft were in one piece, overhanging the chassis on both sides, crash damage to one corner could communicate itself to the other and repair was more difficult than it would have been if separate mounts had been used. Head considered that the rigidity of one-piece construction here simply outweighed the practical penalty.

Within the tub sides, below this bridge arrangement, vertical channel sections enclosed the co-axial Koni damper/coil-spring units which stood on steel feet fitted into the honeycomb floor. Cut-outs in the channels gave access for spring ride-height and damper adjustment.

Steel brackets braced the front corners of the 20-gauge aluminium skinned footbox, picking up the forward legs of the bottom wishbones down below and the bolt-on stays which braced the outboard tips of the front bridge-plate up top. The rear legs of the suspension wishbones picked up on either side of a steel crossbeam in the tub floor.

At the rear, the suspension-pivot crossplates extended the full width of the DFV cam-covers to carry the rear suspension pivots. Top links formed, in effect, a two-piece reversed upper wishbone whose adjustable-length rearward link served to adjust wheel toe-in/toe-out.

The rear suspension rocker arms themselves were mounted close against the foremost sandwich plate, that between the adaptor and final-drive, with their inboard crank arms reacting into vertical coil-spring/Koni damper units standing upon a magnesium casting bolted up beneath the gearbox.

Wide-based lower rear wishbones picked up on lugs in the front of the adaptor oil tank, and on an aluminium beam under the rear of the final-drive.

The magnesium spring/damper brackets were reinforced by vertical stress pillars, which spread their load high into the engine/transmission assembly.

The front rocker arms, front and rear wishbones and uprights were all beautifully fabricated from US aviation-specification '4130' steel alloy while the heavily loaded rear rockers were fabricated in 'S514'. Front uprights were exquisitely crafted magnesium castings. They supported outboard-mounted ventilated cast-iron brake discs, and the uprights featured cast-in cool air intakes and galleries designed to blow across both disc faces

and into its internal ducts. Brake-cooling air intake trunks were fitted to the uprights, facing forward between the suspension links at the front, and over them at the rear.

The brakes used all-outboard 11-in. diameter discs, clasped on both leading and trailing edges by Lockheed aluminium twin-pot 'balanced' callipers, as originated in structural form for Lotus. Disc thickness varied according to circuit. For example, the team would employ 1 in. thick discs for Brands Hatch, but 0.9 in. thick discs for anywhere faster. Zolder's virtually unique braking demands were notorious, and Lockheed provided thicker and stiffer callipers for use there, but they mounted in the same way and had identical pad area. Slots routed into the disc faces swept away debris, to keep the pad-to-disc contact clean and crisp.

The conventional brake balance bar was modified to accept a Smiths tachodrive connected to a knurled knob on the left-side dash frame, lower than the instrument panel. By winding this control to left or right the driver could juggle his brake balance as he pleased while in motion. With his front and rear anti-roll bar adjusters also available for fine tuning one could picture his controls as having more in common with an aircraft pilot's than a road car driver's.

This author has had a lot of exposure to historic racing cars made by Mercedes-Benz, Auto Union, Alfa Romeo and the like. Whenever a more jaundiced elder enthusiast says something like 'They don't make them like they used to', he may be technically right, but he is far off the mark as regards sheer quality. The Grand Prix car may have gone through a low period in the late-1950s and '60s, but by the late-1970s there was no room for slipshod blacksmithery by any team wishing to prove competitive. Frontline modern Formula 1 cars are all very well made.

Returning to the Williams FW07; both its front and rear hubs were machined from 'S514', the live axle at the front being fitted with Timken taper roller bearings fixed in the upright. All suspension pivots used ball-races, the same size fore and aft at the front, but with larger races for the forward pivots at the rear where high tractive torques were applied.

In the suspension rod-ends, Williams normally specified NMB spherical bearings, falling back on Rose joints if NMBs were unavailable.

The rear anti-roll bar clamped against the rearmost suspension pivot plate and was driver-adjustable for stiffness from a left-hand cockpit control. An adjustable front anti-roll bar was also fitted during the 1980 season.

Steering was via a Jack Knight-adapted Lola magnesium rack housing with Knight gears and Williams's own outer housing ends. The assembly mounted above the driver's legs behind the front axle line and was foam-wrapped for his protection, being so close above his shins. The short steering column, universal joints and outboard steering arms were all Williams-made, while the steering wheel was a 10-in. diameter type by Personal.

Slung wide on each side of the slender central monocoque were the all-important side pods with their underwing 'floors' or diffusers. The '07 series cars' underwings were slung from aluminium strong-points inserted into the honeycomb tub sides. The underwings were initially in glass-fibre, but this material was insufficiently rigid, being too easily sucked out of shape by the downloads generated. Through 1980 the underwings would be in bent aluminium honeycomb retained for the '07 cars' life. They became carbon-composite in FW08. Moulded carbon radiator air intakes were used right from the start because their precise shape was so critical.

Along the outer edge of the underwing tray the vertical skirt box was attached. Its inner panel was honeycomb dotted with numerous inserts for it was very highly loaded. In

comparison, the outer skin enclosing the skirts was a lightweight carbon-foam sandwich with solid glass-fibre inserts where bolt-on fixings penetrated. The skirts themselves were of carbon-glass, with three aluminium bottom-edge inserts containing ceramic skids on which the skirt rode against the track surface.

The skirts were of course free to rise and fall as the road dictated. There was a ball-race guide at the rear of each skirt to accept dragging loads, while a simple guide peg rode in a slot at the front. Their motion was smoothed by nylon rollers on aluminium axles fixed to the inner box skin and by nylon rollers on steel axle-pins on the skirts themselves.

Good skirt control, springing and guide systems were absolutely critical in maintaining a constant seal between skirt and roadway to ensure consistent download. As the underwing venturis accelerated airflow and reduced its pressure, so that low pressure area beneath the underwings acted not only on the underwings to draw the car down vertically, but also upon the side skirts to suck them in laterally. A skirt control system which allowed the skirt to skew and bind in its guides would compromise the aerodynamic seal against the track surface, download would be inconsistent and consequently both car and driver would suffer. William's skirt guide system was probably superior to any other team's (except perhaps Brabham's) from 1979 to 1981, and it showed.

Meanwhile, in 1977-78, the fashionable rear wing mounting had been via rigid end plates, mounted at their lower extremities on the ends of a lateral beam across the gearbox.

The formerly conventional centre-pillar mounting had interrupted airflow beneath the wing's working undersurface so end-plate support leaving the entire wing span unfettered offered improved download. Unfortunately, on new-generation ground-effect cars the low-level lateral mounting beam for the end plates themselves then obstructed airstreams exiting from the underwing tunnels so designers reverted to centre-pillar support.

Williams's rear wings were of this type, aluminium skinned over alloy profile-formers, two in the middle and one either side, with aluminium and carbon-fibre end plates.

The team would race only one front wing shape. It used an aluminium pole as a main spar, with the wing sections formed over foam profiles which had been cut to shape by hot wire and template, and then clad with pre-made carbon skins. An aluminium trailing-edge flap was added and the wings were then mounted on the front tub horns.

Where ancillaries were concerned, an aluminium VW Golf diesel water radiator was adopted in the original FW07s. For 1980 a Citroen CX radiator would replace it. This unit, with its aluminium core and plastic header tank, was light and efficient and could have been produced no better and certainly no cheaper to special order. It lay at a shallow angle in the right-hand side pod, gripped between foam rubber pads.

The cooling system included a swirl-pot at the rear of the engine where steam bubbles could be centrifuged out of the coolant before hot water returned to the outboard side of the radiator. Pressure filling was available for rapid topping-up during qualifying or in the race when every split second saved could be vital. The pressure filler itself was actually a converted fire extinguisher canister, coupled to a high-pressure gas bottle.

Oil cooling was by a 44-row Serck aluminium radiator in the left-hand side pod of the 1980 cars, fed from the engine scavenge pumps by 'Aeroquip-16' braided flexible hose. The bell-housing oil tank carried two gallons of Valvoline oil when brimful. For Kyalami 1981 the water and oil systems would be modified, with the water radiator moving to the left side, oil cooler to the right.

Electrically, Williams tried both Lucas and Marelli ignition systems before opting in 1980 for the German Contactless brand which gave better-controlled sparking with less scatter. According to the drivers this gave them 'more power more consistently', although the advantage could not be proved on the dyno. The Contactless system lacked a rev-limiter override for heroics, but the Lucas limiter was in any case considered to be 'a bit iffy'.

With an air-starter, only a tiny battery need be carried – in Williams's case a National Panasonic motor cycle type measuring only some 6 in. x 2½ in.

Several brands of dash panel instruments would be used, with variable success.

The fuel system drew from a collector box in the rear of the solitary bag tank. The system had changed at least twice during the car's original design period.

Initially in 1979, a toothed-belt driven Lucas pump was used, suitably tucked in behind the tub section to clear airflow through the underwing side pod tunnel. Early in 1980 Williams fitted this pump – which is virtually a flat disc, smaller than the palm of your hand – onto the nose of the right-hand inlet camshaft.

Cosworth predictably objected, pointing out that ineffective pump seals could pass neat fuel into the cam-box and dilute the oil pumping through there with disastrous results. They specified instead an apparently Heath Robinson system, with an angle-gear drive from the tail of the left-side inlet camshaft, passing to a tacho-cable which ran forward to a tiny clutch device, then an electric motor, then the pump itself, perched on the tank top.

As described in the Cosworth chapter, the electric motor then powered the pump for starting, and once the engine fired the mechanical tacho-drive would take over.

All fuel lines had standard dry-break links to prevent leaks should an accident separate engine from tub.

Onboard safety systems included two Dreadnought extinguisher bottles, one 5 kg, the other 2.4 kg, mounted either side of the forward cockpit floor crossbeam. One bottle was piped around the cockpit, the other into the titanium tubing of the roll-over bar, down its bracing struts, and thence out through neat nozzles aimed into the engine vee. The Graviner life-support air bottle was mounted on the tank top, protected within the roll-over bar struts. Seat harness was by Willans.

Should the driver stall his engine on circuit, an onboard starter air-pressure bottle was carried, housed in one side pod. A right-hand cockpit lever opened the air-cock via a Bowden cable to give a 12-second churn on the starter. If the engine didn't fire, then it would be time to hop out and start walking . . . the race is over.

The bodywork had to be light yet rigid, and free of drag-inducing flutter. In 1980 Jones's number one team car would use a honeycomb resin cockpit section, the others glass-fibre. In 1979 the engine cover was aluminium honeycomb for the flat sections, with a riveted-in glass fibre hump carrying the induction mesh. The 1980 engine covers were all glass-fibre with some foam and honeycomb stiffening.

Wheels were Dymag one-piece or Speedline bolt-together types, in 13 in. and 15 in. diameters with 11 in. wide front rims as standard and 17¼ in. or 18 in. wide rears.

Wheelbase was 106 in., front track 68 in., rear track notably narrower at 63¾ in., tailoring the wide rear rims to the overall width restriction. Overall height was 42⅞ in., until the tall Carlos Reutemann joined the team as Jones's team-mate in 1980, and his cars were fitted with a taller roll-over hoop to suit. Ground clearance was a nominal 3 in. under the monocoque.

At Zolder in 1979, Jones qualified third fastest in FW07/1 despite having broken a skirt. Regazzoni was shunted out of the race early on in '07/2 but Jones led the very potent Ligiers which had started the season so well. It was the

The FW07C 'clearance car' of 1981 demonstrated here by Jones shows off its blade front wing, rocker-arm suspension, top radiator ducts, high exhausts and brake ducting, here taped over, front and rear.

first time since 1969 that a Williams-entered car had led a Grand Prix, but the spell lasted only until lap 40 when Jones retired with electrical failure.

The Australian was running in third place at Monaco in the new '07/3 until he clipped a barrier but Regazzoni finished second to score Williams's first FW07 points of the 1979 Championship. There followed a gap in the calendar before the French GP and Head used that breathing space to test at Dijon, where FW07 simply murdered the lap record. The Michelin-shod Renault turbocharged cars were to come good in that race, however, and they finished first and third, split by a Ferrari while Jones was fourth – the leading Goodyear runner home in his FW07 – and Regazzoni was sixth.

Then followed a simply stunning test session at Silverstone in preparation for the British Grand Prix. The lap record was 1:18 and Jones had already got down to 1:13.6 when a newly-developed engine under-fairing was attached, and he ended that day clocking 1 minute 12.18 seconds. The sheer grip generated by the Williams cars in the race there enabled them to run 1-2 until the neck of Jones's engine's water pump cracked and dribbled away all the coolant. Out he went, leaving his popular team-mate to score the first victory for both the new cars and the Williams team in chassis '07/2, adding fastest lap along the way.

Jones then underlined Williams superiority by winning the next three GPs in a row; Germany and Austria in the latest '07/4 and Holland in '07/1. In Austria the team cars finished first and second.

Jones and Regazzoni thereafter went on to complete this remarkable season with another superb 1-2 in Canada, using chassis '07/4 and '07/1 respectively but Jones lost a wheel after a fudged tyre change in the US GP at Watkins Glen. He finished only third in the 1979 Drivers' Championship despite having won – like Andretti in 1978 – more Grands Prix than any other driver.

Early-season disappointments with the old FW06 cars and late development of the '07s had clearly cost Williams dear . . . but it would all come right in 1980.

Patrick Head's engineering team now believed they needed a car which would be two seconds per lap quicker to continue winning.

They developed the FW07B with composite undersides extending the underwing back through the rear suspension to generate greater downforce.

They tested extensively at Ricard-Castellet in the south of France and the development seemed very promising, but in practice for the Argentine GP at Buenos Aires Autodrome the new stiffened-monocoque FW07B – available as new chassis '07B/5 and '07B/6 – proved unstable due to 'porpoising'. Consequently, the B-spec components were hastily stripped off and Jones notched his sixth Grand Prix victory.

Jones was third in Brazil but retired the third new FW07B chassis '7 in South Africa where new team-mate Reutemann placed sixth to score his first point for Williams. Both FW07s were sidelined by collisions at Long Beach, while at Didcot the Williams engineers had developed an alternative B-spec package with modified undersides ending short of the tail and with modified cooling systems.

These definitive FW07B cars made their debut in the Belgian GP at Zolder. Pironi's Ligier beat Jones there, the '07B slowed by a blistered tyre, but Reutemann was third and Williams were now leading the Constructors' Championship table.

While the race team operated their cars in the Grand Prix calendar, engineer Dernie presided over a separate test team with its own chassis and engines which conducted the required research and development and reconnaissance testing at whatever venues matched the team's requirements.

The team held a float of 18 available Cosworth DFV engines, priced new at £22,600 each. Thirteen of them were raced regularly, four were earmarked primarily for the R&D unit, and one was maintained exclusively for experimental purposes.

Jones lost the Monaco GP with crownwheel failure in what had become his regular '07B/7 letting Reutemann through for his first Williams victory, in '07B/5. The Argentinian's luck then deserted him in Spain as he was tee-boned by another car and Jones managed to salvage a

very lucky win in a very sick car. But this race was subsequently deleted from the Championship for political reasons, which robbed Jones and the team of nine valuable points.

At Ricard they utterly destroyed both Renault and Ligier hopes with Jones first and Reutemann sixth in '07Bs '7 and '5 . . .

Jones and Williams consequently led their respective World Championship competitions into the British GP at Brands Hatch where, based on practice form, the Ligiers of Pironi and Laffite looked all set to do to Williams what Williams had done to them on their home soil. But this time the Ligiers encountered wheel problems and Jones won yet again, in '07B/7 this time with Reutemann third in '07B/5.

The South African girl driver Desiré Wilson drove FW07/4 at Brands Hatch but she failed to qualify. This car was subsequently written off in a testing accident at Donington Park, with Jones driving. Chassis FW07/5 became the test team car for the rest of the season before going on the North American tour as Jones's spare chassis.

On the fast circuits at Hockenheim and the Österreichring, the turbo Renaults were expected to show off their power. But in the German GP a Ligier won with the '07Bs second – Reutemann who had led before a tyre change in '07B/5 – and third – Jones in new car '07B/9 having started from pole position and setting fastest race lap. In Austria, Jabouille's Renault won at last with the '07Bs accumulating more points, second and third yet again. Reutemann's third place was taken in the debut race of new car '07B/8.

It still managed to go wrong for the Williams team at Zandvoort in Holland, where Jones crashed '07B/5 very heavily in practice when the throttle jammed open, and then in the race he broke a skirt in the spare car '07B/7 by sliding carelessly over a high kerb and finished last. The practice crash damage was very bad and a replacement had been shipped out overnight, but within seven days the damaged '07B/5 was repaired and available. Nelson Piquet's Brabham won there in Holland and suddenly Jones's Championship lead over the Brazilian was cut to only two points.

There were three Championship rounds remaining, and at Imola Piquet beat Jones fair and square to take a one-point lead in the Drivers' Championship.

Williams arrived in Canada with four cars, eight Cosworth engines, 5.5 tonnes of spares and 26 people. They were taking it very seriously, but the effort looked like ending in

farce as Jones and Piquet collided in the first corner of the race and the ensuing multiple pile-up caused the race to be stopped and restarted. Piquet took over his qualifying car with its special 'screamer' Cosworth engine for this restart and he led until the highly-tuned V8 blew apart. This left Jones able to cruise home unconcerned to win the race in '07B/9 and the Drivers' World Championship title.

The team were determined to stay up on their toes for the final race of the season, the US GP at Watkins Glen which followed one week later, and Jones and Reutemann rewarded their efforts by promptly dominating the event and finishing 1-2 yet again; Jones winning his second consecutive GP in '07B/9, while Reutemann drove his regular late-season '07B/8.

Williams Grand Prix Engineering Ltd became undisputed Formula 1 Constructors' World Champion.

Frank Williams himself was still a wheeler-dealer at heart and because team finances were still quite tight he sold some of the obsolete 1979 FW07 cars, just as he had sold FW06s before them. John MacDonald's RAM Racing team bought the cars, FW07/1, '07/2 and '07/3 and they were driven by de Villota and more often by Rupert Keegan although it was always a struggle for them to qualify. Keegan's best finish was ninth at Watkins Glen, where Geoff Lees failed to make the race in the second car after a practice crash.

The service requirements of this private team added workload at the Didcot factory. De Villota managed to damage his car more severely than any works driver had so far achieved in a minor race at Monza, and RAM required a rapid rebuild to continue racing. It was good practice for the Didcot crew and kept the chassis shop busy when it was well abreast of works team needs.

The young American Kevin Cogan rented a RAM drive at Montreal but failed to qualify even after thirty despairing laps in the final practice session there, while Keegan crashed his car '02 heavily in practice and also missed the race. RAM were anxious to have both cars available for the Watkins Glen race one week later, and that Saturday evening they telephoned Didcot works manager Dave Neal at his home – reversing the charges of course – to arrange a lightning monocoque rebuild.

The damaged tub was air-freighted into London and cleared through customs that Monday afternoon, the Didcot crew worked on it through Tuesday night into Wednesday, when it was flown back to New York ready for the start of Watkins Glen practice, and RAM's best finish of the season. This is typical of the pressures in Formula 1 . . . they demand special people to handle them.

During the following winter, Williams ran '07B/7 for Jones in his home Australian GP at Calder – a non-World Championship event which Alan's late father Stan had won many years previously. Now it was his son's turn.

During that winter of 1980/81 the war of the sliding-skirt ban was fought between the constructors and the FISA governing body. The constructors ran the South African GP without FISA sanction, using sliding-skirt cars. The so-called *Grande Costruttori* or *Legalisti* teams – including Ferrari, Renault and Alfa

Top right, secret of success, the WGPE wind tunnel at Didcot. Below, Reutemann at Silverstone, British GP, 1981 in 'FW07C/14' on his way to second place. See the hinged skirts used that season, fine air entry for side pods and overall smoothly integrated shape.

Romeo – stayed away, while Reutemann won for Williams in the last brand new FW07B chassis (number '10) without Championship points being allowed.

The constructors had to accept the skirt ban and the 6 cm minimum ground clearance rule as well as the 585 kg minimum weight limit which went with it, so Williams rapidly produced an unskirted and ballasted 'clearance car'. This FW07C, was ready in time for the official World Championship opening round at Long Beach, California, on 15 March 1981, using new chassis '07C/11 and '07C/12 built to the letter of the new laws.

They instantly finished 1-2 yet again, Jones in chassis '11 leading Reutemann in '12. Another 1-2 promptly followed, this time in reverse order in the same cars, in Brazil, but in Buenos Aires the trick-suspension Brabham driven by Nelson Piquet proved uncatchable.

Although the Brabham's skirts were fixed to the chassis and its ground clearance was legal when measured stationary, the suspension included hydropneumatic jacking devices which lowered the car and therefore its skirts onto the roadway when running, thus regaining the ground-effect sealing which FISA had sought to outlaw . . . *and* the car was legal.

Consequently, Williams developed a lowering suspension set-up of their own, but at Imola Jones unfortunately rammed his team-mate, though Reutemann survived to finish third.

At Zolder, the Argentinian won in '07C/12, after Jones crashed '07C/11 and was running away with the World Drivers' Championship. Up to this point, Reutemann had had an incredible run of 15 consecutive GP finishes, every time in the points – thanks to Williams's competitive reliability. However, at Monaco his car's transmission failed and Jones inherited the lead briefly before losing it with fuel starvation in his new car '07C/15. The Australian driver then threw away a superb lead through driver error in Spain. In these two events alone a very likely potential 18 Championship points had been lost.

From the French GP the '07Cs wore revised side pods to cure an early-season tendency to porpoise, but they could not match Renault's pace. Reutemann raced '07C/14 for the first time at Silverstone, finishing second. The '07Cs were then further altered aerodynamically in time for the German GP and became truly competitive again, but Jones's earlier mysterious fuel starvation fault reappeared and robbed him of yet another probable victory, and nine more points. In this race he gave the intended six-wheeler FW07D chassis '16 its race debut, in four-wheeled form.

This elusive fuel starvation fault was subsequently traced to a flow impediment through a pump union. An angle within the union was cut sharp instead of being radiused, and at that point swirl within the fuel flow promoted local vapourization and caused the problem. It was corrected by the most simple machining operation, merely cutting back that sharp angle into a smooth-radiused curve . . . end of problem, ironically at the cost of only a few pence.

This had taken months to locate and isolate, and had cost Jones Championship points and what could easily have been the first back-to-back double World Championship victory since his great compatriot Jack Brabham had last done the double in 1959-1960 for Cooper Cars.

Reutemann then suffered an uncharacteristic rush of blood at Zandvoort in the debut of the last FW07-series chassis, FW07C/17, where he triggered a collision which robbed him of more points, and which left him and Nelson Piquet now neck-and-neck for the 1981 Championship titles on 45 points apiece. They raced on into the final round at Las Vegas, where Reutemann's always suspect psyche seemed to crack under the pressure and the Brabham driver was able to canter home to secure the Drivers' Championship, although Jones won the race outright in '07D/17 and Williams had long since

secured their second consecutive Constructors' Cup victory.

Head's design team had been well advanced in the design of a new shorter and lighter replacement for the whole FW07 family. This new FW08 was intended originally to be a six-wheeler but would finally emerge in 1982 as a conventional four-wheeler built to run extremely light with an onboard reservoir for its 'water-cooled' brakes which would enable it to be brought up to legal minimum weight post-race for scrutineering, when the hitherto empty reservoirs could be filled with water. This perfectly admissible ploy enabled the team to compensate somewhat for the huge power advantage now being enjoyed by those teams with turbocharged engines, like Renault and Ferrari.

But, disgusted with the hard-ride torture handed out by the lowering-suspension cars fostered by the rules chaos of 1981, Alan Jones had retired from driving after his Las Vegas victory, and for the new season Carlos Reutemann was left heading the team, with the Finnish driver Keke Rosberg as his number two. Then Reutemann abruptly turned his back on motor racing and followed Jones into retirement in early season, and the '07Cs were campaigned thereafter by Keke Rosberg,

Mario Andretti and Derek Daly, before the stubby new FW08s replaced the '07s in time for Zolder and the Belgian GP in early summer.

During the '07s' final races, Reutemann was second in South Africa with Keke Rosberg fifth; the Finn second but disqualified after a terrific performance in Brazil; then second again at Long Beach.

Rosberg would in fact end that season as WGPE's second World Champion driver in three years, but the Formula 1 Constructors' Championship would fall to Ferrari's new turbocharged cars which won more GPs and only failed to give one of their drivers the World title due to Gilles Villeneuve's ghastly fatal accident in Belgium and Didier Pironi's similar career-ending crash at Hockenheim.

During its long frontline run – beginning in the April 1979 Spanish GP and ending in the April 1982 US GP (West) at Long Beach – the Williams-Cosworth FW07 series included no less than 16 individual chassis (no number '13') and they won back-to-back Constructors' World Championship titles in 1980-81, plus 18 races overall, 15 of which were full World Championship-status Grands Prix. They proved themselves classic Grand Prix cars, of which Patrick Head and his men could be justifiably proud.

The Williams Six-Wheeler

In 1977 Robin Herd of March briefly – and cheaply – explored the low-drag aerodynamic advantages of an 0-2-4 six-wheeler layout for Formula 1 using front-size wheels and tyres with the rear four all driven. He simply added a third axle and final-drive behind the standard units but had no budget to develop the idea further.

Then during 1980-81 Renault and Ferrari began to set new performance standards with their turbocharged engines which the Cosworth brigade could not match.

At that time turbocharged engines simply were not available for client teams. Patrick Head of Williams Grand Prix Engineering approached Ferrari to use their V6 but the answer, predictably, was 'No'. Cosworth at that time had a rather negative attitude towards attempting to extract more than their usual 490-500 bhp from the DFV engine on which most specialist teams relied. Williams therefore began a development programme of their own with John Judd's Engine Developments concern of Rugby. Cam and valve specialist Chris Walters assisted, and they eventually saw 535-40 bhp from the DFVs.

Sheer straightline speed was the turbos' greatest single advantage, and they also had an edge on overall acceleration despite this being diminished by the extra equipment weight they carried.

Conventional rear tyres at that time were 29 in. outside diameter on ultra-wide rims, generating some 40 per cent of the car's aerodynamic drag. By using three axles, two driven at the rear, and running small front-size tyres on each, it was possible to reduce drag while at least maintaining, at best improving upon, aggregate rear contact-patch area and traction. And other advantages emerged.

Aerodynamic underwing skirts were restricted to the area within the wheelbase. With an extra axle, skirted underwings could be longer and their working area and total download therefore much larger. A six-wheeled model was made and tested promisingly in the Didcot wind tunnel.

The new 4×4 rear end was centred more or less around the conventional four-wheeled car's rear axle-line, the second-axle wheels now being some four inches ahead of the normal wheelspin safety-valve had been removed by 4×4 startline grip. So Head was advised to use the more robust DG gear forward driveshafts, and the new third axle outrigged just behind from an extension supplementary final-drive.

Hewland Engineering assisted on the transmission. The March 0-2-4 car was being hill-climbed by Roy Lane at that time and its FT gearbox first-gear often stripped because the normal wheelspin safety-valve had been removed by 4×4 startline grip. So Head was advised to use the more robust DG gear

cluster, allied to smaller final-drives.

The FW07D monocoque was prepared for this rear end, and Jones first drove it one week after Las Vegas 1981, but stood by his decision to retire, despite two standing starts in which the new car took off like a bullet without wheelspin. Palmer tested at Silverstone in the wet and was very quick, the team suspecting they could actually run slick tyres on the third axle since the track was so well drained ahead of it by wet tyres on the first two axles. Patrick was concerned however about tight corners, so a test was held at Croix-en-Ternois in northern France, where Palmer lapped as quickly as the new four-wheeled FW08 car. The '08's short tub had actually been tailored to match this 4×4 rear end with those vast underwings.

The six-wheeler was some 120 lb heavier and in this prototype form its aerodynamic download and drag were broadly similar. Because of their great length and considerable width, the underwings could get away with only a modest flare, rising towards the rear, but though this took them beneath the driveshafts, they still passed above the lower wishbones, which interrupted airflow in this crucial area.

Consequently a second-generation six-wheel conversion was then designed, in which fixed-length driveshafts would be used as lower lateral location members (as in the 1960 Lotus 18), leaving the six-wheeler's underwing tunnels completely unobstructed. In this design the conventional high rear wing on its pillar would be replaced by a simple rear-body trim-flap like the Lotus 80's.

Meanwhile water-ballast weight-saving ploys seemed more profitable short-term and Rosberg ultimately won the Drivers' Championship in the four-wheeled FW08, while calendar pressures only slowed progress on the six-wheeler update, tunnel tests suggesting 30 per cent greater download.

How well would it have worked?

With an outside consultant, Williams had by this time developed a very accurate lap-time-simulation computer programme. It predicted a Ricard-Castellet six-wheeler lap of 1:28. Prior to the 1985 Australian GP, on a circuit the team had never even seen, they set up this programme simply on the map provided. The prediction indicated an FW10-Honda best qualifying time of 1:20.4, actually clocking 1:20.5, and a best race lap of 1:23.1, actually clocking 1:23.7 . . . so the prediction programme really was incredibly accurate. By the end of 1985 the powerful Williams-Hondas, albeit flat-bottomed, were still lapping Ricard around 1:32 – four seconds *slower* than the far less powerful Cosworth-engined six-wheeled ground-effects car should have been.

But six-wheelers and four-wheel drive were both then banned for 1983 and perhaps it was as well, for this time everyone must surely have followed the six-wheeled lead and grids full of such exotica might have been too far removed from what the public and sponsors would understand to maintain credibility and interest.

But what a nice try . . .

Chapter 13

THE GORDON MURRAY CHAMPIONSHIP BRABHAMS 1980-83

Nelson Piquet's first World Championship win came in 1981. His BT49C displays hydraulically adjusted pullrod front suspension and smooth overbody form feeding air beneath the rear wing. Bottom, Piola's BT49 sketch shows 1, Girling 4-piston calliper; 2, carbon top; 3, anti-roll bar; 4, steering rack end; 5, carbon skirt; 6, skirtbox inner; 7, dash; 8, machined aluminium tub insert; 9, water container; 10, gear linkage; 11, carbon underwing floor; 12, exhaust heat-shielding; 13, rising-rate geometry suspension pullrod; 14, bell-housing oil tank; 15, Girling 4-piston calliper; 16, rear wing-post; 17, gearbox oil cooler.

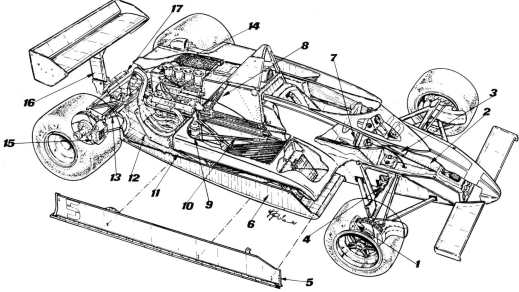

By September 1979 the Brabham-Alfa Romeo co-operative arrangement was drawing to a close, ending on a victorious note with Lauda's BT48 victory in the non-Championship race at Imola.

The decision was taken to revert to Cosworth power since Autodelta were spending more of their time concentrating upon development of their own rival Formula 1 project. A terrific effort by their Chessington workforce enabled Motor Racing Developments to present three still red-liveried BT49-DFVs (two race cars and a spare) at Montreal for the Canadian GP.

The cars used a lengthened version of Gordon Murray's existing BT48 slimline aluminium and carbon-panelled monocoque tub. The cars were 35 lb lighter than the BT48 when empty, 95 lb lighter when fuelled to DFV requirements.

Piquet ran 'BT49/2' third for a long time in the Canadian GP before retiring with gearbox trouble, while Lauda abruptly quit racing after the briefest of practice outings, much to his hard-worked crew's dismay. He was replaced immediately by Ricardo Zunino taking over 'BT49/3' for the race.

Second time out, at Watkins Glen, the new cars ran well, Piquet qualifying on the front row beside Jones's Williams and setting fastest lap before a driveshaft broke, while the novice Zunino qualified ninth-quickest but spun off.

As 1979 ended, Brabham faced their first full Cosworth-powered season for four years. It would see Piquet growing in stature and experience while the team beavered away to develop their new DFV car to winning pitch. By the end of 1980 the BT49 was arguably the fastest Cosworth-powered car, despite Jones's Championship victory in the Williams FW07Bs, for Piquet had come within an ace of denying the Australian driver his title.

As a marque, however, Brabham could not challenge Williams for the Constructors' Cup because both cars in a team could score points in that competition and Brabham was effectively a one-star-driver team with the second seat filled normally by a driver paying for the privilege. Neither Zunino in early-season, nor his replacement Rebaque, could accumulate sufficient points to combat Williams's driver strength.

The two original late-1979 BT49s, chassis '2 and '3, appeared early in 1980. Seven more were built that season, chassis 'BT49/4-5-6-7-8-9-10'. In Argentina, '2 was team spare while Piquet and Zunino raced new cars '4 and '5 which wore revised rear suspension, modified side pod profiles and a new skirt system, and both radiator positioning and fuel system had been modified. They were the fastest cars on the straight, and Piquet finished second while

Zunino drove carefully on the slippery track . . . at the tail of the field.

They had problems in Piquet's native Brazil, and a major development came at Long Beach where the BT49B variant emerged with its rear end modified to use a Weismann transverse-shaft gearbox which was narrow and tall and useful in altering weight distribution. The coil-dampers mounted on the rear of the gearbox side by side.

These mods appeared on chassis '3, the race cars '5 and '6 also using modified side pods, bodywork and rear suspensions though retaining the conventional Brabham gearbox. Piquet, in his regular car, was able to put in the perfect performance, starting on pole, leading throughout and scoring his first Grand Prix win.

New car '49/7 was ready for Zunino in Belgium fitted with the Weismann gearbox, though only in practice. The big Brabham-Alfa rear wing reappeared for the slow-speed circuit at Monaco, where both drivers crashed during first qualifying, damaging their cars' tubs. Piquet raced the spare while Zunino raced development car '3, hastily sent out from Chessington as replacement along with tub '6 unassembled. After a lot of work, the original Monaco cars were repaired in time for Spain, while a stiffened-monocoque new chassis '8 made its debut in France as spare and was finally raced by Piquet. It was very fast on the straight but lack traction.

Larger 15 in. front wheels and the big Monaco wing were used for Brands Hatch, and for Germany reprofiled side pods appeared on Piquet's '49/3 (the team spare which he raced there), while at the Österreichring he crashed his own race car '7 very heavily in practice. Old '49/3 was again prepared for him and he finished in the points for the eighth time that season, as team-mate Rebaque gave '49/6 the Weismann gearbox car's first finish.

Major change came in Holland. Gordon and his number two, David North, had developed a new front suspension sweep, lengthening the wheelbase by three inches, altering the relative positions of the centres of pressure and gravity, and new side pods were profiled to suit. Brabham could now run less wing, gaining on straightline speed while still retaining downforce. Both race cars – '6 for Rebaque and '7 for Piquet – ran Weismann gearboxes and Piquet won after Jones slid over a kerb and damaged a skirt when leading.

Now the Drivers' Championship battle was joined in earnest between Piquet and Jones. A new chassis '9 was available for Nelson at Imola, and with its longer wheelbase and new side pods the BT49 was now superior to the rival Williams FW07B. Seeking reliability, the Weismann gearbox was set aside at this point and the trusty Brabham transmission reinstated, and Piquet won his second GP in a row.

Four cars were taken to Canada; Rebaque's spare '49/10 being brand new. Piquet rammed a Renault in early practice and set his time in his spare car '7. Both drivers preferred the smaller 13 in. diameter front wheels. After a first corner collision with Jones, Piquet had to use the spare car in the restarted race with its practice qualifying engine still installed, and this sprint unit broke when he was leading, losing him the World title.

Gordon told me: 'The car there was dynamite, but then it all went out the window which was really a bitter, bitter disappointment; not so much for me, as for all the effort our chaps had put in over such a long, long period . . .'

During that 1980 season Piquet finished ten of the 14 Championship rounds, placing 2-4-1-3-4-2-4-5-1-1, producing points every time. Zunino attempted seven GPs, failing to qualify at Monaco, retiring three times and placing 7-8-10 in his first three outings, Argentina, Brazil, South Africa. The Mexican, Rebaque, drove in the last seven races, finishing three times, 7-10-6 – scoring his solitary point at the

scene of Piquet's and the team's bitter disappointment in Montreal.

Brabham placed third behind Ligier and Williams in the Constructors' Cup competition.

The application of a ban on sliding skirts marked 1981, which saw the dawn of the so-called 'clearance car' era. The rules insisted on a 6 cm clearance between their lowest suspended part and the road surface. Goodyear had pulled out of racing that winter, much development had been wasted by all teams on sliding-skirted cars, and Brabham turned to Michelin to use their radial-ply racing tyres.

The scene was set for a remarkable season.

Gordon described the situation after FISA's arbitrary application of the clearance rule. 'The hierarchy kept telling us don't worry. Skirts are in. You're OK. But we could see teams testing without skirts and we grew more and more nervous . . . we had been assured skirts were OK, we did absolutely no testing at all without them. Then it all exploded after Kyalami [run by FOCA as a skirted race, losing its Championship status accordingly] and suddenly the 6 cm clearance rule was in. That was a shaker. We had all discussed such a rule and rejected it as unenforceable . . .

'Now we had just a month to build clearance cars before Long Beach. So David and I took the rules and read them closely again . . .'

They were convinced that all teams would simply fit soft springs and allow the natural and inevitable vertical load upon the car at speed to force it down closer to the road surface whereupon its fixed-skirt ground-effect sections would begin to exert their download, despite the absence of sliding skirt seals against infilling around their periphery.

'There was no problem securely attaching any aerodynamic device to the entirely-sprung part of the car but we could not have any device bridging the gap to the ground; fair enough. No part of our car when measured would be closer than 6 cm to the ground except wheels and tyres. Certainly no part would "systematically or permanently touch the ground" as had the old sliding skirts [and as the new rule now prohibited]. Even then, if the car hit a bump or kerb the skirt would leave the ground for a moment, and that would constitute "not permanently touching the ground".

'The rules were unenforceable . . . They said nothing about measuring the car at speed, and we understood the "correction of suspension height" rule to mean anything other than the normal loads experienced by a racing car.

'If you set a Ford Escort, for example, at 6 cm clearance stationary and then drive it on the road it's going to squat down and at some time it'll clear only 5.99 cm, so did that mean we had to set cars at 7 cm static, so they would go no closer than 6 cm when loaded up at speed?

'That's not what the rule said. It was a stupid rule, we told them it would be unpoliceable . . . but we built a system which complied with it to the letter.

'We were confident everyone else would be doing exactly the same thing. We chose a soft air spring, storing the energy by compressing air in a central reservoir through a hydraulic piston, piped to cylinders on each suspension corner. By carefully choosing orifice sizes we could bleed fluid back to the cylinders to pump the suspension back up.

'This way, the car would in effect be blown down as it gained speed away from the pits or startline and download increased. Fluid would be forced out of the cylinders, load the piston and compress air in that central reservoir.

'Then if we got the bleed rate right, the car would stay down through slow corners without springing back up suddenly as download reduced. Once the car slowed on its way in, the compressed air would force back the reservoir piston, fluid would bleed back into the cylinders on each suspension corner and the car would rise to its 6 cm clearance for measurement.'

The lanky, quietly-spoken South African

told me this story at the end of that season, earnestly leaning forward to add 'No bullshit Doug – it was so *obvious* a loophole we thought everyone would be doing it.'

Brabham went to Long Beach with their latest BT49Cs, all agog to see who had the best lowering system, and they had several other tricks up their sleeve just in case. They confidently expected to see everyone running hydropneumatics, but nobody was!

This often happened to Gordon and his team.

At Long Beach they had their problems. 'The car went down and wouldn't come up, then it came up and wouldn't go down, then one end went down and the other jammed up. It was awful. We were using plastic hydraulic lines to save weight. They blew off or melted on hot parts, the fluid leaked, the car sank and stayed sunk. It looked as if Nelson wouldn't qualify so we took the system off his car and ran with conventional twin-rate coil springs.'

In Brazil they were still in trouble but Piquet qualified on pole only for poor tyre choice to cost them the race. Both there and at Long Beach the BT49Cs had worn peripheral plastic skirts with thicker blocks of similar material protecting the bottom edge where it might touch the road.

These skirt devices were governed by the old rule which had applied in the days before sliding skirts. So the Brabhams ran the same fixed-skirt material used then without any complaints at the time. It would not survive if it touched the road surface, but once the car settled to its racing ride-height the skirt would prevent in-fill diminishing ground-effect.

Williams and the opposition protested against the Brabham system to establish what was considered legal and what was not. They objected to the skirts' floppiness, enabling them to suck in and run on an air-bleed bearing which kept them hovering just above the road surface. This was considered to contravene the requirement 'to remain immobile in relation to the sprung part of the car'.

Murray's reaction was natural: 'Everything moves to some degree. How rigid is rigid? Everything flexes to some degree, how do you define it?

'In Argentina everybody had some sort of skirt, bits around the rear wheels to seal them to the side pod, they bent when the wheel hit them, but not everybody had it round the edges of the car like us.'

Eventually he and team patron Ecclestone said they would gladly accede to the protests if everyone ran marker paint on the fixed skirts attached to their cars, and any one found to have touched the ground would be disqualified. Nobody would agree to that, for every car touched the ground or a kerb somewhere around the circuit at some time on a quick lap.

Still, the joke was that the Brabham BT49C lowering system was still troublesome. Gordon flew home between Brazil and Argentina to redesign it. In Argentina the Mark II system was better but still unreliable. It would not stay

Top, *Piquet loads up 'BT49/8' through the S-bends at Ricard in 1980 when sliding skirts – visible here deeply extended between the car's right-side wheels as it rolls – were still legal. The diagonal links in the front suspension are the pullrods actuating levers at the feet of inboard coil-spring/damper units. Above, with DFV, Gordon Murray, Brabham's quietly innovative South African-born Chief Engineer.*

down out of slow corners. Fortunately Piquet picked up enough time round the quick curves to compensate, he won and Rebaque retired after running second in Piquet's wake.

A complete front spring and cylinder were stolen from the team's garage there and they were fascinated to see who would fit similar systems at Imola. There was still much ill-feeling about the Brabham ploy.

'It was a bad feeling – all the blokes you'd always chatted to, all your friends, suddenly not talking to you . . .'

They had redesigned the system again, put the cylinders on the suspension links instead of in the springs and changed the hydraulic lines from plastic to metal. This Mark III system was reliable at last until the race, when for the last ten laps Piquet screamed past the pits like a power boat with the car's nose jammed up and its tail still down.

The Imola scrutineers had examined the hydraulic system and approved it, but then dismissed the skirts.

'We said, "Fine, choose an acceptable material"; offered them a selection and they found one they couldn't bend and we put it on. It didn't make much difference to the downforce, just meant we had to make the suspension stiffer to maintain a more consistent ride-height. So we stiffened the springs, put more packers in the suspension to limit wheel movement and the car was the same – just no wheel movement.'

By this time opposition teams were working desperately to match the Brabham effect. Ligier were believed to have adopted a gearbox-switched lowering system which was clearly illegal under the regulation wording. Murray had told Ecclestone '. . . it wasn't right. All this struggling and work to make our systems operate properly, and now some teams were trying to take short cuts which we had avoided because we knew they were illegal.'

A Paris meeting of FISA then issued one of their famous rule clarifications specifying uniform skirts, not more than 6 cm deep and 6 mm thick. Although lowering switches were blatantly illegal they could not be policed, Murray contracted mumps and missed the Belgian race at Zolder and lay at home agonized as he received 'phone calls every day telling me "so-and-so's got a switch, the scrutineers have washed their hands of it, they say you can do what you like, we can't police it".

'At Monaco we put a switch system on one car and kept the fully legal system on the other with a spare new system in the truck. I wanted to put a big notice on the switch saying "Suspension Height Correction Switch" but Bernie wouldn't let me.'

So the season developed in anarchy with every team running switched systems. Piquet threw a Monaco victory away when he crashed under pressure while leading, in Spain Brabham were off the pace but in the points, then when rain interrupted the French GP at Dijon Brabham dibbed-out on tyres.

In the year the cars had gone from some 6.5 in. total wheel movement to 1.5 in. – half of which was provided by the tyres flexing. What had been brought about allegedly by a drivers' plea to ban sliding skirts so as to obtain slower, safer cars resulted in the cars actually shaking themselves and their drivers apart.

After Zolder, Goodyear had returned to the fray as Michelin were not prepared to service everyone much longer and would not give MRD a contract, so Brabham returned to the American company's tyres. But their temporary withdrawal had left them with no experience of these strange new-generation cars and that cost Brabham their chances at Dijon and Silverstone – the French race because at the

restart Goodyear had no tyres soft enough for the final sprint, and the British race due to a tyre failure which put Piquet into the bank. In Montreal, for the Canadian GP, both hard and soft wet tyres were far too hard for the rainswept and bitterly cold conditions.

However, Brabham had only one mechanical failure on Piquet's car, a probable gudgeon pin failure which saw the engine blow up at Monza. However, 'the number of things broken, bent, cracked and shattered on his car after one race – which formerly would have survived several races under higher but more consistent loads with sliding skirts – was incredible. Lifing procedures had to be dramatically revised.'

During the season seven BT49s were used, chassis '7, '9-10-11-12 and '14-15. Piquet and Zunino ran 49B-spec chassis '10 and '7 at Kyalami last time out with sliding skirts, and the new BT49Cs for Long Beach then were '11 and '12 for Piquet and Rebaque, with '9 spare. At Imola, Piquet raced '9, otherwise running '11 until the British GP where it crashed heavily after that tyre failure. New car '14 was ready for him in Germany, and he used it until Canada where new car '15 made its debut and it was in this car that he clinched his Drivers' title at Las Vegas that October.

He had finished eleven of the 15 races, scoring points every time but one, winning in Buenos Aires, Imola and Germany, and elsewhere placing 3-12-3-3-2-'6'-5-5. Team-mate Rebaque attempted all 15 Championship rounds after Zunino's one-off appearance at Kyalami, failed to qualify for Monaco and could only finish five times, 4-9-5-4-4, his fourth places coming in Imola, Germany and Holland.

Brabham ended the season second in the Constructors' Cup with 61 points compared to 95 for Williams.

Meanwhile, a new BT50 car had been completed in mid-season to track-test BMW's new four-cylinder turbocharged Formula 1 engine. In 1982, Brabham's year was dominated by turbocharged BMW engine development and the high spot was winning three races early in the year – two with the DFV and the Canadian GP with Piquet's BMW car leading Patrese's DFV home. That was a considerable feat because the team had to cater logistically for two entirely different cars, the BT49D and turbo BT50.

There was relatively little chassis development during the season apart from changes to their aerodynamic form, the centre of gravity and centre of pressure being in different places between '49D and '50.

The basic aluminium bathtub cum moulded carbon stiffening panel monocoque chassis was

based still on the age-old Alfa Romeo V12 BT48 design which had been altered progressively in length and height. Brabham built many cars to maintain adequate stiffness, testing them for torsional rigidity at regular intervals and retiring old loose tubs, so 1982 was another hectic season for the Chessington build team.

The early-season DFV-powered BT49Ds used new tubs cut down to lower the bodywork which was new with swallow tail, carbon brakes (by the specialist American Hitco company) as standard, in addition to myriad detail improvements. Gordon described the BT49D as a bigger step from the BT49C than the BT49C had been from the basic BT49.

The team had to concentrate prematurely upon the still-troublesome turbocharged BT50 when BMW publicly insisted they do so. These demanded a 47-gallon race fuel load compared to 38 for the naturally aspirated BT49-DFV. BMW engine problems, which centred mainly on the electronic ignition and injection systems, largely ruined the rest of the year. The new engine was some 30 kg (66 lb) heavier than a DFV with all its radiators, heat exchangers and electrics but it was as well that Munich had a full inventory because Brabham consumed 7-8 engines in the French GP meeting. Even that was not a record; a test session at Ricard used up nine, though I understand that only 'about three of them were really big blow-ups'!

The new power and torque of the turbocharged BMW engines created problems with the faithful old Alfa Romeo-cased part-Brabham, part-Hewland transaxles, which had been designed originally for the flat-12 engine in 1976 and since used with V12, V8 and now in-line turbocharged four-cylinder units.

During the season Gordon developed the pit-stop ploy to start on soft, fast tyres and establish a sufficient time cushion for a stop to refuel and fit fresh soft-compound tyres. This also allowed fuel to be expended on cooling the turbocharger and engine, enabling greater boost and race-tune power to be deployed. But on balance Gordon felt that the tactic failed. That year it was only really successful in 'giving our sponsors exposure in races we weren't going to win . . .'

Using a BT49D-DFV, Piquet won at Rio but was disqualified after Renault protested against the use of 'brake-cooling' post-race water ballast and FISA upheld the complaint. His second and final DFV race of the season was at Long Beach where he retired. With the BMW engine he had started in the opening race at Kyalami, then returned to the fray at Zolder to finish fifth. He retired at Monaco, failed to qualify at Detroit, won at Montreal, was second at Zandvoort, then suffered four retirements before reaching fourth at Dijon, concluding the season with two more retirements.

New team-mate Patrese was third with DFV power at Long Beach, won with luck at Monaco and the DFV brought him second at Montreal. He made ten BMW starts, finishing only twice: 15th at Zandvoort and fifth at Dijon in the 'Swiss' GP. Brabham finished fifth in the 1982 Constructors' Cup.

The 1981 prototype 'BT50/1' had formed part of the new Brabham-BMW team at Kyalami, along with two new 1982 cars, '50/2 for Patrese and '3 for Piquet. When the BMW cars were then set aside for further development, much to BMW's public discomfort, 'BT49C/15' was used as team spare, being raced by Patrese at Long Beach. Two new BT49D chassis, '16 and '17, emerged new at Rio for Piquet and Patrese, the latter subsequently crashing his in practice at Long Beach. Chassis '17 was Patrese's Monaco winner, '16 his second-place car at Montreal where 'BT49D/18' was new as spare and not seen again thereafter. The latter was destined to be, with its ultra-low mileage, the last of the long Brabham BT49 line.

BT50 production proceeded with '4 new at

continued on page 129

Piquet's 'BT52/3' at Rio, 1983 Brazilian GP. Lower monocoque is a folded aluminium sheet, black top is moulded carbon composite. Front suspension pushrods had to be more beefy under compression than pullrods which operate under tension.

Final practice, Monaco GP, 1967. Lorenzo Bandini's low-frontal area Ferrari '312/67 001' at the Station Hairpin showing its in-vee snakepit of tuned-length exhausts, and the deep rear monocoque horns supporting the engine and accommodating fuel closer to the centreline than the podgy 1966 cars. Hot radiator air exits through the nose-top ducts, inboard front dampers are cooled from the intake just ahead of the suspension rocker arm, inboard rear brakes from the intake above the Modenese test plate number which allowed the car to be run on the road in Italy. Times have changed since then. Poor Bandini crashed fatally in the race next day, his car destroyed by fire, ostensibly due to driver fatigue after 82 of the 100 laps. The traditional Monaco race distance was shortened to 80 laps the following year.

Top: Ron Tauranac's 1967 Repco Brabham BT24s were light but not that light. Champion Denny Hulme yumps high over the 13.5 km hump at the Nürburgring, on his way to winning the German GP from his team chief. The BT24s were very much the minimum amount of car for the job, yet carried a lot of Goodyear tyre for the size of car. Note the out-turned lip ahead of the front suspension to create a low-pressure area and so extract hot radiator air sideways. The centre-exhaust Repco 740 engine and side-panelled engine-bay to minimize aerodynamic drag can also be seen. Nice cars. *Above:* Graham Hill's Lotus '49B/6' demonstrates the download power of its strutted rear wing at Watkins Glen during the 1968 US GP. Note waving front Firestone, and 49B's characteristic squat under power here increased by download. *Left:* The way it was – Grand Prix racing in a more genteel age: Jimmy Clark, the leading driver of his day, settles into his brand new Lotus '49/2' for the very first time ready for practice to begin at Zandvoort, Dutch GP 1967, with a crowd of 26 people to see it. On Sunday the new car and its Cosworth engine will win their debut Grand Prix, and a new era will have begun for Formula 1.

Formula 1 engines 1966-70 with (*above*) Gurney-Weslake
V12 in Dan's Eagle at Monaco 1967. Note the use of polythene
and rubber pipe, coiled capillary tube against rear cockpit
bulkhead and sinuous tubular rear anti-roll bar curled below
Lucas fuel injection metering unit; throttle linkage also
visible. The Hewland transaxle is protected by that robust
nerf-bar. *Right, from top left to bottom right:* 1967 Lotus 49's
Ford-backed V8 seen in later-season form, with ignition box
moved in-vee from top of ZF transaxle, cam-box external oil
drains still in place. Note beefy final-drive cheek plates added
after French GP distortion, also solid brake discs replacing
original ventilated type. The ultimate 3-litre box of tricks,
BRM's 1966 BRM H16 shows off its two-storey side inlets,
quad-exhausts and hefty starter ring on gearbox tail. Note
wafer-thin brake discs, copper brake pipes along radius rods
and copious polythene piping. Monaco '68 Matra V12's
Pan-pipe exhausts, inlets between cam-boxes and generous
oil de-aerating and catch-tank provision. 1966 wide 90-degree
Honda RA273 V12 deafening its custodians in the Monza
paddock. BRM H16 headaches continue, Monza '67. Honda's
1968 air-cooled RA302 V8 displays its rear-boom monocoque,
engine suspended beneath. BRM's V12 in McLaren's 1967
M5A at Monza, Aeroquip braided aviation hose is coming in.
Brabham's 4-cam 32-valve Repco 860 V8, Monaco '68.
Boxer: 1970-80 Ferrari 312B flat-12,
this is a 1974 unit with cast front tub mounting
instead of original over-boom pick-up. The gearchange tube
runs above right-side head, inlets on top; starter motor and
suspension pick-ups under gearbox on left.

Monaco 1969, strutted wings abruptly banned after first practice, just as some teams were getting to grips with them. *Above:* John Surtees shows off BRM's latest BAC-developed aerofoil aids at Old Gasworks Hairpin; note slender cigar-shaped 'P138/01' full-monocoque hull, centre-exhaust 48-valve V12 and afterthought extra fuel tank. Wing struts act on suspension uprights to load tyres, not suspension, direct. *Left:* After the ban, Stewart hustles through *Mirabeau Inférieur* in his Matra 'MS80-02' without its strutted rear wing and featuring heavily riveted aeronautical monocoque and bulged centre fuel tankage.

Left: Emerson Fittipaldi ran the Lotus 56B-Pratt & Whitney four-wheel drive gas turbine car in only one Formula 1 Grand Prix, at Monza in September 1971. Here he is, whistling into the *Curva Parabolica* at the end of the long straight which Colin Chapman felt would favour the heavy and fuel-bloated car's sustained high-speed preference. Bulged centre-section was necessary to gain GP duration fuel capacity – nearly 60 gallons. Indianapolis heritage is obvious in the door-stop aerodynamic form. The turbine exhaust chimney is behind Emerson's head, cool-air intakes for the sorely over-taxed rear brakes behind that. The car sports same-size Firestone tyres front and rear. *Below left:* Ronnie Peterson showing how in Colin Crabbe's March '701/8', 1970 French GP, Clermont-Ferrand. The car is rigged with the aerofoil-section supplementary 'wing tank' mouldings recommended to designer Robin Herd by Peter Wright of Specialised Mouldings, who originated the idea with BRM in 1968-69. They held handy extra fuel for the longer, thirstier races without added drag. This is the dawn of ground-effects car thinking eight years before Peter made it happen in the Lotus 78/79 underwing forms.

Left: The most successful individual Formula 1 chassis in history, Jackie Stewart's Tyrrell-Cosworth Ford '003' seen here on its way to winning the 1972 French GP, eighth and last of its Championship GP wins. Derek Gardner's impeccably executed design was a study in well-developed conservatism. Notable features include Matra MS80-like 'Coke bottle' tub with 'midships fuel, broad bluff nose minimizing front-wheel lift, moulded body top 'splitter' deflecting hot radiator air around cockpit, tall engine airbox, and fenced and flapped rear wing. Seat belts have been mandatory for three seasons. Arranging mirror visibility was a problem. *Top:* Classic profile – Fittipaldi's Lotus '72/5' winner of the race at Monza 1972, showing low-profile Firestone tyres, hip radiators, sculptured airbox and far-outrigged rear wing and oil tank giving rearward weight bias. The successful 72s were complex and are recalled by their mechanics as 'sods to work on'. *Above:* Changing circuits: Ricard-Castellet became home of the French GP in 1973 and was regarded at the time as 'utensilar'. In the snow-free south of France it became Formula 1's winter test home. Here, McLaren, Lotus, Tyrrell and Brabham nose treatments and frontal areas may be compared as Scheckter leads Stewart, Peterson (eventual winner), Fittipaldi, Reutemann and the rest from the start.

Above: Niki Lauda's 1975 Ferrari '312T-022' about to open out along Ricard-Castellet's one mile Mistral Straight. The dominant Ferrari displays its full-width nose wing, tall, well-sealed airbox and now regulation-overhang fenced rear wing with the mandatory bad weather tail-light beneath. Hot-air exit and cool-air entry ducts betray water and oil cooler positioning. *Left:* The angular planform of the McLaren 'M23/5' at Zandvoort 1974 as Fittipaldi clambers aboard. Note airbox form to clear optimum airflow onto large rear wing, flexible trunking to cool ventilated inboard rear brakes, and rear coil/damper and suspension pick-up frame. Goodyear slick tyres have been carefully selected, matched and marked for Emerson's use.
Following pages: Glorious start of an inglorious German GP at the Nürburgring in 1975. Tall airboxes and aerodynamic aids were in – compare Ferrari's full-width nose wings with white Brabhams' split-radiator noses, blue Tyrrell 007s' finned chisel nose with tyre-fairing end plates and the on-the-verge March 751's F2-derived full bluff nose. Flinty verges caused a puncture plague, Reutemann's Brabham (7) won, Laffite's Williams was second, ensuring the endangered team's survival to achieve greater things.

Derek Gardner's extraordinary six-wheeled Tyrrell Project 34s caused great excitement as they progressed rapidly towards their first GP win in 1976. Here at the site of the old Gasworks Hairpin at Monaco, Patrick Depailler's 'P34-2' leaps over the hump where new Rascasse circuit section joined the old. Note full-faired small-diameter front wheels, the wheel-sighting window let into the cockpit cowl, and enormous protrusion of the standard-sized Goodyear rear tyres. NACA inlet ducts on nose fed trunkings to cool first-axle brakes, the second-axle set being cooled from snorkel intakes just behind.

Above: James Hunt in his McLaren 'M23/8-2' on the charge, as he was throughout 1976, in the controversial Spanish GP at Jarama. He won the race, was disqualified then subsequently reinstated. New airbox rules have slashed its height, there is a forward roll-over bar ahead of the steering wheel, oil coolers are now in the side pods behind water radiators, and vestigial underbody draught-excluding skirts are just visible.

continued from page 112

Zandvoort for Patrese and the final 1982 car, 'BT50/5', new for Piquet at Dijon.

For 1983, Gordon and David North, then designed a brand new BT51 pit-stop ground-effects underwing car with a small tank. However on 3 November 1982, only three months short of the first 1983 GP date, FISA announced an arbitrary ban on underwing devices within the wheelbase and placed a blanket flat-bottom ruling on Formula 1. Existing plans had to be torn up, the BT51 would be dismantled unraced and Gordon and David decided that the only proper approach to the new regulations would be to design and build a totally new car.

Thus the needle-nosed, spearhead-shaped, hip-radiatored, short side pod Brabham-BMW BT52 came into being. It used a typical modern-series Murray monocoque chassis, formed from a single aluminium sheet folded into a trough-section, tied together by very light but rigid one-piece aluminium bulkheads hogged out of the solid at front and rear, with moulded carbon-fibre scuttle and fuel tank top sections. Wide-track front suspension had inboard-mounted coil-spring/damper units operated by pushrods and rockers, and inboard rear suspension was supported on the slim internally webbed (giving a smooth exterior) Brabham transaxle casing. Delta nose fins trimmed out the effect of a big centre-pillar mounted rear wing, and down below behind the back-axle line were neat underwing diffuser surfaces to add a little ground-effect download.

At the end of the year, Gordon reflected: 'We keep catching ourselves out. We convince ourselves that this is the obvious way to go, this is what everybody will be doing so we go flat out to match them. And when we get to the first race everybody else has settled for the easy option, and we're out there on our own and already worn out by the effort.'

Yet Piquet won on the BT52s' debut at Rio, and thereafter Brabham-BMW had what Gordon describes as 'probably our most consistent season since 1974-75. We weren't uncompetitive anywhere, unless in the race we ran too little power or chose the wrong tyres. One satisfying thing was that after laughing at us in '82 when our cars often didn't last until the scheduled pit stop, everybody scrambled to follow us into the pit-stop routine.

'It was fun developing the new car too, but the low points were the stupid disappointments, like losing the lead with a puncture near the end, or a fuel fire near the end, or the driver falling off the road within sight of the finish . . .'

Early on, the gearbox proved a major weakness. American transmission designer Pete Weismann assisted in beefing it up to survive. In Rio the rear radiator concentration cooked the rear dampers. Rearranged ducting fixed that. Their only testing pre-Rio had been at Brands Hatch in the depths of an English winter, hardly ideal preparation for the height of the Brazilian summer!

Paul Rosche's BMW engine group, meanwhile, had progressed in leaps and bounds, the compact little turbocharged engine with its efficient Bosch electro-mechanical management system being competitive mainly in race-tune only until a major stride forward was made in time for the Dutch GP early in the second half of the season, when the 'turbo circuits' follow each other on the calendar.

With 42 or 43 gallons fuel capacity the BT52s could attack only the street-circuit races non-stop with confidence. They had been planned as pit-stop cars, complete with built-in pneumatic jacks and quick-change wheel fixings amongst other features.

Brabham used six BT52s and during the mid-season calendar gap a new BT52B-spec was developed with myriad detail changes including some to stiffen the tub with a more extensive carbon moulded inner 'bathtub'.

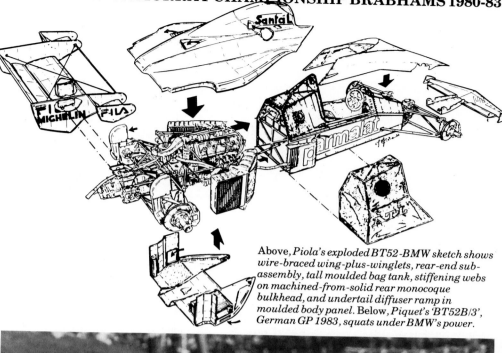

Above, Piola's exploded BT52-BMW sketch shows wire-braced wing-plus-winglets, rear-end sub-assembly, tall moulded bag tank, stiffening webs on machined-from-solid rear monocoque bulkhead, and undertail diffuser ramp in moulded body panel. Below, Piquet's 'BT52B/3', German GP 1983, squats under BMW's power.

Some weight was saved, lighter bulkheads being fitted. New bodywork introduced a revised underbody form and also smoothed out the original body's distinctive front suspension clearance blisters on top of the nose. The early-season dark-blue-on-white livery was also reversed, with white upperworks and dark-blue sides now to emphasize the sponsoring Italian dairy company's 'Parmalat' logos more vividly.

Three original BT52s had been readied in time for their debut in Brazil, in March, while 'BT52/4' was new for Patrese at Imola and was instantly badly bent about the nose moments after taking the race lead. It was repaired within days and raced again at Monaco, performed spare car duties in Montreal and became a show car thereafter.

Meanwhile, 'BT52/1' had been uprated to B-specification after Montreal and was the late-season spare car, being raced by Patrese at Brands Hatch.

The second prototype, 'BT52/2', was new for Patrese at Rio, and became the team's test chassis after the French GP at Ricard which opened the European season. Piquet wrote it off testing at Brands Hatch on 31 August.

Chassis 'BT52/3' was also uprated (like '52/1) to B-spec after Montreal, acting as spare car at Silverstone and Hockenheim where it was raced by Piquet and effectively written off by the fire which ended his race there. BMW had

used an off-the-shelf production type in-line fuel filter and this particular one just happened to have a casting imperfection in its alloy bowl; it split under engine vibration, dribbled fuel out into the airstream and this spray was then ignited by turbo flame on the over-run.

Meanwhile for Silverstone two brand new BT52Bs had been completed. Chassis '5 was Piquet's car, in which he won the Italian and European GPs and clinched his title at Kyalami, while chassis 'BT52B/6' appeared new in late-season for Patrese, in which he won the South African GP.

It had been a dramatic season, with the Brabham-BMWs suffering all kinds of niggling failures, Piquet twice going out with throttle linkage problems. At last at Zandvoort BMW's newfound power and a typically painstakingly prepared Gordon Murray lightweight qualifying special were enough to slam him straight onto pole position, but Prost put him off during the race in a minor collision. Prost had at that stage looked to have the Drivers' title sewn up, but the rest of his season simply fell apart while the BT52-BMWs went from strength to strength.

Brabham and BMW had had their problems, but the Drivers' Championship is the one which the public at large know about, and Ferrari's Constructors' Championship title was small beer in comparison – unless you happened to be Italian.

Brabham Fan-Car

During the early part of 1978 when Lauda and Watson were proving just how competitive the Brabham-Alfa Romeo BT46s could be against all but the new ground-effects Lotus 78/79 series, Gordon Murray and his right-hand man David North wrestled with the problems of designing a ground-effects car around the wide, low-level Alfa '115-12' flat-12 engine. Its heads projected obstructively into the precise area where ground-effect venturi tunnels should be sited.

They investigated mounting the engine in the front, then putting the fuel tank behind the engine, sandwiched ahead of the gearbox. It would have worked that way, but the multiple joints involved would have made it very heavy and handling changes between full and empty would have been spectacular.

In desperation they re-read the regulations, and spotted a loophole under which an extractor fan could be used to reduce air-pressure beneath the car so long as its 'primary function' was not 'aerodynamic' in the Formula 1 sense. In other words, it could be claimed that its primary function was to draw air through a radiator to cool the engine, rather than being intended to affect the performance of the car generated from its motion through the air.

They had already used a small fan in a panic attempt to cool the BT45C's horizontal oil matrices above the engine in South America, though there was no real link between the two ploys.

The fan-car device became a most celebrated case of rule-bending, for drawing air through a radiator is still literally an 'aerodynamic' function, unless my grasp of the English language is at fault, but even today its creator insists it was utterly legal. Indeed, it was declared so by the racing authorities, after its further use had been effectively banned by a change in their regulation wording.

So the famous Brabham BT46B fan-car came about. The initial idea had occurred around Kyalami time, which is very early in the season – hard evidence of Murray's remarkable perception. The team's 40-odd staff at Chessington set about building two cars for Monaco. All the bits were made and ready, but skirt and fan development delayed their race debut. At last, two cars – modified chassis 'BT46/6' and '4 – appeared in the Swedish GP which Lauda won while Watson also shone.

The BT46B emerged with a large horizontal water radiator above its engine, the whole engine bay area being sealed against ambient pressure infill underneath by flexible skirts extending down to the road surface with sections even sealing the slots in which driveshafts and suspension arms rose and fell. Massive effort went into finalizing skirt, fan and radiator.

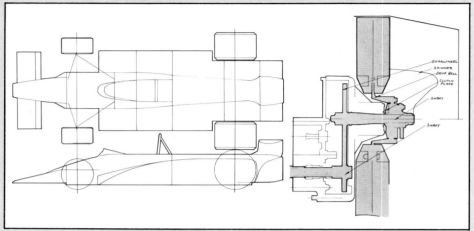

Top left, *fan, exhausts and engine-bay rear sealing skirt at Anderstorp, '78;* top right, *the horizontal water radiator which justified the fan;* above, *schematic drawing of the BT46B fan-car and fan mechanism;* below, *the Dunlop puck-type carbon brakes pioneered in Formula 1 by Brabham in 1976.*

Thermodynamics consultant David Cox calculated the number of fan blades, pitch and optimum rotational speed required. Typically, Murray and North agonized over potential problems and sought to design them out right from the start.

The fan drive was taken from the gearbox lower shaft, but this would have created an H16 BRM-like problem if direct drive had been employed, since the inertia of the fan making the gearbox input shaft run on while the driver fought to slow it down sufficiently to find another gear could create some grief.

Therefore a sprag clutch was fitted at the back of the gearbox to uncouple the fan as the driver kicked-out the clutch proper. To avoid a nasty pit accident a cut-out device was also added to enable the mechanics to disengage the fan with the engine ticking over.

A spur-gear drive train was necessary to raise the fan hub sufficiently to accommodate fan blades of reasonable radius. The problem of a racing start shock-loading the fan drive led to another friction-plate clutch going into the fan-hub assembly.

Brands Hatch testing then showed surprisingly there was *no* need for either the sprag clutch or pit disengagement devices, as the gearchange seemed unaffected even when the sprag locked solid.

But the original plastic fans disintegrated. Glass-fibre filled fans disintegrated as well. Within a week of the Swedish GP magnesium fan blades were cast and new hubs machined from the solid. Only three were ready in time.

Skirt sealing at the sides and rear had caused no problem, but the front lateral skirt ahead of the engine bay caused endless headaches until David North devised a brilliant system involving two stitched sailcloth sausage bags with a system of coinciding edged holes which enabled the 'bags' to be inflated by under-chassis airflow and then remain inflated against pressure and road surface changes which tried to force them clear of the roadway.

The first day's practice at Anderstorp wore away this complex front skirt, but Brabham's men fitted a skid on its leading edge for the second day and thereafter it worked superbly well.

Even sitting in the pit lane the cars would squat down when the throttle was blipped and the fan revved, but five teams protested its legality even before Lauda and Watson qualified 2-3 behind a Lotus 79. The Austrian won the race, showering dust and grit from the fan efflux in his car's wake.

Before the next race, the fabulous fan-car and any and all successors using that system were henceforth banned from competition, although the Swedish result was confirmed and the fan-car itself never declared illegal.

And most regarded Gordon Murray and David North with reconfirmed, rather awed, respect.

Below, *BT46B, showing 1, air-speed pitot; 2, underside ASI; 3, plastic skirts; 4, water radiator; 5, brake cooling; 6, rear upright air-seal slide; 7, engine-bay seal skirts; 8, exhaust efflux; 9, fan.*

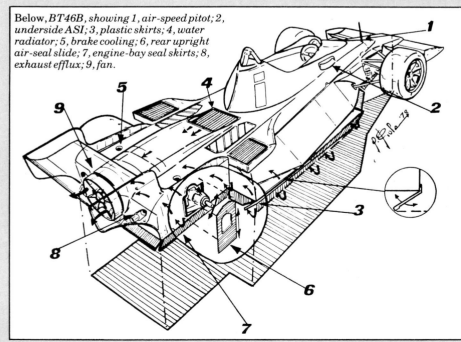

Chapter 14

THE TURBOCHARGED FERRARI 126Cs, 1981-83

While the Ferrari 312T4 was accumulating World Championship points so reliably during 1979, work began at Maranello on its long-term replacement – the first forced-induction Ferrari for nearly 30 years – and on 9 June 1980 the first prototype turbocharged Ferrari 126C was unveiled at the *Pista di Fiorano*. Renault's pioneering efforts to take advantage of the supercharged clause in Formula 1 had – as described in the Team Directory – gone off at half-cock in 1977-78 but, after winning Le Mans and ridding their system of that primary target in 1979, Renault Sport had concentrated its resources on Formula 1 and had begun winning by mid-season. As their turbo V6 became competitive so it became obvious that this was the way to go. Turbocharging, and construction of the specialized racing engines demanded by it for Formula 1, threatened almost prohibitive expense. Yet the potential for 650-plus horsepower when the very best atmospherically aspirated 3-litre could offer little more than perhaps 530 bhp (though Cosworth users talked of much less) was irresistible.

During 1979, Ferrari showed interest in building a turbocharged Formula 1 car, and, in collaboration with Brabham, BMW of Munich would soon follow suit.

Ferrari's engine group at Maranello was headed by veteran engineers Franco Rocchi and Walter Salvarani, assisted by Angiolino Marchetti, all answering to Chief Engineer Mauro Forghieri. Having studied the requirement in detail, they evolved a new 120-degree V6-cylinder engine, on which they tested three alternative forced-induction systems. Two involved conventional exhaust-driven turbochargers made by Kühnle, Kopp und Kausch of Germany, or by Garrett AiResearch of America, while the third featured a Swiss belt-driven mechanical pressure-wave supercharger developed by Brown Boveri & Co.

The new V6 owed only its 120-degree included angle between the cylinder banks to any previous Ferrari V6, while its double overhead camshaft four-valve-per-cylinder, single-plug cylinder heads derived from recent flat-12 practice.

The V6 offered several advantages over alternative V8 and four-cylinder studies. With each cylinder bank only 'three cylinders long' not only the block but also the crankshaft and camshafts could be shorter and much stiffer.

With fewer moving parts than a V8 it offered lower friction loss, while compared to a four-cylinder the reduced surface area of each individual piston promised less thermal trouble yet potentially provided greater piston area in total. The wide-angle vee provided plenty of space between inlet cam covers to accommodate the turbochargers and electronic ignition and fuel injection equipment. In addition, the V6's relatively narrow base chamber left plenty of space each side for unobstructed ground-effects undersurface tunnels, quite unlike the old flat-12.

All engine castings were in light alloy and the four valves per cylinder were actuated by double overhead camshafts per bank, gear-driven from the crankshaft nose. Where the flat-12's bore and stroke dimensions at that time were 80 mm x 49.6 mm, the new V6 had a wider bore and shorter stroke, 81 mm x 48.4 mm, to displace 249.4 cc per cylinder, aggregating 1496.43 cc overall.

To accommodate the boost available from the prototype car's German-made Kühnle, Kopp und Kausch ('KKK') exhaust-driven turbochargers, compression ratio was low, at 6.5:1. Ferrari's published performance figures claimed only 540 bhp at 11,000 rpm, compared to the quoted 510 bhp (but probably more) at 12,000 rpm of the contemporary 'T5-tune flat-12. More significantly, at 7500 rpm the turbocharged 1500 delivered 100 bhp more than the flat-12 at that speed . . .

To provide the unit with accurately metered fuel/air charge throughout the revolution and turbocharger boost ranges, Ferrari had worked closely with Lucas and Magnetti Marelli on their fuel injection and latest 'Digiplex' electronic ignition systems.

Renault had already made two major advances with their turbocharged Formula 1 cars. The first was the age-old step of intercooling the compressed charge before it entered the engine, to retrieve worthwhile density. The second was the adoption of two small turbochargers – one per bank – instead of one big one, to reduce each unit's rotating mass and inertia and so improve its response to throttle

Arnoux at Hockenheim in 1983 with 126C '066', showing its abbreviated flat-bottom era side pods, pit-stop filler, in-line coolers, prominent front brake-ducts and massive rear wing.

131

demand from the driver. This diminished the famous turbocharger problem of throttle lag – the delay between the driver opening the throttle and the turbochargers winding up sufficient boost to answer his call.

Brown Boveri's approach with their 'Comprex' pressure-wave supercharging system was quite different from these conventional turbochargers. Although the Comprex system was aimed mainly at diesel engines, Brown Boveri were at this time interested in promoting its use for small passenger cars, hence the promotional R&D link with Fiat-Ferrari.

The Comprex unit was driven not by exhaust gas flow but by an engine drive-belt and as such its output was directly proportional to instantaneous engine revs rather than exhaust gas flow. The Comprex system did however rely upon interaction with the exhaust gas pressure waves for the charge compression which it then delivered to the induction manifold. Its use by Ferrari was massively publicized, BB looking for widespread adoption of their system by production industry. It didn't happen.

This system displayed far better throttle response than the turbochargers during early testing, but the conventional KKK set-up always offered more power, more reliably, and in this form the car was generally quicker.

The first prototype 126C took chassis number '049' in the long Formula 1 Ferrari chassis series originated in 1969. The chassis monocoque was a slender nacelle skinned in riveted aluminium sheet in Lotus 79/Ferrari 'T5-style. To provide adequate stiffness with the smaller nacelle cross-section, a fairly hefty internal frame structure supported the external skins.

Fuel was carried in a single cell in the rear of this slimline tub, which had an octagonal section, elongated towards the top.

Heavily triangulated lower front wishbone pick-ups were built into the angles of the internal frame diagonal tubes which braced the side bays of the tub's forward section. A cast crossbeam built into the top of the tub provided forward pivots for the fabricated top rocker arms, while the rearward pivot bearings sat in tubular braces just behind.

The new V6 engine formed a fully stressed chassis member, while the *trasversale* transmission casing just behind accepted all rear suspension loads. Not even a radius rod reached forward to load the monocoque directly, although a steady bar on each side linked the rear suspension's forward top link

pivot to the engine.

Rear suspension featured inboard coil-spring/damper units as at the front, here tucked tight against the gearbox flanks and actuated by hefty fabricated top rocker arms. Location was by wide-based lower wishbones with the rocker arm and forward-mounted lateral link providing toe-in adjustment up top.

The gearbox itself was a beefed-up version of the immensely successful *trasversale*, now with a choice of five- or six-speed internals. The very short engine, only three cylinders long instead of six as in the flat-12, meant a lengthy spacer could be accommodated between engine and transaxle, in 'British style'.

Brembo – more familiar in the motor cycle world at that time but keen to break into Formula 1 – provided the heavily ventilated disc brakes, and were capable of lightning-fast reaction to Ferrari requirements. These were mounted all round to clear underwing airflow and were buried within the Speedline bolt-together split-rim wheels.

Bodywork comprised a one-piece top section-cum-cockpit surround, a detachable engine cover shaped as a semi-fin ahead of the centre-strutted rear wing, and a separate needle-nosepiece with the nose wing formed around it rather than sitting on top as had been Ferrari's style for 6½ years.

The side pods housed the water (on the left side) and oil coolers (on the right) in similar raked-forward mounts to those of the 312T4 and 'T5, with the new turbocharger intercooler matrices set square behind them. The outer pod boxes housed fashionable spring-loaded sliding skirts with abrade-resistant bottom edges. Upper pod decks flared out from the nose and windscreen area to mimic the successful 'T4-originated download shape. They were relieved with neat hot air exit ducts serving the various coolers on each side, before running smoothly back alongside the engine to feed clean air beneath the rear wing. Moulded flick-ups did their best to fair-in the rear wheels and their Michelin tyres.

Voluminous cool air intake ducts for the brakes protruded from the front wheels and up above the rear end of the pod upper decks.

Dimensions released at the time of the 126C's launch – Mr Ferrari insisting that the 'C' stood for *Corsa* ('Racing') not *Compressore* ('Supercharger') as would have seemed logical – were as follows: wheelbase, 2719 mm; front track, 1761 mm; rear track, 1626 mm; overall length, 4468 mm; overall width, 2110 mm; height, 1025 mm, weight, 600 kg (1322.76 lb).

In fact the prototype 126C, chassis '049', would not appear in public until that September when it ran in practice for the Italian GP at Imola. By that time it had completed 10 weeks

of serious testing between the Formula 1 team's race commitments with their sadly neglected 'T5 flat-12s. Chassis '049 was driven by Villeneuve during Imola practice, merely to keep him interested and to keep faith with the Italian *tifosi* because there was no intention of racing the car.

The irrepressible Villeneuve gave it all he had, lapping in 1:35.751, faster than in his flat-12 'T5.

The new car had by this time been modified with swept-forward front suspension arms lengthening the wheelbase and increasing rearward weight distribution. Its intercoolers were now mounted vertically rather than raked, a vertical rather than horizontal wastegate nestled into the turbocharger plumbing within the vee, and the original semi-fin engine cover had been replaced by a smoothly faired cover sloping down at the rear like the Boxers'.

During the winter of 1980/81, while the political squabbling between FISA and FOCA intensified, Scheckter had retired and Frenchman Didier Pironi took his place alongside Villeneuve.

Their Fiorano test programme proved that the 126C was extremely fast but hard on brakes, thirsty for fuel and still lacking mechanical reliability. Due to the political storm then raging it was unclear whether or not sliding skirts would be permitted in 1981. Scheckter's skirted Fiorano lap record in a 'T5 stood at 1;08.74, and Villeneuve's best unskirted 126C time, set on 11 January 1981, was 1;10.19. Using Comprex supercharging the French-Canadian clocked 1;10.61, before public testing commenced at Ricard-Castellet.

Ferrari boycotted the South African GP which was run by FOCA as a 'skirted' race, so the 126Cs' career commenced at Long Beach in March. Brown Boveri's Comprex R&D chief Tony Köllbrunner believed his supercharger could shine on this stop-go street circuit where crisp throttle response was more significant than peak power. The Comprex installation could be distinguished externally by its simpler exhaust system with a large oval-section megaphone emerging above a gearbox heat shield just ahead of the rear wing.

Bodywork design had been refined during this preliminary test programme, the 'T4-like forward tray being replaced by a slimmer cockpit surround with simple flares over the top front suspension pivots. The side pods were reprofiled, with top vents formed by three airfoil-section vanes either side of the cockpit before running back into smooth, unbroken decks midway along the tank bay. Unbroken top deck, side-vented side pods had already been tested and they would become standard from the next race in Brazil.

At Fiorano, Pironi established a 'T5 baseline time of 1;08.96, to which Villeneuve responded with 1;08.469 in a skirted 126C, and both drivers managed 1;10.2 in an unskirted Comprex car. Pironi lapped Ricard in 1;05.67 compared to the best time of 1;04.77 set by Giacomelli's skirted Alfa Romeo V12 179C.

Both Comprex and KKK variants were tried during practice at Long Beach, the quieter Comprex versions – known initially by Ferrari as the 126BBC but later reclassified as 126CX – proved slower than the KKK turbocharged 126CK version with its distinctively vicious over-run crackle. Both race cars, chassis '049 and '051, used the German turbos, and while the Comprex would appear again in practice for the Brazilian and Argentine GPs it would never be raced, Ferrari concentrating upon the KKK turbos thereafter.

From the start of practice at Long Beach it was evident that the KKK-turbocharged Ferraris would become a real threat once they were adequately sorted out. Reliability was poor in their first three races, the cars retiring each time, though on one occasion this was due to collision. They were also too heavy at 610 kg (1345 lb) and handling was poor, not matching

Piola reveals details of Postlethwaite's aluminium-honeycomb 1982 126C2; 1, bracketed blade wing; 2, footbox; 3, top rocker-arm; 4, rocker pivot brace; 5, wide-based lower wishbone; 6, pedal access; 7, scuttle top; 8, brake duct; 9, protective high tub side; 10, side pod air-entry cowl; 11, honeycomb composite side panel; 12, intercooler; 13, inlet plenum; 14, fuel cell section; 15, skirtbox; 16, exhaust; 17, turbo intake; 18, KKK turbo; 19, wastegate vent pipe; 20, brake duct; 21, gearbox oil cooler; 22, rear anti-roll bar; 23, rear suspension rocker-pivot support plate; 24, suspension rocker; 25, brake calliper; 26, engine breather; 27, bell-housing; 28, wing-post.

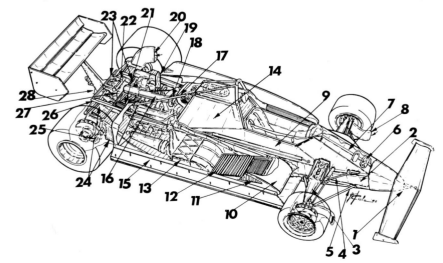

the latest generation of Williams and Brabham 'clearance cars' which by this time were developing lowering suspensions to retrieve ground-effects download.

Six 126C-series cars would be built that season. The first trio numbered '049, '050, '051 were virtually identical in structure, but the follow-up trio of '052, '053, '054 were considerably modified around the front end, with an additional protective box section built ahead of the original pedal-box. Skinning around the inboard coil/damper housings was different and the top rocker arm pivot pick-ups were redesigned and fabricated in weight-saving titanium.

The first batch of three cars was then completely rebuilt, particularly around the front end, into a 'B-specification' which extended the new protective nose crush-structure the full depth of the tub; and raised a completely enclosed scuttle structure high above the driver's shins and feet, right up around the dash panel roll-over bar. Further to stiffen the chassis, sheet fillets were added along either side of the cockpit opening.

The front rocker arm pick-ups were faired into the tub fore and aft with sheet metal. At the end of the season, during final tests at Ricard-Castellet prior to the introduction of the all-new honeycomb structure 126C2 design, the original cars' cockpit area was further stiffened and protected by the addition of higher built-up sides.

The new 126Cs had emerged as follows, '050 and '051 at Long Beach, '052 at Imola – where Pironi scored the type's first Championship points by finishing fifth while Villeneuve qualified on pole and led the race – '053 at Jarama and '054 at Silverstone.

More by luck, plus Villeneuve's intense application and irrepressible competitiveness, the underdeveloped cars actually won two Grand Prix races, at Monaco and in Spain after faster runners had dropped out. Though powerful and quick out of corners, the cars remained notoriously ill-handling and prone to bouncing as Ferrari's efforts to apply lowering suspension systems à la Brabham created untold problems. At Zolder, for example, Villeneuve's suspensions lowered correctly, but during the race the front end popped up and jammed there, the car hurtling round nose-high like a power boat. Its driver persevered apparently unconcerned, foot flat as ever . . . Nor was this problem confined to Ferrari: system-innovators Brabham had suffered similarly while winning at Imola.

The cars made 30 starts in that season's 15 World Championship GPs, winning two, and adding one third place, two fourths, three fifths, a seventh, an eighth, two ninths, a tenth and a fifteenth place finish. The team's 16 retirements included five accidents and 11 mechanical failures – four apparent piston or other internal problems, two turbocharger failures, two driveshaft breakages and one each involving the electrical, injection and lubrication systems.

By midway through 1981, the British brigade were looking enviously at the power and general reliability of the Renault and Ferrari turbo engines, and while they did not fear Renault's fragile organization, they knew how capable Ferrari could be should they climb back onto the competitive tightrope.

Just as Ferrari had caught up with British state-of-the-art Formula 1 chassis manufacture in 1963 by hiring John Surtees and Mike Parkes, so they did it again in 1981-82 by hiring Dr Harvey Postlethwaite, and the opposition's fears crystallized. 'All it needs', they were saying, 'is for Harvey Postlethwaite to give them a halfway decent chassis, and we won't see which way they've gone . . .' In Constructors' Championship terms, that is exactly what happened in 1982.

To hear an Italian trying to pronounce Harvey's surname is to fear for his life as

'Pozelytwyte' tends to cause choking. Consequently he became known in the factory as 'Harraveee', and quaintly elsewhere in nearby Modena as 'Mr Thompson' – his wife Cherry's maiden name.

With Wolf in 1978 he had introduced the folded aluminium-honeycomb sandwich form of construction taken up so notably by his former Wolf-Williams assistant Patrick Head in the Williams FW07 of 1979, and with his knowledge of British carbon-fibre developments and aerodynamic study he would bring Ferrari out of what one other English engineer rather dismissively described as 'the aerodynamic dark ages'.

The honeycombs used were to Ferrari specification: two thin sheets of aluminium stabilized by sandwiching internal foil honeycomb, to which the skins were carefully bonded. Postlethwaite's 1978 Wolf and the descendant Fittipaldi of 1980 had used honeycomb tub panels folded into channel sections like a 'U' laid on its side, the two reclining 'U's then being bonded together down a centreline joint to form the finished tub.

While the 126C series went through its progressive stiffening process, six months or more were spent just establishing facilities for the new technology at Maranello, designing and installing autoclave pressure ovens to cook and cure honeycomb bonds and carbon-fibre composites. The American Hexcel company's European division based in Belgium supplied materials and performed bonding operations on panels too large for Maranello to instal the specialized press tools required. Once set up, production of the first 126C2 chassis at Maranello took about a month. Further into the 1982 season, Ferrari could crack-out a new tub in 1½ days.

The 126C2 tubs emerged using the Postlethwaite form of construction; two channel-section honeycomb folds being united along the centreline, with carbon-fibre bulkheads inserted to stiffen it all.

Again the tub section was octagonal, as in the riveted-sheet 126C, but it was now lower and had a forward-sloping upper half to the rear closing bulkhead behind the central tank cell, whereas on the 126C this bulkhead had been vertical throughout its height. This minor reshaping enabled the heavy in-vee turbochargers and their plumbing to be moved forward.

The cockpit was high-sided, the sides merging into an all-enclosed dash panel surround and forepart which tapered smoothly into the integral footbox-cum-crush structure in the nose to protect the driver.

The various honeycomb panels were bonded together so this was a shiny aluminium Ferrari tub without a rivetline in sight. It was claimed

Top, *Villeneuve demonstrates Ferrari 126CK 052's dreaded bounce in 1981 at Jarama, Spanish GP, which he won by allowing potentially quicker pursuers no room to get by. Above, Villeneuve and '052 again, this time winning at Monaco. This uncomplicated car was intended to free engine development time; what Ferrari needed was a decent chassis to match their powerful V6 engine.*

to be 4.8 kg (10.58 lb) lighter than the 126C's.

At the rear the further developed 126C V6 engine was retained as a fully-stressed structural member accepting rear suspension loads. Suspension mounting was now lighter than before, using a shaped dural plate to pick up the rear ends of the rocker arm pivots and doubling as foundation for the rear wing post.

Front suspension was along broad 126C lines, with top rocker arm pivots sandwiched between lateral beams built into the honeycomb monocoque and braced forward to anchorages on the tub by jointed tubular rods.

Once again, water radiators and incoming-charge air-to-air intercoolers resided in the rear halves of the side pods, with shaped underwings moulded into a one-piece undertray – replacing the original two-piece design – underneath them. Hot air exhausting from the various coolers exited through louvred slots cut into the pod sides.

The nose treatment was new, with the full-width wing neatly strutted above the nose instead of being split by it as in the 126C. The *trasversale* gearbox again had provision for a sixth gear if necessary, and fairing panelling enclosed the bottom of the engine and extended either side of the transmission casing to the rear of the car, with neat slots in it to allow the driveshafts to emerge.

Dimensions released for the prototype 'C2 were as follows: wheelbase, 2657.8 mm; front track, 1787.4 mm; rear track, 1644 mm; overall length, 4333 mm; overall width, 2110 mm; overall height, 1025 mm; weight c. 595 kg (1311.74 lb).

The new car looked superb. It was quite neat and tidy compared to its predecessor and was beautifully made in most details. The team commenced their second full season of turbocharged Formula 1 racing using uprated 126C chassis '049B as spare in the first race at Kyalami, South Africa, where 126C2s '055 and '056 emerged brand new.

During the season, two of the cars were destroyed when Pironi crashed them in testing accidents at Ricard-Castellet, these being '055 soon after its Kyalami debut and its sister '056 later in the year. Both were heavy impacts in which the French driver escaped serious harm. Two new cars '057 and '058 appeared at Rio de Janeiro, the latter being tragically ill-fated. Chassis '059 emerged brand new for Pironi at Zolder and another new car '060 appeared for his use at Zandvoort. French driver Patrick Tambay joined the team in mid-season and he debuted '061 at Brands Hatch.

For the Maranello factory, the early part of the season was spent merely building cars. Engine installation changes were many and varied. Different radiator, heat-exchanger and ancillary mounts absorbed immense time and effort. The spark-box alone, Postlethwaite told me late in the year, 'chased around the cars like a frightened rabbit!'

The season was riven by a fatal accident to Villeneuve during practice for the Belgian GP at Zolder, 13 days after he and team-mate Pironi had fallen out at Imola. There, against meagre opposition – for the race was boycotted by ten FOCA teams in dispute with the FISA governing body – Pironi had won. However, Villeneuve had been leading before, as he saw it, his team-mate had disregarded team

instructions and pit signals and taken over the lead and clung onto it, holding him off.

At Zolder, the still-smarting longer-serving *Ferrarista* was on his last qualifying lap, desperate to better Pironi's time when he collided with a slow-moving March. His 'C2, chassis '058, planed off the March's right-rear wheel and cartwheeled at high speed. Its first impact with the ground saw it jam its nose into yielding sand which trapped the tub's forepart and broke the chassis in two as the massive inertia of engine and gearbox flailed the tail over. The seatback bulkhead ripped out, along with the unfortunate driver's seat harness mounts, and he was fatally injured.

Such chassis disintegration was widely criticized, but Postlethwaite and his Maranello study group subsequently attempted to reproduce similar damage on a tub section test rig, and the forces required to achieve it proved far higher than had ever previously been considered possible in racing. The 126C2 design had already absorbed some extremely heavy, but conventional, horizontal-trajectory impacts at Ricard and what happened at Zolder was one of those killer-freaks which burst upon the scene perhaps once in ten years. It seemed unlikely that anything similar could happen again . . .

Critics of aluminium honeycomb construction held that, in order to save weight compared to conventional alloy-sheet, honeycomb sandwich skins had to be less than half as thick as the standard single-thickness panels. It was thought that these very thin skins would be likely to split and tear under heavy impact. Postlethwaite, Head and the other aluminium users believed otherwise . . .

After Villeneuve's death, Ferrari understandably non-started in the Belgian race, but reappeared at Monaco with a one-car entry for Pironi who raced '059 and almost scored a fortunate win, inheriting the lead on the penultimate lap before last-lap electrical failure then killed his engine and he was classified second. Then came Detroit and the Canadian GP and the debut of the pullrod suspension modification.

One major early problem with the 'C2s was sheer tyre consumption. The team had returned to Goodyear after four seasons with Michelin and initially the contemporary American-made tyres and the Italian chassis did not seem well matched. This was certainly not a weight-related problem as the new cars were tight against the new minimum weight

limit, and with test miles accumulating the problems were rapidly resolved. Meanwhile Brabham and Williams amongst other teams had proved the efficacy of suspension systems in which the inboard coil/damper units were actuated by lightweight pullrods and rocker links in place of the hefty conventional top rocker arm system. Just before the Detroit GP in mid-season, Ferrari adopted their own pullrod system for the front suspension.

The sliding-skirt system ban of 1981 had produced cars in which tyre sidewall deflection was virtually the sum total of suspension travel. Massive aerodynamic forces had to be endured, and in cars of this type the rocker arms themselves had begun to act like undamped springs. They had in any case to be massive fabrications to support enormous downloads, and so they had become both bulky and heavy with their large frontal area generating wasteful aerodynamic drag.

At a stroke, the pullrod system removed the need for this heavy, draggy component and also offered easy and useful rising-rate geometry. Now, upper location of the wheel upright could be entrusted to simple wishbones, which could be formed from aerodynamically-efficient tube if required since there was no longer a massive bending load to be sustained only simple end loads. With these wishbones slim and light to save drag and weight, only the wheel and tyre remained as undamped springs worth worrying about within the suspension system.

This massive increase in front-end rigidity transformed the feel of the 126C2s. If Pironi had not stalled and become involved in a massive startline accident at Montreal the team felt he would have 'walked the race, no problem'. Thereafter, the cars were redesigned around the pullrod suspension as an integral standard fitting rather than a bolt-on go-faster modification.

The first of these so-called 'B-specification' 126C2s was chassis '062 which was built pullrod from the ground up for Tambay in the Swiss GP meeting at Dijon-Prenois, while '063 and '064 followed by year's end.

Meanwhile the transmission study group had produced a new longitudinal gearbox to assist ground-effect underwing devices by replacing the wider but reliable and effective *trasversale*. This new longitudinal gearbox was used extensively in testing and practice late in the year but it was never raced.

Popular French driver Patrick Tambay joined Pironi in the team for the Dutch GP at Zandvoort where Pironi won handsomely in '060's race debut. The cars were consistently competitive now, finishing 2-3 in Britain and 3-4 in France, and Pironi looked to have the Drivers' Championship at his mercy when he suffered grievous career-ending leg injuries in wet practice at Hockenheim, in a near carbon-copy of Villeneuve's accident, which demolished 'C2 '061.

Tambay and the team responded brilliantly by winning the German GP next day, using chassis '060. The new-boy was then fourth in Austria but the G-forces in modern Formula 1 pinched a nerve in his neck and he was unable to start in the Swiss GP at Dijon-Prenois, which ran without Ferrari in consequence.

Mr Ferrari then invited Andretti to rejoin the team for the Italian GP at Monza, and the former World Champion repaid him handsomely by setting '061 on pole there and finishing third behind Tambay's second-placed '062B. The Frenchman was again unable to start the final race, at Las Vegas, where Andretti suffered one of the 'C2's too-prevalent suspension failures and retired in '061.

All development work on the cars suffered a major setback with Pironi's Hockenheim accident. Thereafter the direction changed and the priority was solely to play-in the team's new drivers and generally salvage the best they could from this shattered season. Everybody responded superbly, from Tambay and

This 126C2's trasversale *gearbox was replaced experimentally by the in-line transmission here. Note carbon-composite underwings, rear suspension, 'top-heavy' V6 with turbos in-vee.*

Andretti to the most junior team member at Maranello, and the reward was Ferrari's fifth Formula 1 Constructors' Championship title in eight seasons, and the first ever for a turbocharged engine. They won the title with a total of 61 points to McLaren's 54 – modest consolation after the most bitter adversity.

Overall the team had made only 22 starts in the season's 16 World Championship Grand Prix races, running only a single car in the Monaco, Detroit, Canadian, German, Austrian and Las Vegas GPs and failing to compete at all in the Belgian and 'Swiss' events. Even so, they won three of the 14 GPs which they did start and added four second places, five thirds, two fourths, three eighths and one ninth-place finish. The team's four retirements involved three accidents and Andretti's rear suspension failure at Las Vegas but no engine failures.

During the winter of 1982/83 a major revolution took place within Formula 1. On 3 November 1982 the FISA Technical Commission voted through an instant ban on ground-effects underwing tunnel forms, and slapped a flat-bottom requirement on Formula 1.

Ferrari had been planning their Constructors' Championship title defence around a highly-developed 126C3 design which was intended to replace the successful if ill-starred 'C2. Forghieri's engine group developed a water-injection system in conjunction with the AGIP fuel company, in search of more power. This proved a contentious ploy.

Compressing a gas, as in a turbocharger system, heats it up. Hot gas is less dense than cold, so it is normal for racing engineers to use an intercooler – either gas/air or gas/water – to lower the temperature of the newly-compressed charge on its way into the engine. With water injection, evaporation of the water droplets within the incoming charge cools it still further. Density increases and charge capacity is enhanced. The more charge the engineer can force in and the more the engine can burn, the more power it will produce. By reducing the temperature build-up inevitable with boost compression, water injection permits higher boost to be sustained and really substantial power gains result.

Ferrari and Renault would run their own versions of this system but BMW, whose turbocharged engines were now powering the Brabham cars, were doubtful of its legality, mindful of the Formula 1 regulation which banned fuel additives and regarding water as just that. Ferrari and Renault meanwhile counter-claimed that water injection was not a matter of employing water as an 'additive', merely as a 'coolant'. It was all a question of 'primary function' and Formula 1 had been up that particular path before in 1978 with the Brabham fan-car and the primary function of its 'engine-cooling' fan. Significantly, 'primary function' was a phrase which had been excised from contemporary Formula 1 regulations because of the arguable freedom it could admit on so many factors. The major manufacturers had some political clout, after all . . .

Quite apart from these controversial water-injection developments, Ferrari had built up a ground-effects interim test hack 126C3 prototype, based on an existing 'C2 aluminium-honeycomb monocoque, before the rule changes were confirmed.

This prototype used the longitudinal transaxle developed by the five-man transmission group during 1982. In Fiorano tests it proved 'an absolute *bomba*' according to Postlethwaite. Yet the flat-bottom rule change killed that concept stone dead, and the car was dismantled.

At this point the medium-range strategic decision was taken to modify existing honeycomb 'C2Bs to flat-bottom specification, while the forthcoming new 126C3 design was completely rethought and redrawn around an all-new monocoque which would be moulded in very light, very rigid, carbon-composite mate-

rials. Consequently the first half of 1983 saw Ferrari racing modified 'C2 honeycomb cars, while Postlethwaite's latest carbon-composite 'C3 was finalized.

Through 1982 Ferrari had adopted new technology to produce their honeycomb 'C2s. At Christmas they had moved their *Reparto Corse* – racing division – into its new purpose-built factory and headquarters building, partly on the old works car park directly across the main Formigine-Maranello road from the production car factory. There the administration and drawing office building was combined with its machine- and race-shop complex, while a covered walkway connected with a separate engine design and test house building across the courtyard.

Mr Ferrari had listened patiently to his engineers' requirements for carbon-fibre composite processing plant. To ensure even distribution of the matrix resins through the basic lay-ups of woven cloth, vacuum-bags and pressurized ovens known as 'autoclaves' were necessary. When asked to authorize installation of an autoclave large enough to cook a Formula 1 monocoque, the octogenarian company founder again demonstrated his extraordinary far-sightedness. 'Make it big enough to house a 400', he ordered, specifying the largest of his company's production road cars.

Such an autoclave from a specialist manufacturer would have cost a considerable fortune. But Emilia, the region in which Modena and Maranello are situated, is rightly renowned for the broad spectrum of its industrial skills. An autoclave is essentially just a carefully monitored heated pressure vessel, and just round the corner from the new *Reparto Corse* was a pressure-vessel company by the name of Pannini. It was run by a kindred spirit to Mr Ferrari; they shook hands on a price and Pannini manufactured Ferrari's massive autoclave to the racing department's design in double-quick time. The racing department's staff then installed it in a corner of the workshop, with its computer-controlled heat-cycle system close by, and the oil-fired heating plant in an outhouse through the wall.

While supervizing completion of this enormous oven and learning how to use it and its smaller counterparts, necessary for minor composite components, they also began the new season with 126C2B chassis '063 and '064 modified to flat-bottom specification, alongside new 'C2B/83s '065 and '066 completed as flat-bottom cars from the ground up.

Patrick Tambay had been joined in the team by former Renault driver René Arnoux. In most early season races Arnoux drove '064,

Top, *Postlethwaite's 126C2 aluminium honeycomb tub of 1982 was notable as the first Ferrari monocoque without a rivet in sight. Features visible here in Austria are carbon cockpit insert, raked coolers, pullrod front suspension and long brake ducts. Above, Villeneuve's 126C2 '058' with its Forghieri leg-pull full-width staggered wing at Long Beach 1982.*

Tambay '065.

The interim flat-bottom 'C2Bs did not shine in pre-race testing at Rio, lacking rear-end adhesion and traction. In the Brazilian GP neither car impressed, seeming too heavy and not performing on their Goodyear tyres.

For Long Beach the team found adhesion by harnessing the download of enormous new rear wings with extra winglets projecting forward on both sides, supported by the full-width main airfoils' end plates. Snorts of disgust at this apparition soon turned to murmurs of admiration as the powerful V6 cars proved capable of hauling these high-drag/high-lift devices around the street circuit at a very competitive pace. The turbocharged engines simply had power to burn. Tambay qualified on pole and led easily, opting to conserve his tyres and adapt his pace to that of his pursuers. This was his undoing as he was rammed by Rosberg's Williams when it attempted to duck inside in one of the slow hairpins. Arnoux lacked the sensitivity to conserve his tyres and ruined two sets, changed twice, and was on his third set when the race finished with '064 actually placing third despite all these delays . . . it was that kind of race.

Arnoux ran '063 in the minor Brands Hatch International, the car using a new rising-rate rear suspension system in which the old familiar top rocker arms were replaced by triangular machined upper wishbones, with pullrods actuating the inboard coil/damper units. This proved too nervous for Brands Hatch, and the old system was refitted for the

race. The Ferrari led before burning out three sets of tyres and being forced to retire as no more were available in the pit.

For Ricard-Castellet's long straight in the French GP the 'C2Bs were rigged with more modest rear wings, made now in carbon-fibre. The cars wore lighter bodywork and carried lightened starter systems. Ferrari followed Brabham's lead in adopting pit-stop race strategy, refuelling their car and fitting fresh tyres at around half-distance. A troubled race fell to Renault with the 'C2Bs finishing 4-7.

For the San Marino GP at Imola the pullrod rear suspension had been perfected and was fitted on '062, '064 and '065. Arnoux put his car on pole position but Tambay won with his team-mate third after the leading Brabham-BMW had crashed.

At Monaco, Arnoux had a collision and while the pit crew worked feverishly to put him back into the race, Tambay was waved away despite signalling frantically for a tyre change due to changing weather conditions. He had to run four long, slow laps on unsuitable tyres, Arnoux's bodged-up car retired while Tambay finally finished fourth in a race he might have won with better management. You can't win them all . . .

Arnoux's regular '064 was still being repaired after its Monaco collision when the team left for Spa-Francorchamps and the Belgian GP, so he ran old '062, bouncing wildly over the kerbs and losing a front brake cooling scoop before his engine broke a camshaft. Tambay qualified second fastest behind Prost's Renault and finished a strong second, splitting the French factory cars.

Arnoux felt at home in Detroit and qualified '064 on pole, with Tambay third fastest. But at the start Tambay's engine died due to fuel vapourization somewhere in the critically fine-balanced water injection system and zealous marshals pushed the silent car off course, far beyond the pit crew's reach and leaving no alternative to instant retirement. Arnoux, meanwhile, was running away, with the race apparently well won, until a wire came off a terminal in the Ferrari injection system. It was an uncharacteristic double failure for the reigning World Champion team.

In Canada, however, Arnoux was supreme, starting from pole again in his faithful '064 and leading throughout save for four laps around his scheduled refuelling stop. Tambay was third after having to nurse an overheated rear tyre in the closing stages.

The author discussed the season with *Ing.* Postlethwaite the following week: 'The problem now', he observed, 'is convincing ourselves that the 'C3 is adequately better than the 'C2. After Canada to be adequately better it'll have

to win by a clear lap . . .'

Unusually, there was then a five-week break in the calendar before the British GP at Silverstone in July. This allowed the new carbon-composite 126C3 to be completed and prepared for a tyre test session at Silverstone in late June, the car having been unveiled to the press at Fiorano the previous week. Visually it was only marginally different from the preceding 'C2Bs, but in fact it was a very different beast indeed.

Known in the *Reparto Corse's* thick drawing-office ledger as the *Tipo 632*, the new 126C3 used a unitary integrated tub moulded in carbon-composite reinforced with Kevlar. It was formed in two main sections, upper and lower mouldings, which were bonded together like a plastic construction kit, with machined magnesium bulkheads trapped in between.

While the external form of the 'C2-series had been provided by separate bodyshell mouldings, now the nose and cockpit surround shape of the 'C3 was achieved by the moulded tub itself. The only openings in it – apart from the fuel filler and various cable and pipeways were the cockpit aperture itself, a hatch-covered nose bay containing the master cylinders and giving access to the back of the pedals, and a small circular access hatch enabling steering column and pedal-pad changes to be made.

Ferrari had a minor problem in the differing physiques of their two French drivers, for a spare car set-up for Tambay had to be modified with pedal extensions to allow the diminutive, bird-like Arnoux to drive it properly. Observant journalists would check the spare-car pedal set-up in the race paddocks to see which driver was in favour! The mechanics, under burly, balding Vittorio Bellentani adored Tambay, and on balance he was usually ahead.

Initially the 'C3s' water radiators were housed in smaller, more rearward-confined side pods than those of the 'C2Bs, while suspension employed the proven 'C2B pullrod systems at front and rear.

The older style *trasversale* gearbox was preferred to the new longitudinal design now that the need to clear airflow from underwing tunnels no longer existed. In any case the *trasversale* helped give the required overall length for optimum rear wing overhang.

Forghieri would describe the Silverstone 'C3 as; 'an evolutionary car intended to combine the good points of the 126C2 with improved agility and handling'. Tambay reported that the 'C3 felt much more responsive and precise than the hybrid 'C2, but further development was required, and in that exploratory Silverstone outing the well-sorted 'C2Bs proved slightly quicker, despite Arnoux losing a wheel on his car due to an improperly fastened

After Pironi's Hockenheim practice crash in 1982, new team-mate Tambay won in 126C2 '061'. Note aerodynamic skirt running against road surface and low wing-incidence.

centre-lock nut, which fell off and sent him spinning harmlessly into the catch-fencing.

The 'C3s' turbochargers were still mounted in the vee above the engine, but they were now angled more rearwards to improve airflow to the compressor intakes. After early testing with the abbreviated side pods and rearward-mounted coolers, the longer 'C2B-type pods would be adapted to fit the new carbon tubs due to oil overheating problems.

These new 126C3 cars continued the established 126-series chassis numbering system which itself carried on from the 1969-originated 312 Boxer flat-12 line. For the British GP, Arnoux took over 126C3/066 and Tambay 126C3/067.

Goodyear had a very effective qualifying tyre at this time and Arnoux qualified on pole position with a best lap in 1;09.462, 151.9 mph – something close to the *maximum* speed of Gonzalez's 4.5-litre Ferrari 375 V12 which had first beaten the supercharged Alfa Romeos on this same circuit 32 years earlier . . .

But Goodyear's race rubber was no match for Michelin, and small rear wings fitted to minimize drag diminished rear tyre loadings, compromising the chassis' ability to put power down on the road. Goodyear's race tyre deficiency affected Ferrari and Williams most notably. As a rule of thumb, the 1983 Ferraris performed better the slower the circuit and the cooler the conditions, while they could lose that edge on the faster, hotter courses. At Silverstone, while Tambay's delicate touch nursed his car home third, Arnoux burned his tyres and finished a dispirited fifth.

It was after this race that Tyrrell officially protested against Ferrari's use of the AGIP water injection system. Eventually, and perhaps predictably, defendants Ferrari and Renault (who used a similar system developed in conjunction with Elf) won their case and the Tyrrell protests were dismissed, but it was a long drawn-out business.

Meanwhile the new 'C3s had qualified 1-2 for the German GP at Hockenheim, Tambay ahead, but in the race rough, tough little Arnoux stormed away to win and set fastest lap, while Tambay's engine broke its valvegear – a now rare mechanical failure.

At the Österreichring the team achieved its third successive pole position with Tambay again fastest, but when he was baulked by a back-marker in the race, his team-mate chopped him off and then his engine failed again.

Arnoux inherited the lead, only to be overtaken by Prost's Renault with six laps to run, having lost fourth gear. He finished second, and Renault regained the Constructors' Championship lead which they had just lost to Ferrari in Germany.

The Dutch GP at Zandvoort was usually lucky for Ferrari. The third new 'C3 to be built, '068, was available for Arnoux but he preferred his German GP-winning car and used it for the rest of the season. Until this time Ferrari's personnel were confident that they had the strongest engine, but during Dutch practice it became clear that BMW had taken a significant step forward. When Piquet's now faster Brabham-BMW was taken out of the race by Prost's sliding Renault, Arnoux inherited the lead he then held to the finish, with Tambay second after a slow start and an exemplary recovery drive. This bad day for Renault left Ferrari leading the Constructors' Championship again.

The fourth 126C3 appeared in time for the Italian GP at Monza, '069 as spare car, but Patrese's Brabham-BMW took pole with the Ferraris only 2-3 in its wake. Rear suspensions had been modified slightly to prevent the tyres burning out their inside edges so quickly. Piquet's Brabham-BMW was uncatchable and Arnoux drove typically untidily into second place. Tambay's engine seemed down on power and he could not compete, finishing a distant fourth. Ferrari now led Renault by 17 Championship points but they were losing their grip.

At Brands Hatch for the European GP, Tambay crashed helplessly when his car's rear brake circuit failed leaving him with front brakes only, which locked. Arnoux spun repeatedly and staggered home ninth and dizzy.

In South Africa to decide the World Championship title, Tambay placed '069 on pole in his farewell Ferrari appearance, the announcement having just been made that Alboreto would replace him for 1984. Arnoux raced '066 in a despairing final tilt at the Drivers' Championship title, but the gulf between Goodyear race rubber and the Michelins used by the now dominant Brabham-BMW and Renault teams seemed wider than ever.

Back home in Maranello, Ferrari were sliding into one of their periodic bouts of internal political strife which would harm their performances in the field. At Kyalami, being pressed harder than ever before by the Brabham-BMWs' sheer pace, Ferrari reliability simply evaporated. Tambay retired with ignition failure while Arnoux gave up when a cracked head caused overheating. What had looked such a dominant season to follow the unfortunate but Championship-winning season of 1982, had ended in dismal failure.

This, however, is a relative judgement, for it applies only in the sense that any team is only as good as its last race, for cumulatively Ferrari still emerged from 1983 with yet another victory in the Constructors' Championship, having successfully defended their 1982 title, although their drivers again failed in their personal Championship chase.

During the year Tambay and Arnoux had qualified for every race, making 30 starts and finishing 20 times (Arnoux 11, Tambay nine), winning four GPs (Arnoux three to Tambay's one), taking eight pole positions (four to each driver), and setting three fastest race laps (two to Arnoux). Tambay had retired on six occasions, Arnoux on four, but every time Tambay finished he scored Championship points while Arnoux did not.

The new flat-bottom regulations had been intended largely to make racing safer and, unlike 1982, not one of the four 126C2B and four 126C3 cars built for use that year had been lost in accidents. Ferrari had come close to losing the Constructors' title at the last few fences but had hung on to make it their sixth victory in nine seasons – still a record to beat and absolutely one to envy.

Turbocharging

The idea of using the exhaust gases of an internal-combustion engine to energize an air compressor which in turn boosted the engine's induction was devised by a Swiss, Dr Alfred Büchi, around the turn of the century.

A turbocharger is a small centrifugal compressor which has a radial-inflow turbine mounted on a common axial shaft and propelled by exhaust gases. Boost pressure which it generates is then ducted into the engine's induction; the more charge you can force in, the more the engine can burn and the more power it produces.

Both drive and driven turbine are housed within their own casings which incorporate inducer and diffuser sections for the impeller, and the collector and nozzle ring for the turbine, plus the vital bearings, seals and lubrication feed for the shaft itself.

The complete assembly could weigh as little as 15-20 lb, or even less in recent years. The radial-inflow drive turbine has to survive in 1000-plus degrees centigrade exhaust gas flow. This also indirectly affects the bearings which, in addition, have to sustain turbine rotational speeds of 100,000 to 130,000 rpm in a big charger, maybe up to 180,000 rpm in a small one. The compressor is capable of generating boost as high as 30 or 40 psi.

The great advantage of a turbocharger over an old-style mechanically driven supercharger is that there is little mechanical demand upon the engine to power it. Whereas a gear-driven conventional Roots-type supercharger could demand 65-70 bhp or more just to drive it round, the turbocharger merely creates a back-pressure in the exhaust manifold against which the pistons have to fight on the exhaust stroke.

But this can be balanced by the intake manifold boost pressure being equal to, or higher than, exhaust back-pressure, enabling incoming boost pressure to assist the pistons' return down the bores on the inlet stroke. Thus the engineer can arrange for his design to maintain higher induction boost than exhaust pressure in which case the turbocharger generates relatively free horsepower.

Turbocharger sizes can be selected to generate required maximum boost pressure at medium engine speeds, and at high engine rpm excess boost pressure is then bled away to atmosphere, maintaining constant optimum pressure in the induction system. The valve enabling this to be achieved became known as the 'wastegate', which is a diaphragm valve fitted with its own small tailpipe on the exhaust manifold which begins to open to bleed away excess boost when pressure reaches a pre-set level.

This wastegate or 'blow-off valve' is pre-set by a 'turn of the screw' to govern boost applied to the engine and hence potential power generated by it; high boost for qualifying, lower boost for the race.

Disadvantages of turbocharging include extreme thermodynamic stress involving pistons, rings and valves, the need to contain boost pressures throughout the induction tracts and the increased mechanical loads applied to both engine top and bottom ends.

But the biggest single problem with turbocharging has been controlling and minimizing the delay between the driver opening the throttle to accelerate his engine, and the engine picking up speed, sending increased exhaust flow down the system, accelerating the turbocharger to increase boost and the knock-on effect of all these interactions finally achieving response from the car.

This is the much-discussed problem of 'throttle lag', because unlike a mechanically driven supercharger there is no direct linkage between engine speed and turbocharger speed.

To shorten lag, rotating turbocharger mass – hence its inertia – had to be reduced to a minimum. The lighter the turbine wheels could be made, then the quicker they would react, for acceleration and deceleration. It was also advantageous to arrange

extra fuel flow when first cracking open the throttle to produce an exhaust gas surge to spin up the turbine, and with time other similar ploys were developed to keep the wheels turning and maintain boost 'on tap'.

Early on, ball bearings had a hard time surviving in turbochargers and were replaced by a fully floating plain type, being both lubricated and cooled by high-pressure engine oil. If the bearing collapsed the turbocharger could shatter, pressurized oil flooding the incandescent wreckage causing spectacular ignition and belching trails of blue smoke which signified a 'blown turbo'. Many a piston collapse, however, has been described as a turbo failure.

From Renault's introduction of turbocharged engines to Formula 1 in 1977 to Brabham's introduction of pit-stop strategy in 1982, teams were restricted by car tank capacity on the amount of fuel they ran. With pit-stop strategy employed through 1983 by most teams, unlimited fuel was available and by running very rich the fuel's latent heat of evaporation could be employed to cool the turbos and cut the thermodynamic loads on the engines. Cooling the charge delayed the onset of detonation – uncontrolled burning of fuel within the combustion chamber, which eats pistons in seconds.

This brought a vast increase in race power output from the turbocharged cars, until the application of a 220-litre fuel limit for 1984 and the ban on in-race refuelling.

At this point, fuel management assumed vital significance. It was TAG Turbo by Porsche and Bosch Motronic who found the best solution with their fabulously expensive MS3 system which offered the nicest balance between fuel consumption, temperature control and useable power output.

Pressurized air from the turbocharger compressor section was heated by its compression, thus reducing density. To retrieve some density without diminishing pressure the old Twenties US track-racing ploy of intercooling was adopted, as it had been for years in turbocharged diesel vehicles.

An intercooler is simply a radiator core containing hot air under pressure instead of water or oil, and cooling it by passage of airstream around the car or, in Renault's case for some time, by circulating water. For optimum performance, a turbocharged engine had to be run consistently near optimum temperatures and to control that level engine cooling and intercooling assumed vital significance, dictating many aspects of modern Grand Prix car design and layout.

The air/air intercooler is more bulky than the air/water type but far more efficient. Its internal design is also vital, it must flow efficiently or boost pressure will be lost. Intercoolers have to reduce compressed charge inlet temperatures of around 230-240° C – at some 3.5 ata boost – to around 40° C outlet, again to delay detonation. Some 20-30 bhp will be lost for every 10 degrees' rise in inlet temperature. Compressor outlet temperature is a function of pressure-out over pressure-in (the pressure ratio) and the higher the ratio the hotter the charge, demanding more intercooling as it rises so as to delay detonation.

Both Ferrari and Renault adopted water-injection to increase still further the density of their incoming charge, although BMW eschewed this approach as they considered it constituted the use of a banned additive. FISA, however, effectively kept out of the argument. In retrospect, Ferrari came to believe that they had lost ground by the sideways step into water-injection.

Many extremely able engineers addressed themselves to all these problems in the early-Eighties and the rise in turbocharged 1500 cc Formula 1 power outputs from around 500 bhp in 1980, to 640 bhp minimum in the winter of 1983/84, close on 800 bhp on race boost by the summer of 1984 and on to 850-900 bhp in 1985, testify to the soaring learning curve ending our period.

Chapter 15

THE REMARKABLE McLAREN-TAG TURBO MP4/2s 1984-85

Niki Lauda just pipped his team-mate Alain Prost for the 1984 Drivers' World Championship title in McLaren International's extraordinary 12 GP-winning season. What was more extraordinary was Lauda's use of the same car, 'MP4/2-1', in all his races, winning five to Prost's seven. Note MP4/2's neat lines, pushrod front suspension, rocker-arm rear suspension and vast rear 'foil with winglets.

McLaren International had achieved a remarkable resurgence in the fortunes of that honoured name since their formation – as described in the 'Team Directory' – in September 1980. Their John Barnard-designed Cosworth-engined MP4/1 cars had won the race to introduce carbon-fibre moulded monocoque construction to Formula 1. The new model made its debut in 1981 and, driven by John Watson, gained its maiden victory in that season's British GP. During 1982 he and Niki Lauda then won four World Championship Grands Prix in updated but still Cosworth-powered MP4/1Bs.

McLaren International – MI for brevity's sake – involved a partnership between former Team McLaren directors Teddy Mayer and Tyler Alexander, with the ambitious, less experienced but highly talented former Project 4 team trio of Ron Dennis, Creighton Brown and engineer Barnard.

Early in 1983 their still basically 1980-designed MP4/1Cs with their Cosworth engines carried Watson to victory at Long Beach before the turbocharged engine domination really took hold. Through that late summer the McLarens proved themselves the best of the Cosworth brigade, until on 28 August, the Dutch GP witnessed the race debut of a new TAG Turbo V6-engined McLaren MP4/1E driven by Lauda, while Watson ran the McLaren-Cosworth swansong race to finish a fine third overall.

In the next race, at Monza, both McLarens used the Porsche-engineered TAG Turbo V6 engines, and again in the European GP at Brands Hatch. Then came the South African event at Kyalami, where the new turbo McLaren showed real form as Lauda ran second and looked set to challenge Patrese's leading Brabham-BMW for the lead, only for its electrics to fail near the finish.

There followed a winter's development of

all-new McLaren MP4/2 cars tailored to their custom-made turbocharged engine, and this completed the prelude to what would prove an historic Formula 1 season.

Misgivings about the long-term future of the 3-litre Cosworth V8 engine in Formula 1 had begun even before MI's formation. Renault's introduction of turbocharged 1500 cc engines in 1977 had been a faltering first step, though it was not until 1979 that they really performed. Ferrari, then BMW and Alfa Romeo all followed suit, as did the small British Hart concern, racing with Toleman.

Soon after commencing his carbon-fibre Formula 1 design for Project 4, Barnard had been approached by Heidegger, the Formula 2 BMW engine specialist, who was preparing an in-line six-cylinder turbocharged engine for Formula 1. Heidegger showed Barnard his plans but the hard-nosed Englishman said, 'Look, it might be great from the engine man's point of view, but when it comes to mounting it in a chassis it's a complete non-starter'. As an in-line six it was too long, the drive was taken from the middle of the crankshaft, it was canted to one side and it could not be used as a stressed member like a Cosworth. 'Engine people tend to worry about how to mount their engines on a dyno', Barnard explained, 'and thought stops there. The chassis designer is expected to bolt it in somehow – and that's not good enough.'

After MI's formation, the new board agonized over possible turbocharged engines to replace the ageing and increasingly outclassed Cosworth. Mayer and Alexander's huge experience was based upon building and operating competitive chassis around available proprietary engines. It was the same with Dennis and Barnard, but the engineer always chafed at such restraint because it meant compromising chassis design to match the engine. His idea of nirvana was to be able to dictate an integrated

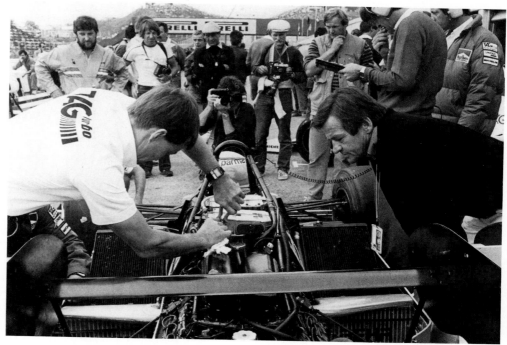

design including both engine and chassis. He wanted to be a Ferrari – or Mercedes-Benz – not merely what Mr Ferrari himself had so often disparaged as a mere *Assemblatore*, or, even more rudely, a *Garagista*.

MI's directors considered what engines were available. It came down to a choice between Renault's V6 or BMW's in-line four-cylinder. Barnard dismissed the Renault as too much of a compromise, having begun life as a 2-litre sports-racing engine, subsequently converted to Formula 2, then turbocharged for Le Mans before being shrunk for Formula 1.

'It hadn't been designed seriously as a stressed member; pumps etcetera seemed untidy . . . There was talk of Cosworth producing them for Formula 1 but I honestly didn't think it was very good. BMW: . . . I personally didn't think an in-line four would do the job reliably. It was another iron block, production based, it wasn't useable as a fully-stressed member – I just thought it was a big compromise . . .'

His discomfort with the available choice became one source of the dawning realization amongst MI's directors that their partnership had little future. Mayer was alarmed by the potential costs of turbocharged Formula 1, but he and Alexander pressed for a decision on available off-the-shelf engines. Barnard had been given technical control and he vetoed such haste. He disagreed that either a BMW or a Renault represented the limit of their options.

'But by that time', he told me, 'Ron was more used to the way I work, which is to start right at the top and work your way down until you get a breakthrough . . .'

It's not a bad philosophy.

They pondered on ways to avoid a compromise. Ferrari's V6 turbo was not available. The Alfa Romeo V8 had not yet been announced, and due to the small size of Brian Hart's operation they did not consider his four-cylinder turbo engine being developed for Toleman. 'No reflection on Brian', Barnard would explain, 'who's done a terrific job with limited resources – but essentially the same objections applied as to the BMW'.

So the question then was 'Who can build us a turbocharged engine?', and at that stage Porsche was suggested. They operated a customer design house and so Dennis arranged a meeting in the winter of 1981/82 with Porsche R&D chief engineer Helmuth Bott.

There had been many rumours of Porsche entering Formula 1 in their own right, but they preferred endurance racing as offering more direct spin-off for their production and customer R&D programmes. They had virtually unrivalled experience in turbocharged road-racing engine design, matched by a reputation for astronomically high pricing of R&D work.

Other Formula 1 teams had asked Porsche before if they would consider developing a turbocharged Formula 1 engine in Cosworth-Ford style for customer purchase. The answer had always been 'No'. Now Dennis asked a subtly different question: 'Would you build me a Formula 1 engine as my sub-contractor if I cover all costs?' – and the answer was a delighted 'Yes of course, step right this way Herr Dennis . . .'

Barnard visited Porsche's Weissach R&D centre outside Stuttgart with a rudimentary sketch of his engine package requirements and extensive specification notes.

At that time ground-effects underwing sections were the ultimate arbiter of racing car performance. He had a vision of a car with completely straight underwing tunnels extending unobstructed from front to rear, angled slightly inwards to avoid the rear wheels. This demanded a narrow engine with a small frontal silhouette, its exhaust plumbing raised high each side to clear the raised underfloors. He had wind-tunnel tested a model of such a car and it produced 30 per cent better lift figures than he had ever seen before. This promised

enormous advantage which, with a custom-made engine of McLaren's own, would not have been available to their rivals.

Barnard set his requirements before Hans Mezger of Porsche's engine design unit, specifying maximum crankcase width and height, and maximum width across the cam-boxes. He utterly ruled out a four-cylinder and declared a preference for a compact V6, only three cylinders long of course, but he asked Porsche's opinion – might a V8 be better? Vee angle itself must certainly not exceed 90-degrees, which would make the cylinder banks obtrude too far into his underbody, but it could with advantage be narrower. Pumps for oil and water had to go to the front of the engine within its crankcase silhouette. Exhaust pipes had to leave the heads horizontally, not downswept, so as to lift the underfloors high on both sides.

The engine had to run as a stressed chassis member like the DFV, and he wanted it to pick up similarly on the chassis. The intercooler lines had to run up under the DFV-like mounting plates on the front of the cam-boxes, between engine and monocoque rear face, to keep within the silhouette.

He even specified a precise crankshaft height, the same as the DFV's, to offer the best design parameters for the whole car. It could have gone lower, but he wanted the ultimate ground-effects car and DFV height avoided potential piping and underbody problems.

Mezger – an excellent engineer in his own right – must have been rather startled by these bluntly specific demands. For years Porsche had rather dismissed Formula 1 as the province of dodgy motor traders and special-builders, not of 'proper' engineers. Their own Formula 1 foray had achieved meagre success before fizzling out in 1962, and they had not returned.

But the deal would go through, and he went away to prepare thoughts and costings. When Porsche's initial response favoured a three-year development programme, MI just laughed; 'They'll have changed the rules by then – do it in a year'.

Dennis came into his own in completing the deal. MI initially funded Porsche's design of the engine and prototype build, after which the design, its production rights, even its type number would be MI's property so that Porsche could not build it for somebody else if MI should fail to raise sufficient cash for more development and production. This six-month 'Phase I' gave Dennis time to raise production finance.

As the valued customer, Barnard was now in overall technical control. He was not too over-awed by Porsche's reputation; it might be

Top, *Hans Mezger (right) watches work on Lauda's TAG Turbo V6 in the Österreichring pits, 1984. Raked-forward radiators vent hot air through the side pod tops, Behr intercoolers just behind. Above, John Barnard, creator of the unprecedentedly successful MP4/2s, quietly celebrates Championship victory in the Estoril garage after the 1984 Portuguese 1-2.*

more in character to describe it as like a red rag to a bull. He would say 'NO' most emphatically when, for good reasons of their own, Mezger's group tried to ease their design straitjacket.

They produced draft layouts which Barnard vetted, and occasionally he would scream when they tried to slide something through his technical filter. One example involved some sump bolts which passed up through the crankcase. Initially Porsche sited the pumps at crank height on the front of the engine, which forced the sump bolts out sideways for clearance so they added a little cast boss to accommodate them, and that boss exceeded Barnard's required silhouette. SCREAM! Bemused German design group amend their design and try again, keeping within the silhouette this time. The pumps dropped below crankshaft height and the offending bolts were brought in closer as required.

Barnard was most concerned with the overall package but he also closely followed its internal design. Decisions on optimum bore and stroke, valve angles, combustion chamber shape and so on were Porsche's alone.

Mezger's team also preferred a V6 to a V8 and produced studies of V6 primary and secondary balance curves at various included angles between 60 and 90 degrees. They could not go tighter than 60 degrees due to space demand for ancillary equipment within the vee, while Barnard would tolerate nothing wider than 90. The final angle of 80 degrees was Porsche's best compromise, identical to Honda's Formula 2 – and soon to be Formula 1 turbocharged – V6 racing engine.

The telling difference between the two units would be Honda's sprawling untidiness compared to MI-Porsche's tight compactness, prompting Barnard to observe: 'That's what will happen when engine men are asked to build a racing engine and there's no thought of asking what the car designers think. Car designers don't come into it . . .'

This was the key to the tight control of the project. MI were the customer and Barnard could state bluntly 'That's not what I want, do it again', and Porsche's design team would either have to convince him of the error of his ways, or do it again. The customer-contractor relationship proved very effective – both parties learned much.

Once the design was complete, the crunch came. MI had to produce the production money.

After approaching several potential backers, Dennis was finally successful in acquiring the support of Mansour Ojjeh's *Techniques d'Avant Garde* (TAG) concern to build and promote the engine. Ojjeh had enthusiastically sponsored the Williams team and when first approached by Dennis he asked its principals their advice. On balance they thought it was a good idea to be involved with a Porsche-engineered Formula 1 turbo engine, but they felt the financial burden could outstrip even such a wealthy private sponsor as TAG.

Porsche's services did not come cheap. Initial production of the engine would merely comprise initial investment. What would happen if it should prove barely competitive and require development of expensive new components like new heads for example? Overnight an investment of hundreds of thousands of pounds in obsolete heads alone could be written off, while new investment would be involved to replace them. A major commercial manufacturer such as Porsche racing on their own account, or Ferrari, or Alfa Romeo, could absorb such costs for the lessons learned, but it made less sense for a private sponsor backing a private customer. Had TAG thought this through?

Ojjeh intimated to Williams that they could have the engine as well as McLaren if he decided to finance it. I dread to think what Barnard and Dennis's reaction would have been to that offer had it been accepted, but Williams declined and eventually teamed-up with Honda instead.

Ojjeh went ahead, forming a company named TAG Turbo Engines with MI personnel involved, and 'Phase 2' – the production contract – was signed between Porsche and TAG Turbo Engines in December 1982, by which time the prototype TTE-PO1 V6 unit was ready, running for the first time on a Weissach dyno on 18 December.

But by that time Barnard's vision of the ideal ground-effects car had been shattered . . .

The FISA ruling which insisted on flat bottoms for Formula 1 cars for 1983 had been announced on 3 November. Barnard was devastated. I vividly recall him spitting blood and venom at the time but didn't quite appreciate why. Overnight his 'no-compromise' engine had lost some of its reason to be.

Its specification '. . . would have been different if we'd been running flat-bottom rules from the start. The exhaust pipes would have swept down instead of sticking out, so we could tuck-in the turbos closer, but otherwise

because of the way we waisted-in the sides of our car for other aerodynamic reasons it was pretty much the way we required, even under flat-bottom rules. I would have tried for a lower crank centreline though, and put the pumps on the sides to shorten it, that would have been useful – although it was already a very short engine . . .'

The prototype unit was shown to the press at the Geneva Salon in April 1983. Mezger explained; 'We consider the V6 configuration is the optimum for the current Formula 1, where we seek good fuel economy in addition to competitive power and a good package. The V6 is more compact, with less internal friction than a V8, and can rev higher than an in-line four-cylinder. We started straight away with six cylinders in mind. You need space in the vee for an intake manifold, injection equipment etc, so we rejected a 60-degree layout immediately as too narrow. A 90-degree offered good rigidity and is conventional, but this makes the engine too wide for our requirements . . . Our calculations on engine balance showed the 80-degree vee to be optimum. Honda has reached the same decision completely independently. Why have we not seen an 80-degree vee before? I can only guess nobody else has done the same calculations', he concluded, smiling broadly.

Few firm details of the engine have been released at the time of writing. McLaren International encouraged their employees not to say anything to anybody which might jeopardize technical advantage and in general they set an example from the top. The new TTE-PO1 V6's water-cooled block was cast in crisp aluminium alloy as were the heads, while the ribbed block itself, using Nikasil liners, was as neat and pretty as it was functional, a piece of technological art. It used a three-pin crankshaft with the pins phased at 120 degrees so when viewed from one end the shaft resembled a Mercedes-Benz three-pointed star. Each head, no wider than the average man's handspan, had two gear-driven camshafts actuating four valves per cylinder disposed at a narrow included angle. The same cam-drive geartrain also powered the water and oil pumps neatly packed into the front of the unit. At the rear, the tail of each exhaust camshaft drove a small three-plug ignition distributor, while the tail of the left-hand inlet camshaft powered the original mechanical fuel injection pump and metering unit via an internal toothed belt. The right-hand camshaft tail powered the fuel pump. A single KKK turbocharger and wastegate matched into each bank's simple but wide-flung exhaust manifolding.

Total weight of the package ready to go was 330 lb, and typical of the thought applied by Barnard was the integral tunnel cast into the left-side of the crankcase into which the McLaren air-starter cartridge could be inserted, saving the weight of an individual casing of its own while the tunnel also provided a useful extra structural feature within the casting.

Mezger's preferred bore and stroke dimensions were published as 82.0 mm x 47.3 mm, displacing 1499 cc, and Porsche claimed 600 bhp, an immediate 75 bhp gain for McLaren compared to its Cosworth DFY V8s. Peak power was produced between 10,000 and 11,500 rpm, though the power band was claimed to be useable from as low as 8500 rpm. At the time of the press conference it was stated that the prototype units had completed some 4000 test miles.

The relationship between MI and Porsche was not without its problems. In some respects it was conducted rather at arm's length and was occasionally adversarial. Barnard's demanding nature and famously short-fuse temper sometimes caused the diplomatic, entrepreneurial Dennis some problems as he tried to hold it all together.

Porsche planned to endurance-test the pilot engine in one of their *Typ* 956 Group C Coupé

test hacks at Weissach. MI said 'Don't', wanting serious testing to begin instead in their Formula 1 mule, but Porsche went ahead regardless. They insisted they learned much from grinding round Weissach in the big Coupé, but the McLaren team drivers, Watson and Lauda, learned little, though Lauda drove very hard, ignoring the meagre safety facilities of the undulating test track. He revelled in the new engine's smoothness after the Cosworth V8's vibration, and there was no doubting its power; 'Incredible, fantastic!', he enthused, 'Just like being hit from behind by a bomb!'

Still, Barnard insisted that fitting the engine in a 956 merely delayed discovery of a more serious throttle lag problem than expected. The engine was mounted unstressed in the multitubular 956, so it was not running under the structural loads which would apply in Formula 1. The 956 was around 250 kg (551 lb), heavier than the Formula 1 McLaren, but Porsche's test team considered throttle response was as good as on their standard turbo Group C V6. The McLaren drivers went to Weissach, tried the car and '. . . just looked blank and said "We don't know either way, funny old car, like a tank, you have to heave it round the corners" . . .' Irrespective, Watson completed some 540 km running, and Lauda around 300, and the embryo engine demonstrated good mechanical reliability.

Back in England, MI modified their old original prototype carbon-fibre Cosworth chassis, 'MP4/1-1', with 1982 straight-sided bodywork, into the turbo test hack model MP4/1D. When testing commenced with this far lighter car the drivers instantly recognized excessive throttle lag. The new engine also displayed an alarming oil breathing problem, emptying the Formula 1 hack's system in only 10 laps or so.

Porsche's men glared at McLaren's oil tank and remarked 'You've got a problem there', while MI's men pointed to the 956 Coupé hack which had a catch tank the size of a dustbin, quite out of the question in a single-seat open-wheeler.

Porsche responded very quickly, changing their KKK turbochargers and exhaust sizes to improve throttle response and investigating the oil-breathing problem. Testing progressed. Early on Lauda was thrilled to exceed 300 km/h (186 mph) at Silverstone. Although his Cosworth-engined car had been 36 mph slower than Arnoux's turbocharged Ferrari along Hangar Straight in the British GP meeting, now he was already within 12 mph of the Ferrari's speed with this heavy and extensively instrumented test hack. He pressed for the opportunity to race the engine as soon as possible, and the team's sponsors backed him, demanding that interim turbocharged cars should be built to replace the contemporary Cosworth race cars before the end of that season.

Barnard refused, but for once was overruled. His design philosophy could not contemplate such a rushed expedient. Whereas the late Bruce McLaren liked to 'build it early, build it well and develop it thoroughly before its first race', Barnard preferred to think deeply through the entire concept, research it in fine detail and only then build as late but as precisely as possible – the emphasis having been on extending the thinking time to a maximum.

Barnard believed the existing MP4/1Cs should complete the season, while background development could continue at a more thoughtful pace on the turbo test hack. Certainly McLaren would have finished the season with more Championship points that way.

But historically there is no substitute for race-testing a Grand Prix car. An hour's racing can highlight problems which could remain hidden despite weeks of private testing, but Barnard remained unrepentant. The test hack had been built merely to run the engine and no more, and when his arm was twisted to race the

The TAG Turbo V6 engine looked like a triumph of packaging, until it was installed in the car with all the necessary accessories attached. But it still set new standards. The low-slung KKK turbochargers are hidden in the side pods, drawing air through the gauzed intakes.

new engine short-term he simply could not bring himself to build two or three more such crude hacks.

'So in six weeks our blokes built two cars – well, one runner and the other 85 per cent complete – ready for Zandvoort. There Niki was unbelievably quick on the straight, but basically the Cosworth wing package download was way deficient with turbo power. We cooked the brakes in the race, a function of the turbo car going about 30 mph faster down the straight than the Cosworth . . .'

The interim turbo cars, chassis 'MP4/1E-01' and '02 were based on the former 'MP4/1C-05' and '06 monocoques, the latter becoming Lauda's regular mount, suitably modified to carry the new engines and their accompanying intercoolers and electronic gear.

Meanwhile, a frustrating new problem had intruded. Bosch had been asked by Porsche to develop an electronic management system to relate the new engine's ignition and fuel injection supply to demand. In 1984, fuel for a Formula 1 Grand Prix race was to be reduced from 250 litres to only 220, while refuelling stops would be outlawed. Consequently fuel economy matched to sheer power became vital, and the new management system was required to balance performance against economy in the most competitive and efficient manner. One Bosch development unit was already working closely with BMW on a semi-mechanical system based upon a Kugelfischer pump and metering unit, but now a separate Bosch team was to develop the 100 per cent electronic 'Motronic MS3' system exclusively for TAG Turbo Engines, via Porsche R&D. The system employed sensors and a processing unit to control solenoids which adjusted the fuel metering jets to govern fuel quantity and to time its delivery to each cylinder in line with demand. This was far from easy to achieve.

On initial test at Weissach the V6 had started perfectly every time, easy as a VW, but now at Zandvoort and on test it refused point-blank to start for hours on end.

The unfortunate Bosch technician would plug in his diagnostic electrickery and its monitor screen would merely flash up 'ERROR', whereupon hours of head-scratching could commence. And there was no communication between McLaren and Bosch, who made it clear they were working with Porsche and regarded McLaren's only function to be settlement of their bills . . . which of course set the veins bulging again on Barnard's forehead.

Very early in the programme this lofty attitude set MI looking for alternative contractors. They talked with Ford who were very interested in production car engine management systems, and also with Lucas and Marelli, but Porsche had age-old links with Bosch and eventually MI bowed to the inevitable.

Initially the engine had run on the Weissach dyno using mechanical injection. But once in the car Bosch decreed otherwise, understandably anxious to develop their own electronic system. Porsche's mechanical injection used a Kugelfisher pump, and Bosch own Kugelfisher, so it was a rather rueful Mezger who one day explained to Barnard that the next time they wanted a three-dimensional cam ground for the Kugelfisher mechanical system they could expect a six-month delivery delay . . .

So Bosch got their way, and the engine went into the cars on electronic management, and it caused untold heartache before coming good.

If anything, the individuals in the project had grown further apart. This was alarming, and it took Dennis's considerable skills – and then major technical problems – to force everyone to pull together. Something deep in the programming or function of the Bosch management system repeatedly prevented the engine from starting at all. Development of the cars was delayed while a third of total testing time could be wasted with silent engines.

Both new interim MP41/E turbocharged cars

raced at Monza in September, with a new double rear flap addition to the rear wing to seek extra download. There were starting problems in qualifying, while Lauda's car, '06, ran poorly in the race but Watson's '05 soared into seventh place before retirement. The V6 suffered its first mechanical failure here when a locating pin in the cam-drive train sheared. It was a feature Porsche had used in many other engine applications without problem, but in the TAG Turbo V6 it failed so they rapidly developed an alternative.

Download was still inadequate. In haste before Brands Hatch a huge new rear wing was designed and made. It collapsed on Watson's car while Lauda had another valvegear failure, after which a subtle piston redesign went through. In practice both cars had starting problems and Bosch's men suffered severe earache in consequence.

Kyalami's South African GP ended the 1983 season, and a third interim MP4/1E was now available as spare, based on chassis 'MP4/1C-07'. MI were thankful for the two-day test session preceding official practice there. Barnard stayed at home to finalize his MP4/2 design for 1984, while race engineers Alan Jenkins and Steve Nicholls wrestled with the interim MP4/1Es at altitude on the Rand plateau.

Again it was near impossible to make the engines start or run properly, and little serious work was possible on the car set-up. Bosch's reprogramming of the management system for altitude proved wrong in practice but they reprogrammed it successfully for the race. The McLaren crew and Porsche engineers fitted the right turbos while the drivers and race engineers made a very fine tyre choice and the new rear wings were built properly this time. Poor Watson made a starting grid line-up error in the new spare car and was disqualified but Lauda was the fastest man on the track near the end of the race before his engine's electrics cut out and stranded him.

Hapless Bosch were blamed again. Their racing experience was very restricted, and they had fitted a humble production car regulator into the MP4/1E's alternator circuit. Its internals just vibrated apart, the alternator ceased charging and the management system was left with insufficient power to operate, so it simply shut down.

Lauda's performance before this failure was a massively morale-boosting high note on which to end the season but the repercussions of the continuing electrical problems were also valuable.

The Germans undoubtedly found their British customers demanding and blunt, but their own early tendency towards self-satisfied omniscience had been whittled away. Now they knew that Formula 1 really was tough and they could not relax.

In January 1984 the old interim cars were taken to Rio for the pre-season tyre test. The trip was catastrophic. The engines would neither start, nor run, nor perform adequately. Bosch returned to Stuttgart considerably shaken, Porsche and MI applied the pressure and a major re-examination began of the super-expensive management system. It paid real dividends.

Meanwhile the new MP4/2 tailor-made turbocharged cars were in production. The interim MP4/1Es' former Cosworth tubs had changed only in minor detail since the design's original inception in 1981.

Barnard's thoughtful approach to design before first cutting metal, or carbon cloth for that matter, had given remarkable stability to his creations. The original MP4/1 tub made by Hercules in 1981 was so successful that only minor modifications were made for the second and subsequent units. The large plan-area ground-effect '4/1s which raced through 1981-82 were hard to tell apart externally, and the flat-bottom MP4/1C which replaced them with Cosworth power for 1983 retained that unmistakable family resemblance.

The MP4/2 made its mark first time out with Prost at Rio, Brazilian GP, 1984. Here we can see the 'McLaren tail' with its aerodynamic diffuser ramps passing through rear suspension.

Barnard's MP4/2 tub redesign was governed by the TAG Turbo V6 being shorter than a Cosworth V8 and by the 220-litre fuel limit/ refuelling ban preventing use of an undersized tank such as Brabham had used in 1983. The complex tub tooling was retrieved from the Hercules Corporation in Salt Lake City, Utah, where they made the McLaren tubs. It was part revised, part replaced, remachined and returned to Hercules.

New tub sections were moulded there, with a lower, longer tank section behind the cockpit. The lower sides of the chassis around the bottom wishbone rear pick-ups flared out to enhance airflow into the side pods, which themselves remained rather longer and more voluminous than was fashionable. The rear end of each pod curved-in elegantly at the rear wheels, exposing a neat ground-effect diffuser panel like a horizontal fin, with both under and upper surfaces active, which swept up either side of the gearbox.

The lower rear wishbones lived beneath this panel, while the driveshafts and redesigned top rocker arms were all that interrupted airflow between wheel and vertical body side, the driveshafts projecting from neat holes in the side panelling which otherwise enclosed engine and gearbox completely. This was the soon-to-be-famous 'McLaren tail' which many other teams would copy with varying degrees of comprehension and success as the season progressed.

Barnard and Dennis impressed upon their team the need for design and technical security. For this reason few concrete details of the cars' construction have ever been released and, with this and other considerations in mind, not one of the carbon-composite McLaren cars has been sold into private hands. Even the Marlboro-liveried MP4-series show cars use wooden mock-up 'SS' – 'static show car' – tubs rather than a production version which might allow detailed examination of the carbon-composite originals.

The carbon-composite tub, however, carried an aluminium nosebox for driver protection and neatly housed its front coil/damper units either side of his shins within the rigid moulded scuttle and forward tub structure. Where the side pod intakes extended amidships on the cockpit sides a neat slot intake sunk into the tub itself bled cooling air back into the engine bay.

The side pods were shorter, set further back than in the 1983 interim cars, but remained larger than most of the rival designs. Dual-purpose radiator cores lay raked steeply forward in each pod, each core's left side cooling water, the right side cooling oil. Two separate cores – set one behind the other, oil ahead of water – had been used in the interim '1E cars' longer pods.

Where the Bosch Motronic system boxes had been mounted in the front of the '1E side pods, they now moved to the top of the tank cell moulding, which itself sat lower and was some 6 cm longer than in the MP4/1-series tubs.

The TAG Turbo V6 engine hung neatly on the rear of this tub via its Cosworth-like four-point mounts. Where in the interim cars the KKK turbochargers hung out on either side at a shallow angle to the centreline to allow the exhaust manifolds to feed into them nicely without tight curves, this set them too far back towards the rear wheels for aerodynamic comfort. In the new MP4/2 Barnard wanted to bring the body waist further forward, so he shifted the turbochargers forward at a tighter angle with the manifolds cramping round towards them, then the tailpipes arching back close against the gearbox. He admitted, 'It's not ideal, and Porsche don't like it, but I think it's the car designer's job to juggle the best compromises, and that's *it*.'

The turbochargers drew their air through a horizontal duct under the high-pressure area on top of the side diffuser surface but this

proved inadequate early on and an additional mesh-covered opening in the side panel was formed.

Plumbing passed pressurized air forward from the turbochargers into the bottom of the large Behr intercooler matrices housed at right-angles to the tub within the side pod. Cooled compressed air was then ducted upwards through big-bore intercooler pipes into the round induction 'logs' on top of the engine. In the interim cars there had been too little space between the back of the old tubs and the front of the engine to pass the intercooler pipes under the cam-box mounting plates as intended. On MP4/2 space was allowed, so the pipes could tuck in neatly within Barnard's original silhouette.

The oil tank was incorporated into the engine/transmission adaptor plate, as on the interim car but now redesigned, while the gearbox itself was the familiar McLaren unit employing modified predominantly Hewland internals as on the old Cosworth cars, and now working overtime to cope with the 750 bhp of the TAG Turbo compared to the 550 bhp-plus of the ultimate Cosworth DFYs! Its oil system had been extensively revised to help, but by mid-season '84 Barnard would be working on an all-new transmission and the team was 'carrying eggs' all year where the gearbox was concerned.

Beneath the tail ramp, which generated valuable ground-effects download, the exhaust and turbocharger wastegate pipes exited in flush vents, playing their gases across the diffuser surface to entrain airflow. This created an early problem as the gearbox shroud suffered under exhaust heat. A metal-sided gearbox shroud was run for a while, which Barnard hated, until a heat-resistant carbon-fibre shroud became available, and survived happily with the exhaust gases playing across its outer surfaces.

His rear suspension redesign retained the same general layout as before, with wide-based flat-section lower wishbones, fabricated top rocker arms actuating inboard coil/damper units and a single raked-back top link each side to control toe-in and camber. But now the rocker arms raked back from inboard, where the coil/damper mounts had moved further forward, as permitted by the shorter V6 engine. This allowed an even slimmer rear bodyline, hugging the engine up top and the gearbox down below and considerably enhancing airflow over both the lower ramp surface and the centre-pillared rear wing above it all.

As the new cars were being completed, just in time for the start of the season, so a production engine specification was frozen for the TAG Turbo unit. To save weight over the ten or so development prototypes used in 1983, it used titanium main crankcase studs and a lightweight cast magnesium inlet manifold which replaced the hefty original bolt-together machined-section type used for shape experimentation.

MI's requirement was for a float of some 15 to 20 complete race engines with some five to ten extra sets of parts available at any time. By June 1984 they would have complete engines Nos. 21-35 in use.

True to Barnard's philosophy of extending the thinking time to the maximum before building late and building right, two new MP4/2s were completed in time only for a brief three-day test at Ricard-Castellet before their Brazilian GP debut at Rio on 25 March. There the opening round of the 1984 World Championship was decided largely on fuel economy and most teams were in trouble towards the end of the hot, thirsty race. Porsche and Bosch had got their sums right, and Prost won after Lauda had looked likely to and profiting from the demise of some quick Ferrari and Renault opposition.

There were 16 Championship rounds in 1984 of which McLaren International won no less

than 12; Prost winning the seven GPs at Rio, Imola, Monaco – rain-shortened, scoring half-points – Hockenheim, Zandvoort, *ersatz* Nürburgring and Estoril; Lauda adding five more victories, at Kyalami, Dijon-Prenois, Brands Hatch, Österreichring and Monza. Crucially, Lauda took four second places, at Montreal, Hockenheim, Zandvoort and Estoril, while Prost was second only once – at Kyalami – then third in Montreal and fourth in Detroit. Lauda accumulated 72 Championship points, compared to his faster team-mate's 71½, to clinch his third title in the final race of the season at Estoril, which Prost actually won with the Austrian second.

Little Prost could have tried no harder, having equalled Jimmy Clark's record number of GP wins in one season, yet he still only finished second to Lauda's reliable skills.

Meanwhile McLaren International scored the most convincing victory in the history of the Constructors' Cup competition with no less than 143.5 points to Ferrari's humble 57.5 in second place. It was a demonstration of crushing superiority unprecedented in modern Formula 1.

McLaren-TAG Turbo-by-Porsche MP4/2s had started 32 times in those 16 GPs and had won 12 of them – 75 per cent – and added five second places, four of them in team 1-2 finishes, plus one third, two fourths and one seventh, retiring 11 times.

The statisticians discovered that Prost had led 34.47 per cent of the seasons' race laps, Lauda ranking third in this respect behind Piquet of Brabham, leading 16.78 per cent. McLaren cars had led 51.25 per cent of the season's Championship race laps, totalling 1440 miles in the lead, against Brabham's 24.08 per cent – 714 miles.

Such were the pressures of race preparation upon the TAG Turbo project that special qualifying 'screamer' engines were not prepared to combat the Brabham-BMW speciality in this field. Even so, Prost took pole position three times against Piquet's nine which included a Brabham-BMW hat-trick of pole positions in the final GPs of the year. Lotus took two pole positions, one to each of their drivers, de Angelis and Mansell, Ferrari one with Alboreto and Renault one with Tambay.

In comparison, however, the McLarens took eight of the season's fastest *race* laps using GP distance boost and power, and perhaps significantly while only two of these fastest laps came

in the first half of the season, the other six were grouped together in the final eight races as Porsche's rebuild programme got into its stride and the team gained turbo experience. Against this octet of McLaren fastest laps, Brabham set only two unequalled, Ferrari two and these two marques shared a third between them; Renault set two, and Toleman one in the rain at Monaco with Senna driving his heart out.

Further examining the results, it could be argued that McLaren were lucky to win at Rio, where the opposition had problems, at Monaco, where Prost seemed set to lose his lead just as the red flag went out, and at Österreichring, where Lauda's gearbox broke but Piquet's pursuing Brabham was in tyre trouble and his team failed to appreciate that the leading McLaren was crippled.

But any team on the crest of a winning wave makes 90 per cent of its own luck. Part of the trick is simply sticking around, fuel-efficiently, until the race ends, and another part is to run fast enough to break the opposition before they can break you.

A new Gleason-type differential was introduced at Monaco and retained thereafter and at the same event the team obtained their first specially-commissioned lightweight turbocharger housings from KKK. These allowed tighter internal clearances for higher boost and effectively were used for the rest of the year.

The team's biggest problem was simply to get parts made quickly enough. Porsche struggled desperately hard to come to terms with the frantic pressures of the Formula 1 calendar and McLaren's taut rebuild schedules.

The team tested different front uprights and other modifications during the year, but frequently found no conclusive advantage so no changes were made to the race cars.

At Detroit both MP4/2s broke their front anti-roll bars, which were not strong enough to withstand the bumps. Barnard had to re-stress the design and ordered new bars in titanium. They were long in coming, so heavier interim bars ran meantime, which grieved him.

In general then, the McLarens ran this fantastic season with incredibly little modification, evidence of how right had been the original thinking. There were in fact only two notable bodywork changes. One came in Austria where they ran a complete new front wing package intended to enhance ground-effect and sensitivity although 'the length of time it takes to do the wind tunnel work and

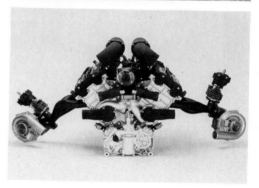

Top, *Prost's 1985 Championship-winning MP4/2B at Imola where it won on the road but was disqualified for being underweight. The rear winglets of 1984 were now illegal; note the large ducts venting radiator/cooler air, louvred vents above turbos. Above, TAG Turbo's V6 shows off its 80-degree vee angle, high-swept exhausts and KKK turbochargers.*

then to tool-up the carbon-fibre wing itself' had delayed even this development.

In Holland came the debut of an enlarged turbocharger air intake on the rear bodywork side, square now in place of the original rectangular vertical slot. The team played around with an assortment of ducts and trunking to cool their McLaren-SEP callipers and carbon brakes, but they ended the season with effectively the same ducts as those they had started with, having never run iron brakes at all in either race or practice.

To make this remarkable team's achievement even more extraordinary, only four complete MP4/2s had been built, with a fifth tub held in reserve, but the fourth car had missed its target completion date in time for the Brands Hatch test just prior to the mid-season US tour, so instead of joining the race team for the trip it went direct into the test team.

Schedules were then so tight that after testing 'MP4/2-4' could never be rebuilt and race-prepared in time to join the race team, so it remained purely a test chassis for the rest of the year. Thus the McLaren-TAG Turbos' transcendant first full season was accomplished with only three race team cars. Lauda became the first driver in modern times to win the World Championship while driving the same car all season: this was chassis 'MP4/2-1'.

Meanwhile, 'MP4/2-2' was Prost's regular assigned car, but he was forced to race the spare chassis '3 in South Africa, and again at Imola and Hockenheim – winning both times – and finally at Monza. This car was also used in testing before the completion of chassis '4.

In Austria where Prost spun off on oil and reported he had been holding-in fourth gear, gearbox strip-down suggested from the condition of the selector mechanism that only fifth had been held-in with any force. The car was not damaged by the spin so his inability to restart its stalled engine was infuriating.

The McLarens were by this time unusual in still carrying onboard starter motors with ring-gear teeth machined into the engine flywheel. But a stalled and hot turbo engine demands a much fiercer churn on the starter than a hot Cosworth before it will fire, and the team's old MP4/1-style aluminium pressure-air bottle had insufficient capacity for the job. However, an aluminium bottle large enough to restart the TAG Turbo would be very heavy. Consequently, Barnard had asked Hercules to spin up some double-capacity half-weight pressure vessels in carbon-fibre. As Prost spun away the Austrian GP so the first batch of these vessels were sitting on Barnard's desk in Woking. They had not been fitted because when tested they leaked air . . .

Through this season the team still experienced engine problems, which fortunately were confined mainly to testing and practice. The V6 was dogged by mysterious water loss, Bosch's electronics eventually came under control, while most engine breakages involved burn-down failures, torching down the side of the piston after early valvegear misbehaviour had been corrected at the end of 1983.

Hans Mezger's team of three engineers, five design-draughtsmen and 27 mechanics divided into two groups for R&D and construction at Porsche Weissach had done a superb job on their demanding customer's behalf.

Rival team drivers raved about the TAG Turbo engine's superb pick-up out of slow corners, while McLaren's men continually bitched about inadequate throttle response and Prost recalled Renault's pick-up with affection. Mezger admitted, 'We can certainly win more easily on fast flowing circuits' but by the end of the season all circuits seemed to come much the same. The engine management system chip was set up for a specific quality fuel, which through a 'fuel company cock-up' was not supplied at Zolder for the Belgian GP. Practice there saw a series of shattering TAG Turbo piston failures, and other problems sidelined both McLarens in the race – a double retirement which would recur only once, in Dallas. Further piston failures punctuated practice for the French GP at Dijon, but Porsche had the fix, and in the race there Lauda won and Prost shone on newly-built V6s flown down overnight from Weissach.

Barnard would admit to having some 750 bhp available in race tune, and only late in the season did McLaren adopt additional intercooler and radiator cooling for their qualifying shots, without besting Brabham-BMW let it be said. Michelin tyres were as consistent as ever while Goodyear's decision to adopt radial-ply construction had put them into a 'catch-up situation' all year. Late on, McLaren felt Michelin's development was lagging, and this was the only prior warning they would receive of the French company's sudden close-season withdrawal from Formula 1.

It is worth considering the context in which these remarkable McLaren-TAG Turbo cars shone so brightly. Were they making the best of 'a bad season' which simultaneously afflicted Brabham, Ferrari, Renault and the rest? Was it really the poor performance of others which made the McLarens look so good? Or was it the clear superiority of the Porsche-produced engine which would have achieved the same

success in any other frontline chassis?

Where so many rival teams had an unreliable year I suspect that, excepting Ferrari which suffered other problems, they really had to run so hard just to keep McLaren in sight that they simply came apart at the seams.

In qualifying, and occasionally in the race, Brabham-BMW had an obvious performance edge and Piquet drove better than ever for them all season. He regularly out-qualified the McLarens and equally often led races before retiring. Some other cars arguably outhandled the McLarens, notably the Lotus-Renaults, but on The Day only Brabham-BMW posed them a consistent and serious threat. On the occasions when McLaren did not win from strength, they were always ready to win on reliability, fuel efficiency and driver wit. And of course they had the finest all-round driver pairing in competition.

It is interesting to ponder the crucial role still being played in the mid-1980s by the dismissively nicknamed *Assemblatori* teams in achieving success for the great constructors through their chassis engineering skills and simple racing wisdom. Where would Porsche have been without McLaren, BMW without Brabham, Honda without Williams or indeed Renault – in what was for their works team a troubled season – without Lotus?

What wins races is possession of the best combination on race day. If any vital ingredient is missing, the chance is lost. The superbly integrated McLaren MP4/2 chassis/engine package proved good enough for its drivers to extract virtually everything the TAG Turbo engine had to offer, and that was plenty. Not only did it have lots of competitive horsepower, it also offered much useable mid-range torque. Bosch's super-expensive tailor-made management system made it the most fuel efficient F1 engine of the year. The cars always finished with quite a lot of fuel left in their tanks. McLaren ran Michelin tyres at a time when they were the class of the field, and in the services of Prost and Lauda they had two of the top four drivers of their day. At most circuits on race day this combination proved just too hot for the opposition to handle.

Some observers, notably in the European press, doubted McLaren's contribution to the equation and put it all down to Porsche know-how. They were deluding themselves. Porsche did a superb job on TAG Turbo's behalf, no question, but McLaren had won the 'Cosworth class' in their last four outings with the DFV/DFY engines through 1983, and they simply continued that dominance at a higher level after receiving their turbocharged engines.

And they were '*their*' engines, for McLaren International had commissioned the design in broad detail and policed the project without compromise while Porsche designed and manufactured the TTE-PO1 units so brilliantly for them.

At the end of 1984, the glory of McLaren-TAG Turbo and Porsche was truly indivisible.

For 1985, Barnard set out to build upon that incredibly successful season of '84, updating the existing MP4/2 design around the existing moulded carbon-fibre chassis with all-new bodywork, a new pushrod rear suspension, new front uprights and a new hub package.

The new year's major regulation change was the banning of the additional winglets on the rear 'foils which had enabled more download to be generated in '83-84. Winter tunnel testing enabled recovery of some lost download with even less aerodynamic drag. This meant an overall increase in aerodynamic efficiency, and with extra power found for '85 by all engine manufacturers, straightline speeds and lap times plummeted.

McLaren's major chassis work centred around Barnard's needs as follows: 'What I wanted to produce was a car which was totally predictable on the servicing side, so we could

say this part does 500 miles and that part does 1000 miles; so we could accurately life all our components and then, apart from accidents, we could accurately predict how many parts we would need for the year's racing. I wanted a gearbox, engine and four suspension corners which we could completely ignore for two races at a time. With two pairs of races spaced only one week apart this was vital. I have nightmares about trying to race-prepare a car away from home in circuit lock-ups . . .'

McLaren MP4/2B cars were built up on chassis '3 (spare), '4 (Lauda) and '5 (Prost) in time for the first of the new World Championship series races at Rio, and old tub number '2 would join the team for Prost from Silverstone. An all-new chassis, '6, was completed for Prost in time for the South African GP at Kyalami, and had the distinction of being the first carbon moulding to be made in Woking rather than by Hercules in Salt Lake City.

Early in the season the new car proved itself as good as the team's 1984 Champion design had been, with Prost winning the majority of the races on the road, but losing on disqualification at Imola where his MP4/2B ended up underweight through over-consumption of fuel, oil, brake pads and tyres.

Then in the middle of the season the McLarens seemed to go off form, suffering especially in Montreal and Detroit, but came back with a vengeance on the fast circuits from the British GP at Silverstone forwards.

There were two main reasons for this. One was a suspension change, the other was the behaviour of McLaren's carbon-fibre brakes on the demanding American courses compared to their behaviour on fast circuits where they were not subjected to such intensive use.

John explained both the suspension and brake problems like this: 'Before we made the front suspension geometry change we were not really *plagued* by anything, no dreadful problems at all, but the drivers complained that the cars seemed to fall into an oversteer in/understeer out condition which was not very predictable and could be improved. They did not have total confidence in their cars' handling. So we just moved the suspension pick-ups and achieved a considerable improvement in feel.'

Prost tested the modification at Silverstone before the British GP, and a few days later Barnard told me: 'Just you wait and see what happens at Silverstone in the British GP, I think we will be in good shape there . . .' And they were, Prost dominant.

Subsequently the MP4/2Bs' rear suspension geometry was also modified to bring the cars into still better balance, Prost's assigned race car at Österreichring having the all-modified suspension though he actually raced and won in his spare car, which lacked the latest rear suspension revision.

The team ran a new design rear wing and different flaps on the '84-style front wings, but most of the year was dominated by incessant work on the brakes. Barnard observed ' . . . our blokes will probably remember 1985 as the Year of the Brake Duct!'

Throughout 1984 McLaren had run carbon brakes with their own design aluminium twin callipers, without problems. Nowhere did they run cast-iron discs. Ending that season John was happy with the brakes and felt they could remain unchanged for 1985 . . . But he was wrong.

They ran higher turbo boost in race trim in cars generating less aerodynamic drag, which meant they ran much faster at the end of the straights.

'The problem with brakes is that in effect they either work OK or don't work at all, giving all kinds of problems. Unless you reach their limit and run into problems you have no way of knowing how close to that limit you are. Although we had no trouble with them in 1984 I suspect now, looking back, that we were using

Alain Prost's McLaren MP4/2B notches the team's eighth consecutive Grand Prix victory. The flag waved in Brazil 1985 completed their unprecedentedly dominant run which had begun at Brands Hatch the previous July.

99 per cent of their capacity! But we had no way of knowing how close to the limit we had come.

'In '85, because we were going quicker between the corners, by mid-season we just lacked sufficient braking capacity.

'We had a real struggle in Canada, we had been on the limit in Monaco even though we won, and suddenly those teams using their Brembo callipers bought off the shelf from your friendly dealer looked in better shape than we were with our specially designed and made McLaren type . . . In Detroit we just ran out of brakes, simple as that, and at that time I got heavily into the braking side and looked at everything in the system.

'Ricard and Silverstone, of course, are no problem for brakes; then we tested at the Nürburgring and were really in deep trouble but by the time of the German GP I'd found the problem and fixed it and that made it all come right again. Before that we had been beaten in Canada and were a complete flop in Detroit, even Monaco was a terrible struggle, and we tried so many different types of brake duct our chaps were going crazy . . .'

During the winter there was evidently some alarm within the team at the apparent lack of direction within the TAG Turbo engine project. However, they got back into gear again, settled their 1985 engine spec in time for Rio and then made few further changes. In race tune on race

day the Porsche-engineered power unit still offered the most consistent combination of power, reliability and economy in Formula 1.

New mirror-image, tailor-made turbochargers, were delivered in mid-season. The original interchangeable type demanded a slightly different exhaust system either side of the engine to feed them which slightly compromised the efficiency of one engine bank, so the new mirror-image KKKs put this right.

The persistent and mysterious water loss which had plagued the engines during 1984 had been cured, while the very compact and talented Bosch Motronic management system development team under Dr Udo Zucker had – in Barnard's words – 'Done a brilliant job of making that system perform really well . . . I think they really do deserve enormous credit for what they have done. Most races have seen us use all our fuel and the Bosch system has enabled us to do that perfectly while other teams have to carry extra fuel weight just in case their management system doesn't quite get consumption right. This allows us to start with a minimum load. We missed out at Imola when the car used more oil and more brake pad and more of everything than we expected, but everywhere else it's been very good.

'Bosch's management system is a marvellous piece of kit – it really has come good and people should be more aware that it's a Bosch development.'

This was a very different attitude to 1984's, but the early stormy days of the McLaren/Bosch partnership were now long gone and relationships were now marked by a healthy air of mutual respect.

Apart from remapping engine performance profiles to match differing circuit demands, and the mirror-turbo introduction, there was little

alteration to the TAG Turbo engine. It remained one which would not accept greatly increased turbocharger boost merely for qualifying, and the team was always at a horsepower disadvantage there against BMW, Renault and Ferrari. But in terms of race distance fuel economy on race day, the McLaren-TAGs were normally right there, leading the pace.

Although McLaren again won races consistently, Prost profited while Lauda's sister car was consistently unreliable, surviving once to beat Prost narrowly at Zandvoort.

The team's change from Michelin to Goodyear for '85 initially found the Goodyear rear tyre was much less durable as a race tyre, which created problems of much less grip at the rear than in the front though that situation later reversed.

Prost's 16 1985 races yielded 13 finishes, all of them supposedly scoring points although his clear victory at Imola was disallowed as his car was underweight at post-race scrutineering. His finishing record read 1-(1)-1-3-3-1-2-1-2-1-3-4-3, including wins at Rio, (Imola), Monaco, Silverstone, Austria and Monza.

In contrast, Lauda's season saw 14 starts, missing two races due to a wrist injury suffered in a minor practice incident at Spa late-season, and he finished only three times, 4-5-1, at Imola, *ersatz* Nürburgring, and Zandvoort – the last victory of his superb career as he announced his intention to retire at the end of the season. He retired after a minor crash in Adelaide caused by locking rear brakes, while leading handsomely.

For 1986 Barnard and McLaren International plus TAG Turbo Engines (by Porsche) found themselves aiming at a third consecutive Constructors' Championship title . . .

Carbon Composite Materials

In recent years the phrase 'composite materials' has assumed almost mystic significance amongst the racing media. However, if we consider the term literally, there's nothing at all new about 'composite materials'. A composite of wattle and daub is an age-old material, as is papier mâché.

But composites in Formula 1 take on a different hue. Robin Herd introduced aerospace Mallite composite in his 1966 M2B monocoque car. This was a sandwich skinned in thin aluminium sheet bonded to end-grain balsa wood filling and offered great rigidity with minimal weight by the standards of the time.

Sandwich panels confining aluminium-foil hexagonal-cell 'honeycomb' infill between aluminium sheet skins had already become popular in the aviation industry during the 1950s. Such material offered light panels of outstanding stiffness. The Ford J-car of 1966 featured an incredibly strong, driver-protecting honeycomb chassis carried over into the Le Mans-winning 1967 Ford Mark IV, but as one crew member told me 'It was a sonofabitch to work with, and *impossible* to repair!'

Similar honeycomb panels were used occasionally in Formula 1 – a little in Herd's Cosworth 4WD car of '69, a little more in Derek Gardner's experimental mid-series Tyrrells, with Kevlar and Nomex paper honeycomb infill in the 1977 McLaren M26.

In 1978, Harvey Postlethwaite made a Wolf chassis around a single sheet of aluminium honeycomb, folded up into a U-section trough, suitably stiffened by interior panels and cross-bulkheads, with the man in the middle and fuel in the back.

Patrick Head's Williams FW07, which was built along similar structural lines, then became the finest aluminium honeycomb racing car ever built.

But others despised the stuff. To make a honeycomb lighter than a comparable-strength structure with simple aluminium sheet panelling its skins had individually to be less than half the thickness of the simple aluminium panel to allow for the weight of the foil infill. Its critics claimed these thin surface skins simply tore like paper in heavy impacts, offering minimal driver protection, whereas heavier-gauge simple aluminium would absorb energy very effectively by progressive deformation.

Like so many contentious issues, much depended on where and how this structural aluminium honeycomb was used. One proven designer told me how aluminium honeycomb was suspect in monocoque use as the epoxy bonding between honeycomb infill and outer skin would fail, allowing the tub to flex.

Yet one of his equally experienced peers assured me the opposite is true, especially when more modern Redux glues have been used. The 1978 Williams FW06, for example, was bonded with Araldite which was attacked by brake fluid. The FW07s were Reduxed instead and one 1979 tub had covered 30,000 miles at the time of writing and was still considered 'tight'.

Compared to old-style riveted aluminium tubs in which the rivet holes used to elongate, allowing the rivets to rattle around and joints to chatter, properly-bonded honeycomb monocoques were good news if made by a good team – production honeycomb tubs perhaps less so as quality control was necessarily less strict. In the old days, to re-rivet and reglue an aluminium tub was to give it a real treat . . .

Glass-fibre body panels as used in racing from the early-Fifties were formed of a composite more in line with the popular meaning of that term into the Eighties.

Drawn fibres of glass spun into yarn, woven into mats and then set into a moulded shape within a cured resin matrix – this is what modern 'composites' are all about.

Young's Modulus puts numbers to the stiffness of any material, and it is most illuminating in this context. The Modulus of steel is about 30 million lb per square inch, of wood about 2 million lb, of rubber about 1000 lb.

From around 1960 Government-backed aerospace development in the USA, Britain and Japan sought a new generation of super-stiff, super-light materials, and they came up with filaments of boron in the US (60 million psi) and carbon in the UK, which I am glad

to report had a Young's Modulus of a staggering 110 million psi!

The American method of producing boron fibres – or the shorter form known as 'whiskers' – involved drawing a 0.013 mm tungsten wire through a reaction chamber part-charged with either boron trichloride or boron hydride. The wire was heated electrically like a light-bulb filament to more than 10,000 degrees centigrade, whereupon a 0.05 mm layer of boron would build up on its surface.

Boron composites in resin and aluminium matrices were produced for aerospace use. They were certainly very light and stiff but as boron fibre cost some $700 a kilogramme – at early-Sixties values – it was unsuitable for inexpensive fabrication processes.

Carbon fibre was more practical. One primitive kind had been produced by Edison when he heated bamboo to make his electric light filaments. Then in 1964 a team under Bill Watt at Britain's Royal Aircraft Establishment, Farnborough, succeeded in carburizing polyacrylonitrile (PAN) fibres – basis of the dress fabric Courtelle – under special conditions to produce a very practical fibre possessing very high Modulus and substantial tensile strength.

These fibres were a little weaker than glass fibres but for their weight they were some eight times stiffer than both glass and conventional engineering metals, and resin-fibre composites made with carbon were extremely light and rigid.

DuPont in America then developed Kevlar which could be made much more simply, without need for the special conditions and intense heat applied in carburizing carbon fibre. Kevlar comes from an organic polymer, similar to a high-grade cellulose like flax, but Kevlar was four times stronger, unlike flax it could not rot and its Modulus was about a third that of carbon. Weight for weight, Kevlar was not quite so stiff as boron or carbon but it was quite close behind and was cheaper . . .

Commercially-available carbon fibre and Kevlar were offered ready-spun into thread, then woven and usually pre-saturated in epoxy resin, as 'pre-preg' cloth. Apply a chemical catalyst or subject the cloth to carefully controlled temperature and pressure in an autoclave pressure oven and the epoxy cures into a rigid matrix taking up whatever shape the mould containing the cloth might dictate.

The technique was similar to glass-fibre lay-up but the end product emerged far stronger and very much stiffer per unit weight.

The resin matrix was the key, locking the cloth fibres relative to one another. Fibre orientation within the structure could be aligned so as to take maximum advantage of their individual tensile strength and great stiffness, also minimizing their weakness in compression, for the strength of composite materials of this type is extremely directional.

Once set within a well-cured resin matrix, individual fibres could fracture without significant reduction in component strength because the resin matrix spreads the load throughout the cloth fibres, and where one might fail there is always another right alongside which will not. Fractures seldom propagate as extensive cracks because the plastic matrix does not transmit cracks, and fibres can be arranged as 'crack stoppers'.

Quite unlike steel or aluminium, any shape holes can be cut into a composite carbon panel or moulded

monocoque with little danger of starting cracks from a sharp corner as you most certainly would if you cut a square hole in an aluminium or steel sheet.

Carbon fibre became available on the open market in the 1970s when Roger Sloman worked on R&D for Fothergill & Harvey of Rochdale who made carbon-fibre pre-preg. He recognized its potential in racing but was alarmed by its misuse, as when he heard that carbon-fibre wheels were being made despite the material's poor compression performance.

He wrote to the specialist motor sporting press to say as much and soon received calls from Harvey Postlethwaite of Hesketh and John Horsman of Gulf-Mirage. He quickly produced stiff and light carbon-fibre wing end plates for Hesketh and airfoils for Gulf. The Hill GH1 wing pillar followed but there was a breakdown in communication and the inadequately braced pillar failed in Stommelen's 1975 Spanish GP accident.

Gordon Murray adopted flat carbon panels in the material's first significant use as a structural Formula 1 chassis element in his 1978 Brabham BT46 as Sloman set up his own Advanced Composite Components company in Heanor, Derby, mainly to produce carbon-fibre racing car wings and skirts.

The extreme lightweight and high-rigidity combination of moulded carbon composites attracted Formula 1 designers in 1979-80 as they sought to reconcile ground-effect car requirements for a very slim, low cross-section monocoque chassis with very high torsional rigidity to resist substantial aerodynamic and suspension loadings.

John Barnard blazed the trail as he joined the Project 4 team in 1979-80 to design a new Formula 1 car which would become the McLaren MP4/1, and Peter Wright of Team Lotus almost simultaneously took them along a similar path for the Lotus 88, though techniques differed in detail. Similarly, Carlo Chiti of Autodelta approached Sloman's ACC company to manufacture moulded carbon monocoques for Alfa Romeo.

While the Hercules Corporation in Utah used internal moulding for the McLaren tub, with the 'good' side's nice shiny surface finish on the inside, Sloman used external moulding for his Alfa tubs – 'It was important they looked nice' – so the good side was on the outside. Lotus sought better material quality control by moulding flat panels, feathering the edges and bonding together a kit of flat parts to form their tubs – using the material as 'black aluminium'.

When Gordon Murray adopted a complete carbon inner moulding to stiffen his BT52-53 series aluminium-outer tubs, the interior seat moulding swept up to form an integral tank top, so in Brabham's case the 'good' side was on both the inside and the outside!

Carbon, as the stiffest of these new materials by weight, is used most extensively in these moulded monocoque tubs, while Kevlar is introduced as a 'tear-stopper', its percentage content progressively being reduced in some cases along with moulding wall-thickness as the teams gained experience and confidence, while Nomex foil cells appeared as void fillers to stabilize the finished structures.

A whole new era of motor car design and construction had dawned. Whereas racing mechanics of the inter-war period could still have recognized the materials and techniques of racing car construction up to 1980, they might well have scratched their heads when shown a roll of floppy cloth and a complicated pressure cooker only two or three years later . . .

The modern moulded carbon-composite: a Lotus 97T at Detroit, 1985.

FORMULA 1 RACING ENGINES 1966–85

Apart from the extraordinary story of the Cosworth DFV, which is related in Chapter 3, we can examine here some details of the leading engines built and used in Formula 1 during our period. I make no apology for majoring on the BMW, BRM and Renault engines which played such a significant, if not always successful, role in the Formula 1 story from 1966 to 1985. Details of the minor engines of little real significance, such as the Coventry-Climax 'Godiva' 3-litre hybrid, the Indy Ford, Serenissima and ATS V8s and the Tecno flat-12 are appended in the Shannon, McLaren, Cooper and Tecno sections of the Team Directory.

Alfa Romeo

Autodelta's basic *Tipo* 33 sports-racing V8 engine was first adopted for significant single-seater racing by Alec Mildren's Australian Tasman Championship Brabham team in 1968, two 2.5-litre versions being acquired for Frank Gardner's use. A similar 32-valve 3-litre Formula 1 engine was then to be developed for Cooper, but completed too late for that team's use, first being raced by McLaren in 1970 then March in 1971.

The V8 was an all-aluminium engine, with bore and stroke of 86.0 mm x 64.4 mm, displacing 2998 cc. With five main-bearings and four overhead camshafts rotating in five bearings and driven from rear-of-engine chains, the 33/3 V8 had four valves per cylinder inclined at 39 degrees 30', inlets 32 mm in diameter and exhausts 27 mm, delivering a claimed 400 bhp at 9000 rpm in sports car form. As uprated in 1970-71 with gear-driven camshafts for Formula 1 use, Autodelta claimed

Alfa Romeo's Tipo 1260 3-litre sports car-derived flat-12 was tipped as a challenger for Ferrari.

430 bhp at 10,500 rpm when the Cosworth DFV was delivering some 440 bhp, the Matra V12 around 445-450 and the flat-12 Ferrari 460 at 12,000 rpm.

It was inevitable that *Ing.* Chiti should look enviously at his former employer Ferrari's engine and, with backing from the Alfa Romeo Board, his Autodelta design team produced a sports-racing flat-12 of their own for the 1973 World Championship of Makes season.

In sports car form this Alfa Romeo '115-12' engine was based on cast magnesium blocks and aluminium crankcase, with aluminium or magnesium heads, carrying twin gear-driven overhead camshafts per bank rotating in seven bearings. They actuated four valves per cylinder inclined at the included angle of 35 degrees, inlets 30 mm and exhausts 25.5 mm diameter. The rear-mounted cam-drive gears also powered the 12-cylinder distributor and Lucas fuel injection pump and metering unit. Dinoplex electronic ignition was used, firing single 10 mm plugs per cylinder, and the balanced crankshaft revolved in only three Clevite main bearings, one fewer than Ferrari. Deep-skirted Mahle pistons were used.

Bore and stroke were 77 mm x 53.6 mm, displacing 2995.125 cc. Compression ratio was 10:1; Autodelta claimed 500 bhp at 11,000 rpm.

As developed for Formula 1 (described in the Brabham Team Directory entry, page 169) the engine ran increased compression – up to 11.5:1, valve sizes increased to 33 mm inlet and 26.7 mm exhaust, with a lift of 8.5 mm, and for a weight claimed to average 385 lb (175 kg) the units delivered a claimed 520 bhp at a raucous 12,000 rpm, plus 324 lb/ft torque.

But the flat-12 was an untidy engine apart from its overall dimensions of 30.7 in. long x 27.3 in. wide, and it took time for it to be more neatly packaged. By late-1977 it had become a potential winner with titanium rods and virtually every internal part altered from original sports-prototype form, saving 5 kg.

When Chiti's team rushed through their crash programme to develop the '1260' V12 engine from the flat-12 for Brabham's 1979 ground-effects car, they adopted bore and stroke dimensions of 78.5 mm x 51.5 mm so it was not a direct 'narrowing' of the flat-12 by any means. Compression ratio was quoted as 12:1, valves were as flat-12 and the engine weighed exactly the same – they say – 375 lb (170 kg). Power output was 525 bhp at 12,300 rpm, slightly more than the flat-12 and indeed the V12 engine would allegedly be the most powerful naturally aspirated engine ever seen in the Formula by 1982 when it was producing

Alfa's V8 was like an untidy DFV and made little impression in the 1970 McLaren M7D and M14D.

an apparently genuine 548 bhp.

By this time Chiti had turned to turbocharging, producing a compact but still characteristically rather untidy V8 Type 182T power unit. This engine had twin turbochargers specially made for it by Alfa Romeo Avio although KKKs and Garretts were also tried.

Bore and stroke were 74 mm x 43.5 mm, displacing 1496 cc and the engine was claimed to be delivering 600 bhp at 11,500 rpm in original 1982 form. But in Formula 1 terms it was a rather crude unit, Autodelta hurling fuel into it to cool it adequately and producing horrendous fuel consumption in return. The Alfa-engined cars were notoriously unlikely to survive race distance as fuel capacity restrictions were applied in 1983-84, although by 1984 the so-called '183T' V8 turbocharged engine was producing a claimed 670 bhp at 11,800 rpm, close to Ferrari's 126C but some 180 bhp behind BMW's fearsome little M12/13 turbo's claimed potential – if we believe all the figures in these days of variable boost – and demonstrably some 80 bhp behind the TAG-Turbo Porsche in race trim.

Only the flat-12 Alfa engines ever won a Championship Grand Prix, and that came after disqualification of the first two cars on the road which were Cosworth and Ferrari flat-12 powered. It is not an impressive record, though the engines were usually better than the works cars which carried them.

Major modifications were made to the V8 engine for 1985, the main objective being to control its thirst for fuel. New Chief Engineer Gianni Tonti from Lancia worked closely with Bosch on fuel injection. Although Renault had left KKK in favour of Garrett turbocharging, Alfa took their place with the German company. Tonti's V8 modifications, which included redesign of both block and heads, were merely to see the Euroracing team through 1985 while an all-new replacement four-cylinder F1 engine was prepared for 1986 and its 195-litre GP-distance fuel restriction.

The Alfa *Tipo* 815-84T V8 in final form remained a 32-valve 4-cam V8; bore and stroke was 74 mm × 43.5 mm, displacing 1497 cc, compression ratio 7.0:1, peak race-tune boost pressure 3.4 bar, peak revs (race) 11,300 rpm. Starting the year, Tonti specified peak power in race-tune as 720 bhp at 11,000 rpm – which proved woefully inadequate as the season progressed. The engine, complete and ready to run, scaled 180 kg (396.8 lb) and Euroracing took 11 of them, including five qualifiers, to Rio for the first race. Bosch Motronic all-electronic engine management systems first appeared on the units at Imola, but the season was catastrophic, and, like Renault, Alfa Romeo announced they would not sanction another F1 car build programme for 1986, although Tonti's new four-cylinder engine would be made available for interested customers.

This Alfa Romeo *Tipo* 415-85T unit was unveiled in November 1985 as a neat 92 mm × 56.4 mm, 1498 cc in-line four aiming at 830 bhp in 1986 race consumption tune. It was difficult to see any worthwhile teams who would be sufficiently impressed by Alfa's record to use it.

BMW

On 24 April 1980, the German BMW company from Munich announced their intention to supply engines for use in Formula 1. They had been very active, and highly successful, in Formula 2 and touring car racing since the late-Sixties and after a brief foray in 1970 had introduced a turbocharged in-line four-cylinder engine early in 1977, mounted in 2002 saloons prepared and entered by the Schnitzer concern of Freilassing.

The performance of these cars persuaded BMW to back a co-operative deal with McLaren Engines of Livonia, Detroit, USA, to develop and race a turbocharged BMW 320 in American events to promote export sales.

Under technical direction of BMW Motorsport's Chief Engineer Paul Rosche and McLaren's Roger Bailey, the 2-litre unit was soon developing 550 bhp, then 600. It was not the most reliable racing engine but it showed what was possible.

Meanwhile, Renault had entered Formula 1 in 1977, leading both the turbocharged way and effectively making it 'respectable' for a major manufacturer to be involved in racing against the *garagistes*.

BMW development chief Karlheinz Radermacher and Sales Director Hans-Erdmann Schönbeck joined the enthusiastic Rosche, plus Motorsport's chief-elect Dieter Stappert and Press Department head Dirk Henning Strassl in advocating an entry into Formula 1, using a production-based turbocharged engine to emphasize the BMW 'M-Power' performance image. Strassl was particularly keen to advertize Formula 1 success using a production block engine 'just like you can buy'.

Having developed his 2-litre four-cylinder BMW M12 Formula 2 engine from a 1972 output of some 270 bhp to over 330 bhp and having won six European Formula 2 Championship titles along the way, Rosche had the track record to back his predictions, and a deal was struck to develop a turbocharged BMW-powered Formula 1 Brabham, working closely with Gordon Murray of Bernard Ecclestone's Motor Racing Developments company.

Paul Rosche's engineering group sat down around a clean sheet of drafting paper in April 1980. They decided to use the standard 'small'

Top, the 4-cylinder BMW M12/13 turbo engine in the 1984 Brabham BT53; left intercooler, right radiator; exhaust could only 'blow' one side of undertail diffuser. Below, factory cutaway.

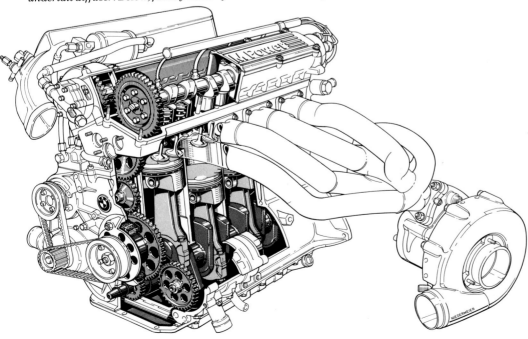

BMW four-cylinder iron block and existing F2-type twin overhead camshaft four-valve-per-cylinder head. BMW Motorsport drew their blocks literally off the shelf from the main production plant. Bore and stroke dimensions were 89 mm x 60 mm displacing 1499 cc.

The finished cast-iron blocks weighed only some 7 kg (15.4 lb) once all machining had been completed. Cylinder bores were glass-polish finished direct into the block without any special surface treatment such as 'Nikasil' lining. But Rosche's men found that a brand new block casting was inadequately stress-relieved for their purposes and preferred well-run blocks with 100,000-odd road kilometres on them as ideally relaxed and stable. An artificial ageing process was therefore applied.

A flat-plane forged-steel, nitrided F2-type crankshaft was retained, carried in five plain Glyco main bearings and incorporating enlarged-flow oilways. It retained the standard production dimensions and bearing shells, 48 mm diameter mains and 45 mm diameter big-ends. The main timing spur gear was pressed onto its nose, a small toughened-steel flywheel bolted onto its tail.

Titanium 153.6 mm long con-rods were used, cut from plate, shot-peened for toughness and with big-ends closed by titanium bolts with

steel nuts. Mahle's pistons were forged aluminium-alloy slipper-type – with very shallow skirts carrying two chromed-steel compression rings and one oil scraper. Hollow-steel fully-floating gudgeon pins attached piston to rod. Each piston assembly complete with pin and circlips weighed only 365 grammes.

Rosche's proven F2-type cylinder head was cast in crisp aluminium alloy with four valves per cylinder inclined in pairs at 30 degrees included angle. They had beryllium-bronze valve seats, the steel-alloy inlet valves themselves being 35.8 mm in diameter, Nimonic exhausts 30.2 mm. Double-valve springs were used, of course.

Copious water supply was galleried around the exhaust valves in particular, and BMW Motorsport were sufficiently confident of the standard production-type head-seal to retain a conventional gasket, tooth-ringed round the cylinders to resist boost pressure there. Head retention was by ten 10 mm bolts.

Cam carriers were in aluminium alloy retained by long studs projecting from the camshaft bearing caps. Bucket-type tappets were used, with shims to set valve clearance. The twin overhead camshafts ran in five plain bearings, obviously less radical cam lobe profiles being employed for the tighter circuits where mid-range torque was more vital than top-end flat-out power.

Camshaft drive was by geartrain from the crankshaft nose, gears running in needle-roller bearings, and also powering the oil pressure and scavenge pumps and alternator while rubber belt-drives were arranged from them for the water injection pumps.

The cast-iron crankcase base was closed by a cast-magnesium sump, with provision for oil/air separation. Four scavenge pumps were provided, two for the bottom end, one for the head and the fourth for the turbocharger lubrication system.

The exhaust manifold was stainless steel carrying a single KKK turbocharger and wastegate. The compressor housing was encased in a carbon-fibre moulding, and an induction tract plenum chamber was another carbon moulding housing the indirect fuel injector nozzles and feeding a cast magnesium induction manifold.

A Bosch electric high-pressure pump was fitted for engine-starting, a Lucas mechanical pump taking over thereafter, driven from the inlet camshaft gear. A Kugelfischer-modified-by Bosch metering unit was used, controlled by a digital electronic management system.

This sensed throttle opening from the main inlet butterfly position, plenum chamber boost pressure, block water temperature, filter fuel temperature, manifold air temperature and engine speed at the flywheel. This data was wired to a carefully chosen pre-set CPU chip whose programme continuously adjusted the injection pump and metering unit fuel flow to match engine supply to demand.

With a compression ratio of 6.7:1 and race boost pressure by 1983 of around 1.9 bar, this engine of relatively humble origin delivered over 650 bhp at 9500 rpm for a weight of 170 kg (374.8 lb) which figure includes the large single Behr intercooler used.

BMW brought Brabham into a more technological era of test and development, using radio link telemetry in track testing to record and permit analysis of both engine and car performance.

Despite continuing unreliability, the early BMW M12/13 turbo engines were very powerful, delivering some 557 bhp at 9500 rpm in 1981-82 when Brabham began using them in anger at Kyalami. Initially, mechanical and turbocharger reliability was very poor and Brabham reverted to Cosworth power to accumulate some points before BMW insisted they bite the bullet and race the M12/13 seriously and soon, and they began winning in mid-season.

During 1982 the M12/13s were producing a genuine 570 bhp at 10,800 rpm in race tune. In 1983, when Piquet won the Drivers' Championship (the important one to BMW's customers), they were turning out a reliable 640 bhp at 11,000 rpm – 426 bhp per litre. In qualifying tune, with higher boost and additional intercooling capacity, there was talk of 750 bhp-plus – 500 bhp per litre. By 1984, when the little engine had become almost grotesquely unreliable in race tune against the economical yet powerful TAG Turbo TTE-P01 V6s, BMW salvaged some of their performance image with some scintillating pole positions, the engine running up to – and very possibly beyond – 850 bhp at 11,000 rpm (556 bhp per litre).

Paul Rosche's humble little in-line four-cylinder production-block BMW M12/13 made a wickedly potent Formula 1 engine into the mid-Eighties. The 1983 World Championship victory with an engine 'based on the one you can buy' certainly brought a smile to Strassl's face – 630 days after the Bavarian project had begun.

Everybody sought more power, torque and economy from their engines for 1985. In qualifying tune BMW's 'specials' would run well into four figures. At Monza, for example, Piquet's Brabham-BMW exceeded 208 mph past the pits, and at Ricard 213 mph on the Mistral Straight, suggesting over 1140 bhp, while over 1270 bhp was reputedly realized on Rosche's Munich dynos.

By the end of '85, 1000 bhp was virtually a minimum requirement for front-row qualifying – 666 bhp per litre – achieved by rapidly improving electronic engine management and highly classified internal engineering to burn specially mixed legal-octane high-aromatic fuel under 4 ata boost or more, with ever-increasing efficiency. BMW's fuels were specially brewed for them by a division of the BASF chemical company, with whom they had been conducting a lengthy development programme.

Only four years previously no more than a reliable 181 bhp per litre from Cosworth had won the Championship. In race-tune in 1985 533 bhp per litre was accepted as normal and the better heat-rejecting iron-block BMWs and Hondas were up around 566.

After the problems of 1984, BMW had tightened up quality control to retrieve engine reliability, and Brabham requested a lower inlet level permitting a lower intake box and new car body giving better airflow to both induction and rear wing. Their float of 25 'works' engines was clearly amongst the most powerful around, but output had to be tailored to Pirelli's available tyres for the Italian

company was still learning through 1985.

Brabham-BMW ran higher race horsepower beginning the year than through mid-season because of this.

BMW's customer engines for Arrows were inevitably in more modest tune aimed at reliability, and were prepared and rebuilt under sub-contract by Heini Mader. That major success eluded BMW during our period's final season was no fault of the German concern, for their apparently humble stock-block in-line four-cylinder remained the most potent engine Grand Prix racing had seen.

British Racing Motors

BRM entered the 1966 Formula with a terrific record behind them in the five seasons of 1.5-litre racing as described in the Team Directory.

The Chief Engineer at Bourne, Tony Rudd, and BRM's remote advanced projects study office attached to Harry Weslake Research in Rye, Sussex, had both studied proposals for a new 3-litre engine. At this time they worked quite well together, each evaluating the other's ideas, and the choice came down to either a 48-valve V12 promoted from Rye, or a two-valve-per-cylinder coupled twin-crankshaft H16-cylinder promoted by Rudd and his men at Bourne.

The more compact if frighteningly complex H16 was chosen as it could use proven 1500 cc V8 components, could be employed handily as a fully-stressed chassis member mated to a monocoque chassis nacelle and had greater theoretical development potential (up to 600 bhp) than the V12. With an initial design target of at least 420 bhp, it should have cleaned up in its first season and should also have been well placed to repeat the performance in 1967.

While design progressed, BRM patron Sir Alfred Owen told his thunderstruck engineers he wanted to run the Formula 1 V8 cars in the 2.5-litre Tasman Championship in January/March 1966, representing important markets for his Rubery Owen industrial group. Rudd and driver Graham Hill argued that the 200-mile tankage Formula 1 cars were unsuitable for 100-mile Tasman races but Sir Alfred would not be moved, and BRM had hastily to enlarge their P56 1500 cc V8 engines to 2-litres.

As quick as they converted them, the enlarged V8s would break their piston rings on the team's test-bed at Folkingham aerodrome. This was thought to be connected with side loads on the piston due to the short con-rod coupled to the increase in stroke.

Matra had been using BRM P80 1-litre Formula 2 engines and they now ordered seven 2-litre V8s for use at Le Mans. Unlike the initial 1916 cc Tasman engines which would also be used in 1966 Formula 1 until the H16 became raceworthy, these were full 1998s. Bourne subsequently decided to go for broke and enlarged their works V8s to the maximum 2070 cc for the 1967 Tasman Championship and subsequent occasional Formula 1 use.

The 1916 cc engines of 1966 appeared with both side- and down-draught port heads, consistently recording 262-265 bhp and 258-260 bhp respectively on the dyno, yet Matra's full 1998s rarely did better and never got above 270 bhp. However, the 2070s shone, most giving 285 bhp and one (engine '5621', ex-Stewart) bellowed out a resounding 292 bhp!

Such is the reality of racing engine production and variation and the engineers were puzzled.

The interim V8s' longer stroke meant that BRM initially limited their drivers to 10,000 rpm in Formula 1 racing but soon they were using 10,500 rpm unconcerned. At Reims, in the French GP, Hill's 1916 was towed along at 10,750 rpm by Parkes's Ferrari V12 and Graham told Tony Rudd, 'The thing was still going and still picking up power', until – inevitably – it broke a camshaft.

In retrospect, Tony told me: 'Had we known how successful the 2-litre was going to be it's quite probable we wouldn't have gone on with the H16 at the expense of the V12. We would have built a two-valve V12 first to get near 400 bhp, and it would have been light and reliable and we could have used a derivative of the very successful 1965 car which would have given us an excellent chance of the World Championship in 1966 and a good chance for '67 as well. We might never have built the H16 at all, in which case motor racing in the late '60s and early '70s would have been very different . . .'

Bourne committed itself to the P75 H16 early in 1965, and having extracted so much from the basic P56 V8 they were looking towards 146-147 bhp per litre from the H16, taking 440 bhp as a starting point.

The H-layout is really a slight misnomer; picture instead the 'H' laid on its side, two flat-eight boxer engines one above the other, their centreline crankshafts geared together. It had been common in wartime aero engine design when Tony himself had headed a Rolls-Royce fault investigation department and was very familiar not only with such engines but also with their designers and trouble-shooters. The 24-cylinder R-R Eagle and Napier Rapier, Dagger and Sabre had all been 'H'-type engines.

Originally there was an idea to use only three camshafts each side of the engine, the centre shaft actuating the inlet valves in both the upper and lower 'eights'. Neat and weight-saving it was found impractical, for extra space was needed between the cranks and Rudd and his assistant Geoffrey Johnson narrowed the angle between the valves and used a slightly larger cylinder bore to accommodate them. Now the H16's bore and stroke became 69.85 mm x 48.89 mm and there was no longer direct interchangeability with the 68.5 mm x 50.8 mm P56 V8's reciprocating components.

Tony had drawn upon Rolls-Royce Eagle H16 aero engine practice in adopting a crankcase cast in light-alloy split along the main bearing cap line, with the coupling gears for the crankshafts in a separate pack bolting onto the back of the engine, connected to the cranks by two alleged quill shafts about an inch in diameter so not very flexible. The cylinder heads were from the 1500 V8s and timing packs from the F2 four-cylinder engines. The oil pumps were to a scaled-up V8 design, passing 32 gallons per minute. Tony himself describes the engine as 'an odd mixture of sophistication and the primitive'.

As an opposed engine, H16 bearing loads would be less than the preceding V8s and there was no reason to suppose individual components would not behave just as they had in those 1500s.

Tony Rudd: 'Of course we did not know there was a malevolent demon hidden in the middle of it.

'We had decided to use the long con-rod of the four-cylinder F2 engine, which had a cylinder block based on one half of the V8 . . . We had terrible trouble with it in the first few F2 races of 1965 and the galling thing was that there seemed no way of coaxing it over 130 bhp. The first few all came out around 125-126 . . .'

Very late in the day, they finally tried shorter con-rods on a lashed-up test engine. The first thing it did was break piston rings and the second thing it did was generate 140 bhp trouble free.

The shorter 1500 cc rods gave a 5.5 per cent reduction in side thrust, which yielded a 7.5 per

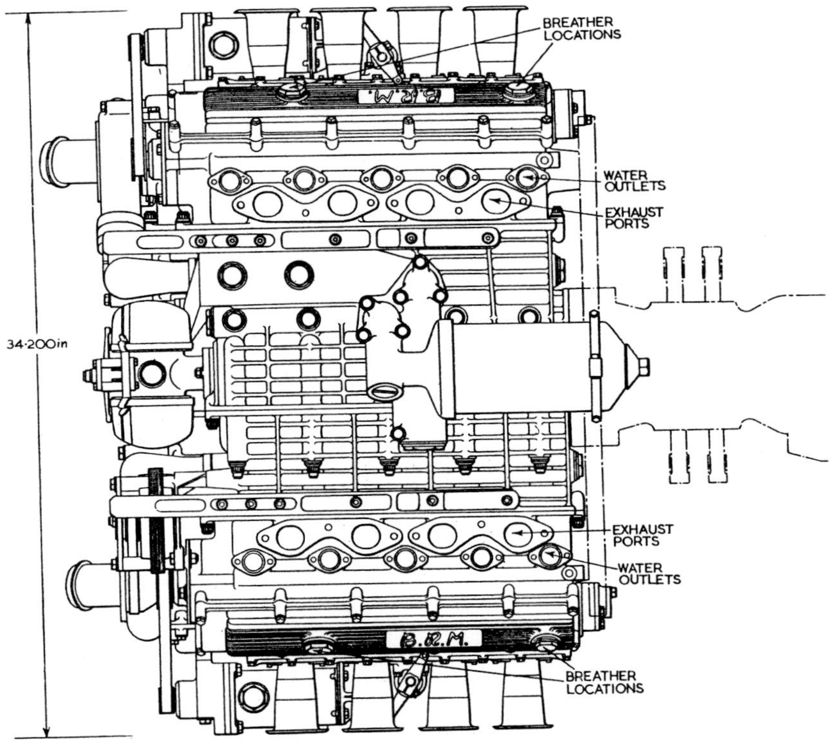

BRM's H16 engine as originally laid out for 1966: above, *planview emphasizes package size;* below, *front-end elevation shows compact coupling of two flat-8s with common vertical gear-pack.*

cent increase in power output. Rudd's team now realized that the difference in piston velocity away from Top Dead Centre between the two rod lengths accounted for the F2 engine's lack of performance, which had always been greater at high rpm than low.

However, by this time the H16 engine was committed to the long F2-type con-rod and when it first ran the approximate 7.5 per cent loss of predicted power became apparent. Instead of the 440 bhp theoretically predicted they were lucky to reach 400, and when in mid-1966 the new 16-cylinder weighed 586 lb compared to the 1500 V8's 260 lb it was obvious 'we had got it wrong somewhere'.

Now there are several legends perpetuated about the shortcomings of the BRM P75 H16. It vibrated, its complex camshaft interconnections allowed drift causing valves to trip over each other, and so on.

Looking at the H16 its creator considers the first and biggest mistake was fitting the longer connecting rod, originally suggested by Charles Goodacre of the Ethyl Corporation, 'and I fell for it'. Hepworth & Grandage, the piston people, also checked the calculations and advised it would work 'but I was the one person who knew about the rate of burning and flame-spread after TDC, and I was the one who should have known better. It was not a good idea for a high-revving engine.

'The geared crankshafts were a mistake from a torsional vibration viewpoint but I don't think there's any evidence that it suffered from that vibration – as distinct from *experiencing* that vibration. It only suffered lack of inertia in its two crankshafts.

'And above all the main problem was that it was just plain 150 lb too heavy. We had calculated a weight of 460-480 lb since it was duplicating most parts of a 260 lb V8.

'The excess arose from castings designed around 3/16 in. thick emerging well over 1/4 in. thick, therefore 25 per cent thicker and 25 per cent heavier, accounting for 40 lb excess overall. Then modifications we added to strengthen the engine, like the flywheels and inertia weights, added another 40 lb and another 30 lb came simply from manufacturing expedience.'

The prototype H16 engine '7501' first fired at 10.45 a.m., 23 January 1966, and its weight quite shattered the engineers. It ran for seven minutes at 2000 rpm until the dyno prop-shaft seized. This was the precursor of a series of failures requiring a strip and rebuild costing a week on each occasion. Rudd suspected the inlet valves were tripping over the exhausts but Geoff Johnson convinced him it was impossible by making a five-times full-size drawing with the valve paths plotted onto it.

'This theory', says Rudd, 'seems to have developed into a legend that this was one of the problems. There was never any evidence of it actually happening . . .'

It took more time to appreciate that the upper crankshaft had no flywheel of its own and relied totally upon the inertia of the gearbox and clutch to carry it from one firing cycle to the next, or upon the inertia of the lower crankshaft to which it was geared.

By April '66 there were still no raceworthy engines. When the inertia problem was recognized, they took large steel discs, split them and slipped them over the balance weights, bolting and tack-welding them together. Each one weighed 2 lb, there were four per crankshaft, another 16 lb in the engine. Now they could run to 10,000-11,000 rpm and the faster it ran the better the H16 looked.

Power remained disappointing, just under 400 bhp, but they were so relieved to find reliability they did not care, and the first engine went into a car for Monaco practice.

The gearchange was fearfully slow and wrecked all the dogs in the gearbox. Lotus had ordered one of the engines and their own was about ready when Colin Chapman had a look and said 'No wonder, you've put the clutch on the wrong way round!'

Instead of the clutch plates – which have no inertia – being connected to the gearbox layshaft, BRM had coupled the heavy outer drum with starter ring connected to it. Thus, when the driver changed gear he would disengage the clutch, the engine would die but the gearbox internals would run on under the inertia of the clutch drum and starter ring, hammering the engagement dogs as he fought to find the next gear. After a few changes the dogs would be damaged and the gearbox in need of a rebuild.

The H16s practised strongly at Reims and Rudd took a spare engine there in his company Rover, which took a poor view of the 500 lb lump in its boot.

Late in 1966 BRM's spare works team engine '7502' won the US GP in Clark's Lotus 43. It was not a heavily salvaged engine at that time, but became so after throwing its inertia weights during practice for the next race in Mexico. New 'eight-throw' two-pin crankshafts were fitted to provide a more permanent vibration cure, and from this point forward the engine fired and sounded like a true 16-cylinder, whereas originally it had fired two cylinders simultaneously so sounded like a loud eight.

Into 1967 the engine was reliable. Engine '7504' turned 400 bhp in March 1967 at 10,500 rpm and weighed some 580 lb with inertia rings on its crankshafts. It was never rebuilt as a two-pin engine. The highest power output recorded from an H16 was seen that March on engine '7506', just topping 420 bhp. Meanwhile, Sir Alfred Owen had authorized construction of a bet-hedging 3-litre V12 engine, not the Weslake 48-valver which in effect had become the Gurney Eagle unit but a sports-prototype oriented 24-valve design by Geoffrey Johnson.

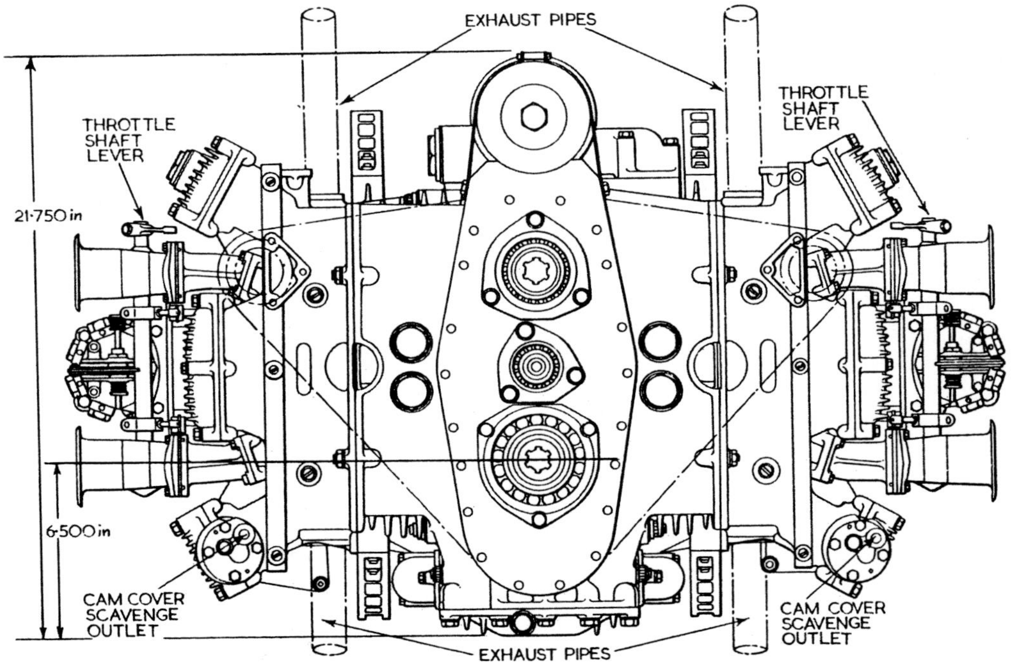

This P101 unit was first employed by McLaren in the 1967 Canadian GP and would be taken up by the works BRM team to replace the H16 for 1968, and on to the end . . .

Bore and stroke were 73.8 mm x 57.2 mm, displacing 2998 cc, compression 12:1, and, after first running on 26 July 1967, engine 'P101-003' had peaked at 369 bhp at 9750 rpm on 14 August. On 3 November 1967, a 2.5-litre Tasman Formula 'P121-001' had its first dyno run, delivering 318 bhp at 10,250 rpm, engine '002 having run earlier on 31 October, delivering 309 bhp at 9900 rpm.

As of 16 November 1967, six BRM V12 engines existed – three P101 24-valve 3-litres and three P121 2.5 Tasman units ready for Len Terry's new P126 monocoque cars and the 1968 Tasman Championship.

Meanwhile the ultimate, much-modified magnesium-block four-valve-per-cylinder H16 engine (yes, 64 valves, 128 valve springs – imagine assembling it all) was completed and tested for 1968 but the policy decision was taken to set it aside and concentrate upon the simpler and lighter V12. The engine continued in test as late as from 13 December 1968 to 25 January 1969. It was number '7541' and the best of its eight runs peaked at only 378 bhp at 10,300 rpm; that was nothing like enough to compete with Cosworth's DFV, which was already beyond 430 bhp.

In comparison, P101 V12s were running as high as 404 bhp at 10,000 rpm (number '019 on 11 January 1969), and Johnson then developed a four-valve-per-cylinder gear-driven camshafts 48-valve P142 unit for 1969; units '142-001' and '002 were available for Oliver and Surtees' in the Spanish GP on 4 May.

The first 48-valver had run on 28 February on the Folkingham bed, recording 453 bhp at 10,350 rpm and '002's first run on 26 March yielded an instant 455 bhp at 10,750 rpm. This was almost 50 bhp more than the best P101 24-valvers and through the season the six P142 engines available to the team averaged 440 bhp at a time when Cosworth were claiming 430 at 10,000 rpm.

In 1970, the P142s powered more adequate Southgate-designed chassis and began winning races, but power was not destined to improve dramatically in the years left to BRM and its V12 engines. After Rudd had gone to

BRM's final serious season in Formula 1 was 1974 when new chief chassis designer Mike Pilbeam (seen here) developed the compact and quick P201s, but tight budgets and muddled management meant their P142 and P192 V12 engines were not man enough to realize the car's potential.

Lotus, Aubrey Woods took over engine development. He considered the chain-driven four-cam centre-exhaust P142 overheated both its water and oil too easily, and suffered badly from detonation. Its relatively long stroke was a limiting factor, new pistons were required and they took a long time to make. He designed new cylinder heads lowering engine CoG with outside exhausts and in-vee inlets with improved ports and enlarged cooling waterways. The crankcase was now cross-bolted and stiffened to allow use as a semi-stressed chassis member.

The BRM V12s would always retain their camshaft chain-drive as the system's last refuge in Formula 1.

Woods subsequently left to join Amon Engines, Peter Windsor-Smith taking over with Rubery-Owen also consulting Walter Hassan and Harry Mundy. Windsor-Smith produced a new P192 V12 for 1974, which carried new heads with narrower-angle valves and altered porting, while the pistons were flatter and lighter, and there were bottom end improvements. Some 13 lb was saved and a shorter stroke and wider bore were mentioned. With minor modifications the lighter short-stroke crankshaft was also intended to fit old P142 crankcases, but ex-BRM staff seem to doubt if the short-stroke crankshaft was ever in fact produced – certainly not in any numbers.

As the team entered its final serious, if even then barely significant, season in 1974, Bourne quality control records indicate that engines '142-008', '009, '017, '018, '021 and '022 as prepared for the Nürburgring on 31 July, 1974 peaked respectively at 454, 444, 430, 444, 435 and 439 bhp. This displayed little, if any, progress over the previous five years, for all engines were run on the same Folkingham dyno, unless that too was growing weary with age.

P192 engine '002 peaked at 453 bhp at 10,750 rpm prior to the British GP at Brands Hatch that season. At 7000 rpm this V12 delivered 284 bhp, at 8000 rpm 352, at 9000 rpm 433 and at 11,000 rpm 447 bhp. Peak torque was 236 lb/ft at 9000 rpm.

A final further Aubrey Woods-revised P202 engine was developed for the Stanley-BRM car of 1977 delivering a claimed 480 bhp at 11,200 rpm but it looked neither conspicuously powerful nor reliable and it failed dismally – a sad and demeaning postcript to the story of a once honoured name. At its peak, BRM had been a superb outfit – an incontrovertible fact which Bourne's many detractors too easily forget.

Anyone who has never made a mistake hasn't done very much and BRM never fell into that category.

Ferrari

The Maranello concern's 1966 V12 F1 engine was a 77 mm × 53.5 mm 60-degree light-alloy V12 with four overhead camshafts. Of modest sports-racing provenance, it was claimed to deliver 380 bhp at 10,000 rpm (probably nearer 360 bhp), with Lucas fuel injection and Marelli coil and distributor ignition.

The elderly but now fuel-injected 2.4-litre four-cam Dino V6 engine used briefly in 1966 was well suited to the more tortuous circuits, but the Ferrari 312 V12s were Maranello's frontline armament.

Major V12 developments have been described in the Team Directory and by the end of its long run in 1969 it had become a roller main-bearing power unit with Lucas electronic transistorized ignition, Lucas fuel injection, compression quoted around 12.0:1 and an output of some 410 bhp at 10,500 rpm. While the DFV V8 had the narrow included valve angle of 32 degrees at this time, the Ferrari V12's valves were still disposed at 50-55 degrees, and BRM's at 61 degrees.

In 1970, the Forghieri/Rocchi/Bussi engine design team produced their splendid *Tipo 312B* flat-12 power unit which in ever-developing form would power their Formula 1 cars for a decade.

The horizontal 'boxer' layout (some people calling it a 180-degree vee!) was adopted to enable a very low centre of gravity to be achieved. It also cleared airflow beneath the rear wing and saved a little weight compared to the V12. Dimensions were 78.5 mm × 51.5 mm, displacing 2991.01 cc. Four-valve-per-cylinder heads borrowed late-series V12 experience.

In initial form piston and crankshaft problems caused a string of testing failures, not least involving lubrication problems solved by the provision of a tilting dyno bed at Maranello to reproduce cornering surge conditions.

The flat-12 was a very high-revving unit and to minimize friction losses its crankshaft revolved in just four main bearings, two plain shell bearings amidships and ball-bearing races at nose and tail. This left the crankshaft with rather dubious support and, after initial breakages, crankshaft torsionals were controlled by the addition of a Pirelli cushion coupling between crankshaft and flywheel, achieving reliability to match 460 bhp between 11,500 and 11,700 rpm power. By 1974, power was up to 495 bhp and by the end of the engine's useful life it was delivering nearer 510 bhp at 12,000 rpm – which few doubted.

The light-alloy block-cum-crankcase was cast in two parts, united on a crankshaft centreline bolted flange. The heads were cast in crisp aluminium alloy disposing four valves per cylinder actuated by double overhead camshafts per bank powered by geartrain from the crankshaft nose.

Light-alloy cylinder liners were used, cooled by water circulation at their upper ends, by oil circulation down below. The crankshaft was machined from a steel forging, each of its six crankpins carrying two con-rods. The crankshaft nose gear drove alternator, ignition distributor and fuel metering unit via gears and pinions. The crankshaft tail drove the valvegear train. A tiny flywheel assembly incorporated a rubber vibration damper. Forged titanium con-rods were used, with plain big-end bearings, although rollers were apparently used experimentally on occasion.

Mahle forged aluminium pistons were used, pocketed for valve clearance and 'squish'.

A single oil pressure pump driven off the rear of the right-hand cylinder-head timing gear fed the oil filter mounted behind the fuel metering unit, then on into the front of the block. The scavenge pump resided in the same housing as the pressure pump, returning oil to the tank which chased around the car in the various 312B, 'B2, 'B3, 'B4, 312T and 'T2-3-4-5 models

in which variations of this power unit featured.

The two cars, the 1973 *Spazzaneve* 'B3 prototype and a 1977-spec 'T2, which were in my care briefly seemed to have nothing interchangeable between their two engines.

The 1979 Championship unit featured an ancillary scavenge pump driven from the exhaust camshaft in one head to clear excess oil from the head chambers into the block. A complex magnesium casting on the front of the engine encased the ancillary drive gears and a solitary water pump.

Water fed into the heads through channels cast integrally into the block covers. The left-side exhaust camshaft drove a high-pressure fuel pump. Engine mounting to the chassis was via lugs on the early units suspending the flat-12 from the rear beam of the 312B and 'B2 series cars, then via four studs in the head covers from the 'B3 model forward.

Internal dimensions of the 312B series engines varied enormously, as did the precise design of their castings and internals, and layout of their ancillaries. Only overall configuration and dimensions, within an inch or so, remained constant through their 11 seasons of competition.

Ferrari listed late-series dimensions as 80 mm × 49.6 mm, giving a unit cylinder capacity of 249.31 cc, or 2999 cc overall. The 1979-80 engine was 650 mm long, 680 mm wide and 300 mm tall and weighed 180 kg with accessories attached.

The turbocharged 120-degree V6 126C power unit developed for 1981 had bore and stroke dimensions of 81 mm × 48.4 mm, displacing 1496.43 cc. With its KKK or Comprex BBC pressure-wave supercharging (although the latter was over-publicized and really hardly significant), this unit had a compression ration of 6.5:1 and delivered a claimed 560 bhp at 11,500 rpm in 1981 form, rising to 580 bhp at 11,800 rpm in 1982, 620 bhp at 11,500 in 1983 and 680 bhp at 11,500 rpm in 1984. It weighed 175 kg (375 lb), as do nearly all Italian Formula 1 engines, if we believe their manufacturers' figures. The flat-

12 in final form was lighter, not carrying turbocharging ancillaries nor having to resist 126C temperatures and pressures, at 160 kg (353 lb).

Ferrari pursued rapid development of their engine, evolving a turbocharger run-on fuel-burning system to keep them wound up on boost ready for the driver to open the throttle again after decelerating on the over-run. With AGIP, an atomized-water injection system was also developed to enhance already intercooled induction charge density, and power output rose progressively to 580 bhp at 11,800 rpm in their first turbocharged Constructors' Championship season of 1982, then 620 bhp at 11,500 rpm in 1983 and finally an alleged 680 bhp at 11,500 rpm – presumably in race trim – in the fuel-conscious season of '84. Subsequently, effort expended upon water-injection would come to be regarded in-house as harmful to

potentially more profitable development elsewhere, and as the 1984 Ferrari season fell apart major changes took place, including the dismissal of *Ing.* Forghieri from direct *Reparto Corse* involvement.

Ings. Ildo Renzetti and Luciano Caruso redesigned the V6 engine for 1985, producing new heads with reversed ports to place the inlet ports in the vee, exhausts outside, manifolding sweeping away through KKK turbochargers low either side. This enabled chassis designer Postlethwaite to create a far neater, lower-bodied car than hitherto, the best-looking in Formula 1. A new digital electronic management system had been developed for the new 156/85 by Weber-Marelli, combined with an AGIP Petroli water-suspension *emulsistem*, and upon release in February '85 Maranello claimed 780 bhp at 11,000 rpm. Development continued rapidly with a quad-turbo engine

Right, *the 120-degree V6 turbocharged Ferrari contrasts with* (below) *a Maranello factory section of the 312B flat-12 engine showing its deep base chamber, roller-bearing mains, narrow included valve angle, induction tracts above the heads, exhausts below and extensive cross-bolting of the split crankcase castings.*

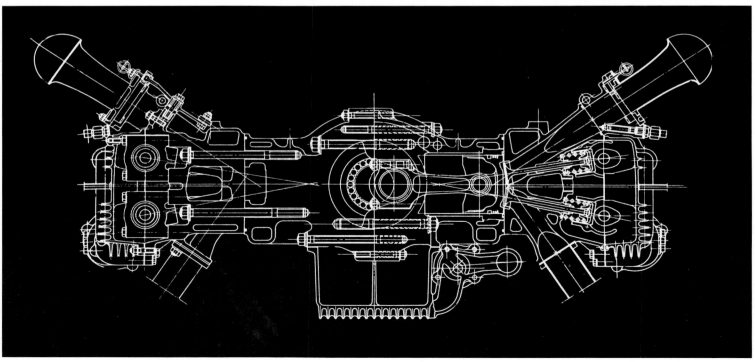

Ferrari's 126C turbocharged 120-degree V6 1.5-litre engine made its debut at Long Beach, 1981. This is the KKK twin-turbocharged version, see the underwing floor curving up beneath the side induction 'log'.

being tested early in the year but remaining unraced. An electronically-controlled waste-gate adjustment, to give fine-adjustable boost while running, was adopted during the season, however.

Nevertheless the V6 engine was near the end of its development life, its original 1980-81 design having itself been trimmed to the bone around an ultimate requirement for perhaps only 700-750 bhp. Forghieri's planned four-cylinder replacement was tested through the 1984-85 winter, but Ferrari's chassis section disliked its slant design as this posed installation problems, and it then proved mechanically unreliable on Caruso's test beds. With Forghieri removed from F1 responsibility, his slant-4 engine was set aside; the V6 went into its fifth racing season with a quoted 780 bhp and at Estoril its times suggested 793 bhp in race-tune. German GP qualifying required a calculated 988 bhp to achieve Ferrari's times, while race-tune there gave around 839 bhp, ostensibly little more than TAG Turbo and BMW, the latter perhaps anxious for reliability and tyre-conservation on home-ground. In Austria, the Ferraris had to run some 881 bhp in race-tune to face BMW, Honda and TAG Turbo and mechanical reliability began to falter.

Thereafter Ferrari's season collapsed as the high boost pressures necessary to keep competitive overwhelmed the 120-degree V6's mechanical reliability. It became obvious that they no longer had the most powerful engine in Formula 1 and ending our period a major rethink and redesign had become necessary.

Gurney-Weslake

Engineer Aubrey Woods had vast BRM experience when he was seconded to the BRM 'think-tank' development group based at Weslake Research in Rye, Sussex. In effect this had been a BRM political device to shuffle their former Chief Engineer, Peter Berthon, sideways away from their Bourne factory, but the Weslake proposal for a 3-litre 48-valve V12 was considered most seriously for 1966 before being rejected in favour of the H16.

This rejected proposal then formed the basis of the Weslake Type 58 V12 engine which appeared in Gurney's Eagle at Monza in 1966. Successful gas-flow specialist Harry Weslake aimed to maintain good power and torque over a very wide speed range by use of a compact combustion chamber mated to carefully chosen port sizes. These had to be large enough to maintain good flow but sufficiently tight for high gas velocities to be maintained, contributing an internal ram effect.

Such theories had worked well on the 2-litre BRM V8 engine with which Woods was familiar, with internal dimensions of 73.3 mm x 59.2 mm; the new Type 58's measurements were 72.8 mm x 60 mm.

The new V12 was very reminiscent of BRM V8 practice, with similar ribbed crankcase castings, seven main bearings instead of the V8's five, the crankcase sides extending below the crankshaft centreline to support two-bolt bearing caps. As in the BRM V8s only the rear main cap was cross-bolted.

Cylinder design was standard BRM, with thinwall cast-iron wet liners secured by a top flange nipped between cylinder head and the closed block top face. Con-rods were identical in length and design to BRM's and piston mechanical design below the crown was the same, with narrow slipper skirts and only two rings.

Valvegear was pure BRM, incorporating twin coil-springs, cup-type tappets above, bolted-in ferrous carriers for each tappet and camshafts rotating in crowded roller bearings, though Woods made both head castings identical to ease manufacture and servicing.

A very narrow included valve angle was adopted, enabling one-piece twin-cam covers to be provided, minimizing weight and width and pre-dating the Cosworth DFV heads to come.

Valve sizes were 1.2 in. and 0.985 in. for inlets and exhausts respectively, valve lifts being 0.375 in. and 0.312 in. Short stub manifolds within the vee connected the inlet ports to a single throat fed with fuel from a Lucas injector nozzle. Camshaft drive was from a train of gears carried in a separate split magnesium casing at the front of the engine. Block and heads were cast in aluminium alloy, and all-up weight was only 390 lb.

The water pump and pressure and scavenge oil pumps were gear-driven from the crankshaft nose, and other accessories were driven from the timing gears; the alternator and twin Lucas distributors. Woods had to move some ancillaries back on the V12 to allow it to fit the space dictated in the Eagle tub by the alternative Indy Ford V8. The left-side exhaust camshaft tail drove the mechanical fuel pump, the right-exhaust camshaft tail operated the Lucas ignition trigger and the fuel injection metering unit was driven by a cogged belt from the right-side inlet camshaft.

The V12s were built for Anglo-American Racers Inc. by a Weslake crew under Michael Daniel's direction. Prototype assembly in August 1966 occupied 1200 man hours and on 18 August it ran for the first time. Within a week it was claimed to produce 364 bhp at 9500 rpm but, as described in the Eagle section of the Team Directory, it suffered numerous problems of overheating, quality-control and rebuilding, and ultimately the project collapsed in recrimination – fortunately not before Gurney had won a minor Formula 1 race and the classic Belgian GP with it in 1967.

The basic design was subsequently revived in 1970 when Harry Weslake discussed a potential long-distance sports car and Formula 1 engine with Stuart Turner and Len Bailey of the Ford Motor Company. The new engine was much modified and revised but in 1972 proved a dreadful flop, despite Weslake and an independent dyno-tester – yes, they had to prove it – recording 464 bhp at 10,750 rpm. One engine was installed in a BRM P160 (it fitted rather nicely!) and run at Ricard without impressing while Brabham built a special car for it which was not considered worthy to be raced and the project petered out.

This was a pity because, apart from anything else, it was a superb-looking power unit.

Hart

Brian Hart, former racing driver turned engine manufacturer, established his fine engineering reputation with a long and successful series of Ford-based engines, most significantly for Formula 2. He followed on from this by manufacturing his own unit from the ground up and aspiring to Formula 1 with a 1500 cc turbocharged 'Hart 415T' version of this unit in conjunction with the Toleman team in 1981. Toleman had used Hart engines to win the previous season's European Formula 2 Championship and it was a bold move for both to plunge into Formula 1.

The alloy-block four-cylinder in-line Hart turbocharged engine had bore and stroke dimensions of 89.2 mm x 60 mm, displacing 1499 cc. Compression ratio was 6.7:1 and with a single KKK turbocharger the unit delivered a claimed 557 bhp at 9500 rpm, compared to the Cosworth DFV V8's contemporary *circa* 500 bhp, the Renault V6's 540, Ferrari's 560, BMW's 557 and Matra's 510 bhp.

The Gurney-Weslake V12 of 1966-68 was the most glamorous Formula 1 power unit of its time, all trumpets, tailpipes and oil filters.

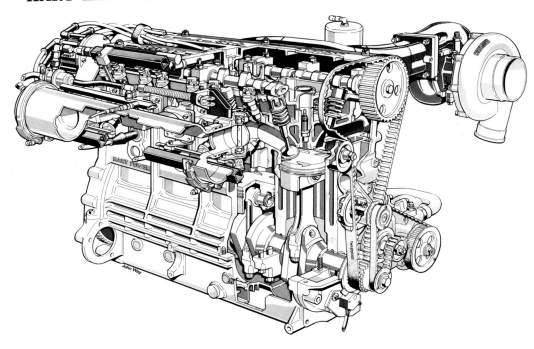

Honda

The Japanese motor cycle colossus had entered production of cars and light vans in 1962, and within two years began promoting its new models by building an ambitious transverse V12-engined 1500 cc Formula 1 car.

It was a motor cycle type engine in its extensive use of roller-bearings and Honda used similar technology in a crushingly successful four-valve-per-cylinder 1-litre four-cylinder Formula 2 engine for 1966, used by Brabham.

That September their monster new Formula 1 four-valve-per-cylinder roller-bearing RA273 V12 appeared in the Italian GP at Monza, as described in the Team Directory. This mighty engine with drive taken from the centre of its crankshaft had dimensions of 78.0 mm x 52.2 mm, displacing 2992 cc. Its published specification included 1.16 in. diameter inlet valves, and 1.02 in. exhausts disposed at an included angle of 75 degrees, 35 degree inlet and 40 degree exhaust. Valve lift was 0.325 in. with Honda timed fuel injection and transistorized electronic ignition this incredibly raucous unit delivered '400-plus' bhp at 10,000 rpm.

As described, development went at best sideways and sometimes backwards in the two seasons' racing which followed. By 1968 Honda were claiming 430 bhp from their RA301 V12 with the narrower included valve angle of 65 degrees, still the most powerful engine in Formula 1.

The ill-fated air-cooled RA302 used a 120-degree V8 with dimensions of 88.00 mm x 61.40 mm, displacing 2987 cc and producing an estimated 380 bhp at 10,500 rpm.

Honda withdrew from Formula 1 at the end of that 1968 season and would not return to four-wheeled single-seater competition until 1980 when they produced their new 80-degree V6 iron-block 2-litre four-cam racing engines intended for contemporary Formula 2.

They were successful in Ron Tauranac's Ralt cars and in 1981 Honda supplied Ralt's works F2 team with 20 updated V6 engines claiming 10 per cent more power than the rival 315 bhp best BMW and Hart units. Team and drivers had their problems but Lees won three races and took the European Championship title for the Honda engine.

The new Spirit team joined Ralt in the Honda camp for 1982 Formula 2 but the anticipated Honda domination failed to materialize, picking up only three race wins. Johansson's Spirit-Honda was on pole for five of the first eight races and there was at least one Spirit on the front row in each of the first nine events. Ralt-Honda suffered development problems on their cars, yet in 1983 they steam-rollered the Formula 2 Championship, with drivers Thackwell and Palmer utterly dominant, the latter winning the last five Championship rounds successively to clinch the title.

Meanwhile, Honda had announced a renewed interest in Formula 1, and modified the basic and rather untidy 80-degree four-cam V6 F2 engine to 1500 cc turbocharged F1 form for Spirit to test as described.

The Honda RA163-E F1 V6 was shrouded in secrecy, no details of internal dimensions being published, merely claiming 600 bhp with twin KKK turbocharging, though Japanese IHI units soon replaced the German turbochargers.

Brian Hart (above) made brilliant use of a tight budget by enabling several smaller teams to compete in turbocharged Formula 1 from 1981 to 1985. His ultimately integral-headed 415T (top) engines sadly ran out of reliability as numbers in use and competitive pressure grew.

potential points-scorer if not a natural front-runner.

Development had included introduction of what Hart calls a 'monobloc' engine configuration, although more properly this is a *testa fissa* (fixed head) design in which there is no separate head joint to be sealed against coolant, boost-pressure and combustion leaks, the head and block being cast in one integral unit. Hart also adopted British Holset turbocharging to benefit from that small and enthusiastic company's flexibility and willingness to pursue special development on his behalf.

There have been any number of small enthusiast chassis builders involved in Formula 1 from 1966 to 1984 but none can compare with the ability and application necessary to manufacture and develop successfully specialist Formula 1 engines. In this respect the popular Brian Hart was unique and very welcome.

Throughout 1984-85, considerable advances in Formula 1 power output were made possible by improvements in engine management systems, cylinder filling and combustion, enabling the restricted amount of fuel then allowed to be burned with increasing efficiency. However, these strides were led by the major manufacturers and the tiny Hart concern was unable to keep pace. When their development partner, Toleman, was unable to run early in 1985, Hart's progress was hampered. Hart engines were also being used by RAM, Spirit and the new Beatrice team. Hamstrung development combined with tight-stretched rebuild capacity, and the need to run ever-higher boost to keep in touch, created very poor reliability. Hart-engined cars were placed healthily only four times from 33 starts in '85: eighth, 12th (twice) and 14th.

Development had picked up rapidly once Toleman's tyre-supply problems had been overcome by buying Spirit's contract as the smaller team bowed out of Formula 1. British Holset turbocharging and Hart/ERA digital management was used, with Marelli CD injection. At 2.5 ata boost Hart quoted 740 bhp at 10,500 rpm which even in Toleman's good TG185 chassis was inadequate until the German GP where the car qualified on pole after second-session times were hampered by rain. There the Hart seemed to be delivering some 822 bhp in qualifying tune, falling to 728 for the race. This was the lowest in Formula 1, but even so reliability had been lost and as Toleman adopted BMW engines for 1986 the respected Brian Hart's brave foray into Formula 1 seemed to be ending.

But the 415T and its Garrett turbocharger proved fragile as the team pursued a painful and frustrating development programme. The in-line four-cylinder, as BMW proved, had some advantages in fewer bearings and piston rings, and smaller friction area hence lower friction losses which in turn meant less thirst for fuel.

In 1984 form, Hart claimed 600 bhp at 10,750 rpm at 2.1 bar boost in race tune and the engine was mechanically very reliable if still a little outclassed by its multi-million budget opposition. It came very close to winning that year's Monaco GP in Senna's Toleman in pouring rain and other good Toleman performances in better conditions proved the Hart 415T a

Honda's Formula 1 engines. Top to bottom: 1967 centre-exhaust V12 as raced by John Surtees; the unfortunate air-cooled V8 slung beneath the RA302's rear boom at Monza, 1968; and the 80-degree F2-based turbocharged unit in the Spirit, 1983.

Honda all-electronic engine management was adopted, and at the end of the season the units were used by new purpose-built Williams FW09 cars in the final race at Kyalami. In 1984, the IHI turbocharged RA163-Es proved wickedly powerful but with abrupt power curves which made them very hard to control and were demanding on chassis performance.

The crankcase and block did not seem adequately stressed for use as an integral chassis component while local cooling hot-spots were blamed for a crippling series of piston collapses.

The bore and stroke of the 1984 D-engines appeared to be massively over-square, at 90 mm × 39.2 mm according to one unconfirmed source, giving a displacement of 1495.5 cc accompanied by the huge piston area of 381.7 cm^2, compared to the Renault EF4B's 348.5, Alfa's 344.1, Porsche's 316.9, Ferrari's 309.2, the Renault EF15's 302.3, BMW's 250.0 and Hart's 243.3 cm^2. These large-area piston crowns were fragile under turbo stress and often failed, while the stroke/bore ration of 0.44 promoted the very narrow useable rev band of which Williams' drivers complained so much. The new E-engine introduced in June 1985 seemed less over-square, 82 mm × 47.2 mm, giving 1494.8 cc and a piston area of 316 cm^2. At Silverstone it was independently calculated that Rosberg had at least 1077 bhp during qualifying and 815 bhp in race-tune, not as much as the rival BMW 'fours' but useable over a wider rev band, and the team admitted those figures were 'about right'. In fact the engines peaked at Ricard, and when bearing problems intruded boost was wound back. Race power was some 850 bhp, however, by late season.

Some observers believed ceramics were being used by Japan's 'Yellow Peril', but team members hotly denied this, pointing out that the poor conductive qualities of ceramics meant unacceptable combustion chamber heat build-up which would aggravate pre-ignition to destroy pistons even more rapidly . . . perhaps significantly, as had been seen in the old D-engines.

Honda's power advance, first with the D-engine through the winter of 1984/85, then with the replacement E-engine in mid-1985, was attributed more to improved filling and burning thanks to combustion chamber design and injection system development. This promoted more complete burning of the fuel/air charge, simultaneously improving both fuel consumption and power output, while Honda's close co-operation with IHI had improved turbocharging efficiency.

Like other teams, William-Honda used dense high-aromatic fuel (in their case produced for them by Mobil) aromatic being heavy hydro-carbon like Toluene to optimize performance, and they ended our period by comfortably winning the last three races in succession.

Maserati

The Maserati V12 engine was an enthusiastic update of a decade-old 60-degree four-cam design as described in the Cooper section of the Team Directory. From new it was already antiquated in many respects and after its maiden season of 1966 when everyone was struggling to develop new cars and engines it was never genuinely competitive.

The 1966 *Tipo* 9 four-cam V12 had bore and stroke dimensions of 70.44 mm x 64 mm, displacing 2989.48 cc, and on Lucas fuel injection with a mixture of either Lucas or Marelli coil and distributor ignition, delivered a healthy 360 bhp at 9000 rpm in 1966 although very heavy and thirsty. Maserati also, strangely, record a 68 mm x 68 mm 'square' version of this engine displacing 2693.7 cc, delivering 340 bhp on carburettors.

The *Tipo* 9 engines had intakes between the

camshafts, while the modified *Tipo* 10 of 1967 featured new Heron heads with three valves per cylinder, twin inlet and one exhaust, and the inlets in-vee.

The *Tipo* 10 Heron head engines had a shorter stroke and bigger bore (75.2 mm x 56 mm) to permit and take advantage of this three-valve-per-cylinder design and with a compression ratio listed as 11.8:1 power output increased to a claimed 380-390 bhp at 9800-10,000 rpm.

But neither Cooper nor Maserati could sustain development pace, there was no money available to finance engineer Giulio Alfieri making a new start with a really modern power unit, and Maserati's interest in Formula 1 ended after the opening race of 1968.

Matra

Much of the Matra V12's development is related in the Team Directory entries for Matra and Ligier. Suffice here to record that Georges Martin's design team sought to maximize piston area and achieve high revolutions to achieve power.

The original 60-degree matra MS9 V12 emerged in 1968 with inlets between the twin camshafts on each head. In this early form it was not capable of being mounted fully-stressed as an integral chassis member; it was also over-thirsty, unreliable and prone to overheating while its average output of some 390 bhp at 10,500 rpm was inadequate in DFV and Ferrari V12 company.

Initially it had produced as much as 420 bhp using a six-tailpipe exhaust system with each six-cylinder bank regarded as a separate in-line engine with cylinders 1 and 6 feeding one tailpipe, 2-5 another and 3-4 the third, each side. But this system have a poor power curve making the car difficult to drive, so a more conventional four-tailpipe system was then adopted, robbing it of some 30 bhp.

After a lay year in 1969 during which the MS12 engine was developed in sports car racing, Matra Sports raced their V12 again in Formula 1 in 1970. The crankcase had been redesigned as a stressed chassis member, and

completely new narrow valve-angle (31.5 degrees) heads were fitted. Inlet ports were now in the valley of the vee and one-piece cam covers concealed both camshafts per bank. The new valve angle provided a shallower and more efficient combustion chamber, and enabled less deep-crowned and hence lighter pistons to be fitted. Inlet valve area was increased, fuel injection revised and each bank fed a single tailpipe, MS12 output rising to a claimed 450 bhp.

In mid-1971 Martin's team introduced further redesigned heads, with still narrower-angle valves and further flattened, lighter pistons. Now Matra adopted year-by-year type numbering, and this type MS71 V12 was used in the MS120B cars that season but oil scavenging problems intruded. Revised lubrication arrangements produced the MS72 engine used in the 1972 MS120B-C and sports-prototype cars and from 1973 to 1975 Matra concentrated upon long-distance sports car competition.

Further redesigning of cylinder head and internals for 1974 sports racing achieved

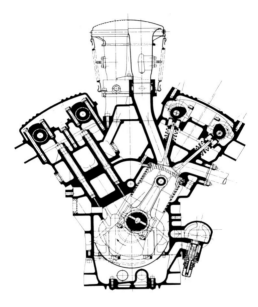

around 480 bhp at 11,200 rpm. This MS73-74 V12 was retired from endurance racing in 1975 but reappeared in the Formula 1 Ligier in 1976-77. In 1978 its crankcase was shortened by 27 mm to fit the Ligier JS7/9, before the units were again withdrawn at the end of that season.

Low priority development continued behind the scenes, and Ligier returned to Matra power for 1981-82, the MS81 unit having been tailored to ground-effects chassis requirements, its crankcase and sump assembly having been narrowed as much as possible with ancillaries repositioned within the cross-section instead of hanging out in the breeze on either side.

The series of Matra V12 engines were based upon a developing design of cast-aluminium block, with a two-part crankcase-cum-sump down below. The earliest 'Type 6W' crankshaft induced vibration problems and the bearing suppliers Vandervell recommended a redesigned shaft, the '4W', which was lighter yet still very stiff, benefiting from the engine's low bore:stroke ratio, 79.7 mm:50 mm, displacing 2993 cc.

In this form the engine won the Le Mans 24-Hours race of 1971, proving itself extremely reliable, but by 1978 as they sought a target of over 12,000 rpm, the 4W crankshafts overstressed the centre main bearing and blocks began to crack. Matra reverted to the original 6W crankshaft, which had identical bearing diameters, and cracking ceased, the engine running its final races operating normally outside the 6W's critical vibration period.

The crankshafts were machined from solid steel billets, nitrided, and slung in seven main bearings with caps both vertically- and cross-bolted for 24-hour reliability. Two titanium or steel con-rods were carried side-by-side on each crank-pin. The crankshaft nose carried a press-fit main pinion driving the cam-geartrain, which also powered the oil pressure pump and two scavenge pumps down below and the water pump immediately above. Each gear ran on needle or roller bearings. The seven plain-bearing camshafts actuated the valves via bucket-type cam followers, with shim clearance adjustment. The entire cam-drive was enclosed by a cast magnesium cover bolting onto the front of the engine.

Forged steel press-fit liners were used, sealed by 'O'-rings at their base, with individual head sealing rings for each cylinder. Piston design evolved as described into a near flat-head form save for valve clearance indents. Heads themselves were cast in the same AS19KG (French norms) as the crankcase and block, incorporating aluminium-bronze/cupro-nickel valve seats, and bronze valve guides. Inlet valve heads were 33 mm diameter, exhausts 27.2 mm, and valve lift around 9 mm, the four valves per cylinder surrounding central threaded bronze inserts carrying the single 10 mm spark plug per cylinder. Slide throttles were used with fuel injectors screwed into the induction trumpets. Lucas injection was used with a mechanical pump identical to the DFV's driven by the left-side inlet camshaft. The mechanical Lucas metering unit was subsequently replaced by an electronic metering control system.

Unusually, Ligier did not use a high-pressure starting pump, preferring instead a small fuel reservoir within the tanks, gently pressurized, feeding the injection system upon command from a dash-panel button. Ligier retained this system on both Cosworth and Matra-engined models.

The French V12s ran a compression ratio of around 11.5:1, and in 1981 form delivered some 525 bhp at 12,200 rpm with peak torque of 33 mkg at 10,000 rpm. The engine weighed 170 kg (374.78 lb) including starter motor, and despite its relatively modest Formula 1 success will always be remembered with affection by all who heard it perform.

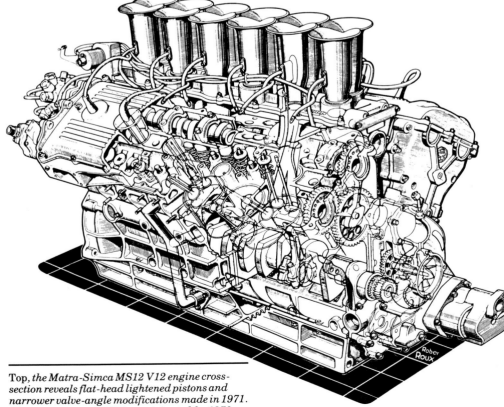

Top, *the Matra-Simca MS12 V12 engine cross-section reveals flat-head lightened pistons and narrower valve-angle modifications made in 1971.* Above, *cutaway of MS12 as originated for 1970.*

Motori Moderni

Early in 1984 Alfa Romeo's managerial unease with their Euroracing satellite team's performances in Formula 1 finally resulted in the dismissal of their long-serving former-Ferrari, then-Autodelta Chief Engineer, 61-year old *Ing*. Carlo Chiti.

In partnership with Piero Mancini, the indefatigable Tuscan promptly set up a new company in Milan named Motori Moderni. The intention was to build pure-bred racing engines for the forthcoming new three-litre Formula 3000 (using the Lamborghini Jalpa V8 as a base) and for 1500 cc turbocharged Formula 1.

For the premier class he laid out a Ferrari-like KKK twin-turbocharged 4-cam V6, and worked as usual with blinding speed, progressing from a blank sheet of paper to running prototype in less than five months. Two engineers, Nicolazzi and Bernardoni, and seven draughtsmen, Villa, Degan, Bollati, Colleta, Pastori, Boldrini and Vigini, made this possible, but Motori Moderni aimed at a potential 800 bhp and even as racing recommenced at the beginning of 1985 this was far from sufficient to perform respectably, never mind competitively.

The F1 engine was to be built in a new factory at Novara and emerged as a 90-degree V6, 80 mm × 49.7 mm, displacing 1498.8 cc, revving to 12,000 rpm and delivering a claimed peak 720 bhp at 11,300 rpm, with peak torque of 46 kgm at 9000. Compression ratio was 7.0:1. It used Bosch-Kugelfischer electro-mechanical fuel injection and two KKK turbochargers gave 2.2 ata boost in race tune. Marelli Raceplex electronic ignition was used. Four valves per cylinder were disposed at an included angle of only 14 degrees and the aluminium-block V6 weighed-in at 147 kg (324 lbs) less clutch, but including other ancillaries and the two heavy turbochargers.

Giancarlo Minardi's new team took up the Motori Moderni engine for their small-budget 1985 Formula 1 programme, giving the new V6 its race debut at Imola. The new engine was underdeveloped, the car and its driver, Martini, unknown quantities and jointly this optimistic Italian venture achieved nothing significant during the season.

Renault

The enormous Régie Renault is one of the world's largest production motor vehicle manufacturers and it returned to Grand Prix racing in 1977, having won the very first Grand Prix in 1906. This was built around an iron-block four-cam (belt-driven) V6 engine originated in 1972-73 as a conventional 2-litre for Alpine-Renault to contest the European Championship for 2-litre sports cars. It was known as the Renault-Gordini Type CH1, apparently initialled in honour of Usine A. Gordini's late Technical Manager Claude Hard (Gordini was Renault's competition and high-performance engine development subsidiary). However, its finalized design was credited to a team headed by the division's contemporary chief, François Castaing.

The compact new V6 powered the Alpine-Renault A440 *Barquette* built for the 1973 European Championship but the combination disappointed, the team withdrawing from the last two rounds without having scored a single point.

A winter's work brought both car and engine on song. The CH1 V6 delivered a claimed 305 bhp at 10,800 rpm and revised A441 *Barquettes* powered by it dominated the 1974 2-Litre Championship. They won all seven races, placing 1-2 four times and once 1-2-3, and driver Serpaggi won the Championship title

from team-mates Larrousse and Jabouille.

Meanwhile, the national oil company Elf fostered the development of French driving talent by backing an extensive Formula 2 programme, which eventually embraced the Renault-Gordini V6 when the regulations admitted racing-block engines in 1976.

More significantly, on 23 March 1975 a new turbocharged A442 V6 *Barquette* shared by Larrousse and Jabouille had won the World Championship of Makes round at Mugello. It was subsequently third at Monza, fourth at the Nürburgring, third at Watkins Glen and third overall in the Championship.

Engineer Bernard Dudot was instrumental in the development of this turbocharged engine which was the first step in a planned Renault assault upon the great promotional prize of the Le Mans 24-Hours classic.

Dudot had graduated as an engineer from the CESTI institute in Paris – 'Like the *Institut des Arts et Métiers*', he says, 'and then I started work with Citroën. But there I was a very small gear in a very big machine so after only one year I joined Alpine at Dieppe, and at the end of 1973 I moved to join Castaing who at that time was still Technical Manager of Usine Amédée Gordini where I started work on 2-litre Formula 3 and rally car engines for him . . .'

Soon after his arrival the then Renault Competitions Manager, Jean Terramorsi, suggested a plan to attack Le Mans in earnest. Alpine-Renault had never been there with a hope of winning outright.

Terramorsi galvanized his technical team. Dudot recalls: 'He was a very futuristic thinker, and he looked at what we were doing already in rallying and Formula 3, and the new V6 was about to begin for 2-litre sports car racing and he wanted to take it to Le Mans. We had just this one real racing engine, and the only way to use it for Le Mans would be to fit a compressor to it and he saw that turbocharging seemed the best way.

'So I was sent off to California – this was still in 1973 – to learn all I could about turbocharging, talking to Garrett AiResearch and other specialist people. While I was there I got a telegram. The project was stopped. Come home. But I had all the information ready for when we could go again and, after five months of no turbocharging, Terramorsi came in and said "OK, we are all go again now". So Jean-Pierre Boudy and I began work seriously, first on a four-valve four-cylinder as used in the production Alpines and Renault 17.

'It was a very long-stroke engine, the volumetric efficiency was not very good, because in the narrow bore there was no space for an adequate inlet valve.

'After that development, which taught us quite a lot, we started work properly in July 1974 on the racing V6 in the 2-litre *Barquette* for the '75 World Championship. The A442 installation had a Garrett turbocharger and wastegate. It looked quite good in testing, we started racing with this engine in Mugello, and we *won!*

'We did two seasons in the Championship 3-litre class with this engine but won no more.'

They had changed the basic V6's compression ratio, pistons, lubrication and injection, having to use an injection system compatible with the boost pressure within the cylinder. The German Kugelfischer pump was used as it could adapt fuel flow relative to boost which the contemporary alternative Lucas pump could not. Water flow was increased to improve exhaust valve-seat cooling and sodium-filled valves were used to keep them cool and hopefully ensure survival.

'Always we had problems with the cars and the engines, but we were learning all the time and Terramorsi's ideal was still Le Mans . . .

'In 1976 we race-tested a European Championship-specification car at Le Mans for the first time. It was a normal 2-litre and it ran nine hours in a good place until a piston

Renault Sport's early EF1 turbocharged V6 engine in 1979; from left to right, chassis designer Michel Tétu, team directors Jean Sage and Gérard Larrousse and engine specialist Bernard Dudot.

problem. Running full-throttle on the long straight caused detonation; it was a temperature problem . . . but we were happy. Now we were sure that a turbocharged special car for Le Mans could win it.

'In 1977 we prepared very hard for Le Mans. We tested very thoroughly at Ricard which has another long straight and three special cars ran in the 24-Hours but again we had a piston problem. They were cracking on the long straight. We were running with Porsche and led them for three hours early on, but our last car stopped at 21 hours, though Mirage ran Renault engines and finished second.

'Now we knew we could win but we had to test the engine at high revolutions on a very long straight. Ricard was not long enough, you cannot test at Le Mans since it is a public road and there was no other track suitable in Europe. So we went to the GM testing ground at Columbus, Ohio, and ran two tests successfully with only one car and one engine, and we learned that we should change a little the height of the block to keep sufficient height above the pin in the piston – to reduce compression ratio the piston had been shaved – we had only 6 mm depth of piston above the pin . . . was too little.

'In 1978 we won Le Mans', he says simply, but it took massive effort. After the 1977 disappointment some 30 modifications had been made to the V6 engine, from valve springs to the position of the plug cable supports. Three marathon tests were run – 3500 km at Ricard, 3000 km in Ohio and another 7000 km at Ricard. A test rig reproduced the stresses of 3½ miles a minute on the Mulsanne Straight. Valve springs were changed to improve reliability; a change of turbocharger widened the power range. The engine now delivered some 500 bhp at 9900 rpm, the Le Mans A442As and 1978 'Bs running 1997 cc units, the new A443 an enlarged 2140 cc engine. The A442s finished first and fourth, with Pironi and Jaussaud winning.

It was slap in the middle of this vast, lengthy and publicly high-profile programme, two years before their eventual Le Mans victory, that Renault's Formula 1 project had begun.

'We were working maximum effort to win Le Mans when the management said "We are going into Formula 1", and we said, "But what about Le Mans?", and they said, "Yes, we are going to win Le Mans *as well!*" This was not really possible.

'In 1976 we actually started the Formula 1 project with just four people, Boudy and two or three mechanics and sometimes part of my time. I was Technical Manager of the Le Mans project. That was vital. Castaing was General Manager of Renault Sport overall. De Cortanze was on chassis and he designed the original Alpine *Laboratoire* test car – a *monoplace*.'

Régie chief executive Bernard Hanon had asked Dudot if he could make a Formula 1 engine of sufficient power to be successful:

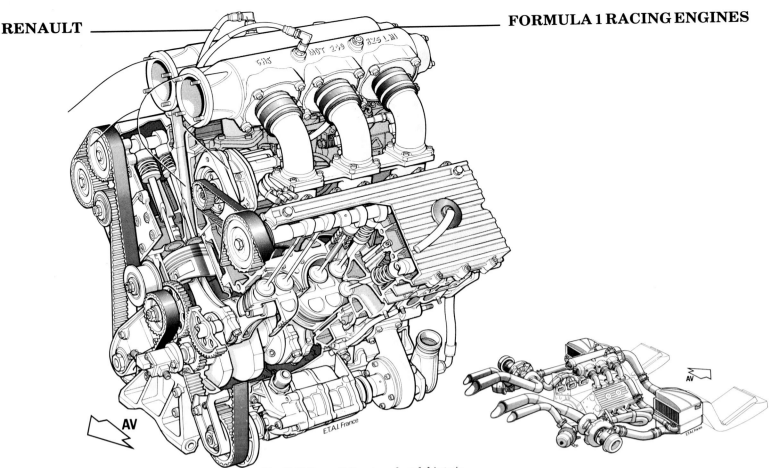

For 1980 Renault Sport produced this twin-turbocharged, twin-intercooled version of their powerful and now reliable V6. These detailed drawings reveal the 4 valves-per-cylinder dohc heads, belt-driven ancillaries tucked against the crankcase flanks, complex KKK turbochargers and wastegate, intercoolers, exhaust pipework and induction path piped from turbochargers to the 'logs' on top of the unit.

'. . . and I said "Yes it is possible" – I knew the potential was there but it was more difficult to have good throttle response with a small 1500 cc engine because the boost has to be higher.

'There was also a big problem because the only engine we could use as a basis was the 2-litre iron-block. We only reduced the stroke for 1500 cc. At the beginning, to get one raceworthy engine we had to build three: two would break and one survive.'

Initially, they tested the Le Mans 2.1-litre Type CHS and putative 1500 cc Formula 1 Type EF1 – 'E' in honour of Elf support – turbo engines back-to-back in a pair of *Barquettes* at Ricard.

'Jabouille found the small engine very good but there was still a lot of work to do. Then we took the new *Laboratoire* to Jarama where there are only short straights between the corners and Jabouille found he could not get back on the boost before having to brake for the next corner. We found we had a BIG disaster about response. Boudy and I were desperate. To go racing we had to reduce boost a little. Boudy went to that first race at Silverstone, not me. At Le Mans we ran about 2 bar boost and in Formula 1 we ran about 2.7 bar and on the test-bed 2.8 bar.'

They learned rapidly. Mahle and Goetze, their piston, liner and ring suppliers, learned with them, as did Garrett, for their original production turbochargers were made to inadequate tolerances for Formula 1. Compressor wheels, turbines and axle bearings all failed: 'At this time they were running 130,000 rpm on plain bearings'.

Then after Le Mans '78, 'everybody worked on Formula 1 and from August '78 we were in Formula 1 seriously'.

The first step of course had been a single Garrett turbocharger engine 'and we made big progress by introducing the smaller twin-turbochargers by KKK at Monaco '79 although the race was a big disaster when intercooler cracks lost boost.

'We could buy small turbochargers easier from KKK while Garrett had to make special small ones for us and now we knew in Formula 1 you have no time to wait.

'The twin-turbocharged engine also used a water intercooler to reduce the temperature of the pressure air. We had tested this at the end of 1978 and the improvement in piston life was very large. Response was also very much better with the two small turbos instead of one big one, though we also improved injection, length of the intake pipes, the turbine wheels, housing and compressor, all to reduce this lag, and for '79 we began spraying oil up under the pistons to help them cool.

'In a turbocharged engine compression ratio is lower but combustion temperatures 500-600 degrees higher. A 1500 can give over 750 bhp and is so small there is little area to lose heat.

'We had our big win at Dijon and through the rest of 1979 worked on reliability. We had a little problem with valve-springs – also in 1980 – due to the cam acceleration being very big because we had very large valve opening and the springs were breaking. We worked out an improvement with Schmitthelm and from 1981 our valve-springs have been reliable.'

The EF1 engine was based upon a fine-cast block in Renault's GS (Spheroidal-Graphite) iron. The original design involving Castaing had specified this material to offer strength and rigidity plus thermal resistance and stability. The Régie's foundry was adept at casting very thin iron sections, enabling weight savings which made the finished block comparable with an aluminium component of similar strength, which would have required thicker sections.

The EF1 iron block had wall thicknesses of 3.5-4.0 mm. See the BRM H16 section to compare technologies (pages 149-150).

The block carried cast aluminium alloy heads and crankcase with integral main bearing supports. Design changes were made to crankcase stiffening ribs during the EF1's life, the basic architecture otherwise being little changed.

Nitrided steel wet-liners were inserted, fixed at the top of the block where thermal stress was most intense, free to expand axially at the bottom, where sealing was by two 'O'-rings. Oil and water passages were sealed by Viton 'O'-rings at head and crankcase joints.

The crankshaft – like all modern racing engine crankshafts – was an almost disappointingly modest-looking 'bit of bent wire'. Nevertheless, it was elegantly machined from a steel billet, including integral bob-weights and was nitrided for toughness. Its three crank-pins were typical V6, spaced 120 degrees from each other; end-on the shaft resembled the Mercedes-Benz three-pointed star symbol. Each pin carried two con-rods, one from each cylinder bank of course.

Nitrided forged steel con-rods were fitted, titanium coming later. Plain bearings were used throughout. The forged aluminium-alloy pistons were by Mahle, with a shallow crown and four valve clearance indents. Three rings were used.

The aluminium heads featured a very shallow pent-roof combustion chamber form with narrow-angle valves, inlets at 10 degrees to the cylinder axis, exhausts 11° 30′ for an included angle of only 21.30, seeking what Renault described as 'a more flexible combustion'.

Cam-carriers, like Cosworth's, were in cast aluminium alloy, supporting the double overhead camshafts in four plain bearings each. Internal-toothed rubber belt drive powered them from the crankshaft nose, the belts also driving such ancillaries as the water and oil pumps and alternator *en route*. This belt-drive system saved the weight of a complete cascade of spur-gears and allowed easier replacement in the rare event of failure, or normal course of maintenance and rebuild.

A single oil pressure pump circulated lubricant at 8-10 kg/cm², and a simple scavenge pump returned it through the oil cooler matrix to the dry-sump system tank.

There were individual centrifugal water pumps for each cylinder bank, all pumps being tucked against the crankcase flanks and driven by the cam-drive belts.

Ignition was by Magnetti-Marelli electronic system, and injection employed the Kugelfischer plunger-type pump already mentioned. There was a throttle device in each of the twin KKK turbochargers, which slung low on the trailing stainless steel or titanium exhaust system and which had their own lubrication arrangement using carefully filtered engine oil.

Bore and stroke of this 90-degree V6 were 86 mm x 42.8 mm, displacing 248.6 cc per cylinder, 1491.6 cc overall. The unit was 680 mm (26.7 in.) wide, 650 mm (25.5 in.) tall and 480 mm (18.8 in.) long *sans* clutch. Weight was listed as 180 kg (396.8 lb). It was designed to be mechanically safe to some 12,000 rpm and the 1980 version would deliver a quoted 500 bhp at 11,000 rpm, plus 38 mkg (000 lb/ft) torque at 9600 rpm.

Major change came quietly in 1981 when the original thinwall cast-iron block was replaced by a redesigned and lighter cast-aluminium unit.

'We had to change the thickness of the casting but it was generally the original Castaing design' – Castaing himself having gone to work in Detroit at the end of '79, and Dudot becoming Technical Manager for both engines and chassis in his place.

Whereas the iron blocks had come from Renault's own foundry which had considerable experience with good-quality thinwall iron castings, the new aluminium blocks were contracted-out to Messier who could deliver more quickly.

Dudot rightly considers 1981 to have been 'generally successful, while 1982 was our best year but we had a problem . . .'

In developing an engine management system for the V6 the original pneumatic device used to adjust the Kugelfischer injection pump's mixture cam was replaced by a microprocessor-controlled 'cheap Japanese electric motor', the system sensing boost, intake temperature, throttle position etc. and the motor then continuously adjusting the mixture cam as required.

The system was introduced at Monaco which Renault led but the electric motor simply could not survive in the heat and vibration of the engine vee. 'Vibration broke the motor's winding, we tried desperately to damp it out but we lost the Championship that year for sure because of this. At Zeltweg and Zandvoort, Prost and Arnoux broke these motors, while it took four months to get a new motor designed and made by an aviation company working with the Renault laboratory.'

In 1983 reliability was much improved by the new Renix management system motors and water injection. Dudot and Jean-Pierre Boudy adopted bigger turbo casings and wheels and Boudy developed his water injection pack on his company Renault 18 saloon!

'But the rest got more power from their engines, specially BMW whose power in the second half of the season left us behind.' Engine performance proved inconsistent after rebuilds; then, 'at Monza we had the first reliability problem, in the turbocharger – the turbine wheel got too hot and broke up, losing Prost the race. The power problem was really about the adaptation of the turbocharging, and in the final race at Kyalami it was worse. It was necessary to improve power. We were running 3.2 bar in the race, 3.4 in practice – no more – we had about 650 bhp at 10,500 rpm in '83, compared to about 550 at the same speed in 1980.'

Through the winter of 1983/84, Dudot's team changed horses again from KKK back to Garrett: 'We felt sure we could use greater potential from Garrett now because they are a bigger company than KKK with the ability and will to develop special turbochargers for our needs . . . At the last race of 1984 we could match the TAG engine on power and after starting the year with a problem on fuel consumption we were now very close to TAG and Ferrari.'

They ditched the heavy water intercooler in favour of an air-to-air intercooler, which also improved aerodynamic performance.

In 1983, customer V6 turbo engines were supplied and maintained for Team Lotus and in 1984-85 also for Ligier. Only the works Renault Sport team's engines were made and serviced by the Gordini plant's 85 staff at Viry-Châtillon, the customer units being handled by a sub-contracted concern named Mecachrome, based near Bourges, where some 15 technicians handled strip and rebuild. Renault Sport maintained a float of 15 works engines, each client team in theory having 12 to choose from to service two cars. These units were drawn from a float at Bourges so that an engine might appear in a Ligier one weekend, a Lotus the next, the British team making by far the better use of it that season.

Asking Dudot what he believed to have been the most significant single steps in the story of Formula 1's first turbocharged engine he thought hard before replying: 'We made a lot of progress – a *lot* of progress – on turbocharger lag, and also on thermal problems with pistons and rings, and Mahle and Goetze who make our pistons and rings learned with us . . . which was good for Ferrari and BMW . . .', he added with a mischievous grin. 'But the obvious big steps were twin turbochargers, intercooling improvements and the improved management system.'

Renault displayed remarkable courage in taking the first pioneering steps into this new Formula 1 technology, and in some ways they paid the price of pioneering while always handicapped by their own labyrinthine management systems. Second-generation turbo engine manufacturers, like Ferrari and BMW, and third generation, like TAG Turbo-Porsche, benefited from lessons learned at the Régie's expense.

For 1985, Dudot's engine team developed a new EF15 variant V6 so as to improve on the existing EF4's fuel consumption at high power outputs. The new engine mounted differently, like a Cosworth DFV this time with cam-box strap plates up top and two points down below, while the EF4 still attached beneath its heads at the front and in Lotus's case was stayed by additional tube-members for additional rigidity. While the EF4B unit's internal dimensions were 86 mm bore × 42.8 mm stroke, displacing 1492 cc, the EF15's were less over-square, with narrower bore and longer stroke at 80.1 mm × 49.4 mm, 1494 cc. Claimed power minima for these units were respectively 760 and 810 bhp. The EF4Bs were more amenable to accepting high qualifying boost than the EF15s, and would seem to have exceeded 1000 bhp in this tune. Lotus made better use of the engines than Renault's own works team which was by this time in final run-down. When customer EF15s became available in quantity from Mecachrome, Lotus regularly qualified on EF4Bs then fitted the more economical EF15s for the race. It paid off, and by late-summer 1985 Viry-Châtillon concentrated upon EF15 production, with Dudot's team studying 195-litre race consumption options for 1986.

TAG-Turbo

Background to the TAG Turbo by Porsche TTE-PO1 engine is described fully in Chapter 15. The engine statistics included a bore and stroke of 82 mm x 47 mm displacing 1482.18 cc. Compression ratio was 7.5:1, block cast in aluminium alloy with Nikasil cylinder lining, pistons and rings were by Mahle and Goetze, bearings by Glyco, and engine management by Bosch Motronic MS3 system. Twin KKK turbochargers were fitted, alternative smaller units with closer clearances permitting higher boost pressures and improved throttle response being developed to McLaren's commission. For a weight of 145 kg (319.61 lb) the 80-degree V6

unit delivered 750 bhp on race boost at 11,500 rpm, a genuine 500 bhp per litre.

Into 1985, TAG Turbo were caught by the opposition as the project seemed frozen by complacency. A new engine spec was decided just in time for the season-opener at Rio, after which few changes were made. TAG Turbo still did not resort to the high-boost, lightweight car qualifying ploys used by some, but come race day the V6's race-tune output was always very competitive in the latest MP4/2B car. This was thanks largely to the Bosch Motronic management system which had now reached reliable maturity.

Dr Udo Zucker's system had emerged at a time when neither Bosch nor any other electronics company had reached that level of complexity on road cars. It is very difficult indeed to match injection and ignition requirements to a turbocharged engine across such an immense range of airflow from idling on zero boost up to 11,500 rpm on full boost. 'Mapping' engine performance across such a wide range is a very complex business and Bosch achieved this brilliantly during most of the '85 season to help McLaren win their second consecutive Formula 1 Constructors' Championship.

Hans Mezger having been seconded now to other projects, Porsche engineer Rolf Hahn took his place working closely with McLaren on the engines. Overall the TAG Turbo V6 remained the most consistent combination of power, reliability and economy in Formula 1.

The engines remained averse to accepting high boost for qualifying, partly because as boost was raised so back-pressure increased to the point where no further advantage could be gained. TAG Turbo also seemed to be lagging on fuel technology until Shell supplied a newly developed high-aromatic fuel for the abortive June meeting at Spa. Engine failures resulted and the fuel situation was reviewed as a high priority, properly tested new recipes being rapidly developed.

Very few details of TAG Turbo engine performance have been released, and Italian press calculations suggesting 890 bhp in qualifying at *ersatz* Nürburgring, falling only marginally to 821 bhp for the race, are scoffed at by the team as being 'exaggerated'. Certainly they said they would have been very happy if published Österreichring figures of 956 bhp (qualifying) and 866 bhp (race) had been anywhere *near* true!

In relative terms, however, the TAG Turbo's fifth place in the qualifying power league improving to a close third place in race tune would seem supportable. For 1986, a hat-trick of Constructors' titles became the immediate target and, generally speaking, the German-engineered V6 remained the engine to beat.

Zakspeed

The German engineer Erich Zakowski set up his Zakspeed tuning company in 1968 and made its name with a long series of very effective competition Ford saloons. They became increasingly Zakspeed, less and less Ford, and the company accumulated vast experience of highly-specialized turbocharged racing engines. Just like Brian Hart in Britain, Zakowski finally decided to build engines of his own from the ground up instead of modifying Ford units virtually beyond recognition, and against this background he made the ambitious move into Formula 1 for 1985.

Although ambitious, he took this step cautiously with distinctly Germanic logic and practicality. A state-of-the-art carbon-composite Formula 1 car was built as described in the Team Directory, while Zakowski and his engineers designed and built a broadly BMW-like 1495 cc 4-cylinder turbocharged engine. With twin KKKs, this alloy unit gave about 700 bhp at 11,500 rpm.

TEAM DIRECTORY

In this section we cover the marques which have not won the Formula 1 Constructors' World Championship, in some cases despite many years of trying, and we also provide some detailed background to the less successful cars built by those teams whose Champion designs are fully described elsewhere in this volume.

In effect, the cars whose story is outlined here divide conveniently into winners, losers and no-hopers, but such clear-cut distinctions are often unfair. Many a slow car has been slow simply because there was insufficient money within its team to provide a competitive engine or a good enough driver. Some very nice-handling chassis never achieved a thing for that very reason, while occasionally a real 'old dog' of a car has won races despite its inferior design, helped towards success by more money in the team, perhaps a better driver and with infinitely better luck.

There is no divine right to be lucky, nor is there any rule which says life will be fair to you; such a brutal truism is seldom more apparent than in Formula 1 . . .

Alfa Romeo

Alfa Romeo is a name rightly revered by racing enthusiasts for its classical years of competition dominance prior to 1952. After a false start with Cooper in 1968, the Milan company returned to Formula 1 in 1970. A 3-litre V8 sports-racing engine was supplied to McLaren 'just to keep in touch', and this engine was also used by March in 1971 before being dropped. By 1975 another sports-racing engine, the 3-litre flat-12, had been developed for use in Formula 1, and after being fitted initially in one of Graham Hill's Embassy team Lola T370s, it ended up with Brabham instead.

Alfa Romeo's modern racing endeavours were handled by a satellite company named Autodelta, which had been founded at Udine in 1963 by ex-Ferrari, ex-ATS* engineer Carlo Chiti in partnership with Ludovico Chizzola. They prepared and modified Alfa Romeo cars for competition, moved to Settimo Milanese in 1964, and became an integral part of Alfa Romeo there in 1966. From 1967 they built and raced the long series of Alfa T33 sports-racing cars; making chassis, bodies, engines, gearboxes, everything – with help where needed from the Alfa production plants.

The Brabham flat-12 relationship was close but largely unsuccessful. As early as 1977 Autodelta were preparing their own Formula 1 car design around the flat-12 engine. This *Tipo* 177 hack was driven by Vittorio Brambilla at Alfa's Balocco test centre during 1978, while Gordon Murray of Brabham had sparked Autodelta's crash programme to redesign the flat-12 as a narrower 60-degree V12 for a new ground-effects Brabham chassis to race in 1979. In parallel, design work began in Milan for a new Alfa Romeo V12 Formula 1 'wing-car'.

Despite Alfa's poor financial state, the Board decided to authorize a factory race programme in Formula 1, essentially for 1980, with race development being pursued during the summer of 1979.

The podgy prototype 177, with its hefty riveted aluminium chassis and bulbous body-work, made its debut in the Belgian GP at Zolder, driven by Giacomelli and tended by

*Automobili Turismo e Sport, not to be confused with the German ATS Wheels company of later date.

engineers Chiti and Marelli plus ten mechanics and a tatty borrowed transporter. The car had originally been developed on Pirelli tyres, but the Italian tyre company felt unready to enter Formula 1 at that time, so the new team made its bow on Goodyear. Giacomelli was quicker than the Renaults at one time and the car ran reliably until a collision caused retirement in the race.

The unique 177 reappeared at Monza alongside the first new V12-engined 179 'wing-car'. With aerodynamic design by Robert Choulet of the SERA wind tunnel facility in Paris, this car was notable for its far-forward cockpit, lateral radiators instead of in-line in the pod sides as on the 177, and for its retention of inboard rear brakes, which impeded airflow from the underwing tunnels. Its oil tank was unusually high on the sloping rear on the monocoque rather than low down between engine and gearbox as conventional. The bulbous bullet nose and general shape were similar to the Arrows A2.

Two 179s ran in Canada with new Williams-like nose sections, slim and finned, and though Giacomelli didn't start, Brambilla was very nearly in the points.

Marlboro sponsored the team for 1980, when the 179 design was revised with outboard rear brakes and new rear suspension with the uprights buried deeper within the wheels to clear underwing airflow. Giacomelli was joined by Depailler to drive the cars, with new 179s chassis '3 and '4 racing in Argentina. The team lacked organization – a wheel change in Brazil costing 53 seconds – while much work was done on side pod aerodynamic development and stiffening the monocoques early in the year, adding 7 kg (some 15 lb) chassis weight, although new partially carbon-fibre body panels saved 30 kg (66 lb). Titanium suspension parts were introduced and at Long Beach chassis '3 and '4 appeared with reinforced footboxes, while at Monaco the fifth chassis emerged as spare with a new 12 kg lighter V12. In Spain, Brambilla joined the team as third driver, though the team reverted to a regular two-car entry thereafter.

New car '179/6' appeared at the British GP where Giacomelli raced it, this tub having carbon-fibre panels in the front of the tub and on top of the fuel cell section. Rear suspension mounts were more robust following breakages at Ricard and extra oil cooling was provided. The team had suffered several apparent

suspension failures during the season, and on test at Hockenheim one seems to have been responsible for the death of Depailler, believed to have been in chassis '4.

Giacomelli ran alone in Germany and Austria until Brambilla joined him in Holland, the 179 producing something over 520 bhp. At Zandvoort chassis '7 emerged, numbered as chassis '4 to use existing paperwork, and featuring a lowered engine. At Imola the new 1500 cc V8 turbo engine was on show in a corner of the Alfa Romeo garage while on circuit Giacomelli disputed second place in chassis '6, proving the 179s' increasing stature, now running flat rear body sections without flip-ups in front of the rear wheels. In Canada, Williams-like underwings were adopted and in the US GP at Watkins Glen 'Panda' Giacomelli qualified on pole and led convincingly until the ignition 'black box' failed.

Having just come to grips with sliding-skirt ground-effects, Autodelta suffered most from the sliding-skirt ban applied for 1981, following superbly fast winter testing at Ricard using skirts.

Andretti joined Giacomelli that season and the existing 179s were updated as lighter 179Cs, although Autodelta were always wary of disclosing chassis details and at best individual car identities are supposition. However, informed Italian sources consider Andretti normally raced '02, Giacomelli '03 early in the season though he took '01 for the Belgian race; a new car '04 became Andretti's regular mount for Monaco and Spain, where Giacomelli drove '02.

The team experimented hopelessly with hydropneumatic lowering suspensions and the immense jounce loads sustained by cars of this type proved too much for the 179Cs which were retired for rebuilding in mid-season. Old cars were raced at Dijon, Andretti taking '03 while Giacomelli was in old '06.

At Silverstone the revised 179C/D emerged, 5 cm lower overall and with new freeflow rear suspension. By the time of the Dutch GP, engineer Gérard Ducarouge had joined from Ligier, and the 179s ran Ligier-like side pods moving the centre of pressure rearwards. In Italy these underwings extended back to the driveshafts, but the cars showed little better form. A new carbon-fibre tub was now under development to add much needed torsional rigidity.

This emerged at the start of 1982, largely designed and completely made by Roger Sloman's Advanced Composite Components company of Derby, England. Built in just three months the new *Tipo* 182 weighed some 535 kg (1179 lb) less ballast. The tub's underbelly was shaped into a venturi form and the bottom of the V12 engine had been narrowed by pump and pipe relocation to improve aerodynamic performance.

Ducarouge – working now in conjunction with engineer Luigi Corbari – had also rede-

Left, *one of racing's longest-serving engineers, Autodelta's Carlo Chiti's designs were impressive for speed of execution though rarely for competiveness. Top, Giacomelli's new Alfa Romeo 177 flat-12 at Zolder 1979.*

signed the gearbox to place the gearchange on top out of the airstream, but the three new 182s in Brazil were troubled by oil surge. At Long Beach, new driver de Cesaris qualified on pole to widespread astonishment, but wrote off his car '182/01' against a wall after leading.

Extra oil tank baffling was added subsequently and a new tub, chassis '4, appeared for de Cesaris at Imola, demanding 40 kg ballast to reach the minimum limit. On the eve of Imola practice, a 179 fitted with the prototype V8 turbo engine was tested for the first time at Monza, driven by Giorgio Francia. An oil pipe broke and it caught fire . . . Alfa Romeo luck.

The tub was still too wide, and a 20 cm narrower 182B moulding appeared in Belgium. This B-spec included revised bodywork and underwings but the parts were very slow to make due to demands on time by race preparation and turbo development. Eventually the team reverted to running the 192s in near-original form. Chassis '4 was written off by de Cesaris in Canada, where a new '182/5' emerged, tailored to the V12's now-reduced fuel consumption with 195 litres capacity instead of 200, but in this long, thirsty race it ran short.

The expensive Signor de Cesaris wrote off chassis '5 in France and '6 replaced it in Austria, where both Alfas were damaged in a startline fracas. By this time the Alfa V12 was clearly the most powerful normally aspirated 3-litre engine around, but a 1500 cc turbocharged unit was necessary to win.

The long-awaited Alfa Romeo 182T finally emerged at Monza, featuring a taller tank section behind the cockpit containing 250 litres of fuel instead of 195-200 litres. The oil tank moved at last from the tub top into the bell-housing adaptor, between engine and new turbocar gearbox. The team had achieved so little, however, that there were rumours it would fold at the end of that year.

It didn't quite happen that way. Instead, Paolo Pavanello's private Euroracing team of Milan took over from Autodelta, which would continue to manufacture their hardware. It was ailing, however, and would be absorbed at the end of 1984 though it continued to produce Euroracing's Formula 1 engines and gearboxes at Settimo Milanese.

Three ACC carbon-composite chassised 183T turbocars ran in Brazil driven by de Cesaris and Baldi, the engines using Italian-

made Sylo turbochargers and the cars running on Michelin tyres. There had been little winter testing but they were of course revised to match the new flat-bottom rules, with shorter side pods.

The fourth new turbo chassis appeared at Ricard for Baldi after he creased '3 at Long Beach. When qualifying times were forfeit at Ricard due to an empty extinguisher – illegally saving weight – being discovered in one of the cars, Ducarouge was fired, moving to Lotus amid dark mutterings that his dismissal had been engineered by upstaged enemies within the team . . .

Luigi Marmiroli took his place under Chiti while engine development forged ahead. At Monaco the Alfa V8s were running 2.2 bar boost at 11,500 rpm, and new engine heads appeared in Detroit – four engines at Montreal one week later being to the new specification. A brand new chassis '5 emerged at Silverstone, while parallel reduction in engine thirst and the adoption of pit stop race strategy to refuel enabled chassis '3 and '4 to have their fuel cells literally cut down to 225 litres capacity. This lowered the centre of gravity and eased airflow

onto the now vital rear wing. Rear suspension was revised and new turbo wastegate pipes emerged from the side pod tops. This 183T B-spec was applied to the latest chassis '5 by the time of the Dutch GP at Zandvoort.

For the European GP at Brands Hatch a pneumatically adjustable wastegate blow-off valve – controlling the pressure at which turbocharger boost vents to atmosphere instead of charging the engine – was introduced. De Cesaris crashed chassis '5 heavily in practice there but it was repaired for the race. Revised radiator designs appeared in South Africa, improving aerodynamic performance, while the latest chassis '6 remained at home, testing its new pushrod suspension at Balocco.

The cars had shown new promise, taking second places in Detroit and at Kyalami, while de Cesaris had led at Spa for 18 extraordinary laps. For 1984 Euroracing Alfa Romeo reappeared with their cars wearing Benetton knitwear's green livery on new Luigi Marmiroli-designed carbon-chassised 184T cars. These slim, rounded-nacelle machines were driven by Patrese and Cheever. Two were available for the opening race at Rio, with '183T/6' as spare, the cars all featuring pushrod front suspension, pullrod rear. A 3-litre water tank for water injection into the engine was carried but there was no sign of the carbon-fibre head and sump covers which had been much remarked upon at the new model's Italian press debut. Ten 183T turbo engines were available to the team in Rio, and they looked determined to do well.

A new car, chassis '3 was available for Cheever at Zolder and a fourth car emerged at Hockenheim, but third place for Patrese at Monza and fourths for him at Kyalami and for Cheever at Rio were the best of another indifferent season.

Pavanello engineered Chiti's removal from the team with Alfa Romeo president Massacesi's approval in mid-season, his place being taken by Ing. Giovanni Tonti, fresh from the Lancia endurance team, but fortunes did not greatly improve.

For 1985 Euroracing Alfa Romeo lured British designer John Gentry away from the Toleman team whose 1984 car had handled notably well when driven by Senna. Gentry produced a new suspension layout in what became the Alfa Romeo 185T design, two of

Top, using side pods and skirts 'borrowed' from Williams, Giacomelli put Alfa 179 V12 '003' on pole for the 1980 US GP and led the race. Alfa had got it right . . . then sliding skirts were banned. Left, de Cesaris's moment of glory, Belgian GP '83, leading in Alfa's 183T V8 turbo '02'.

these new cars going to Rio for the start of the new season, accompanied by an old 184T, chassis '1, as spare. By that time Gentry had already moved on to join his former Toleman team driver Warwick at Renault Sport, and it was left to Tonti to develop the 185Ts towards competitiveness, and that proved impossible.

Three 185Ts were built, the third chassis making its debut for Cheever at Imola, but by mid-season Euroracing gave up in despair, junked the first two 185Ts, rebuilt the third to 184T-spec and wheeled out old 1984 chassis '2 and '3 for Cheever and Patrese to complete the season.

They achieved very little. Both drivers started all 16 Championship rounds, but Patrese finished only four times and Cheever only three, and these placings respectively were 9-9-10-11 and 10-11-17 so Alfa Romeo abjectly failed to score a single World Championship point.

Patrese enhanced his already ugly reputation for dangerous driving during this sad season, Cheever was unable to rise above the quality of his car and more than once the two drivers took each other off the road. The once mighty Alfa Romeo name had been back in Grand Prix racing on its own account for six full seasons by the end of our period without winning a race . . . two pole positions and one fastest lap representing their only superlative performances in all this time.

In World Championship terms, the Alfa Romeo team understandably scored no points in their 1979 part-season, but in 1980 they placed eleventh with only four points; in 1981 they were eighth with ten points, tied with the mere *Assemblatori* teams of Tyrrell and Arrows; in 1982 they were ninth with seven points; in 1983 improved to sixth with 18 points, but in 1984 dropped back to eighth with 11 points and in 1985 scored no points at all and so did not feature in the Formula 1 Constructors' Championship table – results which, in all conscience, were hardly worthy of the risk to Alfa Romeo's once revered name.

Amon

New Zealand driver Chris Amon made his name with Ferrari in 1967-69. He was almost legendarily unlucky, and his fortunes scarcely improved with March in 1970, nor Matra-Simca in 1971-72, nor Tecno in '73. While with Tecno he had insisted upon an improved chassis for their flat-12 engine, which sponsors Martini commissioned from Gordon Fowell and Alan Phillips's 'Goral' concern. Amon was

impressed with engineer Fowell's work, despite the car's performance not being worth a light, and with backing from wealthy enthusiast John Dalton he commissioned a new Formula 1 car for 1974, to be 'like a Lotus 72'.

It was to use a slimline aluminium monocoque chassis with the fuel load concentrated between cockpit and Cosworth DFV engine, hip radiators, simple torsion bar suspension using de Carbon gas-filled front dampers and inboard brakes front and rear. Aerodynamic form was developed by a Professor Tom Boyce, with a scalloped nose profile topped by a shallow-strutted fuselage-width wing, claimed to prevent boundary layer build-up and enhance download, while a broad rear wing was supported by vast swept-back end plates.

One complete car and a spare tub were manufactured by John Thompson in Northampton and assembled in Amon's Reading workshop by former McLaren and Rondel team mechanic Richie Bray.

In an early test at Goodwood a titanium front stub axle broke and the car lost a wheel, crashing quite heavily. Amon was in any case unhappy with intense vibration under braking, possibly connected with torsional flexion in the front brakeshafts, and Amon AF1 chassis '01's only race would be the 1974 Spanish GP at Jarama in April, where it ran a conventional nose cone but broke a brakeshaft in the race. Using a new full-width bluff nose and outboard front brakes, Amon qualified at Monaco, but opted not to start when a hub showed signs of incipient failure. The car was later taken to the Nürburgring for the German GP, where both Amon and Larry Perkins drove it in practice and the latter crashed, knocking off a wheel. Amon had a final try at Monza but failed again; by that time he felt uneasy whenever he sat in it, nothing was going right and the luckless project was abandoned.

Arrows

The Arrows Racing Team was founded by refugees from the Shadow Formula 1 project (see page 234) in the winter of 1977/78. Team manager Alan Rees, sponsorship entrepreneur Jack Oliver, designer Tony Southgate and draughtsman Dave Wass set up on their own with backing from Italian financier Franco Ambrosio. Anxious to qualify for membership of the Formula 1 Constructors' Association for 1979 they could only miss one non-European GP in '78. Since the Argentine and Brazilian races opened the calendar, they had to design and build their first car in just two months, in

time for Rio on 29 January.

Southgate had completed design work for a new Shadow DN9 before leaving that team. Inevitably his new Arrows FA1 was very similar because design thinking cannot change overnight. Southgate was a designer of vast experience – ex-Lola, Eagle, BRM and Shadow – and he had also worked with Team Lotus in 1976-77 at the height of their Lotus 78 development. Consequently, and inevitably, his new DN9/FA1 designs would be ground-effect 'wing-cars', though subtly different to the Lotus concept in using double venturi wing sections bolted one above the other on the flanks of their slim centre-tanked monocoque, although the air exit from the pods was hampered by outboard rear suspension and inboard rear brakes.

As it was, the first Arrows FA1 emerged before the remaining personnel at Shadow managed to complete their first DN9. Patrese easily qualified 'FA1/1' for the Brazilian GP and second time out in South Africa he qualified seventh on the grid and led for over 30 astonishing laps until his Cosworth engine failed. He notched Arrows' first Championship point with sixth place at Long Beach, and was sixth again at Monaco – the Arrows performing well on street circuits – followed by a rough and tough second in Sweden, holding off Peterson's delayed Lotus 79.

However, Shadow patron Don Nichols had his revenge over Arrows that midsummer when Mr Justice Templeman found in his favour in the London High Court and declared that it would not have been possible for Arrows to complete their car within 60 days without the use of drawings which were Shadow's copyright. He declared 40 per cent of the components to have been copied and banned the FA1 from racing, causing the four FA1s built to be dismantled.

Southgate, meanwhile, had designed a replacement Arrows A1 in June and the first of the three built was completed at their Milton Keynes factory in less time than the original FA1! It appeared in Austria and Arrows did not miss a race.

Patrese was vilified by his fellow drivers for some rough tactics, although the assertion that he caused Peterson's fatal accident at Monza was proved groundless. He was still banned from the US GP, so responded by finishing strongly and placing fourth in Canada to end a hectic first season. The cars had won Warsteiner beer sponsorship and were finished in gold livery. From Kyalami, Stommelen had driven the second car, though with very poor results, often non-qualifying. Yet Arrows finished their maiden season ninth-equal in the Constructors' table, tied with Williams on 11 points.

The existing cars were modified as A1Bs for 1979, chassis '3 for Patrese, '2 for Mass, with new rear suspension, side pods, wings, skirts and larger brakes but as the year progressed the thinly-financed team was under strain, their cars heavy and out of date while Southgate developed a new second generation ground-effect car, the A2.

This remarkable heavily faired-in, bullet-nosed device had its engine and gearbox angled upwards to allow full-width aerodynamic underfloor sections to be fitted. The A2s appeared at Dijon, 'A2/1' for Patrese, 'A2/2' for Mass, but they never handled well. In Holland the A2s used revised front suspension and modified rear wings. Patrese crashed '1 heavily and its tub had to be rejigged, while the cars were simply uncompetitive. Mass drove a modified 'A1/5' in Canada in preference to his A2, but failed to qualify in any case.

The drastic measure of angling the entire

Chris Amon's torsion-bar suspended AF1 in the 1974 Spanish GP, Jarama, using conventional nose aerofoils instead of the nose-top wing originally intended.

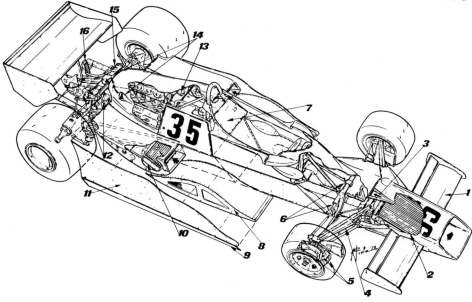

engine and gearbox, so the gearbox end plate was some 3 in. higher than conventional, had raised the car's centre of gravity. This move coincided with the insertion of tight chicanes on many circuits to slow the cars and the A2, tailored to high-speed courses, proved reluctant to change direction tidily. Like the Lotus 80, the Arrows A2 porpoised badly and the experiment had to be abandoned. During the year three more A1Bs had been produced, followed by the unloved brace of A2s, and Arrows again finished ninth in the Constructors' table but with only five points against the 11 of their maiden season. The miscalculation of 1979 was put right with the A3 wing-car introduced in Argentina, 1980, when Patrese was second quickest in the unofficial Saturday morning session and everyone sat up and took notice. The A3 had the shortest wheelbase in Formula 1 and the narrowest rear track after the Ensign, its gearbox was shrouded-in to reduce drag and ease airflow away from the underwing tunnels, but Arrows never seemed to appreciate fully the necessity for a skirt system which sealed adequately both against the road surface and within its own skirt-box, to prevent spillage infilling the low-pressure area which the venturi surfaces were struggling to create to download the car.

In South Africa a new 'A3/3' emerged for Mass, with a 4 cm wider front track to ease airflow into the side pods, and at Long Beach 'A3/4' appeared, with angled suspension for a longer wheelbase though this handled poorly and the team refitted standard suspension. Patrese shunted chassis '1 in Belgium and chassis '5 was completed for him to race at Monaco, Southgate altering its weight bias by moving the extinguisher bottle and other components.

The team appreciated its aerodynamic problems. The A3s understeered all season, and in midsummer Dave Wass spent time at the Imperial College wind tunnel, testing quarter-scale models to find an answer. At the British GP the A3s tested under-nose skirts á la Lotus 80 to find more front-wheel adhesion, but the work was rushed and failed in its purpose. Longer wheelbase form was tried again to load up the front end, but late in the year Southgate left abruptly, leaving Wass as chief designer. A sixth A3 was completed for the North American tour ending the season and Arrows found themselves seventh equal in the Championship with 11 points, just like 1978. But now all eyes were on 1981, and the skirt ban regulations. Over the winter Wass decided the best fix within the team's now very restricted budget would be 'to destroy the rear suspension, make

its adhesion as poor as the front's so that at least the car would come back into balance'.

He reduced rear camber change by some 60 per cent, and in South Africa in FOCA's last skirted race – refused Championship status by FISA – Patrese qualified on row three and finished sixth, while at Long Beach for the first 'clearance car' race, with everyone running on similar Michelin tyres following a temporary Goodyear withdrawal, he promptly qualified on *pole* and led the race until his fuel pressure faltered.

The car was now in balance and competitive, Patrese finishing third in Brazil but as hydro-pneumatic suspension lowering devices became *de rigeur* following Brabham's lead, Arrows found themselves back with skirt problems and fell off the tightrope once more.

Second driver Stohr was unable to contribute much and at Zolder he rammed his stalled team-mate's car at the start, crushing chief mechanic Dave Luckett between the two cars in a gruesome startline misunderstanding, though Luckett happily recovered. In France Patrese ran chassis '5 with a new Arrows-cased gearbox which was some 10 cm narrower with high change linkage out of the airstream, and there were new flatter uprights.

By this time Goodyear were prepared to return to racing, Michelin became alarmed at the prospect of servicing too many teams to remain competitive, so attempted to palm off Arrows to the Ecclestone/Avon tyre supplies

company. Rees and Oliver of Arrows responded by refusing the offer they had been made and going to Pirelli instead, starting with the British GP.

For the rest of that season Arrows were handicapped by poor grip, and by Pirelli's physical weight penalty, each tyre scaling 12 kg (26 lb) more than the comparable Michelin, and 15 kg (33 lb) more than Goodyear. In Holland each of three Arrows A3s on hand had different rear suspension sets to make their tyres work and by the end of the year, when Jacques Villeneuve (Gilles' brother) failed to qualify in Canada and the US, there seemed little point in going to the races with so little chance of success. Even so, the good start to the season gave the team 10 Constructor's Championship points, eighth equal with Tyrrell and Alfa Romeo.

Wass designed new A4 cars for 1982, three being ready in time for Brazil, where they were driven by Henton and Baldi. Arrows were living hand to mouth, picking up local sponsors wherever they could. Wass aimed for ultimate downforce in his A4 wing-car 'but we still ignored the necessity for really sophisticated sealing systems and we ran into constant porpoising troubles'.

New Pirelli tyres, 6 cm narrower than before, improved the cars in Holland, where they were driven notably by Surer and showed higher top speed and lighter steering, but a new A5 – effectively a Williams FW08 copy – emerged at Dijon in the 'Swiss' GP, using an aluminium honeycomb tub and pullrod suspension, very small and light enough. Wass consciously designed it with some 30 per cent less download than the A4 and in practice it proved far easier to control, so lapped faster, Baldi and Surer taking turns to drive it.

Five A4s had been built, chassis '2 being written off in Surer's Kyalami accident, while the A5 remained unique. The team placed tenth in the Championship, with five points from Baldi's two sixth places, in Holland and Austria, plus Surer's fifth in Canada and yet another sixth in Germany ... very much the poor men picking up crumbs from the rich man's table.

The winter of 1982/83 saw the flat-bottom rule change and Wass designed new A6 cars to suit, having returned to Goodyear tyres. They would perform better but now the age of the Cosworth engine had passed and a turbocharged engine was vital for success, and

Top, Piola's sketch of Tony Southgate's original Arrows A1 shows its twin ground-effects sidewing attachments amongst other details. This was the design subsequently judged to infringe Shadow copyright. Left, unsuccessful Arrows A2s, with dramatically angled engines, Zandvoort '79.

ARROWS

Arrows on their slender financing had none available. 'We lost on horsepower, everywhere . . .'

Former World Champion Jones drove for them briefly at Long Beach but they could not afford him long-term. At Imola, shorter underwings appeared in an effort to save the gearbox too much heat embarrassment and at the end of the year a new pullrod rear suspension was tried. Arrows were again tenth in the table, with four meagre points from Surer's early-season fifth at Long Beach, and two sixth places at Rio and Imola. Chico Serra drove the second car in early season, replaced subsequently by Thierry Boutsen who finished seventh in both Detroit and Montreal.

The unique A5 from 1982 had been updated to A6 specification and was used up to Montreal, while four true A6s, numbered '2-5' were built.

In the winter of 1983/84 Oliver negotiated use of BMW four-cylinder turbocharged engines for the coming season, but Arrows had to accept them direct from BMW Motorsport rigged with ATS team standard radiators, intercoolers and turbochargers, far behind Brabham quasi-works team specification. This was a disappointment and severely constrained design of the A7 turbocharged cars, and since the engine deal had only been completed at the last minute, design was

rushed and aluminium honeycomb monocoques were used again, though with a carbon-fibre inner moulding. Wass and the team were now entering an entirely new world of turbocharged power and loadings, and with more time a moulded carbon tub would have been developed, as it was in fact for 1985.

In the A7-BMW cars they tried to keep the A6 suspension, because it had worked well, 'but a Cosworth isn't a turbo' and this proved another enforced misjudgement which would not have happened given more time to test and to think. The A7s ran with pullrod front suspension, rocker rear, and made great use of Italian Brembo brakes before AP balanced callipers reappeared.

Arrows finished ninth in the Championship with six points from Boutsen's Cosworth-powered sixth in Rio and fifth at Imola, and his A7 turbo fifth in Austria. The faithful Surer was sixth behind his team-mate at the Österreichring and earlier in the season, when still Cosworth-powered, he managed three consecutive finishes in the first three GPs, 7-9-8.

Arrows A6 chassis '2 was written off in a startline shunt at Detroit, '4 and '5 being the others raced in this year, while four A7-BMWs replaced them during the season. Dave Wass embarked on a new moulded carbon-composite A8-BMW design for 1985, using pushrod front suspension, pullrod rear, the Heini Mader-prepared BMW four-cylinder turbo engines' exhaust system rising through the rear suspension à la Brabham.

Three A8s had been completed by the time the season opened in Rio, chassis '4' following for Boutsen in Portugal, '5' emerging as a spare, raced by Berger in Austria. Both drivers started all 16 GPs, and Arrows' reliability was quite good, Boutsen finishing 12 times and Berger nine. Boutsen inherited second place in the fuel-consumption derby at Imola, was fourth in Germany and sixth in successive races at Brands Hatch and South Africa ending the year. His other finishes were 11-9-9-7-9-8-9-10. Berger scored points at the end of the year with fifth at Kyalami and sixth in Australia, placing 13-11-8-7-9-9-7-10 elsewhere, so Arrows improvement came just as the season was ending. Until that time BMW had been

Above, Boutsen's Dave Wass-designed turbocharged BMW-engined Arrows A8 at Monaco, 1985, contrasts in shape with (below) Patrese's Wass-developed Arrows A3 clearance car (with dislodged nose wing) at Jarama 1981 during their period of greatest promise.

disappointed that the Milton Keynes-based team had not performed as well as they felt their customer engine merited and it was touch-and-go whether they would retain use of the German unit for 1986.

ATS

This team bears no relationship to *Automobili Turismo e Sport*, also known as ATS, which flopped in Formula 1 in 1963. This ATS is a German specialist wheel company headed by one Hans Gunther Schmid. An enthusiastic but autocratic man, he decided to promote his wheel company by entering Formula 1 in 1977, buying the Penske PC4 cars upon the American-managed team's withdrawal from Grand Prix racing.

One car, chassis 'PC4-002', was driven by Jarier on the team's debut at Long Beach in April '77, qualifying comfortably in midfield and immediately scoring a Championship point by finishing sixth.

The three Geoff Ferris-designed PC4s completed a staccato season with a variety of drivers, but Schmid determined to have his own cars built for 1978. He bought March's Formula 1 interests and their membership of FOCA, and Robin Herd of March developed the existing Penske PC4 design for the German to form the ATS HS-1, later further modified by John Gentry who also evolved a new wing-car design known as the ATS D1. Team drivers included Mass, Jarier, Bleekemoelen and Rosberg but the Bicester-based team found it difficult even to qualify and had a pitiful year, even worse than March's swansong effort in 1977.

Shortly after the D1's debut in practice at Zandvoort, Mass broke his leg testing it at Silverstone, but Rosberg subsequently gave the team some hope with better performances in the D1 in the North American races ending the season.

For 1979 Fred Opert took on team management, and ex-Ferrari aerodynamicist and engineer Giacomo Caliri designed D1 revisions in his Fly Studio bureau. One car would be entered for H-J Stuck to drive. Schmid had rapidly established a reputation as a hire and fire merchant, making few friends. Caliri was out by the time of the Belgian GP but Stuck wrestled his ill-handling car throughout the year, best placing being fifth in the wet final race at Watkins Glen, where the tall German's wet-weather skills did the team proud and they found the reliability for him to finish.

For 1980 ATS confirmed their position as one of the real 'no-hoper' teams. Gustav Brunner and Tim Wardrop were responsible for design and construction of two D3 cars, followed by six D4s which were effective Williams FW07 look-alikes. They were driven notably by Surer and Lammers; Surer broke his legs at Kyalami but Lammers qualified third quickest at Long Beach to widespread amazement. When Surer returned, Lammers moved to Ensign and ATS ended the season as consistent midfield qualifiers but scored no Championship points.

In 1981 the Hervé Guilpin-designed HGS1 appeared, in which the ABBA-backed Swedish drummer-cum-racing driver Slim Borgudd managed to finish sixth at Silverstone!

Schmid persevered in 1982 with two HGS models modified by Don Halliday and now known as the model D5. Two entries were made regularly for Manfred Winkelhock and the Chilean Salazar who was fifth in the small-field race at Imola, while Winkelhock was fifth at Rio.

For 1983 Schmid won use of the BMW four-cylinder turbo engine through BMW's interest in his driver Winkelhock who had formerly shone on BMW power in Formula 2. Gustav Brunner designed a neat new moulded carbon-fibre monocoque to take the engine, designated D6 in the ATS system, and three

Marc Surer at Ricard-Castellet, 1980, in Brunner-Wardrop designed ATS D4 '03' – a Williams FW07 lookalike, sliding skirts clearly visible against the road surface.

such chassis would be built. Winkelhock always showed promise but the team's destructively capricious management repeatedly ruined his chances, making less of the car than it was clearly capable of. Again they scored no points.

For 1984 BMW stood by ATS but it was an even worse year and the team withdrew after BMW refused to support them again in 1985. 'D6-03' had been team spare until written off by Winkelhock in Monaco practice, and two new D7s followed for Winkelhock and Berger.

In Championship terms, Schmid's team had scored no points at all in 1978, 1980 and 1983; they managed two points for eleventh place in the 1979 table, one point for twelfth-equal (with the far less ambitious Theodore team) in 1981, and four points for eleventh place in 1982. It had been an expensive exercise, with minimal return for the intense effort which Schmid's ever-changing staff had unstintingly expended over eight virtually fruitless seasons.

Beatrice-Lola

After relinquishing his interest in McLaren International, American Teddy Mayer developed a CART track-racing operation for the US, using proprietary March cars with Cosworth DFX turbocharged V8 engines. The team performed quite well, technical preparation and direction being controlled by the other former American McLaren director, Tyler Alexander. They missed Formula 1, however, and during 1984 developed plans to return to the World Championship series with a new British-based operation and massive US backing. This came from entrepreneur Carl Haas – for many years Lola Cars' US concessionaire – and from the major Beatrice Corporation, a fast-growing conglomerate with interests in foods, various types of manufacturing and also owners of the Avis car rental empire.

Mayer set up FORCE (Formula One Race Car Engineering) to build the new car, designed by ex-Williams engineer Neil Oatley. Haas's Lola interests emerged in Team Haas-Lola who were to race the car, although Lola Cars had virtually no part in its design. Long-term it would employ a new 1500 cc turbocharged Ford engine developed by Cos-

worth Engineering in Northampton, England. Short-term, just to get the show on the road in '85, Hart four-cylinder engines were employed.

Former World Champion Alan Jones was persuaded out of retirement to drive for the team and two slender carbon-monocoque Beatrice-Lola-Hart THL-1 cars emerged in the final four GPs of 1985, '001 being the spare car raced by Jones – very briefly – at Monza and Brands Hatch, and '002 being his race car for Kyalami, where he non-started, and Adelaide. Hart engine fragility prevented any serious progress, the three races ended in three retirements, and into 1986 the project remained an unknown quantity.

Bellasi

The Italian Formula 3 constructor Vittorio Bellasi was approached by Swiss owner/driver Silvio Moser to build him a Cosworth-engined Formula 1 car for 1970, when a rule change demanding metal fuel tank sheathing logically dictated use of a monocoque to replace the old tubular spaceframe cars. Moser had performed quite well in Charles Vogele's ex-works Brabhams, and now Bellasi made him a bulky, heavy but workmanlike riveted aluminium monocoque to pick-up suspension based on his old Repco Brabham BT24's. The new car was undistinguished, Moser failing to qualify in its debut at Zandvoort 1970 and not making the race until Austria on 16 August, where he started last on the grid and retired with a holed radiator. At Monza he failed to qualify again and did not reappear until the Italian GP 1971, when the podgy Bellasi again failed to qualify. It survives intact today, in the Donington Collection, near Derby, England.

Silvio Moser's 1970 Bellasi-Cosworth special.

Boro

See entry for Ensign (page 180).

Brabham

The detailed story of the twice Constructors' World Championship-winning Repco Brabhams is told in Chapter 2. Their relative failure in 1968 with the four-cam Repco Type 860 engine has also been described.

The first two seasons of the new Formula inevitably saw the use of a number of former 1.5-litre or *Libre* Brabham spaceframe chassis (built by Motor Racing Developments Ltd) with various engines in Formula 1. During 1966 – especially in the early events before the new Formula got into its stride – six of these hybrid cars competed. They were all BT11 chassis of original 1964-5 manufacture; 'F1-1-64' being the works car with 2.7-litre Climax four-cylinder FPF engine entered for Hulme in early-season. Chassis '2-64 was a re-chassised car with this serial originally entered by the South African Scuderia Scribante in the November 1965 Rand GP, which it won driven by Brabham himself, using another big FPF engine. Aldo Scribante subsequently ran the car in South African events, including the International GP, for Dave Charlton. 'F1-4-64' was a BRM V8-engined car originally entered by Bob Gerard, and later David Bridges, for John Taylor, who sadly sustained fatal burns in this car following a German GP collision at the Nürburgring. Rhodesian former motor cyclist Bob Anderson's DW Racing Enterprises team ran his immaculate bright-green BT11 'F1-5-64' with 2.7 FPF power with great success until his fatal testing accident at Silverstone in August 1967. Rob Walker's 1.5-litre BRM V8-powered 'F1-6-64' appeared right at the start of the 1966 season in South Africa, while the final BT11 of this interesting but obscure sextet was the production *Libre* car 'IC-5-64' owned and entered by South African Otelle Nucci for Pieter de Klerk.

At more significant level, in 1969 Jack Brabham and Ron Tauranac bowed to the inevitable, and cut their Repco engine ties and adopted the Cosworth DFV V8.

The existing BT26 hybrid-construction chassis with their part stressed-skin stiffened spaceframe chassis were altered to accommodate the British engine. Two existing ex-Repco BT26s were uprated as DFV-powered works team BT26As, chassis '2 for Brabham himself and '3 for new team driver Ickx.

Old ex-works 'BT24/3' had been sold to Frank Williams and fitted with a 2.5-litre Cosworth DFW V8 engine for Courage's use in the Tasman Championship. After that tour this car was sold to Swiss privateer Moser who fitted it with a 3-litre DFV as a replacement for the Charles Vogèle-owned BT20 which he had campaigned previously. Williams replaced this car with ex-works prototype 'BT26/1' which he also had converted to DFV power for Courage to contest the World Championship GP series.

Jack himself destroyed 'BT26/2' in a pre-French GP testing accident at Silverstone – where he had earlier won the International Trophy in '26/2 running new Goodyear G14 wet-weather tyres and wearing twin strutted wings. He broke an ankle and so missed the mid-season GPs leaving Ickx to uphold team honour alone. A replacement 'BT26/4' was completed in time for the British GP in which it was driven by Ickx to finish second. Subsequently, he won the German GP in this car and the minor Oulton Park Gold Cup race in his early-season regular '26/3. Brabham returned to take over chassis '4 from the Italian GP, these two works cars finishing 1-2 in the Canadian GP at Mosport Park.

The BT26As were arguably the best-handling cars of the 1969 season but they suffered on reliability. Jack himself qualified on pole for the season-opening South African GP at Kyalami and ran second until his car's wing fell off. Ickx also lost his wing. Brabham broke an engine at Barcelona and Ickx broke a wishbone but he was classified sixth. Wing trouble persisted. Courage broke a valve spring.

At Monaco, Brabham collided with a BRM and Ickx disputed second until a rear upright broke, leaving Courage a splendid second place in his private Brabham. Ickx and Brabham placed 5-6 in Holland, Courage suffering clutch trouble.

Ickx shone as he always did when he was undisputed team leader. He was third in France after running second most of the way, second at Silverstone with Courage fifth, as well as adding a new lap record to his win at the Nürburgring where he started on pole. He bent his car during pre-race filming at Monza when he found a barrier erected across the road! A spate of engine failures wrecked his Italian GP practice and race though Brabham himself ran high until a fuel pipe pulled off. Courage drove another fine race and led briefly until fuel starvation began.

Jack qualified on pole before the Canadian 1-2. Courage retired with a fuel leak but at Watkins Glen he was second after holding off both works cars in a spirited duel, Jack having to stop for fuel and finishing fourth, while Ickx was second and set fastest lap. In Mexico, Goodyear tyres shone again; Brabham took pole once more but finished only third after injection problems while Ickx gained second and set fastest lap. Courage bounced his car off

Graham Hill in Ron Tauranac's 1971 'lobster claw' Brabham BT34 at Brands Hatch (below) contrasts with the BT37 (bottom), cobbled together around BT34 bag tanks to keep the team racing in 1972-73. This BT37 is in 1973 form with deformable structure side pods.

Siffert's Lotus and finished tenth.

During the season the Kyalami wing failures had been traced to the omission of a washer on the stays, the bolts subsequently being over-tightened, while those at Silverstone and Barcelona were due to extra loading caused by the adoption of end plates. After Kyalami, Jack's '26/2 was fitted with 2 in. wider track long wishbones, '26/3 being updated accordingly while '26/4 had the wider track from new.

After the Barcelona wing collapses on the Lotus 49s and Brabham BT26As, Ron Tauranac was largely responsible for framing the new wing regulations which took effect at Zandvoort, but he felt chassis-mounted wings were bad in principle as they caused the car to run nose-up under acceleration. The Brabham marque finished second behind Matra-Ford in the Constructors' Championship. 'BT 26/4' went to Tom Wheatcroft, founder of the Donington collection, for 1970, when it would be driven briefly by Bell.

For 1970, fuel tanks had to be metal-sheathed, so Ron built his first monocoque Formula 1 cars, the BT33s.

Three of these handsome, podgy-tubbed machines were built, each slightly different from its predecessor and many detail modifications were made during the season. Jack's turquoise-and-gold 'BT33/2' works car was joined by newcomer Stommelen's sister 'BT33/1' in German magazine livery from the start of the season. Jack's car was consistently the fastest conventional-layout Cosworth-powered car but due to unreliability and some team mistakes his last driving season collapsed as defeats were snatched from the jaws of victory.

He won the South African GP on 'BT33/2's debut. He led the Race of Champions before suffering electrical trouble and was close behind Stewart at Jarama when '33/2's crankshaft broke. At Monaco, Jack made his famous mistake on the very last corner, losing the lead and limping home a thoroughly disgusted second. Punctures hampered his progress at Zandvoort and he crashed Stommelen's car heavily in practice. Clutch trouble was the problem at Spa, while at Clermont he finished a tardy third.

He dominated the British GP only to run out of fuel on the last lap. Thereafter the Brabham season fell apart. At Hockenheim there was an oil leak, in Austria a stone pierced his radiator and in Italy he went off the road when his engine cut. A massive oil leak ended his run in Canada, at Watkins Glen he spun and stalled,

losing much time, and in Mexico – his farewell outing – his engine failed, losing third place. He had scored 25 points in the first part of the season but added none in the second half.

Meanwhile, Stommelen failed to qualify at Monaco but was fifth at Spa, missed the Dutch GP after Jack had bent his car in practice, and then himself wrote off 'BT33/1' in practice at Brands Hatch. A new 'BT33/3' was ready for him to finish fifth in Germany, third in Austria and fifth again in Italy. Brabham placed fourth-equal with McLaren in the Constructors' table.

In 1971 they fell to the foot of the Championship. Jack had gone back to his native Australia, and Tauranac seemed to miss him badly as he ran the team alone on a tight budget. Driver Graham Hill was past his best and number two Schenken's best was not good enough.

Ron's latest 'lobster-claw' BT34 design was little better than the BT33, whereas Hill thought it worse. Its monocoque was squarer in section and to minimize front end lift Ron divided the conventional nose radiator and slung two small cores in faired pods ahead of each front wheel, a tub-width nose wing bridging between them.

Jack's 1970 '33/2 was sold to private entrant Alain de Cadanet for Chris Craft to drive late in 1971. Stommelen's wrecked '33/1 had been rebuilt to accompany '33/3 in the new works team, Hill and Dave Charlton driving them at Kyalami, doing nothing. Schenken managed to reach fourth at Brands Hatch in '33/1 where '34/1 made its debut, Hill encountering engine trouble.

The cars were lucky at Silverstone where Graham won in the BT34 with Schenken third in '33/1, but at Monaco Graham bent '34/1 and Schenken came tenth after bursting a tyre.

The British GP at Silverstone saw Schenken run as high as third until his gearbox failed; in Germany he was sixth in '33/3, then in Austria Schenken and Hill placed 3-5 for the team's first two-car score of the season. They ended the season ninth and last on the Constructors' table with just five points.

At Brands Hatch in the minor final race of the season Schenken finished fifth in '33/3 while the modified '33/1 was driven by Reutemann, making his serious Formula 1 debut, finishing ninth just behind Hill's still-unique '34/1.

During the winter of 1971/72 Tauranac sold MRD to Bernie Ecclestone, businessman, former Formula 1 Connaught private entrant and more recently Rindt's business manager. 1972 was a formative season for the revamped company.

They retained 'BT33/3' and the BT34, while Ralph Bellamy from McLaren handled technical development – which was modest. The BT34 ran in Argentina with revised bodywork and narrower rear track for Reutemann, Hill driving the ex-Schenken BT33 updated with 16-gauge regulation outer skin, strengthened bulkheads, revised bodywork as seen at the end of '71 and new Girling four-pot brake callipers. Reutemann ran Goodyear's latest G52 soft compound tyres there to qualify on pole.

The Bellamy-designed BT37 ran at Silverstone; in effect a BT34 with conventional nose radiator and regulation deformable structure tank protection. Front track was 1.5-in. narrower and it was some 25 lb lighter. Parallel-link rear suspension was adopted on the cars in mid-season.

Ecclestone also backed a test programme, building a one-off BT39 to accommodate the Ford-financed Weslake Type 190 V12 engine which had been intended for sports car use and was based upon 1966-68 Gurney-Weslake V12 experience. The project had similarities with the contemporary March 721G in that it used a basic F2 tub – a BT38 design – completely reskinned with 47-gallon fuel capacity. Hill tested the Brabham-Weslake briefly at Silver-

stone prior to the Italian GP but the claimed '445 bhp' engine was underpowered. The brief test told the team all they wished to know and Ecclestone was not afraid to write off the investment and put the project down to experience.

Brabham made 35 starts in 14 races in 1972, finishing 20 times, winning the minor Interlagos event and adding third there, but had only one fourth, a fifth and two sixths at Championship level.

Ending that year Bellamy moved to Lotus and his quiet young assistant, Gordon Murray, was offered the chance to take his place.

Gordon had been a great fan of the svelte little Lotus 25s of 1962-63 and had an image of a small, light and simple Formula 1 car which Ecclestone allowed him to build. Since the rather pathetic BT37 had been restricted by the decision to use existing BT34 bag tanks, no compromises were to stand in the way of the new 1973 deformable-structure BT42. Nothing current was to be used which could possibly limit it.

Gordon wanted to gain on top speed by making a smaller hole in the air than the preceding BT33-34-37 cars, so adopted a triangular pyramid-section monocoque design. The idea for this had been 'kicked around' with Bellamy before he left, and the intention was to keep centre of gravity low, maintain airflow on top of the chassis and to match the DFV cam-cover slope, thus providing nice straight load paths for the top engine mountings.

Gordon adopted a short wheelbase and very simple fuel system, employing only three tanks – a large one amidships pushing the driver quite far forward plus one on each side. He used Tauranac's BT34 split-radiator position just ahead of the front wheels which faired into a full-width nose, streamlining the front wheels and minimizing lift. These split radiators in the nose could be made some 50 per cent smaller than mid-mounted radiators because they received cleaner direct airflow, and could also be made any shape.

The BT42 emerged some 10 per cent smaller on frontal area than some cars but was still not the quickest along the straight. There were also shortcomings in stiffness and geometry which would later be corrected on the BT44.

During 1973 the team campaigned 'BT37/1' and '2 in early events before the first 'BT42/1' was written off on its Race of Champions debut by the unfortunate Watson, its throttle jamming open at Stirling's Bend. Ceramica Pagnossin-sponsored Italian driver de Adamich destroyed '37/1 in Spain. Five more BT42s were built that year: chassis '4 was destroyed by the luckless de Adamich – neither of his write-offs really being his fault – in the Scheckter collision during the British GP at Silverstone, '3 became Reutemann's usual mount, '2 and later '5 allocated to Wilson Fittipaldi, while '6 appeared late in the year driven by Stommelen and then the recovered Watson.

After brief elation and final disappointment when Reutemann led in Barcelona, Brabham's results showed Reutemann third at Ricard and Watkins Glen, fourth in Sweden and Austria, and sixth at Silverstone and Monza. Wilson Fittipaldi was fifth at the Nürburgring to add to his sixth in Argentina, and de Adamich was fourth in Belgium and seventh at Monaco in the remaining BT37. Brabham cars had made 42 starts in the 15 GPs and scored nine times, taking fourth in the Constructors' table.

For 1974, Murray began work on the improved BT44 and the prototype emerged just in time to be shipped to Argentina for the first race, not turning a wheel in England before it left. Gordon, Team Manager Herbie Blash and their long-serving team members rate the BT44 as one of his 'nicest' cars – a honey both to work on and to drive.

Gordon recalls: 'I tried to keep the good points of the 42 in the new car. What I wanted

to do really necessitated starting with a new tub. I built in rising-rate suspension, while the wheelbase was one inch longer . . . it was generally a neater car in detail, simple and without a great deal of fabricated work, the kind of stuff which gives trouble.'

He introduced pullrod rising-rate front suspension linkages in this BT44, using semi-inboard coil/dampers standing on pivoting feet, tensioned by rods attached to the outboard top wishbone tip. This obviated the need for massive top rocker arms, 'beams in bending', which Gordon called 'Nasty, horrible things'.

Subsequently, pullrod suspensions would be widely adopted, as were pushrods which Gordon also evolved – 'Pullrods the other way up, they needed to be heavier of course, being in compression rather than tension'.

In his native Argentina, Reutemann shone again and led until the airbox ripped away around its retaining bolts, losing 200 rpm on the straight. Five laps from the end while still leading handsomely, a plug lead came loose so the engine ran on seven cylinders, before finally stopping during the last lap . . . out of fuel. 'We had had a panic on race morning with a wheel seized on, and although 39 gallons of fuel should have gone in the tanks, one churn didn't go in . . .'

Many Grand Prix races, much prize money and an awful lot of glory have been squandered this way.

The four surviving BT42s, chassis '2-3-5-6, were raced early in the year, four new BT44s '1-2-3-4 replacing them.

The BT44s had a new, less drag-inducive nose and smoother cockpit area cleaning up airflow onto the rear wing. BT44s '1 and '2 ran for Reutemann and rent-a-driver Robarts in Argentina, with 'BT42/3' spare, while motor trader John Goldie's Hexagon of Highgate team ran the ex-Fittipaldi 'BT42/2' for Watson in its chocolate livery. 'BT44/1' used the underbelly chevron air dam discussed on page 94.

In South Africa, new tapered-wire progressive-rate rear springs were introduced on Reutemann's car. In Spain, old 'BT42/5' and '6 appeared for Swiss driver Moser, entered by Bretscher Racing, but did not run as he had been fatally injured in the Monza 1000 km. These cars subsequently raced under the Scuderia Martino Finotto banner for Larrousse.

In Sweden, the '44s toyed briefly with 12 in. diameter front wheels and in Holland Goodyear tried their latest 24 in. outside diameter rear tyres on 10 in. diameter rims against the normal 26 in. OD on 13s. This was an attempt to combine smaller frontal area

Gordon Murray, who succeeded Colin Chapman as the most innovative F1 design engineer, ponders his BT44's pullrod front suspension.

with contemporary deep and soft sidewall construction, improving straightline speed and incidentally driveshaft angularity, but after a brief run in practice the BT44s reverted to normal trim.

These rims and tyres were tried again at Dijon and in Austria, while at Monza 10 in. rims were tested with 18 in. wide rear tyres, 2.5 in. wider than normal. Spare chassis '3 was used, then returned to standard for Watson to race after crashing his own Hexagon 'BT44/4'. This car had made its debut in Germany, replacing old '42/2 which Ian Ashley failed to qualify in the USA at the end of the season.

Von Opel had briefly replaced Robarts as second MRD driver but was superseded from mid-season by Pace.

The Brabham BT44s at some stage led each of the season's first five races. Suspension geometry and stiffness deficiencies were corrected to enable Reutemann to score the Ecclestone and Murray team's first victory in the South African GP, then winning again in Austria and the US where Pace and Watson completed a works team 1-2 and Brabham 1-2-5 result.

Reutemann finished nine of his 16 GPs, placing 7-7-1-12-6-3-1-9-1, while von Opel's neat if brief MRD career comprised two non-qualifications, two retirements and two ninth places. Pace had an unlucky debut, non-qualifying at Brands Hatch due to a car problem, and thereafter started six races, finishing five of them – 9-12-5-8-2. Brabham ended the season fifth in the Constructors' table.

For 1975, Martini and Fina sponsorship coloured the formerly virgin-white Brabhams' flanks, and Gordon developed his successful BT44s as BT44Bs with stiffened tubs, revised narrower front suspension though still rising-rate, and redesigned bodies with greater downforce nose sections. Chassis '44B/1 was new in Argentina, 'B2 was built from '44/3, 'B3 from '44/1 and 'B4 from '44/4.

The underbelly air dams reappeared for the partly high-speed circuit of Kyalami and in Spain small 'whisker' foils appeared on the nose sides, greater downforce now balanced by deeper banana section rear wings offering minimal frontal area. Pace tried the underbelly air dam in Holland and thought it was terrific; Reutemann tried it and preferred to run without.

At Ricard, cycle-type front wheel mudguard fairings were attached, ostensibly to deflect

flying grit and gravel. Gordon always loved a try-on. After first practice they were removed.

Pace crashed '44B/2 in the rain at the British GP, though nevertheless was classified second, and '44B/4 which had been completed earlier in the year made its race debut under him at the Nürburgring.

Reutemann scored in eight of the year's 14 GPs, won in Germany and was third in the Driver's Championship. His record included only two retirements from 14 GPs, placing 3-8-2-3-9-3-2-4-14 before his first failure in Britain, then 1-14-4 at the end of season. Pace won his home GP in Brazil, being classified as a finisher six times, 1-4-3-8-5-2. Brabham finished second to Ferrari in the Constructors' table.

It had been their best season but could have been better still, for the BT44Bs' development stagnated as Gordon concentrated upon a new Alfa Romeo-engined project. Ecclestone had first made contact with Autodelta (Alfa's competitions wing) as early as June 1974 to discuss use of their 3-litre flat-12 sports car engine. The deal was agreed late that year and Gordon spent much of the summer of '75 engrossed in designing a new car around this large, heavy and thirsty but powerful unit.

It could offer some 510 bhp, compared to the DFV with perhaps 480 bhp, but as a sports car unit it had untidy ancillaries and was some 40 kg (88 lb) heavier. Additionally it needed 8 to 12 gallons more fuel depending on the circuit, greater cooling surface and more oil; it was also 11 in. longer than a DFV and some 3 in. wider.

Consequently the 1976 Brabham-Alfa Romeo BT45s were hefty brutes. Gordon had to abandon his preferred pyramidal tub section to accommodate sufficient fuel and the flat-12 engine in a broader, more squared-off tub. Autodelta fought to reduce consumption and weight, while MRD developed the chassis.

As early in the season as Kyalami, weight was being saved by using more titanium in the tubs and more magnesium in the engines. Chassis '45/3 emerged at Long Beach, 10 kg (22 lb) lighter than '1 and '2 with still more weight saved in the engine. In Spain, Reutemann bent '45/2 badly in practice; it was rebuilt for Belgium but there Pace demolished the latest '45/3.

At Monaco, the latest Brabham-Alfa Romeo six-speed gearboxes appeared, though raced only by Pace. The RAM Racing team fielded 44Bs '1 and '2 for Nelleman and Kessel, though without luck, '42/2 being their spare.

In France, a stride was made with modified front suspension rising-rate geometry, deep skirting all round the bottom of the chassis, new airbox design, brake fans and streamlining wheel discs in the front wheel centres. Rear suspension settings were also revised and Pace was timed at 177.36 mph on the Mistral Straight. Power was never a problem.

A new 5 kg (11 lb) lighter '45/4 emerged for Pace at the British GP, using lighter gauges and more titanium, and in Germany it used an air-starter like McLaren's, plus experimental Dunlop disc brakes with carbon-fibre insert pucks as friction surfaces, potentially saving weight and offering better retardation as they could endure higher temperatures than conventional brakes. Reutemann moved to Ferrari, unable to cope with the BT45s' development, RAM driver Stommelen taking his place.

in '45/1 with carbon-fibre brakes. Meanwhile, RAM ran into litigation with driver Kessel and did not start.

Stommelen finished sixth, but Pace ran the carbon brakes in Austria and had the discs expand on the straight – the fluid boiled as he touched the pedal and he entered the *Glatz-kurve* brakeless at 180 mph, destroying '45/4. The carbon brakes gave endless trouble with boiling fluid, vibration, wear, inconsistency and snapping bolts. However, the system's day would come.

In Holland, lower rear wishbones were tried instead of parallel links in practice, reverting to normal for the race, but the new centre-pivot suspension was used throughout in Italy (where Pace qualified faster than the Ferraris!) and in America. Perkins joined Pace in the American races and a new '45/5, lighter still by 6 kg (14 lb), made its debut.

Initially, communication with Autodelta was poor: without warning such vital items as engine mountings could vary by up to half an inch from one engine to another, causing nightmares in assembly and preparation.

During 1976, the cars had been quite reliable, Pace finishing nine of his 16 GPs, 10-9-6-9-8-4-8-4-7, his fourth places coming in France and Germany. Reutemann had a miserable time in contrast with nine retirements in his twelve races, finishing 12-4-11, Spain providing his best placing, where there was a promising Brabham-Alfa 4-6 finish. But Brabham tumbled to ninth in the Constructors' Championship.

Into 1977 the Brabham BT45s scaled some 620 kg (1366.8 lb), though a lighter B-spec was on the way and with Pace's unstinting faith the team were showing real progress.

Pace damaged '45/1 heavily in Argentine practice and it was rebuilt as the first BT45B in time for Kyalami with its engine lowered by 1.5 in., parallel-link rear suspension and Brabham-Alfa six-speed gearbox, saving around 55 kg (122 lb). Pace qualified second, Watson was on pole for the Race of Champions but news of Pace's death in a flying accident broke later that day and there was no joy in Watson's third place.

Stuck joined Watson at Long Beach where three BT45Bs ran, Watson qualified on pole at Monaco and in Sweden – where the last new 'BT45/6' emerged for Watson – he might have won but for a collision. In France, again in '6, he led only to run out of fuel within a mile of the finish, and in the British GP in '1 he led again until another fuel system malfunction.

He qualified on the front row in Germany, but the second half of his season slumped. Stuck raised morale with third in Germany and Austria and led the flooded US GP before crashing.

Pace had run only three races before his tragic death, finishing second in Argentina, going out in Brazil and 12th at Kyalami after again showing well. Watson finished only five of the 17 GPs, 6-5-2-8-12, while Stuck finished eight of his 14 Brabham-Alfa GPs, 6-6-10-5-3-3-7-7, scoring more points. Brabham-Alfa finished fifth in the Constructors' table.

In mid-season '77, Gordon had begun work on a pyramidal monocoque replacement for the BT45s, using surface cooling to minimize aerodynamic drag, and featuring greater driver protection. The tub sides rose to shoulder height, while nose box and wing occupied a separate foam-filled monocoque structure. A double-skinned panel went up to the dash panel and supported the now mandatory front roll hoop. Dunlop carbon-fibre brakes reappeared after a year's absence and sophisticated instrumentation was adopted. Digital displays enabled the driver to select read-outs on whatever function he required, including instantaneous lap times, saving reliance upon pit signals which are inevitably one lap out of date upon reception. The BT46 also had integral air jacks to facilitate speedy tyre

changing in practice and race, activated by an external pressurized air supply. More weight was saved on the six-speed Brabham-Alfa gearbox, and rising-rate Murray suspensions appeared front and rear.

Unfortunately, the surface coolers towed still air with them and overheated, the digital instrumentation vibrated itself into failure and the BT46 was not raceworthy as the new season began. So Brabham raced new BT45Cs chassis '7 and '8 with shallow full-width nose radiators. The BT46 was redesigned with nose radiators and chassis '46/3 and '4 made the model's debut at Kyalami. Chassis '2 became team spare, replaced by '5 at Monaco where they qualified 2-3 and Watson led – having started from pole there the previous year only to lose the lead into the first corner. But his brakes faded, Lauda set fastest lap and Gordon twigged the significance of Lotus 79 ground-effects and told Ecclestone they were finished unless they did something drastic to keep in touch.

As the Lotus 79s came on song, Gordon and his assistant, David North, developed the legendary Brabham BT46B fan-car (see page 130).

In Spain, '46/6 emerged for Lauda while Watson retained '4 and these machines were reworked as fan-cars for their unique victory in Sweden. Following the British GP, Watson drove '5 and in Holland Lauda took new car '7, while for the American trip Watson used chassis '8.

The fan-car was banned and a second-generation BT47 which had already been designed had to be shelved, so BT46s completed the season. The BT46C variant for the Austrian GP had its water radiators faired into the monocoque just behind the front wheels, thus enabling the original needle nose to return and improving weight distribution. They placed 1-2 at Monza after the on-road 1-2 Lotus and Ferrari had been penalized for jumping the start.

Both Lauda and Watson ran all 16 GPs, the Austrian finishing excellently the seven times he managed to finish at all: 2-3-2-1-2-3-1. Watson was overshadowed, finishing ten times 8-3-4-5-4-3-7-7-4-2 and the marque reached third place in the Championship. This was more encouraging.

Autodelta had made a bewildering range of changes to their flat-12 engine. Only the basic head and block castings remained unaltered; all the internals were different from the original 1976-spec, the layout was more tidy, there were titanium rods and exhausts, and the flat-12 was within 25 kg (55 lb) of the Cosworth DFV.

But after the Lotus 79s' dominance, Gordon knew that ground-effects showed the only way to go; to arrange underwing tunnels the flat-12 engine must be replaced by a V12. Autodelta built a suitable Alfa Romeo '1260' engine within three months of MRD's request. By the end of 1978 Gordon felt robbed of probably two Drivers' titles. The Italian engines had been strong and reliable in '78. Take the Lotuses out of the equation and Brabham would have won many races.

The new Alfa 1260 was available a few weeks ahead of the BT48 Brabham chassis designed to accept it. With 525 bhp at 12,300 rpm it was slung as a stressed engine on a narrow and neat aluminium sheet tub which incorporated moulded carbon-composite structural panels in the scuttle and around the fuel cell, forming some 30 per cent of the tub. Pullrod suspension used totally inboard coil/dampers and there were full-length underwing side pods.

Gordon and David North had felt it was vital to build a second-generation ground-effects car rather than merely copy the Lotus 79 layout, simply to keep contact with Lotus themselves. Consequently they developed a full-length underwing car with low-level rear wing in Lotus 80 style. At this stage Gordon still did not

Four Murray Brabhams: opposite top left, 1973 BT42 which introduced the pyramid-section, low frontal area, low centre of gravity tub; top right, 1974 BT44 retained split nose radiators but added aerodynamic improvements; bottom left, the much-maligned surface-cooled 1978 BT46 which became such a fine car with its Alfa Romeo flat-12 engine; bottom right, Piquet in his 1985 BT54-BMW turbo at Rio, racing for the first time on Pirelli tyres.

use a wind tunnel, his work was intuitive.

Like the Lotus 80, it was a disaster, but Brabham instantly recognized it as such during practice in Argentina and hastily ripped off the offending surfaces, cut back the under-wings and were soon able to run – at Kyalami – in aerodynamic balance without nose foils.

Gordon Murray: 'We didn't understand centres of pressure. In Argentina the springs were far too soft and the skirts sticking up. Any dynamic input – acceleration, braking or cornering – simply upset the whole thing and the centre of pressure went rocketing up and down the car two or three feet one way or the other!'

Like the Lotus 80 the Brabham BT48 in original full-length underwing form suffered the dreaded 'porpoising', and at one point in Argentine practice Lauda felt the front wheels lift off as it attempted to fly . . .

Thus began a miserable Brabham season. Four BT48s were built, '48/1 and '2 appearing in Buenos Aires as spare and race car for Lauda, while new team-mate Piquet drove old 'BT46/7'. At Kyalami, Piquet used '48/3 with '1 spare and Lauda took over chassis '4 in Belgium where Piquet qualified faster. However, the Austrian crashed '4 at Monaco, the rebuilt car being used as spare in France where Lauda raced '2 but returned to the latest car at Silverstone. At Monza, Piquet tore '48/3 in two in an almighty accident, while in the Dino Ferrari GP at Imola Lauda won in '48/2.

Not only was this the Alfa Romeo 1260 V12's only victory, it also marked the end of the Brabham-Alfa relationship, for at Chessington three brand new BT49-Cosworth DFVs were being completed hastily for the trip to Canada and Watkins Glen. Autodelta would be concentrating upon their own Formula 1 cars hereafter, and the Brabham BT49s' story is related in Chapter 13.

During 1979 Lauda had started an unlucky thirteen GPs in the Brabham-Alfa BT48s, finishing only twice, sixth in South Africa and fourth in Italy. Piquet made four finishes from his 13 Brabham-Alfa starts, placing 7-8-'12' and fourth in Holland.

Brabham ended the season eighth in the Constructors' table but now at last they were beginning their run towards World Championship success, as described in Chapter 13.

With first Cosworth DFV and later turbo-

charged BMW power the team rode their World Championship-winning wave to the end of 1983, until reliability sank in 1984.

For that season, extensive winter testing of BT52C and then BT52D development specs finally formed the basis of a shapely and still essentially spearhead-form BT53. The prototype chassis 'BT53/1' was retained as test car, while five new BT53s were built during the season, employing a folded aluminium outer tub skin with moulded carbon-composite inner-cum-tank top and fully machined solid aluminium bulkheads.

Drivers for the season were Piquet and the Fabi brothers, usually Teo, sometimes Corrado. Chassis 'BT53/2' was new for Teo at Rio and was raced by him at Kyalami, Zolder, Imola and Dijon, then driven by Corrado at Monaco, Montreal and Dallas, returning to Teo for the middle of the season until Hockenheim.

Spare car duties were performed by 'BT53/3' from Rio to Monza, being raced by Piquet at Detroit after the startline collision and restart.

Piquet's usual car was 'BT53/5' new at Rio, though he raced '4 in the autumn from Brands Hatch to Monza, then took over new car '6 at *ersatz* Nürburgring.

Gordon described 1984 as ' . . . a disaster for Brabham results, really worse than when we were using Alfa Romeo engines, but on the other hand, though exasperating, it's been quite satisfying to see your car on pole and leading races against such serious opposition.'

The Brabham-BMWs were the only cars to challenge McLaren seriously that year but the pattern of failures was frustrating, each one being different, without an established pattern. Perhaps it was symptomatic of overstressing an engine near the limit of its possible development. BMW uprated their engines for Brabham's 25-unit pool, claiming 770 bhp in race tune, ending the season with more than 850 bhp in qualifying.

An early spate of turbocharger failures abated for the American mid-season tour when the BT53s' weight distribution was changed with the relocation of 'hot elements', siting the oil cooler in a nose-top duct. The team had bearings fail, seals go, bad welding, wrong fuel, timing problems, an overheating turbo. At Zolder, bad fuel destroyed ten engines.

A revised BT53B aerodynamic package for Brands Hatch was a disaster because it refused to heat its tyres adequately despite handling well. The B-spec was shelved although its underwing and rear suspension modifications were retained.

BMW attributed early-season turbo troubles in part to running too hot in the new car layout. Non-engine failures included a pinion-bearing collapse stopping Piquet in Germany and an oil union coming undone at Zandvoort. At Monza a radiator punctured, possibly due to Piquet hitting a kerb early on.

Piquet finished only seven of the season's 16 GPs, winning twice in Montreal and Detroit, finishing '9'-7-2-3-6 otherwise. Teo Fabi drove 12 GPs between CART commitments in the USA, finishing four times (9-3-4-5) and scoring three times, while younger brother Corrado drove at Monaco, Montreal and Dallas, finishing just once – a pointless seventh in Texas.

Brabham finished the season fourth in the Constructors' Championship.

At the end of 1984 Michelin withdrew from Formula 1, and Ecclestone signed with Pirelli, who had hitherto been uncompetitive, instead.

That change, combined with the need to improve BMW engine reliability, involved some 12,000 miles winter testing, much of it in the heat of Kyalami. This was like finishing one race season then immediately doing another, only more concentrated, through the winter.

They emerged with a more reliable engine but it was not enough and the team's gearboxes would also be unreliable through '85. Brabham had asked Pirelli to develop a competitive race tyre first, then qualifying tyres later. They had competitive hot-weather tyres for Rio only for a gearbox to fail.

The 1985 Pirellis were always very weather sensitive. If the appropriate tyres for whatever ambient conditions happened to be available, the Brabhams ran well. It was like that at Ricard, with a new tyre good in very hot weather. That new tyre was a big change, and from half-way through the season a competitive Pirelli qualifying tyre also emerged. Tyre testing proceeded continuously, and the Brabhams were very quick in a cold test at the Nürburgring and quickest in a freezing test at Zandvoort, then looked potential winners at Brands Hatch on a cool grey day . . . contradicting a popular impression that Brabham's Pirellis only performed in a heatwave.

Gordon Murray's BT54 design was the last in Formula 1 to retain an aluminium outer skin, stiffened by a complex moulded carbon-composite inner-cum-scuttle-and-tank-top. Like the BT52s/53s, it used modular construction with the entire front suspension hung on a machined-from-solid nose bulkhead plugged into the front of the tub structure, and a similar engine/gearbox/rear suspension module at the rear. Continuous torsional tests throughout the season monitored each chassis' health, weakening ones being retired, which explains why no less than nine BT54s were built.

Whereas in 1983/84 it had become standard Brabham practice to produce a B-spec update mid-season, their intensive winter testing for '85 left the BT54 broadly settled all year. Gordon at last abandoned the American Hitco carbon brakes for French SEPs with modified Girling callipers which tested well and whose manufacturers offered 'a good deal'.

Three of the longer-side pod BT54s were now in Rio for Piquet and new driver Hesnault, but the young Frenchman was replaced by Surer from Spa in June when the Belgian GP was postponed due to the relaid road surface breaking up. Chassis '4 was new for Piquet at Estoril, round two of the series, '5 new as spare at Monaco and later burned-out in a fire at *ersatz* Nürburgring testing, '6 new for Piquet on the return to Spa, '7 a new spare at Silverstone, '8 emerging for Surer in Austria and '9 new for Piquet at Brands Hatch.

Piquet started all 16 races, finishing only seven: 8-6-1-4-8-2-5. The win came in blistering heat – hence the Pirelli legend – at Ricard, placing second at Monza, fourth at Silverstone, fifth at Spa and sixth in Detroit.

Hesnault had only three races, retiring each

Patrese demonstrates pit-stop race strategy in 1982. The ploy worked for the first time here in Austria but three laps later BT50/4's engine broke.

time and failing to qualify at Monaco, while Surer did well in his 12 races, being placed eight times: 15-8-8-6-6-10*-4-8. His points scores, in sequence, came at Silverstone, the Österreichring and Monza, while he looked a likely winner at Brands Hatch until his car caught fire.

The Brabham-BMWs were handicapped mainly by their tyres which were generally inferior to Goodyear all season. They ran higher race horsepower beginning the year than through mid-season in deference to the tyre situation. A computer failure at Imola saw them burn all their fuel while at Silverstone 'We cocked-up completely and were just utterly uncompetitive and finished with a lot of fuel left over'.

The end of the season and the end of our period was also the end of a Brabham era, for Nelson Piquet swopped seats with Keke Rosberg and left the team which had brought him two World Championship titles, to join Williams-Honda.

BRM

Founded as a trust intended to organize a cooperative industrial Grand Prix car venture in 1945-46, British Racing Motors – BRM – had been a subsidiary of the privately owned Owen Organisation since 1952. From its base at Bourne in Lincolnshire it had campaigned Formula 1 cars in three Formulae from 1950 and finally won the World Championship with its 1500 cc V8-engined cars driven by Graham Hill in 1962.

BRM was, in effect, a British Ferrari, making its own chassis, engines and gearboxes while all around were specialist 'kit car' teams buying engines from one supplier (often BRM itself) buying gearboxes from another and merely engineering and operating their own chassis.

Through the last three seasons of 1½-litre racing, 1963-4-5, BRM was a magnificent team with not a weak link in the chain. It was immensely consistent and Hill came within an ace of winning a second title in 1964 but had actually scored too many times. To comply with contemporary rules, he had to drop his lowest-scoring finishes, allowing Surtees and Ferrari to pick up the titles instead. BRM was second in the Constructors' table in each of those three seasons.

For the start of the new 3-litre Formula in 1966, Chief Engineer Tony Rudd opted to build an H16-cylinder engine. It began life as a pair of the successful P56 1500 V8 engines with their cylinder banks laid horizontal, mounted one above the other with their crankshafts geared together, though it did not quite emerge like that after development. Until it became raceworthy, BRM ran Tasman Formula 1.9-litre versions of its highly-successful P261 1964-65 Formula 1 cars. Engine development is outlined on pages 149-51.

These very neat cigar-like full-monocoque cars were on the minimum weight limit and had available some 275 bhp at 9750 rpm.

Chassis '2616' and '2617' were driven by Hill and Stewart as the European season began seriously at Monaco, Stewart winning and Hill finishing third. Both crashed in the first-lap rainstorm at Spa in which Stewart broke his collarbone and destroyed chassis '7'; Hill, however, later ran high in the French GP until a camshaft broke.

Stewart returned for the British GP, in '2614', but the V8 BRMs were slower than the Repco Brabhams and even Gurney's merely four-cylinder Eagle. Hill was third; a week later he came second in Holland with Stewart fourth, they achieved 4-5 at the Nürburgring, but after this the 2-litre cars were pensioned off as the H16s took precedence.

The BRM used a bulky P83-design forward-monocoque nacelle with the compact but heavy P75 H16 engine and gearbox bolted rigidly onto its rear bulkhead as a load-bearing structural member. In this respect, it anticipated the Cosworth DFV but was itself pre-dated by the 1965 flat-12 Ferrari model 1512.

The factory H16 did not actually race until September 1966, although it had made one very brief appearance at Reims in a Lotus 43 and was given practice runs at Monaco, Spa and Reims – where it had first shown promise. A variety of mechanical problems, mostly with clutch and gearchange, made it unraceworthy until Monza.

Both works H16s ('8302' for Hill and '8303' for Stewart) retired early, Hill's engine disintegrating internally and Stewart's car developing an incurable fuel leak. Clark's Lotus 43-H16 ran strongly between pit stops, and the hope which this engendered seemed justified two weeks later when first Stewart then Hill led the Oulton Park Gold Cup before engine trouble intruded.

The US GP at Watkins Glen followed, where the spare works H16 engine, '7505', won, but as it was fitted in Clark's Lotus 43, Chief Engineer

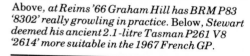

Above, at Reims '66 Graham Hill has BRM P83 '8302' really growling in practice. Below, Stewart deemed his ancient 2.1-litre Tasman P261 V8 '2614' more suitable in the 1967 French GP.

Tony Rudd had a little explaining to do when he returned home . . .

The works engines also ran well – for a time – until Hill's car broke its final-drive and Stewart's its engine. Mexico was an anticlimax, as Clark's US-winning H16 exploded in practice and the substitute failed to perform in the race. Stewart's ran third until its engine grenaded, throwing a crankshaft counterweight, but Hill's refused to run properly and this was worrying for it had the latest eight-pin crankshaft intended as frontline armament for 1967.

That formative season also saw a private Tasman P261 '2615' with former 1½-litre 1960 cc V8 engines entered by Bernard White, notably for Bondurant. Other BRM V8 engines powered Lotus 25/33, Brabham BT11 and even old Cooper and BRP chassis during the season for Ireland, Siffert, Hobbs, Bonnier, Wicky and John Taylor.

The Bourne works team made 19 starts and finished seven times, all with the Tasman V8s; placing 3-1, 2, 2-4 and 4-5, scoring 22 points for fourth place in the Constructors' Championship.

Had BRM's planning worked out, 1967 would have been the year of the H16. In dyno testing before Monaco, '66 engine '7504' had delivered 395 bhp at 10,250 rpm and it remained consistently the most potent unit, exceeding 400 bhp that winter. But Rudd planned a new four-valve-per-cylinder unit and Geoffrey Johnson was designing a new P101 24-valve 3-litre V12 which BRM hoped to market for sports car racing. McLaren ordered the prototype for Formula 1, while running Tasman V8s in their own chassis in the interim.

The H16 cars' main problem was excessive weight. Except at Monaco where Stewart led for a time in '2616' V8, BRM was handicapped by the H16 being nearly 300 lb overweight, even in magnesium-skinned P115 lightweight form, while the earlier conventional skin cars were 350 lb overweight. After the Race of Champions a wide-based upper rear wishbone replaced the original single link system, and it was some time before the solitary '1151' handled as well as the P83s.

The season began badly when Stewart's engine in '8303' blew up on lap 2 in South Africa, and new team-mate Spence ran 32 laps in '8302' until an oil pipe broke. At Monaco, Stewart's 2.1-litre uncharacteristically broke its final-drive (having already won three

BRM

Monaco GPs) but Spence's '8302' finished sixth, albeit four laps behind.

At Zandvoort, Stewart practised '1151', which was three inches narrower and incorporated a top-ducted radiator, and raced '8303' but lost brake fluid; Spence, meanwhile, was eighth. However, Stewart showed his class by leading at Spa until the car started jumping out of gear and finished second in '8303', with Spence's '8302' fifth. Stewart's car was geared for 198 mph at 11,000 rpm.

Stewart preferred '2614' for the French GP at Le Mans, finishing third. Irwin's '8302' placed fifth despite a last-lap engine cut but Spence retired '8303' early with the gearbox output shaft broken. Stewart's new '8304' broke at Silverstone, where Spence had ignition failure. At the Nürburgring, the cars chewed up five crown-wheels and pinions – Irwin having finished seventh in the Parnell team-entered '8301'. Mosport saw McLaren's debut for the new BRM V12 engine, while Stewart spun '1151' out of its maiden race, Irwin spun '8302' clogging its throttle slides with mud and Spence finished fifth in '8303'. Stewart and Irwin retired at Monza and all three BRM H16s failed at Watkins Glen, though Spence was able to salvage some pride

Top right, BRM's 3-litre V12 emerged in works cars in 1968 but Bourne was losing its grip by this time. Left, Richard Attwood during his brilliant 1968 Monaco GP drive in '126/03'. Below, the V12 came good in Tony Southgate's 1970 P153 design, here with Rodriguez's '02 winning at Spa.

with fifth in Mexico. As Stewart departed for 1968 and V12 engines were introduced, BRM would start anew, leaving the lightweight magnesium 64-valve H16 to be abandoned, unraced.

Spence drove the H16's farewell race at Kyalami on New Year's Day 1968, but both his '1151' and team-mate Rodriguez's new P126 V12 were dogged by fuel vapourization.

In its entire career the BRM H16 engine started only 20 races, 16 at Championship level, winning once in a non-works client's car. BRM's 1967 record included 32 works-car starts but only 12 finishes; their 17 points gave them sixth place in the Constructors' table.

The new P126 V12 cars used elegant monocoque tubs stress-skinned 360 degrees through the scuttle area and carrying the V12 mated to a Hewland DG300 gearbox. They were designed and built by freelance Len Terry's consultancy to ease pressure on Bourne. Three of the cars were built by Terry's Transatlantic Automotive Consultants concern and used his parallel-link rear suspension layout.

Chassis '126/03' used a Formula 1 3-litre V12 engine for Kyalami, chassis '01 and '02 using 2.5-litre V12s for the 1968 Tasman Championship, later being re-engined to Formula 1 form for the European season. The Bourne-built version of the P126 was known as the P133; '01 made the type's debut in Rodriguez's hands at the minor Brands Hatch meeting in March, '133/02' being written off by him at Monaco. A lightweight full-monocoque P138 emerged with BRM gearbox for the Italian GP but had hardly been used by the season's end.

Early on, Rodriguez's '133/01' was second in the Race of Champions after Spence qualified '126/03' on the front row, but bottomed through an oil pipe in the race. Spence was second fastest again at Silverstone, the engine timing chain breaking as he was in second place. Just over a week later, Spence was killed in a Lotus turbine car at Indianapolis, devastating his friends at BRM.

Rodriguez drove '133/01' at Jarama, led 11 laps and was fighting to retain the lead when he crashed, while Courage's quasi-works 'B-team' Parnell-entered '126/01' broke its meter-

ing unit drive belt.

Attwood joined the team at Monaco, finishing second and setting fastest lap in '126/03'. At Watkins Glen, Indy star Bobby Unser drove the P138 which had first appeared at Monza with a new BRM gearbox in place of the Hewland and with the rear suspension mounted on extended monocoque rear horns, but its engine blew. From Rouen, top-ducted nose cones were adopted McLaren fashion, and a variety of wings arose.

They made 38 starts that season, finishing 19 times, and after that early-season promise in the non-Championship races and at Monaco, Rodriguez placed second in Belgium, third in Holland and Canada, and fourth in Mexico – all in '133/01' – but the cars never challenged on equal terms and the relatively modest 24-valve V12 engine was no match for the 32-valve Cosworth V8s. On 18 February 1969, the prototype 'P142-001' 48-valve engine had its first run, delivering 441 bhp at 9300 rpm, while P101 24-valve units '003, '006 and '009 gave respectively 390, 393 and 383 bhp at 9750 rpm when tested at about the same time.

Surtees joined for the 1969 season but the 48-valve V12s lacked reliability and torque. The trouble began at Kyalami where the new engine broke a valve guide in practice and did not even race in Surtees '138/02'. The 48-valve units were still not ready for Silverstone and the works cars were withdrawn, but at Barcelona Surtees finished fifth with engine '142-002' and team-mate Oliver retired '133/01' with engine '142-001'.

While concentrating on combating Cosworth engine power, BRM lost its way over chassis design. Their monocoque cars were always beautifully built but were dated, featuring slim low-frontal area forms in an era when aerodynamic demands dictated flatter, broader shapes.

Alec Osborne was responsible for the circular-section P139 which incorporated new-geometry suspension, low rear-mounted oil coolers, reduced weight, and 45 instead of 38 gallons fuel capacity – as in the P138 but now contained in a multitude of small cells. It appeared in practice at Zandvoort but was not considered raceworthy. Oliver retired '133/01' early with gear selector trouble and Surtees trailed round in '138/01' to finish ninth. At this point there was a great upheaval at Bourne and Rudd was dismissed, Tony Southgate having been brought in from Eagle as chief chassis designer.

BRM missed the French GP but reappeared at Silverstone for the British race. Surtees drove '139/01' modified with one of his own Surtees TS5 F5000 nose cones to improve aerodynamic performance, increased fuel capacity and revised exhaust system to find more mid-range power, but after qualifying sixth a front wishbone broke when third on the opening lap and Oliver retired soon after with another transmission failure. At the Nürburgring, Surtees' '139/01' was withdrawn after practice failures and Oliver retired '138/01' which had bottomed so badly that it had holed its sump.

A complete redesign of the lubrication system finally brought Surtees third at Watkins Glen but the cars were obsolescent and

By 1971 BRM's latest Southgate-designed P160s were true front-runners; however, Bourne's management were being tempted to run too large a team. Here is the 'onion-monocoque' Southgate car sporting aerodynamic nose aerofoil end fences.

Southgate's new broom would make a clean sweep for 1970.

During this sad 1969 season, BRM made 27 starts, finishing nine times, with only seven points for fifth-equal place with Ferrari in a Constructors' table which included only six scoring teams.

Work on a new P153 chassis began on 1 October 1969, and the prototype was completed in three months. Its shallow 'onion-shaped' aluminium-skinned forward tub carried the engine in a tubular rear truss. Testing was limited to around 150 miles at a damp Silverstone before two P153s went to Kyalami for the South African GP. There a rear axle broke and Southgate rushed out with bolt-on modifications; Rodriguez finished ninth in '02.

Larger, redesigned back axles were introduced at the Race of Champions, where the BRMs ran sponsorship livery for the first time – the white, gold, russet and black of Yardley cosmetics – and Oliver led in '153/01' until a rear axle sheared again. The forging cores were soft, not having been heat-treated properly due to a sub-contractor's error.

Tony Matthews' skill unveils the 1971 BRM P160. Note the large oil tank and ducted oil coolers beneath the rear wing; rearward weight bias was increasing.

New rear axles had been fitted in time for the Spanish GP, and new car '153/03' for Canadian driver George Eaton had also been provided with redesigned front axles although thus far they had given no trouble – whereupon Rodriguez's '02 broke a front stub-axle in practice! Eaton didn't qualify, so his car's new-design stubs were fitted one each to the left front of the Rodriguez and Oliver cars. Oliver apparently had one snap on the first lap, '153/01' being consumed in the ensuing fire, as was the Ferrari which it had rammed.

A major engine development came at Monaco where Marelli ignition replaced the original Lucas system, and new car '153/04' appeared for Oliver. Southgate and the team were confident for Spa where their top-endy V12 and good aerodynamics should count; Rodriguez promptly won in '02.

At Zandvoort the BRMs suffered three punctures and Rodriguez wrote off his Spa-winning '02 in a practice accident. One Dunlop tyre actually jumped the four bolsters fitted to retain it, so BRM fitted eight in their wheels thereafter. Rodriguez raced new car '05 after his crash, a sixth P153 emerging as spare at Hockenheim. Reliability was poor mid-season with oil surge, indicating that a new lubrication system was needed, which unfortunately increased drag. At Monza, where great things were expected, Rodriguez's '05 threw a rod and Oliver's '04 popped-off its watercap – both after leading. Eaton had a new bifurcated-port engine, '142-007', which went well there until it overheated due to porous casting.

At St Jovite in Canada fuel consumption proved a major problem, having fallen from some 6 mpg to only 4.8 mpg; the P153s had insufficient capacity to survive race distance and were forced to make a pit stop. Despite this handicap, Rodriguez finished fourth in Canada, second at Watkins Glen where he had looked set to win before his enforced pit stop, then sixth in Mexico, where Oliver was seventh.

BRM had finished 16 times from 37 starts and placed sixth in the Constructors' table, with 23 points.

Southgate produced the finest 3-litre BRM in 1971: the definitive chisel-nosed P160, a cleaner, lower, lighter development of the P153, though actually incorporating few interchangeable parts. At the end of 1970, a seventh P153 had been completed, to race early in '71. Four new P160s would be built that year: '01 making its debut with Rodriguez at Kyalami, '02 for new team member Siffert at Ontario in March, '03 for Rodriguez at Zandvoort and '04 for new driver Ganley in Austria.

The P160s were very fast and proved it by winning the Austrian and Italian GPs; they handled very well and also became reliable. There were chassis problems early on and the Firestone tyre vibration that season also caused coil failures which were not avoided quickly enough. But in mid-season the team lost Rodriguez – killed in an insignificant little German sports car meeting – and the year ended with their other star driver, Siffert, dying in BRM's first, and only, fatal accident – at Brands Hatch, in which '160/02' was burned out.

During that season, BRM had run a regular three-car team, which expanded to four at the Nürburgring, while in Canada and the USA they ran five cars, all five finishing at Watkins Glen, 2-4-9-13-14. The season's record showed 59 starts yielding 43 finishes, with Ganley failing to qualify at Monaco and non-starting in Canada. The team won two minor races in addition to their two GPs, adding five second places, a third, five fourths, three fifths and a sixth. They were second in the Constructors' table, with 36 points, their best result since 1965 and the end of 1½-litre Formula 1. From here on it was all downhill.

Successfully running those five cars at Watkins Glen influenced the thinking of team Chief Executive Louis Stanley, the self-styled patrician husband of Jean Owen, part-owner of the Owen Organisation itself.

He concluded a new sponsorship deal with Marlboro for 1972-73, and planned a full season with a five- or even six-car team, magnifying

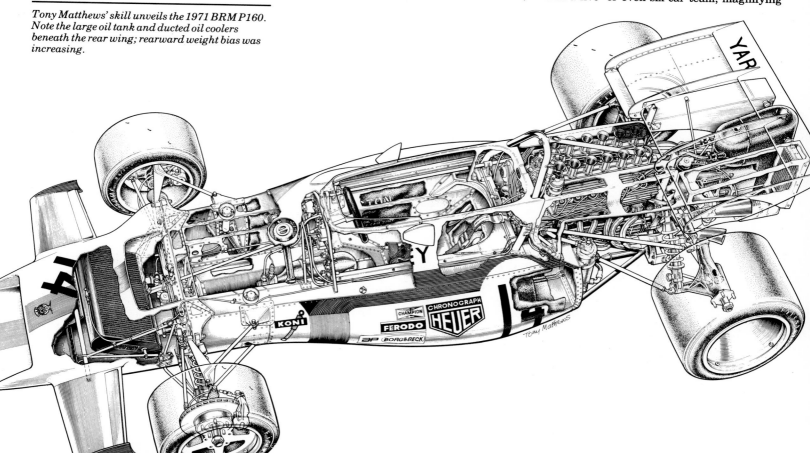

Beltoise's P180 with its extreme rearward weight bias and Southgate 'ladybird-section' hull at Monza, Italian GP, 1972.

the team's potential earning power and the exposure it could offer its sponsor.

Stanley told Southgate: 'If you can run one car you can run ten, you just employ ten times as many people'. In motor racing, it doesn't work like that. His diktat demonstrated a lack of understanding of epic proportions.

BRM launched no less than 63 starts overall, 50 in Championship races, from which they finished in the points on only four occasions. Compared, for example, to McLaren's 16 places from 25 starts, such return was dismal. No fewer than ten different drivers appeared. Team manager Tim Parnell had the task of running four and five cars at a time and everything suffered. The V12 lost its edge as both engine and chassis preparation was over-stretched.

Southgate recalled: 'Tim and I kept losing our way. There'd always be two cars in the pits so I'd talk to the drivers, make changes to the cars and by half-way through the session I'd be having hysterics. We'd lose track of which car was which. I'd say to this white helmet: "Ah Pete, er, no – it's not Pete, it's Howden isn't it? Now then, what did we do to your car last time you were in . . .?" I took a tape recorder with me eventually so I could note all the changes down at the end of the day.'

The initial driver line-up included Beltoise, Gethin, Ganley, Marko and Soler-Roig, with Wisell and Schuppan in reserve. Soler-Roig left, Wisell won a more established place, then poor Marko was blinded in one eye by a flying

Beltoise again, this time winning at Monaco, 1972, handling '160B/01', tail light aglow.

stone at Clermont, ending his career. Redman, Oliver and Canadian Bill Brack all drove and a motley selection of old P153s, 1971 P160s and the two latest Southgate P180s was campaigned.

Beltoise's heart gave the team a rare high-spot in pouring rain at Monaco where he won in '160B/01'; at Brands Hatch at the end of the year in changeable weather Parnell made the right tyre choice, helping Beltoise to win in '180/02', Schuppan coming fourth in '160C/05' and Gethin fifth in '160C/06'. The P160s had been built new for the season along with the two Southgate 'ladybird section' P180s.

These dragster-like cars experimented with more rearward weight bias, 30:70 front:rear, with radiators hung under the tail wing. They made their debut in Spain, but Ganley retired '02 at Monaco and Wisell at Oulton Park. Their handling was poor and they were shelved because, as Southgate admitted: 'we got the 160 going better which only made the 180 look worse; we fitted 180 suspension parts to the 160s and later in the season got it running, but the drivers wouldn't look at it. Didn't want to know . . .' – until Beltoise was eighth in '180/02' at Monza and ran it thereafter.

Parnell and Southgate went over Stanley's head to Marlboro to persuade them to reduce the team to three cars. Five days before the British GP Stanley relented, but although he approved the move there was insufficient time to prepare those three cars properly. Two retired, Beltoise was 11th and Stanley asked coldly, 'If running three cars means none of them finish, why don't we run five?'

Engine man Aubrey Woods had been replaced by Peter Windsor-Smith, who struggled to keep the V12 competitive and at the end of the year Southgate moved to Shadow. This left gearbox designer Alec Stokes as the sole survivor of the old-time BRM senior engineers, Mike Pilbeam taking chassis responsibility.

Throughout 1973, the P160's third season proved it was still as good as any of its rivals. A new deformable-structure P160E version appeared, with new chassis '07 first running in Spain, '08 in Belgium and '09 in the British GP.

They braked and handled as well as any but the V12 engines could no longer compete with Cosworth. BRM development had stagnated. They were hard-pressed to reproduce 1972 times on some circuits. Fifty starts were made in Formula 1, yielding 26 finishes; Regazzoni third at Silverstone in the minor meeting, sixth in Austria and Brazil and seventh in Argentina; Beltoise fourth in Canada, fifth in Spain, Austria and Holland, and new-boy Lauda fifth

at Silverstone and in Belgium.

BRM predictably lost its major sponsor for 1974, the Owen Organisation was itself in trouble but French Motul oil support secured drives for three French drivers; Beltoise, Pescarolo and Migault – the first being past his best, the latter not having a best and Pescarolo ranking somewhere in between. Amon joined at the end of the year and cheered the Frenchmen by assuring them the cars really were as gutless as they believed, then proving his own ability by qualifying in mid-grid at Watkins Glen.

Stanley had been trumpeting about 'regaining one's self-respect', running 'British Racing Green' and being 'unsponsored' for 1974 and criticizing major sponsors for the power they were attempting to wield in Formula 1. His tune had changed so often, with little reduction in volume, few took any notice.

Above, *significant swansong: Mike Pilbeam's angular 1974 P201 design. Opposite,* BRM's *3-litre zenith, autumn 1971: Siffert's '160/03' (top) and Gethin's '160/01' (centre) win consecutive Austrian and Italian GPs. Opposite bottom, Peter Connew's special, British GP, 1972.*

Still, Bourne was staffed by some excellent people who made the best of limited funds and eccentric management. Pilbeam produced a new pyramid-section, mid-radiator, short-wheelbase chassis in the new P201, which handled excellently. Four were used that season but they were too heavy and underpowered with the now much-patched and ancient V12 engines.

Old P160Es '05 and '09 were joined by a new car, '160E/10', while '201/01' made a superb but flash-in-the-pan debut at Kyalami where Beltoise finished second on 'qualifying' tyres. Beltoise had two P201s available at Monaco, '03 emerged for Pescarolo at the Nürburgring, and at Monza Beltoise drove this car, while Pescarolo debuted '04 and Migault inherited '01. Running engines '008, '021 and '007, they each retired – Beltoise and Migault on the opening lap and Pescarolo surviving three laps. Beltoise demolished '03's front end in practice at Watkins Glen and non-started, while Amon's run home ninth in '201/04' may be regarded as the end of the long and sometimes noble BRM saga.

Irrespective, Team BRM had made 42 starts that season, with most of their 24 finishes in the early part of the year. Beltoise added fifths in Argentina and Belgium to his second in South Africa, while Pescarolo and Migault were 4-5 in the minor Silverstone race. Thanks to Beltoise's results, BRM finished seventh in the Constructors' Championship with the last ten points they would ever score.

Promises of ever more power had proved empty on track and, ending the year, Stanley publicly blamed Bourne's loyal and highly competent staff for 'shoddy' work, making many redundant after years of service. Parnell resigned in disgust, his men having been asked to make bricks without straw.

The ailing Owen Organisation divested itself of Team BRM for 1975, Stanley taking it on and entering the old P201s one at a time as Stanley-BRMs, initially with Mike Wilds retiring '201/04' from his two races in South

Cooper

Early in 1965 John Cooper sold his Cooper Car Company to the Chipstead Motor Group. One of their executives was the Italian Mario Tozzi-Condivi. He was an old acquaintance of Adolfo and Omer Orsi who owned Maserati, and when Cooper's existing engine suppliers Coventry Climax refused to support the forthcoming 3-litre Formula, Tozzi-Condivi approached the Orsis instead.

They were keen to sell Cooper a Formula 1 engine but Tozzi-Condivi would not commission Maserati development at Chipstead's expense. Instead he proposed Cooper becoming sole concessionaires for a 3-litre engine to be developed by Maserati, which would be sold to private owners in custom-made Cooper cars. The Cooper works team engines would remain Maserati's property and they would commit themselves to providing sufficient units for three works cars, to competitive development and to all necessary servicing, for which Cooper would pay a flat rate per rebuild . . . of around £700 a time.

Cooper paid seed money to launch the project and *Ing.* Giulio Alfieri began to update and enlarge his nine-year old 2.5-litre V12 engine which had been introduced in the front-engined era.

Cooper completed their T80 spaceframe chassis – built for the still-born flat-16 Climax engine – as a V12 test hack. It was completed late in 1965 and during that winter Cooper's ex-Connaught, ex-Jaguar chassis engineer Derrick White designed a robust and practical monocoque chassis – Cooper's first – to carry the hefty, thirsty and bulky V12.

He noted that it would take '14 weeks to design and build. 15 weeks to develop design & build 5 [cars].' Cooper took on ex-BRP team engineer Tony Robinson, who had been building aluminium monocoques since 1963, to oversee the work and the new Cooper T81s were beautifully made.

The prototype made its debut at the London Racing Car Show in January 1966 as the first fully fledged British 3-litre F1 car. By 1500 Formula standards it was enormous. Its twin-boom tub was skinned in duralumin for rigidity and housed 50 gallons of fuel to satisfy the big V12 engine. Front coil-spring/damper units were inboard, rears outboard and an ingenious inboard-of-the-upright front disc brake system exposed them to direct cooling airstream. The Maserati engine drove via a heavy ZF 5DS25 transaxle identical to the Ford GT40's.

Private entrant R.R.C. 'Rob' Walker bought chassis 'F1-2-66' for Siffert's use, French owner/driver Guy Ligier bought 'F1-4-66' and Swedish veteran Bonnier had 'F1-5-66'. Chassis '1, '3 and '6 were retained as works cars for Rindt and Ginther, the latter loaned by Honda pending completion of their own car.

In mid-season Surtees joined from Ferrari, new chassis '7 being completed to accommodate him although he would regularly race chassis '6, while Amon had a one-off drive in '7 at Reims, finishing eighth.

The big cars handled indifferently until sorted out after the arrival of Surtees but they were fast enough, Rindt finishing second to a Ferrari at Spa after leading. In Germany, Ligier wrote off chassis '4 while Surtees and Rindt finished 2-3 in cars '6 and '3 and Surtees clocked fastest lap.

With something like 360 bhp the hefty Coopers were now manageable and handling well, nicely built, very strong. Surtees might have won the US GP but was barged off course by a back-marker and could only finish behind Rindt in another good team 2-3, having set fastest lap.

The V12 ran well at altitude in Mexico City. Surtees qualified chassis '6 on pole and won, Bonnier sixth in chassis '5.

The big T81s had made a total 39 starts,

America, then Bob Evans persevering in the now feeble '201/05' – except in Belgium where he ran '02 – failing to qualify at Monaco but finishing four of his other eight races, 15-9-13-17, plus sixth in the Race of Champions and tenth at Silverstone.

Starting 1976, Stanley-BRM sent their re-nosed P201B, '04, to Brazil with Ian Ashley strapped into the cold seat; they retired. The team then retreated to Bourne until the following winter when Stanley announced plans for a grand return in 1977. It happened, linked to the extraordinary story of the Stanley-BRM P207, a bulky, vaguely Ferrari-like vehicle designed by freelance Len Terry.

Two were built, with revised P200 V12 engine by Aubrey Woods and an improved Alec Stokes gearbox. Stanley-BRM were sponsored by Rotary Watches, who had been foolish enough to believe prophecies of Grand Prix-winning glory. The tiny remaining Bourne staff under Alan Challis and Alec Stokes were happy just to be back. Larry Perkins was to drive. He was in Buenos Aires awaiting his car's arrival by air when he was told it was not coming, because it proved too big to fit through the freight-plane's door at Gatwick Airport – the fault of the shipper, who had subsequently to compensate Stanley-BRM.

The team did get the car to Brazil where, amongst other problems, it was unable to run more than two consecutive laps without over-heating – Interlagos being rather hotter than Lincolnshire in January! Perkins drove old '201B/04' at Kyalami, finishing 15th, but '207/01' non-started the Race of Champions and Perkins walked out in disgust.

Conny Andersson was unable to qualify for the Spanish, Belgian, Swedish and French GPs, Edwards could not even pre-qualify for the British race, and Teddy Pilette failed in Germany, Holland and Monza. This was a rather different picture to that painted for Rotary, and their partnership with Stanley-BRM collapsed amid acrimony and litigation.

Even so, Stanley-BRM stumbled on into 1978. Though out of serious Formula 1, a P207C was run for Pilette in glorified club racing, and was uncompetitive even there.

Activity ceased during 1979 but in 1980, and then again in 1982, the enthusiastic John Jordan, who had bought much BRM material, entered cars under the Jordan-BRM name in

bush-league Formula 1 'clubbies'. British Racing Motors had been founded by ordinary enthusiasm and it was there in the early-Eighties that it all ended . . .

Connew

Peter Connew was a draughtsman working for Team Surtees when they entered Formula 1 racing in 1970 and he developed ambitions to have a go himself. With absolutely zero finance, he designed a single-curvature riveted aluminium monocoque to take a Cosworth/Hewland power pack. He built the tub with help from some friends in an Essex lock-up and was gratified to find component suppliers as helpful as they were. This was probably the most under-financed of all true Formula 1 specials, and perhaps 'Connew' itself was an unfortunate name when seeking sponsors.

A pilot-build tub and one complete car, '002', were completed and with French Darnval seafood sponsorship the team entered the 1972 British GP at Brands Hatch, only for François Migault to fail in qualifying due to a suspension collapse.

The damage was repaired in time for the German GP but although they arrived at the Nürburgring they could not gain an entry due to Migault's inexperience. They started in Austria but rear suspension problems retired Migault after 22 laps.

David Purley qualified the PC1 for the end-of-season Brands Hatch race but was unable to start due to electrical trouble. It was then converted to Formula 5000 trim with a 5-litre V8 engine. It had been fun while it lasted . . .

winning once, with three second places, two thirds, three fourths, three fifths and three sixths in 23 finishes. Surtees and Rindt finished 2-3 in the Driver's Championship, Cooper second in the Constructors' Cup, their best season for four years.

Surtees moved to Honda for 1967 but Rindt had to serve another year with Cooper. Rodriguez had a one-off drive in South Africa in Surtees's Mexican-winning chassis '6 and won on reliability with local driver John Love second in his old ex-McLaren Tasman Cooper-Climax 2.7 4-cylinder T76, 'FL-1-65'. From this point it was all downhill . . .

At Monaco, Alfieri's latest engine emerged, using the 1966 *Tipo* 9 bottom end with new *Tipo* 10 three-valve-per-cylinder Heron heads. A new narrower valve angle permitted lighter single covers enclosing both camshafts. Inlets were resited within the vee in true crossflow form with the exhausts outboard. Twin spark plugs per cylinder lay beneath the exhausts in the side of the combustion chamber, rather than more conventionally. Three-plug heads were also tried. Internal-toothed flexible belts drove from the front of each inlet camshaft to 12-pole distributors fed by Lucas transistors.

White and assistant Bob Marston had developed an experimental lighter and smaller radiator as well as new fabricated magnesium disc wheels but they remained unused at Monaco.

A new lightweight T81B car had been completed using aluminium instead of duralumin skins and a Hewland instead of ZF gearbox, plus the new disc wheels. This chassis, 'F1-1-67', was first used by Rindt in this finalized form in the Dutch GP. While the Lotus 49s set new standards there, the Cooper-Maseratis of Rindt and Rodriguez lined up on row two. But reliability faltered that summer.

For the British GP the new T86 appeared, chassis 'F1-2-67' with magnesium-elektron skinned shallow monocoque to compensate for the still massive overweight of the engine and fuel load. Suspension was T81B-style, while the flat-scuttled car had quite the ugliest nose treatment ever seen in Formula 1! It used a *Tipo* 10 36-valve engine mated to a Hewland gearbox, saving some 112 lb compared to the T81.

For the Nürburgring, both this T86 and its T81B sisters used Hewlands, but the engines suffered a plague of disintegrating starter rings, which damaged engines, gearboxes and tubs. In testing, the T86 lifted its nose at speed and after adding 30 lb of lead (!) a chin-spoiler

was fitted for Monza. Ickx made his Formula 1 debut there in the T81B, both machines using 36-valve engines with revised combustion chambers, Hewland gearboxes and rear suspension which now placed the rear brake discs inboard of the uprights, as at the front. Rindt finished fourth, Ickx sixth, both ahead of Ferrari to delight Maserati's men.

In America, both 36-valve 24-plug and 36-valve 36-plug engines were in use, prompting Keith Duckworth, the designer of the 8-cylinder, 8-plug Cosworth DFV, to remark that if one spark wasn't enough to set fire to the charge then something was radically wrong. It was really the technology of the 1950s breathing its last. Not only was the 36-plug engine heavier than the 24-plug, it also required extra ignition coils, room for which had to be found on the already crowded cars.

The privateers, Siffert and Bonnier, soldiered on to the end in their T81s, while Ligier had replaced his wrecked 'F1-4-66' with ex-works chassis 'F1-7-66' before buying a Repco Brabham BT20 after the 1967 French GP.

Two elderly spaceframe Cooper Specials ran in some 1966-67 events: Pearce's 'F1-1-64' with a two-cam Ferrari 250GT V12 for Chris Lawrence, and Fritz Baumann's 'F1-1-65' with an ATS V8 sports car engine for Bonnier in France '66 and for Moser later in 1967.

By the end of that season the Maserati deal had run its course and would not be renewed. In the South African GP on 1 January 1968, Siffert drove Walker's faithful old 'F1-2-66' – affectionately nicknamed *Torrey Canyon* after the wrecked and oil-oozing Land's End supertanker – into seventh place. Scarfiotti and Redman respectively retired the works team's T86 'F1-2-67' and T81B 'F1-1-67'; Bonnier retired his T81 '5-66' and local driver van Rooyen had the Climax 4-cylinder engine break in the even older T76 Tasman car, 'FL-1-65', to mark the end of Cooper's penultimate Formula 1 season.

Tony Robinson had left after the original T81 build programme but now returned at John Cooper's invitation to supervise construction of the latest T86B cars for the new BRM V12 engine. Cooper had wanted to use the Cosworth-Ford V8 but was unable to because of his BMC/BMH tie on the Mini-Cooper saloons.

The new T86B tub was skinned principally in 18-gauge NS4 malleable aluminium sheet formed over three mild-steel bulkheads fabricated around 22-gauge tube. The BRM engine was smaller, narrower and lighter than Maserati's and was less thirsty, so there was no need

for magnesium skinning to save weight. Over 40 gallons of fuel was still carried, however, alongside the cockpit, in the rear horns supporting the engine and in a 6-gallon scuttle tank. Suspension used many T86/81B parts, with pronounced front anti-dive. The BRM V12 cooled better than the Maserati, so the T86B's nose was slimmer.

Chipstead's marketing interests extended to Alfa Romeo. A deal was struck with Autodelta (Alfa Romeo competitions) to run a 3-litre Alfa T33 sports car-based V8 in Formula 1, copying the Maserati deal. The third T86B-style tub was actually classified T86C (serialled 'F1-3-68') and was prepared with 4 in. shorter rear booms for the V8. Bianchi tested it at Silverstone with a 2.5 V8, but the 3-litre would never come.

Meanwhile the T86B-BRMs were still some 118 lb overweight. Three of the cars were built, Redman giving the type its debut at Brands Hatch in March where he placed fifth in the prototype 'F1-1-68'. Two cars, chassis '1 and '2, were driven by Gardner and Scarfiotti at Silverstone, placing reliably 3-4, and the same cars then inherited consecutive Championship GP 3-4 finishes at Jarama and Monaco, driven by Redman, Scarfiotti and Bianchi. Bianchi was sixth for another point at Spa where Redman's chassis '2 was destroyed when a lower front wishbone snapped.

A new chassis '4 was driven by Elford into fourth place at Rouen – his single-seater debut – but in the team's final 11 starts that year they only finished once in the points, Elford fifth at Mt Tremblant in Canada.

The T86Bs had been modified with stronger wishbones after the Spa accident, and for the British GP chassis '5 used a top-ducted radiator to kill nose lift. At the Nürburgring both T86Bs had strutted rear wings. Elford's circuit knowledge gave him fifth spot on the grid but he crashed heavily in spray on the opening lap, ripping two wheels off chassis '4. The repaired car was fitted with a spring-loaded trimming rear wing for Monza where he crashed again, due to brake failure.

The team simply faded away at the end of that season, their final appearance being in Mexico where Elford finished eighth in 'F1-4-68' while Bianchi retired '1-68'.

Cooper never really recovered from the loss of their BP sponsorship in 1967. Although they abandoned the BRM engine as underpowered at the end of 1968 and a new Cosworth car was designed, negotiations for Wilkinson Sword sponsorship failed and this famous team withdrew.

The old Cooper-Maserati T86 'F1-2-67' survived in Colin Crabbe's Antique Automobiles team in early-1969, using a 36-valve 24-plug engine. Elford finished 12th in it at Silverstone, while historic racer Neil Corner was fourth in the F1/F5000 Madrid GP at Jarama amongst a thin field. At Monaco there was no need to qualify and Elford started last on the grid, 8.2 secs slower than Stewart's Matra on pole, finishing seventh, six times lapped. This was Cooper's last outing in a Grand Prix, the team's assets being auctioned off on 11 June 1969 to end a noble story

Copersucar

See 'Fittipaldi', pages 187-8.

The Beast – Cooper-Maserati T81 at Brands Hatch, 1967, driven by Rodriguez and demonstrating its beefy shape, front brakes exposed to direct airstream and cranked lower wishbone-ends.

Cosworth

In 1969 Cosworth Engineering set out to produce an advanced four-wheel drive Formula 1 car of their own design and manufacture which would overcome the traction problems which so many of their client teams were experiencing with the abrupt power delivery characteristics of their DFV V8 engine.

Design had commenced early in 1968 when youthful McLaren Chief Engineer, Robin Herd, had been invited to join the Keith Duckworth/ Mike Costin company in Northampton. Robin recalls how thrilled he was to be offered 'the chance to sit at the feet of Duckworth and learn' and in that respect it was a valuable exercise reaching ultimate fruition in his March cars.

Short-term, however, the advent of strutted wing aerodynamic aids during the summer of '68 sidestepped the very problems to which the excess weight and complication of four-wheel drive had been addressed.

Robin's strikingly unconventional design used the body with broad-set monocoque tub to generate aerodynamic download which was trimmed out by wedge-section nosepieces ahead of each front wheel and a modest strutted wing above the tail. The nose radiator was top-ducted and a unique lightweight magnesium-block DFV was used to compensate for 4WD system weight, turned about-face to drive to front and rear axles.

In extensive testing with drivers like Costin himself – no mean performer – and Redman, it became clear that putting worthwhile power through the front wheels overwhelmed the capabilities of contemporary tyres. The massive understeer which this induced could be minimized only, it seemed, by reducing the torque-split bias to that end. The message was that more power should be transmitted through the rear wheels; ideally they should use rear-drive only, which made the entire system redundant.

Robin told the author: 'Bruce McLaren described it best when he said driving a four-wheel drive Formula 1 car was like trying to sign your autograph with someone jogging your elbow all the time'. He considered a limited-slip front differential was needed, but effectively the requirement for four-wheel drive had in any case been overtaken by far more effective aerodynamic development, 'so what was the point?'

The one complete Cosworth car was sold unraced to collector Tom Wheatcroft and survives today in his magnificent Donington Collection at Donington Park near Derby, while its uncompleted sister pilot-build is in a museum in Australia.

De Tomaso

Argentinian entrepreneur Alessandro de Tomaso made his name as an amateur racing driver in the Fifties, with OSCA, Maserati and Ferrari cars. He subsequently set up a specialist company manufacturing high-performance cars in Modena, Italy. By 1969 *Automobili de Tomaso* was building a Ford V8-powered mid-engined Coupé named the Mangusta for US sale, and development began of a new US-oriented Coupé, the Pantera.

To promote the company name and indulge his own enthusiasm, de Tomaso authorized production of a monocoque Formula 2 car in 1969, designed by *Ing.* GianPaolo Dallara – co-creator of the remarkable Lamborghini Miura – and for 1970 he agreed with British private entrant Frank Williams to enter Formula 1. Dallara was briefed to design a new chassis to carry the standard Cosworth-Hewland power pack.

A single car entry would be made for Piers

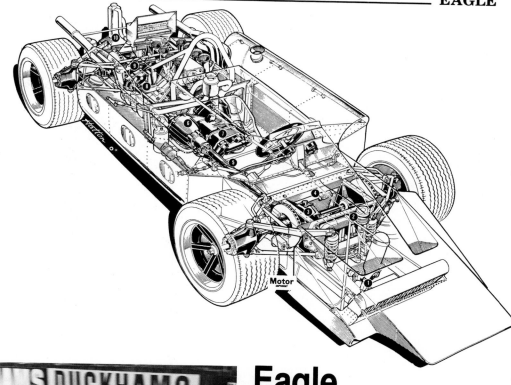

Top, *Brian Hatton's* Motor *drawing of Robin Herd's 1969 Cosworth tells all.* Above, *Mike Costin testing the stillborn but fascinating 4WD car at Silverstone. A low-level rear wing was later fitted.*

Courage who had scored two second places in Williams's private Brabham BT26 the previous season. Three de Tomaso *Tipo* 308 cars were built, chassis serials '505/1-2-3'. Initial outings showed promise, though car '505/1' was at least 120 lb too heavy and track initially too narrow. Engine shortages slowed development. Courage had to retire chassis '1 at Kyalami after hitting a kerb too hard, and at Jarama he wrote it off after qualifying on the third row of the grid, being unable to start. A lighter chassis '2 ran at Silverstone, where Courage finished third; Stewart drove it in practice and declared 'It's quite good'. At Monaco, Courage ran seventh before the steering tightened and at Spa his engine failed. A still lighter third chassis was now available as spare but, while lying seventh in the Dutch GP at Zandvoort, de Tomaso '505/2' crashed and burned furiously, Courage losing his life. This was shattering.

De Tomaso totally lost interest and the tiny team missed the French GP but returned at Brands Hatch with '505/3' driven by Redman. A hub failed after qualifying and he non-started. He then failed to qualify at Hockenheim with more car trouble, and due to his sports car commitments Schenken then took over, retiring from the Austrian GP with engine trouble, finishing in Canada after a long stop to change a damper, having the suspension break at Watkins Glen and being refused an entry for Mexico. De Tomaso took chassis '3 back to Modena, and still has it, derelict, today, while Williams would buy March cars for 1971, before beginning to build his own (see page 241).

Eagle

American driver Dan Gurney and his fellow former Le Mans winner Carroll Shelby – creator of the Cobra sports car project – formed All-American Racers essentially to win the Indianapolis 500-Miles on Goodyear tyres.

The team began its career by entering a Lotus and two Halibrand Shrikes in the 1965 Indy race, while Gurney was still driving Brabham cars in Formula 1 and AAR's new purpose-built factory was being completed at Santa Ana, south of Los Angeles in California.

Gurney wanted to fly the All-American flag in Formula 1 with the start of the new Formula in 1966, so to design his new cars both for Indy and Formula 1 he hired Lotus engineer Len Terry, whose Type 38 had just won at Indy driven by Clark.

Terry designed a Lotus 38-like Indy car for AAR, to be named the Eagle and to carry a handsome beak-like nose treatment. He then adapted this design to Formula 1 road racing, with less fuel capacity. In fact the Indy design was compromised slightly to enable conversion to road racing, low roll-centre heights featuring in the suspension geometry, though Terry believed a higher roll axis would suit Indy better. Furthermore, despite asymmetrical suspension offset being common at Indy, Terry adopted symmetrical suspension for the track car to generate development experience for the road racer.

Four Type T1G Formula 1 monocoques would be completed in 1966, skinned in 18-gauge aluminium unlike the 16-gauge skinned track cars, saving 50 lb weight. These were full monocoque tubs, with 360-degree stressed-skin scuttle and seatback sections either end of the cockpit opening.

In his suspension and other tube component design Len Terry went up in diameter and down in wall thickness compared to the Lotus 38 to gain strength without weight penalty. He also planned fitting a second brake disc and calliper on the inboard end of each live front stub axle to add braking power at the front, but this idea would be shelved.

AAR adopted the 'Anglo-American Racers' title for Formula 1 and were to use an all-new 3-litre V12 Eagle-Weslake engine, built by Weslake & Co., of Rye, Sussex, on England's south-east coast. The design was by ex-BRM engineer Aubrey Woods, who had worked with Gurney when he was a BRM team driver in 1960. A Weslake V12 design with four-valve-

per-cylinder heads had been rejected by BRM in favour of their own H16, yet by the summer of 1965 a twin-cylinder test engine to this design was giving good results, so Gurney became interested. An engine contract had been signed in October 1965 for six engines, and space for AAR's British base was provided beside Weslake's premises.

The new V12 would not be available for the start of the new season so AAR bought four stop-gap 2.75-litre Coventry Climax FPF four-cylinder engines to put miles on at least one chassis. Outputs ranged from 190 to 235 bhp, and the best of these 'old nails' was dropped into chassis 'AAR-101' and tested at Goodwood on 8 May 1966. Gurney was stunned by the four-cylinder engine's frantic vibration.

Maiden race was in the Belgian GP at Spa, Dan qualifying last for this power circuit and finishing seventh after a mid-race stop to relieve himself in the roadside ditch, wedging a rock under the Eagle's wheel and leaving the engine ticking over! 'The vibration got to me', he explained, 'I was fearful something was going to burst inside . . .' At Reims, in a more continent performance, he finished fifth in the French GP for his new marque's first World Championship points.

The need for better steering lock had led to the rear lower wishbone legs being kinked to give space, anti-dive was taken out of the front geometry and at Brands Hatch Gurney qualified third and held second place until broken piston-ring lands retired '101. Engine problems grounded the Eagle again at Zandvoort where Gurney both qualified and ran fourth.

AAR engine specialist John Miller rebuilt and developed at least one of the Climax units at Santa Ana with American forged pistons to produce 255 bhp. Gurney ran fourth at the Nürburgring using this engine but a broken condenser bracket dropped him to seventh at the finish.

At Monza he qualified with the Climax engine but raced the first Weslake Type 58 V12-powered car instead. A week after first dyno test the engine gave a claimed 364 bhp so, with Monza only one week away, it was rushed to Italy and installed in 'AAR-102' in the paddock there. Phil Hill practised Eagle-Climax '101, while Dan found problems with the new car's fuel system and with oil temperature soaring in the race he switched off

after 17 laps.

Both Climax and V12 cars ran in the US and Mexican GPs – the V12 overheating and throwing out its oil at Watkins Glen, then being retired by Bondurant in Mexico because of fuel feed problems. Bondurant's '101 had been disqualified for receiving outside assistance in the USA, and Gurney drove it into fifth place in Mexico with its Climax engine ailing.

Old '101 appeared once more in Gurney's hands, in the 1967 South African GP where it was retired again, before being sold to Castrol for Canadian Al Pease to drive.

Castrol support for 1967 replaced AAR's original sponsor Mobil, whose departure left the Formula 1 team grossly under-financed. Oil blow-by in the engine had been traced to excessive clearance in cylinder liner fit.

Gurney had a new '413 bhp' engine in '102 for the minor Race of Champions at Brands Hatch, accompanied by new team-mate Ginther in chassis '103 with its prototype V12 claimed to be capable of producing 409 bhp. They ran 1-2 in the final before experimental brake pad trouble retired Ginther, and Gurney won narrowly from a Ferrari.

The Eagle had landed . . .

Though undeniably beautiful, it was a heavy car, some 180 lb over the minimum limit. The cars were lettered 'Harvey Titanium' after California's Harvey Aluminum company had advised replacement of the design's aluminium skins with magnesium and substituting tita-

Deep monocoque, beak nose and gorgeous finish typified the AAR Eagle-Weslakes; 'T1G-102' at Le Mans 1967. Below, Bill Bennett's drawing of the 1966-67 Eagle-Weslake.

nium for steel components to save weight in a new chassis.

Ginther failed to qualify at Monaco and Indy; at Zandvoort he felt unable to compete in modern racing and abruptly bowed out of the sport. Gurney, meanwhile, ran third briefly at Monaco only for '103's Lucas fuel metering unit drive belt to break.

Chassis 'AAR-104', nicknamed the 'mag-ti Eagle', was visibly different from its sisters with its close-spaced magnesium skin riveting. All suspension links were titanium, leading to a reduction in weight for the top front wishbone alone from 3⅜ lb in steel to under 2 lb in titanium. Exhaust manifolds in titanium saved 20 lb; a total 88 lb being saved as '104 scaled 1192 lb. Chassis '103 was subsequently fitted with a titanium suspension set and some of Weslake's V12 castings were changed from aluminium to magnesium to reduce weight still further.

In '104, Gurney was fast at Zandvoort only for the metering unit to fail again, but at Spa he set a new lap record despite low fuel pressure causing a top-end misfire and won the Belgian GP in grand style, one week after winning Le Mans for Ford. It was the zenith of Dan's fine career.

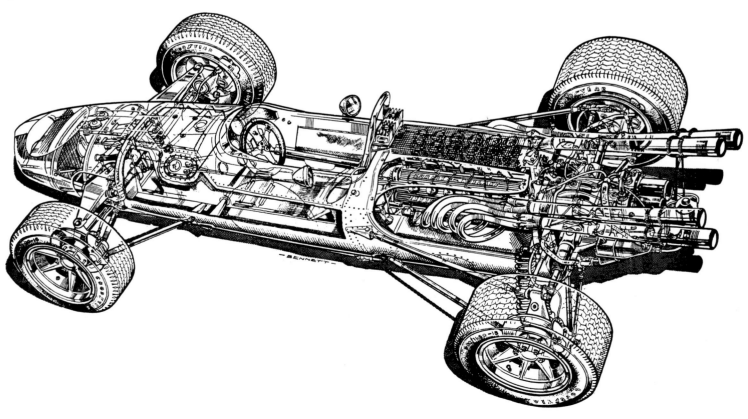

McLaren joined the team as second driver for the French GP, driving '102 and Dan using '104 on the front row, but both retired with minor failures. In Britain massive engine failures intruded, three V12s breaking that weekend. In Germany Gurney nearly won. With three laps to run, a 45-second lead and a new lap record to his name, a UJ cross sheared – McLaren having already retired with another engine failure.

In Canada Dan was third in '103, and at Monza three Weslake V12s failed, one in practice, one in Gurney's '104 while leading and one in guest driver Scarfiotti's '103, within the opening six laps. Gurney ran '104 as a lone entry in the US, where its suspension failed, and Mexico, where he holed its radiator at the start.

By this time AAR were dubious of Weslake's ability to sustain manufacturing and assembly quality under Formula 1 pressures. AAR hired ex-Vanwall fitter Doug Orchard to assemble engines drawn from Weslake parts on a new monthly basis for 1968.

In South Africa Gurney retired with oil leaks and overheating, quite uncompetitive, and a spare engine installed for a post-race Goodyear tyre test then proved in poorer shape than the race engine! Gurney severed his Weslake tie thereafter and set up a new shop in Ashford, Kent, to build and test the engines. Woods joined them, and from 1 May AAR's entire UK operation, engine and race shop were concentrated there. One V12 was tested on the BRM dyno at Folkingham where it gave no more than 390 bhp – another rude shock after Weslake's claims, for the BRM dyno was hardly considered pessimistic.

An improved Eagle Mark 1A V12 was under development, the team missing Spain and appearing at Monaco, where Gurney started from the back of the grid and was an early retirement. More races were missed before reappearance at the British GP, but although running quicker Gurney again retired. He was ninth at the Nürburgring, having run third early on before a tyre was damaged. Monza was hot, and fast, and the V12 wilted under the strain of climbing from 13th to seventh as oil pressure disappeared.

There, Gurney tried a works McLaren M7A with Cosworth engine, and next day he arranged to drive it for the rest of the season, setting aside the never completely developed Eagle-Weslake.

At Santa Ana new ex-Lola designer Tony Southgate was drawing the 1969 Formula 1 Eagle, with all-magnesium skins. It was to be a neat slim car with outboard front suspension aiming at minimum limit weight and, in view of the V12's continued problems and insufficient budget for further serious development, they thought of building a similar alternative Cosworth car.

But funds were very short, Gurney was not too happy at the fire risk in a magnesium car –

Dying days: Dan Gurney sports his new-fangled Bell Star helmet in his only finish with the aerodynamically modified Eagle-Weslake '104, Nürburgring, 1968.

mindful of Schlesser's death in the air-cooled magnesium Honda at Rouen – and in November 1968 further Formula 1 plans were abandoned. Henceforth, All-American Racers would concentrate upon US racing, Anglo-American Racers as such being wound up. Woods returned to BRM and a buyer was sought for the V12, Honda expressing brief but unfulfilled interest, and the most gorgeous of all 3-litre Formula 1 cars would be raced no more.

Ensign

Former Lotus sports and Formula 3 driver Morris Nunn built the Ensign F3 cars before being approached by one of his customers, wealthy Liechtensteiner Rikki von Opel, to produce a Cosworth/Hewland Formula 1 car for 1973.

Ensign-Cosworth N173 chassis 'MN01' made its debut in the French GP at Ricard, using a simple made-out aluminium monocoque clad in strikingly-styled Specialised Mouldings glass-fibre bodywork with a full-width chisel nose, hip radiators and a spectacular rear wing supported on its end plates. It was all finished in bright green with yellow pinstriping and was beautifully made and well prepared. Peter Gethin helped with initial development.

Von Opel was little more than a cheerfully amateur driver and placed 15th in France, 17th in Britain and ignored the Dutch and German GPs. He then returned for the Austrian, Italian, Canadian and US events, finishing only in Canada, 20th and too far behind to be classified. Never mind, it was fun, Mo Nunn had a taste for Formula 1 and they were learning fast.

But into 1974 von Opel considered his car uncompetitive and he drove briefly for Brabham before leaving motor racing altogether. Despite having lost his banker, Nunn was determined, somehow, to stay in Formula 1. A second chassis, the more conventionally bodied N174 'MN02', had been completed and guest driver Redman tried both at Silverstone before racing '02 and finishing eighth.

Having abandoned Formula 3 customer car production, all Nunn's eggs were in the Formula 1 basket. He needed an angel to finance survival and one appeared in the diminutive form of Hong Kong/Macau mil-

Heyday: Dan Gurney takes '102 off from pole position alongside team-mate Richie Ginther's new '103 in the 1967 Race of Champions at Brands Hatch, which the Eagle-Weslake pair dominated.

lionaire Theodore 'Teddy' Yip who injected finance to give his Australian driver Schuppan the ride.

He drove 'MN02' five times and failed to qualify twice, from the Belgian to German GPs. Yip then withdrew, and Nunn arrived in Austria with F5000 driver Mike Wilds and old 'MN01' with revised cockpit section and altered engine cover and airbox. Poor Wilds had little chance, and failed to qualify three times, eventually making the grid at Watkins Glen, where he was 14th, unclassified.

For 1975 the Dutch HB Bewaking alarm systems company bought the Ensign drive for Roelof Wunderink. Wunderink first drove '02 at Brands Hatch in March, qualified for the Spanish GP, but failed to qualify at Monaco and missed the Belgian and Swedish races. Wunderink had hurt himself in a Formula 5000 accident and Gijs van Lennep drove in the Dutch GP, comfortably finishing tenth, while a new Bewaking-financed Dave Baldwin-designed LNF75 – or N175 – model 'MN04' appeared there as unused spare.

It used rising-rate front suspension and inboard brakes all round and again was very nicely made, belying the Walsall team's humble facilities.

Lennep drove it in the French GP, Wunderink failed to qualify it in Britain, then Lennep was sixth in Germany to score Ensign's first Championship point.

Meanwhile, Amon joined Nunn to drive 'MN04' in Austria alongside Wunderink in '02. After his misfortunes in his own Amon AF1 the previous year, the newcomer had reservations about the LNF75's inboard front brakes but he ran well in the car, without worthwhile results, for the rest of the season.

Nunn fell out with HB Bewaking, so for 1976 they took 'MN04' away and he was left to race two-year-old 'MN02' which was updated as far as possible for Amon at Kyalami, Long Beach and in two minor British events, finishing fifth at Brands Hatch. At Long Beach, '02 – which had been advertized for sale for £4000 in the winter – ran 12th fastest in first practice and was eighth in the race, which proved either how good a car it was or how brilliant Amon could be.

Meanwhile, a new Dave Baldwin-designed LNF76 chassis 'MN05' was being completed to conform to the latest airbox and roll-over bar regulations in force from the Spanish GP. Again, it looked beautifully made with AP Lockheed balanced calliper front brakes mounted outboard partly in deference to Amon. At Jarama he qualified tenth and finished fifth for two Championship points, and at last Ensign seemed to be going somewhere. HB meanwhile allowed Australian driver Larry Perkins – who acted as his own mechanic, transporter driver, chief cook and bottle washer – to enter their old 'MN04' under the 'Boro' name, and he finished 13th.

Amon drove well at Zolder, running fifth until 'MN05's left-rear suspension broke and it crashed very heavily. Perkins finished eighth. Amon finished at Monaco in his repaired car, while Perkins was unable to qualify on his minimal budget.

In Sweden Amon was sensational, qualifying third, but when challenging for third place in the race the Ensign's left-front wheel broke loose, causing another heavy accident, painfully bruising Amon who was lucky to escape so lightly.

While he recovered, Patrick Neve drove the rebuilt 'MN05' in France, hopelessly off the pace and finishing 18th. Amon was back for the British GP but in Germany he withdrew from the race and from the team after witnessing Lauda's crash. Roland Binder drove in Austria, Ickx joining the team at this point, though without result beyond qualifying comfortably. Subsequently, he destroyed the car in a massive accident at Watkins Glen, apparently caused by another structural failure, which tore 'MN05' in two and injured the Belgian's legs and feet.

Perkins meanwhile crashed 'MN04' at Zandvoort but rebuilt it in time to qualify strongly in the middle of the Italian GP grid, only for the engine to disintegrate, ending his season.

Nunn, indefatigable, now planned to rebuild his car and his team for 1977 with sponsorship from Tissot and Castrol. A brand new N177 chassis 'MN06' was completed for new driver Regazzoni who ran it in the first six races, finishing sixth for another point in Argentina and apparently surviving the culture shock of changing from Ferrari to Ensign quite well. After qualifying on row four of the 2-by-2 grid in Spain, Regazzoni damaged the car in a race collision. He went off to Indy in the midst of Monaco practice, Ickx racing '06 in his place, finishing tenth, while new car 'MN07' was available as spare in the paddock.

Regazzoni was seventh in both Sweden and France, while at Silverstone for the British GP

two Ensigns appeared, '06 for Regazzoni and new car '08 entered by Yip's Theodore team for Patrick Tambay, who qualified easily while Regazzoni did not.

Both Ensigns completed the season, Regazzoni driving '07, Tambay '08; the works driver fifth in Italy and the US, Tambay showing promise with sixth in Germany, while third place was in the bag at Zandvoort when the Theodore Ensign ran out of fuel. Tambay was fifth in Canada and Ensign ended the season tenth in the Constructors' Championship, with ten points.

This marked the high tide of Ensign fortunes.

For 1978 Nunn had to do his best with his basically three-year-old cars, using chassis 'MN06-7-8' with a variety of rent-a-drivers, including Lamberto Leoni and Danny Ongais but settling finally on Ickx and Daly. British-based entrant Mario Deliotti bought old 'MN04' for Geoff Lees's use in British national Formula 1 races, and it was also handled by Giancarlo Martini and Desiré Wilson. Piquet and Harald Ertl featured in late-season events as did Lunger, but Daly was Ensign's most regular pilot. An 'MN09' car was built for David Price Racing for Val Musetti to drive in national Formula 1, both this car and old '04 subsequently coming under the Deliotti umbrella. Only in the final race of the season, at Montreal, did it all come good for Nunn, Daly finishing sixth to score a point at last.

This struggle for survival continued in 1979; construction of 'MN10' was started but later abandoned, followed by an extraordinary new Theodore-sponsored '179/01' or 'MN11' which emerged in South Africa. It incorporated a huge radiator built into the scuttle ahead of the cockpit but this proved a miscalculation and the radiators were split back into the side pods for Long Beach. For Spain, Nunn modified old '06 with ground-effect side pods lashed on, since the new 179 was late returning from California.

179 as a wing-car ran at Monaco but it had become a regular non-qualifier by this time. In France Patrick Gaillard drove, then qualified for the British GP but Surer replaced him at Monza. There, Nunn announced new plans for 1980 but, overall, Ensign had only qualified for two races with Daly, two races with Gaillard and one with Surer, while the only finishes had been one 11th and two 13ths . . . a literally pointless season.

Regardless, Nunn had won Unipart backing for 1980, running Regazzoni again in an all-new 180 car designed by former Lotus

engineers Ralph Bellamy and Nigel Bennett. The riveted aluminium monocoque car was a virtual Williams FW07 copy but differed in its side pods and its ultra-narrow rear track. At Kyalami a spare car '02 became available but in Long Beach Regazzoni crashed very badly when apparently assured of fourth place, ramming another car parked in an escape road. He was paralyzed by his injuries, ending his career and ruining Ensign's hopes of a bright future; chassis '180/01' was destroyed.

In the remainder of the season first Tiff Needell, then Lammers drove; Ensign failed to qualify for six GPs and placed 14th and 12th in only two finishes. There was no 'MN13' but 'MN14', the third N180, was completed in time to be Needell's spare at Monaco. Gaillard drove in Spain . . . no joy.

Into 1981, Nunn clung onto Formula 1 by his finger nails, 'MN14' was updated to B-spec and renumbered N180B 'MN15', to be driven by Surer. A second N180B tub was brought to Hockenheim and was on its wheels by Österreichring but was never actually completed. Surer drove six times and saved the team at a time when Nunn was staring down the gun barrel in Rio.

There the car felt comfortable in heavy rain and Surer drove very competently to place fourth, remarkably setting fastest lap as well as earning Ensign precious survival money. He did it again with sixth at Monaco, but Chilean Eliseo Salazar then rented the drive for himself in the last nine races, failed to qualify once and finished sixth in Holland on reliability. This compensated for other shortcomings and Ensign ended the season 11th in their Championship, with five points.

The final season under the Ensign name came in 1982 when 'MN15' was updated while waiting for new car N181, 'MN16' (a Brabham look-alike wing-car), to be completed. Roberto Guerrero drove 'MN15' at Kyalami then took the new 'MN16' at Long Beach. A second N181 was started but never finished, while Guerrero failed to qualify five times, his only finish placing him eighth at Hockenheim. The earnings from this season had been minimal but a faint glimmer of hope came when Guerrero qualified respectably for the last race, at Las Vegas. That hope was cruelly dashed when a jubilee clip on a cooling system hose worked loose, gushing water, just before the start and they could not race.

Nunn's old sparring partner, Teddy Yip, had for some time held an interest in the team, and after that unfortunate finale to 1982 he combined his recently acquired Shadow team with Nunn's, using the Ensign cars and his own Theodore Racing title, and persevered for '83. See under 'Theodore', page 237.

Ferrari

Maranello's first 3-litre Formula 1 car used a four-cam 24-valve V12 derived from their 3.3-litre 275P sports-prototype unit, uprated with Lucas fuel injection. Ferrari claimed 360 bhp at 10,000 rpm but, upon first acquaintance, driver Surtees was unconvinced – it felt like 'no more than 270'!

The engine was also thirsty, demanding a voluminous monocoque chassis which used Ferrari's 'Aero' hybrid construction, with a tubular internal frame stiffened by riveted-on aluminium stressed skins. It was a full-length tub with projecting rear horns supporting the engine, transaxle and rear suspension. Front suspension used top rocker arms and inboard springs, rear suspension outboard springs but inboard disc brakes.

Clay Regazzoni in the neat Ensign-DFV N180 'MN11' on its debut at Buenos Aires, 1980. Later that year he would crash badly at Long Beach to end his fine career.

Three of these model 312 cars would be built, numbers '0010-11-12. The latter was a special long-chassis/long-cockpit car for the tall Mike Parkes after Surtees left in mid-season, having just won the Belgian GP in '0010.

Chassis '0011 raced only once that year, in the Italian GP at Monza, where Ferrari fielded three 312s powered by reheated 36-valve V12s offering perhaps 370 bhp and which dominated thoroughly. Bandini had led at Reims in '0010 until a missing throttle stop caused the cable to break, wrecking Ferrari chances.

In addition they used a 1965 monocoque, '0006, fitted with a 2.4-litre four-cam Dino V6 engine early in the season, the engine as used in Formula 1 from 1958-60 and in the 1961 246SP sports-prototypes, now modernized with fuel injection. This light, nimble and powerful special had been intended for Surtees's use in the winter Tasman Championship but injuries prevented him from going.

He won at Syracuse and Spa in '0010, while Scarfiotti won the Italian GP at Monza – imagine the noise! – in '0011, with Parkes second in '0012. The hybrid Dino 246T was second at Syracuse and Monaco then third at Spa driven by Bandini. It reappeared unsuccessfully in Scarfiotti's hands at the Nürburgring – for which it should have been very well-suited – and finally as a private Parnell Racing team replacement entry at Monza, driven by Giancarlo Baghetti. It was ideal for Monaco and Surtees should have driven it there, but it was handed instead to Bandini, contributing towards the departure of Surtees from the team.

Thereafter Ferrari concentrated upon sports-prototype development to beat Ford at Le Mans in 1967. Bandini drove '0010 as a lone team entry in the US GP, therefore, and led before either a spark plug electrode smashed a piston, or a piston smashed the spark-plug electrode. He retired and the team cancelled its Mexican GP entry.

In essence Ferrari should have walked the 1966 Championship, and would surely have done so had they looked after Surtees. The engineers were doing their job but the team's internal politics simply threw it all away. They experimented with both Dunlop and Firestone tyres during the season, opting for an American dollar contract in the end. They would use Firestone tyres until changing to Goodyear for 1974-77, to Michelin for 1978-81, returning to Goodyear thereafter.

Into 1967, despite their heavy endurance racing commitment, Ferrari ran a three-car Formula 1 team for a choice of four drivers – Bandini, Parkes, Scarfiotti and new-boy Chris Amon.

Franco Rocchi uprated the V12 with new reversed-flow cylinder heads. The inlet ports were still between the camshafts but the exhausts now exited in the vee, gathering the pipework within the roll-over bar cross-section, clearing the airstream either side. A new lightened magnesium-zirconium alloy crankcase was on the way, while Walter Salvarani completed a new weight-saving five-speed transmission, based on his latest 1600 cc Formula 2 design.

The 312-67 prototype car '0001 used 1966-block engines with centre-exhaust heads in original form, installed in a slim new 'Aero' type pseudo-monocoque chassis whose engine bay horns rose taller and stiffer than before. They carried fuel now displaced from what had been the bloated centre section of the 312-66 model tubs. This low-frontal area Ferrari looked superb and an output of 390 bhp at 10,000 rpm was claimed from its revised 36-valve engine, though the drivers again suggested this was optimistic . . .

Ferrari missed South Africa due to sports car commitments, their Formula 1 season commencing instead in the minor Brands Hatch meeting where Bandini drove '0001 into second place just 0.4 second behind the winning Eagle-Weslake V12, Amon had a road accident so non-started old '0010 and Scarfiotti was fifth

Lorenzo Bandini, Monaco, 1966, in the hybrid Ferrari 246T 2.4-litre Tasman V6 'special' with which he began the season in support of Surtees's full 3-litre V12 cars.

in his Monza-winning '0011.

Parkes won at Silverstone using his long-cockpit 312-66 '0012 with centre-exhaust engine; two 312-67s ran at Monaco, where Bandini qualified second fastest but crashed '0001 fatally late in the race, and Amon was third in brand new '0003 after a pit stop to change a punctured tyre had lost him a certain second place.

Ferrari then scored a dead-heat victory at Syracuse, where Parkes started on pole with '0012 centre-exhaust engine, and Scarfiotti set fastest lap in his '66 specification '0011.

There was to be no longer-cockpit 312-67 car for Parkes so he again raced his '66 special, finishing fifth sandwiched between Amon's '0003 and Scarfiotti's brand new '0005. In Belgium, Parkes destroyed his elderly special in a first lap accident which ended his own Grand Prix career, Scarfiotti saw it all and subsequently opted out while Amon again soldiered round to finish third.

In the following six races Ferrari made singleton entries for Amon, normally in chassis '0005 with '0003 spare.

Once they had got the endurance races out of their system, Ferrari could concentrate more effort upon Formula 1 in the second half of the year. Their new lightweight-block V12 and F2-based gearbox appeared at the Nürburgring, and for Monza the all-new lightweight car '0007 emerged with the latest block and gearbox plus four-valve-per-cylinder heads. The four valves were disposed at a slight radial angle in planview, giving a semi-hemispheric pent-roof combustion chamber though the angle between the valves was narrow, cramping the camshafts too tightly together to allow the inlets to remain between them. They were moved to outside the heads, therefore, while

exhausts remained within the vee and single spark plugs fired the mixture.

Now Forghieri's claims of 390 bhp seemed realistic, and since the chassis, according to Amon, was already 'an absolute dream' to drive, Ferrari were set to win races again. It could have happened at Watkins Glen, where the Lotus 49s proved fragile, but Amon's engine blew up 12 laps from the finish and the limping Lotuses finished 1-2. In Mexico, Amon qualified second to Clark's Lotus 49 in '0007 but ran low on fuel, finishing ninth behind his once-only team-mate, Jonathan Williams in '0003.

A low-key finale to the season came at the new Jarama Autodrome, in Spain, where Andrea de Adamich drove '0005 quietly into a lowly ninth place in the Madrid GP.

In 1967, Ferrari had made 22 Formula 1 starts, 15 of them in Championship GPs, winning none but taking four third places. Bandini's death and Parkes's injuries had coincided with excessive pressure upon the racing department and so made this an indifferent season.

For 1968 Ferrari abandoned endurance racing in displeasure over a rule change and concentrated upon Formula 1. It paid off. The 48-valve engines now gave around 410 bhp but compared to the minimum 408 bhp Cosworth DFVs they lacked mid-range torque, with 'nothing at home below 9800 rpm' according to Amon, who was joined by Ickx and de Adamich.

The cars suffered high water and oil temperatures, and associated power loss. The V12 was still thirsty, Ferrari having to start most races carrying 8-10 gallons (56-70 lb) more fuel than their Cosworth rivals.

Three 1967 chassis, '0003-5-7 (Ferrari's system skipped even numbers at this time), were used in South Africa and at Brands Hatch, where the unfortunate de Adamich crashed '0005 very badly, hurting himself and ending the car's career.

A new 312-68 chassis '0009 appeared for Ickx at Silverstone with its engine lowered in the chassis. Amon was third there in '0007 and Ickx fourth in the new car. Amon raced '0007 in the first six events of the season, before taking new chassis '0011 at Rouen and using it in the next five events, eventually destroying it in a heavy race crash at Monza. Ickx used '0009 in his summer races, apart from Spa where he drove old '0003, but in Germany he put new car '0015 – even the Italians missing out '0013 – on pole position.

For the American races Amon drove '0009 while Ickx crashed '0015 heavily in Canadian GP practice, breaking his leg and ruining his chance of the Drivers' Championship.

At Spa, as described on page 72, Forghieri introduced a strutted aerofoil mounted above the gearbox and the cars handled superbly well there. Forghieri subsequently moved the aerofoil forward, closer to the centre of gravity to distribute download more evenly front to rear but the drivers found it less effective, preferring sheer traction to this theoretically better balance.

Amon built his legendarily unlucky reputation this season. He qualified on three consecutive pole positions – Spain, Spa and Zandvoort (the team having refused to enter Monaco after Bandini's death there) – and he led the first two handsomely until fused fuel pumps and a holed oil cooler respectively robbed him of victory. It rained in Holland, where Firestone's wet-weather tyres proved no match for Dunlop, and the peaky V12 rev band made the Ferrari tricky to control. Amon was worse affected than Ickx in these conditions, and when it rained again at Rouen, Ickx won unconcerned.

Ickx and Amon qualified 1-2 on the grid at the Nürburgring but by this time the Cosworth cars were far ahead aerodynamically and were quicker away from slow corners. Derek Bell joined the team in the minor race at Oulton Park, driving '0007, while Forghieri devised an ingenious moveable wing system for Monza, energized by engine oil under pressure. The wing dropped into a high attack-angle for maximum download in first, second and third gears, but feathered for low-drag, high-speed with the throttle open in fourth and fifth. It returned to the download position in those gears when the brakes were applied. An over-ride switch was also provided, which Amon preferred but which Ickx disliked and had it removed from his car.

Amon qualified on the front row at Monza with this system but an oil leak onto a rear tyre caused an almighty accident which destroyed his '0011 in the race. Ickx was third and was

Top, Amon at Spa in his Ferari 312/67 during the 1967 Belgian GP, these low-frontal area centre-exhaust V12s now being mouth-watering collector's items.

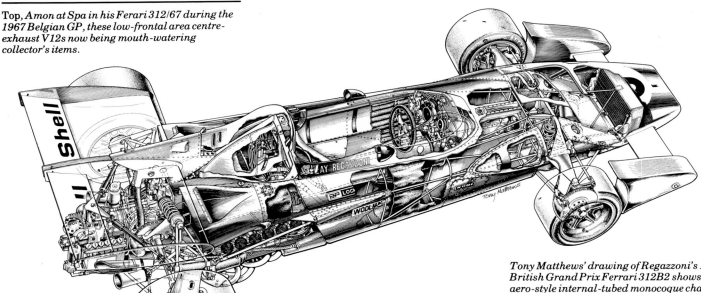

Tony Matthews' drawing of Regazzoni's 1971 British Grand Prix Ferrari 312B2 shows its aero-style internal-tubed monocoque chassis with its inboard semi-rising rate rear springs. Firestone's slick racing tyres were first tested during practice for the early season Questor Grand Prix at Ontario, California, and were introduced to championship racing in the Spanish GP. They were in response to Goodyear's introduction of a slick tyre in the South African Grand Prix which had opened that season.

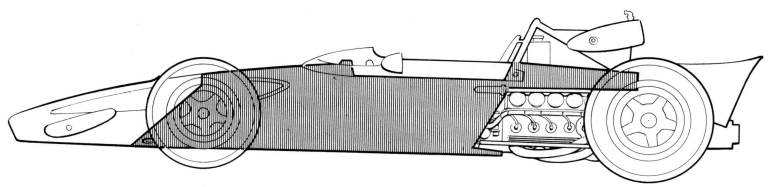

The shaded area above shows the structural form of the 1970-71 Ferrari 312B semi-monocoque chassis, with its flat-12 engine suspended beneath the protruding rear horn, after the style of the 1968 Honda RA302.

still in contention for the World Championship title before having '0015's throttle jam open, breaking his leg in the Canadian accident. Amon was able to dominate that long race imperiously in '0009 running with extra fuel tankage outrigged alongside its engine bay, despite losing the clutch as early as lap 12. Sadly the final-drive suffered under clutchless gear-changing, and failed with 17 laps to run, robbing the New Zealander and Ferrari of their third probable victory that season.

Ferrari had made 30 Formula 1 starts, winning just one Grand Prix, taking one second place and three thirds. But their cars were on the front row nine times, eight to Amon, and they took four pole positions, three of them his. Three of the six cars used were effectively written off, while unreliability robbed Ferrari of those three probable GP wins and the title.

The company encountered financial crisis in 1969 but still returned to endurance racing, if low-key, while Mr Ferrari took the long-term strategic decision for Forghieri's men to develop the new 312B flat-12 for 1970 while *Ing.* Stefano Jacoponi took Formula 1 team responsibility to do his best with the obsolescent V12. Only three cars would be used in the new season: '0009 from 1968, plus two new cars '0017 and '0019.

They used very similar monocoques to the successful 312-68 cars, but new flattened nose cones gave them a totally different, more podgy appearance.

Despite protestations that the further-revised 48-valve V12s now delivered 435 bhp, Amon could not believe they had even 1968 power. New heads reversed the porting once more, returning the exhausts to the outside of the vee, lowering the car's centre of gravity and reducing airflow turbulence around the rear wing. Inlets were in the vee, more radical new camshafts were fitted, and disastrous efforts were made to reduce internal friction by reducing main bearing area.

Except for the minor Silverstone meeting, where Bell drove '0009, Amon raced alone until the British GP, initially with new 312-69 '0017 introduced at Kyalami, then taking '0019 brand new at Monaco. At Barcelona, the Ferrari was equipped with a low-reciprocating mass V12 featuring new titanium con-rods and further revised valve timing. Amon found difficulty in gearing the car properly due to a massive flat-spot in the engine's output between 9800 and 10,400 rpm, but still qualified second quickest in practice. After the works Lotus 49Bs had crashed due to wing collapses, '0017 led by over 30 seconds only for its engine to seize. At Monaco, Amon was second when the diff failed. Pedro Rodriguez joined him for the British GP but gearbox and engine failures sidelined them both.

Ferrari withdrew from the German GP to prepare the new 312B for a debut at Monza, but the new engine failed repeatedly in testing and this was the final straw for Amon, who left in disgust. Rodriguez ran out the stub end of the season, easing '0019 home sixth in the Italian GP, then driving '0017 within its capabilities in Canada, the US and Mexico, finishing latterly

fifth and seventh.

Ferrari had made only 13 Formula 1 starts and achieved just six finishes, three of them by Rodriguez at the end of the year when it didn't matter. Amon finished only one race, with a good third place in Holland, but he had been in a winning position in Spain and was well placed at Monaco before it all went wrong . . .

The 312B came on song in 1970. Its flat-12 engine is discussed elsewhere, but when the car first appeared its 'Aero' style chassis suspending the engine beneath a rearward-projecting beam – reminiscent of the air-cooled Honda V8 – was the best-integrated 3-litre Formula 1 package yet created. It would remain the best packaged of all Ferraris until the Postlethwaite 156 appeared in 1985, after our period had ended.

Five 312Bs were built that first season; chassis '002 being destroyed by fire at Jarama and replaced by a completely new car taking the same number.

Ickx returned as number one, and 312B development may be judged by results: the new design's first finishes occurred in its fourth race, placing 4-8 in the Belgian GP; then qualifying on the front row and setting fastest lap in its fifth race, in Holland; able to take pole position for its sixth race, in France; followed up by qualifying on pole for four of the next seven races while placing on the front row in *all* seven.

The cars set fastest lap in six races, including five of the season's last six. From 25 starts in 1970 they recorded 17 finishes, won four of the last five races of the year and were first and second in three of them, 1-2-7 with their three-car entry in Austria.

It rocked the Cosworth brigade to the last locknut and washer but the cars had come on song just too late that season to win the World Championship titles. Ickx, who won the Austrian, Canadian and Mexican GPs in '001, had a chance of the Drivers' title until a fuel pipe broke at Watkins Glen, where Rindt's posthumous crown in the Lotus was assured. Regazzoni won the Italian GP in '004 while the other team driver was another newcomer, Ignazio Giunti.

For 1971, three revised new 312B2 models were built, serialled '005-6-7, while existing 'B1s '001-2-3-4 would appear in 1970 form before at least one was modified to 'B2 trim, if we believe the chassis numbering. Since such a total conversion would have entailed one of the new squarer-section monocoques replacing the rounded 312B section, we can take the numbers with a pinch of salt – never mind the history, let's make the customs carnets fit . . .

The definitive 'B2 tub had a reduced frontal area and adopted a more wedgy flat-topped, vertical-sided form. The inboard front suspension of 1970 was retained, but at the rear Forghieri mounted the coil/dampers above the gearbox, actuated by bell-crank extensions of the upper suspension links. Engine improvements were made in search of better combustion.

Ickx, Regazzoni and Andretti drove, and Ferrari won the first three races – Andretti the

South African and non-Championship Questor GPs in '002 and Regazzoni at Brands Hatch in the new 312B2 '005. Later, Ickx won a minor Hockenheim race in '003, but the new 'B2's only win other than at Brands Hatch would be Ickx's masterly wet-race performance in the Dutch GP.

Overall, the flat-12 Ferraris made 31 starts in 1971, finishing 16 times and notching five wins but only two at Championship level, one each for 'B1 and 'B2, while their three non-Championship wins split 2-1; 'B1, 'B2.

Yet in that first half-season the Ferraris had won five of the seven races held, qualifying on the front row every time, on pole three times and setting four fastest race laps.

In the second half they made 17 starts in seven races and finished only five times, though achieving 3-4 in the German GP. They were four times on the front row, took one pole position – at Silverstone – but Ickx was responsible for the only fastest lap, in the US GP.

So a season which had started so well simply fell apart in ill-handling and unreliability. Had Ferrari's run been concentrated in one calendar season, instead of being split back-end of 1970/front-end of '71, the cars would have made history indeed!

The 'B2's ill-handling, especially upon bumpy surfaces, was exacerbated by Firestone's development of new ultra low-profile tyres which encountered harmonic vibration problems shaking the cars to pieces, both Ferrari and BRM losing races for this reason (see page 87).

For 1972 the 'B2s' inboard-mounted rear coil/dampers were resited outboard with conventional linkages, and wider tracks were adopted at the front and rear. Aerodynamic changes were made to nose section and wings but only one new chassis was made, namely 'B2 '008. The 1971 drivers were retained but Andretti missed much of mid-season with other

Team Manager Peter Schetty wears Regazzoni's helmet to test an interim 312B2 at Modena, October 1971. Note rear springs now outboard.

commitments, then Regazzoni broke his wrist, so Galli and Merzario ran as stand-ins until The Men reappeared in Austria and Italy.

The 1972 Ferrari record shows 29 starts, 19 finishes, only one victory – though a most convincing one – and 10 more finishes in the points. Team achievements included 2-3 in Spain, 3-4 in Argentina, and second at Monaco. Ickx drove '006 in five early races, '005 for seven races thereafter including the German GP at the Nürburgring in which he was inspired, qualifying on pole, setting fastest lap and winning so handsomely. But the 'B2 was heavy, aerodynamically ineffective and could not match Lotus 72 handling that year.

Ferrari then ran aground on internal bickering. Forghieri completed a prototype deformable structure car aimed at the forthcoming 1973 regulations, using a very brief wheelbase, low polar moment central weight concentration and side radiators fed through NACA ducts cut into a full-width snowplough nose. On test the car was horrible. It would never be raced. It lived with the author for some weeks in 1983, still looking horrible, its aluminium body panels were incredibly heavy, but nonetheless Forghieri was on the right track with this central mass concentration, and would still have the last laugh . . .

Short-term, driver criticism of this 'Spazzaneve' (snowplough) prototype, '009, plus relative failure through 1972 saw Forghieri assigned to future project development, out of the racing team as in 1969 when his group had developed the 312B to revive Ferrari's racing fortunes.

Ex-Innocenti engineer Sandro Colombo was given technical charge of Formula 1, now running Goodyear tyres for the first time. Ferrari began the year with the obsolescent 'B2s '005-6-8, while a new deformable-structure 312B3 was completed. Due to continuing metal-working union unrest, Ferrari sub-contracted John Thompson's TC Prototypes company of Weedon, near Northampton, England, to build three bare aluminium-sheet monocoque chassis to Maranello drawings. The engine-suspending rear beam was now dispensed with, the revised flat-12 engines instead bolting fully-stressed onto a cast magnesium sandwich plate fitted against the tub's rear bulkhead. The tub itself was broad, rectangular in section and slightly wedge-form towards the nose. Inboard front coil/dampers were retained, actuated now by fabricated rather than forged top rocker arms; the rear

was conventional, feeding major loads into a cast-alloy bridge bolted over the transaxle.

The three 'Thompson monocoque' 'B3 Ferraris were chassis '010, '011 and '012 in the 312B series. Ickx tested '011 with side radiators at Fiorano just before the Spanish GP at which the new deformable-structure regulations would take effect. It overheated and the team fell back on '010 rigged with a conventional nose radiator. Both cars ran in Barcelona practice, Ickx concentrating upon '010, as a lone entry. He ran alone in Spain, Belgium, Sweden and the British GP; Merzario, his early-season team-mate in the 'B2s, rejoined him at Monaco and in France. The only worthwhile results were sixth at Anderstorp and a 5-7 finish in France but the cars were uncompetitive and Ferrari withdrew entries for the Dutch and German races.

Reputedly under Fiat pressure to improve fortunes, Ferrari had summoned Forghieri to return to Formula 1. He reworked '312B3 010' in 20 days in time for Merzario to drive it in Austria, the car now using lengthy radiators raked forward in the hull sides, air being ducted through them from underneath and out through vents on the side pod upper decks. The oil tank was sited at the rear of the tub to the right of the engine, the oil cooler on the opposite side, and Forghieri had applied his low polar moment theories as in the hapless Spazzaneve to transform the 'B3 into a more raceworthy proposition by season's end.

Merzario was seventh on the revised car's debut in Austria. Ickx returned to run '010 suitably modified at Monza, finishing eighth while Merzario shunted '011; then the Italian driver completed the season in Canada and the USA, driving '011 in singleton entries, 15-16. Meanwhile at Maranello work progressed on an all-new Forghieri 312B3 for 1974.

This agonized season had seen Ferrari make only 19 Formula 1 starts, with 14 finishes but only four in the points, all with the 'B2s in the three early-season races at Buenos Aires, São Paulo and Kyalami. Ickx had driven '005 home fourth and fifth in the former pair, qualifying on the front row in Brazil, while Merzario's results were 9-4-4 in '008 and (at Kyalami) in

Above left, Ferrari 312B2s under preparation, showing the squarer tub shape of these cars (background) and the suspended mounting of the flat-12 engine beneath that rear monocoque horn. Left, Ickx at Monaco 1972 in the 312B2 with rear spring/damper units conventionally outboard again.

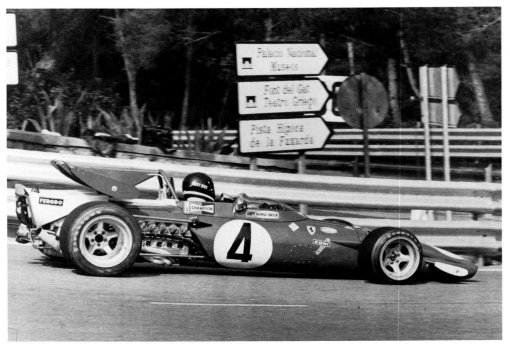

Classical beauty: Ickx's Ferrari 312B '003' on its way to second place in the 1971 Spanish GP, Barcelona. This car is preserved today in Britain in the Donington Collection.

'005, while Ickx crashed '006 in the South African race.

There was little joy in the rest of the season, the best 'B3 finish being 5-7 in France, never looking competitive.

For 1974 the team was reorganized under the management of Luca di Montezemolo, Forghieri in charge of technical direction, and with drivers Regazzoni and new-boy Lauda. The 312B3s were developed with tubs remade though initially retaining the interim 'B3 chassis numbers for paperwork convenience. The revised monocoque had the cockpit moved forward some five inches in the wheelbase, revised cylinder heads boosted flat-12 output to some 495 bhp at 12,600 rpm, and with Lauda and Regazzoni forming an excellent driving team they would return to the winner's rostrum.

Six 1974 312B3s were produced, under the numbers '010-11-12-14-15-16, recording 32 starts, 30 of them in Championship GPs, 20 finishes, 18 in GPs, and returning three wins – Lauda in Spain and Holland, Regazzoni in Germany – seven seconds, two thirds, three fourths, two fifths and a lowly 11th in Championship events. All but one Grand Prix finish scored points, while in the minor Brands Hatch race they finished 2-5.

In addition, the new car's pace was emphasized by its nine pole positions, eight to Lauda, including six in a row from the Dutch to the Italian GPs . . . they were quick.

Driver immaturity and an extraordinary race organizers' error in the British GP caused Lauda to become boxed-in by a scrum of hangers-on after a late-race pit stop and he was unable to rejoin a race which he had been leading, foiling Ferrari's best Championship hopes since 1970. But the record would be put right in 1975-76-77 (see pages 88-93).

For 1978, aiming at a fourth consecutive World title, Ferrari ran existing 312T2 cars '027 and '031 for Reutemann and Villeneuve in the South American races before introducing all-new model 312T3s at Kyalami, chassis '032-033. These had been specifically tailored to the team's new Michelin radial-ply tyres, which demanded more camber change in the suspension geometry. Tubular front rocker arms actuated coil/dampers, which were larger than before and were now mounted outside the tub footwell. The body was completely redesigned, with a shapely spearhead planform shell, full-width wing and smooth flow onto the delta-form rear wing.

This was the season of the Lotus 79s and ground-effects, which Ferrari could not harness comfortably due to the width of their flat-12 engine. Considering this handicap, they had another very good season, making 32 starts in the 16 GPs, finishing 21 times, with five victories – Reutemann in Brazil with 'T2 '031, Long Beach in '032, Britain '033 and the USA '035; Villeneuve won in great style on home soil in Montreal, driving '034 with Reutemann third in '035 behind him. They had two pole positions, Reutemann on the street circuits at Long Beach and Monaco, and were four times on the front row, that at Long Beach seeing the 'T3s side by side.

Ferrari ended the season second in the Constructors' Cup, but in 1979 they would win it again (see pages 102-3).

In 1980 the hapless 312T5 was a makeshift ground-effects flat-12 car which was never adequately developed, and which in truth was run virtually as a spare time effort while everyone who mattered (excluding the drivers) concentrated upon development of a new turbocharged engine and car for '81.

The result was Ferrari's worst season in many years. They made 27 starts in the 14 GPs, Scheckter actually failing to qualify for his penultimate race, in Canada, and they were classified as finishers 18 times. Their only points were scored from three fifth places – Scheckter in Long Beach, and the irrepressible Villeneuve in Monaco and Canada. Additionally, Villeneuve finished sixth in Belgium and Germany.

The 'T5 chassis were '042-43-44-45-46-48, '047 never being raced if it existed at all.

The ungainly cars simply destroyed their Michelin tyres and pit stops to change tyres were a normal part of their days' racing. It was like the old days of tortoise and hare – unblown

cars versus thirsty, refuel-stopping, super-charged machinery – but in relative terms the unfortunate 'T5s were never capable of haring anywhere. The long-term investment in turbo-charged development of the new 126C, however, would pay off handsomely – and the failures of 1980 must be seen as Ferrari's investment in a brighter future.

Ferrari fell apart as a Formula 1 force with a terrible season in 1984. The new 126C4 cars were effectively revised 1983 Constructors' Championship-winning 'C3s (see Chapter 14). The bottom of the 'C4 moulded carbon tub was identical to the 'C3's, although the upper

Niki Lauda dominating the 1974 Dutch GP at Zandvoort in Ferrari 312B3 '015'; engine, fuel, radiators and coolers are all now within the wheelbase.

section was a little different, the two sections went together differently and were a little stiffer. Some 10 per cent was trimmed off engine weight, eight per cent off gearbox and the centre of gravity was slightly lower.

Nine 'C4s were built, the team taking four to most races but only seven ('071-077) were used, the eighth tub being ready for build-up just before the penultimate race and the ninth at

Matthews again, this time depicting the Ferrari 312B3 in which Lauda came to fame in 1974.

Shapes of the Eighties: top, Alboreto in the Ferrari 126C at Monaco 1984, Postlethwaite carbon-composite tub, pullrod suspension, twin-turbocharged V6 engine and huge rear wing with abbreviated side pods. Above, backs to the wall at Monza 1984; note reshaped side pods.

that time fresh out of the tooling but not bonded together.

An early arrowhead shape was tried with the radiators upright and angled back but this discharged hot air against the tub and boiled the fuel. Changes were made, while at Maranello the senior engineers were restless and Forghieri's highly personal theorizing had

left him in an isolated position. In-house politicking would play a major part in this poor season (by Ferrari standards), with a fall to *only* second place in the Constructors' Championship, accumulating a measly 57.5 points to McLaren's 143.5.

Worst thing of all, perhaps, was Ferrari's win at Zolder, which led to an assumption that everything had come right. The drivers had been on form there, Goodyear's tyres had excelled in heat *and* a rogue fuel batch had decimated the opposition, while the troublesome electronic ignition had been replaced by a Lucas-Ferrari mechanical system. But then the team slipped into the abyss.

In the first 13 GPs up to Zandvoort, Arnoux finished nine times: 3-2-4-3-5-2-6-6-7. This was acceptable, but Alboreto finished only four times: winning in Belgium, then 6-5-3. If the cars finished they scored (all but once) but what was so serious was that they no longer looked likely winners that mid-season.

Just before the British GP, crisis management prevailed. At Brands Hatch two of their four 'C4s, '075 and '076, were revised with new radiators and intercoolers in top-ducted side pods. Pushrod suspension then replaced pullrod as development progressed. In Austria these 126C4/M (for *Modificato*) cars tried a 13 cm (5.1 in.) wheelbase stretch with altered underwing, but if run in anything other than high-download tune they just did not perform.

At Monza, '075 had been testing a side-ducted body. A similar 'K4 solution was tried in Austria but abandoned. In the Italian race, Ferrari were out-performed by *green* Alfa Romeos but salvaged a lucky second place.

There two McLaren-waisted 'C4/M2s appeared, on chassis '072 and '074 but 'C4/M1s '076 and '077 raced. The 'M2s ('074 for Alboreto, '077 updated for Arnoux) ran far more effectively in the final two races. Alboreto's final three GPs of the year yielded 2-2-4 finishes, while Arnoux clocked up a

retirement, a fifth and a ninth in the same period.

In the vast and clinical new *Reparto Corse* at Maranello, *Ing.* Renzetti had joined Tomaini's race team, while long-serving Forghieri had been removed from racing and seconded to the *Reparto Ursa* (*Ufficio Ricerche Studi Avanzati*) to develop long-term advance projects.

That winter, work progressed on Forghieri's last hurrah, a slant-four 1500 cc turbo engine which gave the chassis engineers installation nightmares. As 1985 approached it appeared to be still-born as the most complete team in Formula 1 looked towards a new 1200 cc turbocharged Formula 1 for the late Eighties.

For Ferrari 1985 was a season much like '83 with one exception. This time they lost the Constructors' Championship *as well as* the Drivers' title when their form fell apart at the year's end.

Nine new 156/85 chassis were built, numbered '078-086, each one a little different from its predecessor, but '078-082 were more similar to each other than to chassis '083-086. Design and construction used CAD-CAM computer-aided design and modelling technology with co-operation from Aermacchi aeronautics and Gould computers. New low-mounted turbochargers were adopted instead of the earlier in-vee layout. The smooth, long-tailed, low-slung 156s were the year's best-looking cars and performed well for two-thirds of the season. For Monaco rear suspension geometry was modified, and the front was revised for the first fruitless visit to Spa, where electronic wastegate control was also featured. Still chassis balance was not quite right and new tubs at Ricard had revised front suspension but events suggested a team in increasing trouble. Intercooler, oil radiator and water radiator positions were all revised for Germany but this was the last occasion on which Ferrari had competitive horsepower.

Chassis '078 had been the winter test car

then team spare raced by Alboreto at Spa; '079 was new for the Italian at Rio and was raced by both drivers subsequently; '080 was new for Arnoux's swansong at Rio; '081 new at Imola for Alboreto; '082 new for newcomer Johansson at Spa in June; '083 new for Alboreto at Ricard; '084 emerged for Johansson there in practice only, later becoming team spare; '085 was new for Alboreto at Monza and finally '086 made its debut for Johansson at Brands Hatch.

Balancing race-tune power against fuel consumption had always been a nice trick which Ferrari seemed to have well under control. McLaren regarded the 156s as their TAG Turbo engine's equal in race-tune economy, but the pressure of the new E-Type Honda engine and also Brabham-BMW's four-cylinder late in the year simply broke Ferrari's heart.

The awful realization that they were beaten on sheer horsepower hit Maranello like an ice-cold shower. It was a difficult, *difficult*, thing to swallow. In the later races their attempts to match even Renault and TAG-Porsche power saw Ferrari having to run boost-levels which blew their alloy-block V6 apart. It had become thermodynamically unreliable, and it looked as if a formerly excellent 1982 engine designed for, say, 700 bhp, was now being asked to contain 850-900 bhp or more.

From the mid-season American tour forward, the 156 chassis seemed not to perform as well as previously. It was very efficient but much too sensitive to different types of track; fine at *ersatz* Nürburgring, in trouble at bumpy Zandvoort and Brands Hatch. It seemed suited best to circuits which were like Ferrari's Fiorano test track, but modern Formula 1 had outgrown Fiorano, which lacked very high-speed corners.

The 156s for Monza were extensively reworked, Harvey Postlethwaite's section having swopped downforce generated by ground-effects for downforce generated by wings. They ran minimum download, minimum drag in qualifying and even then were demolished by BMW and Honda and even struggled against Renault. That was the point, on the holy ground of Monza, at which the cold shower hit poor Ildo Renzetti's engine section.

Team leader Alboreto contested all 16 GPs, finishing nine of the first 11, then significantly being merely classified after retirement at Monza and subsequently failing in each of the last four races of the season. His finishing record read 2-2-2-1-3-2-1-3-4-13*, which was good enough to give him the Drivers' Championship lead for most of the season, until Prost forged ahead for McLaren. Alboreto's victories were in Canada and Germany. Team-mate Arnoux was fired after Rio (where he finished fourth) and his replacement Johansson did the remaining 15 GPs, finishing ten of them – 8-6*-2-2-4-9-4-5-4-5 – looking set to win at Imola before running out of fuel and generally doing a fine job.

Until their late-season slump, Ferrari had led McLaren comfortably in the Constructors' Championship, but they were unable to resist the British team's pressure, and a major rethink began in the *Gestione Sportiva* for 1986.

Fittipaldi

After an indifferent career as a Formula 1 driver, Wilson Fittipaldi – the elder of the Brazilian brothers – set up his own team to build a car sponsored by Brazil's Copersucar sugar marketing organization, which he would drive in 1975. There was much money involved and, with former mechanic Richard Divila, the elder Fittipaldi developed a Cosworth-powered 'special' built in São Paulo.

The prototype Copersucar-Cosworth FD01 had a deep, shapely monocoque, nose radiator ducted under a full-width blade wing and rear-mounted radiator, and was regarded pretty much as a joke through '75. Wilson tackled 13 GPs, failed to qualify twice, non-started once and finished six times with tenth as his best at Watkins Glen. The prototype crashed heavily on its debut in Buenos Aires, and '02 ran in Brazil, now with twin rear radiators and more robust rear suspension to obviate the cause of the Argentinian crash. New chassis '03 appeared in France and was used for the rest of the year.

The car was quite hopeless, Wilson mediocre, and for 1976 his double World Champion brother Emerson was persuaded to join him, reputedly for a ton of Copersucar money. All Brazil held its breath . . . but to no avail, for the Copersucar team achieved less than Emerson's potential.

Four Divila-designed FD04 types were now produced, using in-line hip radiators cowled into shapely flaring side pods and featuring a full-width chisel nose with wide airfoil ahead of it, like the Hesketh 308B. Emerson was sixth on luck and reliability at Long Beach and Monaco but failed to qualify in Belgium. Another sixth came in the British GP but hopeful Brazilian team-mate Ingo Hoffman had only four drives, failing to qualify in three of them and reaching 11th in his home GP, driving 'FD01/3'. Emerson drove 'FD04/2' in Spain, '1 again until France where '3 appeared, and '4 from Holland to the end of the season.

The FD04s ran on into 1977 before ex-Ensign designer Dave Baldwin produced his replacement Fittipaldi F5 (no 'D' for Divila here), three being built. They looked like developed Ensign LNF75s, but Baldwin left abruptly just before his first F5's debut in the French GP and development stalled. Emerson's driving and the cars' reliability won fourth places in Argentina and Brazil as well as fifth at Long Beach; later another fourth came in Holland but he failed to qualify in Germany and Italy. Poor Hoffman ran only in South America, retiring and finishing seventh. They drove old 'FD04/3' and '1 in those races, Emerson using 'F5/1' from France and 'F5/2' from Germany on.

The brothers hired Giacomo Caliri's Fly Studio consultancy to update the Baldwin design as the F5A wing-car for 1978. At last Emerson became almost competitive – second in Brazil, fourth in Germany and Austria, fifth in Holland and the USA and sixth in Sweden, gaining 17 points and seventh place in the Constructors' Championship – although the car never looked a potential race winner.

For 1979 the Fittipaldis hired ex-Lotus designer Ralph Bellamy to build them a second-generation wing-car and he produced the rearward-podded needle-nosed F6A for them in São Paulo, which looked sensational but flopped. It was discarded and the old Caliri aerodynamic-pack F5As were updated instead. Subsequently, the two F6As built were modified for use later in the year.

Emerson started all 15 GPs, retired from seven, his only score being sixth in Argentina, though he was eighth in Italy and Canada, and seventh in the USA. Alex Ribeiro failed to qualify the second car in the North American races.

For 1980 Fittipaldi Automotive merged with the remnants of Wolf with Harvey Postlethwaite designing new F8 cars for Emerson and Rosberg, after beginning the season with ex-Wolf honeycomb cars. The new year's 'F7/1' was ex-Wolf 'WR8' and 'F7/2' ex-Wolf 'WR7' while chassis 'F7/3' was completely new. Emerson normally raced '1, Rosberg '2, with '3 the spare car raced by the Finn at Long Beach.

The completely new, long-podded, short-nosed 'F8/1' made its bow in the British GP driven by Emerson, was crashed by Rosberg at the Österreichring and quickly rebuilt around a new tub. Chassis 'F8/2' was new in Germany, Rosberg racing it twice, Emerson five times. Rosberg placed third in Argentina and fifth in Italy, while he was also seventh at Zolder but non-qualified for three other races. Emerson, meanwhile, inherited third at Long Beach and was sixth at Monaco, starting all 14 GPs and retiring from six.

Emerson hung up his helmet at this point; sponsorship was drying up and Postlethwaite joined Ferrari. Gary Thomas developed the F8C for 1981, three chassis running for Rosberg and Chico Serra; 'F8C/2' using a 1980 tub, 'F8C/3' being built new and a third chassis, 'F8C/4', first appearing as a spare tub at Kyalami and later completed for Serra to drive from Long Beach. With poor backing, poor engines and poorer tyres Fittipaldi stood no chance. Rosberg retired from six of the first nine GPs, finished 9-12 and non-qualifying in the others. In the last six races his entry was scratched once, he non-qualified four times and was tenth at Las Vegas to end the year. Serra had two finishes, 7-11, retired from his three

Alboreto's 1985 Ferrari 156 in Austria when the team suffered several engine failures but salvaged third place.

The Caliri-styled Copersucar-Fittipaldi F5A worked reasonably well in the former double-World Champion's hands, here leading de Angelis's Shadow DN9B, Buenos Aires, 1979.

other races and non-qualified eight times, non-started once and was scratched from the Austrian GP.

In Fittipaldi's case there was life after death. They floundered through 1982, making a one-car entry for Serra, stripping their 1981 cars, rebuilding '3 and the latest '5 to F8D specification, while '4 remained in their Reading works as a spare tub. One Richard Divila/Tim Wright-designed F9 emerged at the British GP to be driven subsequently by Serra as the team's swansong. The Cosworth era was gone, and a turbocharged engine was vital for success. Serra fought his qualification battles well, starting in nine races, finishing six and placing sixth for a point at Zolder and seventh, just out of the points, in Austria.

Through the winter of 1982/83, the brothers tried to raise new sponsorship, but failed; early in the new year the author bought a DFV from them and it seemed like the kiss of death, for they took the money and closed their Reading works within the hour . . . was it something I said?

Hesketh

Lord Alexander Fermor-Hesketh was a very young, very wealthy enthusiast who entered Formula 3 racing with a Dastle car in the early Seventies, his little team full of knock-about if rather juvenile fun, but run by the experienced Anthony 'Bubbles' Horsley. They provided James Hunt with Formula 2 and Formula 1 Surtees experience in 1972, and he made their name in 1973 driving a new Formula 1 March engineered by Dr Harvey Postlethwaite, previously with March.

The team was based at Hesketh's stately home, Easton Neston, near Towcester, Northamptonshire, within earshot of Silverstone circuit. Elated by their March success, Hesketh Racing built an all-new Postlethwaite-designed Cosworth/Hewland car for 1974. He drew on his considerable aerodynamic knowledge and produced a shapely wedge-elevation, Coke bottle planform monocoque car known as the Hesketh 308. In initial form it used a nose radiator but would subsequently be revised, introducing in-line hip radiators and a wide blade nose with full-width wing ahead.

Hunt tested '308-1' in Brazil early in 1974, it

qualified on pole at Brands Hatch but retired with bad handling in the race. At Kyalami a driveshaft joint failed but on home ground at Silverstone Hunt put '308-1' on pole again, set fastest lap and won the International Trophy on merit. In the next five GPs he drove '308-2', finishing only once, third in Sweden. This car was badly damaged in the French GP and was rebuilt around a new tub in late-1974 with rubber-controlled front suspension and new bodywork.

The 308s were competitive in Hunt's hands but the question became 'Is it the car, or is it the driver?', for they seldom qualified well at GP level and were unreliable. Chassis '308-3' was used from the German GP, finishing third in Austria but chassis '2 with blade nose raced in Canada and the USA, finishing fourth and third respectively.

This promising debut season left Hesketh sixth in the Constructors' Championship with 15 points, and for 1975 Postlethwaite further developed the 308B, while a replacement all-new 308C was under development. He had experimented briefly with rubber cone suspen-

sion medium but would alternate with conventional coil-springs after the 1975 season had begun. Hesketh sought reliability in '308-3', Hunt finishing second and sixth in Argentina and Brazil, using rubber suspension medium, while he usually raced '308-2' thereafter.

Hesketh had no external sponsor and now — despite the continuing parties and high jinks — money was very tight. For the Spanish GP, '308-1' was sold to private entrant Harry Stiller for Alan Jones to drive; both Heskeths, works and private, crashed. Rob Walker entered the Jones car later, while Horsley rented '308-3' to Torsten Palm for Monaco (non-qualifying) and Sweden (tenth).

Jones showed promise but achieved little. Hunt's '308-2' was the sole Hesketh representative at Zandvoort and Horsley's team actually won on tyre-change strategy in a wet-dry race, after qualifying on row two. Hunt qualified there again in the next race, the French GP, finishing second, but was out of luck until Österreichring where he qualified on the front row and finished second. In the latter race, rent-a-driver Brett Lunger was 13th in '308-3'.

The all-new shallow-chassis, in-line hip radiator 308C made its race debut in the 'Swiss' GP at Dijon, but rigidity, in suspension as well as chassis, was deficient. Hunt could only finish eighth. The car felt queasy under him; despite this, he finished fifth at Monza, where Lunger reached tenth in '308-3', and at Watkins Glen, where Hunt always went well, the 308C finished fourth but Lunger crashed.

Meanwhile old '308-1' had been sold to German privateer Harald Ertl, who performed most respectably on a tight budget, eighth in Germany, ninth at Monza.

Lord Hesketh decided to cut his losses and withdrew from Formula 1 at the end of '75, selling the 308Cs to Walter Wolf who also took some of the staff and Dr Postlethwaite's services. Hunt went to McLaren, becoming World Champion but Horsley preserved the Easton Neston company as Cosworth DFV engine-preparation specialists and continued to prepare and enter the old 308B or updated-spec 308D cars for paying customers.

Ertl raced '308/3' throughout 1976 achieving reliable results, including seventh in the British GP and eighths in Austria and Japan. Hesketh Racing ran Guy Edwards in '308/2', without distinction, until it was written off in the Lauda crash at the Nürburgring. New chassis '308/4' was used by Stommelen in Austria, then by Edwards, and Alex Ribeiro in the USA.

The irrepressible Horsley found new rent-a-drive customers for 1977 and young engineer Frank Dernie produced five distinctively tapered new 308Es for them. Hopeful drivers included Rupert Keegan; Ertl, who was going no further after a good run and who left in mid-season; Hector Rebaque, who had great difficulty qualifying; and Ian Ashley, who suffered similarly and was badly hurt in a terrible practice accident in Canada, which destroyed '308E-3'. Keegan demolished 'E-1 in the race, ending Hesketh's season.

Into 1978 Divina Galica, the girl driver, non-qualified for the South American GPs and crashed at Silverstone, as did Daly in old 'E-1. Cheever qualified 'E-5 for Kyalami but had an oil pipe fail after only eight laps, and Daly tried and failed to qualify chassis '5 at Long Beach and Belgium, and 'E4 in Monaco. By May, chassis '5 had been sold to John Cooper, already owning an ex-Wolf-Williams 308C, for national British Formula 1, and Hesketh's racing days were over.

James Hunt's Hesketh 308 at Zandvoort, Dutch GP 1974, shows off its flat-topped, curve-sided tub form, bluff nose with large horizontal splitter and rear wing.

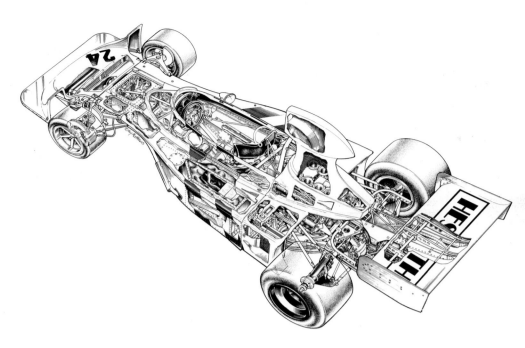

The Postlethwaite-designed Hesketh 308, in 1974 form with nose radiator and hip oil cooler, was subsequently modified to run with in-line hip water radiators.

Hill

Former double World Champion driver Graham Hill had established his Embassy Racing team in 1973 driving a Shadow DN1 and in 1974 commissioned construction of the Lola T370s. During the 1974/75 winter he then backed design and construction of a developed version of the T370, known initially as the Lola T371 but which was very quickly and more logically renamed the Hill GH1.

It was Lola-like, with water radiators podded just behind the front wheels *à la* Ferrari, but the monocoque was slightly triangular in section with inward-sloping side panels. It was Cosworth-powered of course. Design was by youthful Andy Smallman, a former Lola employee who had been seconded to the team. The new cars' tubs were made by John Thompson's TC Prototypes company, four being completed. The prototype 'GH1/1' made its debut in South Africa '75, where Stommelen finished seventh.

Hill himself was no longer driving seriously and for the Spanish GP at Barcelona Migault drove 'GH1/1' and Stommelen took brand new 'GH1/2'. This car ran a new experimental carbon-fibre rear wing post, against its manufacturer's recommendation on this rugged circuit, and after an early field-decimating multiple accident Stommelen actually led under heavy pressure. Over the severe hump into the first corner where the famous Lotus 49B wing collapses had occurred in 1969, the Hill's wing post failed, pitching Stommelen into a huge accident which killed five bystanders, demolished the car and caused the race to be abandoned.

Graham failed to qualify in his swansong outing at Monaco, and thereafter ran his cars for newcomer Tony Brise, Jones, Migault, Schuppan and – later in the year – the recovered Stommelen. Brise ran nine races, finishing five times, 6-7-7-'15'-15. His sixth place came second time out, in Sweden. The car by no means set the world on fire but it was a competent design while Brise showed great promise.

Jones drove four times, with a 100 per cent record of finishes, 13-16-10-5. His fifth place in Germany added two more team points, giving an aggregate of three to put the Hill team into

11th place in that season's Constructors' Cup competition. Migault drove only once more after Spain, at Zolder; Schuppan retired in Sweden and Stommelen was 16th in Austria before retiring in Italy.

Smallman designed a new part-pyramid section tub for 1976, the Hill GH2. It reputedly had many problems in initial testing at Ricard that November, and Graham flew Brise, Smallman and other team members home that evening contemplating some weeks of hard work to put it all right. Arriving over London in fog, their private aircraft struck the grasping branches of a tree on Arkley golf course and crashed – all on board were killed. 'GH2/1' rests today in the National Motor Museum at Beaulieu, Hampshire, as a memorial to one of Britain's best-loved racing drivers and his unfortunate team.

Honda

The Japanese Honda Motor Company had rapidly spreadeagled all opposition in motor cycle racing after a tentative start, and in 1964 set out to do the same in Formula 1 with an unusual transverse V12-engined spaceframe-chassised RA271 design. A regular two-car works team then ran improved RA272 machines during 1965 and by the end of that season they had clearly the most powerful engine, and Ginther easily won the Mexican GP for them.

Unfortunately for Honda, this was the final race of the 1500 cc Formula, so their potentially dominant RA272 was left obsolescent, all dressed up with nowhere to go.

Undismayed, indeed greatly encouraged, Honda R&D headed by engineer Yoshio Nakamura concentrated intense effort upon 3-litre development for 1966.

The new 3-litre RA273 V12 was late appearing and made its debut in the Italian GP at Monza in September, where it instantly impressed as the largest and most powerful car in Formula 1. Ginther drove bravely, the car may have been rather slow and unwieldy through the corners, but it accelerated fiercely and was very fast at the end of the straights.

The V12 engine had its power take-off amidships, geared down to an output shaft, so in effect it was actually two V6 engines in tandem. If it had used the conventional 60-degree vee angle, the take-off shaft under the crank would have made it uncomfortably tall, but Honda chose a 90-degree angle (unusual for a V12) instead, which made it

uncomfortably wide. They then applied their motor cycle engine experience to the full, by using roller bearings everywhere rather than plain bearings, which offered theoretical advantages in decreased friction but which physically made the engine uncomfortably big and heavy. Motor cycle practice also extended to the four-valve-per-cylinder combustion chamber design, which itself was being tried very successfully in their contemporary 1-litre Formula 2 racing engine, which would dominate the class in Brabham's factory cars.

Overall, the Honda RA273 V12 is a classic example of 'an engine man's engine', with little practical thought devoted to the kind of chassis necessary to carry it.

Also in accordance with motor cycle practice, in which low all-up weights and multi-speed gearboxes were common, the V12's peak power and torque were confined to a narrow band at the top of its rev range, making the five-speed gearbox inadequate for the driver to keep the engine working at its optimum speed on the tighter road circuits. Power circuits like Spa, Reims and Monza were an increasingly endangered species, yet with the massive excess weight which the Honda had to brake and accelerate in every corner these would be the very circuits to which it was best suited.

The full-length aluminium monocoque had to carry a huge fuel load and was stiffened by a fully stressed scuttle section above the driver's legs. The completed car when dry weighed no less than 740 kg (1631 lb) – nearly 40 per cent more than the legal minimum. It was claimed to possess 420 bhp at 10,000 rpm, yet that was only some 25 per cent more than the average of its opposition, all of which were at least 15 per cent lighter. In fact it seems doubtful if in Monza form the engine had more than 380 bhp and though the V12s seemed to begin life with great power, they then deteriorated markedly with age despite Honda's best rebuild efforts.

At Monza the prototype RA273 chassis 'F-101', with its spectacular snake pit of exhausts within the engine vee, qualified on the second row of the grid and was running second in the race – deafening everyone present – when a rear tyre deflated and pitched Ginther into an almighty accident in the high-speed *Curva Grande*. Chassis 'F-101' was used-up . . .

Two new cars, 'F-102' and 'F-103' appeared in the next race at Watkins Glen, driven by Ginther and Bucknum, '102' featuring a 7.75 in. wider track. In Mexico, Ginther led for the first two laps in this car but progressively lost power – a habit typical of the old RA272 transverse V12 cars – and finished fourth.

For 1967 Honda R&D ceded racing responsibility for their cars to former multiple motor cycle World Champion, and 1964 motor racing Champion Driver, John Surtees. He set up Honda Racing in Slough, England, to campaign the developed V12s. Unfortunately, his faith in Honda doing to the Formula 1 world what they had done to motor cycling was misplaced. His two seasons with them coincided with a major expansion in their production car programmes which diverted attention from Formula 1 development, at Honda Racing's expense.

During negotiation, he had recognized limitations of their existing design, as they themselves had, and the 500 lb engine plus the giant chassis needed to carry it just had to go.

Modern advances in lubricant and plain bearing technology made roller bearings unnecessary. Honda had an all-new 360 lb plain-bearing V12 on the drawing board but it would clearly be a long time coming. Meanwhile, by using elektron castings in place of aluminium 90 lb was saved, while power was allegedly up to 412 bhp and 450 was considered within reach. A further 50 lb was saved by design of a two-shaft gearbox to replace the original three-shaft version.

Surtees began 1967 race-developing old 'F-102' with any worthwhile results regarded as a bonus. He took two third places although the car was slow in '67 company, while passenger car demands siphoned-off Honda's best R&D men, leaving him with an untried, inexperienced crew and the Formula 1 programme suffered while they learned. For example, at Kyalami two engines disintegrated in practice because fragments of broken file had been left inside them during assembly, Surtees finishing third with a bitsa engine lashed together from salvaged parts.

High-mileage chassis 'F-102' was rested at Monaco where Surtees raced 'F-103' but a wrong-specification and inadequate hose burst on the grid. 'F-103' was retired from further competition, having run only three races in its life, as Surtees concentrated development upon '102'.

Honda power showed at Spa, but there the engine blew up; then in its last two outings, at the British and German GPs, despite running poorly, Surtees was able to salvage sixth- and fourth-place finishes on mechanical sympathy.

This was the Formula 1 car with everything – excessive weight, indifferent road-holding, what Surtees described as 'hellish differential trouble' causing serious tyre wear, and chronic difficulties with Honda's own low-pressure fuel-injection system.

On slower circuits Surtees could gear it to keep between 8750 and 10,000 rpm in the meat of the narrow torque band, though it was marginal even then. On faster circuits a higher top gear increased ratio gaps so at various points around the circuit the Honda was right 'off the cam' with poor response until it came back into its working range. And at low engine speeds, fuel was drawn so slowly through the injection system that it was prone to heating up and evaporation, which caused the unmistakable and characteristic Honda misfire.

At Spa in 1966 Surtees had geared his Ferrari 312 for 176 mph and in 1967 there he geared the Honda for 190 mph at its peak power engine speed of 9500 rpm. It steadfastly refused to pull more than 8000 in practice . . .

Due to chassis structure limitations it had not been possible to change suspension pick-up points and the 1967 RA273 suspension was a compromise demanding spring rates some 30 per cent higher than ideal. This caused wheel patter at high speed when the car would wander and skip on Spa's super-fast straights. The two-shaft gearbox was successful but the elektron engine tried at Monaco and Zandvoort had expansion and pressurization problems, blowing out its oil, while the original-spec V12s were down to 408 bhp at Monaco and 385 again

thereafter. In Germany the fuel mixture became over-enriched, giving 4.5 mpg consumption, thereby using nearly 46 gallons for race distance or some 460 lb of fuel . . .

Surtees had gained approval to build a lighter chassis at Slough. He raced Lola CanAm cars in between Formula 1 commitments and had a close engineering relationship with the neighbouring Lola company and its founder, Eric Broadley. Now he drew heavily upon Lola's T190 Indianapolis car design. Honda chassis designer Sano came to Europe to assist and, to rush the car through, they adapted existing T190 tub sections wherever possible. The tub terminated behind the cockpit, where the engine would be slung in a multi-tubular subframe also supporting the gearbox and rear suspension.

This hybrid Honda RA300 was skinned on Lola's chassis jig, modified to Honda Racing requirements. The front bulkhead was identical, as were certain pressings, while radiator, pedals and so on came off the shelf and they also used the Lola T190 nose cone mould. But from the front bulkhead back the tub matched Sano's and Surtees's suspension requirements, quite different from the offset Indy Lola layout.

Every conceivable corner was cut to get the car ready but the team had to miss the Canadian GP and aim for the Italian at Monza in September. The car emerged weighing 1340 lb dry – a saving of 228 lb, 150 lb off the chassis alone – and the old system of six fuel tanks and six separate pumps was simplified to just three tanks and one pump, arranged to drain completely in contrast to the old system which always left four gallons unuseable. Because the car was lighter, consumption would be less, so tank capacity was cut from 50 gallons to 44. Back in Tokyo 'Naka-San' made the elektron engine reliable, got power back to 395 bhp (more than since Monaco), and by playing with exhaust pipes on the dyno improved power down around 8000 rpm.

The new car 'RA300/1' – dubbed the 'Hondola' by the press – won on its debut in a sensational finish at Monza.

It was used again in the US, with stronger wishbones, but fuel injection problems persisted; yet, despite diff trouble, Surtees finished fourth in Mexico.

Through the 1967/68 winter Honda decided to continue although Surtees had lost his major sponsor when BP pulled out. The RA300 was raced for the last time in South Africa but was now two seconds off the pace and could only finish eighth.

Honda's promised new lightweight RA301 chassis 'F-801' emerged at Jarama, flatter and lower than the RA273 but now with outboard front springs à la Brabham. But it was 90 lb heavier than the RA300. The revised engine used Formula 2 type valvegear with torsion bar valve springs, the inlets were in the vee, exhausts now outside, handling and fuel injection troubles persisted, yet Surtees ran third before gear selection failed. However, when we talk of anyone running in high-sounding positions in 1968, one must remember how thin the grids were that year. Only 13 cars started the Spanish GP.

At Monaco the RA301 gearbox broke again; at Spa Surtees had the power to lead until the rear suspension broke. He was second in the French GP, fifth in the British after a newly-fitted strutted wing collapsed and third in the US, but with whole-hearted factory involvement it would surely have been so much better.

A second RA301 chassis, 'F-802', was assembled at Slough, redesigned by Len Terry with

Top left, Ginther's Honda RA273 V12 challenges Parkes' Ferrari 312 V12, Monza 1966. Left, Surtees at Monza 1968 in the unsuccessful air-cooled RA302 V8 Honda's last run. The jury-rig oil cooler on top superseded the original internal oil/air mist cooling system.

parts made at his Poole works. It was skinned in magnesium instead of '801's aluminium to save precious weight, and the rear suspension was improved. Hobbs drove it at Monza, running sixth until a valve dropped, wrecking the engine. Surtees used '802 as his training car in the US and Canada but it was afflicted by various problems. It ended its career fifth in Mexico driven by Bonnier.

Meanwhile in mid-season an entirely new Honda RA302 had appeared, chassis 'F-801', tested by Surtees at Silverstone just prior to the French GP. He found it not yet raceworthy, but Mr Soichiro Honda himself was on a trade mission to France at that time and both he and the GP organizers wanted it to run, driven by Jo Schlesser.

The RA302 was extraordinary. It used an *air-cooled* 120-degree V8 engine with four valves per cylinder, all torsion-bar sprung. The engine was slung beneath a high-level extension boom protruding from the rear bulkhead of a truncated magnesium-skinned forward monocoque and driving via a new five-speed gearbox. Suspension was the only conventional part of this wholly Japanese designed and built newcomer.

Surtees still felt it was too new to be raced but Honda's visiting management insisted. The twitchy-handling RA302 was misfiring from the start, possibly due to rain being drawn into its gaping induction and cooling intakes and finding a way into the electrics, and poor Schlesser lost control when the V8 cut completely; the car climbed a bank and somersaulted, exploding into a furious magnesium blaze which killed its unfortunate driver.

A replacement RA302 chassis 'F-802' emerged in time for the Italian GP at Monza, lacking the oil-mist cooling of the prototype though the engine itself was still air-cooled. But Surtees used the V12's top end power to the utmost in practice to qualify on pole position only to go off the road in the race when Amon crashed the Ferrari in his path.

Honda withdrew from this enforcedly half-hearted and ultimately tragic Formula 1 programme at the end of 1968 but would return as a supplier of turbocharged 1500 cc engines in 1983.

Kauhsen

The German sports car driver-cum-entrant Willibald Kauhsen launched a Formula 1 project for 1978, commissioning Ford Cologne engineer Klaus Kapitza in conjunction with Professors Cramer, Gerhardt and Jaeger of the technical high school at Aachen. They conceived an advanced wing-car along Lotus 78 lines, while former Porsche engineer Kurt Chabek designed an aluminium monocoque using titanium extensively in its suspension and bracketry. It would use the Cosworth/Hewland power pack but Kauhsen and his driver Brancatelli got into a muddle with FISA's red tape, had to pay $30,000 merely to join the Championship series, and upon their debut in Spain found it was forfeit as a fine for failing to join in the correct manner at the start of the season.

Two Kauhsen WKs were at Jarama, '005' with fuel concentrated in a single cell behind the cockpit, the older '004' with extra side tanks like a Lotus 78. Kauhsen claimed three prototypes had been built and scrapped during development. If that was true, this was indeed an expensive and wasteful project, for in Jarama practice the WK was five seconds off the pace and failed to qualify.

The original flowing body style had been abandoned in favour of a flat rear-decked form with end-plate mounted rear wing. Lotus-like radiators sat in the side pod leading edges, while a large oil cooler resided in a lengthy nose-top duct.

Brancatelli reappeared in '005' to non-qualify for the Belgian GP. Thereupon Herr Kauhsen cut his losses and retired from Formula 1, leaving Brancatelli to fail to pre-qualify at Monaco, in the Merzario. Little Arturo Merzario subsequently negotiated to buy the Kauhsen wing-car hardware for his own specials, which hardly improved their class . . .

Kojima

The inaugural World Championship-qualifying Japanese Grand Prix in 1976 saw the debut of the Kojima KE007.

Matsuhisa Kojima was a former works Suzuki moto-cross rider. His Kojima Engineering company produced a series of nicely made, generally successful cars for national competition.

The KE007 used the standard Cosworth/Hewland power pack, hung on the rear of a neat riveted aluminium tub with hip radiators, semi-inboard top rocker arm front suspension and parallel link rear suspension. Front brakes were outboard, rears inboard, the black-liveried bodywork highly stylized with Ferrari-like engine-air ducting moulded around the cockpit. Design was largely by engineer Masao Ono, whose name had been connected with the hapless Maki, yet 'KE007-001' proved quite competitive driven at Fuji by Masahiro Hasemi – one of Japan's leading drivers.

He set fourth fastest time on Japanese Dunlop tyres in first practice but crashed heavily in the second session, severely damaging the tub. Kojima promptly completed a second tub overnight around which the car was rebuilt in time for the race, starting tenth on the grid. Determined to do well for Japan on race day, Hasemi was delayed by a stop to replace worn wet-weather tyres, then another stop – with nothing to lose – to fit qualifiers on which he set fastest race lap on the way to finishing eleventh and last.

For the 1977 Fuji race, two Kojima KE009s were developed and driven by Noritake Takahara and Kazuyoshi Hoshino, using Bridgestone tyres. At one stage during practice Hoshino was sixth quickest in '009/2 but the pair finally qualified 11th (Hoshino) and 19th. Takahara crashed '009/1 avoiding someone else's opening lap accident and Hoshino survived to finish 11th.

The German would-be Formula 1 entrant Willi Kauhsen showed interest in a Kojima to be driven by his Italian protégé Gianfranco Brancatelli in 1978 but opted to build his own Kauhsen cars instead – which proved to be his second mistake.

LEC

Another standard Cosworth/Hewland private-entry Formula 1 car, in this case financed by Charlie Purley – head of the LEC Refrigeration business in Bognor Regis, England – whose son David had raced Formula 1 March cars in 1973-74. The Purleys commissioned a design from ex-BRM engineer Mike Pilbeam, which was known as the LEC CRP1. It featured a distinctive angular riveted aluminium monocoque chassis, side radiators and inboard front suspension, and made its debut in the 1977 Race of Champions at Brands Hatch, where Purley finished respectably sixth, one lap down on the winning McLaren M23.

LEC failed to qualify for the Spanish GP but started in Belgium, finishing 13th, then placed 14th in Sweden, before crashing in the French GP at Dijon. During practice for the next race, the British GP at Silverstone, the CRP1 crashed violently when its throttles jammed open, apparently on extinguisher powder residue left in the system after an earlier minor incident.

David Purley survived the massive head-on impact despite severe injuries, and another LEC car was later built up with which he entered bush-league Formula 1 in 1979, but no significant progress would be made.

Ligier

Rugged French industrialist Guy Ligier spent some of his construction company fortunes to indulge his enthusiasm in motor racing, first as driver, later as performance and competition car constructor. He founded *Automobiles Ligier* at Vichy in 1969, producing a competition coupé powered by a 1.8 Cosworth FVC engine and known as the model JS1 in memory of Ligier's great friend and former team-mate Jo Schlesser – killed in the air-cooled Honda during the previous year's French GP.

In 1971 the Michel Têtu-designed Ligier JS2 appeared with 2.6 German Ford V6 engine, intended for production and in 1972 the racing JS3 ran successfully at Le Mans with mid-mounted Cosworth DFV engine.

Ligier was keen to re-enter Formula 1 and in December 1974 work was able to begin because he won sponsorship from SEITA, the French tobacco company marketing Gitanes brand cigarettes which had formerly backed the Matra-Simca sports car programmes.

SEITA enabled Ligier to use the Matra V12 engine, while Matra engineer Gérard Ducarouge moved to Ligier to assist on overall design and operation. Ligier chassis designer Michel Beaujon was also joined at Vichy by former Matra draughtsman Paul Carillo, and Charles Deutsch's SERA (*Société d'Etudes et de la Réalisation Automobile*) concern was commissioned to assist, represented by aerodynamicist Robert Choulet, working in their Eiffel wind tunnel facility.

Negotiations for supply of the V12 engine were settled in May 1975, even before Shadow's DN7-V12 had raced. Ducarouge had a good grasp 'on what not to do', Beaujon briefed Carillo and they produced the Ligier-Matra JS5 with a conventional monocoque which can be regarded as the logical development of the 1972 Matra MS120D, in line with 1975 state-of-the-art and rules. JS5 was a long-wheelbase, wide-track car, with inboard rocker arm front suspension and conventional rear end. Tub manufacture was sub-contracted to the Hurel-Dubois aerospace company at Vélizy, who would later assist Renault's entry to carbon-fibre technology.

Despite having been out of Formula 1 for three seasons, Matra Sports had kept contact through sports car racing into 1974. Georges Martin and Jean-François Robin had continued development of what was now their MS73 V12 engine.

On 29 October 1975, the Ligier-Gitanes JS5 prototype was unveiled at SEITA's Parisian HQ, where it was notable for its enormous airbox, brief full-width nose, and looked like a teapot on wheels. Ligier tested at Ricard on 5 November, SEITA's preferred driver Beltoise being overshadowed by Laffite whom Ligier signed up.

The new Ligier-Matra made its debut in Brazil '76 and Laffite finished fourth at Long Beach for the team's first points. New airbox restrictions from Spain onwards forced Ligier to abandon that huge airbox and pull the rear wing forward. At Zolder Laffite finished third behind the Ferrari 312T2s, three 12-cylinders in a row humbling the Cosworths.

Chassis 'JS5-02' made its race debut in Austria, this car having straight sides unlike the curvaceous prototype, Laffite finishing second with the best result of the season. At Monza he qualified on pole and finished third. He was seventh in the Drivers' table that year; Ligier fifth in the Constructors' Cup.

That December, a new JS7 tested at Ricard,

while the new Matra-Simca MS76 V12 engine
emerged. It had lost 27 mm in height between
the crankshaft centreline and sump floor, this
lowered engine taking the suspension pivots
lower with it. Oil radiators were repositioned
behind the front wheels, altering weight bias
forward, and the SERA-modified bodywork
was more rounded than JS5's, using a full-
width Ferrari-like front wing. The monocoque
itself was little changed. Norev sponsored the
team, allowing them to build a second JS7
ready for Kyalami to give Laffite an up-to-date
spare. He could choose between long and short
wheelbases and five- or six-speed gearboxes.

The new MS76 engine gave early trouble,
but on 19 June at Anderstorp Laffite started
from row four, settled for second behind
Andretti's Lotus 78, and was able to win when
the Lotus ran low on fuel.

A third JS7 became available at the German
GP, with its 20 cm narrower track raising top
speed. Laffite was second in Holland, unable to
catch Lauda's Ferrari, but the absence of a real
engineer on circuit was a handicap and the
engine did not reach expectations. Laffite
ended the season sixth in Japan.

SEITA were slow in confirming continued
support for 1978 due to restrictions on tobacco
advertizing in sport. Matra also considered
ending V12 development. The JS7 was therefore updated for the new year while the JS9
completed slowly, having long stabilizing rear
fins and Hewland FGA six-speed gearbox in
place of the heavier, slower-changing TL200
used previously.

These modifications were made to 'JS7-01' in
which Laffite came fifth at Kyalami, while '03
also reached fifth place at Long Beach. The first
true JS9 ran at Monaco where its lightweight
gearbox broke. Laffite had to drive the hybrid
'JS7/9-01' in Belgium, finishing fifth and
France, finishing seventh; while in the prototype JS9 he was third in Spain, seventh in
Sweden, third in Germany and eighth in
Holland.

A brand new 'JS9-02' appeared at Hockenheim with revised suspension geometry and
it was fifth in Austria and fourth at Monza
where the wailing Matra V12 was heard for the
last time in Europe, since Matra were withdrawing it at the end of the season. Development had ceased long-since, otherwise Ligier's
results might have been better. As it was, the
car was very reliable, Laffite retiring only twice
in the 16 races, and taking 19 Championship
points to give the team sixth place in their
Championship.

Beaujon and Ducarouge designed new
Cosworth-powered JS11s for 1979 and
developed a ground-effects form which would
set the early-season standard. For the first
time Ligier operated a two-car team. Three of
the new cars were ready for the Argentine GP,
Laffite racing chassis '02 and team-mate
Depailler '03 with '01 as spare.

The design featured deep venturi side pods
with sharp flip-ups ahead of the rear wheels,
against which they were closely sealed to use
the high rotation of the wheel as an extractor,
accelerating airflow below the underwings and
increasing download. Laffite promptly won in
Argentina and Brazil where Depailler was
second in a total Ligier demonstration.

The JS11s were immensely strongly constructed, looking like real blacksmith's cars,
but Ducarouge had appreciated better than
most how vital stiff structures would be when
downloaded as severely as the new ground-
effects era would permit. His moulded underwings, however, were too flexible.

It was surprising that Ligier failed to win the
1979 Championship. But their drivers had joint
number one status, and they would race each
other. Depailler hurt himself hang-gliding and
did not race again after Monaco. SEITA
insisted upon a French-speaking replacement,
accepting Ickx who had not driven a competitive F1 car for several years and who was no

longer 'hungry'. He proved unable to rob
Ligier's rivals of valuable points which might
assist Ligier and Laffite.

Before filing his vertical flight plan, Depailler, anxious to keep his own Drivers' title hopes
alive, knew it was crucial to win at Jarama, and
so he held off Laffite there who already had two
early-season wins behind him. Running in his
team-mate's turbulence, Laffite found his car
skittish, he missed a gearchange, and broke his
engine.

But in any case Ligier were unable to
maintain competitiveness in every race. They
say their setting-up instruments had become
inaccurate, and following Depailler's Belgian
crash they were unable to rebuild his car
accurately. It sounds as if they had also
distorted their chassis jig. Worse still, they
abandoned their SERA wind tunnel contract in
mid-season to move to the Government's
Institute des Arts et Métiers St Cyr facility – the
irascible and autocratic Guy Ligier being
well-connected in French political circles – and
the cars lost adhesion in July-August which
cost them dear, presumably because they had
lost their comparative baselines established in
the Eiffel tunnel.

They ran new side pods at the Österreichring
but it then took three races to support that
download with revised suspension geometry,
and although the JS11 ended the season as a
quicker car than early on, they would end up
only third in the Constructors' Championship,
Laffite fourth in the Drivers' table.

The JS11s were reworked for 1980 to
produce JS15s chassis '01-02-03-04. These
emerged in Argentina using a redesigned rear
end, new wing profiles, new skirt system and
revised suspension with the rear dampers
tucked tight against the Hewland FGB gearbox casing. For the faster circuit at Kyalami
new smaller side pods and rear wings were used
to improve straightline speed, while the larger
pod/wing 'slow circuit' set-up reappeared at
Long Beach. This fast circuit/slow circuit spec
set the style for the rest of the year. At Monaco
new extractors appeared in the side pods, and
in practice there a new wing and carbon-fibre
brake discs were tried but set aside. Further
modified side pods helped make the cars very
competitive at Jarama, while for Ricard the
cars were provided with low-drag small rear
wings and a new Williams-like engine cover,
being beaten only by Jones's heart and
Williams team forethought.

The JS15s ran at Brands Hatch in Monaco
trim, save for new 15 in. wheels which were
3 kg heavier than the original 13 in. type and

*Jaques Laffite's robust 1980 Ligier JS11/15-DFV
'01' at Ricard during another season when the
French team could easily have emerged as World
Champions.*

which caused tyre deflations wrecking their
race performance. A carbon-fibre tank
appeared on one car there.

A new fast circuit set-up appeared at
Hockenheim, using narrow 16 in. instead of the
normal 19 in. wide rear Goodyear tyres, and
with lowered but otherwise Kyalami-like side
pods. In Austria the narrow rear tyres overheated so had to be replaced and the Kyalami
standard pods replaced the lower Hockenheim
type. At Imola, Ligier returned to Long Beach
slow circuit set-up and the drivers complained
of poor grip. Brakes were modified for the
demands of Montreal, while in the US a device
was used to regulate download and make it
more consistent.

Ligier again tended to self-destruct. Their
tyre choice was seldom as good as Williams or
Brabham, they had preparation problems and
the two drivers, Laffite and Pironi, seemed to
rob each other of points rather than work
towards a common goal. The cars dominated in
France and Britain before delays, they could
have won Argentina, Brazil, Monaco and
Canada, but only won in Belgium – where
Pironi shone – and Germany, which went to
Laffite.

Both drivers made 14 GP starts, Laffite
finishing ten times to Pironi's eight, winning
the German GP and placing second at Kyalami
and Monaco, third at Ricard and Zandvoort.
Pironi won at Zolder, was second in France and
third at Kyalami, Montreal and Watkins Glen.
Ligier ended the season second to Williams in

*Cheever's Talbot-Ligier-Matra JS17-04 heads for
second place, Detroit 1982. The car was big and
heavy but got away from the tight corners very well.*

the Constructors' Championship, while Laffite was fourth, Pironi fifth in their competition.

For 1981, after two seasons with British Cosworth V8 power, Guy Ligier completed a new deal with Talbot to return to the Martin-designed Matra V12 engine. The revised and latest MS81 V12 averaged something over 510 bhp at 12,500 rpm and reintroduced that spine-tingling exhaust note to Formula 1 after a two-year absence.

Ducarouge and Beaujon designed a new JS17 car to carry the revised engine, and five cars would be built. The JS17 was the only contemporary Formula 1 car still to retain its oil tank between cockpit and engine. Unfortunately for Talbot-Ligier, this was the year of the sliding-skirt ban and lowering suspensions.

They set out with strictly legal cars which were soon rendered uncompetitive as others exploited the gaping loopholes in the law. Ligier tried lowering suspension first with two springs end-to-end on the same damper, the softer spring collapsing as speed and download rose to provide the required low-level ride height. At Imola they adopted a hydropneumatic system like Brabham's but ran into problems with suitable skirts.

For Spain, Matra provided a revised new engine, peaking now at 12,800 rpm instead of the 12,300 rpm they started the season with in South America. New suspension worked well there and Laffite enjoyed himself.

Laffite and Jabouille had been contracted to drive the cars but Jabouille had injured his legs severely in a Renault crash at the end of 1980 and he was not fit to drive starting the new season, Jarier standing in at Long Beach. Jabouille tried to drive 'JS17-03' at Rio but was unfit to race so Jarier stood in again while Laffite handled '02. In Argentina Jabouille raced his car, but both Talbot-Ligiers lacked grip and the engines were 800 rpm down due to ignition coil trouble.

At Imola, Jean-François Robin of Matra was explaining the engines were not reproducing their test-bed power in the cars. In Belgium

lighter Campagnolo wheels were adopted in place of the team's original Gottis, three-piece rear wings were fitted and the Citroen-developed lowering suspension – controlled by a gearbox sensor – began to work better, controlling pitch and porpoising in addition to ride height alone.

New skirts and an improved Matra injection pump appeared at Monaco while for Spain Laffite's car was the new chassis '04. This would be Jabouille's last race, Ligier persuading him to bow to the inevitable, give up driving and concentrate upon technical direction of the team.

In France, Tambay took Jabouille's place and both cars raced with 10 cm narrower front

The rugged Ligier chassis performed well with Matra-Talbot V12 engines in 1981-82. Note the massive centre fuel cell, slender engine, carbon cockpit stiffening.

track. By the time of the British GP Ducarouge had gone, moving to Autodelta Alfa Romeo. Tambay's chassis '03 sported revised bodywork around the radiator outlet ducts on top of the side pods. Wheel bearing problems troubled the team around this time, but in Austria Robin provided engines capable of an ear-splitting 13,000 rpm and, with Jabouille's sage advice selecting the right tyres and skirts, Laffite won. It was Ligier's first victory in over a year.

Tambay's new '05 was stiffened around the

Piola's breakdown of the 1980 Ligier JS15-DFV shows: 1, wing mounts; 2, brake master-cylinder; 3, front suspension fairing; 4, footbox; 5, brake duct; 6, Girling single calliper; 7, stub axle; 8, aluminium brake shroud; 9, floor bridge; 10, oil cooler; 11, water radiator; 12, skirt; 13, louvres, 14, water pot; 15, fuel pumps shield; 16, side pod frames; 17, emergency driver air; 18, water; 19, tank hatch; 20, body moulding; 21, underwing; 22, tyre fairing; 23, tank; 24, engine mount; 25, exhausts; 26, side plate; 27, engine cowl; 28, tailpipes; 29, bell-housing; 30, brake ducts; 31, Girling balanced callipers; 32, inboard spring/dampers; 33, crossbeams; 34, wing.

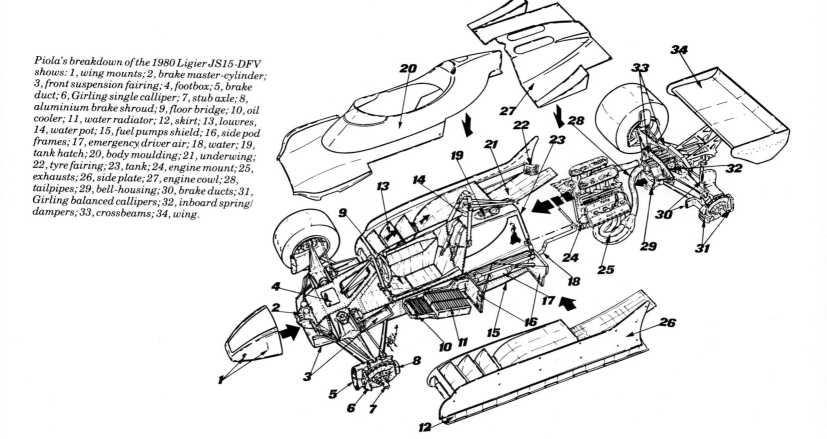

cockpit and through the rear end in time for Zandvoort, where Laffite was bundled off the road by his fellow Championship contender Reutemann's Williams. For Monza, cowls on top of the side pods enabled the team to run less rear wing incidence, gaining top speed. Yet another skirt change had been made and Laffite's brand-new '06 was stiffened like Tambay's, but he took over '05 for the race.

In Canada, Laffite strengthened his Championship challenge by racing from tenth on the grid to victory, and from having had a single point at the time of Imola, he went into the final round at Las Vegas with an outside chance of becoming World Champion. He ran second but had to change tyres, then recovered sixth place on the last corner of the last lap. Tambay had worked faithfully in Laffite's shadow but suffered an almighty accident on lap 3 at Las Vegas, completely destroying '06's forepart.

Both Talbot-Ligier and Laffite ended the season fourth in their respective Championships and continued to campaign the V12 engine in 1982 when Cheever joined the team. Initially the existing JS17s '02-4-5 and rebuilt '06 were updated and stiffened but the long-awaited Talbot turbocharged V6 was shelved.

A new JS19 design was introduced at Monaco, '01 for Cheever, '02 for Laffite, tailored to the regulations as Ligier read them, using full-length pod sections and skirts extending right to the tail, but the scrutineers ordered the sections aft of the rear wheels to be excised, so there went four months' development and 30 per cent download. The veins bulged on Guy Ligier's bald head . . .

A third new JS19, '03, appeared for Laffite at Brands Hatch; the team ended the season with Laffite's sixth at Detroit and third at the Österreichring, in addition to Cheever's second with luck on his side in Detroit, thirds at Zolder and Las Vegas and sixth at Monza, giving a total of 20 Constructors' Championship points and leaving Ligier eighth in the table.

Early in the season the JS17s were heavy cars amongst 1982 company. Their track was widened after Kyalami, Aerospatiale-made carbon-fibre discs were tried during practice at Zolder but again set aside. At Monaco the scrutineers forced them to remove nearly one metre of active section from the new JS19s. Their rear suspension links were completely enclosed within side pod panelling, leaving airflow uninterrupted, unlike the Lotus 80 in which the lower wishbone interrupted flow. At Detroit the American scrutineers followed Monaco's lead and ordered the skirts to be cut back to the centre of the rear wheels so the

solitary JS19 there, '01, never ran. Chassis '02 was in France at this time undergoing further wind tunnel testing at St Cyr, supervised by engineer Jean-Claude Guenard.

The JS19s with cut-back pods ran in Holland, where '02 was crashed, new car '03 replacing it at Brands Hatch, but the team was still in skirt sealing trouble and for the French race Guy Ligier decreed they should concentrate on the JS19s rather than waste further effort on the now uncompetitive JS17s. Altered side pods and suspension pick-ups appeared at Hockenheim, changed again for the 'Swiss' race at Dijon on Laffite's car, and again for Monza, while at Las Vegas the carbon-fibre centre section of the car had been reinforced. But that race saw the last appearance of the V12 engine in Formula 1, and this time it would not return.

The Talbot deal had ended and Ligier reverted to Cosworth power for 1983, starting the season with two hack cars converted from JS19 tubs '01 (used for testing only) and '02 which was raced by new driver Raoul Boesel at Spa but generally performed spare car duties. Chassis 'JS19-03' was also modified to Cosworth power and was raced regularly by Boesel while his team-mate Jarier ran brand new 'JS21-04' throughout the year, these cars being tailored by Michel Beaujon and Claude Galopin to new flat-bottom regulations with much-diminished side pods and slender stiletto lines.

In a turbocharged season, the Ligier JS21s – both hybrid and genuine – stood little chance and could only expect to pick up the crumbs. Boesel qualified for 13 of the 15 races, failing in Austria and Italy, and his best result was seventh at Long Beach, while Jarier started every race, but retired nine times and could only finish seventh at best, in Austria.

So the respected Ligier team, for the first time in their Formula 1 history, failed to score any points at all.

Ligier then won use of Renault's turbocharged V6 engine for 1984. New carbon-composite JS23 slimline chassis were designed by Beaujon and Galopin and three were ready for the start of the season, to be driven by de Cesaris and newcomer François Hesnault. They were unsuccessful and did nothing to impress. A fourth standard JS23 was ready for de Cesaris's use at Zolder. The old Ligier glory days were long past, and even when 'JS23-03' was updated to JS23B specification with pushrod suspension and revised inter-cooling in time for de Cesaris to race it in the last two events of the season, the modification work looked clumsy and ill-conceived; Ligier was a team which had lost its way.

Meanwhile Renault Sport had been forcibly reorganized, team director Gérard Larrousse carried the can for their lack of success and was dismissed, moving to Ligier and – to Renault's dismay – being accompanied by chassis designer Michel Tétu, himself an ex-Ligier engineer returning to the fold.

A new JS25 chassis for the Renault V6 engine was already on the stocks and Tétu developed it progressively during 1985 to achieve some good results although the French-blue cars would not look likely winners. Drivers were Laffite and de Cesaris and three new JS25s were ready for Rio where they were the heaviest in Formula 1, short of the Osella!

A fourth chassis was available for de Cesaris at Imola and '05 followed for Laffite at Ricard. The Italian driver had a chequered season, with too many accidents for Guy Ligier's taste, and after a spectacular somersault in Austria – much re-run worldwide on TV – he was dismissed and replaced by Philippe Streiff.

De Cesaris's 11 outings yielded only three finishes: fourth at Monaco, 14th and 10th. Nevertheless, the team's gradual re-emergence as a competitive force was evidenced by Laffite's eight reliable finishes from his 15 races (South Africa being boycotted on political grounds) and his finishing record read 6-6-8-12-3-3-11*-2; points scores in turn being at Rio, Monaco, in Britain, Germany and Australia.

Streiff's four races each yielded a reliable finish, he qualified well and even had the temerity to punt his team leader in the tail at Adelaide, attempting to turn his inherited third place for a team 2-3 into a second for himself and third for Laffite. As it was it very nearly spelled the end of the team's hopes, for he smashed his left-front suspension and only just limped past the flag, his antics being something unmatched even by de Cesaris at his wildest. His placings were 10-9-8-3, and Ligier ended the season in justifiably optimistic mood.

Having once fallen off the tightrope, the hardest act is to climb back onto it. Ligier looked close to having achieved that by the end of our period.

Lola

Eric Broadley's Lola Cars company built spaceframe Climax V8-engined Formula 1 cars for John Surtees's Bowmaker team in 1962 but did not return to Formula 1 until 1974. In that year, they were commissioned by Graham Hill to build Cosworth/Hewland cars to replace his Embassy-sponsored team's Shadow DN1 of 1973.

Edwards hurt his arm in a Formula 5000 crash so Gethin drove the second car in the British GP at Brands Hatch. However, its engine broke on the warm-up lap so he took over the spare, set up for Hill, but after rattling around the cockpit like a pea in a drum for one lap, he quit. By the Austrian GP, Hill admitted: 'The more we experiment the more we come back to Lola's original design!' Edwards' replacement, Stommelen, crashed chassis '1 when a tyre deflated. They drove for the rest of the year, Hill eighth in Italy and the US, Stommelen 14th in Canada and 12th in the US.

Hill almost pulled off a deal to use the Alfa Romeo flat-12 engine in 1975, spare chassis '1 being fitted with a slave unit before negotiations collapsed and the engines went to Brabham instead.

The Lolas were reliably uncompetitive. A new Hill GH1 was built for 1975, but the old T370s appeared at the start of that season, Hill and Stommelen 10-13 in Argentina, 12-14 in

The 1985 Ligier-Renault JS25 turbo at Rio, an overweight original design developed to late-season competitiveness by Michel Tétu, prodigal returnee from Renault.

Lotus

Brazil, while Stommelen inherited seventh at Kyalami where Hill crashed in practice and did not start. Thereafter the ill-fated team concentrated upon their own Hill chassis. See also entry for Beatrice, page 165.

Colin Chapman's Team Lotus entered the new Formula in 1966 with little hope of defending successfully their 1965 World Championship titles, which had been won with Clark. The BRM H16-engined Type 43 which they slowly developed through 1966 is described in the Lotus 49 chapter (4), Lotus 72s are covered in Chapter 6, while the 78s and 79s are described in Chapter 10.

Meanwhile, early-1966 saw several elderly Lotuses competing, not least in Team's own hands, for they ran their monocoque Type 33s 'R9' and 'R11' with 2-litre BRM P56 and Coventry Climax V8 engines. Spence, Clark and Arundell drove them, while a completely new 33, 'R14', was completed for Clark in the British GP, pending raceworthiness of the 43-H16.

The private Parnell team's own built-from-parts 25/33, nicknamed *Percy*, was fitted with a 2-litre BRM V8 and performed well in Spence's hands, while their older 25s, 'R3' and 'R7', appeared briefly with 2.7 Climax four-cylinder power and even unmodified 1500 cc V8s from the old Formula.

Spence won the non-Championship South African GP in Team's 'R9', powered by the first of two stretched 2-litre Climax V8s specially built for Lotus. Arundell was fourth in this comeback race after grievous racing injuries, driving 'R11' with a 1500 Climax V8.

For the British GP, a BRM V8 went into 'R11' for Arundell but the mechanics left a rag in an oil-line and it blew up as soon as it started. The 2-litre Climaxes were reserved for Clark's spanking new 'R14', which finished fourth after losing brake fluid. In Holland he challenged the Repco Brabhams hard until a coolant leak left him third, and Spence was fifth in *Percy*. Clark set 'R14' on pole at the Nürburgring but crashed, and at Monza he drove '43/R1' while Spence was fifth in Parnell's 'R13', Arundell eighth in the outclassed 'R11'-BRM and local man 'Geki' ninth in 'R14'. Clark was third in the Gold Cup, Arundell sixth in 'R14' at Watkins Glen and seventh in 'R11' at Mexico City.

A second 43-H16 was ready for the 1967 South African GP when Hill joined Clark in what would become the Cosworth-powered superteam. Both 43s failed. *Percy* was driven by Irwin in the Race of Champions and by Courage in the Oulton Spring Trophy, before Irwin took him for Silverstone to finish seventh.

Team Lotus reappeared at Monaco where Clark ran 'R14' for the last time, retiring with a broken damper mounting, and Hill finished second in 'R11'-BRM.

Next time out, at Zandvoort, the Lotus 49 legend was born. Irwin was seventh there in *Percy*, Parnell concentrating on quasi-works BRM P261 and P83 H16 cars thereafter. Old 'R11', meanwhile, had been sold to Craig Fisher in Canada, placing 11th at Mosport but non-starting in Mexico due to a faulty fuel metering unit.

While the Lotus 49s ran their successful course, Colin tried to replace them in 1969 with a sophisticated four-wheel drive design, the Type 63. Traction had become a problem early in 1968 with Cosworth V8 power and abrupt mid-range torque, and four-wheel drive was considered the cure-all.

Coincidentally, the wing era dawned, solving the traction problem more cheaply, with less complication and significantly less weight.

The engineers interested in 4WD were unconvinced, Colin and his people amongst

them. Two Type 63s were built, using a broad, shallow, full-length monocoque tub, whose DFV engine was turned about-face and drove thence to front and rear final-drives. The experiment flopped, though Rindt was finally persuaded to take it seriously enough to place '63/1' second in the minor Oulton Park Gold Cup, which would be the best performance of the 1969 4WD crop.

Cadet driver John Miles made most of the 63, while Bonnier drove one briefly at Silverstone. But putting power through the steerable front wheels overwhelmed contemporary tyre technology, and Formula 1 4WD evaporated in terminal understeer, excess weight and complication.

Meanwhile, in 1968, Hill had qualified fastest in practice for a USAC road race at Mosport in Canada driving one of the Indianapolis 4WD Lotus 56 turbine cars. He enthused about how fabulous the smooth-riding turbo car felt for road racing.

Colin discussed a plan with Pratt & Whitney to produce 3-litre equivalency gas turbine engines for Formula 1. Three cars would have been built for 1969 but P&W's prime interest was Indy, rather than European Formula 1, and development lagged.

At Monaco in 1970, Colin had a chance encounter with his P&W contact and heard that a 3-litre equivalent turbine was nearly ready at last. The fourth Indy Type 56 tub was lying in store at Hethel, and it was rigged with the prototype '3-litre' engine and tested that autumn. It was hoped to startle the opposition on the high-speed track at Monza but braking and throttle lag were still problematic for road racing, so the Type 56B as it was known was held back for '71.

Its debut came at the Race of Champions, Fittipaldi driving. It bottomed very badly and finally wiped off its right-rear suspension. Wisell ran briefly fifth at Oulton Park, then Fittipaldi qualified on the front row at Silverstone (using bigger brakes) and finished third in heat two.

The taper-sided hull was then bulged to carry extra fuel for full-length GP racing. Dave Walker drove at Hockenheim in June but the engine failed in practice and it did not race.

A replacement engine was available for the Dutch GP; it rained and Walker had a real chance in the smooth 4WD car, only to crash. Wisell ran in the British GP, then for Monza the 56B was sprayed gold and black to form Lotus's sole entry since legal problems following Rindt's fatal crash there in 1970 prevented them entering under their own name and livery.

Fittipaldi drove, ambient temperatures were too high for the turbine to generate peak power and he soldiered home eighth. One week later, in the *Preis der Nationen* F5000 race at Hockenheim, Fittipaldi qualified on the front row and finished second after setting fastest lap – end of experiment, on a fairly high note.

The Type 72s remained centre-stage and their remarkable performance on new Goodyear tyres in Brazil '73 persuaded Chapman that all they needed to stay ahead was a '100 lb lighter 72'. Ex-Brabham and McLaren designer Ralph Bellamy was detailed to design it, which involved 72-type suspensions and geometries being attached to an all-new tub incorporating some innovations.

The new Type 76 tub's shape was a shallow and slender delta-form. Initially, electro-magnetic clutch operation featured, controlled from a gear-knob button. The idea was to enable the driver to brake with his left foot and maintain engine revs with the other, Lotus having learned the value of such techniques at Indianapolis. Driver Peterson was particularly enthusiastic but the system proved more trouble than it was worth and was scrapped.

The Type 76 was the first Lotus to be designed and built entirely under the John Player Special sponsorship regime and a new

numbering system was henceforth used for this 'Mark I' chassis type. Chassis '76/1' carried a plate reading 'JPS/9', to follow on from the existing Lotus 72 series after '72/8' (which was plated 'JPS/8') . . . still with me? The second new car, '76/2', became 'JPS/10' but the specialist press would not play ball and preferred to use their own, more logical manner of indicating who did what with which.

The 76s' systems played up and Peterson eventually persuaded Chapman that the proven old 72s would be more effective; so they were. The 76s were relegated to spare-car duties at Monaco and Anderstorp, though on the way home from Anderstorp, Team tested at Zandvoort where Peterson crashed '76/1' heavily, knocking himself out when some experimental brake pads gave trouble.

For the Dutch GP there, Ickx's spare '76/2' ran with its water radiators far forward behind the front wheels, shrouded in new side panelling. Colin told me: 'When we got the 76s their systems didn't work – fuel, oil, cooling and brakes didn't work, and the steering wasn't very good. Nothing very serious . . . half-way through the programme neither Ronnie nor Ickx would drive them and then we put one on the scales and it weighed the same as the old 72! Its rear hubs were cracking and I had this terrible fear of a wheel coming off. I just couldn't live with that so I said to Ralph, "Look there's no point in sorting it all out; if we do, all we've got is a car the same weight as the 72 with fifty new problems . . ."'

The repaired '76/1' went to North America as spare at the end of 1974, Schenken qualifying it as second alternate and taking off after the field at Watkins Glen. He was disqualified on lap 6: a fitting finale to the Type 76's brief career.

Early in 1975 a new design team was set up at Hethel under Team Manager Peter Warr, including Mike Cooke, Geoff Aldridge and Martin Ogilvie, briefed to translate Colin's latest Formula 1 concept into metal, while in parallel Ralph Bellamy worked on a new Lotus 'queerbox' transmission for Chapman's pet theories about two-pedal driving.

He wanted to learn about the effects of long and short wheelbases, wide and narrow tracks, and the Type 77 was designed in effect as an experimental interim car, working towards the Type 78 which would hopefully put Lotus back on top in 1977.

The new Type 77, or John Player Special Mark II, featured an Aldridge-designed slender aluminium tub, to which Martin Ogilvie attached a structural calliper inboard brake system in which the callipers doubled as pick-ups for the suspension links and wishbones. Hip radiators appeared in neat side pods.

Brazil opened the World Championship, Peterson crashed '77/2' ('JPS/12') after coolant leaked onto a rear tyre, and after an overnight rebuild it developed steering trouble. Andretti had a one-off drive in '77/1' ('JPS/11') and in the race the two collided, as had the luckless 76s on their Kyalami debut two years before.

Peterson heeded the omen and joined March, Team Lotus engaging the inexperienced Bob Evans and Gunnar Nilsson for South Africa, Brands Hatch and Long Beach; Nilsson drove alone at Silverstone.

Like the 72 before it, the 77 failed to heat its front tyres adequately, so freelance Len Terry did a quick redesign to outboard front brakes, using production Ralt F2/F3 uprights. The first set was fitted to '72/2' then became standard.

Andretti joined full-time from the Spanish GP onwards and Tony Southgate moved to the team from Shadow immediately that race was over. He found himself being flown by Colin straight to the Chapman holiday home in Ibiza where he was grilled for three days solid by the Lotus boss.

Tony described the experience: 'After the steady plod at Shadow it was like being dragged from a convalescent home and dropped in the middle of a mad 'ouse . . .'

Lotus thinking on weight distribution, for example, was very outdated. Nevertheless, they caught up, stiffened the 77's structures and Andretti won the Japanese GP in 'JPS/11' ending the year.

Although 'JPS/14' ('77/3', there being no '13' in the JPS numbering series) had been crashed heavily in testing at Anderstorp by Andretti, he qualified on the front row for the Swedish GP and led 45 laps until his engine exploded. The damaged car was rebuilt with more forward weight bias, a Southgate nose oil cooler mount like the Shadow's, while, later, a cockpit-adjustable rear anti-roll bar (Andretti Indy practice) and a lightweight air starter like McLaren's became standard.

Revised front suspension geometry appeared at Monza, as did deeper aerodynamic skirts to control airflow beneath the hull. In North America the 77s ran a 4 in. shorter wheelbase and brush skirts as a Type 78 development. Andretti's win at Fuji was supported by Nilsson finishing sixth; Team were back in business.

The Type 78/79s set new performance standards and began the ground-effects car revolution through 1977-78 but in 1979 the opposition raced ahead as Lotus became bogged down in development of their Type 80, which flopped.

The thinking behind the 80's design was to maximize underwing area to capitalize upon the download generated by ground-effect side pods fringed with sliding skirts. In the 80, the underwings extended back through the rear suspension to the car's tail, download acting around the car's notional centre of gravity in order to dispense with conventional nose and tail aerofoils to trim it out.

Gordon Murray of Brabham had anticipated this Lotus development in his original BT48-Alfa V12 design but encountered immediate 'porpoising' problems in practice for the Argentinian race, then ripping off most of the underwing. At Kyalami, the BT48s ran safely without nose fins and found the way ahead, while Lotus's Type 80 had yet to emerge.

This was based around a slim honeycomb aluminium monocoque tub, with side pods curving inside the rear wheels and the sliding skirts rashly following this curve. Additional skirts hung beneath the nose section, and air passing underneath was encouraged to exit upwards through a duct with an adjustable trim-tab sitting inside. In this way the tab was masked by the nose section in frontal area, yet could trim the car front to rear. The whole Type 80 rear end was new, the gearbox/clutch/oil tank casting being beautifully made, like the rest of the car.

The prototype, known as '80/1' to enthusiasts or 'ML23' in the new Martini-sponsored team's latest system, gave trouble in testing. Its under-nose skirts could not survive pitch, which ground them off against the road surface as the car porpoised. They were removed and conventional nose fins appeared each side. It had been intended that when the original nose section became effective, the separate rear wing between its tall end plates could be deleted, leaving just the full-width rear trim-tab on the bodywork to do the job alone.

The 80 made a decent race debut at Jarama, where Andretti finished third and set fastest lap. However, in testing at Dijon, Peter Wright recalls: 'we suddenly encountered the most dreadful bouncing problems', possibly exacerbated by the S-bend main skirts skewing and jamming in their slides to break suction against the road, then freeing and remaking the seal to slam on high download again. Stiffening the suspension to control this pitch made the car skittish and again uncontrollable in an agonizing descending spiral of failure and frustration.

Left, the complexities of the 1969 Lotus 63 4WD car uncovered in the Silverstone pits. Below, the Lotus 76 as unveiled to the press in 1974 with multi-wedge forms, twin rear wings, hip radiators and two-pedal control beneath the skin. As a 100-lb lighter 72 it was an abject failure.

At the height of the season the 80's problems could not be solved, so it was set aside after the French GP and another Team Lotus failure passed into history. Three Type 80s had been built.

For 1980, the 'ML' Martini-Lotus prefix became 'EL' for Essex-Lotus after another sponsorship change, and tests during the winter with a heavily modified 79X, which was a cross between the 79 and 80, led to construction of a new Type 81. The prototype was run by new team driver de Angelis in Buenos Aires, while '2 ran there driven by Andretti.

Three more Type 81s emerged during the season: '3 was new in South Africa as spare before being crashed mightily by de Angelis at Long Beach and subsequently completely rebuilt; chassis '4 emerged new in Monaco as spare and was promptly written off by Andretti in practice.

Lessons learned were incorporated in the Type 81B which used a new monocoque and '81/4's chassis-plate. It was completed in the paddock at Hockenheim, being raced first by newcomer Mansell in Austria and Holland, then crashed by him in Monza practice.

These tubby short-nosed Type 81s did not impress and Lotus struggled all season. Andretti was classified as a finisher only five times, 12-7-7-8-6, his only point being scored in the USA as the season ended. De Angelis was finding his feet in Formula 1 after his move to Lotus from Shadow amidst litigation and he did better, similarly being classified only five times but inheriting second in Brazil and placing fourth in Italy and the USA. Cadet driver Mansell retired in Austria and Holland, learning about the 81B but failing to qualify after his accident at Monza.

From their fourth position in the Constructors' table with 39 points in their troubled 1979 season, Team Lotus slipped to fifth with just 14 points in 1980.

Faced with the problem of massive ground-effects download now demanding ultra-stiff suspensions to support it, making both cars and drivers prone to physical failure, Team experimented late in 1980 with a Type 86 hack using a Type 81-like aluminium monocoque chassis. Colin's team conceived an effective twin-chassis design which would form the basis of the controversial Lotus 88.

Initially, Wright, Ogilvie and the other engineers appreciated that very light yet stiff bodywork was required and therefore used carbon panels with Nomex honeycomb sandwiched between. In search of further weight saving without compromising stiffness in a very confined cross-section monocoque hull, they made the next logical step – discarding aluminium sheet or honeycomb tub construction in favour of inherently stiffer but lighter, moulded carbon-composite.

Whereas McLaren was having its carbon tub set up for moulding at this time, Lotus formed their version from flat moulded sheets, the flat panels then being cut to shape, edges feathered, then seamed and bonded together to form the monocoque. The whole thing was done in about 12 weeks from start to finish, to form the basis of a conventional Type 87 and alternative 'twin-chassis' Type 88. This was the plot . . .

The 88's primary chassis consisted of the bodywork, supporting side pods, wings and radiators while riding independently within that structure was a secondary chassis composed of the monocoque tub, engine, gearbox and front and rear suspensions.

The outer or primary chassis could be seen as a massive one-piece, full-length, full-width enveloping wing acting direct upon the suspension uprights at all four corners. This was the way FISA would see it . . . though Lotus argued long and hard against their intention being construed in this way.

This 'primary' chassis was actually suspended on four coil/damper units coupled to the

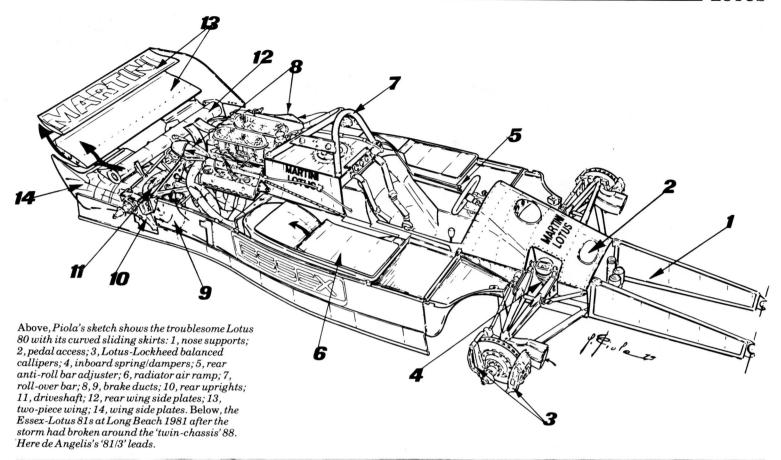

Above, *Piola's sketch shows the troublesome Lotus 80 with its curved sliding skirts: 1, nose supports; 2, pedal access; 3, Lotus-Lockheed balanced callipers; 4, inboard spring/dampers; 5, rear anti-roll bar adjuster; 6, radiator air ramp; 7, roll-over bar; 8, 9, brake ducts; 10, rear uprights; 11, driveshaft; 12, rear wing side plates; 13, two-piece wing; 14, wing side plates. Below, the Essex-Lotus 81s at Long Beach 1981 after the storm had broken around the 'twin-chassis' 88. Here de Angelis's '81/3' leads.*

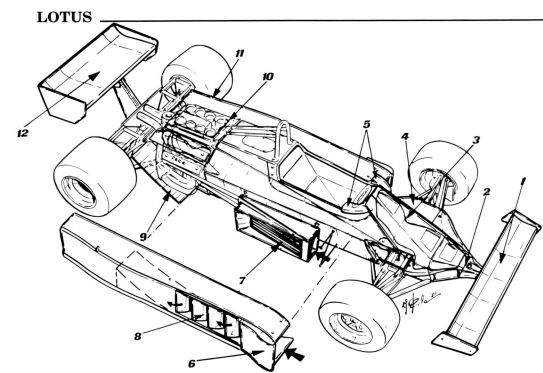

bottom of the wheel uprights. Dynamic loads were handled by the conventional rocker-arm/wishbone layout of the inner monocoque which was by the same token insulated from high aerodynamic loading. It was claimed to be the inner or secondary chassis.

This novel layout had much to commend it, as it harnessed ground-effect download yet protected the driver from its worst effects.

The prototype '88/1' was used by de Angelis in between vociferous protests at Long Beach, Rio and Buenos Aires, but was eventually ruled illegal and the rules changed to make it clear.

Had the 88 been accepted, at least one great driver might still be alive today and another's career might not have been ended . . .

Faced with the rejection of the 88 concept, Colin gained the support of the British RAC who said they would accept the concept in modified 88B form for the British GP at Silverstone. Consequently Type 88Bs were produced, but Ferrari, Talbot-Ligier and Alfa Romeo protested again, and FISA horned-in from Paris by stating flatly that the 88 concept and all derivatives *were* illegal and the RAC had no option but to agree, sending Team's mechanics into a 12-hour conversion job to strip the 88Bs and return them to 87 'single-chassis' specification.

Team had introduced these effective stand-by Type 87s '1 and '2 for Mansell and de Angelis in Monaco, '87/3' running at Silverstone for de Angelis, and '87/4' converted from '88B/4' for Mansell in the autumn fast-circuit races. New '87/5' was spare car at Monza. Meanwhile '88B/2' was converted from '87/2' for Mansell at Silverstone and then converted back to 87 form for second practice, while '88B/4' was completed for de Angelis at Silverstone but converted to '87/4' for Mansell at Hockenheim.

Amidst all this controversy, de Angelis put together a decent season, being withdrawn from Imola but otherwise starting all 14 GPs, and finishing ten times, 5-6-5-5-6-7-7-5-4-6, all but twice in the points in a consistent display of the Type 87's natural level.

Mansell was less consistent, failing to qualify at Silverstone after all the practice hullabaloo, finishing five of his 13 races, 11-3-6-7-4, three times scoring points. Team's seventh place in the Constructors' table was their lowest since 1975, but their 22 points showed an improvement over 1980.

The old Type 87s '2-3-4-5 appeared at Kyalami in 1982, '5 becoming a pullrod-suspension car. The new much-tidied Type 91 emerged at Rio and followed on from the 87-sequence chassis numbers, the prototype

tub '6 going to de Angelis, with '7 for Mansell. In tidying up the design, Peter Wright told me, 'We tried to take ten per cent weight off *everything.*'

Car '91/8' was new as spare at Zolder and '9 new as spare at Monaco, though the latter was not a successful tub and suffered relegation to show car duties (Team nicknaming it 'The Flexi-Flyer'). Chassis '10 was new, therefore, for Mansell ending the season at Las Vegas. Chassis '91/5' was a conversion from old '87/5' which had last been seen at Kyalami and served as team spare in mid-season.

The Type 91 was a handsome, stub-nosed car with a long downswept engine cover behind the far-forward cockpit, and it featured variable front track and wheelbase like the old Type 77s from the last period when Team had lost their way and were floundering about, in 1975-76.

De Angelis missed Imola in the FOCA boycott, but his 15 races yielded eight finishes, 8-5-4-5-4-4-6, and he actually won the Austrian GP in '91/8' after a fearsome final dash to the line, just 0.05 second in front of Rosberg's Williams after the turbocharged cars had all struck trouble.

This was also the 150th GP win for the Cosworth DFV engine, and the last Lotus race victory which Colin Chapman would see.

Mansell again was fated, missing both the Dutch and French GPs with minor injury, and his 13 races saw six finishes, 3-7-4-9-8-7. Team's total of 30 points gave them sixth place in the Championship between Brabham and Tyrrell. Things were improving, but slowly.

For much of 1982 the Lotuses suffered two main problems – porpoising over bumps and understeering on slower circuits. In practice for the British GP they toyed with pullrod suspension, but raced rocker arms to the end of the year. The cars were more effective on fast circuits than slow. It proved difficult to set them up, demanding many miles of testing before they were considered 'right there' and in a race it was then hard to maintain the car within its competitive 'working area' between full tanks and empty.

Before his tragically premature death that winter Colin had signed a deal with Renault Sport to use their turbocharged V6 engines in 1983. Peter Warr was now in sole executive charge of Team Lotus. Until sufficient French engines became available Team began the new year with two Cosworth cars, known as Type 92s but based on '91/5' and '10 which had been converted to the recently introduced flat-bottom rules. Chassis '5 was used as a spare until Montreal then pensioned-off, while '10 was raced by Mansell from Rio to Montreal before his turbocharged Type 93T appeared.

The prototype Lotus-Renault 93T chassis '1 appeared for de Angelis at Rio and was retired at the conclusion of spare car duty at the Österreichring having been replaced by the much improved Gérard Ducarouge-designed 94Ts. Chassis '93/2' ran from the Race of Champions to Silverstone, where it was a spare, being retired thereafter. The 93Ts had been far too great, gormless and cumbersome to be successful and early active-suspension experiments were shelved.

Chapman had been impressed by Ducarouge ever since his Matra-Simca sports car team days and the French engineer was taken on in June after being dismissed by Alfa Romeo. He used old rocker-arm suspension Type 91 tubs as the basis of his new 94Ts, and the revised weight bias of this much lighter model gave the Pirelli-shod cars hope at last.

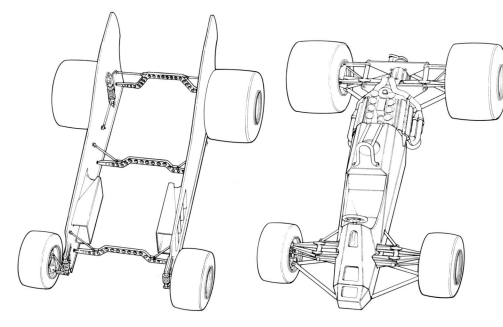

Top, Team's 1981 substitute for the 88 was the carbon-tub Lotus 87. Piola shows 1, wing; 2, nosebox/wingframe; 3, carbon tub; 4, fairings; 5, mirrors; 6, radiator 'airflow activator'; 7, radiator; 8, exit louvres; 9, rear diffuser; 10, engine; 11, side pod; 12, wing. Left, the sketches of the Type 88's two 'chassis' fail to show how the crossbeams fitted around the tub.

Above left, *the big idea – the 'twin-chassis' Type 88 shows its quite handsome if bulky lines at Long Beach '81, enveloping de Angelis, while (above) in Brazil '84 his new Gérard Ducarouge-designed Lotus-Renault 95T showed real signs of coming very good indeed, back on Goodyear tyres.*

The two 94Ts at Silverstone were '1 for de Angelis, which used '91/7's tub, and '2 for Mansell, using '91/8's, while '3 appeared for the Italian driver at Zandvoort.

De Angelis ran 14 Renault-powered races but finished only twice, reaching ninth at Spa and fifth at Monza for two meagre Championship points. Mansell raced the Cosworth car eight times, finishing 12-12-'12'-6, the point being scored at Detroit in Lotus's penultimate race with the engine which they had introduced 16 years earlier to Formula 1.

Mansell drove the revised and much-improved 94Ts seven times, sparkling in the British GP to make fourth place for the type's debut, then adding fifth in Austria, eighth at Monza and third at Brands Hatch to show some real form at last, scoring ten points and boosting Team's Constructors' Cup total to 12, seventh-equal with Tyrrell.

Ducarouge and Team then did a fine job on their 1984 Lotus 95T, only four being built, all brand new and set up to clearly defined specifications, and operating well now that Lotus were back on Goodyear tyres after their sorry Pirelli period. Old '94T/1' was used in Rio as spare, while '95T/1' was a test and spare chassis, raced only at Imola by Mansell. Chassis '95T/2' was new for Mansell at Rio and was his regular car thereafter, de Angelis drove '3, while '4 was a new team spare, raced by de Angelis at Montreal, Detroit and Estoril after its introduction at Dijon-Prenois.

The 95T was arguably the best-handling chassis of 1984. Only one tub was lightly damaged all year (by hitting a kerb) and Team had never lost one of the 17 carbon-composite tubs made since 1981. Ducarouge introduced a slow-speed aerodynamic package and a high-speed one and these were effectively the only changes to be made.

With both Ferrari and Williams in trouble, Goodyear gave Team terrific testing commitment, but their American-made race tyres could never match Michelin's grip so the Lotuses were unable to compete on even terms. In part this was due to tyres, in part the effect of Renault's fuel consumption problems.

Renault engineer Bruno Mauduit was attached to Team and he had a lovely time with his cars consistently out-performing Renault's own . . .

De Angelis might have won Rio but for a misfire, Mansell could have won when leading Monaco in heavy rain but lost control and crashed; at Detroit de Angelis had a gearbox failure when catching the leader at a second a lap, and at Dallas more gearbox trouble and

another driver error wrecked bright Lotus hopes after another fine qualifying performance. At Hockenheim, de Angelis was leading the McLarens when the car failed again. A new gearbox was ready for the end of the season, carbon brakes were tried but not raced seriously.

At one stage de Angelis looked as though he would win the Drivers' title on reliability, as McLaren's two star drivers split the winning between them. He finished 12 of his 16 GPs, the first ten consecutively: 3-7-5-3-5-5-4-2-3-4. With his fourth in Holland and fifth in Portugal, he was able to accumulate 34 points to reach third in the Championship. Mansell in comparison finished only five times, but actually scored every time, 3-6-6-4-3, for another 13 points. This gave Lotus third place in the Constructors' Cup with 37 points, compared to Ferrari's 57.5 and McLaren's staggering 143.5.

For Lotus 1985 was only satisfying in that every year since Colin Chapman's untimely death their results had improved. Four of Ducarouge's latest Type 97T-Renaults were built for the new year, closely based upon the promising 95T of 1984, the Type 96 having been a stillborn Indy project. The 97T had small winglets on the rear of each side pod to compensate for the banning of rear wing extensions as used in '84, and also adopted the CART-racing idea of vertical vanes in the front suspension to clean-up turbulence and reduce drag. Others would copy where Ducarouge led with varying degrees of comprehension and success.

Once again, Team's tiny car inventory was sufficient as not one was written off and each of the 21 carbon-composite series tubs built over five seasons had survived.

They used a mixture of Renault's old EF4 and revised new EF15 V6 engines. The EF4s were in qualifying-boost tune which the customer EF15s would not accept to the same degree. After qualifying, EF15s would be fitted for warm-up and the race, along with new drive trains/rear ends to replace those freshly-compromised by qualifying loads. Essentially the spare car was EF15-powered throughout, being used in practice to assess appropriate race-tune consumption. An average 270 miles went onto each engine before it was due for service.

The 97Ts saw more changes than the 95Ts, partly due to 1985 Goodyear tyre development. First they improved rear tyres, then fronts, and so on, to-and-fro but generally moving forward all the time.

Three of the new cars had been ready in time for Rio: '97T/1 acted as spare but raced by de Angelis at Imola and Monaco and becoming the test car thereafter; '2 was new driver Senna's regular mount up to Detroit, then spare raced by de Angelis in Austria; '3 acted as the Italian's regular race car; while '4 came in new at Monaco and was Senna's race car from Ricard onwards.

Newcomer Senna was Team's greatest attribute, taking seven pole positions, leading 10 of the 16 GPs for a total 270 laps, 38 more than his nearest rival, Rosberg of Williams, but only winning two, often hitting trouble. Between victory at Estoril and at Spa and good placings elsewhere, Senna's first eight retirements effectively broke down as: two due to Team's chassis, five to Renault's engine and its ancillaries, and one driver error.

De Angelis did his usual reliable job and was given first place at Imola after Prost's McLaren disqualification.

Senna's season included nine classified finishes from 16 starts, placing 1-7*-16-10*-2-3-3-1-2; while de Angelis finished from 11 of his 16 starts, once being unclassified and once disqualified, placing 3-4-1-3-5-5-5-5-6-5 – as usual scoring every time he finished.

For Peter Warr one significant landmark was reached at Monza. 'There in 1970', he said, 'Team used a 200 mph final-drive for the first time, in a Lotus 72 running low-drag configuration. It's taken us 15 years, but this year at Monza we were back up to 200 mph again'. And in safety.

Team had begun to win again; Colin Chapman himself would have been delighted.

Lyncar

This was another Cosworth/Hewland 'kit-car', built in 1974 for McLaren engine builder John Nicholson to drive as a private entry and sponsored by the enthusiastic Bruno Drury's Pinch Plant hire company. Amongst his other racing designs, manufacturer Martin Slater had built a highly successful Formula Atlantic car which Nicholson raced, and the Formula 1 car became chassis '007' in his Lyncar series – which was named in his wife's honour.

Nicholson made his debut in '007' in the 1974 Race of Champions at Brands Hatch, being classified 16th, but at Silverstone he finished as high as sixth in the International Trophy. The British GP meeting then saw him up against the big guns and he failed to qualify. He brought the car out again in 1975, retiring from the Race of Champions, finishing 13th at Silverstone in the non-Championship meeting but qualifying successfully for the Grand Prix there in July, where he was classified 17th after crashing in the downpour which caused the race to be cut short. Thereafter he concentrated upon power boat racing while continuing his highly successful Nicholson-McLaren engine business.

Maki

This tiny, enthusiastic and rather misguided Japanese Formula 1 project was the brainchild of Kenji Mimura who designed a bulkily unconventional-bodied Cosworth/Hewland 'kit-car' in conjunction with Masao Ono. The F-101 was unveiled with considerable fanfare and was to be driven by former McLaren and BRM driver Ganley. He was unable to qualify for the British GP, and in the attempt to qualify for the German GP at the Nürburgring where he said the car was 'actually feeling very good' he suddenly found himself wildly out of control at high speed as something in the suspension apparently broke. The car rammed the guardrail and its entire front end, including suspension and pedals, was ripped away, Ganley's legs and feet being injured as they were dragged along the ground while the wreck spun to a halt.

The opinion was expressed that most Formula 1 teams 'wouldn't even make a water tank that way', and the car was seen no more that season.

It returned, however, in 1975 when the much modified 'F101-02' was entered for ex-Lotus driver Dave Walker for the Belgian and Swedish GPs. However, it did not appear, then did not start and was way off the pace in Holland driven by Hiroshi Fuchida. The Japanese driver failed to qualify for the British GP at Silverstone, and Tony Trimmer then tried and failed to qualify it in Austria and Italy. Nevertheless, he started the non-Championship Swiss GP at Dijon-Prenois, five seconds off the pace and finished 13th, six times lapped.

Maki's last chance came in the 1976 Japanese GP, when an allegedly new car, serialled 'F102A-1' and driven by Trimmer, again failed to qualify.

Enthusiasm alone was never enough . . . exit the Maki.

March

March Engineering was formed in 1969 by Max Mosley, Alan Rees, Graham Coaker and Robin Herd to build production racing cars. It was a fine time to begin, for in addition to a healthy market for Formula 2 and Formula 3 chassis several teams were also at a loss to find chassis for Formula 1, including Ken Tyrrell's World Champion team. What's more there were several sponsors seeking involvement.

March won backing from the American Granatelli brothers' STP Corporation for a two-car works team plus a single sister car for STP's own driver Andretti. Tyrrell bought three cars for Stewart and Cevert and Crabbe's Antique Automobiles team would run another car for works appointee Peterson's Formula 1 debut.

Robin Herd's 1972 March 721X was intended to set new standards but passed into history as a flop. Its low polar moment design concentrated mass within the wheelbase.

Howden Ganley braving the Maki at Brands Hatch, British GP 1974, before the ill-fated trip to the Nürburgring.

Herd had to design a simple, easy-to-build car which would perform respectably without lengthy development. His March 701 featured a simple straight-sided aluminium monocoque, with a cast magnesium front bulkhead and two smaller castings providing suspension pick-ups at the front. The nose radiator, fire extinguisher and battery lay in a projecting forward tray, and the Cosworth/Hewland DG300 pack bolted on conventionally at the rear. Suspension was conventional, outboard all round. Robin reflects, 'There was hardly time to build the cars let alone use inboard suspension and do it properly'.

However, in conjunction with ex-BRM engineer and aerodynamicist Peter Wright – at that time running the Specialised Mouldings wind tunnel at Huntingdon – Robin adopted moulded glass-fibre low aspect ratio wing-shaped auxiliary tanks bolted on either side of the tub; a precursor of Wright's later ground-effect underwing side pods introduced on the Lotus 78/79s.

'At that time', Robin explains, 'there was a terrific differential in the amount of fuel required from race to race so add-on tanks were a good idea. Peter recommended this idea, and it worked – we might have found a little extra downforce and it certainly carried extra fuel without a drag penalty.'

March had to build at least six 701s in three months, and they succeeded. The car was initially effective, but there were so many fundamental compromises in its design that once Lotus and Ferrari sorted themselves out the 701s could no longer cope.

Tyrrell bought 701 chassis '2-4-7 for his drivers Stewart and Servoz-Gavin, though the latter abruptly opted out of racing at Monaco and was replaced by Cevert. Works drivers Amon and Siffert drove '701/1' and '701/5', the former machine receiving a new tub under the same number in mid-season, thus setting a March fashion which has confounded and confused those who try to keep track of these things ever since. History mattered less than retaining the same chassis number as the available customs papers when a car had to be rebuilt and another race was looming next weekend.

Andretti's STP team car was chassis '3 – wrecked in Austria and seen no more – and

Formula 2-derived F1 March cars: top, James Hunt making his name in the 1973 British GP at Silverstone in the Postlethwaite-developed Hesketh team 731. Above, British GP 1975 – Mark Donohue in Penske's March 751.

Peterson's Crabbe car '701/8'.

March made a fantastic start to their Formula 1 career with five cars running at Kyalami and Stewart on pole alongside Amon; only Stewart and Siffert finished, 3-10. Stewart won the minor Race of Champions from pole in '701/2' – the cars looking awkwardly high-set when they ran without the wing tanks on their rolled-under tub sides. In Spain, he qualified on the front row and won March's maiden Grand Prix victory, Andretti and Servoz-Gavin 3-5 behind him, though Siffert had not qualified. Amon then took the International Trophy at Silverstone on aggregate, winning from pole and setting fastest lap; Stewart won his heat and was placed second overall.

Thus, March won three of their first four Formula 1 races . . .

It was extraordinary and it could not last, even though Stewart and Amon qualified 1-2 at Monaco and Spa, where Amon set fastest lap and finished second behind a BRM. Stewart put '701/4' on the front row in Holland and was second again, but thereafter the 701s fell off the pace, with Amon coming second in the French GP and Stewart second in Italy. By this time the chance had passed as Tyrrell built his own cars for 1971 and March thereby lost a customer.

Robin 'had a proper go at Formula 1' in 1971 with the model 711 design, an unconventional device with its aerodynamic form based on advice from Frank Costin; an elliptical centre-strutted nose wing, compact hip-radiator aluminium monocoque, and all-inboard brakes to minimize unsprung weight. The distinctive nose wing proved incredibly incidence-sensitive. As they attempted to reduce incidence to minimize drag and find better straightline speed at the Österreichring, the 711s would exhibit terrific understeer and lap slower, marring Lauda's maiden GP.

The 711s lost much of their originally extensive aerodynamic bodywork early on, and outboard front brakes were fitted after a brakeshaft snapped on the Williams car '711/3', driven by Peterson at the minor Brands Hatch meeting. Subsequently, there were few structural faults, except to the private Williams cars for Pescarolo. The experiment of playing Alfa Romeo's V8 off against Cosworth's was unprofitable in results.

Old 701s ran on into the first part of 1971, in the Williams team for Pescarolo, Bell and others using chassis '6; new chassis '11 in the new Mordaunt-Guthrie team for Beuttler, while chassis '10 had been sold to John Love for use in southern African Formula 1. Car '701/9' emerged, owned by Hubert Hahne and driven by Jarier at Oulton Park late in the year, and entered for the Frenchman by the Shell-Arnold team at Monza.

Six 711s appeared, Peterson heading the works team initially in '711/2', for most of the season in '6, and finally in the Brands Hatch Victory race in '4. Normally his car was Cosworth-powered but March toyed with Alfa Romeos V8; sponsored rides for Galli and de Adamich, normally in chassis '711/1'. Peterson wrote off this car at the minor Silverstone meeting when the Alfa V8's throttles jammed open but it was rebuilt around a refabricated tub. The top-endy Alfa engine was fitted in '711/6' – if we believe the numbers – for the French GP at Ricard. However, Peterson retired and thereafter used DFVs exclusively.

All four 711s in Spain ran outboard front brakes and nose-mounted batteries were provided for the STP works entries to improve their sprung:unsprung weight ratio. For Monaco, Peterson's '711/2' was provided with strengthened rear suspension, and the Alfa-engined car which Galli failed to qualify there was a brand new replacement for Ronnie's Silverstone write-off, albeit still wearing '711/1's chassis-plate. A low-drag nose was tested at Monza but the 711s raced with standard nose cones shorn of their elliptical wings. In Canada, the Gene Mason Racing '711/5' appeared for American club driver Skip Barber.

Peterson drove brilliantly all year, placing second at Monaco, Hockenheim, Silverstone, Monza – just 0.01 second behind the winner! – and Mosport Park; as well as achieving a third at Watkins Glen, fourth at Zandvoort and finishing second in the Drivers' Championship behind Stewart. March Engineering were third-equal in the Constructors' table, tied with Ferrari behind BRM and Tyrrell, maintaining their 1970 position.

Now Herd was determined to win the Championship in 1972, and invested much time and effort in a highly mass-concentrated low-polar moment March 721X.

Initially, a lighter 711 development known as the March 721 contested the early-season races, losing its 711-like nose-top wing after Argentina and adopting a bluff nose form with moulded-in planes ahead of the front wheels either side. Peterson drove '721/1' and new team-mate Lauda took '721/2' which did only two races before being withdrawn. Meanwhile, an Alfa Romeo sports car drive had been arranged for Peterson in the 1971 Watkins Glen 6-Hours race. He used a car fitted with Alfa's gearbox-ahead-of-final-drive transmission which pushed the engine far forward to concentrate mass within the wheelbase, whereas a conventional gearbox like the Hewland waved in the breeze out behind the back axle. Peterson found the Alfa T33 to his liking, encouraging Robin to make his biggest mistake.

Alfa Romeo provided gearbox components for the 721X, which also introduced new rear suspension with inboard coil/dampers at the rear. But the 721X's weight distribution did not suit the Goodyear tyres which March had just adopted, having previously run Firestones. Space was very tight and restricted the differentials useable; the 721X was dogged by understeer when entering corners and suffered vicious oversteer leaving them, though otherwise handling well on fast curves. Although Peterson quite liked the 'X, team-mate Lauda tried it for the first time and grunted 'No vay', and he was right.

March talked to Firestone who felt they could provide tyres which would improve behaviour, but races were being lost, the season was

passing by and an instant 'fix' had to be found.

Consequently, the two 721X cars were withdrawn after contesting only the Spanish, Monaco, Oulton Gold Cup (where Peterson's '721X/2' used a conventional Hewland FG400 transaxle) and Belgian races, and hastily built production Formula 2-chassised 721G cars replaced them for the French round.

The first 721G had been built in just nine days prior to the Spanish GP for Beuttler's private entry, the 'G' standing for *Guinness Book of Records* because it had been devised and built so quickly. He liked it, and works 721Gs, chassis '2 initially for Lauda and '3 for Peterson, rapidly followed; the team leader finishing fifth at Clermont. He was third in Germany, qualified on the front row in Canada but was disqualified for reversing in the pit lane having overshot his marks, Lauda being disqualified from the same race in '721G/4' for receiving outside assistance. Few F1 teams share with March the distinction of having had both entries disqualified in the same Grand Prix . . .

At Watkins Glen Peterson was fourth, and he qualified on the front row for the final race of the year at Brands Hatch, where Migault debuted the Ecurie Volant Shell '721G/5' intended for hill-climber Daniel Rouveyran, and bent it badly.

Meanwhile, private entrant Frank Williams had run '711/3' for Pace and '721/3' for Pescarolo. The latter had a hectic time as he crashed the long-suffering car at Monaco, Clermont – where it was badly damaged so the Frenchman instead wrote off the new Williams FX/3 in the next race at Brands Hatch – then at the Nürburgring, (writing off '721/3' again), Austria (writing it off a third time) and at Monza. In the last race the car appeared with a unicorn nose wing, possibly indicating that it was the ex-Lauda '721/2' revived under '3's serial. Between destructive accidents, '721/3's tub had been remade in Williams's own workshops, then replaced by a brand new tub from Bicester.

Of more eccentric note was the 'Eifelland-Cosworth Type 21' *née* March '721/4'. The German driver Stommelen's long-time sponsors Eifelland Wohnwagenbau (Caravans) backed walrus-moustached artist Lutz 'Luigi' Colani to style florid body panels including an integral periscope mirror on the centreline ahead of the cockpit but most were quickly replaced by standard panelling. Stommelen had nine outings, finishing seven times, 13-10-10-11-16-10-15, which record tells its own story. Stommelen sold the car to the London Hexagon car dealership and they entered it for Watson at the final Brands Hatch meeting, where he finished sixth in a promising Formula 1 debut.

After this 1972 season, March Engineering merely toyed with Formula 1. Robin explains: 'After that season we merely converted our production Formula 2 designs to Formula 1, providing cars where drivers or sponsors wanted to pay us for the privilege and generally tackled Formula 1 on Formula 2 budgets.

'Our bank had got whingy, telling us "You must take life more seriously".'

Team manager Rees had left to create Shadow while Mosley and Herd ran their 'team', such as it was, alone as March's production Formula 2 and 3 cars dominated their classes. The outstanding March of 1973 was the Hesketh entry for Hunt, developed and tended by former March engineer Harvey Postlethwaite, which made its debut at Monaco, then finished 6-4-3-7-2 in its next five successful GP outings in France, Britain, Holland, Canada and the USA. There, at Watkins Glen, Hunt challenged hard for the lead, set fastest lap and was beaten by just 0.312 second.

With such a driver there was little wrong with a well-developed converted Formula 2 car. In fact the 1972 works 721G chassis numbers were used in these updated 1973 '731' versions which looked totally different with their deformable structure tank-protecting side pods and narrower rear tracks.

Beuttler ran his original '721G/1' into the new season at Kyalami, then returned it to the Bicester works, taking over a new 731 numbered '721G/2'. David Purley acquired a sister 731 reputedly based on the ex-Beuttler '721G/1' tub. The Hesketh car carried ex-works plate '721G/3' but was definitely all-new; Dr Postlethwaite made sure of it – no tired, stretched old tub for *his* driver.

Jarier, March's 1972 Formula 2 star, normally drove a solitary works entered 731 numbered '721G/4', though newcomer Roger Williamson took over for the British and Dutch GPs, being involved in the Scheckter collision through no fault of his own at Silverstone before crashing fatally at Zandvoort after a suspension failure.

For 1974 the F2 monocoque 741s emerged with hip radiators angled almost in-line each side of the engine, sheet magnesium end plate mounted rear wings and spatular bluff noses derived from 1973 F1 and F2 experience. Stuck and Ganley drove in early season, Vittorio Brambilla replacing Ganley with Beta Tools orange livery on his often-battered tubs thereafter. Stuck showed terrific car control almost in the Peterson mould and was fifth at Kyalami, fourth in Spain, while Brambilla was sixth in Austria to highlight a season which saw the Marches performing respectably, all things considered.

Brambilla wrote off his '741/2' at Jarama when the rear wing swayed forward under braking, its stays cramped a brake hose against a disc, which sawed through it, leaving Brambilla with front wheels locked and no retardation at all on the rear. A new tub replaced the damaged original on '741/2' in Belgium. A second new tub went into the car for the German GP but, like George Washington's axe, it was still 'the same car'.

The same happened to Stuck's '741/1' after it was heavily damaged at Monaco. Both 741s had begun the season painted British Racing

Green. Brambilla brought orange *Beta Utensili* livery and Stuck's car progressively changed colour to match, appearing as a green and orange patchwork at one stage 'as he progressively wrote off the green panels'.

An F2-derived extra long nose section appeared in Sweden, adding download leverage, while narrow track gave good straightline speed on the fast end-of-season courses.

In 1975, Brambilla began the season alone in an old 741 modified with new regulation engine-bay extinguisher and battery moved from tail to nose, but in Spain his lighter '751/3' was supported by Lella Lombardi's new '751/2' and they finished 5-6 for the best March result in years. Better would follow.

Brambilla was very quick at Zolder until the circuit burned out his Formula 2 brakes – 'because we literally couldn't afford to buy proper Formula 1 brakes'.

At Anderstorp for the Swedish GP nearly all the geometric corners suited the 751, where the team ran Brambilla on new 20 in. wide rear wheels to add tyre stability and stripped all excess weight out of the car. In a meteoric qualifying shot on extremely stiff springs making the car handle like a kart, he qualified on pole and led the race until a UJ failed.

Penske bought '751/5' new for Donohue in time for the British GP where he was classified fifth and Brambilla sixth after accidents in the rainstorm which stopped that race. The works 751 there had new geometry suspension and horizontal rear winglets projecting from the side plates low down just behind the rear wheels. They were judged legal and gave 200 rpm more along the straight by cleaning up turbulence from the wide rear tyres. They were a forerunner of the rear diffuser underwings used in 1983-84 but, again, Herd did not pursue the idea.

The Penske car was rebuilt after its Silverstone crash with new bulkhead castings and some reskinning, but in morning warm-up in Austria Donohue was fatally injured as its left-front tyre collapsed at speed. The race was stopped by torrential rain, at a time when Brambilla's narrow-track '751/3' was leading,

so he was declared winner, subsequently celebrating by smashing the nose cone in a victory-lap incident.

The Italian GP was a disaster, as Brambilla's clutch failed and both Stuck (whose '751/2' sported a new tub following a crash in Austria) and Lombardi crashed again; however, in the USA Brambilla and Stuck finished 7-8.

For 1976 Peterson left Lotus after the season had begun and returned to his old friends at March, whom he loved and where he was immensely popular. They ran the whole season that year on a budget of just £35,000. The developed 761 cars were very agile, quick on the straights, immensely fast in damp conditions but unreliable.

At Ricard a speed trap on the long Mistral Straight showed Peterson quickest at 182.56 mph, with Brambilla next up at 179.43 mph, in the two March 761s . . .

Peterson ran 15 races for the team, being classified as a finisher only six times but featuring prominently – crashing out of second place on spilled oil at Monaco, leading in Austria, starting from pole and heading the field in Holland and surviving 43 laps in the lead to win the Italian GP at Monza, where spasmodic rain showers cooled the car's brakes just enough to finish.

He started on the front row in Canada and led eight laps, then at Watkins Glen qualified on row two but started the race with a fractured front bulkhead allowing the suspension mounts to move about, and understandably did not feature. His sixth in Austria was Peterson's only other points score.

Brambilla finished five races but his only score was sixth in Holland; Lombardi was 14th in her solitary race in Brazil; while Merzario finished twice out of five starts before moving to Wolf-Williams for the end of the year, never finishing another race.

One Karl Oppitzhauser failed to practice for the Austrian race, while in contrast the reliable Stuck finished five of his 16 GPs, 4-12-4-7-5, his placings in Brazil, Monaco and the USA bringing him and the team eight points.

March ended the season seventh in the Cup

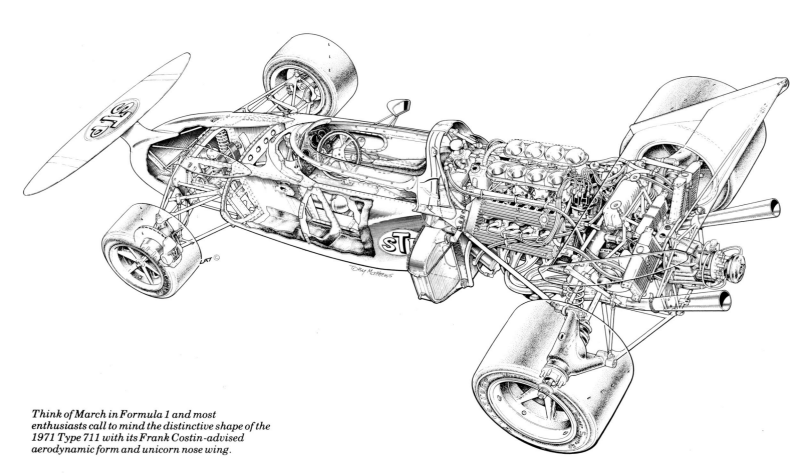

Think of March in Formula 1 and most enthusiasts call to mind the distinctive shape of the 1971 Type 711 with its Frank Costin-advised aerodynamic form and unicorn nose wing.

table, the neat rounded-arrowhead tub 761s with their in-line hip radiators and bluff nosepieces with forward-thrust splitter tray doing wonders on such a tight budget.

For 1977, improved 761B and nose-radiator 771 cars were produced by Herd and his assistant Martin Walters, three of each running during the season. Mosley (law graduate son of Sir Oswald) acted as field engineer that year because March's Formula 2 programme backers BMW had threatened to withdraw if Herd, the real engineer, 'did not stop playing around with Formula 1 and concentrate upon their Formula 2 programme. So I had to do Formula 2 and Max set up the Formula 1 cars for Ribeiro and Ian Scheckter, and that was it.'

Frank Williams bought an ex-works March tub – said to have traces of orange paint on it – for Neve to drive in Williams Grand Prix Engineering's maiden season. Eight GPs were started, finishing 12-10-15-9-7-18 and failing to qualify in France, Germany and Holland. Merzario ran his private car seven times, failing to qualify in Monaco, Germany and Holland, his only finish being 14th in Belgium. Other private March drivers that year included Michael Bleekemoelen, Bernard de Dryver, Boy Hayje, Brian Henton, Brett Lunger, Stuck (one race only in South Africa before joining Brabham) and Andy Sutcliffe – jointly achieving nothing. Seven cars had been built.

The Rothmans-sponsored Mosley team for Ribeiro and Ian Scheckter meanwhile started 22 times, finishing six races whose best placings were eighths for Ribeiro in Germany and Canada. They non-qualified nine times.

At the end of that season March sold their FOCA membership to Schmid's ATS team and left Formula 1 to continue their highly successful minor-Formula production programmes. March cars raced on in bush-league Formula 1, with drivers like Guy Edwards, Jurg Zaborowski, Bruce Allison, Gerd Biechteler, Geoff Lees and Dennis Leech.

The 1978-79-80 seasons saw March racing elsewhere. Then in 1981 they returned, being commissioned to build customer cars for the RAM team. These modest March 811 wing-cars with Cosworth power were driven by Daly and Salazar, failing to qualify twelve times with 16-7-11-8 representing their only finishes, seventh being in the British GP. No less than six of these new March 811s, numbered 'RM01' to 'RM06', were built and for 1982 RAM updated chassis '05 as spare car to support new 821 models, chassis '07-08-09-10-11 for drivers Mass and Boesel. As would become characteristic of RAM, they suffered a series of accidents.

Boesel destroyed 'RM08' testing at Snetterton, '09 was written off in the startline collision at Detroit and '10 featured in Mass's potentially horrifying high-speed accident at Ricard during the French GP when it hurdled the catch-fences and somersaulted into a spectator area and caught fire, miraculously without anyone being seriously harmed. This accident perhaps was the last nail in the coffin of the clearance ground-effect wing-cars, making the latter-day March significant in at least that unhappy respect.

For 1983 RAM Automotive manufactured their own new Cosworth cars, initially retaining the March tag (see RAM, page 228).

Martini

Unrelated to Martini & Rossi, Tico Martini was a Channel Islander who made his name hill-climbing a kart-like special in the early-Sixties before settling down as a French-based Formula 3 and eventually European Championship-winning Formula 2 manufacturer, with workshops at the Magny-Cours circuit.

For 1978 he built a one-off Cosworth/Hewland monocoque car, its slim arrow-head chassis reminiscent of the contemporary Williams FW06, to be driven by Arnoux. It featured inboard top rocker arm front suspension with a parallel link system at the rear and used a six-speed FGA gearbox. The project was sponsored by RMO, a temporary-staff agency, Silver Match, manufacturers of lighters and pens, and by Elf, the French oil company. It was known as the model MK23 in Martini's system, MK being the initials of Martini-Knight – the Knight family running the Magny-Cours driving school – rather than an abbreviation for 'Mark'.

The MK23 made its debut at Kyalami where Arnoux failed to qualify. Loss of oil pressure prevented him starting at Silverstone and at Monaco he failed even to pre-qualify. In Belgium he finally made the race, finishing a reliable but uncompetitive ninth, and he was then 14th in his home GP at Ricard. The fast circuit at Hockenheim saw him fail to pre-qualify again but in Austria he was ninth. The car's only race retirement came at Zandvoort where its wing mount failed but that was the end and Martini opted out of Formula 1 thereafter.

Matra

The emergence of Matra Sports as a Formula 1 force and their World Championship victory of 1969 is related elsewhere (see pages 61-5). They experimented rather half-heartedly with a spaceframe four-wheel drive car named the MS84. It was the cheapest and simplest of the 1969 crop and the only one to score a Championship point with Servoz-Gavin's sixth place in Canada. For the last race in Mexico the engineers split torque 100 per cent to the rear wheels and the driver reported a great improvement in handling and 'feel'! After that Championship season Matra Sports had to shelve their Cosworth-Ford interest in view of their own takeover by Chrysler's French subsidiary Simca.

For 1970 Georges Martin revised his V12 engine, stiffening its crankcase sufficiently to act as a stressed chassis member like the Cosworth DFV, and designing new cylinder heads with a narrower valve angle and shallower combustion chamber, offering enlarged inlet area while demanding less deep-crowned, and therefore lighter, pistons. Inlet ports were now within the vee instead of between the camshafts, which were themselves closer together, thanks to the narrower valve angle, and that permitted generally narrower and hence lighter head assembly castings. This new MS12 engine's bottom end was unchanged. A Boulogne company named *Moteur Moderne* helped in this development.

Bernard Boyer had to design a new monocoque to comply with 1970 regulations, and he chose a rectilinear configuration, heavily riveted with sloping upper faces on fuel tank panniers each side, offering downthrust planes to the airstream. Wheelbase was longer than the Champion MS80 but suspension geometry was similar with a narrower track front end. Citroen power-assisted steering was tried but not raced, while the car carried a large rear wing and wide spatular nose cone with canard fins either side.

The first two chassis, 'MS120-01' and '02, were raced by team drivers Beltoise and Pescarolo in South Africa, finishing 4-7, but at Brands Hatch for the minor International

The 'Matra-Matra': Beltoise in the MS10 V12 at Rouen during the 1968 French GP meeting, shows off the car's F2-derived cigar shape and its Georges Martin-designed wailing multi-piped V12 engine.

Beltoise crashed '01 in practice, amputating two wheels and damaging the tub. It was repaired for Pescarolo's use in Monaco practice and was then crashed by him back at Brands in the British GP. It was repaired again in time for the American tour as spare and was retired from competition thereafter.

Meanwhile Pescarolo normally drove '02 and his 11 starts in it yielded nine finishes, including third at Monaco for Matra's first four 1970 Championship points, and fifth in the French GP at Clermont. There it was dogged by low oil pressure, then crashed mildly, as well as suffering a damper failure – after all of which fifth place was a terrific bonus. The tub was in fact distorted in this accident and after being straightened it finished sixth for another point in Germany and seventh in Canada.

The glorious-sounding French V12 cars were far more difficult to work on than their Cosworth-engined opposition, a Matra engine change taking seven or eight hours against the DFVs' ninety minutes.

Beltoise concentrated upon chassis '03 in which he started 12 races, finishing six times; third in Belgium and Italy, fifth in Holland and Mexico and sixth in Austria. This vehicle was an improved car which first appeared in Spain with 13 in. front wheels instead of the 15 in. type, better brakes, wings and lightweight titanium rear hubs. Integral front upright callipers appeared on both '02 and '03 there while V12 development extracted more power, now claimed to be around 435 bhp at 11,000 ear-splitting rpm. The 13 in. wheel experiment was unsuccessful as the smaller new brakes were cooking, so 15 in. wheels reappeared for Monaco. Nevertheless, Spa saw another outing for the low-drag 13 in. type. The 15in. wheels and better cooled brakes would be used for the slower, tighter courses but the cars were dogged all season by persistent understeer so revised anti-roll bars and camber angles were adopted at Clermont, where Beltoise was able

to lead his home race until a puncture and fuel starvation spoiled France's day.

At Monza, a new MS12T engine with further stiffened crankcase and 'special' (presumably titanium) lightweight rods appeared, but reliability suffered in Canada and the USA.

Much of the cars' handling deficiency was attributed to torsional flexion in the chassis structure. Certainly now that Matra had to use bag tanks instead of carrying their fuel direct in the hull boxes they were robbed of the extreme monocoque sub-division which had made their 1968-69 cars so rigid.

For 1971, Pescarolo was replaced by Amon, who drove '02 in the minor Argentine GP that

Top, the Matra MS10 V12 set everyone's spines tingling upon its debut at Monaco 1968. Bottom, the other end of the Matra story, Chris Amon's brand new rounded-tub MS120D '07' at Clermont, French GP, 1972 – their final F1 season.

January and won on aggregate! This was to be Matra's one and only Formula 1 victory.

The winning car became team spare before final retirement when '06 was completed for that year's Monaco GP.

Meanwhile, Amon drove '03 – wearing a new full-width wheel fairing nose – to finish fifth at Kyalami, fourth at Ontario and California, and third in the Spanish GP.

In the latter race, Beltoise drove the revised new MS120B prototype '05, using Boyer's latest stiffened tub design with laterally down-sloping side tank upper surfaces. Martin's latest engine mods included a new exhaust system, more radical camshafts and a modified crankshaft.

For Beltoise this was a difficult season as he had been judged culpable for a fatal accident in an early-season Argentine sports car race, being suspended until Spain, and later in the year suffered a further suspension. He would make only eight starts, all in '05, and his only Championship point came in Spain, though he finished five times and was seventh in France and England.

Chassis '06 – last of the MS120Bs – appeared as Amon's spare at Monaco. In time for the Dutch GP it was fitted with the latest MS71 reheaded V12 but was used only in practice, Amon then racing it in France where he finished fifth despite breaking several valve springs. In face of continuing MS71 troubles Amon persevered in the German GP but crashed the car, which there included the entire rear end assembly of '04 bolted onto '06's tub.

Tyre deflations were traced to wheel problems; the team tried running on higher pressures which caused excessive understeer. Matra development had slowed as their long-distance sports-racing programme gained precedence. They missed the Austrian GP to catch their breath, '06 being modified with extra chassis stiffening between driver and engine,

The angular-chassised MS120C in Amon's hands at Monza 1971, showing off its bluff nose and smoothly tailored aerodynamic upper surfaces leading back onto that rear wing. Cam-drive geartrain of the French V12 as in 1968 (below) and as developed for Ligier, 1981 (bottom).

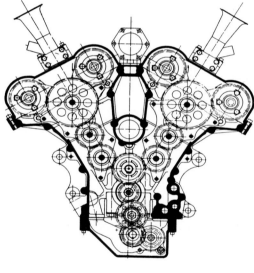

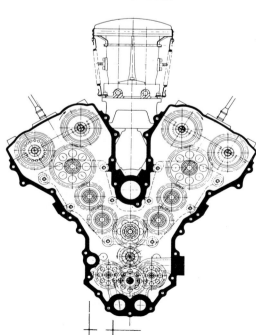

while engine porting was again altered to find more power. At Monza, Amon promptly qualified '06 on pole and led before his visor was ripped off and he dropped back to finish sixth.

Matra achieved nothing more that season but through the 1971/72 winter, Martin, development chief Loze and engine test manager René Fortin succeeded in boosting the MS71 V12 from 440 to 450 bhp at 11,500 rpm.

Boyer further modified his cars' front suspension to suit the latest-generation Goodyear tyres, and a smoother wide nose was adopted with twin top ducts to vent hot radiator air instead of the broad single duct of '71, these changes forming the MS120C specification.

Now they would enter just one car, for Amon, but the MS120C changes proved insufficiently radical to remain competitive. A preparation problem forced Amon to non-start in Argentina. By Kyalami the oil tank was moved to the rear, altering weight distribution, while 35 kg (77 lb) was pruned away in time for the Spanish GP by using titanium exhausts in conjunction with a lighter honeycomb core rear wing and new light alloy wheels. All this work was carried out on chassis '06, but at Monaco Amon found he preferred his old spare MS120B '04 so the latest engine and other parts were transferred from '06 and he raced the older car, finishing sixth after four stops to clear a misting visor in the heavy rain which marred that race.

The new MS120D chassis '07 finally appeared in the French GP, using a totally redesigned tub, scrapping the original rectilinear form in favour of a rounded centre section more reminiscent of the old MS80. Weight was concentrated further rearward, the oil tank was permanently in the tail, its old housing behind the seat in the back of the tub now being taken by fuel. Amon promptly qualified on the front row and for 19 laps the French crowd believed in miracles, Amon leading in the blue Matra. Unfortunately, road work in preparing the Clermont course had left the verges strewn with sharp stone chippings and many competitors suffered punctures; Amon was one, falling back to ninth before charging through the field to finish third.

He then crashed '07 in practice at Brands Hatch, racing '04, and finishing fourth after an early collision. Thereafter '07 suffered various mechanical *ennuis*, but ended the season with a fifth to its credit in Germany and sixth in Canada.

Meanwhile, Matra-Simca had won Le Mans, a victory provoking immense adulation in France, and the management decided sports car racing like this offered far better value than

Formula 1, so the Formula 1 programme was abandoned forthwith. They would return as an engine supplier – experimentally to Shadow in 1975, then more seriously for Ligier in 1976, and again in 1981 – but would build no further Formula 1 cars of their own.

McGuire

Australian amateur driver Brian McGuire made the long trip to England with fellow hopeful Alan Jones in the early '70s to race Formula 3 cars. Jones made his name and fortune, McGuire did not. In 1976 he bought ex-'works' Williams FW04 chassis '1 and won the Thruxton Shellsport club race in it. For 1977 he had the old car updated in a vain attempt to make it competitive enough to run in serious Formula 1. He called it the McGuire BM1 and entered for the British GP at Silverstone. He failed to pre-qualify, lapping nearly 3.5 seconds slower than the quickest of those who also failed to pre-qualify.

No other GPs were entered, and later that year, while practising in 'BM1-1' for the August Monday meeting at Brands Hatch, a mechanical failure caused an awful accident in which McGuire himself and two unfortunate marshals were killed as it somersaulted onto their post at Stirling's Bend.

McLaren

New Zealand racing driver Bruce McLaren left the Cooper Car Company after seven seasons as team driver to go his own way with the start of the new Formula in 1966. He based his tiny team at Colnbrook, near London's Heathrow Airport, and ran it in partnership with American Teddy Mayer.

Robin Herd, a youthful but brilliant engineer previously at the Royal Aircraft Establishment in Farnborough, Hampshire, designed an advanced monocoque F1 chassis for that first season, known as the M2B and skinned in Mallite composite sheet, an aerospace sandwich material comprising end-grain balsa filling between thin sheets of aluminium. The Mallite McLaren full monocoque tub possessed almost legendary torsional rigidity, around 11,000 lb/ft per degree deflection at a time when conventional tubs claimed perhaps 4-5000 lb/ft per degree, and the otherwise very rigid Eagle achieved 6200 lb/ft.

Sadly, McLaren's choice of a modified Indy

Ford four-cam V8 centre-exhaust engine was catastrophic. It was over-valved and over-ported and had a very narrow useable rev band. For the record, it was a 95.3 × 52.4 mm unit, 2999 cc, and producing 300 bhp at 9000 rpm. McLaren hastily adopted a humble Serenissima sports car V8, cutting down the rear chassis horns of 'M2B/2' to accommodate the Italian unit's side exhausts. The 'M166' engine's dimensions were as follows: 91.5 × 57.0 mm, displacing 2996 cc and giving an alleged 350 bhp at 8600 rpm. This gave them their first point-scoring finish, sixth at Brands Hatch, the team then concentrating upon their CanAm sports cars while the Italian V8's actual output was only some 260 bhp.

Three M2Bs had been laid down and two completed, the Serenissima car failing to start after practising in Holland, 'M2B/1' then being prepared with a revised Ford V8 engine fitted with Chrysler 'Hemi' induction tracts coaxing output to some 321 bhp at 9500 rpm for the US and Mexican GPs. Bruce finished fifth on reliability and retired with engine failure respectively, his team's four starts having yielded two finishes, both in the points, though not as securely as it may sound.

McLaren used BRM's new V12 (intended for use in sports cars) in 1967, starting the year with a 2.1 Tasman V8 until the new V12 was ready. The V8 mounted in a Formula 2 McLaren M4A aluminium bathtub monocoque, rigged with extra fuel tankage, known as the M4B – not to be confused with the Trojan-built production McLaren M4Bs for American 'Formula B' racing at that time. The rear of the tub had been cut away to accommodate the V8.

Bruce tackled five races in 'M4B/1', three of them non-Championship; fifth at Oulton Park and Silverstone, fourth for three Championship points at Monaco (for which the little car was admirably suited) and then crashing heavily in the Dutch GP, the car subsequently being burned out when testing.

Through that mid-season Bruce accepted an Eagle team drive and the prototype BRM P101 V12 engine became available enabling the new monocoque M5A to be completed as a runner in time for the Canadian GP in August. Mallite had been abandoned as too complex and heavy in favour of sheet aluminium, the rounded

Bruce McLaren himself in his F2-based M4B with 2.1-litre BRM V8 engine at Oulton Park early in 1967. This hybrid special did well before being burned out in a testing incident.

M5A having a fully-stressed section enclosing the driver's shins for'ard, leaving the area above his knees open for maintenance. Behind the seat-back two rear horns carried the V12, claimed to deliver 370 bhp at 9750 rpm, driving via a Hewland five-speed DG gearbox.

The engine as delivered was a little longer than anticipated, with water pump and distributors encroaching upon the cockpit. To save weight the alternator was omitted. The Varley battery lay on its side under the seat-back and the oil tank.

During the Canadian race, the hot oil tank cooked the battery. It was a rainy race and Bruce gained on the leaders before spinning but recovered to run second until the road began to dry. A Lotus 49 retook second place, then the new BRM engine began to misfire as the cooked battery ran flat. Without an alternator to recharge it Bruce had to stop for a fresh battery, finishing seventh.

At Monza, McLaren flew. Having qualified on the front row and with 20 laps to go he and Surtees's Honda were wheel-to-wheel ready for a final dash to the flag when a BRM cylinder liner collapsed. They had found another 19 bhp and both McLaren car and driver shone. But M5A then retired in both the USA and Mexico, the four starts having yielded just that debut finish.

Old 'M5A/1' was driven by new team driver Hulme in South Africa to start the 1968 season,

finishing fifth, and subsequently was sold to Bonnier to replace his Cooper-Maserati. The McLaren-BRM was outgunned even in the dry there by the Repco Brabhams supposedly producing 340 bhp. The new Cosworth-Ford DFV now offered customers a minimum 408.

Backed by Gulf Oil sponsorship McLaren had ordered five DFVs and Herd designed a new M7A bathtub aluminium monocoque to match. Shortly afterwards he left to join Cosworth, leaving assistant Gordon Coppuck to complete the new cars.

Chassis 'M7A/1' driven by McLaren and '2 for Hulme made a terrific debut, winning the Race of Champions from pole position and setting fastest lap, 1-3, followed by 1-2 at Silverstone with Hulme winning from pole. He was second in Spain, fifth at Monaco where Bruce crashed '1 heavily, leading up to a sensational Belgian GP where Bruce won after last-lap fuel shortage had felled the leaders.

Hulme won the Italian GP with Bonnier sixth in the M5A-BRM. Hulme and McLaren were then 1-2 in Canada, where Gurney rented 'M7A/3' but retired with overheating, and in the USA Gurney and McLaren placed 4-6 while Hulme crashed 'M7A/2' heavily after a half-shaft broke. The wreck was rebuilt frantically in time for Mexico where the Championships would be decided between Hulme, Stewart and Hill – McLaren, Matra-Cosworth and Lotus.

The rebuilt car's suspension broke early in the race and it crashed again, leaving Bruce to finish second in 'M7A/1'.

In all, the M7s started 29 times that season, 25 of them at Championship level, finishing 20 times, 16 at Championship level, winning five times (three GPs), and taking four seconds, a third, two fourths, two fifths and two sixths.

These simple, competitive cars continued racing throughout 1969 when old 'M7A/1' was sold to South African privateer Basil van Rooyen. Bruce experimented with wide pannier tanks to reproduce the better handling of his sill-tanked CanAm sports cars – and failing. This pannier car was 'M7A/3', also known as model M7B, which Bruce drove in South Africa and at Brands Hatch before taking over the Formula 5000-chassised M7C chassis 'A/4' at Silverstone.

This car featured a tall structural monocoque rear bulkhead rising behind the driver's shoulders, unlike the shallow tubs of the true M7A. Where the production F5000 M10A tub supported its American V8 engines on rear horns,

Denny Hulme winning the 1968 Italian GP at Monza in his wingless M7A, rigged here with a supplementary right-side fuel tank for this long race. These cars initiated McLaren's F1 reputation for outstanding workmanship and preparation.

M7C had these horns amputated to provide the conventional Cosworth mounting.

The M7B was sold to Colin Crabbe's Antique Automobiles team for Vic Elford; reaching tenth in Holland, fifth at Clermont, sixth in the British GP and then being written off at the Nürburgring.

McLaren's major effort for the early part of the season involved the hapless M9A four-wheel drive car. It would race only once, in the British GP, being driven by Bell until its suspension collapsed. This Jo Marquardt-designed car was one of the better 1969 4WD cars but like the others it did nothing but absorb time and money.

Tyres were decisive in Formula 1, as Firestone and Dunlop were both ahead of Goodyear (which McLaren used) until the latter rounds of 1969, when the latest G18 and G20 compounds excelled, allowing Hulme to win handsomely in Mexico, racing faithful 'M7A/2' for the 26th time.

McLaren's 1969 F1 record totalled 26 starts, with one victory, one second place, four thirds, four fourths, four fifths, three sixths, a seventh and an eighth comprising their 19 finishes. It should be noted that although Bruce McLaren finished fourth at Monza, his time was only 0.14 second behind the winner. *That* was a motor race . . .

In January 1970 the expected rear-wheel drive replacement for the now obsolescent M7-series was introduced. Known as the M14A it was improvement by evolution, not revolution. Where the M7s' front suspension had rearward legs demanding extra internal bulkheads within the monocoque sides to provide an anchorage, the M14 front suspension was forward braced to offer both better steering lock and enabling longer fuel tanks to be housed within the tub. The monocoque wrapped round 360 degrees in the scuttle.

Two M14As were built, plus an M14D tailored to accept the Alfa Romeo V8 sports car based Formula 1 engine which appeared at last, having first been mooted for Cooper in 1968. Alfa's driver de Adamich handled this car and an older M7D tub similarly converted. The McLaren-Alfa never matched the McLaren-Cosworth. Old 'M7A/2' still survived in works hands.

Bruce McLaren was killed in a CanAm car testing accident at Goodwood that June, Gurney replacing him as works driver with Hulme and Gethin. Surtees had bought the M7C, chassis '4, making four starts but never finishing before his own new car made its bow.

Best performances were Hulme's second in South Africa in 'M14A/2', McLaren's second in Spain in '14A/1', while Hulme was third in the British GP, driving 'M14D/1' fitted with a Cosworth in place of the Alfa, third in Germany in his usual 'M14A/2', and third in the same car in Mexico to end this sad season.

For 1971, ex-Brabham designer Ralph Bellamy produced his new 'Coke bottle' monocoque M19A design with geometrical linkage rising-rate suspensions at front and rear. This encountered severe development problems after a promising debut at Kyalami where Hulme led handsomely in chassis '1 until a bolt fell out of its rear suspension with only four laps to run, finishing sixth. In Championship races that season, the two regular cars '1 and '2 carried Hulme to fifth in Spain, fourth at Monaco and 12th at Zandvoort, where the second car emerged for Hulme and where Gethin in 'M19A/1' was 15th though not classified.

Gethin was ninth in France, then Oliver drove '1 for ninth in Austria, and Donohue used it to gain a tardy third place behind Hulme's chassis '2 in Canada. The Donohue car was painted in the Penske team's Sunoco dark-blue and yellow livery; Hobbs was tenth in this car at Watkins Glen, while Hulme crashed '2. The best showing even in minor races was Hulme's third in the Questor GP at Ontario and after

those heady early races the season fell apart.

Bellamy told me: 'The rising-rate suspension offered many theoretical advantages but in practice worked well enough at the front end of the car and less well at the back. Trying to sort it all out and set up the system so the driver felt happy and could understand what was going on proved rather tricky . . .'

Tyre vibration troubled everyone that season; by fitting far stiffer rear springs this was controlled but grip alas then destroyed. Donohue, the master car-developer, came to conclude later in the year that the M19s' problems were more to do with poor wing forms than trick suspension. Irrespective, Bellamy left the team during the 1971/72 winter to return to Brabham, thence to Lotus.

The M19s were modified for 1972, featuring improved wings and conventional rear suspension. Hulme's chassis '2 in new Yardley livery then won at Kyalami, as if in compensation for 1971.

A new lightened 'M19C/1' – ostensibly the last of the series – was completed for Hulme in the Race of Champions. Redman later deputized for new team driver Revson (absent at USAC races in America) and he crashed 'M19A/2' heavily at Clermont after which it was rebuilt around a new tub. The damaged original was subsequently rebuilt as a show car, renumbered 'R4' as a replica. The M19s' best result followed in the Austrian GP with Hulme and Revson 2-3 in pursuit of Fittipaldi's dominant Lotus 72; Hulme in 'C/1 and Revson in the re-chassised simpler and lighter 'A/2. Old 'M19A/1' was reworked with 49 gallons fuel capacity for the 312-mile Rothmans 50,000 Libre race at Brands Hatch, Redman finishing second.

Scheckter made his Formula 1 debut in 'A/1 at Watkins Glen. It had been a better year and the M19s would reappear in the early races of 1973 – Hulme and Revson 5-8 in Argentina, third and retired in Brazil and then, while Hulme gave the new M23 its debut in South Africa, Revson and Scheckter placed 2-9. Scheckter finally crashed 'M19C/1' in the minor Brands Hatch meeting, the Coke bottle cars' farewell appearance.

The new M23s' story is detailed on pages 80-6, and it in turn was replaced by the extensively honeycomb-chassised M26 designed by Gordon Coppuck as a lower, lighter, hip-radiator version of the M23. It made its debut during 1976 but was set aside as McLaren concentrated upon its M23s.

Second team driver Mass had given 'M26/1' its race debut at Zandvoort that August, placing ninth, then retired it from the Italian GP. The brief closed season prior to the

Unveiling the Coke-bottle rising-rate suspension 1971 M19 outside the Colnbrook factory are (l to r), Ralph Bellamy, Denny Hulme and Team Manager Phil Kerr.

new 1977 season saw extensive M26 testing. However, McLaren continued to run its faithful M23s until the Spanish GP because as 'M26/1' was being tested by Hunt at Kyalami a bolt on one of the balanced front brake callipers backed out and machined its way through the wheel rim, deflating the tyre and causing a comprehensive accident which virtually wrote off the car.

A new 'M26/2' was ready for Hunt at Jarama but it handled erratically and retired. M23s were raced at Monaco, then the M26 returned at Zolder with revised wings and an oil cooler in a nose duct to improve balance. It was well suited to the constant-radius corners at Anderstorp, qualifying third and running second before a stop for fresh tyres. The M26 was improving with every race and at Dijon Hunt put 'M26/2' on the front row and finished third. The Kyalami-damaged 'M26/1' was rebuilt for Mass to drive at Silverstone, Hunt placed '2 on pole and won luckily after the leading Brabham-Alfa faltered.

Mass ran a new 'M26/3' at Zandvoort, Hunt won again in 'M26/2' at Watkins Glen and was thundered out of the race in Canada by Mass! Poor 'M26/2' was bent severely against a wall. Hunt took over Mass's '3 in Japan and at one stage the two M26s, Mass in '1, ran 1-2 before the German's engine failed and Hunt won comfortably; the third Grand Prix victory of the season for this driver and the M26.

Three of the cars went to South America for the start of the 1978 season, with Tambay joining Hunt. 'M26/4' for Hunt was new, Tambay drove old 'M26/3', and they placed 4-6. Hunt was on the front row in Brazil but spun out of the race. New 'M26/5' was ready for Tambay at Kyalami, while another new M26 was being completed as a customer car for Brett Lunger, chassis '6. Giacomelli appeared in an effective McLaren 'B' team at Zolder in a new 'M26/7'. Later in the season the M26s fell off the pace as the new wing-cars forged ahead.

Chassis '4 was reworked after a practice collision at Jarama with rectangular side pods, sliding skirts and a cowled-in rear deck. This so-called M26E did nothing worthwhile.

On 17 October, Coppuck's new ground-effects M28 prototype was tested by Tambay, ready for 1979, and McLaren were entering a long, dark tunnel.

The M28 Nomex honeycomb monocoque formed the basis of a new large plan area car seeking to improve upon Lotus 79 download

James Hunt en-route to winning the 1977 British GP in his Coppuck-designed McLaren M26, notable for its shallow tub, extensive use of composite structural materials and neat cuneiform aerodynamics. Left, later McLarens sketched by Giorgio Piola: the 1979 M28 and its replacement M29.

1, Kevlar nose; 2, chassis front bulkhead; 3, steering rack; 4, suspension rocker clearance hole; 5, front rocker pick-up beam; 6, suspension rocker; 7, sliding skirt; 8, engine oil cooler; 9, water radiator; 10, honeycomb underwing side panel, Kevlar top bodywork; 11, titanium rear roll-over hoop; 12, inboard spring/dampers; 13, engine exhaust primary pipes; 14, cast-magnesium upright; 15, airbox; 16, integral rear wing side plates; 17, exhaust tailpipes ramp; a, top and bottom facing skins; b, honeycomb core; c, film adhesives.

1, front wings; 2, aluminium nose frame; 3, brake cylinder; 4, all-aluminium chassis; 5, front calliper; 6, bottom wishbone; 7, roll-over hoop stays; 8, water radiator; 9, water radiator air exit louvres; 10, oil-water intercooler; 11, fuel tank; 12,

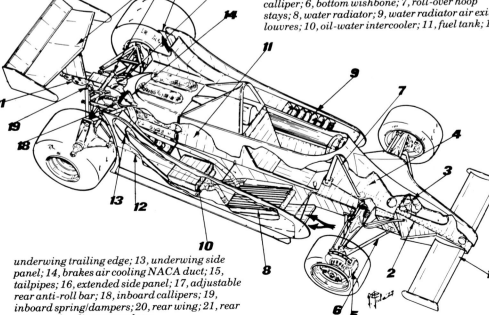

underwing trailing edge; 13, underwing side panel; 14, brakes air cooling NACA duct; 15, tailpipes; 16, extended side panel; 17, adjustable rear anti-roll bar; 18, inboard callipers; 19, inboard spring/dampers; 20, rear wing; 21, rear wing angle adjustment plates.

values by using increased area underwings. The result was one of the largest modern Formula 1 cars, with inboard suspensions front and rear, a 113 in. wheelbase, 70 in. front track and 64 in. rear track. It was tested in Lockheed's Atlanta wind tunnel and seemed to show potential.

Tambay was joined by Watson but the M28 was a disaster. The prototype structure failed, the bonding between its cast magnesium beams and honeycomb skins rending, and it had to be reworked. It was available to join 'M28/2', which had been more strongly constructed from the start, in Buenos Aires, and the cars ran through the first part of that season with insufficient grip, slow straightline speeds, as well as excess size and weight. Initial tests had seemed promising, probably because Goodyear offered McLaren a particularly good test tyre, but thereafter the awful truth dawned . . .

At Jarama a more compact M28B appeared, five inches shorter and some 50 lb lighter with new rear spring location behind the axle instead of ahead of it, in addition to revised front suspension geometry. Tambay drove 'M28/3' and 'M28/2' became team spare.

At Monaco an M28C-spec emerged, chassis '3, incorporating entirely inboard front suspension, revised bodywork and reprofiled side pods. Two M28Cs ran at Dijon but meanwhile on 1 May serious design had begun on a replacement M29.

It was virtually a Williams FW07 clone, with slender tub, single central fuel cell, VW water radiators in the side pod leading edges, oil cooled by radiator water in a heat-exchanger – another idea borrowed from Williams but used by BRM back in the '50s. The M29 saved some 125 lb under M28, and it featured hefty footbox driver protection which contemporary wing-cars lacked; its rear brakes were still inboard and thus continued to obstruct side pod airflow; it had a centre post rear wing, rear suspension elements behind the discs; and single instead of twin calliper brakes. John Thompson's TC Prototypes company in Northampton built the first M29 and two more followed from Colnbrook. An interim outboard rear brake variant was employed in winter Ricard tests, which saw newcomer Prost signed on for 1980.

A variant known as the M29C started the new season, with revised weight distribution, but Prost crashed it in practice at Kyalami, the first of several confidence-sapping incidents which he survived while Watson sank from indifferent to worse and was overshadowed.

A new M30 emerged, 50 per cent stiffer with all-inboard suspension, all-outboard brakes, making its debut at Zandvoort but being crashed in practice at Watkins Glen, destroying the last of the Colnbrook McLaren line.

A new McLaren International company was formed (as described in Chapter 15) late in 1980, Coppuck packed his bags and new Chief Engineer John Barnard improved the M30 before the end of the 1980 season, then concentrated upon development of his new carbon-fibre MP4/1 cars for 1981. These would bring success at last. The old M29Cs chassis '2-4-5 went to Kyalami for the first race, uprated to M29F spec thereafter.

The first Hercules-moulded (see page 146) MP4/1 made its debut at Long Beach, though for practice only, being driven by Watson and the improvement was instant. Chassis '2 emerged for Watson at Imola, '3 as spare from Dijon and '4 brand new for Watson in Montreal and Las Vegas.

Continued on page 225.

Previous page: The right racing line demonstrated by three very different designs at Monaco 1976: Lauda's Ferrari 312T2 leading the rush from *Mirabeau Inférieur* into *Le Portier* from Ronnie Peterson's shoe-string budget F2-based March 761, Regazzoni's second Ferrari and the Tyrrell-twin P34 six-wheelers of Depailler and Scheckter. *Above:* Gordon Murray's Brabhams have all been beautifully built, few more popular with the team than the 1975 BT44B seen here, showing off its broad nose with horizontal sacrificial 'air-splitter' protruding forward which prompted early Brabham ground-effects experiments, split water radiators inside, rising-rate pullrod suspension, and pyramid section tub. Black grip on tub side was a hand-hold so the driver could lever himself out of cockpit, otherwise his hands would just slide down the sloping surface! Goodyear treaded tyres are unusual in such a sunny scene. The air-hose is evidence that compressed-air power tools were gaining popularity. *Right:* The Right One – in this case Lauda's Ferrari '312T2-030' hounding Hans Stuck Jnr's Martini-backed Brabham-Alfa Romeo 'BT45/1' down into the Old Station Hairpin at Monaco, 1977. The Martini-Brabham's flat-12 Alfa engine demanded a lot of fuel and cooling.

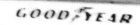

Above: New dawn, Mario Andretti's Lotus 78 'wing car' heralded the harnessing of ground-effect aerodynamics in Formula 1 during 1977. Here, with the improved Type 79 (*right*) under development back home, Mario is on his way to winning the 1978 Argentine GP at Buenos Aires in '78/3'. The 78's underwings generated their download rather far forward due to protruding wing tanks, engine exhaust and outboard rear suspension obstructing side pod air-exit, and grip from its wide-track front end always overwhelmed the rear. The Lotus 79, seen here with Andretti at home and the Guv'nor, Colin Chapman, alongside, had over-the-gearbox exhausts, all its fuel in a single tub tank, centred its download further aft and went as well as it looked in 1978. The following year showed up its system and stiffness inadequacies.

WASTE
OIL
VALVOLINE
OLYMPUS
CAMERAS
Valvoline
5
Valvoline
GOODYEAR

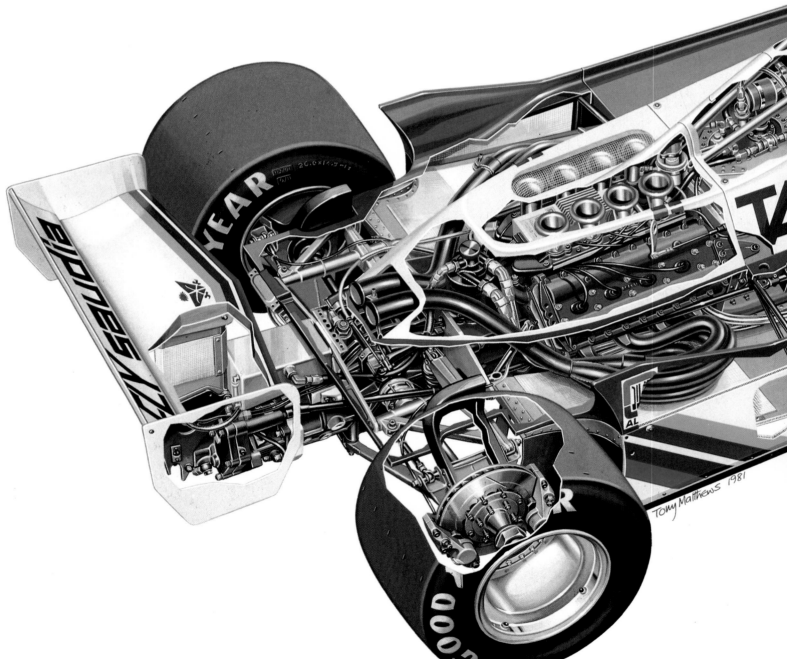

Tony Matthews 1981

Left: Scheckter's 1979 Ferrari 312T4 'lawn-mower' which made effective use of overbody air to achieve aerodynamic performance when Ferrari were increasingly confused by new ground-effects technology. Note clean airflow onto front wing, around cockpit and over low rear deck to that highly cambered, low frontal area wing. Some pressure loss was inevitable on the wing centre due to masking by high cowl ahead, hence Ferrari's increase in wing-chord there to increase active area in the blind spot. *Below:* Ultimate expression of the ground-effects car era, Alan Jones actually unsticking his Williams 'FW07/7' for a change, Long Beach 1980. Over the hump here the left-side skirt with its abrade-resistant edge can be seen just clearing the dipping roadway. The aerial is a timing trigger. *Left:* Tony Matthews' artistry unveils some of the secrets of the 1981 Williams FW07C 'clearance car'.

215

Top left: Gilles Villeneuve coming to grips with Ferrari's new 1.5-litre 126C2 turbocharged cars, in this case '055, at a rainy Kyalami, South African GP, 1982. The Postlethwaite-designed aluminium honeycomb cars gave Ferrari the handling to match their turbocharged power. The fixed skirt should be noted, with its resistant edge running against the road, and clean over-body airflow. *Left:* 'All Ferrari need', the British said, 'is a half-way decent chassis and we won't see which way they've gone'. Dr Harvey Postlethwaite was imported to deliver the goods which he did with the carbon-composite mid-1983 'C3, as seen here at Silverstone with René Arnoux installed. Flat-bottom regs have led to abbreviated side pods, mid-ship tub tank forces driver forward, pullrod front suspension is used, tub moulding forms external 'body'. *Above:* Gordon Murray's approach to flat-bottom rules was the all-new spearhead Brabham BT52 BMW turbo. Nelson Piquet is seen here at Monaco — despite a draggy rear end it was a striking and Drivers' title-winning package. Michelin radial-ply tyres were inherently consistent in manufacture, and the bad old days of team tyre specialists painstakingly selecting and matching inconsistent covers were a fading memory.

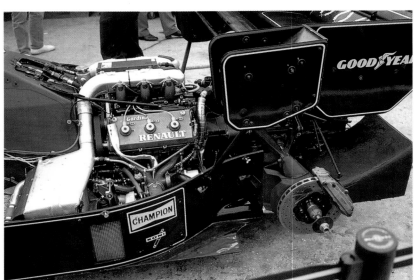

Loss of innocence. When a late-1970s Cosworth car was taken back to its manufacturers for service the mechanics scratched their heads and wondered if half of it was missing because the 3-litre naturally aspirated cars were so simple compared to the turbos. *Opposite, top left to bottom right:* Lotus 79 stripped out, 1978, showing spidery tub, up-and-over exhausts, inboard brakes and rear coil/dampers tucked within DFV section, Aeroquip everywhere and the red-cased rear anti-roll bar adjuster cable clearly visible. Brabham's Alfa Romeo V12 was produced with incredible speed for 1978 but reliability suggested as much. Underbody floor is visible sweeping up in that left-side pod, Alfa still demanded a lot of cooling. BMW's M12/13 turbo made its Brabham bow in 1982 and became the most potent unit in Formula 1, with over 1270 bhp in 1985 test-trim. Heat insulation was copious, and vital. Renault pioneered the turbo option from 1977 – here's an EF4 V6 in the 1984 Lotus 95T. Left-side manifolds feed one charger, pressure air then passing through the intercooler ahead, into engine-top induction log. Note seamed carbon tub, waisted-in 'McLaren tail', rear ground-effects diffuser moulding 'blown' by exhaust below, and sidestep winglet ahead of axle line up top. In Renault's cars the V6 displays its array of electronics, vital for mid-1980s 950 bhp. Ferrari's 1981 126C V6 shows off its in-vee twin turbochargers, centre wastegate with vertical flue, hip-mounted intercoolers feeding side induction logs direct. Water radiators recline out ahead, underwing floors below. The curved-tube rear suspension truss would have done Cooper credit. Note tiny rear anti-roll bar on top of the excellent *trasversale* gearbox. *Right:* Dominant 1984 engine: McLaren's Porsche-engineered TAG Turbo V6 was reliable, powerful and, thanks to John Barnard, stringently well-packaged. Just two hand-spans cover the cam-box length, V6 mounts in the DFV strap-plate manner; note McLaren tail, inboard rocker-arm rear suspension, large de-aerating oil tank, low-slung KKK turbocharger, carefully sealed intercooler and carbon tub. By courtesy of McLaren International and TAG Turbo Engines, here's the first published section through the double-Championship-winning TTE-PO1 V6.

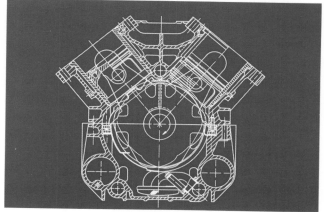

Planform of the flat-bottomed Formula 1 car, 1984 – in this case Tambay's Renault RE50. Pushrod links operating the inboard coil-spring/damper units extend from the front upright feet to their high-mounted chassis rockers, sidepods are abbreviated with intakes in relatively clean air, the driver's feet being down between front suspensions. The dayglo rear winglets add download just ahead of rear axle line, behind which wing width is restricted. For 1985 tighter regulations made such devices illegal.

Alain Prost gave Marlboro-McLaren and Unipart maximum exposure at Zandvoort '84. Here the standard-setting MP4/2-TAG Turbo-by-Porsche shows off its beautifully conceived and well-packaged low-drag, high-download form, diagonal front suspension pushrod links, hip turbocharger air intake just ahead of that rear wheel and well-fenced rear winglets and wing. Prost's carbon-composite chassis 'MP4/2-2' led 61 of the 71 laps after qualifying on pole and beat team-mate Lauda's 'MP4/2-1' by 10 seconds into second place.

Overleaf top: Rising sun – after delivery of latest-spec Honda V6 engines, the Williams FW10s emerged as the most potent performers in Formula 1. Here at Detroit Rosberg won in 'FW10/4'; note pushrod front suspension, narrow regulation two-tier rear wing and 'McLaren tail' waisting within rear wheels. The tall engine cover was lowered later in the season after engine modifications, improving airflow onto rear wing which, with revised rear suspension, greatly enhanced performance.

Overleaf bottom: Over the hill and far away – Ayrton Senna's Lotus-Renault 97T dominated the 1985 San Marino GP at Imola until it ran out of fuel. The vertical deflector vane inboard of the front wheel cleans up turbulent drag-inducing airflow there, while beneath the centre-strut rear wing can be seen the behind-the-rear-axle legal underwing diffuser assembly, retrieving ground-effects download with the aid of high-energy exhaust gases 'blowing' the diffuser underside.

In 1979 the vast M28 caused McLaren deep trouble and they responded mid-season with this hastily concocted M29 'Williams FW07 clone' in which John Watson salvaged a little pride for the team.

continued from page 208

His results from the Spanish to the British GPs ran 3-2-1 and thereafter he placed sixth in the German and Austrian races, second in Canada and seventh in Las Vegas. His young team-mate de Cesaris was less consistent, crashing too often and having only one worthwhile finish, classified seventh after retirement in Italy.

Barnard's bold stroke in giving a very slender tub vital rigidity by moulding it in lightweight high-stiffness carbon-fibre was condemned in some quarters because the poor impact and crush resistance of carbon structures had received great publicity. 'Wait until that McLaren hits something hard', they said, the present author included. De Cesaris put the moulded tub to the test repeatedly and finally Watson crumped into the Lesmo barriers at Monza very violently during the Italian GP, smashing 'MP4/1-3' in two as engine and gearbox tore away from the monocoque.

Perhaps it was fortunate the impact was rear-end first but Watson survived unharmed, as had de Cesaris every time, and the Monza tub could almost have been repaired though badly crazed and sporting a fine maze of cracks.

Barnard considered Dijon, where Watson was second, their best race that year because the car was quick with minimal practice changes, having been set up properly in the new Woking factory before departure. Paradoxically, he was not so happy in Britain where Watson won, since in testing there Watson had found the car would do anything and everything he wanted it to, while for the GP it was not quite so well balanced.

Running very stiff suspension made McLaren re-examine package stiffness. There were some damper troubles and a major bounce problem. The McLarens were the only Cosworth runners contracted to Michelin tyres and in some ways suffered because of it. Whereas Renault and Ferrari demanded traction for their turbocharged engines, McLaren had other requirements. Sometimes they could minimize bounce by using different construction tyres; they had more downforce than Renault and far more than Ferrari but less power.

For 1982 the existing cars were updated to MP4/1B specification, starting the season at Kyalami with chassis '2 and '4 from 1981 plus a brand new chassis '5. Chassis '6 emerged new for joint number one driver Lauda at Zolder and chassis '7 emerged as spare at Brands Hatch. 'MP4/1-1B' was the old original prototype tub moulding and it was uprated to B-spec and used as test and development car throughout '82.

Towards the end of 1981, McLaren Interna-

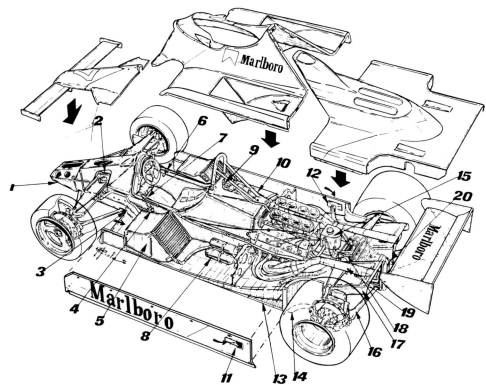

John Barnard's carbon-monocoque MP4/1 of 1981, dissected by Piola.
1, aluminium nose; 2, front anti-roll bar blade; 3, bottom wishbone, rear leg inboard pick-up; 4, air starter action lever; 5, honeycomb oil radiator air duct; 6, gearlever; 7, rear anti-roll bar adjusting lever; 8, air starter bottles; 9, fuel tank quick filler; 10, titanium roll bar; 11, left rear shock absorber cooling duct; 12, right rear shock absorber cooling duct; 13, carbon-fibre underwing; 14, rear wheel sealing to underwing; 15, engine oil filler and catch tank; 16, rear bottom wishbone; 17, underwing extension; 18, adjustable rear anti-roll bar; 19, left tailpipe; 20, gearbox oil tank.

tional had developed an efficient wind tunnel research programme, fitting their own moving ground gear in the National Maritime Institute tunnel at Feltham. Testing full size at Michelin's Ladoux centre near Clermont-Ferrand confirmed model results, the track having in-built weight balances to record load as a vehicle passed over them. The MP4/1s changed very little outwardly during the season though Barnard pared-off some weight, modified the suspensions and tried to improve stiffness in everything.

Early-season success – winning at Long Beach – saw Michelin build special 15 in. front tyres which reacted better than the 13s and intermediate 'TRX' sizes formerly used, though the TRX 340 mm rear rim size remained virtually standard. Michelin traction was always very good. On many circuits McLaren could run narrow rears for a useful drag reduction – tyres which Renault with their greater power could not nurse through race distance. During the year McLaren also varied both track and wheelbase, mostly running front track as wide as possible, adding 3½-4 in. to wheelbase at one point, then pulling back to 2 in. longer than original.

Carbon brakes were tried in Brazil and California, then set aside for further development.

In 1982, Lauda started 14 of the 16 GPs – the team withdrawing from Imola and Lauda injuring himself in practice at Hockenheim. He finished eight times: 4-1-(3)-4-1-8-5-3, but he was disqualified from the third place at Zolder because his car was underweight, having consumed more consumables than expected.

Watson started 15 GPs, finished ten, placing 6-2-6-1-1-3-9-13-4-2. They won the Long Beach and British GPs (Lauda) and at Zolder and Detroit (Watson), MI placing second only to Ferrari in the Constructors' table.

In 1983 the existing MP4/1Bs were further updated as flat-bottom MP4/1Cs, chassis '2-4-5-6 all being thus modified while '6 would be converted to accept the TAG Turbo engine (as described on page 159) late in the year. New chassis '7 and '8 emerged respectively for Lauda at Rio and Watson at Monaco, the latter being destroyed in a workshop accident hilarious to outsiders when, against Barnard's instructions, higher-pressure refuelling was tested; incoming fluid splashed up into the breather, blocking it temporarily, whereupon excess back-pressure applied over the considerable wall area of the tank simply blew it apart.

The original old prototype tub '1 became the TAG turbo test hack MP4/1D while '5-6-7' became the TAG Turbo MP4/1E interim cars introduced at Zandvoort – '5 as incomplete second car, '6 as Lauda's race car, '7 as a spare in time for Kyalami, ending the season. The rest of the story is related in Chapter 15.

Merzario

The Italian Arturo Merzario was primarily a sports car and road racing ace, but he was also competent in Formula 1. When the offers of drives dried up he promptly built a car of his own based on the old March 751.

This was in 1978, and he attempted to run the complete season with his Merzario A1 specials, chassis '01 and '02. They were very hefty-looking cars, the effect heightened by the spindly Merzario's extraordinarily low driving position, the top of his head barely visible over the high cockpit coaming. He tried wider tracks at Kyalami and had a fright in Long Beach qualifying when the steering column dropped loose. Chassis '02 appeared in Austria, finished in the paddock with revised front suspension and many titanium parts. He qualified for eight of the 16 races but finished none.

Merzario pressed on in 1979, first with his updated A1B then with the new A2 designed in conjunction with his mechanic Simon Hadfield.

Neither were proper wing-cars, though by Kyalami the A2 had everything necessary bar the slender tub. A new '03 car appeared at Long Beach which was too fragile to race, and after Merzario fell down the stairs at his workshop and broke his right arm Gianfranco Brancatelli attempted to pre-qualify at Monaco, following the withdrawal of his Kauhsen team. He failed, but Merzario had bought some of the Kauhsen hardware.

For the British GP, the remarkable Merzario ran the Kauhsen-based A4 co-designed by GiamPaolo Dallara of Lamborghini, and de Tomaso fame, this being a proper wing-car with single fuel cell behind the cockpit, underwing side pods and slender, high scuttled riveted aluminium monocoque, rocker-arm suspensions and outboard brakes, but it was not enough.

At Monza, Merzario became probably the first Grand Prix driver to be sponsored by an undertaker but his hopes had been buried by the season's end. He tackled 14 GPs, non-qualified for 12 of them, and retired in Argentina and Long Beach.

There was no longer a place for 'specials' in modern Formula 1 and the tyre supply situation, with hot 'qualifiers' rationed for the major teams and only 'wooden' tyres left over for the non-FOCA teams, negated the last chance the little men might have had.

Minardi

Giancarlo Minardi had been running various Formula 2 teams for several years when he decided to make the step into Formula 1 for 1985. It was a product more of enthusiasm and available sponsorship than of technical excellence, and team driver would be a wealthy newcomer, former Italian Formula 3 Champion, Pierluigi Martini.

A Giacomo Caliri-designed F3000/F1 car was built by Minardi in their Faenza plant, the prototype being intended for Alfa Romeo V8 turbo power. However, during 1984 Carlo Chiti was dismissed from Alfa Romeo and set up his own Motori Moderni concern to build an all-new turbocharged V6 intended for customer sale à la Cosworth DFV. Inevitably, with Chiti's reputation, there would be few takers, and Minardi emerged as the initial and, at the time of writing, only customer.

Four carbon-composite M85 chassis were built and Chiti's new V6 was not raceworthy in time for the opening races at Rio and Estoril, so chassis 'M85/1's engine mounts were revised and a shorter spacer inserted between engine

and gearbox to carry a Cosworth V8 engine without disturbing the designed wheelbase. The car ran near-horizontal rear dampers over the gearbox, and unfortunately looked as hopeless as its driver.

Both its 3-litre races ended in retirement; the new Motori Moderni V6 emerged at Imola after 700 km trouble-free testing, but it proved desperately underpowered and Martini retired again. He failed to qualify at Monaco and in the next 12 GPs retired or crashed nine times, was classified 11th in Germany though not running at the finish, and took the chequered flag 12th in Belgium and eighth and last in Australia. Nevertheless, Minardi announced plans for a two-car team in 1986.

Osella

In the 1970s Italian Enzo Osella bought the Abarth company and made a series of small-capacity sports-racing cars which achieved considerable Italian national success; then from 1976 he embarked upon Formula 2, winning three races in 1979 with Cheever driving. Osella and Giorgio Stirano then designed and built a bulky Cosworth-powered FA1 wing-car which initially weighed over 650 kg (1433 lb) but which was trimmed down subsequently, for Cheever. Neither team nor driver had an easy time, failing to qualify four times through 1980 and finishing only once, 12th, with a new FA1B car, at Imola of course!

Two FA1s had been built in Osella's Turin factory, using Ferrari 'Aero' hybrid monocoque construction, with a tubular-steel internal frame stiffened by the aluminium stressed skins. Chassis 'FA1/1' ran most of the season, chassis '2 appearing brand new as Cheever's spare from Monaco. The revised FA1B had a much lighter and 8 cm (3.1 in.) narrower aluminium tub allowing larger-area underwings and Cheever drove this in the last three events.

Osella ran a proper two-car team in 1981. Beppe Gabbiani became regular driver, with a notable string of 12 non-qualifications to his name and he finished not one of the three GPs he did start. Giorgio Francia had one outing, failing to qualify in Spain, Piercarlo Ghinzani two outings, finishing 13th at Zolder after his only qualification. Angel Guerra failed to qualify three times and retired at Imola, before

PierCarlo Ghinzani demonstrating the flat-bottom regulations needleform of Enzo Osella's Southgate-designed FA1E '003' at Kyalami, 1983.

Osella hired the experienced and able Jarier for the last seven GPs, for which he qualified 100 per cent and finished four times – 8-8-10-9.

Two new regulation 'clearance cars' had been built under *Ingegnere* Giorgio Valentini's direction, namely FA1Bs '3 and '4. The prototype 'FA1B/1' was uprated and retained as spare, while a new FA1C model emerged at Monza for Jarier.

This was lighter and stiffer, like an Arrows A3 up front, Brabham BT49 at the rear, and it dispensed with the 'Aero' hybrid structure, using aluminium sheet with honeycomb outer skins for driver protection. It had the shortest wheelbase in Formula 1, its aerodynamic form developed by *Ing* Beccio in Fiat's Orbassano wind tunnel.

Osella retained Jarier for 1982; he started 13 races, failed to qualify at Monaco and Österreichring, and did not start in Las Vegas. He finished three times, placing 9-4-14, the fourth place being at Imola where there were only a dozen starters due to FOCA's boycott.

A young Italian Formula 2 driver, Riccardo Paletti, was given his Formula 1 chance, but anyone with a Cosworth engine could have only limited hopes in '82 and he failed to qualify five times. He raced in the thin Imola field but failed to start due to a practice accident after qualifying in Detroit. A week later he qualified on the back of the grid at Montreal but at the start he was unsighted by the pack ahead and smashed flat-out into the stalled pole-position Ferrari, dying later while 'FA1C/002' was destroyed. This tragedy left Jarier to race alone thereafter.

Osella's season began with FA1Cs '001-2-3, Jarier damaging '001 heavily during Las Vegas practice at the other end of the year, '003 being bent at Detroit in practice and not reappearing, and '004 being Paletti's warm-up crash car at Detroit, repaired for Jarier's use in Montreal and subsequent races.

For the German GP Osella perversely adopted new wide-track rear suspension – odd, because most people tried to run narrow track on the faster circuits to find more speed – and with engine and gearbox undertrays the cars became known as FA1Ds.

Osella persevered into 1983, starting with FA1Ds, updated by Giuseppe Peirotta to conform to flat bottom rules with very abbreviated hip radiator pods exposing slender forward tub nacelles and numbered as new, awaiting a new Alfa Romeo 1260 V12-engined car in mid-season. This FA1E prototype was actually a Cosworth tub converted for the longer Alfa unit, and it was driven by Ghinzani from Imola onwards, a second FA1E '02 emerging with Alfa power for team-mate Corrado Fabi and a third car following.

These later FA1Es were designed by Tony Southgate and built by a company he had formed with John Thompson, the well-known jobbing monocoque specialist, named Auto Racing Technology Ltd, originally set up to build the aborted Ford C100 endurance cars. Their Osella chassis used a slender aluminium-sided, carbon-topped tub with unusual pushrod front suspension in which the rods fed direct into the feet of coil/dampers mounted high on the scuttle spine, reacting either side of a common mounting.

In the early-season Cosworth cars, Fabi posted three non-qualifications and five race retirements, while Ghinzani simply non-qualified in his three Cosworth outings. In the Alfa cars Fabi non-qualified three times more, and his four races included two finishes, 10-11. Ghinzani's Alfa-powered races included five non-qualifications, six retirements and just one finish, 11th at the Österreichring. By this time Autodelta were concentrating upon their 183T turbo V8 engines for the Alfa Romeo 'works' team and the V12 was a forgotten quantity, hardly any better than a decent off-the-shelf Cosworth.

Chassis used were 'FA1D/001' and '002 for

Fabi and Ghinzani respectively early in the year, then the Alfa-powered FA1Es '001 from Imola, '002 new for Fabi at Silverstone and '003 new for Ghinzani there.

The Alfa V8 turbo was available to Osella with the prospect of being competitive at last in 1984. Osella actually took over an ACC British-made ex-Alfa Romeo 183T carbon-composite chassised car, slightly remodelled and repainted in their 'Kelémata' sponsor's colours for Ghinzani. He survived an almighty accident in it pre-race at Kyalami, which cannot be said for the car . . .

After 'FA1F/01's demise in this manner, three more 'proper' Osella-Alfa V8s emerged, with design credited to Enzo Osella and Southgate no longer consulting: '02 was new for Ghinzani at Zolder, '03 new at Monaco as team spare and '04 new at Brands Hatch for new team number two Jo Gartner. He had driven old Alfa V12 'FA1E/02' at Imola and retired, then ran the last seven races, retiring four times and finishing 13-5-'16'. The points-scoring fifth place was achieved on Osella's home soil at Monza where the aces ran out of fuel in the closing laps and Gartner was too slow to be that thirsty, despite the Alfa engine being a desperately dypsomaniac unit.

Ghinzani, meanwhile, understandably did not start at Kyalami and failed to qualify at Imola – which stung – but his 14 races yielded five finishes – 12-7-5-9-'7' – his fifth place being at Dallas where the disintegrating state of the track, the heat and fuel economy decimated the field and again the slow Osella survived when most around had not.

For 1985 Osella engineer Nino Petrotta modified the 1984 FA1F chassis '01 and '02 for Ghinzani's lone-entry use as spare and race cars in Rio and Estoril, opening the new season, then introduced his improved FA1G design at Imola. It weighed-in at 568 kg, 10 kg lighter than the '1F, with altered aerodynamic form, side radiator and vertical intercooler like a Toleman, a wider front track and now an '85-spec Alfa Romeo V8 turbo engine.

Ghinzani subsequently took the second Toleman driver's seat, making room at Osella for Dutch driver Rothengatter from the German GP.

Both drivers did seven races for the team (based in Volpiano, Turin), Ghinzani failing to qualify at Monaco and Rothengatter at Brands Hatch. The Italian finished three times, the Dutchman only twice; placing respectively 12-9-15 at Rio, Estoril and Ricard, and 9-7 in Austria and – very much on inheritance – in Adelaide.

It was always difficult to understand what a team like Osella could gain from Formula 1, particularly as they were always handicapped by their uncompetitive Pirelli tyres; nevertheless, it has always been good for racing that such teams will contribute colour and quantity, and cheerful enthusiasm.

Parnelli

Serbo-American Velco Miletich, together with his former Indianapolis-winning USAC Champion driver friend Rufus Parnelli Jones, had formed Vel's Parnelli Jones Racing in 1969 after the track Champion's retirement from driving. They were very successful in USAC and also embraced drag racing, Formula 5000 and even off-road events like the Baja classic. They were heavily backed by Firestone tyres and for 1974 decided to enter Formula 1 by building a Firestone-shod car to be driven by Andretti.

This was a natural step, for VPJ had a number of ex-Team Lotus Formula 1 personnel who would include Chief Engineer Maurice Phillippe, Crew Chief Dick Scammell and Team Administrator Andrew Ferguson.

Their new Formula 1 Parnelli VPJ4 was a development of Phillippe's work on the Lotus

72; wedge-form, hip radiators alongside its Cosworth engine, rearward weight bias, torsion bar suspension and all-inboard brakes. The debut of the car (carrying Viceroy cigarettes livery) came in the late-1974 Canadian GP, where Andretti finished seventh. It also qualified third quickest at Watkins Glen, only for an electrical problem to intrude at the start.

The sophisticated new car showed great promise but Firestone abruptly withdrew from racing, leaving Vel's Parnelli to rely on outdated stock tyres for 1975, without hope of competitive development. Worse, Jones had no interest in Formula 1 and was not carried along by Miletich's enthusiasm.

Andretti began the new season in Argentina with 'VPJ4/002' on Firestones, but for the second race in Brazil it was Goodyear-shod. He placed third in 'Team USA's entry in the minor Silverstone race and led the Spanish GP in '002 after the field had been decimated by an early collision. Sadly his car had also been damaged in that shunt and as its rear suspension progressively failed he eventually crashed. He missed the Belgian race (away at Indianapolis) and the Dutch GP; his 12 Championship outings saw four proper finishes, 7-4-6-12, which was not bad, all things considered . . .

His consecutive fourth and sixth place points scores came in the Swedish and French GPs. He had shunted '001 during practice in Sweden, new noses were tried in France and outboard front brakes appeared at the Nürburgring to load up the latest generation Goodyear tyres – the same problem afflicting the 'genuine' Lotus 72s at that time. Chassis '001 was also on outboard brakes at Monza, and one of the two cars at Watkins Glen ran coil-spring rear suspension in place of torsion bar, so curing a much-criticized tendency to spin the inside wheel under power. Andretti had driven '002 in early season races until new car '003 appeared at Monaco, then took charge of '001 in the French and British GPs, '002 at the Nürburgring, '003 in Austria, '001 in Italy, '002 in the USA. But his team owners had quite lost interest: winning was not easy, there was minimal return and they had other business problems in the USA.

Early in 1976 Andretti carried the project on his shoulders. Chassis 'VPJ4B/002' appeared with coil-spring suspension all round and redesigned rear bodywork to finish sixth at Kyalami. The same chassis, with '75-style rear body, shorter nose and 'All American Racing Wheels' lettering, retired at Long Beach. Vel's Parnelli abandoned Formula 1 thereafter, and the team was disbanded.

Only the crew and that beautiful car would be missed, and Andretti was outspokenly bitter at this wasted opportunity.

Pearce

Wheeler-dealer J. A. Pearce, based in Southall, West London, was a skilled welder who had built Chris Lawrence's Deep Sanderson chassis, before emerging as head of a considerable wheel and tyre and motor trading business. He built a Formula 1 Cooper-Ferrari 250 GT V12 special in 1966 which Lawrence raced for him. Following this relative success – it earned some start money – Pearce manufactured two new Formula 1 spaceframe chassis to be powered by the Martin V8 engine, manufactured by Ted Martin's tiny engineering and tuning workshop in Haddenham, Buckinghamshire.

Most of the circuit development for this two-cam light-alloy V8 had been done by Roy Thomas of Lucas Engineering. This Formula 2 team fitted one in a Lotus 35 F2 chassis, which was raced at Mallory Park on Boxing Day 1966, driven by Roy Pike and finishing third. Courage then drove it at Brands Hatch in March 1967 but an overnight head change had been botched and a rocker bent as it was started just before the race, forcing it to non-start. Sadly Courage then crashed heavily in Snetterton testing and it was seen no more.

Meanwhile, the prototype Pearce Formula 1 chassis had been exhibited at the London Racing Car Show, for which the Ferrari engine from the older, heavier Cooper had been earmarked. However, three more compact cars were to be built, only two of which were ever completed, tailored to the more compact Martin V8. Lawrence lapped the Brands Hatch short circuit in the 52 second bracket in an early test, only to crash heavily, severely damaging the prototype car. The two complete Pearce-Martins and the old Cooper-Ferrari, all in the team's metallic pale green colours, were in the team transporter parked at Silverstone on the Wednesday before the International Trophy meeting, when the vehicle caught fire. Everything was totally destroyed.

Penske

The patrician Philadelphian businessman Roger Penske made his name in SCCA sports car racing in the early-Sixties, before concentrating his sporting interests upon running CanAm, long-distance sports, TransAm and Indy cars, mainly for the very accomplished engineer-driver Mark Donohue.

After winning the 1972 CanAm Championship in his Penske-entered turbocharged Porsche 917/30, Donohue retired from driving. During 1974, however, Penske laid plans to enter Formula 1 and Donohue was tempted back into the cockpit.

Penske appreciated that he could not tackle Formula 1 from a US base, and he took over the former McRae Formula 5000 workshops in Poole, Dorset, on the south coast of England, to have his cars designed, built and prepared. Even after his Formula 1 team's eventual demise, this facility would continue to produce highly successful Penske track racing cars for years to come.

The prototype Penske PC1 made its debut in the 1974 Canadian GP at Mosport Park. It was designed by former Brabham draughtsman Geoff Ferris, featuring a very clean wedge profile with hip radiators. Front suspension had semi-inboard springs actuated by rocker arms extending from large planform faired-in fabricated top links, parallel links were used at the rear and there was talk of fitting cockpit-adjustable anti-roll bars for 1975, as planned by March in 1972 but not used.

Donohue easily qualified for the race and finished 11th, then retired from the US GP.

For 1975, a second PC1 was completed, with a wider track than '01, new rocker-arm inboard front suspension and modified airbox and wing. Donohue was seventh in Argentina but retired in Brazil with handling problems.

The PC1 was not really competitive and Donohue was unhappy with both his own form and the car's. He was a distant eighth at Kyalami where 'PC1-02' ran a three-inch wider rear track and five-inch spacer between engine and gearbox, lengthening its wheelbase. He crashed at Brands Hatch but was sixth at Silverstone.

Some progress was clearly being made but then Donohue crashed at Barcelona. At Monte Carlo, where '01 ran a five-inch narrower front track and short wheelbase for the tight circuit, he crashed heavily yet again in practice. Nevertheless, it was rebuilt in time to race once more uncompetitively, finishing 11th.

The Swedish GP saw a decent result at last, Donohue reaching fifth to gain his first two Championship points. A new chassis '3 appeared at Zandvoort in narrow-track form, but eighth place there and retirement with driveshaft joint failure in France convinced Penske – used to success – to cut his losses in the short term by dropping the PC1 and trying a March 751 customer car instead.

One of the works 751s was tested by Donohue at Silverstone, instantly some two seconds per lap quicker than the PC1, so a brand new Penske March was built up. Donohue crashed fatally due to a front tyre failure on race morning at the Österreichring in August.

After the March's destruction, Penske missed the Italian GP but Ferris was joined at Poole by the team's American engineer Don Cox and between them they developed a new PC3 design based on the March, though the PC3 retained the successful PC1 rear end and Hewland FGA gearbox unlike March's preferred FG.

When questioned on the PC3's similarity to the March 751, team manager Heinz Hofer remarked sagely; 'When you don't know the neighbourhood, you don't stray many streets away from home . . .'

New team driver Watson qualified 'PC3-01' safely in mid-field at Watkins Glen, but a severe misfire on the warm-up lap caused the PC1 prototype to be hastily substituted. Watson's reliable ninth came as a surprise, because the car had not been race-prepared, having been merely a sponsor's display-piece in the paddock.

This was the prelude to a much better year for Penske's Formula 1 hopes in 1976, with Watson starting the PC3 cars in 16 races, 15 of them Championship rounds, and finishing 11 of them. Three PC3 chassis were built and results included fifth at Kyalami in chassis '1, while Watson crashed '02 in the minor Brands Hatch meeting, was seventh in Belgium and 10th in Monaco in '01. The PC3 still wasn't quite 'there'.

A new PC4 appeared at Anderstorp in June, but its throttles jammed open on the first lap and it crashed. This machine had a very low-built tapered-planform monocoque. Its Ferrari-like nose wing used in Sweden was replaced by a slim chisel affair with side fins for the next race at Ricard, where a longer wheelbase was used. PC4 featured in-line hip mounted radiators and a very slim and neat cockpit surround and engine cover, intake ducts for the engine induction being moulded into its shoulders.

It proved fundamentally better than the PC3s. Watson was third at Ricard – only to be disqualified because the leading edge of the rear wing side plates proved to be a centimetre above the legal maximum height, the whole assembly having bent backwards on its mounting during the race.

Repositioned oil coolers improved balance for Brands Hatch, Watson finishing fourth, then seventh in Germany and winning on merit after qualifying on the front row in Austria.

In Holland, Watson qualified on the second row and duelled for the lead until gearbox trouble intervened. Local driver Boy Hayje rented old 'PC3-02' there but suffered driveshaft failure. In the US GP, Watson finished sixth and in Japan qualified on row two but retired with engine failure.

Chassis 'PC4-02' had been raced in Canada and the US and was then returned to Poole for strip-down while only '01 went to Japan. Penske had decided to withdraw from Formula 1 and concentrate upon American track racing which promised a better return. The Penske PC4 cars were bought by Hans Gunther Schmid for his ATS team's Formula 1 programme in 1977 (see page 164), while the old PC3s went into other hands.

Pilbeam

See entry for LEC, page 191.

RAM

John MacDonald and Mick Ralph's RAM team entered Formula 1 with immaculately prepared Brabham and March cars from 1976, but they were run for no-hoper drivers and achieved nothing significant. RAM persevered regardless, always with support from FOCA supremo Bernard Ecclestone, who is generally very good to the smaller teams. In 1981 they brought March back into Formula 1 and then began building their own cars for 1983.

Initially they retained the March name for their Dave Kelly-designed Cosworth-engined RAM model 01. Three such chassis were built, '01-2-3 of course, and they were campaigned through that season by drivers Salazar, Jean-Louis Schlesser, Jacques Villeneuve and Kenny Acheson.

They achieved little. Schlesser placed sixth (second to last) in the minor Race of Champions at Brands Hatch in '02's debut, Salazar was 15th in '01 at Rio and Acheson 12th at Kyalami to end the season. They failed to qualify 12 times, their car simply not up to the job.

For 1984, however, MacDonald obtained Hart 415T four-cylinder turbo engines as proven by Toleman, and the still impecunious team converted RAM '01/01' from Cosworth to Hart power as a pilot exercise while new carbon-composite chassised RAM 02 cars were built.

The prototype RAM '02/01' made its bow at Rio driven by Philippe Alliot, hybrid '01/03' running there for his team-mate Jonathan Palmer. Alliot drove '02/01' regularly until effectively writing it off in Dallas practice and therefore non-started in the race. RAM '02/02' was new for Palmer at Zolder, crashed heavily following a chassis failure thereby stopping the British GP at Brands Hatch, and was then rebuilt for the final races of the season.

RAM '02/03' made its debut in the British GP for Alliot and was badly bent by a multiple accident – with little blame attaching to its unfortunate driver – within its first mile of racing there.

After its Dallas wounds had been repaired, '02/01' re-emerged as '02/04' in time for Alliot to race again in Austria.

The sum total of this demanding and fraught season included 13 starts for Alliot yielding only three finishes, 10-11-11, and 14 starts for Palmer, with six finishes, 8-10-9-13-9-10, which impressed nobody, unlike the preparation of these pretty little cars. Alliot failed to qualify twice and was unable to start after the Dallas crash, while Palmer failed to qualify only once but too often proved a baulky back-marker when the leaders were lapping him. Mike Thackwell qualified for his lone race with the team in Montreal, but failed to finish.

RAM Automotive girded its loins and prepared regardless for 1985 . . .

For 1985, RAM produced four new 03-series carbon-monocoque cars designed by Gustav Brunner, but they suffered a desperately uncompetitive and unhappy season culminating in dire financial straits and missing the last two races, which left the Oxfordshire team in jeopardy.

Initially, two new Hart-powered 03s were ready for drivers Alliot and Winkelhock in Rio, chassis '3 being introduced for the German at Imola, and '4 for him at Silverstone. Tragically he would be killed in a Canadian Group C endurance race and his death seemed to sap team morale even more than their dreadful reliability and accident record.

Alliot did 13 races for the team, failing to qualify at Monaco; RAM opted out of Kyalami and Adelaide at season's end. He finished only once: eighth in the 03's Rio debut.

Poor Winkelhock started eight GPs, also failed to qualify at Monaco, was unclassified in Portugal but finished 13th at Rio and 12th at

Ricard.

Kenny Acheson took his place for Austria, Monza and Zandvoort, retiring at the former races and failing to qualify in Holland.

By the end of the period the indefatigable RAM team had lost its sponsor (Skoal tobacco substitute) and the future of the now-uncompetitive Hart engine itself seemed in doubt. They were heading into the dark . . .

Rebaque

Wealthy Mexican privateer Hector Rebaque bought Lotus 78s and a 79 from Team Lotus and ran them with variable success into 1979. The cars were always immaculately prepared for him by Ian Dawson's organization but Lotus had little in the way of spares and less development to offer as 1979 progressed.

Rebaque normally raced his 79 with the 78 as spare, but at Zandvoort for the Dutch GP a new Lotus 79 clone was delivered on the Mexican's transporter as spare car. It was the Rebaque HR100, chassis '01', using a Lotus-like slender tub flanked by Williams-copy side pods and skirts, with modified suspension, a water radiator in the right-hand side pod and oil coolers for engine and gearbox in the left.

Design and construction was by Penske Racing at Poole, Dorset, the project supervised by Geoff Ferris and Derrick Walker. Rebaque talked of a second all-new design which would appear for 1980.

He drove HR100 at Monza but failed to qualify, then made the race in Canada only for the engine mounting to fail. He failed to qualify at Watkins Glen, the season ended and through the following winter, after John Barnard had tried briefly to help the team, the project was shelved. Rebaque drove the number two works Brabham in the last seven GPs of 1980 and nothing more would be heard of the first, and so far the last, Mexican Formula 1 car.

Renault

The nationalized French Régie Renault became the largest motor manufacturer involved in Formula 1 when they took the brave decision to enter the first 1500 cc turbocharged contender, in 1977. Renault had a long competition involvement behind them, notably with Amédée Gordini's engine development programmes and with Jean Redelé's Dieppe-based Alpine concern.

Once the Régie's chief executive Bernard Hanon authorized Formula 1 research, an experimental Alpine *Laboratoire* single-seater was built at Dieppe, designed by André de Cortanze. Aerodynamicist Marcel Hubert developed a sleek body with Ferrari-like full-width nose wing, while the sheet aluminium tub itself was slab-sided Coke bottle in planform, carrying in-line hip radiators either side of its engine bay.

At the Gordini workshops, technical head François Castaing with Bernard Dudot and Jean-Pierre Boudy developed a turbocharged version of their existing essentially 2-litre Formula 2 and sports-racing V6 engine (see pages 157-9).

Michelin had achieved considerable competition success with Renault and Alpine and now decided to support their Formula 1 venture, so as to promote their radial-ply tyre technology internationally and steal some of Goodyear's glory. Consequently, the *Laboratoire* Alpine Type A500 turned a wheel for the first time on Michelin's Ladoux test track near Clermont-Ferrand on 21 May 1976. Works F2 and sports car driver Jabouille ran an extensive A500 turbo test programme that summer, and approval was given to go racing in 1977.

Meanwhile, in April '76, Alpine had been absorbed as a Renault subsidiary, while Renault Sport was founded to handle the Régie's wide-ranging competition interests, run by ex-driver Gérard Larrousse. Renault-

Gordini at Viry-Châtillon, south of Paris, would prepare the new Formula 1 car and develop its turbocharged engine.

Renault announced their Formula 1 plans in December 1976; but the finalized car itself would not appear until the following May.

This yellow-liveried Renault RS01 was neatly packaged, reminiscent of the Formula 2 Alpines, its Hubert body remodelled and developed from its A500 basis in the St Cyr wind tunnel. The aluminium tub was folded from two large alloy panels, stiffened by internal steel strap plates. It was designed as a simple car, minimizing potential chassis problems to enable engine and tyre development to proceed unhindered. Turbocharger plumbing was neater than on the A500 jury rig, and included a block-type intercooler nestled between engine and rear of the tub to cool the boost charge between turbo compressor and the induction 'log' on top of the engine. Oil and water radiators by Chausson were slung in-line just ahead of the rear wheels, and transmission was via a six-speed Hewland FGA400 gearbox. Bodywork was elegantly styled, made by Moch in moulded Kevlar.

The new car's debut came on 16 July 1977, at Silverstone, which was well suited to the characteristics of the turbo engine. A maiden outing public failure in France would have been hard to justify and in some respects Renault still had more to lose than gain by participation, for they could only be beaten by far smaller concerns.

Jabouille qualified 21st and retired early after the induction manifold split, venting boost to atmosphere and leaving him with a simple low-compression 1500 in a 3-litre race.

After a break for further development, Jabouille ran in four more GPs that season – Holland, Italy, the USA and Canada, failing to qualify in Canada and never finishing.

Renault Sport were still trying to win Le Mans with their turbocharged sports-prototype cars so their 1978 Formula 1 effort was still confined to a single car for Jabouille,

Turbocharged monocoque tubs had to be strong. Renault's primitive-looking heavily riveted early-series chassis is under assembly at Viry-Châtillon in December 1979. In the preceding season the

Régie's team at last came good and proved that turbocharged 1500 cc engines were to become essential in Formula 1.

commencing in South Africa after ignoring the South American overture. Jabouille normally drove 'RS01/2', racing '3 instead only at Long Beach and Zolder. The car's qualifying record reads 6-13-12-10-11-10-11-12-9-3-9-3-9-22 as development progressed – note the late season improvement after Le Mans.

It was of course most at home on fast circuits, and at altitude as at Kyalami. The first finish came at Monaco, tenth, but in France the engine failed after one lap. At Watkins Glen, Jabouille actually finished fourth to score Renault's first points, then in Canada he was only 12th but reliability was improving. In all the RS01s made 14 starts, being classified as a finisher five times.

At Kyalami, revised bodywork placed the oil cooler in a nose duct and Jabouille did few laps at full speed. When he did, he was quick. At Long Beach, an old-style airbox had been attached just to cool the single large Garrett turbocharger, while mixture adjustments had unlocked more power. One early problem had been overheating the left-rear brake calliper, simply because it was close by the turbo. For the Monaco race, Jabouille made the best of his Michelin tyres and good brakes, despite the low-revving engine keeping him busy on the gears, and achieved 12th on the grid by a fine effort.

Jabouille was fifth fastest in first qualifying at Anderstorp, looking more stable than the Ferraris on the same tyres, but his final practice was spoiled by engine problems in one car and a flat battery in the spare. In France he said: 'Throttle response, power, everything has to be better before I can challenge for the front row . . .' It would come . . . However, the RS01s were encouragingly less destructive of their tyres than the Ferrari 'T3s.

In qualifying at Hockenheim, the radiators were packed with ice to combat hot weather, and in Austria a new water-cooled intercooler was introduced. Jabouille tested his two cars back to back, one with water intercooling, the other without, and the new system was consistently faster as the engine no longer lost power when it got hot.

At Monza many drivers were shaken by the Renault's straightline speed. Villeneuve reported, 'It's incredible, it passed me on the straight like you can't believe. It must be 10 km/h faster than anything else here.' Both Renaults there were fitted with improved

René Arnoux's RS12 in the rain at Watkins Glen, 1979, demonstrates the shape of French Formula 1 thinking at that time, the turbo engine pulling big wings plus sliding-skirted ground-effect loads.

intercoolers and new pistons and rings.

But the season ended mutedly in Canada where Jabouille only just made the grid after rain prevented him setting up the chassis adequately, then finding himself with pick-up problems out of the slow corners. Renault Sport still lacked race-wise experience compared to their rivals, most of whom expected to set up their cars fairly accurately in the factory before revisiting a circuit.

Now Renault made their serious debut in Formula 1 with a proper two-car team for 1979, Arnoux joining the veteran Jabouille, who now had by far the most experience of turbocharged engines of any road racing driver in the world.

Chassis designer Michel Tétu, previously with Ligier, completed a new RS10 ground-effect car in time for the Spanish GP, featuring a slender aluminium centre monocoque, extensively top-louvred side pods and an elegantly designed rear wing supported on curvaceous end plates.

Spain followed a disappointment at Long Beach where Arnoux's 'RS01/3' broke a driveshaft on race morning after Jabouille had crashed at 170 mph following a similar practice failure. Rather than risk a repetition, team manager Jean Sage wisely withdrew from the race.

Both drivers were equipped with RS10-series wing-cars for Monaco, but Renault changed their system so that while 'RS10' was driven by Arnoux, Jabouille's broadly similar sister car was chassis 'RS11'. It was slightly lighter with a new front wing and other detail changes. Both cars used twin KKK turbochargers, one per bank instead of relying upon a single large 'charger feeding both banks. This greatly improved both throttle response and mid-range punch; at last the Renaults were to become competitive and could set new standards. After Monaco there was a month's break before the French GP at Dijon-Prenois.

During this hiatus a general tyre test session was held at Dijon, during which Harvey Postlethwaite of the Wolf team was watching a speed trap on the top straight, while a Renault was running.

'I'll never forget it', he says. 'Suddenly it read out a speed about 20 mph faster than anything we'd ever seen before . . . That was it, the Renault was coming good. Soon we would all need turbos . . .'

In 1977 at Dijon Andretti had taken pole in the Lotus 78 at 1:12.21; now, two years later, Jabouille took it in 'RS11' at 1:07.19, while Arnoux in the new 'RS12' qualified alongside him to make it a bright-yellow Renault turbo front row.

In Monaco their intercoolers had leaked, here at Dijon they were strengthened and Sage and his men merely hoped for a cool race day; they got it, Jabouille winning while only Villeneuve's combative driving in the Ferrari could bundle Arnoux back into third place for a 1-3 finish, Arnoux setting fastest lap.

Jabouille qualified on the front row at Silverstone but misfortune and mismanagement wrecked his race before a valve-spring failed while Arnoux finished second in 'RS12'. The Renaults were on pole for the next four races in Europe, but rather fell off the tightrope in North America where their only finish was Arnoux's second at Watkins Glen. In Italy it was an all-Renault front row, which mightily concentrated Ferrari's mind on turbocharger plans for 1980-81! But reliability continued to handicap the Régie's team.

A fourth wing-car, 'RS14', ran in North America. Water-spray brake cooling was employed at Montreal for that circuit is very hard on brakes and the turbo engine's relative lack of overrun braking gives the brakes a hard time. At Watkins Glen where the weather was cold and wet the Renaults, traditionally light on Michelin's rubber, were unable to heat the tyres adequately and grip was lacking.

Renault Sport ended this first successful Formula 1 season with a record of 28 starts in 14 GPs – discounting the non-starts in Long Beach – and they finished only eight times, the 1-3 in France backed by seconds in Britain and the USA, sixth in Austria and one each 8-9-10. They did not finish in the Dutch, Italian and Canadian GPs, making it a fruitless autumn; reliability was still poor.

For 1980 Renault devoted a massive budget to their World Championship quest, and began brilliantly with Arnoux winning in Brazil and South Africa – both times thanks in part to team-mate Jabouille's grotesque misfortune when leading – but fortunes declined as the season progressed. Michelin tyres caused some headaches and a bad batch of valve-springs ruined mid-season, while Jabouille's sole reward in a season of disappointment and frustration came when he won in Austria. Arnoux had performed brilliantly in practice at Long Beach, Zolder and Ricard.

A new RE20 chassis design emerged, featuring improved new side pods, new skirt system, gearbox spacer, new intercoolers and a modified cooling system. The 'RE' signified 'Renault-Elf' in honour of the main external sponsor.

In Argentina the team ran new car 'RE22' for Jabouille, '21 for Arnoux with '20 spare. In Brazil victory should have been Jabouille's but for a broken turbo; in South Africa the cars featured cable clutch linkage for the first time, lighter and more sensitive in operation, and while a puncture deprived Jabouille of victory, Arnoux won again in 'RE21'.

For Long Beach, Arnoux had a new 'RE24' fitted with Italian Brembo brakes, Jabouille's '23 featured integral bodywork around the tail and a wider rear track in search of improved traction. The spare 'RE22' had hydraulic servo brakes, tested by Arnoux as a continuation of a Ricard test programme. But the Brembos were dropped due to disc cracking, AP Lockheed being used instead. Further brake problems handicapped their race.

For Zolder, larger discs and bigger Girling instead of Lockheed callipers were tried, necessitating 15 in. instead of 13 in. diameter front wheels. Jabouille's clutch broke at the start and Arnoux finished fourth. Monaco did not smile on the Régie, while the FOCA/FISA battle saw the Spanish GP run without 'Grandee' team participation, Renault being one to opt out.

Michelin's tyres did not work well in France and engines began breaking; at Brands Hatch a big new rear wing appeared, proof of the power the French V6 turbos could now afford to dissipate in search of download. A new 'RE25'

emerged at Hockenheim, driven by Arnoux, but both cars there were sidelined by valve-spring failures. Some weight was saved by lighter carbon-fibre side pod end plates on both cars.

For the Italian GP at Imola, brakes would again be crucial and different types of standard discs, AP ventilated discs and special brake pads were tested. Large cooling ducts were fitted, and there was also a new engine cover on each car. In Canada, Jabouille crashed 'RE23' very heavily, injuring his legs, and Arnoux was left to run alone at Watkins Glen in 'RE25', finishing seventh after a skirt had broken and thereby diminished download.

Through 1980, the Renaults had made 27 starts, being classified as finishers 12 times, winning three GPs, placing second (Arnoux in Holland), fourth (Arnoux in Belgium) and fifth (Arnoux again, in France), which was little concrete result compared to their five pole positions and three fastest laps. The two Renaults had filled the front row at Kyalami early in the season, then consecutively in the Austrian, Dutch and Italian GPs in the autumn.

Now they were provenly competitive, Renault looked seriously towards 1981 as being their season. Sliding skirts which had enabled the Cosworth teams to maintain competitiveness against the turbos had been banned, power would surely tell. However, FISA's variable rulings embarrassed Renault Sport just as seriously as any of the British teams.

Renault set out with the long-wheelbase RE20B models, developed from the 1980 RE20 to run without sliding skirts while the new RE30 design, tailor-made for the new regulations, was being completed. Renault would have been happy to continue with skirted ground-effect side pods to harness their power, but in the first fixed-skirt 'clearance car' races Brabham introduced their hydropneumatic suspension lowering devices. Renault felt certain FISA would ban such a ploy but in April it was declared legal, and Renault were horrified.

Now the cars could run fixed skirts against the ground, the new RE30 had been tailored as an unskirted car and they were instantly behind the field.

They ignored FOCA's unofficial sliding-skirt South African GP, testing at Ricard instead with enlarged side pods and even bigger front and rear wings. Chassis 'RE26B' was driven by Jabouille's replacement, Prost, and 'RE27B' was used by Arnoux without success at Long Beach.

In Brazil, the servo-assisted brakes gave trouble, contributing to practice incidents, and the system was removed from the race cars, both having suffered race collisions. A new monocoque was flown out to Buenos Aires to replace Arnoux's damaged tub. The cars were fast but the Brabhams were faster; Prost and Arnoux placed 3-5 on reliability but both were troubled by vibration due to a flat-spotted tyre and imperfect wheel rims.

Where the RE20 had been a simple development of the original RS10, the new RE30 marked a new beginning for Renault Sport. Michel Tétu had to save chassis weight to compensate for the extra poundage of turbocharger ancillaries such as the intercoolers and increased fuel load. Where there had been five fabricated bulkheads in the RE20, there were three machined castings and two fabricated bulkheads in the RE30. The latter was still aluminium skinned since Renault fought shy of carbon composites, mistrusting their impact resistance. The RE30 also featured lighter bodywork, with a new gearbox enclosing FG400 internals in a Renault casing which incorporated the oil tank (formerly located in the spacer between engine and gearbox, which had now been dispensed with). The wheelbase was 13 cm (5.2 in.) shorter and the rear dampers which had previously been hung on the spacer now picked up on the gearbox.

Intercoolers raked forward behind the radiators in each side pod, while Bosch electronic fuel metering had been adopted. The AP brake servo and hydropneumatic suspension systems were driven from gearbox pumps, the suspension circuits not interconnecting all four wheels. They were instead paired front and rear to combat differing aerodynamic loadings fore and aft. The car generally was lower than the RE20-series, its side pods lower and the revised centre tank cell longer and lower than before, while the winkle-picker nose was more slender.

However, at Zolder Arnoux failed to qualify after numerous problems while Prost broke old 'RE22's clutch as the race was stopped and restarted – it could not endure two turbo-charged standing starts.

Post-Zolder testing of the new cars produced raceworthy 'RE31' and 'RE32' at Monaco, these cars and the spare using servo brakes, and seven new engines were made available, revving to 11,500 rpm. Prost's new 'RE32' had hydropneumatic suspension, which also went onto Arnoux's car during practice, but the extra pump load affected the gearbox so the system was removed again. Both race cars were damaged early on and retired later.

Two RE30s ran at Jarama: 'RE33' was new for Arnoux in place of his '31 shunted at Monaco, 'RE32' being used again for Prost after he had demolished '30 when a wheel broke during Dijon testing.

The Monaco-damaged '31 was repaired in time for the French GP at Dijon, all three Renaults there having modified side pods with undersurfaces around the gearbox like the unsuccessful Williams FW07B at Buenos Aires '80. Air venting was tidied up with superfluous flaps removed, and rear wings of a new design appeared on the race cars. Prost in 'RE32' won on aggregate after a rainstorm stopped the race, and he took the restart on soft tyres with turbo boost wound up.

New, narrower rear wing stays appeared at Silverstone, Prost took pole and the Renaults dominated until fuel feed trouble stopped Prost and burned valves deleted Arnoux from the race.

At Hockenheim new side pod end plates merging into the rear wing appeared, Arnoux's rear tyre was punctured by another car's nose wing on the first lap, and a skirt damaged in the drag back to the pits caused bad handling thereafter. Prost was handicapped by his engine's rev limiter cutting in 600 rpm too early. After running 2.7 ata boost at Hockenheim, they fell back to 2.6 at the Österreichring. Underwing extensions then appeared at Zandvoort, where Prost's 'RE34' sported further revised bodywork with one-piece nose wing support and he won from pole, whereas Arnoux crashed after starting from the front row alongside his team-mate.

For Monza, Arnoux's 'RE33' was in similar trim to '34 as at Zandvoort and he took Renault's fourth consecutive pole position but Prost led throughout, saying his car's handling on race tyres was better than on qualifiers. Arnoux spun and stalled.

In Canada changes included new injectors, intercoolers, lightweight honeycomb side pods, 13 in. front wheels, different brake ducts and new carbon-fibre front and rear wings, taking the Renaults below 600 kg for the first time. Prost's 'RE34' scaled 595 kg (1311.6 lb) Arnoux's 'RE33' 598 kg (1318.4 lb).

At Las Vegas, 'RE30' replaced Arnoux's 'RE33' crashed in Montreal, and the team was fresh from full-size wind tunnel testing in the Lockheed facility at Atlanta, Georgia. The long-awaited new electronic ignition system disappointed during practice and was set aside.

Just one more win would have given Prost the Championship but they had had that win within their grasp and had lost it at Silverstone due to their faulty valve batch; at the Österreichring due to a broken suspension rocker;

and in Spain, where Prost had been faster than eventual winner Villeneuve but fell off. The Renaults had none the less dominated for sheer pace in the UK, Germany and Austria, but could not finish until Holland. At least the car was now competitive on all kinds of circuits.

They had made 29 starts in the 15 1981 GPs, finishing 14 times, winning three, with three second places, a third, a fourth, a fifth, two eighths, two ninths and one 13th. They sat on pole for six consecutive races: France, Britain, Germany, Austria, Holland and Italy – four times to Arnoux, twice to Prost. Renault were setting standards, but still not winning that elusive Championship.

In 1982, Prost and Arnoux set off 1-3 with RE30Bs at Kyalami. Lighter underbody panels and SEP carbon discs were tried on the T-car, new carbon wing mounts being replaced by metal after Arnoux and Prost both broke them pre-race. Water ballast was added to a hollow seat moulding at Long Beach where the cars were allegedly underweight for the first time. At Imola, Prost had new chassis 'RE30B-8' (the system being restyled). Then new side pods appeared for Monaco.

In Holland, new wastegate ventilation appeared after turbo failure had been caused by lack of it in Canada. New front suspension appeared at Ricard and hydraulic suspension provided at Brands Hatch, both being removed for Zandvoort, where Arnoux crashed '7. Chassis '8 was badly damaged by Arnoux at Dijon and a new chassis '9 was brought to the UK, with reinforced lower front wishbones to prevent another wheel loss as at Zandvoort. In Germany, chassis '10 was new and carbon-fibre brake discs were tried briefly.

Overall, this was another disappointing season, riven by failure of a tiny electric motor within the injection system which combined electronic control with a Bosch-Kugelfischer mechanical pump to produce a considerable performance advantage.

When the new system came on song at Monaco, Prost led to within two laps of the finish when he crashed due to brain-fade when under pressure, destroying his favourite chassis '4. Thereafter the electro-mechanical fuel injection system repeatedly betrayed the cars. Running conventional injection cost two seconds per lap at the Österreichring, the electro-mechanical system was refitted for the race and its tiny motor failed again. It was a humble proprietary unit which was being expected to survive in the heat and vibration of the engine vee, and could not. They tried alternatives without success before finally issuing a custom specification to a specialist sub-contractor who tailor-made what they wanted. This was used in the last race of 1982 at Las Vegas and ran reliably through '83.

Renault also suffered a series of accidents and had to use four replacement chassis. While much effort concentrated upon the EF1 engines, the cars were surprisingly conventional, with all-aluminium tubs, some carbon-fibre side pod panels to save weight, but no raceworthy carbon-fibre brakes (unlike Brabham), nor pullrod suspensions, and the wheelbase was unchanged all year. Track was enlarged 6 cm (2.4 in.) to the maximum 215 cm. Porpoising at speed was a problem, Renault's fore-and-aft split hydraulic damping system controlling this effect with variable success. Sage felt that the 150 km/h wind tunnel at St Cyr was perhaps a contributory factor; it might have been better to use a 300 km/h tunnel.

During 1982 they had made 32 starts in the 16 GPs, finishing only 12 times, but winning four GPs – Prost two, Arnoux two (including the French GP in which he held Prost out of a victory which might have won him the World Championship) – plus three second places, a third, a fourth and one sixth place.

Having come so close, Renault had two goals for '83: more power and adequate reliability. Tétu drew a new RE40 carbon-composite chassis but the management decided that an interim flat-bottomed RE30C would suffice for the opening races. Time had been short since the imposition of the new rule and they felt confident everyone would be running interim cars, reckoning without the reaction speed of teams like Brabham who built all-new. So Renault entered 1983 with a disadvantage and the RE40 programme had to be accelerated.

Engineer Jean-Pierre Boudy wrung more power from the ageing V6, adopting bigger turbo casings and impeller wheels and developing a water-injection pack to use their extra boost. In the winter of 1982/83 he developed water-injection on his Renault 18 saloon.

Three interim RE30Cs ran at Rio. The prototype RE40 emerged at Long Beach. The logistics of running two different types caused Sage deep grief, while electrical problems wrecked the new model's debut. It was new, it was carbon-composite and 'we just couldn't find a good earth'.

Renault got a grip until Zandvoort and by the penultimate race Prost seemed all but assured of the Championship. Six RE40s had been built, the prototype retiring to static test and mock-up duties.

Prost's engine suffered significantly at Imola, Montreal and Monza. They had problems with inconsistent performance quality after rebuilds. The 700 rpm rev loss from the normal 11,000 rpm to only 10,300 at Imola was never explained, even the works' strip-down report finding nothing amiss. At Monza there was no mystery, the device regulating turbo heat build-up was faulty when fitted, allowing the turbos to overheat and damage the impeller wheels, thereby losing boost.

Three wing forms were run, plus a fourth barn-door like Ferrari's at Brands Hatch, the penultimate round. It was ironic that the team should again miss out on the Constructors' Championship where both cars could score points, for new team driver Cheever's misfortunes in the second car cost the largest motor manufacturer in Formula 1 dear indeed.

At Rio, the RE30C chassis '11 and '12 were new, using cast magnesium front uprights and fabricated rears ready for the RE40. Italian Brembo brakes were tried again, the inlet manifold had been redesigned and Boudy's water injection made its debut. For Long Beach the 12 kg (26.5 lb) lighter RE40 prototype chassis '00 made its debut, the tub moulded by Hurel-Dubois at Vélizy.

Three RE40s went to Ricard for the early-season French GP: '00 the spare, now superseded by '01 for Prost and '02 for Cheever, the latter two both equipped with rapid refuelling non-spill fillers for pit-stop race strategy. 'RE40/03' was new at Imola for Prost, a higher carbon content in its composite moulded tub making it distinctively darker in colour than its predecessors. Cheever ran radially drilled carbon discs there, as at Ricard, saving 7 kg (15.4 lb) weight.

For Monaco a greatly extended full-width rear underwing or 'diffuser' was fitted, terminating below the trailing edge of the rear wing. It lay beneath the rear suspension and had four-pipe exhausts playing across the underside to entrain airflow across the diffuser undersurface and add useful extra download. Renault actually claimed the device was to reduce local exhaust heating of the tyres, but their rivals grumbled . . . and at Spa protested that the system harnessed a moveable aerodynamic device, the engine internals, to entrain air. FISA declared the system legal and everyone adopted it subsequently.

New tubs '04 and '05 appeared at Silverstone, to '03 standard but saving 10 kg (22 lb). The four-pipe engines had been found to overheat during Hockenheim testing so for Silverstone they reverted to the original style. Shorter rear bodywork was adopted for Hockenheim where ultimate download is less important than low drag and top speed.

Prost had to drive T-car '03 in the race there with longer rear bodywork after his assigned race car overheated on its way to the grid. In Austria, '03 had short bodywork fitted. Overheating persisted, apparently due to poor separation of steam entrained in the water flow, a problem which also affected other users of Renault engines.

By Holland, '03 had been lightened to the standard of the later cars. Chassis '05 was damaged there in Prost's accident, new chassis '06 replacing it for Monza. A single spray-nozzle intercooler 'super-cooler' system was used there in qualifying, and at Monza a twin-nozzle system cooled both sides of the matrix to find still more power. New car '06 was down to 545 kg (1201.5 lb) and had first run in Brands Hatch tyre testing. At Brands, '05 returned, and they sent to South Africa four Renaults instead of three as well as nine engines in a vain effort to clinch the Championship which Prost had dominated for so much of the year. Running the big Brands Hatch rear wings and special qualifying engines for the first time with larger turbochargers, the Renaults were still over 5 mph slower than the Brabham-BMWs on the straight. They tried narrow near tyres to gain speed but nothing would work. Prost retired '05 with turbo failure, while Cheever finished a distant sixth in '04 . . . and Renault's best-ever chance of the Championship title had gone.

Prost left to be snapped up by McLaren for 1984, Warwick joining Tambay in the rebuilt Renault team to drive a new Tétu-designed model RE50. After prototype '01 had completed initial testing it then, unraced, became a show car. RE50s '02-3-4' were new at Rio, the latter pair being race cars for Tambay and Warwick. '05 was new for Tambay at Zolder and was written off like its new sister '06 in a first-corner collision at Monaco, when the two collided!

Chassis '07 was new for Warwick as a spare at Montreal, where he raced '04 repaired after a heavy accident at Dijon, '08 was new at Brands Hatch and was raced by him late season, while '09 was new for Tambay at Hockenheim and completed the season in his hands, save for one drive by Warwick at *ersatz* Nürburgring.

These eight carbon-Kevlar race cars were a profound disappointment. After reservations about their KKK turbochargers in 1983, Dudot adopted large American Garrett AiResearch 'chargers for the new season. Plans were laid for a spring-time split in Renault Sport's factories, Dudot's engine plant with its 100

Above, a new tub form for Renault in the 1981 Belgian GP where Michel Tétu's simplified, lighter RE30 made its unfortunate debut, Arnoux failing to qualify. Opposite right, low-key farewell season in 1985 saw Patrick Tambay (here at Rio) and Derek Warwick uncompetitive in RE60s.

employees taking over the whole of the original premises at Viry-Châtillon, while Jean Sage took his chassis and gearbox race shop and its staff down the road to new premises at Evry.

The alloy-block engines were now standard, initially suffering some flexion problems which were corrected, though costs soared as the alloy blocks had to be changed twice a year whereas the old iron blocks ran for ever. The latest 'EF4' power unit featured revised heads.

Warwick gave the team a strong start by nearly winning in Rio. The main problem under the new 220-litre fuel restriction was sheer consumption. This was especially serious at Imola but they did much work with the latest Marelli-Weber injection system and with the Renix ('Renault Electronics') management system so that by the end of the season the cars could run race distance without the drivers progressively reducing boost pressure.

Early on in Rio, Warwick's new RE50 was struck by a McLaren and bent a wishbone, which broke and robbed him of a potential win near the finish. Stronger wishbones were adopted thereafter but at Monaco and Dijon they proved so strong that they transmitted shock-loads direct into the carbon-Kevlar tub and punched the pick-ups straight through into the cockpit, injuring the drivers. Thereafter the tub pick-ups were reinforced, adding weight until 'RE50/08' emerged redesigned in carbon – they said without Kevlar – from Brands Hatch.

The greater engine power compromised gearbox reliability which became very marginal by season's end. Intensive SEP-Renault carbon-fibre brake tests continued all year but they were not raced until Monza, when management prevailed upon the drivers to race them despite their lack of progressive feel and tendency therefore to lock. Both drivers quite liked them in the race, where revised high-compression engines proved strong.

Overall, Renault Sport felt they had not achieved their potential for they failed to win a single race and were often struggling to match Lotus performances with their V6 engine.

They started 31 times and were classified as finishers only twelve times. Warwick's finish record read 3-2-4-2-3-11, and Tambay's 5-7-2-8-5-6-7, aggregating 34 points for just fifth place in the Constructors' Cup. From 1978 to

1983 Renault Sport had placed in sequence 12th, 6th, 4th, 3rd, 3rd and 2nd in the Constructors' competition, so the drop to fifth in 1984 was indeed a fall from grace.

The mighty French *Régie*'s decline accelerated into 1985. The production company had been suffering huge trading losses and had to shed many employees, so the Board decided that their expenditure on Formula 1 should be closely scrutinized in light of poor results. Gérard Larrousse was shouldered aside and a new man, Toth, put in his place; the popular former Le Mans winner moved to Ligier and, significantly, chassis designer Tétu went with him, leaving his new RE60 design allegedly complete but the cars unbuilt and obviously undeveloped. The team's labyrinthine management practices had always handicapped progress and now things merely seemed to get worse.

At Viry-Chatillon, Bernard Dudot was completing his new EF15 V6 engine to complement the existing EF4s, while drivers Tambay and Warwick were unchanged. But Renault Sport 1985 was a shadow of what had gone before, and it would be left to Lotus and Ligier to make the best use of Dudot's fine engines.

One test RE60 chassis had been completed and three new team cars then followed in time for Rio where chassis '2 was the spare raced by Tambay, '3 new for Warwick and '4 Tambay's originally-assigned car. Chassis '5 would follow as spare at Monaco where Tambay again raced it first time out, this machine being updated to modified RE60B-spec in time for the German GP. New RE60Bs, chassis '6 and '7, had appeared at Ricard for Tambay and at Silverstone for Warwick.

They were down to the 540 kg limit, using RE60 chassis mouldings but with the electrics moved from above the fuel cell into the cockpit to allow a 15 cm lower engine cover. Smaller radiators permitted shorter side pods, the nose cone was slimmer, new uprights and wishbones were fitted, and brake callipers moved ahead of the rear discs. An EF15 qualifying engine had to be developed since the normal EF4B 'qualifier' would not mount on the '60B tub. Renault's qualifying showed little notable change.

Chassis '7 was written off in a practice accident in Holland. Chassis '8 was new as spare car in Austria, raced by Warwick at Zandvoort and then, after creasing '6 in practice at Monza, Tambay took over '8 as his regular mount for the balance of Renault's final Formula 1 season.

The team boycotted Kyalami on political grounds, so both drivers contested 15 of the 16 GPs. Their cars were not very reliable, and even less competitive; it was pathetic to see, agonizing to experience.

Tambay notched eight finishes, scoring points 5-3-3-6 at Rio, Estoril, Imola and in France, 7-10*-7-12 elsewhere; Warwick finished only seven times, 5-5-6 at Monaco, Silverstone and Spa, 10-7-10-7 elsewhere, which was poor. Evidence that Renault were losing all intent of retrieving Formula 1 competitiveness came in the *ersatz* Nürburgring where 'RE60/4' was prepared as a TV camera car for ex-Brabham Elf protegé Hesnault, inevitably diverting attention from the 'serious' race cars. Thus it was no surprise when Renault's F1 withdrawal was announced soon after, and the team merely went through the motions for the few GPs left to them.

Their defection was a serious blow not only to company and national pride, but also to Formula 1 itself, which could ill-afford to lose the support of such an industrial giant. Fortunately Renault would continue to supply Lotus, Ligier and Tyrrell with engines and into 1986 it remained to be seen if they could achieve the Championship victory on Renault's behalf which in nine seasons' competition had eluded the *Régie* itself.

Renault Sport had always been forced to fight its war with one arm tied behind its back, for French labour laws and social requirements forced them to observe rigid working hours and for overtime and weekend working to be tightly controlled. Even with enthusiastic union support, they could never exploit the seven days a week, 24 hours a day commitment of the British teams' people, nor their flexibility and speed of response. The speed at which urgently required modifications can be made can win or lose the next race, and neither did Renault have on hand the myriad small specialist sub-contractors available in the UK, or on the Emilian plain in Italy.

Nothing is easy in Formula 1, but right from the start it had been harder for the largest manufacturer in the business. Renault's decision to take on the specialists with a largely untried engine concept and to pay the price of their pioneering was a brave one which had changed the face of Grand Prix racing.

Safir

See entry for Token (page 237).

Shadow

American entrepreneur Don Nicholls founded his Advanced Vehicle Systems company to build and race an extraordinary small-wheeled CanAm sports car known as the Shadow in 1970. He subsequently turned his attention to Formula 1, having won major sponsorship from the huge Universal Oil Products (UOP) company, in part to publicise their lead-free fuel products. Former March team manager Alan Rees was interested, as were former BRM driver Jack Oliver and chief chassis engineer Tony Southgate. They would form the nucleus of Nicholls's British-based AVS Shadow company which would build brand new Cosworth/Hewland Formula 1 cars for 1973.

Southgate designed the first car largely in his home at Bourne near BRM. It was his first non-V12 Formula 1 car and he misjudged the destructive vibration of the Cosworth V8. When the first shapely, chisel-nosed, hip-radiatored, squared-off 'Coke bottle' Shadow DN1 appeared – chassis 'DN1-1A' – it literally shook itself apart.

Team drivers were to be Oliver and the American Follmer, whose enormous sports car experience included the 1000 hp Porsche 917 turbocharged cars so Formula 1 held few fears for him. Follmer enjoyed all the luck going in

his Formula 1 debut, for his chassis '2A survived race distance while Oliver's prototype retired to place sixth at Kyalami – immediately scoring a Championship point – and at Silverstone, and then third at Barcelona. At Zolder, for the Belgian GP, the newly laid track surface disintegrated and Oliver wrote off '1A. Follmer, meanwhile, crashed '2A in practice; it was repaired for the race but sand jammed the throttle slides open and he went off and was stranded in a sand-trap. At Monaco, '2A's luck ran out and it was written off in a collision.

Oliver ran a new car, 'DN1-4A', there and finished 10th, but he was dogged by misfortune, becoming involved in the multiple pile-up which stopped the British GP and crashing again in Holland. Follmer drove 'DN1-5A' to replace '2 but achieved little despite five more finishes that season. Oliver took 'DN1-6A' home eighth in Germany and third in Canada where he led that chaotic race during changeable weather, a flurry of tyre-change stops and muddled lap charting. Redman drove chassis '4 in Follmer's place at Watkins Glen. For 1974, new team drivers Revson and Jarier took over as Oliver retired to management duties while the much improved Shadow DN3 made its debut.

Jarier drove 'DN1-7A' in Argentina but destroyed it on the first lap in a collision with Revson's prototype DN3. He then raced '5A in Brazil, where this last DN1 works entry ended with a seized wheel bearing.

One other DN1 had been built in 1973, chassis '3, bought as a kit by Graham Hill for his new Embassy-backed one-car team. The car fell to bits at Monaco, and Hill furiously strengthened it subsequently, ending the season with seven finishes. However, none was worth a candle and the 9-10-12-13-14-16-13 finishes were sad to see.

Hill bought Lolas for 1974, while Shadow's new DN3 proved competitive. Southgate learned from the mistakes of DN1, stretched DN3 with a spacer between engine and gearbox, revised its aerodynamics with a long nose (top-ducted to enclose the oil cooler) and provided a slimmer engine airbox and centre-strutted 'banana' wing.

Revson qualified 'DN3-1A' on row two in its debut at Buenos Aires, ran sixth in Brazil, finished sixth at Brands Hatch, but then in pre-race testing at Kyalami crashed fatally due to failure of a poorly-machined titanium suspension part.

Jarier drove 'DN3-2A' for the rest of the season, finishing nine times, including thirds at Silverstone and Monaco, with a fifth in Sweden. Redman drove 'DN3-3A' in Spain, Belgium and Monaco but could not endure the 'bullshit' of Formula 1 and opted out. Bertil Roos drove once in Sweden, followed by ex-Token driver Pryce who joined Shadow from the Dutch GP. There he damaged '3A in a startline collision, and in France he qualified on the second row and had another startline accident. A new tub had just been finished in Shadow's Northampton factory, which was hastily completed, taking '3A's chassis-plate to keep the customs paperwork tidy.

Meanwhile, 'DN3-4A' had been in use since Monaco as a spare car until Pryce wrote it off in Austrian practice. Since the original '3A had been repaired in time for the Italian GP, where the 'fake' '3A was also to run, the obvious thing to do was to put '4A's plate on the French GP-damaged chassis (the original '3A). The proper plate would be restored to this car for the South American trip at the start of 1975 . . .

Chassis '5A (currently numbered '3A) carried Pryce to his first Championship point, sixth in Germany.

For 1975, Southgate further modified his original DN1 concept, which had been fine-tuned in the DN3, to an even more refined state in the DN5. In this, he sought improved aerodynamic form and cooling, different weight distribution and less weight.

233

Old 'DN3-3A' had been updated with some DN5 bits to form a '3B interim car which Pryce drove in South America alongside Jarier's new DN5. Five DN5s would be built, and the first shone brilliantly in Argentina and Brazil. Jarier qualified on pole both times, only for 'DN5-1A' to shear its final-drive on the warm-up lap in Argentina, then have its fuel metering unit fail after leading for 28 laps in Brazil.

Despite suspicious muttering about UOP's special lead-free fuel supplied for these cars, the new DN5 was clearly very competitive, with excellent handling. Pryce had 'DN5-2A' at Kyalami after crashing his DN3B in Brazil, and at Brands Hatch he qualified on pole and won handsomely – Shadow's first Formula 1 victory.

Pryce and Jarier qualified 2-3 at Monaco, where Jarier crashed '1A heavily, but he reappeared in a new car, '4A, in Belgium. Pryce qualified sensationally on pole at Silverstone for the British GP but both he and Jarier crashed when leading the race.

The fast circuits like the Österreichring and Monza came in the autumn, and Nicholls arranged use of Matra's MS71 V12 engine in a new tailor-made DN7 chassis. It was driven by Jarier in Austria, who reported: 'It's very smooth; it will pull strongly from low in the range, from about 6000 rpm, up to 11,900'. Fuel-injection problems sidelined it in the race, and at Monza the DN7 again retired with fuel pump problems as well as proving to have insufficient fuel capacity to survive race distance in any case.

Matra preferred to supply Ligier for 1976, so 'DN7-1A' was set aside.

It had not been a rewarding season despite the great promise shown. Jarier finished only once in the points, fourth (for half-points) in the red-flagged Spanish GP; Pryce salvaged third in Austria, fourth in Germany, and three sixths in Belgium, Holland, and Italy for eight Championship points. Shadow finished sixth in the Constructors' table.

Unfortunately, UOP abruptly decided it did not appreciate Nicholls' methods and withdrew sponsorship for '76. This was a body blow which crippled Shadow's chances of building on the DN5's undoubted promise.

The old cars were updated as '5Bs for '76 and remained competitive early on, Pryce reaching third in Brazil where Jarier fought hard for the lead, only to crash 'DN5/6A' heavily and write it off. He never tried as hard again for Shadow. Jarier normally drove chassis '4A while Pryce's mount was '5A until Holland when the new Southgate-conceived, Dave Wass-completed 'DN8-1A' made its bow, qualified third on the grid and finished fourth in the race.

Had finance been available, DN8s would have raced from the start of the year, but Southgate had walked out to join Lotus R&D, leaving Wass in technical charge. The DN8 was a neat, lightened and further-refined example of Southgate thinking with a notably low new monocoque tub, high-sided cockpit surround and new AP Lockheed balanced twin-calliper brakes. The nose cone was still distinctively Shadow with the familiar oil cooler in its duct, the car retaining neatly cowled hip radiators.

Jarier ended the season without a single Championship point, but Pryce was third in Brazil and fourth in the British and Dutch GPs, the team eighth in the Constructors' Cup.

Finances were still desperately tight-stretched at the start of 1977. Renzo Zorzi in 'DN5-5A' joined Pryce in the DN8 in Argentina and Brazil finishing sixth in the latter event but proving as slow as his car. A new sponsor enabled a second DN8 to be completed for Kyalami where Pryce was killed in 'DN8-2A' in a stupid accident after Zorzi's car stopped beside the main straight smoking around the tail. A teenage marshal ran across to him carrying a heavy extinguisher just as Pryce arrived flat-out; he struck and killed the

marshal and lost his own life when the extinguisher hit him in the face.

After this appalling incident, Alan Jones, driving 'DN8-3A', joined Zorzi at Long Beach, while Riccardo Patrese subsequently replaced Zorzi. Oliver returned from retirement to handle '8-1A in Sweden while Patrese returned to the team from France to Germany, Merzario driving in Austria, then Patrese at Monza and Jarier joining Jones in the USA when Patrese was engaged in Formula 2.

Southgate returned in mid-summer and development instantly accelerated. A new 'DN8-4A' ran in practice at Hockenheim with slimmer centre section and flared in-line radiator pods ahead of the rear wheels, plus an oil cooler back in the nose, from which it had earlier been removed. Jones had already accumulated places – sixth at Monaco and fifth in Belgium – but his drive in Austria was rewarded by a win in '4A after the team had chosen the right set-up and the opposition faltered. New car '5A was driven by Merzario and was then bent at Monza by Patrese. Jarier drove 'DN8-6A' brand new at Watkins Glen.

Shadow ended the season seventh in the Constructors' Championship with a very respectable 23 points. This was despite parting company with prime sponsor Ambrosio after the German GP, just before the revised DN8 came good, so earnings from the Austrian victory and Jones's subsequent third in Italy and fourths in Canada and Japan were very handy.

During that winter, however, team principals Rees, Oliver, Southgate and Wass abandoned ship to form Arrows, thus leaving virtual absentee landlord Nicholls to pick up the pieces and to pursue them to the High Court . . .

A new DN9 Southgate wing-car design was completed for 1978 by John Baldwin (see Arrows entry page 162). New drivers were Regazzoni and Stuck; the Ticinese finishing fifth in Brazil and Sweden but otherwise having a dreadful season, non-qualifying five times. Stuck only non-qualified once – though he failed to start at Long Beach – but he retired ten times and only had one worthwhile finish, namely fifth in the British GP. Danny Ongais drove Ted Field's Interscope team 'DN9-3A' at Long Beach and the Österreichring, failing to pre-qualify both times. Five DN9s and the three early-season DN8s were employed during this awful season.

For 1979 Shadow struggled with updated DN9s driven by young hopefuls de Angelis and Lammers. Richard Owen and John Gentry had modified the cars to B specification, three B-spec cars appearing in the early season races, de Angelis ramming the new Alfa Romeo at Zolder, bending '3B in the middle, and having a new tub for Monaco.

Shadow DN9B chassis '3 and '4 were available for de Angelis as race car and spare in the British GP, '2 and '5 for Lammers, one car with revised rocker-arm suspension which went onto both cars at Hockenheim to stop de Angelis whining about his team-mate being favoured. But the Shadows were heavy and never able to make best use of the second-division Goodyear tyres to which they were entitled. At Monza '3B and '4B were fitted with new side pods to little effect.

De Angelis qualified for 14 of the 15 GPs, retired from seven of them but finished fourth at Watkins Glen, having been seventh, just out of the points, in Argentina and Long Beach. Lammers qualified for 12 of the races, retiring five times and returning no worthwhile finishes. Shadow were 10th in the Constructors' table, with de Angelis's three points from that last race of the season.

John Gentry initiated design of a new DN11 for 1980, which was completed by Vic Morris, three being built for Stefan Johansson, David Kennedy and Geoff Lees as the season developed. But the cars were never developed, and only Lees managed to qualify for a race, at

Kyalami, being classified 13th after writing off chassis '2. Johansson failed to qualify for both the Argentine and Brazilian GPs, and Kennedy for the first seven races on the calendar.

But the DN11 was recognized early on as a flop and a new little DN12 was designed by Morris with help from Swiss specialist Chuck Graemiger. It had the shortest wheelbase in Formula 1 but was a hefty looking device and again its preparation and development left much to be desired. The prototype DN12 emerged in Belgium, and chassis '2 in Spain.

Just before the Belgian GP, Teddy Yip, who was already an Ensign shareholder, bought Shadow in partnership with enthusiasts Jack Kallay and John Cooper (no relation to *the* John Cooper). Nicholls disappeared into the shadows whence he came. The team was renamed Theodore Racing but Yip felt there was little sense in throwing good money after bad. When both Lees (in 'DN12/1') and Kennedy (in 'DN12/2') failed to qualify for the French GP on 29 June 1980, the team returned sadly to England and quietly closed down. Yip was to use its nucleus as the basis of his Theodore team for 1981, when Lees would race 'DN12/2' for the first and last time at Kyalami – where he crashed again to end his own Formula 1 aspirations. See entry for Theodore, p. 237.

Shannon

Veteran racing mechanic Aiden Jones joined forces with even more experienced inveterate special builder Paul Emery to produce an obscure little no-hoper Formula 1 car which ran once only at this level, in the 1966 British GP at Brands Hatch.

Jones produced a spidery-looking, exceptionally slim, riveted aluminium monocoque chassis, into the rear of which he and Emery persuaded an enlarged version of one of the rare, hitherto unraced and supposedly stillborn 2.5-litre Coventry Climax FPE V8 engines. These had originally been produced for the start of the then-new 2½-litre Formula twelve years before.

Climax had believed media reports of the fantastic power then being obtained by Mercedes-Benz, Ferrari and Maserati and with a remarkable lack of self-confidence – or even of practical research on their own part – shelved their plans, believing that 264 bhp at 7900 rpm on fuel injection was inadequate – which it was not.

Now the remaining FPE stock, said to include four complete engines and many spares, had been sold to Emery, who proposed to fit Tecalemit-Jackson fuel injection. The V8s had meaty wet liners facilitating easy conversion to larger capacity, but they had been designed and developed to run on alcohol fuel rather than straight pump petrol.

Emery and Jones forged ahead regardless, otherwise redundant former Lotus and BRP driver Trevor Taylor took the cold seat, and the ratty-looking little Shannon retired on the first lap of the race, with a split fuel tank – or so they said. The car was seen again, but not with the V8 engine installed. End of story.

Spirit

Ex-March Formula 2 team manager John Wickham and ex-McLaren and March designer Gordon Coppuck – of Championship-winning McLaren M23 fame – formed Spirit Racing to tackle 1982 Formula 2 with the 2-litre Honda 80-degree V6 engine.

After some success they aspired to Formula 1 in 1983, bringing Honda with them. They converted one of their Spirit 201 chassis, number '4, to accept a prototype 1500 cc turbocharged Honda engine and after promising tests in California in the 1982/83 winter they entered the hybrid car at Brands Hatch for their Swedish driver Johansson. It was a modest effort with a slender budget, but Johansson raced it again in the British GP at Silverstone, and at the Österreichring, Monza and Brands Hatch. He also drove another converted-F2 Spirit, '201/6', at Hockenheim and Zandvoort as the improved model 201C, while the small team's first pure Formula 1 car, '101/1', was spare for the European GP at Brands Hatch.

Spirit finished three of those six GPs, 12th at Hockenheim, seventh at Zandvoort and 14th at Brands Hatch, but effectively proved the Honda F1 engine.

It was therefore a bitter blow when Honda pulled the rug from under Spirit to support Williams for 1984. To sweeten the pill they helped finance Spirit's survival in Formula 1 using Hart 415T four-cylinder turbo engines. The 101 chassis was converted to '1B spec for the Hart unit and tested by Emerson Fittipaldi who was considering a return to Formula 1. He thought better of it, Italian driver Baldi's sponsors then buying the drive at Rio, Kyalami, Zolder, Imola and Dijon. Baldi finished eighth at both Kyalami and Imola. At Monaco, Baldi failed to qualify a new car '101/2B', Dutch driver Huub Rothengatter taking the drive mid-season but non-qualifying at Montreal, Brands Hatch and the Österreichring. A Cosworth had to be used in Detroit due to a Hart engine famine but Spirit non-qualified again, best finishes for Rothengatter being tenth at Hockenheim in '1B and eighth at Monza in '2B. Baldi returned for the final races at the Nürburgring and Estoril, finishing 8-15 but Spirit had barely survived a thankless season.

For the little teams it is as hard merely to qualify as it is for the major teams to qualify on pole or win the race. Spirit ended 1984 virtually *sans* hope and future.

They persevered into 1985 but finances were stretched crucially taut. The 1984 chassis were remodelled as Spirit-Hart 101Ds, chassis '2 and '3, featuring resited radiators and intercooler in new side pods, plus a change to pushrod front suspension. Mauro Baldi drove '2 in Rio and at Estoril, where he crashed, then retired '3 at Imola. Spirit then sold their tyre contract to Toleman, their 1985 results being 'unclassified' at Rio, then twice retired. Spirit survived the rest of the season rebuilding '70s F1 cars for private collectors, but their Formula 1 aspirations seemed to be over.

Surtees

After a long and brilliant career as a racing motor cyclist John Surtees took up motor racing in 1960, became World Champion with Ferrari in 1964 and subsequently drove for Cooper, Honda and BRM. As early as his third season, in 1962, he commissioned construction of a special Lola in what was virtually his own team. He was never a man to suffer fools gladly and never delegated if he felt he could do the job better. Ultimately this perfectionism proved counter-productive.

He maintained a close association with Lola into 1967-68, running his own Team Surtees sports car team, and in 1969 Team Surtees built a series of Len Terry-designed TS5 full-monocoque cars for this class while Surtees himself was serving his unhappy season with BRM. At the end of that year he determined to take up Cosworth power for 1970, buying an ex-works McLaren M7 to tide him over.

The new Surtees-Cosworth TS7 design was by Surtees himself, building on experience from the TS5. Chassis '001 appeared at the British GP, using a distinctively small and neat arch-topped, vertical-sided aluminium tub, with inboard front suspension, outboard rear. Surtees held seventh before the engine ran its bearings. Cosworth problems in fact ruined

Mike Hailwood enters one of the Monza chicanes in Surtees TS9 '005', 1972 Italian GP, on his way to second place. Car retains TS7-style angular tub but has hip radiators, pierced bluff nose.

that first half-season, but at Oulton Park Surtees dominated, winning heat one and overall.

A second TS7, lower and lighter with titanium hubs, was available at the Österreichring and at Monza, where '001 suffered a rear suspension failure in practice and the rear end of '002 was grafted on for the race, but electrical trouble and a bad fuel leak sidelined the car after only one lap.

Surtees scored his first points in his own cars at St Jovite, Canada, fifth in '001, and he was sixth when the flywheel disintegrated at Watkins Glen, and in Mexico finished a clutchless eighth. Bell drove '002 at Watkins Glen, scoring a point for sixth place.

Early in 1972 new rent-a-driver Stommelen led heat one of the non-Championship Argentine GP from start to finish in his TS7 but retired after a collision in heat two. The type had its farewell race at Kyalami where a new TS9 appeared. This was a still lower, more robust car generally similar to the TS7 until side radiators were adopted later in the year, together with a full-width bluff nose, pierced to allow cooling air through the front suspension area into the side pods. It used a Hewland FG400 instead of DG300 transmission. Surtees ran second in 'TS9/001' on its debut before a gearbox oil cooler pipe parted and the transmission seized. New 'TS9/002' was ready for Stommelen for the Spanish GP, '003 was sold direct to Team Gunston in South Africa for John Love's use in national Championship racing, while '004 emerged at the French GP as a spare. For the Italian GP at Monza that September, new car 'TS9/005' appeared with side-mounted radiators, but these were replaced by a conventional nose radiator after practice. The side radiators were made to perform satisfactorily in time for the US GP and retained thereafter.

At Monza, Surtees's old motor cycling chum Hailwood came into the team and he promptly finished fourth in '004, just 0.18 s behind the winner . . . it was a close finish. Surtees had won the Gold Cup race again in this same chassis.

For 1972, Hailwood became a regular team driver, Surtees went into virtual retirement from driving and cars were also entered for de Adamich and Schenken. Hailwood came second in the minor race at Brands Hatch and in the Italian GP, as well as fourth in the Belgian and Austrian races, driving 'TS9/005'.

Pace joined in Schenken's place for the final Brands Hatch race and was second, in Schenken's former regular mount 'TS9/006'. This car raced only once more, when it was hired to

Hesketh for their driver Hunt's Formula 1 debut in the 1973 Race of Champions, where he finished strongly in second place.

Surtees made his last appearance as a driver at Monza in 1972, handling his brand new prototype TS14 car built to 1973 deformable structure requirements, with the tub skinned in a sandwich of aluminium, foam and glass-fibre, side radiators, broad pierced nose but now having outboard suspension at the front as well as the rear. Surtees retired '001 with brake trouble and tyre problems – their Firestone tyres would remain a problem throughout 1973, when vibration caused much grief.

Early in 1973 Hailwood led the Race of Champions majestically in '001 until either a tyre or suspension failure hurled him into the bank near the end of the main straight. The car was repaired in time for Mass to drive it in the British GP where all three Surtees cars were heavily damaged in the legendary 'Scheckter shunt' ending lap one. '001 was repaired again for Mass to finish seventh in the German GP.

The second TS14, '002, had been ready for Hailwood in Argentina and was written off in the Regazzoni collision at Kyalami in which Hailwood won the George Medal for rescuing the Swiss BRM driver from his blazing car. New regular team member Pace appeared in 'TS14/003' from Argentina and after serving occasional spare car duties this machine was totally written off in the Silverstone collision. Chassis '004 was Hailwood's mid-season car; it was unreliable and in the US GP its rear suspension collapsed, and Hailwood would leave to drive for McLaren in '74. Chassis '005 was driven by Pace at the Nürburgring to set fastest lap in the German GP, finishing fourth, and he was third in Austria, but the tail-end of the season slumped and like Hailwood he suffered a suspension collapse at Watkins Glen.

For 1974, new TS16 cars emerged, similar to the TS14s in configuration but some 60 lb lighter. Five were built and raced by Pace and Mass, while Leo Kinnunen handled the prototype for AAW Racing mid-season, non-qualifying and getting nowhere. Pace abruptly walked out on Surtees after the Swedish GP, joining Brabham to Surtees's intense disgust, and as the team slid down the tubes Dolhem, Bell and Jabouille all variously tried the cars and failed to qualify. BMW's Austrian veteran Dieter Quester drove 'TS16/005' in Austria and finished ninth, but Bell, Dolhem and Kinnunen all failed to qualify at Monza where Surtees is a folk hero and that really hurt.

Austrian F2 driver Helmuth Koinigg was given a drive alongside Bell in Canada and though Bell again failed to qualify, the uncomplicated newcomer drove very well in 'TS16/005' to finish 10th. Next time out, at Watkins Glen, poor Koinigg crashed '003 – apparently due to a tyre failure – and was killed, and Dolhem's sister car '004 was withdrawn when the sad news reached the pits.

This was a tragic end to a season in which Team Surtees had almost sunk without trace. Earlier, Pace had finished fourth in his native Brazil, Mass was second and set fastest lap in the minor Silverstone meeting but from the Belgian GP, where Kinnunen non-qualified, the cars recorded 16 race starts, 11 non-qualifications, only four finishes (9-10-11-14) and no points.

Surtees was spent as a serious force. In 1975 he ran modified TS16s as a one-car team for Watson, who started 14 races including the Race of Champions and the minor Silverstone event, (the team not going to Germany, Italy or the USA). He finished 10 times, reaching second in the Race of Champions in 'TS16/004' and fourth at Silverstone, fifth in the 'Swiss' GP but never scoring a Championship point.

For 1976 the Edenbridge works developed new TS19 cars, featuring a double-angle pyramid-section chassis reminiscent of the Brabham BT42-44 series. Very small and very nicely made, two works cars with different sponsors were run, essentially for Jones and Lunger and fortunes improved.

The American gave 'TS19/001' its debut alone in South Africa and Jones was second sensationally in '002 on its debut at the Race of Champions. Thereafter a new '003 appeared for Lunger in Sweden while Pescarolo occasionally raced '001 under Team Norev Racing colours. The cars made a total 37 starts, Lunger non-qualifying at Long Beach and Jarama, Pescarolo at Monaco and the Nürburgring. The revived team achieved remarkable reliability as the cars finished 26 times and their last four GPs – the Italian, Canadian, US and Japanese – saw 11 Surtees starts and no retirements. Lunger, Pescarolo and Jones ran cars '002, '004 and '001 in the first three events, Jones taking '004 in Japan while Lunger and Pescarolo stayed home and Noritake Takahara drove '002. Best results were Jones's fourth in Japan and fifths in the British and Belgian GPs.

Surtees was one of the teams picking up crumbs in 1977, when TS19s were campaigned for Brambilla, supported most often by Binder but also occasionally when rent was offered by Perkins, Tambay, Trimmer, Divina Galica, Schuppan and Leoni. The gritty Perkins finished fourth in Belgium to score the team's first points of the year, Brambilla and Schuppan 5-7 in Germany and Brambilla sixth in Canada.

With improved Beta Tools and British Air Ferries backing in 1978, the TS19s were at last superseded by the improved TS20 – another distinctive pyramid-section Surtees – in mid-season, drivers Brambilla and Keegan setting out to do the whole season, never scoring a point and Brambilla being injured in the Monza collision which led to Peterson's death.

Arnoux and Gabbiani drove 'TS20/003' and '001 in the final US and Canadian races of that season, which marked Surtees's swansong, for without Championship points his team's FOCA membership was in jeopardy along with travel savings this entailed outside Europe. John was in any case also unhappy with the handling of Formula 1 finances where the minor teams were concerned, and when he could find no adequate sponsor for his new TS21 design he withdrew from World Championship racing.

Some recent Surtees cars raced on in bush-league Shellsport Formula 1, but drivers like Phillip Bullman, Claude Bourgoignie, Robin Smith, Richard Jones, Gordon Smiley, and Branco Abdul-Halik were hardly expected to build any legends.

Tecno

The Pederzani brothers of Bologna made their company's name with a long line of highly successful racing karts, followed by a series of ultra-short-wheelbase spaceframe Formula 3, and eventually Formula 2, cars. By 1971, they felt sufficiently confident in their own capabilities to embark upon a comprehensive and costly Formula 1 project, developing a flat-12 *boxer* engine broadly similar to Ferrari's superb 312B. The brothers won backing from Martini & Rossi, and after many delays their prototype *Tipo* PA123 chassis 'T-001' made its public debut in the Belgian GP at Nivelles-Baulers. The ugly flat-topped, tumblehome-sided aluminium monocoque used similar hybrid construction to Ferrari, with a tubular infra-frame stiffened by the riveted-on aluminium stress skins. The Tecno engine was stressed and bolted rigidly to the monocoque's rear bulkhead, whereas Ferrari's was still suspended from an overhead beam at that time.

The Pederzanis had planned to use side-mounted radiators, but testing proved the flat-12's cooling demand was so high that a huge nose radiator was necessary, cowled by a full-width bluff nose.

Suspension was unusual only in placing its coil-spring/dampers almost vertically, while track was the narrowest in Formula 1.

Two spare engines were in the Tecno truck at Nivelles and snide comments upon the car's untidy appearance faded as driver Galli hurtled past the pits, the flat-12's exhaust howling a higher, more piercing note than Ferrari's. The green anodized induction trumpets added an unusual sartorial touch, while Galli qualified second to last and ran respectably before spinning in front of a Ferrari causing a collision.

The Tecno reappeared in the minor race at Vallelunga, Rome, Galli finishing third amongst five finishers from only seven starters. Great race, that one . . .

Second driver Bell ran '002 at Clermont-Ferrand but did not start as the chassis cracked in practice. Galli tackled the British GP with '002 which had a new rear suspension crossbeam over the gearbox and coil/dampers more conventionally angled to improve their working efficiency, redesign being by Ron Tauranac of Brabham fame.

Nürburgring expert Bell drove '002 in Germany, the car having widened front suspension and revised oil tankage. Its engine failed. Suspension development continued but in Austria Galli was '17th' (unclassified) and for the Italian GP at Monza a second chassis '005 [sic] emerged with neater front suspension and Matra-like full-width chisel nose for Galli alongside regular '002 for Bell who failed to qualify, while Galli completed only seven laps before the engine failed again.

Only '005, for Bell, was taken to North America but this was a wasted journey as it crashed on the warm-up lap in Canada, while at Watkins Glen the engine failed after only eight laps.

The project had made little progress but continued into 1973 with continued Martini & Rossi support. Ex-McLaren mechanic and F2 Tui constructor Alan McCall was commissioned by Luciano Pederzani to design a new state-of-the-art chassis for the car. Meanwhile, new driver Amon's complaints to Martini persuaded them to contract the Goral consultancy formed by engineer Gordon Fowell and enthusiast Alan Phillips to produce an alternative chassis built by sheet metal specialist John

Thompson in Northampton, England.

The McCall Tecno 'PA123 T-006' was tested in the wet at Misano-Adriatico at the end of March, but within days McCall had fallen out with Luciano Pederzani and departed. Amon disliked the new chassis but felt the engine had potential – like the flat-12 Ferrari on which he had turned his back in 1969 . . .

The McCall car then made its public bow in the Belgian GP at Zolder. It employed a triangular planform monocoque tub, with a fenced twin-entry bluff nose, tubular rocker-arm front suspension and wishbone rear end. It still looked unfinished, the suspension neither plated nor painted, and the engine was tired after extensive testing. Amon's ex-BRM engineer Aubrey Woods was present, fresh from Amon's catastrophic Formula 2 engine project – everything Amon touched seemed to turn to dust.

Yet he finished that race, utterly exhausted, but in sixth place to score Tecno's first-ever World Championship point. At Monaco he qualified comfortably in mid-field, but retired with brake and chassis problems after running seventh before a front tyre punctured.

Thereafter Tecno withdrew, pending completion of the new Goral E731 chassis, causing Amon to miss the Swedish and French GPs before he reappeared at Silverstone for the British race.

There, both McCall and Goral chassis were available, the latter being a remarkably low, parallel-sided, wedgy affair with a rounded-off flat nose and top-ducted radiator fed from an intake underneath. It was so new that Amon could not even fit properly into its cockpit and its tired old engine made it clearly unraceworthy. Accordingly, he started the race in '006 and retired with fuel pressure problems, which recurred in the next, very poor, downfield performance in Holland.

Both cars were present for the Austrian GP, the McCall device arriving in Tecno's transporter while the Goral was towed in on a trailer behind Fowell's road car. Amon qualified both – just – but flew home before the GP in disgust, opting out of the team. The project simply petered out in acrimony and back-biting and the flat-12 Tecnos would not race again. Martini & Rossi's Formula 1 money found a far more sensible home with Brabham for 1974, while Amon again demonstrated his appalling judgement by commissioning Fowell to build a Cosworth Formula 1 car of his own for that season.

Theodore

The Macau-based millionaire Theodore 'Teddy' Yip had sponsored several teams and drivers before launching his own Formula 1 project for 1978. The little team would be managed by Irish former racing driver and entrant Sidney Taylor, and former Brabham creator Ron Tauranac was commissioned to design and build them a Cosworth/Hewland kit car which would be called the Theodore TR1.

Ron designed quite one of the ugliest contemporary cars, reasoning that airflow between the wheels of any racing car will be turbulent, so one might as well fill that space with bodywork. He pursued this theory very successfully with his Ralt production cars built in Snelgar Road, Woking, Surrey, and now Theodore Racing took over those premises while Ralt moved to Brabham's – and Tauranac's – old home at New Haw, near Byfleet, Surrey.

Theodore-Cosworth 'TR1/1' made its debut in Argentina '78 where driver Cheever failed to qualify. The same thing happened in Brazil. Rosberg then took the drive in a new second chassis 'TR1/2' for the minor Silverstone race, qualifying 12th on the 17-strong grid and *winning* in torrential rain which decimated the field and made the most of his car control.

This freak result was really just reward for Yip's years of racing support. The second chassis was used for Long Beach, Monaco and the Belgian GPs but now Rosberg and the team came down to earth with a bump, for they never once managed to qualify. By the time of the British GP, Yip had abandoned the car and was negotiating to buy Wolf machines instead.

Three years later, in 1981, Yip commissioned another Formula 1 Theodore-Cosworth to be designed by Tony Southgate, having since bought the moribund Shadow team. The season began at Kyalami with ex-Shadow equipment, chassis 'DN12/1' being renumbered 'TR2' for Lees to drive, but he had a collision and later crashed.

Southgate's new 'TY01/1' was a distinctive new wing-car with centre pylon-mounted full-width nose wing, which Tambay debuted in Long Beach, qualifying easily and finishing sixth for an immediate Championship point. Two more chassis were built, modified during the season with progressively abbreviated side pods to make download more manageable, lowering suspensions and eventually sporting conventional canard wings each side of the nose. When Tambay joined Talbot-Ligier in mid-season, Surer took his place. Tambay's seven Theodore races included one non-qualification at Zolder and four finishes apart from Long Beach, his best place being seventh at Monaco. Surer drove eight times, failing to qualify only for the Italian GP, while he finished five times, best placing eighth in Holland. Having scored a Championship point, Theodore placed 12th in the Constructors' table, tied with ATS.

Yip entered a TY01 for Daly at Kyalami opening the 1982 season, while two new aluminium-honeycomb monocoque TY02 cars were built, to be driven by Daly – before his entry into the Williams team – then by Lees, Lammers and, ultimately, the promising Irish newcomer Tommy Byrne.

They achieved nothing. Daly had three races, finishing once at Kyalami, 14th. Lees's entry was withdrawn at Imola in concert with other FOCA teams, and he retired from the Canadian GP, his only other appearance. Lammers failed to qualify five times, made the Dutch GP on his native soil but retired, and Byrne failed to qualify three times late-season, and retired in both Austria and Las Vegas.

Yip's struggling Theodore team and Morris Nunn's moribund Ensign outfit then combined for 1983, using the former's name and the latter's cars, continuing the Ensign type and chassis numberings – see 'Ensign' – becoming N183 variants of the original N181 design. Chassis 'MN16' was an uprated '82 car, while 'MN17' was the uncompleted spare tub that season. The third car, 'MN18', was brand new for Rio '83, both these later cars using carbon-fibre cockpit-stiffening inserts in honeycomb tubs. Team drivers starting the season, and paying for their drives, were Roberto Guerrero and former motor cycle star Johnny Cecotto, while Henton had a one-off drive in '18 at the thinly supported Race of Champions, finishing fourth.

Cecotto tackled all but the last two races of the season, failing to qualify for four, finishing six with a best of sixth at Long Beach for the team's only point.

Guerrero tackled every race but the Championship decider at Kyalami, failing to qualify only once but failing to finish seven times, being too far behind to be classified as a finisher on two occasions and placing 12-13-12 in his last three outings.

At the end of the year it was obvious a turbocharged engine was necessary to survive in Formula 1. Theodore could hope for none, designer Nigel Bennett had already moved to Lola to help design a US CART Championship-winning track-racing car so Yip and Nunn turned to CART racing in search of a smaller pond in which to be big fish . . .

Token

In the early-Seventies former Brabham Formula 1 mechanics Ron Dennis and Neil Trundle founded their own Formula 2 team, named Rondel Racing. During 1973 they laid ambitious plans to graduate to Formula 1, building a car designed by Ray Jessop, a former BAC aviation engineer who had worked closely with Brabham in earlier years. Coincidentally, the oil crisis frightened many major companies away from sports sponsorship. In that commercial atmosphere Rondel shelved their plans, but the project was taken up thereafter by businessmen enthusiasts Tony Vlassopoulo and Ken Grob – hence the name Token.

Their Cosworth/Hewland RJ02 'kit car' used a slim, parallel-sided monocoque faintly reminiscent of a Lotus 63 4WD car's, and after a prototype pilot-build, chassis '02' was prepared for racing, making its debut with Pryce driving in the early-1974 Silverstone meeting. It showed quite respectably before its gear linkage went awry. Pryce qualified for the Belgian GP but crashed there, subsequently being taken into the Shadow team.

An entry for Laffite in the French GP was withdrawn and Purley (of LEC fame) then attempted to qualify the car for the British GP but failed. Ian Ashley was another hopeful to drive the Token, finishing 14th and last in the German GP, and being classified 13th in Austria.

Early in 1975 the old car reappeared, entered for fun by John Thorpe's Safir Engineering company which specialized in Range Rover conversions and eventually manufactured the Mark V Ford GTs. Trimmer drove the car twice, being classified 12th (and last) in the Race of Champions and 14th (and last) at Silverstone, after which the RJ02 raced no more.

Toleman

Ted Toleman had built up the largest car-transporter company in Britain and indulged his wealth by racing power boats and entering motor racing. He set up his racing team under the management of Alex Hawkridge to campaign and then to build and race cars under his own name. They won the European Formula 2 Championship with Hart power in 1980, using self-built chassis designed by Rory Byrne and John Gentry, and for 1981 took the immensely bold but perilous step of embarking upon Formula 1, not only using untried new Toleman TG181 chassis of their own design and manufacture, but also commissioning a new Hart 415T turbocharged engine based on the successful F2 four-cylinder unit, and untried new Pirelli tyres.

That maiden season was fraught and frustrating. Both team and engine manufacturer operated on tight budgets, though in their Formula 2 star drivers Henton and Warwick they had at least one known quantity. But the pair qualified only once each and only Henton finished his race – 10th in Italy. They joined Formula 1 at Imola with new chassis 'TG181-01' and '02, '03 appearing for Warwick at Jarama, '04 for him at Silverstone and '05 for Henton at Zandvoort.

In 1982 Toleman continued with their ungainly and ugly TG181C aluminium monocoque cars, now sponsored by Candy, the Italian domestic machinery manufacturers, and drivers were Warwick and the Italian Teo Fabi. One 1981 B-spec car '05 was retained, and two new C-spec cars '06 and '07 were completed. An all-new carbon-fibre TG183 emerged at Monza for Warwick. The carbon moulded tub was reinforced by Kevlar rods, used pullrod suspension in place of the '181's familiarly awful tube-stayed rocker arm sys-

The Toleman-Hart TG181s in their garage at Imola 1981 display a monocoque shape whose complexity contrasts with the neat 4-cylinder Hart engine in its stern.

tem, and was a far nicer package. The nose-mounted oil cooler was retained within much prettier bodywork and the steadily improving Hart engine was now semi-stressed.

It was hoped this car would be a great improvement over the old 'Belgrano' as the TG181s had been dubbed, but first time out at Monza it was appalling. Warwick's season included three non-qualifications, two withdrawn entries (Detroit and Montreal) but 11 starts, much better than '81 despite only two finishes – 15-10 in France and Germany. Fabi's year saw seven non-qualifications, the two scratched entries in North America and only seven races, never finishing.

After two years of barely relieved struggle, Toleman became established in 1983. Unfortunately their Hart engine turbochargers gave more trouble than the engine itself, Garrett were disinclined to assist adequate development so Brian Hart adopted British Holset turbochargers instead, pursuing vigorous development with them.

New flat-bottom TG183B cars were developed for that season, the prototype '01 being updated and '02-3-4 appearing new as the season progressed. Giacomelli and Warwick drove. Warwick qualified for all 15 GPs, finishing six and came eighth in Rio and seventh at Spa. Then, with reliability and the driving ability he had always displayed, he finished 4-6-5-4 in the season-ending series of GPs at Zandvoort, Monza, Brands Hatch and Kyalami. Giacomelli was less successful overall, failing to qualify at Monaco, but his 14 GPs included five finishes, reaching seventh at Monza and sixth at Brands Hatch to place both Tolemans in the points.

Toleman were unable to progress properly in 1984, however. They ran the four TG183Bs, '02-3-4-5, into early season for new drivers Senna and Cecotto, and Senna more than compensated for the loss of Warwick to Renault Sport. Cecotto destroyed '04 during practice in South Africa, and the all-new TG184 then emerged; three being built ('01-2-3) ready for Dijon. A new car '04 was ready for Cecotto at Brands Hatch but within its first lap it was utterly demolished as the throttle jammed open and Cecotto was severely injured when the carbon tub shattered against the barriers. Final car '05 was new for Senna at Hockenheim, the young Brazilian star being joined by Swede Johansson for season's end.

Cecotto made nine starts for the team, before his British accident, but finished only once, ninth in Montreal. Senna non-qualified at Imola but started 14 other GPs, being suspended from the Italian race after breaking his Toleman contract option by signing with Team Lotus for 1985. He finished six times and made the most of his car, with a rousing second place in pouring rain – coming within an ace of winning – at Monaco, third at Estoril and Brands Hatch, sixth in both Kyalami and Zolder, then seventh at Montreal. Johansson finished fourth at Monza and 11th at Estoril from his three late-season starts.

While he began winning GPs for Lotus in

1985, Toleman found themselves in a dreadful tangle after Michelin pulled out of Formula 1 at the end of '84. Hawkridge's raucous criticism of Pirelli in the past hung about the team's neck like an albatross.

Goodyear were fully extended and would service no more teams and while Rory Byrne had a very promising new TG185 Hart-powered chassis ready there were no serious tyres on which to run it. This was a body-blow to both team and winter development of the Hart engine, agonizing for signed-up drivers Watson and Johansson. It was only corrected when they bought out Spirit's F1 tyre contract as that tiny team's exit gambit, and with Benetton sponsorship Teo Fabi emerged to drive a single Toleman entry from Monaco. Watson left without any drive, while Johansson had been summoned to Ferrari.

Four TG185s were ready in time for Monaco, Fabi racing '3 then '4 being damaged in practice at Nürburgring before becoming new number two Ghinzani's car, while '5 was new for Fabi at the Österreichring, completing the season thereafter.

The Byrne cars again operated very effectively relative to the restricted power of their Hart engines, a stepped tub underside generating useful extra aerodynamic download and creating great interest. Fabi took a popular pole position in Germany, but the cars were unreliable, being classified only twice in 13 starts – 12th at Monza, 14th (not running) at Ricard. Ghinzani did not start in his Toleman debut at Österreichring, then contested the next six GPs, retiring each time.

It has always been hard for such a small team using such an effectively shoestring engine but the promise of BMW power for 1986 made the future look brighter, for in recent years Toleman's chassis had promised better results than could be achieved without reliable horsepower.

Trojan

Peter Agg's Trojan group of companies built production McLaren racing cars until McLaren abandoned minor-Formula design at the end of 1972. Ron Tauranac, late of Brabham, was then hired to redesign Trojan's basically McLaren M21 Formula 2 monocoque to form the Trojan T101 Formula 5000 customer car for 1973. Agg was keen to enter Formula 1 and, after completing a T102 F5000 design for 1974, Tauranac was asked to produce a Cosworth-engined T103 Formula 1 car for Schenken to

drive that season.

Tauranac produced a very simple, ugly car, with split nose radiators fairing the front wheels and a broad centre-section filling the area between the wheels 'where the air's going to be all messed-up and turbulent anyway'. Oil coolers were suspended behind the rear wheels to provide a radiator at each corner of the Suzuki motor cycles and Homelite chainsaws-logoed car.

Budget was minimal and 'T103/1' ran in nine of the season's European GPs, being refused an entry in Sweden and failing to qualify in Holland and Germany. It finished three of its seven starts, 14-10-10 in Spain, Belgium and Austria, and was withdrawn thereafter. It was not a design to be proud of but as a car that had been built very quickly and very cheaply indeed it actually did rather well for itself.

Tyrrell

After Stewart's retirement and Cevert's tragic death at the end of 1973, Tyrrell Racing Organisation designer Derek Gardner abandoned a new very short-wheelbase, low-polar moment car for 1974 and substituted instead a longer wheelbase car, still advanced with torsion bar suspension, all-inboard brakes and hip radiators slung on a slender monocoque – the Tyrrell 007. New drivers Scheckter and Depailler began the season in the ex-Stewart '005' and '006-2' cars (see Chapter 7), making six starts in Argentina, Brazil and South Africa, and finishing five times, including Depailler's 6-4 placings at Buenos Aires and Kyalami.

'007-/1' made its debut at Jarama with Scheckter fifth. At Zolder, two 007s ran, Scheckter on the front row, third in the race. Depailler reverted to '006-2' for Monaco and also at Dijon mid-season after crumpling his 007 in practice, otherwise it was 007s throughout.

In all, four were built, and Scheckter used the prototype until Canada. There, as he drove '3, its right-front inboard brake straps broke one by one; he felt the first go but pressed on because he was racing and crashed only when the last finally parted. Chassis '007/2' was flown out for the final race at Watkins Glen. Depailler's normal mount was '2 until new car '4 ran in North America.

At Monaco the cars had run with doubled straps on the inboard brake disc mountings to control a recent spate of breakages. At Zandvoort, experiments on Depailler's car tested

different rear suspension geometry and extended radiator pod cowling in an attempt to enhance airflow through the cores, which was unsuccessful. New '007/3' made its bow at Brands Hatch, where Scheckter suffered failures of a rear suspension top link and a front brake strap in practice, before winning the race to compensate.

Car '007/4' emerged at the Österreichring with the revised rear suspension, but it did not run, Gardner explaining that its geometry would show better on a bumpier course.

At Monza he experimented with in-line water radiators, parallel to the car's longitudinal axis. They were fitted to Depailler's car in addition to the standard face-on podded cores, and piped separately during practice. March had worked towards this mounting with shallow-angled radiators in their 741, and Postlethwaite's Hesketh would run in-line hip radiators in the next race, in Canada. They would become common. Scheckter's car featured an adjustable sliding windscreen to arrive at the most comfortable height without cutting.

The Tyrrell 007s made 21 starts, finishing 15 times, including Scheckter and Depailler achieving 1-2 at Anderstorp. Scheckter finished a lucky first in the British GP, was second in Monaco and Germany, third in Belgium and Italy, fourth in France, fifth in Spain and Holland and could have won the Drivers' title at the last round at Watkins Glen, only for a fuel system fault to dash his hopes.

The 007s continued through 1975, though now with an outboard front brake conversion to load up Goodyear's latest generation tyres; after Kyalami, coil/dampers replaced the difficult to adjust torsion bars, being mounted inboard front, outboard rear, and making the cars more comfortable to drive.

New chassis '007/5' for Scheckter at Kyalami introduced abbreviated delta pods with angled radiators, a new airbox and rear coil-springs. Depailler's '007/2' sported a similar system. Stronger lower front wishbones were fitted after a failure to Depailler's car at Interlagos. In Spain both race cars ran slanted radiators.

At Ricard new chassis '007/6' emerged, whose use of thinner gauge in places saved some 30 lb, which allowed the team to run a third entry for Jabouille. Scheckter crashed this car in the rainstorm at Silverstone, and a new chassis was hastily completed for the Nürburgring, taking the same number '6 even though it was actually the eighth 007 tub built. A tyre deflated and Scheckter crashed again, the third '007/6' emerging brand new in Austria! At Watkins Glen the 007s ran glass-fibre under-skirt strips as pioneered by Brabham and McLaren, Leclère driving a third entry, retiring with engine failure.

Scheckter and Depailler made 28 starts in the 1975 Championship rounds – all 14 GPs – but were inconsistent, though reliable. Scheckter finished 11 times, results running 11-1-7-2-7-'16'-9-'3'-8-8-6; winning at Kyalami, second at Zolder and classified third after crashing at Silverstone. He placed seventh in the Drivers' table, with 20 points. Depailler also finished 11 times, 5-3-5-4-12-9-6-'9'-9-11-7, his first four finishes scoring points in Argentina, South Africa, Monaco and Belgium but tailing off thereafter. Depailler was ninth in the Drivers' table while Tyrrell came fifth with 25 points in the Constructors' Cup.

Through 1976 Gardner developed his remarkable six-wheeled Project 34 design detailed elsewhere, but the team began the season with 007s '4 and '6. Both chassis were started in three GPs, then one (chassis '6 for Scheckter) was used at Silverstone, and again in Spain where Depailler gave P34 chassis '2 its debut.

Jody Scheckter shows off the clean lines of Derek Gardner's 1975 Tyrrell 007, having challenged hard for the World Championship title in 1974.

Scheckter and Depailler finished 5-2 in Brazil, 4-9 at Kyalami and, respectively, retired with suspension failure and placed third at Long Beach in 007s. Scheckter was third at Silverstone and suffered an engine problem at Jarama, where the six-wheeler's debut ended with a crash due to brake problems, after qualifying third.

Both Tyrrell drivers had P34s for Zolder – Scheckter taking '3, Depailler in '2 – and they would run these same cars until Österreichring in August where 'P34/4' appeared as spare and Scheckter destroyed '3 after suspension failure. A replacement '3-2 was completed but Scheckter drove new chassis '4 late-season, Depailler driving '3-2 for the first time at Fuji.

In all, the new P34s made 27 starts and finished 19 times, making remarkable early-season progress. Their results included, consecutively: fourth and engine failure at Zolder, 2-3 at Monaco, and 1-2 at Anderstorp where Tyrrell had achieved similar success with the 007s two years before. Thereafter, from the French to the Japanese GPs, the six-wheelers' results read 6-2, 2-R, 2-crashed, crashed-R, 5-7, 5-6, 4-2, 2-R, R-2.

Meanwhile, old '007/4' had been sold to the Italian Scuderia Gulf-Rondini for Alessandro Pesenti-Rossi, who made his debut in the German GP finishing 14th, last and lapped. He placed 11th in Austria, where '007/6' had been entered by OEASC Racing for Otto Stuppacher who was not allowed to start. Pesenti-Rossi failed to qualify at Zandvoort but was 18th at Monza. Stuppacher did not start in the latter race, packing up and going home before it began. He then made the long trip to non-qualify in Canada and the USA. Chassis '007/5' emerged in Japan, entered by Heros Racing for Kazuyoshi Hoshino, and retiring as weather conditions changed and no spare tyres were available to the little local team.

The Tyrrell P34s had given Scheckter 12 races and ten finishes, 4-2-1-6-2-2-5-5-4-2, finishing third in the Drivers' table, while Depailler's 13 P34 drives yielded only seven finishes, 3-2-2-7-6-2-2, building his reputation as the eternal second in Sweden, France, Canada and Japan. He was fourth behind his team-mate in the Championship, and Tyrrell third in the Constructors' Cup.

Depailler was probably the strongest 'number two' in the Formula. He could have won in Canada where he was challenging for the lead until intoxicated by a fuel leak and in Japan he led briefly until tyre trouble intervened.

For 1977 it all went wrong: the updated P34s were bulkier, heavier and unwieldy, while their tyres were off the pace, lacking development and ignored by Goodyear who had to concentrate upon their more numerous four-wheeled clients. Peterson joined Depailler as Scheckter had moved to Wolf. New chassis '5 emerged for Peterson at Kyalami, '7 being raced by Depailler from Spain and the Frenchman pressing spare car '6 into active service from Austria to season's end.

They made 34 starts, finishing only 15 times, the best being Depailler's second in Canada after qualifying sixth quickest, while Peterson qualified third there but retired with a fuel leak. Depailler was also third in Japan, Argentina and South Africa; Peterson came third in Belgium in the wet, Depailler reached fourth at Long Beach and in Sweden, Peterson was fifth in Austria and sixth in Italy. The Swede ended the year and his brief Tyrrell career with fastest race lap and fifth on the grid at Watkins Glen, before being rammed up the tail by Villeneuve's Ferrari at Fuji.

Otherwise reliability and competitiveness had gone out the window. It was a sad Tyrrell season, with the drivers 8-14 in their Championship and the team placed fifth with only 27 points in its Championship.

The cars had been heavy and difficult to drive, and the drivers became frustrated and disappointed. Derek Gardner returned to the motor industry and Maurice Phillippe took over as Tyrrell's Chief Designer.

In 1978 Phillippe produced a typically minimum-limit four-wheeled P34 replacement, trimmed to the bone but beautifully built. It was based on an extremely shallow aluminium bathtub monocoque and was outclassed against the latest ground-effect cars but none the less proved consistently competitive, if only winning once – Depailler, at last, at Monaco. Meanwhile, new team-mate Pironi started gently but showed promise.

Depailler started all 16 GPs, finishing eight, 3-2-3-1-4-2-11-5; thus all but one finish scored points, his second places being in South Africa and Austria, thirds in Argentina and Long Beach. Pironi's 16 starts yielded ten finishes, half of which scored points 6-6-5-6-5; the fifths were at Monaco and Hockenheim, sixths in Brazil, South Africa, and Belgium. Tyrrell ended their first 'Phillippe' season placed fourth in the Constructors' Championship.

Five 008 cars had been built, Depailler commencing the season in the prototype while Pironi drove chassis '2; '008/3' making its bow for Depailler in South Africa and '008/4' for Pironi at Long Beach. Chassis '3 and '2 ran mid-season, while Depailler drove a new chassis '5 for the first and only time at Monza in September.

During this period Tyrrell had taken on ex-Goodyear boffin Dr Karl Kempf. A highly qualified polymer scientist, he had been largely responsible for Goodyear's own vehicle dynamics research programme. Now he had painstakingly instrumented Tyrrell's cars to discover in detail from electronic recording just what did go on within a Formula 1 car at speed. The programme had produced an active-jacked suspension system, in which onboard microprocessors sensed attitude and demand, so as to add virtually instantaneously positive camber to the inside wheels and negative camber to the outside wheels to resist tyre up-edging.

Much was promised by all this work, and an 008 tested the system with very encouraging results before the season ended. However, Tyrrell then lost their major sponsors and with money very tight into 1979 Ken had to let Kempf go, so this innovative programme never reached public fruition.

For 1979 Phillippe produced an improved Lotus 79-clone ground-effects design – Tyrrell 009 – which was described as an 'undramatically effective racing car', and it proved its points-accumulating value more competently than the updated real 79s that season. But it never looked likely to win, nor did it.

New team driver Jarier ran '009/1' and Pironi had '009/2' in South America, both being damaged in Argentina but repaired hastily for Brazil; Jarier taking new chassis '3 at Kyalami where Pironi inherited '1. New chassis '4 was ready for Pironi at Monaco, where he crashed comprehensively in a desperate overtaking manoeuvre which predictably failed; chassis '6 was available for him at Brands Hatch, and '5 finally ran in the non-Championship event at Imola in September.

Depailler had departed to join Ligier, though Pironi drove the entire season in the Candy-sponsored cars. He finished ten of the 16 GPs but his only scoring finishes were 4-6-3-5-3 respectively in Brazil, Spain, Belgium, Canada and the USA. Jarier drove in 12 GPs, non-starting Brazil and missing the German and Austrian events where Lees and Daly deputized, finishing 7-8. Jarier finished seven times, scoring 3-6-5-5-3-6 at Kyalami, Long Beach and in Spain, France, Britain and Italy. This points-accumulation placed Jarier and Pironi tenth-equal in the drivers' table and Tyrrell fifth again in the Constructors' Cup.

In 1980 new Tyrrell 010s, this time effective Williams FW07 clones, looked good. Jarier fought for a place in the top six on the type's debut at Kyalami and the pair finished 4-5 at Brands Hatch, but for once reliability was poor and component failures twice launched new driver Daly into heavy accidents.

Three modified 009s were used to start the season in Argentina and Brazil; '009/2' as team spare was in fact the fifth 009 tub built, '3 being raced by Jarier and '6 by Daly. The new 010 cars introduced before the South African GP were chassis '1 and '2, the latter crashing spectacularly after brake and suspension failure robbed Daly of control at Zandvoort. The tub was repaired and used as the basis of a race car for Daly at Watkins Glen, known as '010/2-2'.

New chassis '010/3' appeared at Long Beach as spare and was crashed by Daly just after the start at Monaco, appearing no more. Chassis '010/4' was new as spare in Spain and was crashed in German practice, being rebuilt with components from '010/2', known as '4-2 and being crashed by Daly in Canada. Finally '010/5' was completed in the Hockenheim paddock using salvage from '4 and became Jarier's late-season race car.

Complicated, isn't it?

Both Jarier and Daly ran the full 14-GP season, Daly finishing seven times, at best fourth in Argentina and Britain to score a total of six points, while Jarier finished eight times, being too far behind to be classified in the USA. His best results were fifths in Belgium, Britain and Holland, again for six points in all, and for the second year running Tyrrell's drivers tied for tenth place in their table – no favouritism there – but Team Tyrrell fell to sixth in the Cup competition.

Money was short into 1981, a new 011 model only appearing in mid-season, 010s running otherwise for Cheever and newcomer Alboreto. The new car was not markedly superior.

The 010 series chassis '1, '2-2 and '5 ran much of the season. '011/1', whose driver safety cell complied with regulations due for 1982, made its debut at Silverstone but Cheever had declared its extra rigidity made it nervous to drive, and he lost control and crashed in practice. Chassis '011/2' was new for Alboreto at Zandvoort, Cheever taking preference thereafter, while the Italian inherited the prototype.

Cheever finished six of the 15 GPs, but failed to qualify in Austria – Tyrrell had come to this. His best finishes ran 5-6-5-4-5 in the Long Beach, Belgian, Monaco, British and German GPs, so the team could still earn its keep. Kevin Cogan failed to qualify at Long Beach and Desiré Wilson crashed out of the non-Championship South African GP after a respectable drive. Ricardo Zunino handled the second car in Brazil and Argentina, finishing 13th both times, before Alboreto cornered the drive from Imola onwards, finishing four times, failing to qualify in Spain and Germany, not being classified at Las Vegas and finishing 12-16-9-11 where he was classified. This did not look much on paper but he appeared more promising on circuit.

Tyrrell flopped to eighth-equal with Arrows and Alfa Romeo in the Cup table, on 10 points – but Alfa's budget was some 20 times greater for the same result, so there at least was something to cheer about . . .

Ken himself was anxious and frustrated by his inability to provide Alboreto, so full of promise, with an adequate car. During the winter of 1981/82 the team tested to the new fixed-skirt regulations and adopted pullrod suspension. Early in the year the emphasis was on qualifying weight-saving with the water bottle ploy. The cars would often run relatively competitively, but would always be handicapped by qualifying poorly against the high-boost turbos.

Brief team member Borgudd drove '011/1' to start the year but ended its career at Long Beach, while old '011/2' ran the full year. Chassis '011/3' was not used until Detroit, where Alboreto raced it, and it was set aside after Montreal. '011/4' was new for Alboreto at

Kyalami, and he crashed it at the Öster-reichring, having already damaged '5 during practice there. Chassis '6 was new for him at Dijon and was his Las Vegas race car.

By the end of 1981 the Tyrrell 011 cars' wheelbase had grown from its original 106 in. to 108 in. by raking the front suspension forward; a new rear suspension for 1982 now gave a 109 in. wheelbase. Towards the end of '82 a narrow-track variant was developed for the faster circuits – 68 in. against the original 71 front and 61 in. against 65 rear. A NACA-duct ram-air induction engine cover and tail also emerged, but the impoverished team could afford no serious wind tunnel work – merely empirical full-scale testing, mainly close to home at Silverstone.

As Alboreto's experience grew in 1982 so Tyrrell regained confidence. They felt optimistic about the Österreichring, but Alboreto made uncharacteristic errors in qualifying and the race and hit the barriers. They went to Las Vegas quietly confident but wondering, as Phillippe told me, 'if as usual we'd go quite well early in the meeting and then taper off. In fact Michele qualified brilliantly and we held that level for the race . . .'

As it was the Italian qualified comfortably for all 16 races and finished 12 – his best finishes running 4-4-3-6-4-5-1. His Las Vegas win was backed by the third at Imola, three fourths at Rio, Long Beach and Hockenheim, fifth at Monza and sixth at Ricard and his 25 points did the team proud.

Second driver Borgudd's three start-of-season races yielded 16-7-'10' finishes, and Henton's 13 subsequent team drives saw him finish seven times, with a best of seventh at Hockenheim in a Tyrrell 4-7 finish.

So the team, despite financial strictures and the handicap of still running an atmospheric-induction engine, finished seventh in the Cup competition with 25 points, Alboreto seventh equal in the Drivers' Championship.

But by 1983 a turbo engine was necessary to be competitive and Tyrrell had none. They rebuilt and modified the 1982 011 chassis, and ran them for regular drivers Alboreto and Sullivan. Chassis '2-4-5-6 were used, while the new carbon 012 emerged in Austria, a second 012 emerging for Sullivan at Brands Hatch.

By mid-season it was obvious the Cosworth was on its deathbed. Cosworth offered two new DFY variants (see page 53), and Tyrrell alone took the longer-term option with totally redesigned, externally different heads, new angle valves, new throttle slides, manifolds and so on. Tyrrell had seven and Phillippe initially converted the 011s to flat-bottom format while the smaller, more penetrative 012 emerged as a putative turbo car for '84.

Alboreto's '011/4' was junked after his Austrian collision with Johansson, having distorted the tub underside far more seriously than an apparently heavier testing accident earlier in the year at Spa which wrote off '011/2'. The prototype '011/1' was cut up during the season as a wind tunnel test hack, with cut-about centre sections allowing it to telescope for research purposes. Old chassis '5 had been raced again, as was '6, which was stripped and extensively rebuilt after Long Beach and re-used later in the season.

The all-new moulded carbon-fibre chassised prototype model 012 made its debut at the Österreichring in August, being used only in practice, while its sister '012/2' appeared new for Sullivan at Brands Hatch, the penultimate round.

Flat-bottom regs had slashed total download by some two-thirds compared to 1982 ground-effect values and the atmospherically aspirated engine's inability to haul big wings became marked. Phillippe: 'We lost our old advantage over the turbos in pick-up out of the corners . . . we also lost our old advantage in the wet, where they can pull a big sail of a wing and still cut

through the water . . .' However, a fortunate combination of factors still gave Alboreto the Cosworth's farewell win around the street circuit at Detroit.

His 15 races yielded only seven finishes, and his only other points score apart from Detroit was Zandvoort where he was sixth. Team-mate Sullivan ran well in the minor Brands Hatch meeting but it was a freak; he showed nothing more in the rest of the season, started all 15 races, and finished eight with a best of fifth for two points at Monaco.

He was disqualified from ninth in Montreal when his car was found to be underweight after an exhaust pipe fell off and all the coolant leaked away leaving it 4 kg below the legal minimum, topping up fluid now utterly *verboten*, so he was out. Tyrrell ended the season seventh equal to Team Lotus with their 12 points. How two mighty names had fallen . . .

Still unable to arrange turbo power for '84, Tyrrell became the last significant refuge of the Cosworth engine. Drivers were newcomers Martin Brundle and Stefan Bellof. The carbon-fibre 012 cars ran the season, five being used: '1 and '2 starting out, chassis '2 being crashed heavily by Brundle in practice at Dallas, demolishing its front end and injuring his legs; '3 emerging for Brundle at Rio and being destroyed by him in an almighty practice shunt at Monaco from which, save for concussion, he escaped unhurt; '4 for Bellof at Dijon, later being driven by Johansson in four races while Brundle was recovering from his Dallas injuries; and '5 being completed in Dallas for Bellof and later driven by Mike Thackwell at Hockenheim.

Bellof drove in 12 of the 16 meetings, missing some due to endurance racing Porsche ties, but failing to qualify at the Österreichring. However, he was excluded in any case after his car was found to be (rashly) 3 kg underweight in a final qualifying check. In the 11 races he started he finished five times, including 6-5-3 at Zolder, Imola and Monaco for five points. Brundle tackled the first nine races, having failed to qualify for Monaco and Dallas after his two heavy crashes. Of the six races he started, he finished all six – 5-11-'11'-12-10 and second in Detroit, where luck was on his and Tyrrell's side and he drove a fine race, just as had Alboreto two years before.

Sadly, this meeting was Tyrrell's undoing, in an unprecedented manner, for analysis of water drawn from the car's water injection system was held to include hydrocarbon material suggesting use of an illegal fuel additive. Tyrrell explained its presence adequately but he had not, perhaps, made many friends over

Brian Hart inspects Maurice Phillippe's largely carbon-composite, DFY-powered Tyrrell 012 prototype at its debut, Österreichring, 1983. Its reversed-sweep rear wing was soon discarded.

his years of struggle in recent Formula 1, and that July the FISA Executive Committee banned Tyrrell from the 1984 Championship; all results and points thus far being forfeit. A High Court injunction enabled Tyrrell to enter the British GP, and FISA then lifted the ban pending appeal, enabling them to complete the year's racing.

Johansson drove in the British, German, Austrian and Dutch meetings, failing to qualify understandably at the Österreichring, retiring once and finishing 9-8 otherwise. Thackwell failed to qualify at Hockenheim, the team lost its appeal and was banned from the last three races.

Ken Tyrrell announced use of Renault turbocharged engines which would come 'on stream' in mid-1985. While Phillippe embarked on a new type 014 Tyrrell-Renault design to suit, the first two existing 012-Cosworth chassis were sold to Baron Racing for Formula 3000 and '2 and '3 having been destroyed in 1984, only old chassis '5 was retained for the new year, while '6 and '7 were built new for Brundle and Johansson at Rio. The Swede then moved to Ferrari, replacing Arnoux, and Bellof returned to Tyrrell. Tragically he would be killed in a Group C Porsche at Spa after the Dutch GP.

Two new Tyrrell-Renault 014s made their debut at Ricard, Brundle racing '1, with '2 as spare. Bellof, meanwhile, drove an 012-Cosworth, then took over the lone turbo entry in his native Germany and Austria, where Brundle reverted to the 012-Cosworth. He predictably failed to qualify despite immense efforts at the Österreichring, and thereafter Tyrrell concentrated upon the Renault model at Zandvoort so the *ersatz* Nürburgring had witnessed the swansong of the Cosworth V8 in Formula 1.

Chassis '014/3' was new for Brundle at Monza and '4 appeared in the final race at Adelaide.

Brundle had seven 012-Cosworth races, yielding five finishes (9-9-10-12-10) but was very unlucky to be shunted out of a potentially fine finish in Detroit, when lapping an unobservant tail-ender. His eight 014-Renault outings saw Team Tyrrell still feeling their way into a turbocharged world but taking five reliable finishes – 7-7-8-13-7 – closing the season by running at the finish but unclassified in Australia.

Bellof had six Cosworth races apart from

failing to qualify at Monaco, and finishing five times: sixth at Estoril in the rain, fourth at Detroit, 11-13-11 elsewhere. His three Renault races saw two finishes, 8-7 in Germany and Austria, retiring in Holland.

Ken Tyrrell's team had been through both zenith and nadir in its long Formula 1 life, and into 1986 looked to build upon their newfound knowledge of turbocharged race engineering.

Williams

Frank Williams, sometime Formula 3 racing driver turned racing car dealer-cum-team patron, graduated very successfully from running a Formula 2 Brabham into Formula 1 in 1969, entering a Cosworth-powered Brabham BT26 for his great friend Piers Courage. For 1970 he ran de Tomasos – Courage losing his life in one – and in 1971-72 March cars. There were many disadvantages in running proprietary cars, so when FOCA began organizing charter travel and race promoters introduced sensible start and prize money, the time was clearly ripe for Williams to build his own Formula 1 cars.

One of his sponsors, the Italian Politoys toy company, put up £40,000 towards the construction of a Len Bailey-designed car. Bailey had worked formerly on the Ford GT40 project, and his new 'Coke bottle' aluminium tub was made by Gomm Metal Developments of Old Woking, Surrey. Williams based his team in Bennett Road, Reading, Berkshire.

Former Brabham constructor Ron Tauranac acted briefly as Williams's technical consultant and the Politoys-Cosworth FX3 made its debut in the 1972 British GP at Brands Hatch. Like all Bailey creations, it was very pretty with shallow bulbous tub and chisel front-radiator nose, but Pescarolo destroyed it early in the race. Amon drove the rebuilt car back at Brands Hatch for the final Formula 1 race of the year but retired, misfiring.

For 1973, Williams cars were backed by Piero Rivolta, of Iso-Rivolta, and Marlboro, being known as Iso-Marlboros. Three of these modified FX3s were completed, driven initially by Ganley and Galli, then by other rent-a-drivers paying for the privilege. John Clarke, ex-March, designed new Iso-Marlboro IR cars to match the new deformable structure regulations, in force from the Spanish GP. These were nice cars and handled well but suffered oil system problems which broke many engines. Williams called in de Tomaso designer Giam-Paolo Dallara, who changed the rear suspension geometry; Clarke left in an understandable huff, for the cars' results reflected budget more than design quality.

During 1973 the early-season FX3s made nine starts, finishing only four times, the best being Trimmer's fourth in 'FX3B-3' at Brands Hatch. The IR cars made their debut at Barcelona, chassis '3 in Austria, totalling 24 starts with 12 finishes, including sixths in Holland and Canada, driven by van Lennep and Ganley. Ickx was seventh in a guest drive at Watkins Glen, commenting favourably on the car.

Merzario joined for 1974, making a vivid impression in Buenos Aires as he blew two DFVs, leaving the tachometer needle lodged at 13,000 rpm! Since the rev-limiter made this impossible under normal acceleration he must merely have changed down as he would normally have done in his previous flat-12 Ferrari, thereby punching the V8 through the roof on the over-run . . .

Williams ran modified Iso-Marlboros in this season. Driving alongside Merzario were Tom Belso, Gijs van Lennep, Richard Robarts, Jabouille and, ultimately, Laffite, the latter winning a regular place in the last five races. Merzario gave new heart, qualifying brilliantly in South Africa, finishing sixth and going well

Frank Williams struggled to keep his team afloat during the early-1970s. His essentially John Clarke-designed 1974 IR-series cars like this one had much to commend them.

until a crash at Jarama damped his ardour. He was his old self again at Monza for fourth in his home GP. Overall, the team tackled 16 races, failed to qualify four times and finished only six times, placing 3-6-14-8-9-4, which was not too bad.

Ex-McLaren engineer Ray Stokoe updated the ageing cars and designed a square-cut new monocoque for 1975 designated 'FW04', old IR's becoming FWs. IR02 was rebuilt on a new tub as FW02. With shoestring finance, in part from a tough Swiss businessman named Ambrozium, Williams ran two cars for Merzario and Laffite, though when they had sports car commitments with Alfa Romeo, alternative drivers included Flammini, Brise, Damien Magee, Ian Scheckter, Ian Ashley, Jo Vonlanthen, Renzo Zorzi and Signorina Lella Lombardi.

Williams survived, buying discarded wings and bits from other teams, like Hesketh, to keep running. During 1975 they made 24 starts and finished ten times. It looked hopeless, finishes being 11-7-7-14-12-11 up to the German GP. However, punctures decimated the field there and Laffite finished second – Williams's best finish since 1969 with Courage and the Brabham BT26.

That was worth some £5500 and assured Williams of continued FOCA membership for 1976 with the travel savings that this involved. Frank had met an Austro-Canadian oil-man named Walter Wolf, and when Wolf looked for a Formula 1 team to buy into, Williams gave him 60 per cent in return for liabilities of around £140,000 (see entry for Wolf, page 243).

Late in 1976 Frank was shouldered out of Wolf's racing plans. Ex-Lola engineer Patrick Head had joined him in Reading just before the Wolf take-over, and had stayed on under Dr Postlethwaite through the catastrophic Wolf-Williams season of '76. When Frank left, he took Patrick with him to be Chief Engineer in his new team, Williams Grand Prix Engineering, based in tiny premises in Didcot, Berkshire.

With backing from the sponsors of Belgian driver Patrick Neve, he bought a much-used March 761, chassis '7, for £14,000, and added four Cosworth engines.

WGPE ran the March through 1977, and for 1978 Head designed his first Formula 1 car – the Williams FW06. This arrowhead shaped car was small, light and simple, with in-line hip radiators, nose-duct oil cooler and full-width

front wing. Backing came from Saudia Airlines, it was driven by ex-Shadow man Jones, and the Head car worked.

Through 1978 Williams built three FW06s, Jones starting all 16 GPs, finishing nine; fourth at Kyalami, seventh (after running second until a nose wing collapse) at Long Beach, fifth at Ricard, and second on merit in the US GP at Watkins Glen. Before retiring, Jones also ran fourth in Sweden, second at Brands Hatch, third at Hockenheim and looked set for another second place end-of-season at Montreal before suffering a puncture.

WGPE placed ninth-equal in the Constructors' table with this one-car entry and clearly had one of the best non-wing cars of the year. This assured backing for Head to build the FW07 wing-car for 1979 (pages 104-9). After ten seasons trying, Williams was about to dominate Formula 1.

At the end of the FW07 period in 1981, Head set out to design a six-wheeler but had also developed reservoirs which helped save startline weight as they could legitimately be topped-up after the race to meet the legal minimum weight requirement in scrutineering.

The six-wheeler ploy would continue development but only slowly.

Consequently, the FW07 replacement FW08 emerged at Zolder in 1982 as an ultra-short wheelbase, short chassis car designed around a weight-limit water tank and incorporating a short, tall fuel cell abaft the cockpit.

From the back of the tub it was virtually pure FW07, little changed from 1979 form. Six FW08s were run, a mid-season misfiring problem in Rosberg's car being cured by moving the fuel tank outlet. Rosberg built a good working relationship with the team, and his number two, Daly, was very popular as well as a super race driver but qualified poorly and therefore was prone to startline collisions.

Now Williams were aiming at their third consecutive Cup title. Apart from the change from FW07C to FW08 after Long Beach, little new was tried. Only two different side pod profiles were used, effectively one for fast circuits and one for slow. Later in the year, the wheelbase was lengthened 1½ in. by raking the front suspension forward, altering weight distribution by around 1.5 per cent. Generally, the cars felt more at home on the faster circuits, and for the final race at Las Vegas they reverted to short wheelbase form.

There was experimentation with skirt materials and spasmodic trials of carbon-fibre brakes, but wear rate with the French SEP-made brakes and heat-soak boiling the fluid when the cars stopped precluded their use in anger.

All aerodynamic study was undertaken in Williams's own wind tunnel at Didcot. Much of the expense of Formula 1 disappears into parts never used and some idea of this 'wastage' can be gained from experimental engineer Frank Dernie's wind tunnel programme. Of all the underwing profiles designed, developed and tested, only Marks 1, 4, 6, 7, 13, 18 and 24 were actually raced; the rest just 'weren't good enough'. Mark 18 formed the original FW08 spec, the late-1982 Mark 24 underwing matching a smaller rear wing for faster circuits. The Mark 24 wing gave a four per cent shift in the centre of pressure and by the end of the season Mark 31 was already under test.

Four FW07Cs were used early in 1982, numbers '14-15-16-17, the latter effectively written off by Rosberg at Rio.

The new 'FW08/1' was normally spare, being raced by Rosberg in Montreal, Hockenheim and the Österreichring. Chassis '2 was essentially Dernie's test-team car, spare at Monaco, and performing show and spare car duties at Las Vegas. Chassis '3 was Rosberg's new mid-season race car introduced at Zolder, and he raced it three times to Montreal. Chassis '4 was Daly's debutante at Zolder, and he raced it to Ricard, after which it was retired. Chassis '5 was new for Rosberg at Zandvoort and he raced it eight times, winning the 'Swiss' GP (a Championship round that season) at Dijon. Finally, chassis '6 was new for Daly at Hockenheim.

Rosberg won the World Drivers' Championship, but Williams failed to secure their potential Constructors' Cup hat-trick, placing only fourth in the table behind McLaren and Renault with 58 points. Constructors' Cup success requires not only a fast and reliable car but also two potential winners to drive them.

Rosberg's season included 15 of the 16 GPs as Williams had joined other FOCA teams in the ill-advised boycott of Imola. He finished 12, his record running 5-2*-2-2-4-3-5-3-2-1-8-5 (*disqualified). He scored in every finish save that eighth place in Italy when the rear wing pillar snapped.

In contrast, the record for Daly, who had joined Williams after Reutemann's abrupt retirement from racing, included only the last 12 races, and he was classified only eight times: 6-5-7-5-5-7-9-6. Although five of those finishes scored Championship points, it was not good enough and Williams did not retain him for 1983.

The new year saw Head's design team rejig FW08 to suit new flat-bottom regulations, one 1982 chassis 'FW08-6' being updated while two were completed brand new to C-spec for Rio, chassis 'FW08C/7' and '8. Chassis '9 emerged new at Ricard as a spare car, old chassis '2 was brought to Brands Hatch as a spare following a practice accident to Rosberg, and tubs '10 and '11 were also completed but not required.

Laffite joined Rosberg, but by now the age of the Cosworth had passed.

Early in the year the FW08Cs showed the other Cosworth cars the way, but later McLaren forged ahead on the faster circuits. Extended footbox protection was grafted on to the original tubs to match new 1983 requirements and these early tubs also retained the attachment inserts originally demanded for the old side pods and underwings (which the true 1983 FW08C tubs lacked while featuring integral footbox protection).

One major development programme produced a new Williams six-speed gearbox.

The cars worked quite well wherever they could run a lot of wing, which means slower circuits, but Head admitted 'it was pretty mediocre' elsewhere.

Tyres, again, were dominant, Goodyear's bias-belted 'radials' causing heartache because without turbo power the team could not afford the aerodynamic loads to prevent them 'going

doughnut-shaped' at high speed. Towards the end of the year, Laffite's form caused serious concern as he was a shadow of his former self, though prospects looked rosy for the new turbocharged Honda FW09 cars which were prepared hastily for the finale race in South Africa.

These FW09s retained the Head folded aluminium honeycomb chassis form of the FW07-08 series, and in 1984 no less than nine would be used.

Williams had originally concluded a deal with Honda in 1982 for a development car, but Honda wanted to see how the Spirit Formula 1 venture for which they were providing engines would evolve. In mid-summer '83 Head began FW09 design and the prototype was tested at Donington Park prior to the Italian GP. At the time there was no thought of racing a Honda-powered car that season but at Monza Patrick remarked to Frank Williams that if they were to challenge seriously for the Championship in '84 they should race FW09-Hondas in South Africa.

First time out on test both drivers commented how nicely the new Williams-Hondas handled, but initially they had insufficient intercooler capacity to handle full boost at Kyalami, despite qualifying well.

That November, WGPE moved into a stunning new custom-built factory at Didcot, and began stiffening FW09, and producing a complete new gearbox with pullrod rear suspension. In South Africa, the car was quick but showed the dominant understeer which would dog it in 1984.

Starting the new year in Rio, Rosberg fulminated about this understeer, but WGPE could not revert to the old set-up because parts were not available. The pullrod rear end cars had to run unhappily up to Dijon, the new gearbox gave trouble due to a crownwheel cutting problem, and Head now wished to waist-in the rear bodywork à la McLaren MP4/2 to seek a useful download advantage without additional drag. This layout demanded rocker-arm rear suspension which the new gearbox could not accept, so the tailored FW09 gearbox had to be set aside and replaced by the old, basically Hewland, FGB as used on the FW07-08 cars.

They ran in this rear rocker-arm form from Monaco. An FW09B used the new bobbed-in tail on test prior to the mid-season American tour, one such running in Canada but suffering an engine failure related to exhaust pipe form so everything was then hurriedly modified to original.

The definitive FW09B emerged thereafter

with a five-inch longer wheelbase, long rear adaptor, new exhaust system, altered bodywork and side panels, FGB gearbox and FW08-like wider track rocker-arm rear suspension. The cars ran essentially in this form for the rest of the year while a new FW10 began design for 1985, nine 1984 cars having been built.

Understeer dominated the season. Some of this appeared to be traceable to the Goodyear radial tyres, but normal palliatives destroyed traction. This was aggravated by the Honda engine's vicious power curve.

Through these problems, Laffite had a miserable season. He retired 11 times and his five finishes (8-8-5-4-14) were the worst WGPE record since the team's first cars ran in 1978. Rosberg fought harder, retiring on 10 occasions, but winning the very hot race at Dallas on personal fortitude and car control, aided by team forethought as he had been provided with a driver cooling device. Elsewhere he placed 2-4-6-5-'9' (having retired but being classified as a finisher) in the other five GPs, and always running in the top four.

Williams-Honda ended the season sixth in the Constructors' Championship, after a difficult first turbocharged season.

Late in '84, Patrick decided to adopt moulded carbon-composite chassis construction for his 1985 FW10-Honda, the first 'black Williams'. After one pilot-build prototype shell, eight more followed, seven being completed. Chassis '1 and '2 were new at Rio, '3 for Rosberg at Imola. 'FW10/2' was effectively written off at Detroit by new driver Mansell, then a tyre explosion at Ricard destroyed his new 'FW10/5' on its debut. Chassis 'FW10/4' went to Japan for Honda's engine development test programme, driven by Satoru Nakajima.

Chassis '6 was new for Mansell at Silverstone and would win two late-season GPs in his hands, while '7 emerged for Rosberg in Austria and would win the Australian GP season finale.

In early-1985 Williams ran modified D-Type Honda V6s, then from Montreal the revamped E-Type. D engines were given the improved engine mounts of the forthcoming Es to match the FW10 tubs, and were further modified to sidestep early IHI turbocharger problems. A new transmission, still six-speed, had been adopted for the D's narrow rev-band where power was enough '. . . to break traction in second and third . . . [sigh, then a rather rueful chuckle] . . . and fourth and fifth as well . . .'

The E engines emerged at Montreal where Rosberg finished 25 seconds behind the winning Ferrari despite two stops; Mansell had a boost problem and effectively ran a 185-litre consumption race. Rosberg won the next race, in Detroit – the Williams-Honda had come good. It would fall back briefly with engine bearing problems, then dominate the end of the season.

The FW10s were mechanically acceptable at Ricard but the heat and speeds there aggravated their ferocious hunger for tyres. A spell of unreliability followed – the car at Silverstone, largely the engine bottom-end subsequently – until Spa's team 2-3 finish. Before Brands Hatch, the engine induction and rear of the body were lowered to improve airflow to the rear wing with redesigned transmission and new pullrod instead of rocker-arm rear suspension. Now the FW10 could handle Honda's reliable power well enough for a convincing team 1-3 in Mansell's maiden GP win, and he then led a team 1-2 at Kyalami, and Rosberg was victorious in Adelaide.

Rosberg started all 16 GPs, finishing nine, 8-4-1-2-12*-4-3-2-1; Mansell started 15 (missing the French after his monstrous practice

The stubby Williams FW08's tub was originally intended for a six-wheeler, hence its brevity. Rosberg (here at Hockenheim) brought the team their second Drivers' World Championship success, in 1982.

accident) and finished ten, 5-5-7-6-6-6-11*-2-1-1, scoring points eight times.

Williams used French SEP carbon brakes everywhere but Detroit and Adelaide where they ran iron, with supreme success.

Their three successive victories in the last three 1985 GPs left Williams looking best-placed for the 1986 season to come.

Wolf

Austrian-born Canadian Walter Wolf made a fortune in the oil equipment business. He part-sponsored Williams until at the end of 1975 he bought Hesketh's equipment and plant for a reputed £450,000. He then took on Williams's liabilities for a 60 per cent share in the business. At a stroke he had gained full FOCA (Formula One Constructors' Association) membership for two cars which he would not have had with Hesketh alone, worth around £150,000 a year in saved travelling expenses outside Europe. His Hesketh material and some personnel, including designer Harvey Postlethwaite, moved into Williams's workshop in Bennett Road, Reading, Berkshire.

Marlboro money came into this new Wolf-Williams team, bringing driver Ickx and F2 hopeful Michel Leclère. But the Wolf-Williams season of 1976 was a catastrophe.

The Hesketh 308C – known now as the Wolf-Williams FW05 – was aerodynamically and structurally mediocre, and as it was strengthened and continuously modified so it became some 120 lb overweight, creating a built-in penalty of a second a lap. Ickx was quite incapable of sorting it out and was fired after non-qualifying for the British GP. Poor Leclère was utterly bemused by the desolation around him, Merzario filled in for the last seven GPs but whereas the first part of the year saw the cars qualify for nine starts and retire only once, Merzario never finished at all. Warwick Brown was 14th in the second-string car at Watkins Glen. Three FW05s were campaigned, two originally built by Hesketh. In September, Williams was dismissed from what had been his team, Peter Warr joined from Lotus to manage affairs for 1977 and Postlethwaite designed an all-new car for a one-driver team built around Scheckter, previously with Tyrrell.

The new Wolf-Cosworth 'WR1' emerged as a neat and attractive arrow-head car, with curvaciously wedgy bodywork enclosing the rugged monocoque. Postlethwaite concentrated upon reliability. Three of these cars were built that season, 'WR1-2-3', and while most rivals concentrated upon twin-calliper balanced brakes, Postlethwaite relied upon a fully-floating conventional system, which performed superbly. Whenever Scheckter finished, Japanese GP aside, he was never lower than third. He started 17 races, won – luckily – on his Wolf debut in Argentina, and again at Monaco and in Canada, was second at Kyalami and Hockenheim and third at Long Beach, Jarama, Zandvoort and Watkins Glen. He retired seven times, but never due to mechanical failure on the chassis. A perpetual fuel pressure problem bothered the team but paradoxically it profited from being too new to qualify for Cosworth's hot 'development' engines, which wrecked the Lotus 78's season. At Monaco, Scheckter scored the DFV's 100th victory on a Hesketh-built unit, rejecting Ford's offer of support. All wins were in 'WR1/1' and Scheckter was runner-up in his Championship; Wolf fourth in their own, with 55 points.

In 1978 Lotus completed their ground-effects car revolution and the old 'WR1-4' series – a fourth car having since been completed – were patently outclassed in South America. Postlethwaite rushed out his own wing-car design, the unusually ugly Wolf 'WR5' and 'WR6' duo.

The new wedge-monocoque 'WR5-6' design

Jody Scheckter's Postlethwaite-designed Wolf WR1 notches Cosworth-Ford's 100th GP victory, Monaco, 1977.

with its massive cooler sunk into the front cockpit fairing made its bow in practice at Monaco and was first raced at Zolder, 'WR6' being ready in time for the French GP. Old cars 'WR3-4' were sold to Theodore for Rosberg. Scheckter led the British GP for a while and raced through the field to claim second at Hockenheim. He raced 'WR6' for the first time in Holland, but destroyed it at Monza, a total rebuild producing another car using the same number for the US GP where he finished third and Canada, placing second. Bobby Rahal drove 'WR5' at Watkins Glen finishing 12th, then raced elderly 'WR1' in Canada where – that's right – the fuel system played up, just as it had done with Scheckter in '77. Wolf finished fifth in the Championship, with Scheckter's 24 points; Rosberg achieved nothing in the Theodore cars.

Scheckter signed for Ferrari for 1979 as Walter Wolf progressively lost interest in his team. Hunt joined them as driver but seemed equally disinterested and quite suddenly retired from racing after seven races which yielded only one place, eighth at Kyalami.

Three new cars, chassis 'WR7-8-9' were built, introducing Postlethwaite's folded aluminium honeycomb sheet construction. 'WR7' caused uproar in Buenos Aires when it featured clutch impeller vanes drawing air through the oil cooler. Rivals construed this as a moveable aerodynamic device now excluded by the 'anti-fan-car' regulations and its ducting had to be altered to prevent download advantage being gained. Wolf then had to mount a secondary oil cooler behind the water radiator.

After Hunt's defection, Rosberg briefly breathed new life into the team, proving the car could perform by running fifth for some time at Zandvoort, but ambition was draining from the team despite best efforts of Postlethwaite and

Warr. Reliability slumped and Rosberg non-qualified in Canada and only finished on his team debut, ninth in France.

During the winter of 1979/80 Walter Wolf agreed to a team merger with Fittipaldi, the Brazilian brothers putting their name on Postlethwaite's cars and the Reading premises, 'WR9' becoming the basis for the 1980 Fittipaldi F7s.

Zakspeed

The German tuning wizard Erich Zakowski had made his name with all manner of Ford-based racing saloons and had extensive experience of turbocharging in them when he decided to enter Formula 1 for 1985. His Niederzissen-based team developed a neat little four-cylinder alloy-block turbo engine of 1495 cc, claimed to deliver 700 bhp at 11,500 rpm, intended to match an exceptionally well-packaged moulded carbon-composite chassis designed for them by ex-Chevron engineer Paul Brown. They made their debut at Estoril in round two of the Championship series, with Dr Jonathan Palmer driving Zakspeed 'ZAK841/1', while chassis '2 was ready for him to adopt as his regular car at Ricard. After the Dutch GP he unfortunately broke a leg in a Group C Porsche crash at the Spa meeting in which Tyrrell driver Bellof lost his life, so Zakowski invited Formula 3000 driver Christian Danner to take his place for the Belgian and Brands Hatch races, the little team not travelling outside Europe.

In all they contested nine races, Palmer non-starting at Imola, while his only finish was 11th at Monaco. Both Danner's outings ended in retirement, so the little German team had little to show for their first foray into Formula 1. But they impressed many not only with their tightly financed car's neat design but also its turn-out.

Formula 1 Factory Drawings

General Arrangement

LOTUS TYPE 49

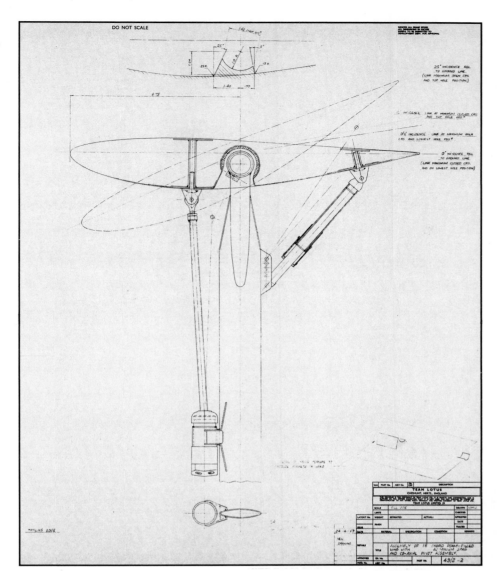

Simplicity which set the standard: Maurice Phillippe's general arrangement for the Lotus 49, dated 5 May 1967.

The era of tall strutted wings was spectacular but brief. Here is a Team Lotus Type 49B wing-mount section. 24 April 1969.

One of the long-lived and successful Lotus 72's unconventional features — the compound torsion-bar suspension spring. Drawing dated 14 November 1973.

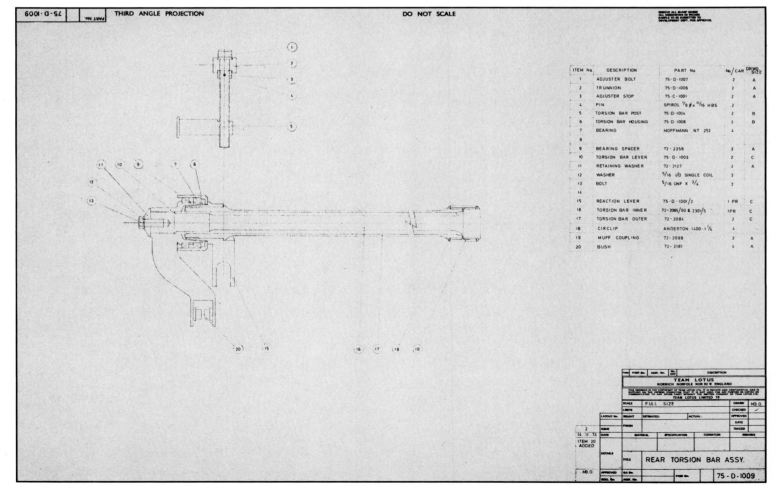

ITEM No.	DESCRIPTION	PART No	No/CAR	DRWG SIZE
1	ADJUSTER BOLT	75·D·1007	2	A
2	TRUNNION	75·D·1006	2	A
3	ADJUSTER STOP	75·C·1001	2	A
4	PIN	SPIROL 1/8 ⌀ x 11/16 HBS	2	
5	TORSION BAR POST	75·D·1004	2	B
6	TORSION BAR HOUSING	75·D·1008	2	B
7	BEARING	HOFFMANN N7 253	4	
8				
9	BEARING SPACER	72·2358	2	A
10	TORSION BAR LEVER	75·D·1003	2	C
11	RETAINING WASHER	72·2127	2	A
12	WASHER	5/16 I/D SINGLE COIL	2	
13	BOLT	5/16 UNF X 3/4	2	
14				
15	REACTION LEVER	75·D·1001/2	1 PR	C
16	TORSION BAR INNER	72·2085/90 & 2301/5	1PR	C
17	TORSION BAR OUTER	72·2084	2	C
18	CIRCLIP	ANDERTON 1400-1 1/4	2	
19	MUFF COUPLING	72·2098	2	A
20	BUSH	72·2181	4	A

REAR TORSION BAR ASSY.

75 - D - 1009

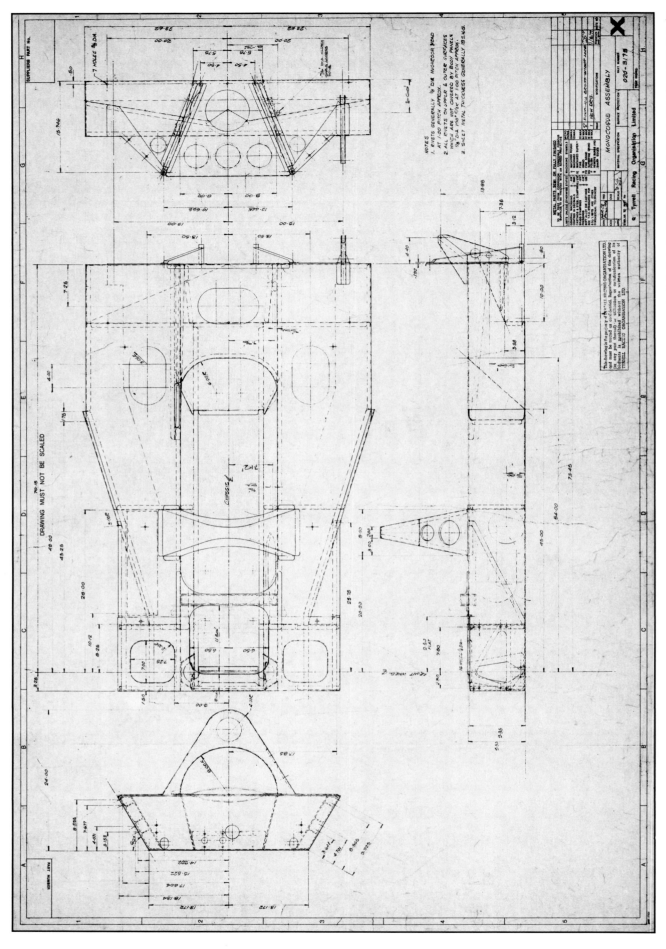

Extremely shallow and broad aluminium monocoque tubs became popular in the late-Seventies. Maurice Phillippe's Tyrrell 008 tub is typical. 1 August 1977. Opposite top, the ground-effects aerodynamic revolution was born in Ralph Bellamy's Lotus 78 general arrangement drawing, dated 15 November 1976. Opposite bottom, Formula 1 rear suspension, in this case Patrick Head's 1978 Williams FW06, 20 January 1978.

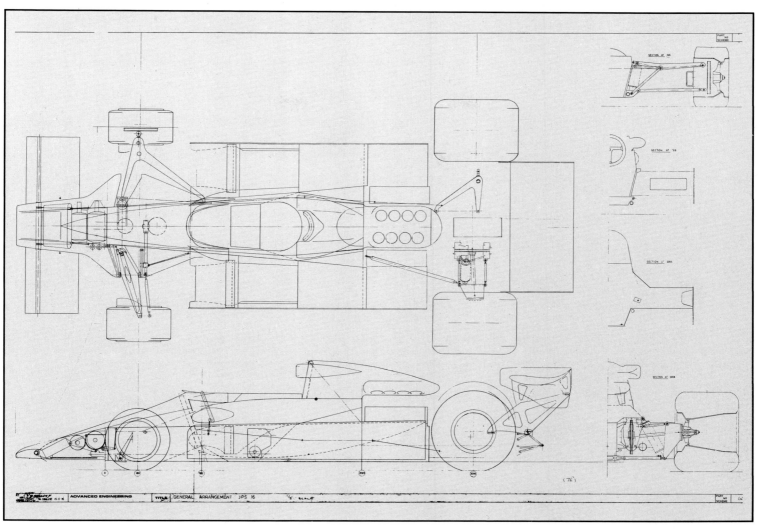

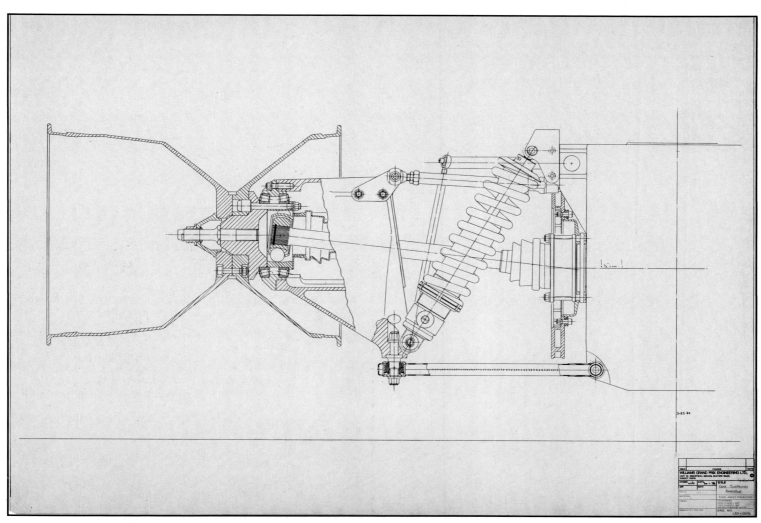

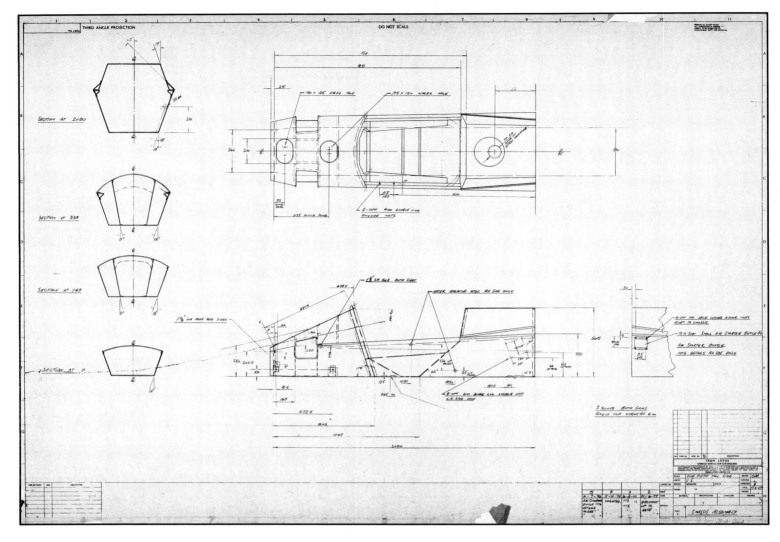

This page, a slimline tub became necessary to clear side pod airflow in the true ground-effects Lotus 79. Martin Ogilvie's drawings (dated 13 June 1977) show monocoque and side pod layout and constructional detail.

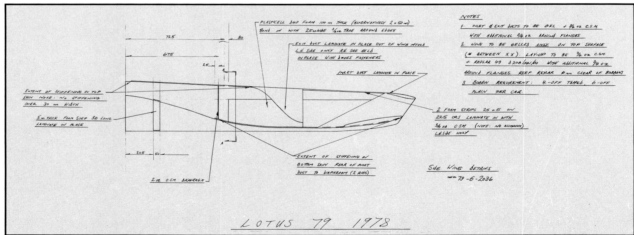

LOTUS 79 1978

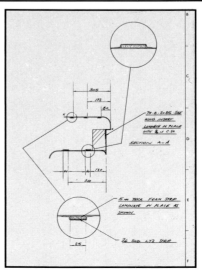

Opposite top, *Lotus and Getrag co-developed this gearbox which was a little jewel but was sadly not robust enough for Formula 1. Opposite bottom, Williams set aerodynamic standards to beat from 1979 to 1981. Skirt-box sealing and sliding-skirt control were vital and even this FW07-series side panel required multiple mounting inserts. Drawing dated 6 March 1979.*

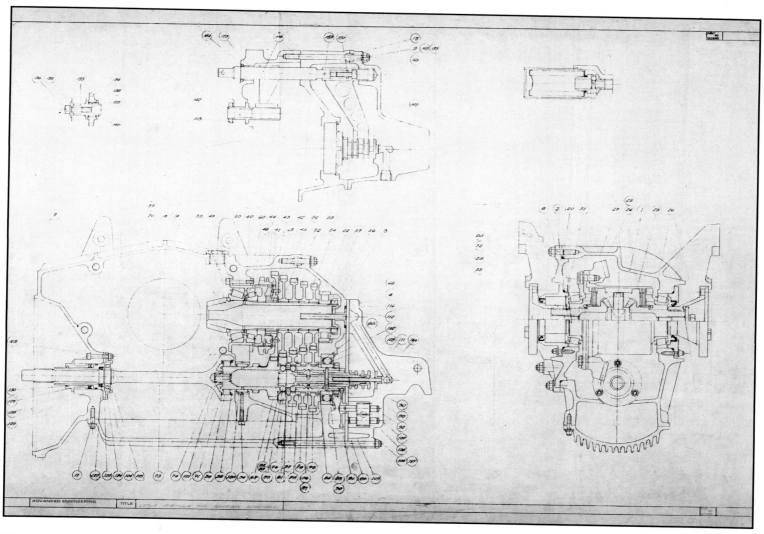

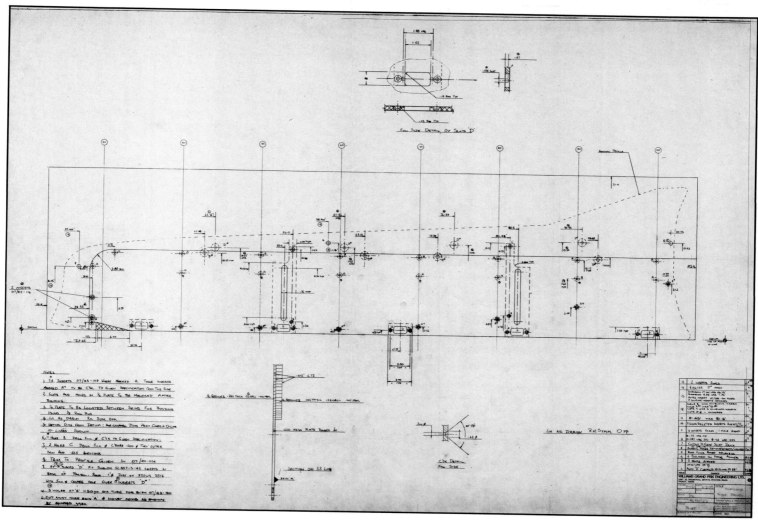

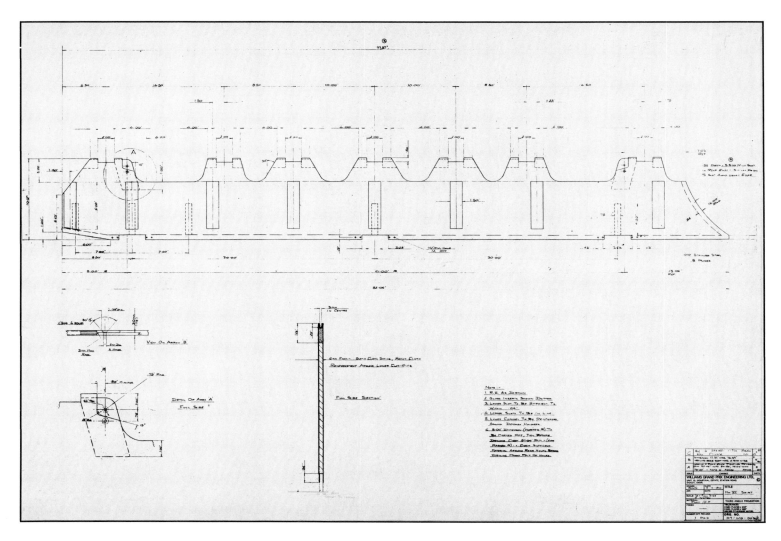

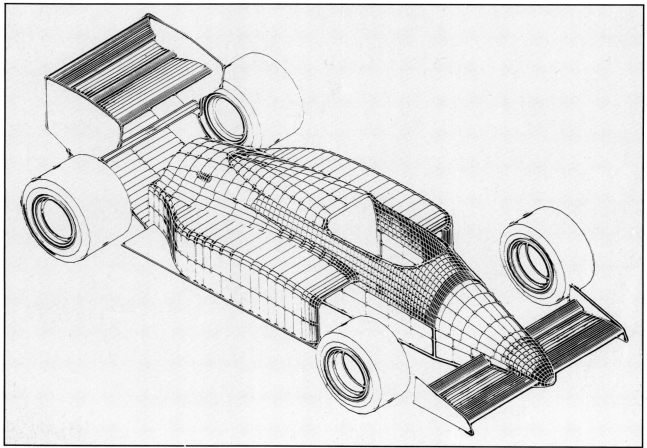

Above, *the sliding skirt itself had to be rigid as well as precisely controlled within its guides. Williams did it better than most — this FW07 skirt drawing is dated 8 April 1980. Left, towards the future: Ferrari's CAD/CAM modelling for their 1985 126C. Gould computers and Piaggio aerospace design company co-developed a system which created and cut patterns from resin block without a line being drawn on paper.*

Torsional strength ▶ *became more crucial in the slimmer modern chassis and this helped to accelerate the use of moulded carbon-composite materials in the early-Eighties. Maurice Phillippe's Tyrrell 012 chassis is shown here in a drawing dated 27 April 1983.*

250

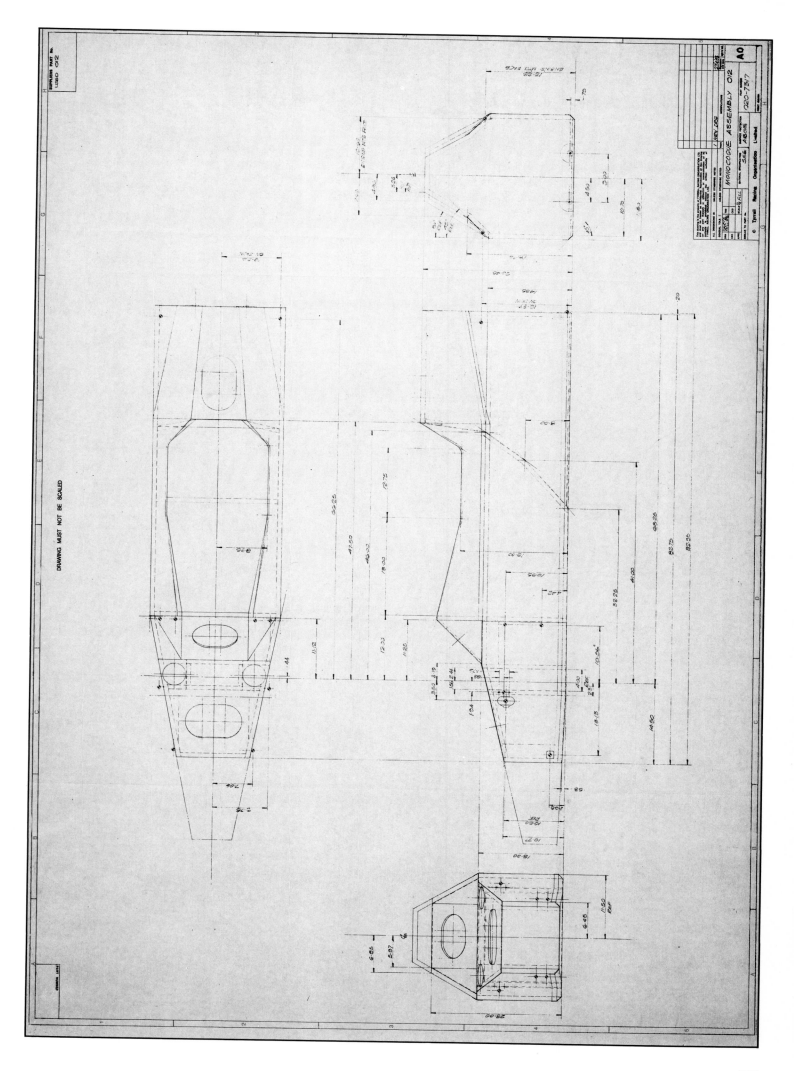

DRAWING MUST NOT BE SCALED

MONOCOQUE ASSEMBLY 012

Tyrrell Racing Organisation Limited

A0

Appendix
The Racing Record

Within these pages it is quite impossible to reproduce in full results of all Formula 1 races held under the so-called '3-litre Formula' since 1966. However, here we do our best, listing the first six in each of the events held, and adding details of pole position, fastest lap and brief summary of the event. This allows us to record fine performances which failed to achieve solid results. The bald record book itself can never reflect credit on those who led, perhaps from start to penultimate lap, only for some often obscure failure to rob them of victory so close to the finish. This listing begins with the non-Championship Rand GP at Kyalami circuit, outside Johannesburg, on 4 December 1965, which was run to the new regulations although they did not formally take effect until 1 January 1966. The listing to the end of the 1985 season includes 331 individual races, 279 Championship GPs and 52 non-Championship events, and it gives us all the bare statistics of success, failure, and relative performance from 1966 to 1985.

Driver, engine capacity, car-engine manufacturer, type and individual car chassis number are all listed, and we hope that the enthusiast will browse happily in this unique record of 20 hectic years of motor racing's premier Formula. A magnifying glass is recommended . . .

4-12-65 Rand GP,
Kyalami, ZA – 50 laps, 127.20 miles
1. Jack Brabham (2.7 Brabham-Climax FPF BT11 F1-2-64/2), 50 laps in 1:18;11.2, 97.69 mph.
2. Pieter de Klerk (2.5 Brabham-Climax FPF BT11 IC-5-64), 50, 1:18;17.1.
3. Paul Hawkins (2.7 Lotus-Climax FPF 25 R3), 50. **4.** John Love (2.7 Cooper-Climax FPF T79 FL-1-65), 49. **5.** Jo Siffert (1.5 Brabham-BRM V8 BT11 F1-6-64), 49. **6.** Innes Ireland (1.5 Lotus-BRM V8 25 R4), 49.
PP – Brabham, 1;30.8; FL – Brabham, 1;31.5, 100.11 mph.
Fine race dominated by effectively Tasman Formula cars with Brabham and Love battling wheel-to-wheel until the latter's rear suspension gave trouble after he had often led.

1966

1-1-66 South African GP,
East London – 60 laps, 145.98 miles
1. Mike Spence (2.0 Lotus-Climax V8 33 R11), 60 laps in 1:29;39.4, 97.75 mph.
2. Jo Siffert (1.5 Brabham-BRM V8 BT11 F1-6-64), 58, 1:29;59.8.
3. Peter Arundell (1.5 Lotus-Climax 33 R9), 58. **4.** Dave Charlton (2.7 Brabham-Climax FPF BT11 F1-2-64/2), 58. **5.** Sam Tingle (2.7 LDS-Climax FPF LDS 3), 57. **6.** John Love (2.7 Cooper-Climax FPF T79 FL-1-65), 56.
PP – Jack Brabham (Repco-Brabham V8 BT19 F1-1-65), 1;25.1; FL – Brabham, 1;25.2, 102.91 mph.
Jack Brabham led from lap 2 in his brand new Repco V8-engined car until lap 51 when he spun and engine refused to restart because injection pump drive belt had snapped.

1-5-66 Syracuse GP,
Sicily, I – 56 laps, 195.27 miles
1. John Surtees (3.0 Ferrari 312 V12 0010), 56 laps in 1:40;08.3, 114.67 mph.
2. Lorenzo Bandini (2.4 Ferrari Dino 246 V6 0006), 56, 1:40;32.9.
3. David Hobbs (1.9 Lotus-BRM V8 25 R13), 54. **4.** Vic Wilson (1.9 BRM V8 P261 2615), 53. **5.** Jo Bonnier (1.9 Brabham-BRM V8 BT11 F1-6-64), 52. UNC **'6th'.** Guy Ligier (3.0 Cooper-Maserati V12 T81 F1-4-66), 39.
PP – Surtees, 1;42.3; FL – Surtées, 1;43.4, 118.99 mph.
Surtees took the lead from Bandini on lap 4 and the Ferraris won virtually unopposed.

14-5-66 BRDC International Trophy,
Silverstone, GB – 35 laps, 102.45 miles
1. Jack Brabham (Repco-Brabham V8 BT19 F1-1-65), 35 laps in 52;57.6, 116.06 mph.
2. John Surtees (3.0 Ferrari V12 312 0010), 35 in 53;05.0.
3. Jo Bonnier (3.0 Cooper-Maserati V12 T81 F1-5-66), 35. **4.** Denny Hulme (2.7 Brabham-Climax FPF BT11 F1-1-64), 35. **5.** Jochen Rindt (3.0 Cooper-Maserati V12 T81 F1-3-66), 34. **6.** John Taylor (1.9 Brabham-BRM V8 BT11 F1-4-64), 33.
PP – Brabham, 1;29.8; FL – Brabham, 1;29.8, 117.34 mph.
Small entry but Surtees' new Ferrari could do nothing about Brabham, who led throughout.

22-5-66 MONACO GP,
Monte Carlo – 100 laps, 195.41 miles
1. Jackie Stewart (1.9 BRM V8 P261 2617), 100 laps in 2:33;10.5, 76.50 mph.
2. Lorenzo Bandini (2.4 Ferrari Dino V6 246 0006), 100 in 2:33;50.7.
3. Graham Hill (1.9 BRM V8 P261 2616), 99. **4.** Bob Bondurant (1.9 BRM V8 P261 2615), 95. UNC **'5th'.** Richie Ginther (3.0 Cooper-Maserati V12 T81 F1-6-66), 80. UNC **'6th'.** Guy Ligier (3.0 Cooper-Maserati V12 T81 F1-4-66), 75.
PP – Jim Clark (2.0 Lotus-Climax V8 33 R11); FL – Bandini, 1;29.8, 78.35 mph.
Stewart duelled with Surtees' Ferrari until its diff failed, then led from lap 14 to finish.

NOTE – *All cars listed hereafter are 3-litres unless otherwise marked.*

13-6-66 BELGIAN GP,
Spa-Francorchamps – 28 laps, 24.8 miles
1. John Surtees (Ferrari V12 312 0010), 28 laps in 2:09;11.3, 113.39 mph.
2. Jochen Rindt (Cooper-Maserati V12 T81 F1-3-66), 28 in 2:09;53.4.
3. Lorenzo Bandini (2.4 Ferrari Dino V6 246 0006), 27. **4.** Jack Brabham (Repco-Brabham V8 BT19 F1-1-65), 26. **5.** Richie Ginther (Cooper-Maserati V12 T81 F1-6-66), 25. UNC **'6th'.** Guy Ligier (Cooper-Maserati V12 F1-4-66), 24.
PP – Surtees, 3;38.0; FL – Surtees, 4;18.7, 121.93 mph.
Field decimated by opening lap accident in torrential rain, Rindt led Surtees' fuel pump-afflicted Ferrari until Cooper's diff played up five laps from finish.

3-7-66 FRENCH GP,
Reims-Gueux – 48 laps, 247.58 miles
1. Jack Brabham (Repco-Brabham V8 BT19 F1-1-65), 48 laps in 1:48;31.3, 124.55 mph.
2. Mike Parkes (Ferrari V12 312 0012), 48 in 1:48;40.8.
3. Denny Hulme (Repco-Brabham V8 BT20 F1-2-66), 46. **4.** Jochen Rindt (Cooper-Maserati V12 T81 F1-3-66), 46. **5.** Dan Gurney (2.7 Eagle-Climax FPF T1G 101), 45. **6.** John Taylor (2.0 Brabham-BRM V8 BT11 F1-4-64), 45.
PP – Lorenzo Bandini (Ferrari V12 312 0010), 2;09.1; FL – Bandini, 2;11.3, 142.09 mph.
Bandini's Ferrari led for 31 laps until throttle cable broke, Brabham scored first *Grande Epreuve* victory for driver in a car bearing his own name. Gurney's new interim Eagle scored its first points.

16-7-66 BRITISH GP,
Brands Hatch – 80 laps, 211.92 miles
1. Jack Brabham (Repco-Brabham V8 BT19 F1-1-65), 80 laps in 2:13;13.4, 95.48 mph.
2. Denny Hulme (Repco-Brabham V8 BT20 F1-2-66, 80 in 2:13;23.0.
3 Graham Hill (1.9 BRM V8 P261 2616), 79. **4** Jim Clark (2.0 Lotus-Climax V8 33 R14), 79. **5** Jochen Rindt (Cooper-Maserati V12 T81 F-3-66), 79. **6** Bruce McLaren (McLaren-Serenissima V8 M2B M2B/2), 78.
PP – Brabham, 1;34.5; FL – Brabham, 1;37.0, 98.35 mph.
Brabham led from start to finish, superb drive by Clark spoiled by stop to top up brake fluid.

24-7-66 DUTCH GP,
Zandvoort – 90 laps, 234.54 miles
1. Jack Brabham (Repco-Brabham V8 BT19 F1-1-65), 90 laps in 2:20;32.5, 100.10 mph.
2. Graham Hill (1.9 BRM V8 P261 2616), 89 laps.
3. Jim Clark (2.0 Lotus-Climax V8 33 R14), 88.
4. Jackie Stewart (1.9 BRM V8 P261 2614), 88.
5. Mike Spence (1.9 Lotus-BRM V8 25 R13), 87.
6. Lorenzo Bandini (Ferrari V12 312 0010), 87.
PP – Brabham, 1;28.1; FL – Denny Hulme (Repco-Brabham V8 BT20 F1-2-66), 1;30.6, 103.53 mph.
Great race between the Brabhams and Clark's Lotus which took lead, then lost it in a stop to add water.

7-8-66 GERMAN GP,
Nürburgring – 15 laps, 212.69 miles
1. Jack Brabham (Repco-Brabham V8 BT19 F1-1-65), 15 laps in 2:27;03.0, 86.75 mph.
2. John Surtees (Cooper-Maserati V12 T81 F1-6-66), 15 in 2:27;47.4.
3. Jochen Rindt (Cooper-Maserati V12 T81 F1-3-66), 15. **4.** Graham Hill (1.9 BRM V8 P261 2616), 15. **5.** Jackie Stewart (1.9 BRM V8 P261 2614), 15. **6.** Lorenzo Bandini (Ferrari V12 312 0010), 15.
PP – Jim Clark (2.0 Lotus-Climax V8 33 R14), 8;16.5; FL – Surtees, 8;49.0, 96.45 mph.
Long duel for lead between Brabham and Surtees decided when the latter's clutch failed.

4-9-66 ITALIAN GP,
Monza – 68 laps, 243.44 miles
1. Ludovico Scarfiotti (Ferrari V12 312 0011), 68 laps in 1:47;14.3, 135.93 mph.
2. Mike Parkes (Ferrari V12 312 0012), 68 in 1:47;20.6.
3. Denny Hulme (Repco-Brabham V8 BT20 F1-2-66), 68. **4.** Jochen Rindt (Cooper-Maserati V12 T81 F1-3-66), 67. **5.** Mike Spence (1.9 Lotus-BRM V8 25 R13), 67. **6.** Bob Anderson (2.7 Brabham-Climax FPF BT11 F1-5-64), 66.
PP – Parkes, 1;31.3; FL – Scarfiotti, 1;32.4, 139.19 mph.
Ferraris uncatchable on home soil, Scarfiotti leading from lap 13, new 36-valve V12 engines being used in the Ferraris. Honda written off in its debut race.

17-9-66 International Gold Cup,
Oulton Park, GB – 40 laps, 110.44 miles
1. Jack Brabham (Repco-Brabham V8 BT19 F1-1-65), 40 laps in 1:06;14.2, 100.04 mph.
2. Denny Hulme (Repco-Brabham V8 BT20 F1-2-66), 40 in 1:06;14.2.
3. Jim Clark (2.0 Lotus-Climax V8 33 R14), 40.
4. Innes Ireland (1.9 BRM V8 P261 2615), 40.
5. Chris Lawrence (Cooper-Ferrari V12 Spl T71 F1-1-64), 38.
No other finishers.
PP – Brabham, 1;34.2; FL – Brabham & Hulme, 1;36.6, 102.89 mph.
BRM H16s fought exciting battle with Brabhams, Stewart led but both he and team-mate Hill retired.

2-10-66 UNITED STATES GP,
Watkins Glen, NY – 108 laps, 248.40 miles
1. Jim Clark (Lotus-BRM H16 43 R1), 108 laps in 2:09;40.1, 114.94 mph.
2. Jochen Rindt (Cooper-Maserati V12 T81 F1-3-66), 108 in 2:11;26.9.
3. John Surtees (Cooper-Maserati V12 T81 F1-6-66), 107. **4.** Jo Siffert (Cooper-Maserati V12 T81 F1-2-66), 105. **5.** Bruce McLaren (McLaren-Ford Indy V8 M2B M2B/1), 105. **6.** Peter Arundell (2.0 Lotus-Climax V8 33 R14), 101.
PP – Jack Brabham (Repco-Brabham V8 BT20 F1-1-66), 1;08.48; FL – Surtees, 1;09.67, 118.85 mph.
Bandini's Ferrari led and broke, Brabham's Repco V8 broke its cam followers, Surtees spun while lapping a back-marker to spoil Cooper's great chance and Clark won using BRM's high-mileage spare works H16 engine. It would prove to be the H16's only victory.

23-10-66 MEXICAN GP,
Mexico City – 65 laps, 201.93 miles
1. John Surtees (Cooper-Maserati V12 T81 F1-6-66), 65 laps in 2:06;35.34, 95.72 mph.
2. Jack Brabham (Repco-Brabham V8 BT20 F1-1-66), 65 in 2:06;43.22.
3. Denny Hulme (Repco-Brabham V8 BT20 F1-2-66), 64. **4.** Richie Ginther (Honda V12 RA273 F-102), 64. **5.** Dan Gurney (2.7 Eagle-Climax FPF T1G 101), 64. **6.** Jo Bonnier (Cooper-Maserati V12 T81 F1-5-66), 63.
PP – Surtees, 1;53.18; FL – Ginther, 1;53.75, 98.33 mph.
Ginther's Honda led briefly until Surtees' Maserati V12 engine warmed up and he proved unbeatable, Rindt was third behind Brabham in second Cooper until sidelined by suspension failure.

1967

2-1-67 SOUTH AFRICAN GP,
Kyalami – 80 laps, 203.52 miles
1. Pedro Rodriguez (Cooper-Maserati V12 T81 F1-6-66), 80 laps in 2:05;45.9, 97.10 mph.
2. John Love (2.7 Cooper-Climax FPF T79 FL-1-65*), 80 in 2:06;12.3.
3. John Surtees (Honda V12 RA273 F-102), 79.
4. Denny Hulme (Repco-Brabham V8 BT20 F1-2-66), 78. **5.** Bob Anderson (2.7 Brabham-Climax FPF BT11 F1-5-64), 78. **6.** Jack Brabham (Repco-Brabham V8 BT20 F1-1-66), 76.
**FL: Formula Libre (Tasman car).*
PP – Brabham, 1;28.3; FL – Hulme, 1;29.9, 101.88 mph.
Works Brabhams dominant in practice; Hulme led majority of race until forced to stop for brake fluid. Love took lead in private Tasman Cooper only to stop for fuel 6 laps from finish, Rodriguez inheriting another Cooper victory.

12-3-67 Race of Champions,
Brands Hatch, GB – 2 x 10-lap heats,
40-lap Final, 26.49 miles/105.98 miles
HEAT ONE: **1.** Gurney; **2.** Surtees; **3.** Ginther; **4.** McLaren; **5.** Spence; **6.** Scarfiotti.
HEAT TWO: **1.** Gurney; **2.** Ginther; **3.** Surtees; **4.** Scarfiotti; **5.** Rodriguez; **6.** McLaren.
FINAL:
1. Dan Gurney (Eagle-Weslake V12 T1G 102), 40 laps in 1:04;30.6, 98.66 mph.
2. Lorenzo Bandini (Ferrari V12 312 0001), 40 in 1:04;31.0.
3. Jo Siffert (Cooper-Maserati V12 T81 F1-2-66), 40. **4.** Pedro Rodriguez (Cooper-Maserati V12 T81 F1-6-66), 40. **5.** Ludovico Scarfiotti (Ferrari V12 312 0011), 40. **6.** Chris Irwin (2.1 Lotus-BRM V8 25 R13), 39.
PP – Heat One, Gurney, 1;32.2; Heat Two, Gurney (result of first heat); Final, Gurney (ditto). FL – Heat One, Gurney, 1;32.6, 103.02 mph; Heat Two, Gurney 1;32.6, 103.02 mph; Final, Jack Brabham (Repco-Brabham V8 BT20 F1-1-66), 1;34.4, 101.06 mph.
Gurney's Eagle V12s uncatchable in heats but pressed hard in final, first by Brabham until ignition wire came adrift, then by Bandini who closed right up in new 24-plug, 36-valve 1967 Ferrari.

15-4-67 Spring Trophy,
Oulton Park, GB – 2 x 10-lap heats,
30-lap Final, 27.61 miles/82.83 miles
HEAT ONE: **1.** Hulme; **2.** Surtees; **3.** Spence; **4.** Hill; **5.** McLaren; **6.** Oliver.
HEAT TWO: **1.** Hulme; **2.** Surtees; **3.** Brabham; **4.** Stewart; **5.** McLaren; **6.** Spence.
FINAL:
1. Jack Brabham (Repco-Brabham V8 BT20 F1-1-66), 30 laps in 47;21.4, 104.94 mph.

2. Denny Hulme (Repco-Brabham V8 BT20 F1-2-66), 30 in 47;21.8. **3.** John Surtees (Honda V12 RA273 F-102), 30. **4.** Jack Oliver (1.6 Formula 2 Lotus-Cosworth 41B), 30. **5.** Bruce McLaren (2.1 McLaren-BRM V8 M4B M4B/1), 29. **6.** Mike Spence (BRM H16 P83 8302), 29.
PP – Heat One, Jackie Stewart (BRM H16 P83 8303), 1;32.2, Heat Two, Hulme (result of Heat One); Final, Hulme (ditto). FL – Heat One, Brabham, 1;32.4, 107.57 mph; Heat Two, Hulme/Spence 1;32.8, 107.11 mph; Final, Brabham/Hulme, 1;33.4, 106.42 mph.
Brabhams dominant in charity event; Stewart's practice pace in BRM H16 not reproduced in race – he crashed in Final when running fourth.

29-4-67 BRDC International Trophy, Silverstone, GB – 52 laps, 152.20 miles
1. Mike Parkes (Ferrari V12 312 0012), 52 laps in 1:19;39.2, 114.65 mph. **2.** Jack Brabham (Repco-Brabham V8 BT20 F1-1-66), 52 in 1:19;56.8. **3.** Jo Siffert (Cooper-Maserati V12 T81 F1-2-66), 52. **4.** Graham Hill (2.1 Lotus-BRM V8 33 R11), 51. **5.** Bruce McLaren (2.1 McLaren-BRM V8 M4B M4B/1), 51. **6.** Mike Spence (2.1 BRM V8 P261 2614), 50.
PP – Jackie Stewart (BRM H16 P83 8303), 1;27.8; FL – Hill, 1;30.0, 117.08 mph.
Tiny 12-car field, Parkes led from start to finish for his first F1 victory.

7-5-67 MONACO GP, Monte Carlo – 100 laps, 195.41 miles
1. Denny Hulme (Repco-Brabham V8 BT20 F1-2-66), 100 laps in 2:34;34.3, 76.69 mph. **2.** Graham Hill (2.1 Lotus-BRM V8 33 R11), 99 laps. **3.** Chris Amon (Ferrari V12 312 0003), 98. **4.** Bruce McLaren (2.1 McLaren-BRM V8 M4B M4B/1), 97. **5.** Pedro Rodriguez (Cooper-Maserati V12 T81 F1-6-66), 96. **6.** Mike Spence (BRM H16 P83 8302), 96.
PP – Jack Brabham (Repco-Brabham V8 BT19 F1-1-65), 1;27.6.
FL – Jim Clark (2.0 Lotus-Climax V8 33 R14), 1;29.5, 78.60 mph.
Stewart's 2.1-litre BRM led briefly, otherwise entirely Hulme's race; Bandini killed in Ferrari accident when closing in second place.

21-5-67 Syracuse GP, Sicily, I – 56 laps, 194.77 miles
1. *DEAD-HEAT* – Mike Parkes (Ferrari V12 312 0012) and Ludovico Scarfiotti (Ferrari 312 V12 0011), 56 laps in 1:40;58.4, 113.73 mph. **3.** Jo Siffert (Cooper-Maserati V12 T81 F1-2-66), 54. **4.** Chris Irwin (2.1 Lotus-BRM V8 25 R13), 53. **5.** Jo Bonnier (Cooper-Maserati V12 T81 F1-5-66), 53.
No other finishers.
PP – Parkes, 1;41.6; FL – Scarfiotti, 1;41.0, 121.82 mph.
Staged finish, only seven starters!

4-6-67 DUTCH GP, Zandvoort – 90 laps, 234.45 miles
1. Jim Clark (Lotus-Cosworth V8 49 R2), 90 laps in 2:14;45.1, 104.49 mph. **2.** Jack Brabham (Repco-Brabham V8 BT19 F1-1-65), 90 in 2:15;08.7. **3.** Denny Hulme (Repco-Brabham V8 BT20 F1-2-66), 90. **4.** Chris Amon (Ferrari V12 312 0003), 90. **5.** Mike Parkes (Ferrari V12 312 0012), 89. **6.** Ludovico Scarfiotti (Ferrari V12 312 0005), 89.
PP – Graham Hill (Lotus-Cosworth V8 49 R1), 1;24.6; FL – Clark, 1;28.08, 106.49 mph.
The fairytale debut of the Cosworth-Ford DFV V8 engine in the Lotus 49s, rewriting the performance standards of their day. Hill led for 10 laps until timing gear failure, trimming 3 secs off lap record before team-mate Clark took over.

18-6-67 BELGIAN GP, Spa-Francorchamps – 28 laps, 245.36 miles
1. Dan Gurney (Eagle-Weslake V12 T1G 104), 28 laps in 1:40;49.4, 145.74 mph. **2.** Jackie Stewart (BRM H16 P83 8303), 28 in 1:41;52.4. **3.** Chris Amon (Ferrari V12 312 0003), 28. **4.** Jochen Rindt (Cooper-Maserati V12 T81B F1-1-67), 28. **5.** Mike Spence (BRM H16 P83 8302), 27. **6.** Jim Clark (Lotus-Cosworth V8 49 R2), 27.
PP – Clark, 3;28.1; FL – Gurney, 3;31.9, 148.85 mph.
Clark led 12 laps before plug trouble after making first 150 mph Spa lap for pole in practice, Stewart's BRM H16 led until lap 20 but was slowed by gearbox problem, Gurney won despite fuel pressure problem with his Weslake V12.

1-7-67 FRENCH GP, Circuit Bugatti, Le Mans – 80 laps, 219.20 miles
1. Jack Brabham (Repco-Brabham V8 BT24/1), 80 laps in 2:13;21.3, 98.90 mph. **2.** Denny Hulme (Repco-Brabham V8 BT24/2), 80 in 2:14;20.8. **3.** Jackie Stewart (2.1 BRM V8 P261 2614), 79. **4.** Jo Siffert (Cooper-Maserati V12 T81 F1-2-66), 77. **5.** Chris Irwin (BRM H16 P83 8302), 76. **6.** Pedro Rodriguez (Cooper-Maserati V12 T81 F1-6-66), 76.
PP – Graham Hill (Lotus-Cosworth V8 49 R1), 1;36.2; FL – Hill, 1;36.7, 102.30 mph.
Lotus 49s briefly dominant until final-drives failed due to case flexion, allowing new F2-based Brabhams to take command.

15-7-67 BRITISH GP, Silverstone – 80 laps, 234.17 miles
1. Jim Clark (Lotus-Cosworth V8 49 R2), 80 laps in 1:59;25.6, 117.64 mph. **2.** Denny Hulme (Repco-Brabham V8 BT24/2), 80 in 1:59;38.4. **3.** Chris Amon (Ferrari V12 312 0003), 80. **4.** Jack Brabham (Repco-Brabham V8 BT24/1), 80. **5.** Pedro Rodriguez (Cooper-Maserati V12 T81 F1-6-66), 79. **6.** John Surtees (Honda V12 RA273 F-102), 78.
PP – Clark, 1;25.3; FL – Hulme, 1;27.0, 121.12 mph.
Lotus 49s dominant, Hill's a replacement car built overnight after practice crash, still led until rear suspension bolt dropped out, leaving victory to Clark.

6-8-67 GERMAN GP, Nürburgring – 15 laps, 212.60 miles
1. Denny Hulme (Repco-Brabham V8 BT24/2), 15 laps in 2:05;55.7, 101.47 mph. **2.** Jack Brabham (Repco-Brabham V8 BT24/1), 15 in 2:06;34.8. **3.** Chris Amon (Ferrari V12 312 0005), 15. **4.** John Surtees (Honda V12 RA273 F-102), 15. **5.** Jo Bonnier (Cooper-Maserati V12 T81 F-5-66), 15. **6.** Guy Ligier (Repco-Brabham V8 BT20 F1-2-66), 14.
PP – Jim Clark (Lotus-Cosworth V8 49 R2), 8;04.1; FL – Dan Gurney (Eagle-Weslake V12 T1G 104), 8;15.1, 103.15 mph.
Clark's Lotus led until suspension failed, Gurney's Eagle led dominantly until halfshaft UJ broke with two laps to go.

27-8-67 CANADIAN GP, Mosport Park, Ontario – 90 laps, 220.50 miles
1. Jack Brabham (Repco-Brabham V8 BT24/1), 90 laps in 2:40;40.0, 82.65 mph. **2.** Denny Hulme (Repco-Brabham V8 BT24/2), 90 in 2:41;41.9. **3.** Dan Gurney (Eagle-Weslake V12 T1G 103), 89. **4.** Graham Hill (Lotus-Cosworth V8 49 R3), 88. **5.** Mike Spence (BRM H16 P83 8302), 87. **6.** Chris Amon (Ferrari V12 312 0005), 87.
PP – Jim Clark (Lotus-Cosworth V8 49 R2), 1;22.4; FL – Clark, 1;23.1, 106.53 mph.
Rain-swept race, Clark's Lotus took lead from Hulme before his ignition drowned, allowing two Brabhams another 1-2 victory. McLaren made fine debut in new M5A car introducing BRM V12 engine.

10-9-67 ITALIAN GP, Monza – 68 laps, 243.44 miles
1. John Surtees (Honda V12 RA300 RA-300/1), 68 laps in 1:43;45.0, 140.50 mph. **2.** Jack Brabham (Repco-Brabham V8 BT24/1), 68 in 1:43;45.2. **3.** Jim Clark (Lotus-Cosworth V8 49 R2), 68. **4.** Jochen Rindt (Cooper-Maserati V12 T86 F1-2-67), 68. **5.** Mike Spence (BRM H16 P83 8302), 67. **6.** Jacky Ickx (Cooper-Maserati V12 T81B F1-1-67), 66.
PP – Clark, 1;28.5; FL – Clark, 1;28.5, 145.35 mph.
Sensational race, Clark led until puncture, Hill until DFV engine failed, leaving Clark set to win, having regained a whole lap deficit from 15th place after pit stop. Clark's engine starved on last lap, leaving Surtees and Brabham racing side by side to the line.

16-9-67 International Gold Cup, Oulton Park, GB – 45 laps, 124.25 miles
1. Jack Brabham (Repco-Brabham V8 BT24/1), 45 laps in 1:10;07.0, 106.37 mph.
No other F1 finishers in first six – all 1.6-litre F2 cars.
PP – Brabham, 1;30.6. FL – 1;31.6, 108.51 mph.
Wholly inconsequential minor event.

1-10-67 UNITED STATES GP, Watkins Glen, NY – 108 laps, 249.40 miles
1. Jim Clark (Lotus-Cosworth V8 49 R2), 108 laps in 2:03;13.2, 120.95 mph. **2.** Graham Hill (Lotus-Cosworth V8 49 R3), 108 in 2:03;19.5. **3.** Denny Hulme (Repco-Brabham V8 BT24/2), 107. **4.** Jo Siffert (Cooper-Maserati V12 T81 F1-2-66), 106. **5.** Jack Brabham (Repco-Brabham V8 BT24/1), 104. **6.** Jo Bonnier (Cooper-Maserati V12 T81 F1-5-66), 101.
PP – Hill, 1;05.48; FL – Hill, 1;06.0, 125.46 mph.
Staged 1-2 by Lotus 49s went wrong as Hill suffered clutch problems and Clark's rear suspension partially collapsed. Amon's Ferrari passed Hill but lost oil pressure, Clark limped home to win.

2-10-67 MEXICAN GP, Mexico City – 65 laps, 201.95 miles
1. Jim Clark (Lotus-Cosworth V8 49 R1), 65 laps in 1:59;28.70, 101.42 mph. **2.** Jack Brabham (Repco-Brabham V8 BT24/1), 65 in 2:00;54.06. **3.** Denny Hulme (Repco-Brabham V8 BT24/2), 64. **4.** John Surtees (Honda V12 RA 300 RA-300/1), 63. **5.** Mike Spence (BRM H16 P83 8302), 63. **6.** Pedro Rodriguez (Cooper-Maserati V12 T81B F1-1-67), 63.
PP – Clark, 1;47.56; FL – Clark, 1;48.13, 103.44 mph.
Clark led lap 3 to finish, unchallengeable.

12-11-67 Spanish GP, Jarama, Madrid – 90 laps, 190.35 miles
1. Jim Clark (Lotus-Cosworth V8 49 R1), 60 laps in 1:31;10.4, 83.60 mph. **2.** Graham Hill (Lotus-Cosworth V8 49 R2), 60 in 1:31;25.6. **3.** Jack Brabham (Repco-Brabham V8 BT19 F1-1-65), 60.
No other F1 finishers in first six – all 1.6-litre Formula 2 cars.
PP – Clark, 1;28.2. FL – Clark, 1;28.8, 86.40 mph.
Only four F1 cars in hybrid F1/F2 field, de Adamich's Ferrari retired, elderly works Brabham not man enough to trouble the Lotuses.

1968

1-1-68 SOUTH AFRICAN GP, Kyalami – 80 laps, 203.52 miles
1. Jim Clark (Lotus-Cosworth V8 49 R4), 80 laps in 1:53;56.6, 107.42 mph. **2.** Graham Hill (Lotus-Cosworth V8 49 R3), 80 in 1:54;21.9. **3.** Jochen Rindt (Repco-Brabham V8 BT24/2), 80. **4.** Chris Amon (Ferrari V12 312 0007), 78. **5.** Denny Hulme (McLaren-BRM V12 M5A/1), 78. **6.** Jean-Pierre Beltoise (1.6 Matra-Cosworth FVA MS7-03*), 77.
**Ballasted Formula 2 car complying with Formula 1 regulations.*
PP – Clark, 1;21.6; FL – Clark, 1;23.7, 109.68 mph.
Most significant race, marking Clark's 25th GP victory, breaking the Fangio record, and also the dawn of the general Cosworth-Ford DFV V8 engine era, with customers like Tyrrell Matra now using them in addition to Lotus. Clark led from lap 2 to the finish at record pace, circuit improvements assisting his record-breaking.

17-3-68 Race of Champions, Brands Hatch, GB – 50 laps, 132.45 miles
1. Bruce McLaren (McLaren-Cosworth V8 M7A/1), 50 laps in 1:18;53.4, 100.77 mph. **2.** Pedro Rodriguez (BRM V12 P133 133-01), 50 in 1:19;07.6. **3.** Denny Hulme (McLaren-Cosworth V8 M7A/2), 50. **4.** Chris Amon (Ferrari V12 312 0007), 50. **5.** Brian Redman (Cooper-BRM V12 T86B F1-1-68), 50. **6.** Jackie Stewart (Matra-Cosworth V8 MS10-01), 49.
PP – McLaren, 1;30.0; FL – McLaren, 1;31.6, 104.15 mph.
McLaren led from start to finish in his new Cosworth-powered car; BRM V12s showed good pace.

25-4-68 BRDC International Trophy, Silverstone, GB – 52 laps, 154.49 miles
1. Denny Hulme (McLaren-Cosworth V8 M7A/2), 52 laps, 1:14;44.8, 122.17 mph. **2.** Bruce McLaren (McLaren-Cosworth V8 M7A/1), 52 in 1:14;55.7. **3.** Chris Amon (Ferrari V12 312 0007), 52. **4.** Jacky Ickx (Ferrari V12 312 0009), 52. **5.** Piers Courage (BRM V12 P126 126-01), 51. **6.** David Hobbs (BRM V12 P261 Spl 2615), 50.
PP – Hulme, 1;24.3; FL – Amon, 1;25.1, 123.82 mph.
The new McLarens dominant again, BRM V12s competed fiercely but did not last long.

12-5-68 SPANISH GP, Jarama, Madrid – 90 laps, 190.35 miles
1. Graham Hill (Lotus-Cosworth V8 49 R1), 90 laps in 2:15;20.1, 84.41 mph. **2.** Denny Hulme (McLaren-Cosworth V8 M7A/2), 90 in 2:15;36.0. **3.** Brian Redman (Cooper-BRM V12 T86B F1-1-68), 89. **4.** Ludovico Scarfiotti (Cooper-BRM V12 T86B F1-2-68), 89. **5.** Jean-Pierre Beltoise (Matra-Cosworth V8 MS10-01), 81.
No other finishers.
PP – Chris Amon (Ferrari V12 312 0007), 1;27.9; FL – Beltoise, 1;28.3, 86.25 mph.
Beltoise's Matra led early on until oil leak developed, Amon's Ferrari led until lap 52 when fuel pump failed, and Hill then inherited victory, Hulme falling back affected by fumes and McLaren retiring when well placed.

26-5-68 MONACO GP, Monte Carlo – 80 laps, 155.33 miles
1. Graham Hill (Lotus-Cosworth V8 49B R5), 80 laps in 2:00;32.3, 77.82 mph. **2.** Richard Attwood (BRM V12 P126 126-03), 80 in 2:00;34.5. **3.** Lucien Bianchi (Cooper-BRM V12 T86B F1-1-68), 76. **4.** Ludovico Scarfiotti (Cooper-BRM V12 T86B F1-2-68), 76. **5.** Denny Hulme (McLaren-Cosworth V8 M7A/2), 73.
No other finishers.
PP – Hill, 1;28.2; FL – Attwood, 1;28.1, 79.86 mph.
Servoz-Gavin's Tyrrell Matra led opening lap – in Stewart's absence – but hit barrier, Hill leading thereafter to take his fifth Monaco victory; debut win for the modified Lotus 49B.

9-6-68 BELGIAN GP, Spa-Francorchamps – 28 laps, 245.32 miles
1. Bruce McLaren (McLaren-Cosworth V8 M7A/3), 28 laps in 1:40;02.1, 147.14 mph. **2.** Pedro Rodriguez (BRM V12 P133 133-01), 28 in 1:40;14.2. **3.** Jacky Ickx (Ferrari V12 312 0003), 28. **4.** Jackie Stewart (Matra-Cosworth V8 MS10-01), 27. **5.** Jack Oliver (Lotus-Cosworth V8 49B R6), 26. **6.** Lucien Bianchi (Cooper-BRM V12 T86B F1-1-68), 26.
PP – Chris Amon (Ferrari V12 312 0007), 3;28.6; FL – John Surtees (Honda V12 RA301 F-801), 3;30.5, 149.83 mph.
Aerofoil aids appeared on Ferrari and Brabham; Amon's Ferrari and Surtees' Honda fought early battle until stone punctured Ferrari's radiator. Honda chassis failure on lap 10, Hulme/Stewart battle for lead then resolved when Hulme had UJ failure. Stewart's Matra ran short of fuel on penultimate lap and McLaren inherited sudden victory!

23-6-68 DUTCH GP, Zandvoort – 90 laps, 234.45 miles
1. Jackie Stewart (Matra-Cosworth V8 MS10-02), 90 laps in 2:46;11.26, 84.66 mph. **2.** Jean-Pierre Beltoise (Matra V12 MS11-01), 90 laps, 2:47;45.19. **3.** Pedro Rodriguez (BRM V12 P133 133-01), 89. **4.** Jacky Ickx (Ferrari V12 312 0009), 88. **5.** Silvio Moser (Repco-Brabham V8 BT20 F1-2-66), 87. **6.** Chris Amon (Ferrari V12 312 0009), 85.
PP – Amon, 1;23.54; FL – Beltoise, 1;45.91, 87.56 mph.
Stewart took wet-race lead from Hill's Lotus on lap 4 and lapped entire field before two-thirds distance, later allowing Beltoise to unlap himself. Triumph for Dunlop rain tyres on the Matras.

7-7-68 FRENCH GP, Rouen-les-Essarts – 60 laps, 243.89 miles
1. Jacky Ickx (Ferrari V12 312 0009), 60 laps in 2:25;40.9, 100.45 mph. **2.** John Surtees (Honda V12 RA301 F-801), 60 in 2:27; 39.5. **3.** Jackie Stewart (Matra-Cosworth V8 MS10-02), 59. **4.** Vic Elford (Cooper-BRM V12 T86B F1-4-68), 58. **5.** Denny Hulme (McLaren-Cosworth V8 M7A/2), 58. **6.** Piers Courage (BRM V12 P126 126-01), 57.
PP – Jochen Rindt (Repco-Brabham V8 BT26/2), 1;56.1; FL – Pedro Rodriguez (BRM V12 P133 133-01), 2;11.5, 111.28 mph.
Heavy rain, Ickx superb in Firestone rain-tyred Ferrari, Rodriguez second in BRM until lap 46 retirement, Surtees also on intermediate tyres. Race marred by Jo Schlesser's fatal accident in new air-cooled Honda V8.

20-7-68 BRITISH GP, Brands Hatch – 80 laps, 211.95 miles
1. Jo Siffert (Lotus-Cosworth V8 49B R7), 80 laps in 2:01;20.3, 104.83 mph. **2.** Chris Amon (Ferrari V12 312 0011), 80 in 2:01;24.7. **3.** Jacky Ickx (Ferrari V12 312 0009), 79. **4.** Denny Hulme (McLaren-Cosworth M7A/2), 79. **5.** John Surtees (Honda V12 RA301 F-801), 78. **6.** Jackie Stewart (Matra-Cosworth V8 MS10-02), 77.
PP – Graham Hill (Lotus-Cosworth V8 49B R5), 1;28.9; FL – Siffert, 1;29.7, 106.35 mph.
Lotus 49Bs dominant, Hill's works car leading for 23 laps, Oliver in sister car for further 17 laps until retirement, Siffert in Rob Walker's new private 49B taking over to hold off Amon until the end. Tall strutted aerofoil aids proliferate.

4-8-68 GERMAN GP, Nürburgring – 14 laps, 198.64 miles
1. Jackie Stewart (Matra-Cosworth V8 MS10-02), 14 laps in 2:19;03.2, 86.86 mph. **2.** Graham Hill (Lotus-Cosworth V8 49B R5), 14 in 2:23;06.4. **3.** Jochen Rindt (Repco-Brabham V8 BT26/2), 14. **4.** Jacky Ickx (Ferrari V12 312 0015), 14. **5.** Jack Brabham (Repco-Brabham V8 BT26/1), 14. **6.** Pedro Rodriguez (BRM V12 P133 133-01), 14.
PP – Ickx, 9;04.0; FL – Stewart, 9;36.0, 88.67 mph.
Yet another rain-swept race, mist adding another hazard, Dunlop tyres and Jackie Stewart triumphant, extending their lead throughout. A classic performance.

17-8-68 International Gold Cup, Oulton Park, GB – 40 laps, 110.44 miles
1. Jackie Stewart (Matra-Cosworth V8 MS10-02), 40 laps in 1:00;39.0, 109.29 mph. **2.** Chris Amon (Ferrari V12 312 0011), 40 in 1:00;43.6. **3.** Jack Oliver (Lotus-Cosworth V8 49B R2), 40. **4.** Pedro Rodriguez (BRM V12 P126 126-03), 39. UNC **'5th'.** Tony Lanfranchi (2.1 BRM V8 P261 2614), 34. UNC **'6th'.** David Hobbs (BRM V12 Spl P261 2615), 34.
PP – Graham Hill (Lotus-Cosworth V8 49B R5), 1;29.2; FL – Stewart and Amon, 1;30.0, 110.44 mph.
Stewart led start to finish amidst great mechanical carnage.

8-9-68 ITALIAN GP, Monza – 68 laps, 242.95 miles
1. Denny Hulme (McLaren-Cosworth V8 M7A/2), 68 laps in 1:40;14.8, 145.41 mph. **2.** Johnny Servoz-Gavin (Matra-Cosworth V8 MS10-02), 68 in 1:41;43.2. **3.** Jacky Ickx (Ferrari V12 312 0015), 68. **4.** Piers Courage (BRM V12 P126 126-01), 67. **5.** Jean-Pierre Beltoise (Matra V12 MS11-02), 66. **6.** Jo Bonnier (McLaren-BRM V12 M5A/1), 64.
PP – John Surtees (Honda V12 RA301 F-801), 1;26.07; FL – Ickx, 1;26.6, 148.52 mph.
Only six finishers from 20 starters, Surtees' Honda dominated practice, McLarens more competitive on new Goodyear rubber, slip-streaming battle punctuated by Amon crashing Ferrari heavily on oil; McLaren and Siffert both featured prominently before retiring.

22-9-68 CANADIAN GP, Ste Jovite-Mont Tremblant – 90 laps, 238.50 miles
1. Denny Hulme (McLaren-Cosworth V8 M7A/2), 90 laps in 2:27;11.2, 96.96 mph. **2.** Bruce McLaren (McLaren-Cosworth V8 M7A/1), 89 laps. **3.** Pedro Rodriguez (BRM V12 P133 133-01), 88. **4.** Graham Hill (Lotus-Cosworth V8 49B R6), 86. **5.** Vic Elford (Cooper-BRM V12 T86B F1-4-68), 86. **6.** Jackie Stewart (Matra-Cosworth V8 MS10-01), 83.
PP – Jochen Rindt (Repco-Brabham V8 BT26/3), 1;33.8; FL – Jo Siffert (Lotus-Cosworth V8 49B R7), 1;35.1, 100.32 mph.
The luckless Amon's Ferrari equalled Rindt's pole time in practice and dominated race despite inoperative clutch, until lap 72 when final-drive failed after strong challenges by Rindt and Siffert ended in their retirement – McLarens running 1-2 for final 17 laps.

6-10-68 UNITED STATES GP, Watkins Glen, NY – 108 laps, 248.40 miles
1. Jackie Stewart (Matra-Cosworth V8 MS10-02), 108 laps in 1:59;20.29, 124.89 mph. **2.** Graham Hill (Lotus-Cosworth V8 49B R6), 108 in 1:59;44.97. **3.** John Surtees (Honda RA301 F-801), 107. **4.** Dan Gurney (McLaren-Cosworth V8 M7A/3), 107. **5.** Jo Siffert (Lotus-Cosworth V8 49B R7), 105. **6.** Bruce McLaren (McLaren-Cosworth V8 M7A/1), 103.
PP – Mario Andretti (Lotus-Cosworth V8 49B R5), 1;04.20; FL – Stewart, 1;05.22, 126.96 mph.
Andretti's Lotus debut on pole sensation of practice, but Stewart took lead from him on lap 1 and held it thereafter.

3-11-68 MEXICAN GP, Mexico City – 65 laps, 201.94 miles
1. Graham Hill (Lotus-Cosworth V8 49B R6), 65 laps in 1:56;43.95, 103.80 mph. **2.** Bruce McLaren (McLaren-Cosworth V8 M7A/1), 65 in 1:58;03.27. **3.** Jack Oliver (Lotus-Cosworth V8 49B R5), 65. **4.** Pedro Rodriguez (BRM V12 P133 133-01), 65. **5.** Jo Bonnier (Honda V12 RA301 F-802), 64. **6.** Jo Siffert (Lotus-Cosworth V8 49B R7), 64.
PP – Siffert, 1;45.22; FL – Siffert, 1;44.23, 107.26 mph.

Stewart's Matra failed in duel with Hill's Lotus for World Championship while third contender Hulme's McLaren, hastily rebuilt after US GP crash, broke suspension and crashed again. Siffert's private Lotus very fast before and after pit stop to repair throttle linkage, shattering lap record by 2.9 secs in climb back through field.

1969

1-3-69 SOUTH AFRICAN GP,
Kyalami – 80 laps, 203.52 miles
1. Jackie Stewart (Matra-Cosworth V8 MS10-02), 80 laps in 1:50;39.1, 110.62 mph.
2. Graham Hill (Lotus-Cosworth V8 49B R6), 80 in 1:50;57.9.
3. Denny Hulme (McLaren-Cosworth V8 M7A/2), 80. **4.** Jo Siffert (Lotus-Cosworth V8 49B R7), 80. **5.** Bruce McLaren (McLaren-Cosworth V8 M7A/3), 79. **6.** Jean-Pierre Beltoise (Matra-Cosworth V8 MS10-01), 78.
PP – Jack Brabham (Brabham-Cosworth V8 BT26A/2), 1;20.0; FL – Stewart, 1;21.6, 112.50 mph.
Stewart's bi-winged Matra led from start to finish, set new lap and race records. Brabham's new Cosworth-powered BT26A took pole, ran second early on until wing collapsed, team-mate Ickx suffering similarly.

NOTE – *From this point only non-Cosworth DFV engines are specified.*

16-3-69 Race of Champions,
Brands Hatch, GB – 50 laps, 132.50 miles
1. Jackie Stewart (Matra MS80-01), 50 laps in 1:13;10.4, 108.65 mph.
2. Graham Hill (Lotus 49B R6), 50 in 1:13; 17.4.
3. Denny Hulme (McLaren M7A/2), 50. **4.** Jo Siffert (Lotus 49B R7), 50. **5.** Jack Oliver (BRM V12 P133 133-01), 48. **6.** Pete Lovely (Lotus 49B R11), 46.
PP – Hill, 1;28.2; FL – Jochen Rindt (Lotus 49B R9), 1;26.8, 109.91 mph.
Stewart start to finish again, this time in new Matra MS80 and, in freezing weather, he and Hill set faster race average speed than old lap record. First four same as in South Africa, but only 12 starters.

30-3-69 BRDC International Trophy,
Silverstone, GB – 52 laps, 154.49 miles
1. Jack Brabham (Brabham BT26A/2), 52 laps in 1:25;20.8, 107.00 mph.
2. Jochen Rindt (Lotus 49B R9), 52 in 1:25;23.0.
3. Jackie Stewart (Matra MS10-02), 52. **4.** Jacky Ickx (Brabham BT26A/3), 52. **5.** Piers Courage (Brabham BT26 Spl BT26/1), 51. **6.** Bruce McLaren (McLaren M7C 'M7A/4'), 51.
PP – Stewart (driving Matra MS80-01, took spare MS10 for race, starting from tail of grid), 1;20.9; FL – Rindt, 1;30.6, 116.30 mph.
Brabham's new Cosworth car came of age and led start to finish, running bi-winged; Stewart practised MS80 but raced older MS10 in awful weather due to more suitable rim availability, starting from back of grid. Brabham's engine cut out due to low fuel on final lap which allowed Rindt's Lotus to close in exciting finish.

13-4-69 Madrid GP,
Jarama, E – 40 laps, 84.63 miles
1. Keith Holland (Lola-Chevrolet V8 T142 Formula 5000), 40 laps in 1:03;29.8, 80.0 mph.
2. Tony Dean (BRM V12 P261 Spl 2615), 39 laps.
3. Jock Russell (Lotus-Ford V8 43 Spl R1 Formula 5000), 38. **4.** Neil Corner (Cooper-Maserati V12 T86 F1-2-67), 38.
No other serious finishers.
PP – Peter Gethin (McLaren-Chevrolet V8 M10A Formula 5000), 1;31.9; FL (F1) – Dean, 1;34.2, 83.78 mph.
The most minor and inconsequential of 'F1' races.

4-5-69 SPANISH GP,
Montjuich Pk, Barcelona – 90 laps, 211.98 miles
1. Jackie Stewart (Matra MS80-01), 90 laps in 2:16;53.99, 93.89 mph.
2. Bruce McLaren (McLaren M7C 'M7A/4'), 88 in 2:17;40.0.
3. Jean-Pierre Beltoise (Matra MS80-02), 87. **4.** Denny Hulme (McLaren M7A/2), 87. **5.** John Surtees (BRM V12 P138 138-01), 84. **'6'.** Jacky Ickx (Brabham BT26A/3), 83.
PP – Jochen Rindt (Lotus 49B R9), 1;25.7; FL – Rindt, 1;28.3, 96.03 mph.
High-winged Lotus 49Bs dominant but both crashed mightily due to wing collapses; Amon's Ferrari inherited lead until lap 56 when engine failed, a lucky win for Stewart. Ickx's Brabham second for while until wing failure, ran third after stop until wishbone broke five laps from finish.

18-5-69 MONACO GP,
Monte Carlo – 80 laps, 155.33 miles
1. Graham Hill (Lotus-Cosworth V8 49B R10), 80 laps in 1:56;59.4, 80.18 mph.
2. Piers Courage (Brabham BT26 Spl BT26/1), 80 in 1:57;16.7.
3. Jo Siffert (Lotus 49B R7), 80. **4.** Richard Attwood (Lotus 49B R8), 80. **5.** Bruce McLaren (McLaren M7C 'M7A/4'), 79. **6.** Denny Hulme (McLaren M7A/2), 78.
PP – Jackie Stewart (Matra MS80-02), 1;24.6; FL – Stewart, 1;25.1, 82.67 mph.
Hill first man to win five Monaco GPs after Stewart's Matra led until UJ broke and Amon's new Ferrari then led until diff failed. CSI ban on high wings came abruptly during practice.

21-6-69 DUTCH GP,
Zandvoort – 90 laps, 234.45 miles
1. Jackie Stewart (Matra MS80-02), 90 laps in 2:06;42.08, 111.04 mph.
2. Jo Siffert (Lotus 49B R7), 90 in 2:07;06.60.
3. Chris Amon (Ferrari V12 312 0019), 90. **4.** Denny Hulme (McLaren M7A/2), 90. **5.** Jacky Ickx (Brabham BT26A/3), 90. **6.** Jack Brabham (Brabham BT26A/2), 90.
PP – Jochen Rindt (Lotus 49B R6), 1;20.85; FL – Stewart, 1;22.94, 113.08 mph.
Stewart took lead on lap 16 when Rindt's Lotus broke UJ, Hill's Lotus having led the opening two laps before handling deteriorated. Great drive through field by Siffert and close battle for third won by Amon's Ferrari.

6-7-69 FRENCH GP,
Clermont-Ferrand – 38 laps, 190.19 miles
1. Jackie Stewart (Matra MS80-02), 38 laps in 1:56;47.4, 97.71 mph.
2. Jean-Pierre Beltoise (Matra MS80-01), 38 in 1:57;44.5.
3. Jacky Ickx (Brabham BT26A/3), 38. **4.** Bruce McLaren (McLaren M7C 'M7A/4'), 37. **5.** Vic Elford (McLaren M7A/3), 37. **6.** Graham Hill (Lotus 49B R10), 37.
PP – Stewart, 3;00.6; FL – Stewart, 3;02.7, 98.62.
Stewart's most convincing victory thus far, leading from start to finish, Beltoise making it Matra 1-2 after desperate race-long duel with Ickx.

19-7-69 BRITISH GP,
Silverstone – 84 laps, 245.96 miles
1. Jackie Stewart (Matra MS80-01), 84 laps, 1:55;55.6, 127.25 mph.
2. Jacky Ickx (Brabham BT26A/4), 83 in 1:56;36.1.
3. Bruce McLaren (McLaren M7C 'M7A/4'), 83. **4.** Jochen Rindt (Lotus 49B R6), 83. **5.** Piers Courage (Brabham BT26 Spl BT26/1), 83. **6.** Vic Elford (McLaren M7A/3), 82.
PP – Rindt, 1;20.8; FL – Stewart, 1;21.3, 129.61 mph.
Great Rindt Lotus/Stewart Tyrrell battle until lap 62 when wing end-plate cut into Lotus rear tyre and Rindt had to make a stop, Ickx coasted across finish line out of fuel.

3-8-69 GERMAN GP,
Nürburgring – 14 laps, 198.64 miles
1. Jacky Ickx (Brabham BT26A/4), 14 laps in 1:49;55.4, 108.43 mph.
2. Jackie Stewart (Matra MS80-02), 14 in 1:50;53.1.
3. Bruce McLaren (McLaren M7C 'M7A/4'), 14. **4.** Graham Hill (Lotus 49B R10), 14. **5.** Jo Siffert (Lotus 49B R7), 12. **6.** Jean-Pierre Beltoise (Matra MS80-01), 12.
PP – Ickx, 7;42.1; FL – Ickx, 7;43.8, 110.13 mph.
After slow start Ickx broke lap record, caught Stewart, duelled for three laps then won as he pleased while Matra allegedly lost all gears but third. Only four F1 finishers, Siffert being classified despite having crashed heavily and Beltoise retiring with suspension failure.

16-8-69 International Gold Cup,
Oulton Park, GB – 40 laps, 110.44 miles
1. Jacky Ickx (Brabham BT26A/3), 1:00;28.6, 109.57 mph.
2. Jochen Rindt (Lotus 63 [4WD] R1), 40 in 1:01;50.8.
3. Andrea de Adamich (Surtees-Chevrolet TS5 Formula 5000), 39. **4.** Trevor Taylor (Surtees-Chevrolet TS5 Formula 5000), 39. **5.** Mike Hailwood (Lola-Chevrolet T142 Formula 5000), 39. **6.** Alan Rollinson (Brabham-Cosworth FVA BT30 Formula 2), 38.
PP – Jackie Stewart (Matra MS80-02), 1;27.2; FL – Stewart, 1;28.6, 112.19 mph.
Second successive win for lone works Brabham, but Stewart's Matra took lead from lap 2 until broken battery terminal caused pit stop which cost him three laps.

7-9-69 ITALIAN GP,
Monza – 68 laps, 242.95 miles
1. Jackie Stewart (Matra MS80-02), 68 laps in 1:39;11.26, 146.96 mph.
2. Jochen Rindt (Lotus 49B R6), 68 in 1:39;11.34.
3. Jean-Pierre Beltoise (Matra MS80-01), 68 in 1:39;11.43. **4.** Bruce McLaren (McLaren M7C 'M7A/4'), 68 in 1:39;11.45. **5.** Piers Courage (Brabham BT26 Spl BT26/1), 68. **6.** Pedro Rodriguez (Ferrari V12 312 0019), 66.
PP – Rindt, 1;25.48; FL – Beltoise, 1;25.2, 150.96 mph.
Classic race to decide 1969 Championship, eight cars in slipstreaming battle for lead thinned to four in final charge, Rindt, Beltoise and Stewart in turn led during final half-lap – study the first four finishing times above!

20-9-69 CANADIAN GP,
Mosport Park, Toronto – 90 laps, 221.31 miles
1. Jacky Ickx (Brabham BT26A/3), 90 laps in 1:59;25.7, 112.76 mph.
2. Jack Brabham (Brabham BT26A/4), 90 in 2:00;11.9.
3. Jochen Rindt (Lotus 49B R6), 90. **4.** Jean-Pierre Beltoise (Matra MS80-01), 89. **5.** Bruce McLaren (McLaren M7C 'M7A/4'), 87. **6.** Johnny Servoz-Gavin (Matra [4WD] MS84-01), 84.
PP – Ickx, 1;17.4; FL – Ickx, 1;18.1, 114.78 mph.
Stewart just led Ickx until lap 33 when their cars collided and both spun, Ickx quickly regained track but Matra would not restart, excellent Brabham 1-2 result, Rindt's Lotus held initial lead, first points for 4WD.

5-10-69 UNITED STATES GP,
Watkins Glen, NY – 108 laps, 248.40 miles
1. Jochen Rindt (Lotus 49B R6), 108 laps in 1:57;56.84, 126.36 mph.
2. Piers Courage (Brabham BT26 Spl BT26/1), 108 in 1:58;43.83.
3. John Surtees (BRM V12 P139 139-01), 106. **4.** Jack Brabham (Brabham BT26A/4), 106. **5.** Pedro Rodriguez (Ferrari V12 312 0017), 101. **6.** Silvio Moser (Brabham BT24/3), 98.
PP – Rindt, 1;03.62; FL – Rindt, 1;04.34, 128.69 mph.
Season's sixth pole and first-ever GP win for Rindt in Lotus 49B, Stewart led just briefly before engine failed, fierce battle between works Brabhams and Courage's private entry sister car. Wet practice proved 4WD approach delusory.

19-10-69 MEXICAN GP,
Mexico City – 65 laps, 201.94 miles
1. Denny Hulme (McLaren M7A/2), 65 laps in 1:54;08.80, 106.15 mph.
2. Jacky Ickx (Brabham BT26A/3), 65 in 1:54;11.36.
3. Jack Brabham (Brabham BT26A/4), 65. **4.** Jackie Stewart (Matra MS80-02), 65. **5.** Jean-Pierre Beltoise (Matra MS80-01), 65. **6.** Jack Oliver (BRM V12 P139 139-02), 63.
PP – Brabham, 1:42.90; FL – Ickx, 1;43.05, 108.53 mph.
New compound Goodyear G20 tyres dictated race, Hulme took lead from Ickx on lap 10 in veteran McLaren chassis and held it despite record-breaking Brabham lap.

1970

7-3-70 SOUTH AFRICAN GP,
Kyalami – 80 laps, 203.52 miles
1. Jack Brabham (Brabham BT33/2), 80 laps in 1:49;34.6, 111.70 mph.
2. Denny Hulme (McLaren M14A/2), 80 in 1:49;42.7.
3. Jackie Stewart (March 701/2), 80. **4.** Jean-Pierre Beltoise (Matra V12 MS120-01), 80. **5.** John Miles (Lotus 49C R10), 79. **6.** Graham Hill (Lotus 49C R7), 79.
PP – Stewart, 1;19.3; FL – Brabham & John Surtees (McLaren M7C 'M7A/4'), 1;20.8, 113.61 mph.
New March 701s performed well, Brabham in his first monocoque F1 car took lead from Stewart's 701 at quarter-distance to win unchallenged.

22-3-70 Race of Champions,
Brands Hatch, GB – 50 laps, 132.50 miles
1. Jackie Stewart (March 701/2), 50 laps in 1:12;51.8, 109.11 mph.
2. Jochen Rindt (Lotus 49C R6), 50 in 1:13;28.0.
3. Denny Hulme (McLaren M14A/2), 50. **4.** Jack Brabham (Brabham BT33/2), 49. **5.** Graham Hill (Lotus 49C R7), 49. **6.** Peter Gethin (McLaren M7A/2), 49.
PP – Stewart, 1;25.8; FL – Brabham, 1;25.8, 111.19 mph.
Brabham's fine BT33 set for dominant win when ignition failed three laps from finish. Stewart's win rewarded hard drive in ill-handling March, Oliver's new BRM P153 led sensationally before falling back to eventual transmission failure.

19-4-70 SPANISH GP,
Jarama, Madrid – 90 laps, 190.15 miles
1. Jackie Stewart (March 701/2), 90 laps in 2:10;58.2, 87.21 mph.
2. Bruce McLaren (McLaren M14A/1), 89.
3. Mario Andretti (March 701/3), 89. **4.** Graham Hill (Lotus 49C R7), 89. **5.** Johnny Servoz-Gavin (March 701/7), 88.
No other finishers.
PP – Jack Brabham (Brabham BT33/2), 1;23.9; FL – Brabham, 1;24.3, 90.33 mph.
Stewart led throughout while field delayed by new flat-12 Ferrari/BRM collision and fire on first lap. Brabham caught Stewart and seemed set to pass when his engine failed. Fine but fortunate result for March. Poor debut of new Lotus 72.

26-4-70 BRDC International Trophy
Silverstone, GB – 2 x 26-lap heats, 154.49 miles
HEAT ONE: 1. Amon; **2.** Stewart; **3.** Courage; **4.** McLaren; **5.** Rindt; **6.** Hulme.
HEAT TWO: 1. Stewart; **2.** Amon; **3.** Courage; **4.** Hill; **5.** McLaren; **6.** Wisell.
AGGREGATE:
1. Chris Amon (March 701/1), 52 laps in 1:13;32.2, 124.19 mph.
2. Jackie Stewart (March 701/2), 52 in 1:13;42.2.
3. Piers Courage (de Tomaso 308 505/3), 52. **4.** Bruce McLaren (McLaren M14A/1), 52. **5.** Reine Wisell (McLaren M7A/2), 51. **6.** Denny Hulme (McLaren M14A/2), 50.
PP – Heat One, Amon, 1;21.4; Heat Two, Amon (result of first heat). FL – Heat One, Amon, 1;22.1, 128.35 mph; Heat Two, Stewart, 1;23.3, 126.50 mph.
In absence of BRM, Matra and Ferrari, Amon's works March roundly beat Stewart's in Heat One and kept pace with it in Heat Two for aggregate victory. Courage promising in new de Tomaso.

10-5-70 MONACO GP,
Monte Carlo – 80 laps, 156.33 miles
1. Jochen Rindt (Lotus 49C R6), 80 laps in 1:54;36.6, 81.84 mph.
2. Jack Brabham (Brabham BT33/2), 80 in 1:54;59.7.
3. Henri Pescarolo (Matra V12 MS120-02), 80. **4.** Denny Hulme (McLaren M14A/2), 80. **5.** Graham Hill (Lotus 49C R10), 79. **6.** Pedro Rodriguez (BRM V12 P153 153-02), 78.
PP – Jackie Stewart (March 701/2), 1;24.0; FL – Rindt, 1;23.2, 84.56 mph.
Stewart's March led convincingly but failed on lap 28 leaving Brabham to hold off strong challenge from Amon's works 701 until its suspension failed. Rindt in old Lotus 49C started racing near half-distance, caught Brabham and pressured veteran into final corner mistake, stealing classic win.

7-6-70 BELGIAN GP,
Spa-Francorchamps – 28 laps, 245.32 miles
1. Pedro Rodriguez (BRM V12 P153 153-02), 28 laps in 1:38;09.9, 149.94 mph.
2. Chris Amon (March 701/1), 28 in 1;38;11.0.
3. Jean-Pierre Beltoise (Matra V12 MS120-03), 28. **4.** Ignazio Giunti (Ferrari 312B 002[2]), 28. **5.** Rolf Stommelen (Brabham BT33/1), 28. **6.** Henri Pescarolo (Matra V12 MS120-02), 27.
PP – Jackie Stewart (March 701/2), 3;28.0; FL – Amon, 3;27.4, 152.07 mph.
Super-fast circuit permits 12-cylinders to overturn usual Cosworth domination, though Stewart's Matra and Rindt's Lotus 72 both led briefly before engine failures, strong BRM uncatchable thereafter; Matras and Ferraris also shone.

21-6-70 DUTCH GP,
Zandvoort – 80 laps, 208.80 miles
1. Jochen Rindt (Lotus 72 R2), 80 laps in 1:50;43.41, 112.95 mph.
2. Jackie Stewart (March 701/2), 80 in 1:51;13.41.
3. Jacky Ickx (Ferrari 312B 001), 79. **4.** Clay Regazzoni (Ferrari 312B 003), 79. **5.** Jean-Pierre Beltoise (Matra V12 MS120-03), 79. **6.** John Surtees (McLaren M7C 'M7A/4'), 79.
PP – Rindt, 1;18.50; FL – Ickx, 1;19.23, 118.38 mph.
Revised Lotus 72 proved its class, Ickx's Ferrari delayed by puncture.

5-7-70 FRENCH GP,
Clermont-Ferrand – 38 laps, 190.19 miles
1. Jochen Rindt (Lotus 72 R2), 38 laps in 1:55; 57.00, 98.42 mph.
2. Chris Amon (March 701/1), 38 in 1:56;04.61.
3. Jack Brabham (Brabham BT33/2), 38. **4.** Denny Hulme (McLaren M14D/1), 38. **5.** Henri Pescarolo (Matra V12 MS120-02), 38. **6.** Dan Gurney (McLaren M14A/1), 38.
PP – Jacky Ickx (Ferrari 312B 003), 2;58.22; FL – Brabham, 3;00.75, 99.68 mph.
Ickx's flat-12 Ferrari led 14 laps until engine failed, Beltoise's Matra 11 laps until tyre punctured; Lotus 72 inherited second win in row.

19-7-70 BRITISH GP,
Brands Hatch – 80 laps, 212.00 miles
1. Jochen Rindt (Lotus 72 R2), 80 laps in 1:57;02.0, 108.69 mph.
2. Jack Brabham (Brabham BT33/2), 80 in 1:57;34.9.
3. Denny Hulme (McLaren M14D/1), 80. **4.** Clay Regazzoni (Ferrari 312B 002[2]), 80. **5.** Chris Amon (March 701/1), 79. **6.** Graham Hill (Lotus 49C R7), 79.
PP – Rindt, 1;24.8; FL – Brabham, 1;25.9, 111.06 mph.
Ickx's Ferrari left field for dead but broke transmission after only six laps; Rindt's Lotus led narrowly until lap 69 when constant shadow Brabham easily took lead, only to have engine starve of fuel on last lap, handing another lucky win to Lotus.

2-8-70 GERMAN GP,
Hockenheim – 50 laps, 210.89 miles
1. Jochen Rindt (Lotus 72 R2), 50 laps in 1:42;00.3, 123.90 mph.
2. Jacky Ickx (Ferrari 312B 003), 50 in 1:42;01.0.
3. Denny Hulme (McLaren M14A/2), 50. **4.** Emerson Fittipaldi (Lotus 49C R10), 50. **5.** Rolf Stommelen (Brabham BT33/3), 49. **6.** Henri Pescarolo (Matra V12 MS120-02), 49.
PP – Ickx, 1;59.5; FL – Ickx, 2;00.5, 126.02 mph.
Race-long sheer speed battle between flat-12 Ferrari and Lotus 72 resolved in latter's favour.

16-8-70 AUSTRIAN GP,
Österreichring – 60 laps, 220.39 miles
1. Jacky Ickx (Ferrari 312B 001), 60 laps in 1:42;17.32, 129.27 mph.
2. Clay Regazzoni (Ferrari 312B 003), 60 in 1:42;17.93.
3. Rolf Stommelen (Brabham BT33/3), 60. **4.** Pedro Rodriguez (BRM V12 P153 153-05), 59. **5.** Jack Oliver (BRM V12 P153-153-04), 59. **6.** Jean-Pierre Beltoise (Matra V12 MS120-03), 59.
PP – Jochen Rindt (Lotus 72 R2), 1;39.23; FL – Ickx & Regazzoni, 1;40.4, 131.70 mph.
Total Ferrari domination, Ignazio Giunti also featuring in third 312B, only one V8 in top six.

22-8-70 International Gold Cup,
Oulton Pk, GB – 2 x 20-lap heats, 110.44 miles
HEAT ONE: 1. Surtees; **2.** Oliver; **3.** Rindt; **4.** Hailwood; **5.** Ganley; **6.** Taylor.
HEAT TWO: 1. Rindt; **2.** Surtees; **3.** Oliver; **4.** Gardner; **5.** Ganley; **6.** Taylor.
AGGREGATE:
1. John Surtees (Surtees TS7-01), 40 laps in 59;48.2, 110.8 mph.
2. Jochen Rindt (Lotus 72 R2), 40 in 59;51.6.
3. Jack Oliver (BRM V12 P153-04), 40. **4.** Howden Ganley (McLaren-Chevrolet M10B 400-05 Formula 5000), 40. **5.** Trevor Taylor (Lola-Chevrolet T190 F1/7 Formula 5000), 38. **6.** Fred Saunders (Crosslé-Rover V8 15F 70-04 Formula 5000), 36.
PP – Heat One, Surtees, 1;36.2; Heat Two, result of first heat. FL – Heat One, Jackie Stewart (Tyrrell 001), 1;26.6, 114.78 mph; Heat Two Rindt, 1;27.6, 113.47 mph.
Surtees able to pace himself in Heat 2 after comfortable win in Heat 1 when Rindt's Lotus handicapped by gear ratio choice. Stewart gave new Tyrrell-Cosworth fine debut despite minor troubles – note his record lap.

6-7-70 ITALIAN GP,
Monza – 68 laps, 242.95 miles
1. Clay Regazzoni (Ferrari 312B 004), 68 laps in 1:39;06.88, 147.07 mph.
2. Jackie Stewart (March 701/4), 68 in 1:39;12.61.
3. Jean-Pierre Beltoise (Matra V12 MS120-03), 68. **4.** Denny Hulme (McLaren M14A/2), 68. **5.** Rolf Stommelen (Brabham BT33/3), 68. **6.** François Cevert (March 701/7), 68.
PP – Jacky Ickx (Ferrari 312B 001), 1;24.10; FL – Regazzoni, 1;25.2, 150.96 mph.
Hectic race followed sombre practice in which Rindt died when Lotus 72 crashed; BRM V12s and Ferrari flat-12s most prominent in initial 12-car slipstreaming leading bunch.

20-9-70 CANADIAN GP,
Ste Jovite-Mt Tremblant – 90 laps, 238.50 miles
1. Jacky Ickx (Ferrari 312B 001), 90 laps in 2:21;18.4, 101.27 mph.
2. Clay Regazzoni (Ferrari 312B 004), 90 in 2:21;33.2.
3. Chris Amon (March 701/1), 90. **4.** Pedro Rodriguez (BRM V12 P153 153-06), 89. **5.** John Surtees (Surtees TS7-001), 89. **6.** Peter Gethin (McLaren

M14A/1), 88.
PP – Jackie Stewart (Tyrrell 001), 1;31.5; FL – Regazzoni, 1;32.2, 103.47 mph.
Stewart established dominant 17 sec lead in new Tyrrell 001 until stub axle failed after 31 laps, flat-12 Ferraris uncatchable thereafter.

4-10-70 UNITED STATES GP,
Watkins Glen, NY – 108 laps, 248.40 miles
1. Emerson Fittipaldi (Lotus 72 R5), 108 laps in 1:57;32.79, 129.79 mph.
2. Pedro Rodriguez (BRM V12 P153 153-05), 108 in 1:58;09.18.
3. Reine Wisell (Lotus 72 R3), 108. 4. Jacky Ickx (Ferrari 312B 001), 107. 5. Chris Amon (March 701/1), 107. 6. Derek Bell (Surtees TS7-002), 107.
PP – Ickx, 1;03.07; FL – Ickx, 1;02.74, 131.97 mph.
Stewart's Tyrrell dominated until lap 62 when oil-line burned through on exhaust, Rodriguez's BRM looked set to win until lap 100 when he had to add fuel, Fittipaldi's maiden Lotus win clinched their own and Rindt's World titles.

25-10-70 MEXICAN GP,
Mexico City – 65 laps, 201.94 miles
1. Jacky Ickx (Ferrari 312B 001), 65 laps in 1:53;28.36, 106.78 mph.
2. Clay Regazzoni (Ferrari 312B 004), 65 in 1:54;13.82.
3. Denny Hulme (McLaren M14A/2), 65. 4. Chris Amon (March 701/1), 65. 5. Jean-Pierre Beltoise (Matra V12 MS120-03), 65. 6. Pedro Rodriguez (BRM P153 153-05), 65.
PP – Regazzoni, 1;41.86; FL – Ickx, 1;43.11, 108.49 mph.
Ferrari/new Tyrrell battle evaporated when Stewart's steering column worked loose, he later hit stray dog; race marred by crowd encroaching on track. Jack Brabham third in his farewell race when engine blew, 13 laps from finish.

1971

24-1-71 Argentine GP,
Buenos Aires – 2 x 50-lap heats, 211.90 miles
HEAT ONE: 1. Stommelen; **2.** Siffert; **3.** Pescarolo; **4.** Amon; **5.** Wisell; **6.** Reutemann.
HEAT TWO: 1. Amon, **2.** Pescarolo; **3.** Reutemann; **4.** Prophet; **5.** Spice; **6.** Marincovich/Young.
AGGREGATE:
1. Chris Amon (Matra V12 MS120-02), 100 laps in 2:08;19.29, 99.18 mph.
2. Henri Pescarolo (March 701/6), 100 in 2:08;41.15.
3. Carlos Reutemann (McLaren M7C 'M7A/4'), 100. 4. David Prophet (McLaren-Chevrolet M10B 400-04 Formula 5000), 96. UNC **'5th'**. Derek Bell (March 701/1), 88. 6. Jo Siffert (March 701/5), 86. (Drivers not featured overall but named in first 6 in heats drove the following cars: Rolf Stommelen, Surtees TS7-002; Reine Wisell, Lotus 72 R3; Gordon Spice, McLaren M10B 400-05 Formula 5000; Carlos Marincovich/Greg Young, McLaren M10B Formula 5000.
PP – Heat One, Stommelen, 1;15.85; Heat Two, result of Heat One. FL – Heat One, Wisell, 1;15.10, 101.68 mph; Heat Two, Amon, 1;15.05, 101.75 mph.
New Surtees driver Stommelen dominant until pushed off in Heat Two by rather desperate Amon's Matra, Siffert having led Heat Two until suspension failure – first F1 win for Matra V12.

6-3-71 SOUTH AFRICAN GP,
Kyalami – 79 laps, 203.52 miles
1. Mario Andretti (Ferrari 312B 002[2]), 79 laps in 1:47;35.5, 112.36 mph.
2. Jackie Stewart (Tyrrell 001), 79 in 1:47;56.4.
3. Clay Regazzoni (Ferrari 312B 004), 79. 4. Reine Wisell (Lotus 72 R3), 79. 5. Chris Amon (Matra V12 MS120-03), 78. 6. Denny Hulme (McLaren M19A/1), 78.
PP – Stewart, 1;17.8; FL – Andretti, 1;20.3, 114.32.
Regazzoni led initially for Ferrari until wheels lost balance, Hulme took over in brand new McLaren M19 until suspension failure four laps from finish gave Andretti and Ferrari victory.

21-3-71 Race of Champions,
Brands Hatch, GB – 50 laps, 132.50 miles
1. Clay Regazzoni (Ferrari 312B2 005), 50 laps in 1;13;35.0, 108.04 mph.
2. Jackie Stewart (Tyrrell 001), 50 in 1:13;58.6.
3. John Surtees (Surtees TS9 001), 49. 4. Tim Schenken (Brabham BT33/1), 48. 5. Howden Ganley (BRM V12 P153 153-03), 48. 6. Ray Allen (March 701/6), 48.
PP – Stewart, 1;24.6; FL – Graham Hill (Brabham BT34/1), 1;26.7, 110.03 mph.
Wet/dry weather decided minor event. Stewart's Tyrrell led on 'semi-wet' Goodyears until track dried and dry Firestone-tyred Ferrari took over from lap 25. Tyrrell with new 11-series DFV engine clearly the faster car; debut of Lotus 56B turbine car.

28-3-71 Questor GP,
Ontario Speedway, California – 2 x 32-lap heats, 204.42 miles
HEAT ONE: 1. Andretti; **2.** Stewart; **3.** Siffert; **4.** Hulme; **5.** Ickx; **6.** Amon.
HEAT TWO: 1. Andretti; **2.** Stewart; **3.** Amon; **4.** Rodriguez; **5.** Hulme; **6.** Schenken.
AGGREGATE:
1. Mario Andretti (Ferrari 312B 002[2]), 64 laps in 1:51;48.410, 109.70 mph.
2. Jackie Stewart (Tyrrell 001), 64 in 1:52;04.324.
3. Denny Hulme (McLaren M19A/1), 64. 4. Chris Amon (Matra MS120-03), 64. 5. Tim Schenken (Brabham BT33/1), 63. 6. Peter Gethin (McLaren M14A/1), 63.
PP – Heat One, Stewart, 1;41.257; Heat Two result of first heat. FL – Heat One, Amon, 1;43.088, 111.54 mph; Heat Two, Pedro Rodriguez (BRM V12 P160-01), 1;42.777, 111.88 mph.
Stewart's Tyrrell led both heats, and was passed in both by Andretti's Ferrari, while Amon's Matra challenged the Tyrrell strongly in both heats but punctured tyre in the first.

9-4-71 Spring Trophy,
Oulton Park, GB – 40 laps, 110.44 miles
1. Pedro Rodriguez (BRM V12 P160-01), 40 laps in 57;33.4, 115.11 mph.
2. Peter Gethin (McLaren M14A/2), 40 in 57;38.0.
3. Jackie Stewart (Tyrrell 002), 40. 4. Howden Ganley (BRM V12 P153-03), 39. 5. Allan Rollinson (March 701/5), 36. UNC **'6th'**. Tony Trimmer (Lotus 49C R6), 31.
PP – Stewart, 1;25.8; FL – Rodriguez & Gethin, 1;25.06, 118.93 mph.
Latest BRM led throughout, Gethin and Stewart fought fierce duel in its wake, lap record shattered, despite only 11 starters.

18-4-71 SPANISH GP,
Montjuich Pk, Barcelona – 75 laps, 176.62 miles
1. Jackie Stewart (Tyrrell 003), 75 laps in 1:49;03.4, 97.19 mph.
2. Jacky Ickx (Ferrari 312B 003), 75 in 1:49;06.8.
3. Chris Amon (Matra V12 MS120-03), 75. 4. Pedro Rodriguez (BRM V12 P160-01). 5. Denny Hulme (McLaren M19A/1), 75. 6. Jean-Pierre Beltoise (Matra V12 MS120-05), 74.
PP – Ickx, 1;25.9; FL – Ickx, 1;25.1, 99.64 mph.
Ickx's Ferrari led first five laps before Stewart dominated, Ickx closed up at finish, lowering his pole practice record time; 12-cylinder cars all looked strong.

8-5-71 BRDC International Trophy,
Silverstone, GB – 2 x 26-lap heats, 150.80 miles
HEAT ONE: 1. Stewart; **2.** Rodriguez; **3.** Hill; **4.** Surtees; **5.** Beltoise; **6.** Gethin.
HEAT TWO: 1. Hill; **2.** Amon; **3.** Fittipaldi; **4.** Gethin; **5.** Pescarolo; **6.** Hailwood.
AGGREGATE:
1. Graham Hill (Brabham BT34/1), 52 laps in 1:11;03.2, 128.50 mph.
2. Peter Gethin (McLaren M14A/2), 52 in 1:12;37.0.
3. Tim Schenken (Brabham BT33/1), 52. 4. Pedro Rodriguez (BRM V12 P160-01), 51. 5. Mike Hailwood (Surtees-Chevrolet TS8-005 Formula 5000), 51. 6. Henri Pescarolo (March 711/3), 51.
PP – Heat One, Chris Amon (Matra V12 MS120-04), 1;20.0; Heat Two, result of first heat. FL – Heat One, Jackie Stewart (Tyrrell 003), 1;20.5, 130.90 mph: Heat Two, John Surtees (Surtees TS9-001), 1;20.6, 130.73 mph.
Stewart crashed Tyrrell 003 first corner Heat Two, Rodriguez's BRM punctured on debris from blown Matra engine, Hill inherited popular win for new 'Lobster Claw' Brabham.

23-5-71 MONACO GP,
Monte Carlo – 80 laps, 153.33 miles
1. Jackie Stewart (Tyrrell 003), 80 laps in 1:52;21.3, 83.49 mph.
2. Ronnie Peterson (March 711/2), 80 in 1:52;46.9.
3. Jacky Ickx (Ferrari 312B2 006), 80. 4. Denny Hulme (McLaren M19A/1), 80. 5. Emerson Fittipaldi (Lotus 72 R5), 79. 6. Rolf Stommelen (Surtees TS9-002), 79.
PP – Stewart, 1;23.2; FL – Stewart, 1;22.2, 85.58 mph.
Staggering Stewart/Tyrrell performance, driver superb as car lost rear brakes before start yet he led start-to-finish and set new record lap on this demanding circuit. Peterson's driving put March 711 in second place.

13-6-71 Rindt Memorial Race,
Hockenheim, D – 35 laps, 146.64 miles
1. Jacky Ickx (Ferrari 312B 003), 35 laps in 1:10;11.7, 126.20 mph.
2. Ronnie Peterson (March 711/2), 35 in 1:11.05.5.
3. John Surtees (Surtees TS9-001), 35. 4. Howden Ganley (BRM V12 P153-07), 35. 5. Nanni Galli (March 711/1), 35. 6. Skip Barber (March 711/5), 34.
PP – Ickx, 1;56.8; FL – Ickx, 1;58.8, 127.82 mph.
Easy win for Ickx's Ferrari, both team-mate Regazzoni and Wisell in Lotus 72 held second early on before suffering electrical and brake trouble respectively.

26-6-71 DUTCH GP,
Zandvoort – 70 laps, 182.70 miles
1. Jacky Ickx (Ferrari 312B2 006), 70 laps in 1:56;20.09, 94.06 mph.
2. Pedro Rodriguez (BRM V12 P160-01), 70 in 1:56;28.08.
3. Clay Regazzoni (Ferrari 312B2 005), 69. 4. Ronnie Peterson (March 711/2), 68. 5. John Surtees (Surtees TS9-001), 68. 6. Jo Siffert (BRM V12 P160-02), 68.
PP – Ickx, 1;17.42; FL – Ickx, 1;34.95, 98.78 mph.
Wet race dominated by acknowledged wet-weather drivers in smooth 12-cylinder cars, new Firestone rain tyres on first eight cars home. Dave Walker's Lotus 56B 4WD turbine car crashed after five fast early laps climbing through field, 4WD's last great chance wasted.

4-7-71 FRENCH GP,
Ricard-Castellet – 55 laps, 198.22 miles
1. Jackie Stewart (Tyrrell 003), 55 laps in 1:46;41.68, 111.66 mph.
2. François Cevert (Tyrrell 002), 55 in 1:47;09.80.
3. Emerson Fittipaldi (Lotus 72 R5), 55. 4. Jo Siffert (BRM V12 P160-02), 55. 5. Chris Amon (Matra V12 MS120-06), 55. 6. Reine Wisell (Lotus 72 R3), 55.
PP – Stewart, 1;50.71; FL – Stewart, 1;54.09, 113.91 mph.
Tyrrells pulverized opposition, Regazzoni's Ferrari and Rodriguez's BRM both held second place but failed to maintain the pace.

17-7-71 BRITISH GP,
Silverstone – 68 laps, 199.04 miles
1. Jackie Stewart (Tyrrell 003), 68 laps in 1:31;31.5, 130.48 mph.
2. Ronnie Peterson (March 711/6), 68 in 1:32;07.6.
3. Emerson Fittipaldi (Lotus 72 R5), 68. 4. Henri Pescarolo (March 711/3), 67. 5. Rolf Stommelen (Surtees TS9-002), 67. 6. John Surtees (Surtees TS9-002), 67.
PP – Clay Regazzoni (Ferrari 312B2 005), 1;18.1; FL – Stewart, 1;19.9, 131.88 mph.
Ferraris led from chaotic start but Stewart's Tyrrell again uncatchable once in front; strong pursuit by Siffert's BRM foiled by severe low-profile Firestone tyre vibration.

1-8-71 GERMAN GP,
Nürburgring – 12 laps, 170.27 miles
1. Jackie Stewart (Tyrrell 003), 12 laps in 1:29;15.7, 114.46 mph.
2. François Cevert (Tyrrell 002), 12 in 1:29;45.8.
3. Clay Regazzoni (Ferrari 312B2 005), 12. 4. Mario Andretti (Ferrari 312B2 007), 12. 5. Ronnie Peterson (March 711/6), 12. 6. Tim Schenken (Brabham BT33/3), 12.
PP – Stewart, 7;19.0; FL – Cevert, 7;20.1, 116.07 mph.
Stewart took lead at second corner, Ickx spun Ferrari out of second place, Siffert's BRM looked capable of catching Stewart but vibration ruined ignition coil leaving only Ferrari close to Tyrrells' speed and durability. Cevert took 20 secs off lap record on modernized circuit.

15-8-71 AUSTRIAN GP,
Österreichring – 54 laps, 198.34 miles
1. Jo Siffert (BRM V12 P160-02), 54 laps in 1:30;23.91, 132.30 mph.
2. Emerson Fittipaldi (Lotus 72 R5), 54 in 1:30;28.03.
3. Tim Schenken (Brabham BT33/3), 54. 4. Reine Wisell (Lotus 72 R6), 54. 5. Graham Hill (Brabham BT34/1), 54. 6. Henry Pescarolo (March 711/3), 54.
PP – Siffert, 1;37.44; FL – Siffert, 1;38.47, 134.39 mph.
The perfect performance from Siffert's BRM – pole, fastest lap, led throughout – deflating tyre allowed Lotus to close at finish. Tyrrells both retired, Stewart became Champion by trackside.

22-8-71 International Gold Cup,
Oulton Pk, GB – 2 x 20-lap heats, 110.44 miles
HEAT ONE: 1. Pescarolo; **2.** Ganley; **3.** Surtees; **4.** Gardner; **5.** Gethin; **6.** Hailwood.
HEAT TWO: 1. Surtees; **2.** Ganley; **3.** Gardner; **4.** Rollinson; **5.** Craft; **6.** McRae.
AGGREGATE:
1. John Surtees (Surtees TS9-004), 40 laps in 57;38.6, 114.96 mph.
2. Howden Ganley (BRM V12 P153-06), 40 in 57;50.0.
3. Frank Gardner (Lola-Chevrolet T300 300-F1-1 Formula 5000), 40. 4. Alan Rollinson (Surtees-Chevrolet TS8-007 Formula 5000), 40. 5. Chris Craft (Brabham BT33/2), 40. 6. Mike Walker (Lola-Chevrolet T192 192/F1/26 Formula 5000), 40.
PP – Heat One, Peter Gethin (BRM V12 P160-01), 1;24.6; Heat Two, result of Heat One. FL – Heat One, Henri Pescarolo (March 711/3) & Surtees, 1;25.0, 116.93 mph; Heat Two, Surtees, 1;24.8, 117.21 mph.
Gethin's BRM and Pescarolo's March collided in Heat Two removing Surtees' likeliest rivals as he won poorly-supported race at record speed.

5-9-71 ITALIAN GP,
Monza – 55 laps, 196.35 miles
1. Peter Gethin (BRM V12 P160-01), 55 laps in 1:18;12.60, 150.75 mph.
2. Ronnie Peterson (March 711/6), 55 in 1:18;12.61.
3. François Cevert (Tyrrell 002), 55 in 1:18;12.69.
4. Mike Hailwood (Surtees TS9-004), 55 in 1:18;12.78. 5. Howden Ganley (BRM V12 P160-04), 55 in 1:18;13.21. 6. Chris Amon (Matra V12 MS120-06), 55.
PP – Amon, 1:22.40; FL – Henri Pescarolo (March 711/3).
Five cars left in final leading bunch and while Peterson and Cevert eyed each other Gethin slammed past both to steal BRM victory, 0.61 sec covering first five home! Stewart, Ferraris and Amon's Matra all had troubles after featuring strongly.

19-9-71 CANADIAN GP,
Mosport Park, Toronto – 64 laps, 157.38 miles
1. Jackie Stewart (Tyrrell 003), 64 laps in 1:55;12.9, 81.96 mph.
2. Ronnie Peterson (March 711/6), 64 in 1:55;51.2.
3. Mark Donohue (McLaren M19A/1), 64. 4. Denny Hulme (McLaren M19A/2), 63. 5. Reine Wisell (Lotus 72 R6), 62. 6. François Cevert (Tyrrell 002), 62.
PP – Stewart, 1;15.3; FL – Hulme, 1;43.5, 85.53 mph.
Wet, misty race dominated by Stewart although Peterson led twice before nudging a backmarker and having to settle for second.

3-10-71 UNITED STATES GP,
Watkins Glen, NY – 59 laps, 199.24 miles
1. François Cevert (Tyrrell 002), 59 laps in 1:43;57.991, 115.09 mph.
2. Jo Siffert (BRM V12 P160-02), 59 in 1:44;32.053.
3. Ronnie Peterson (March 711/6), 59. 4. Howden Ganley (BRM V12 P160-04), 59. 5. Jackie Stewart (Tyrrell 003), 59. 6. Clay Regazzoni (Ferrari 312B2 005), 59.
PP – Stewart, 1;42.642; FL – Jacky Ickx (Ferrari 312B2 006), 1;43.474, 117.50 mph.
Stewart led until lap 14 when understeer allowed team-mate ahead to win, the Champion falling back; Ickx's old B1-model Ferrari was closing on Cevert mid-race until alternator failed.

24-10-71 Victory Race,
Brands Hatch, GB – 40 laps, 105.96 miles*
**Race stopped after Siffert's fatal BRM accident on lap 15, results declared at 14 laps.*
1. Peter Gethin (BRM V12 P160-03), 14 laps in 19;54.4, 111.82 mph.
2. Emerson Fittipaldi (Lotus 72 R5), 14 in 19;54.6.
3. Jackie Stewart (Tyrrell 003), 14. 4. Jo Siffert (BRM V12 P160-02), 14. 5. Tim Schenken (Brabham BT33/3), 14. 6. John Surtees (Surtees TS9-002), 14.
PP – Siffert, 1;22.8; FL – Fittipaldi, 1;24.0, 113.57 mph.
Tragic minor event to celebrate Stewart's title. BRMs dominant in practice with Gethin equalling Siffert's pole time, Gethin led throughout.

1972

23-1-72 ARGENTINE GP,
Buenos Aires – 95 laps, 201.40 miles
1. Jackie Stewart (Tyrrell 003), 95 laps in 1:57;58.82, 100.33 mph.
2. Denny Hulme (McLaren M19A/2), 95 in 1:58;24.78.
3. Jacky Ickx (Ferrari 312B2 006), 95. 4. Clay Regazzoni (Ferrari 312B2 005), 95. 5. Tim Schenken (Surtees TS9-006), 95. 6. Ronnie Peterson (March 721/1), 94.
PP – Carlos Reutemann (Brabham BT34/1), 1;12.46; FL – Stewart, 1;13.66, 101.59 mph.
Stewart led throughout but newcomer Reutemann challenged strongly on home ground until sticky Goodyear tyres on which he gambled deteriorated and he had to make tyre-change stop, Fittipaldi's Lotus held second place until its suspension failed.

4-3-72 SOUTH AFRICAN GP,
Kyalami – 79 laps, 201.45 miles
1. Denny Hulme (McLaren M19A/2), 79 laps in 1:45;49.1, 114.23 mph.
2. Emerson Fittipaldi (Lotus 72 R5), 79 in 1:46;03.2.
3. Peter Revson (McLaren M19A/1), 79. 4. Mario Andretti (Ferrari 312B2 007), 79. 5. Ronnie Peterson (March 721/1), 79. 6. Graham Hill (Brabham BT33/3), 78.
PP – Jackie Stewart (Tyrrell 003), 1;17.0; FL – Mike Hailwood (Surtees TS9-005), 1;18.9, 116.35 mph.
Fine race – Hulme led lap 1 before Stewart opened a lead; Hulme/Fittipaldi/Hailwood (Surtees) battle then closed gap, latter looking set to take lead for Surtees when rear suspension bolt broke. Hulme eased off to cool engine and Fittipaldi pressed Stewart until Tyrrell gearbox seized on lap 44. Lotus inherited lead but oversteered on light tanks and Hulme went by on lap 57 to win; Hill just held off March newcomer Lauda for 6th by 0.3 sec.

19-3-72 Race of Champions,
Brands Hatch, GB – 40 laps, 105.96 miles
1. Emerson Fittipaldi (Lotus 72 R5), 40 laps in 56;40.6, 112.22 mph.
2. Mike Hailwood (Surtees TS9-005), 40 in 56;54.0
3. Denny Hulme (McLaren M19A/2), 40. 4. Peter Gethin (BRM P160-03), 40. 5. Tim Schenken (Surtees TS9-006), 40. 6. Jean-Pierre Beltoise (BRM P160-05), 40.
PP – Fittipaldi, 1;23.9; FL – Fittipaldi, 1;23.8, 112.84 mph.
Effortless 13 sec win by Fittipaldi's Lotus, another fine Surtees performance by Hailwood, Gethin prominent throughout but lost places as race progressed.

30-3-72 Grande Prêmio do Brasil,
Interlagos – 37 laps, 182.02 miles
1. Carlos Reutemann (Brabham BT34/1), 37 laps in 1:37;16.248, 112.91 mph.
2. Ronnie Peterson (March 721/1), 37 in 1:38;43.904.
3. Wilson Fittipaldi (Brabham BT33/3), 37.
4. Helmut Marko (BRM V12 P160-01) 36. 5. Dave Walker (Lotus 72 R6), 36. 6. Luiz Bueno (March 711/6), 35.
PP – Emerson Fittipaldi (Lotus 72 R7), 2;32.4; FL – E. Fittipaldi, 2;35.2, 119.74 mph.
Moral victory for Emerson Fittipaldi who led until suspension failure, 5 laps from end. Only 11 starters, three retiring with dust jamming throttles in first corner.

23-4-72 BRDC International Trophy,
Silverstone, GB – 40 laps, 117.08 miles
1. Emerson Fittipaldi (Lotus 72 R7), 40 laps in 53;17.8, 131.81 mph.
2. Jean-Pierre Beltoise (BRM V12 P160-01), 40 in 53;19.6.
3. John Surtees (Surtees TS9-006), 40. 4. Denny Hulme (McLaren M19C/1), 40. 5. Peter Revson (McLaren M19A/2), 40. 6. Peter Gethin (BRM V12 P160-03), 40.
PP – Fittipaldi, 1;18.1; FL – Mike Hailwood (Surtees TS9-005), 1;18.8, 133.72 mph.
Hailwood's Surtees led until engine failure 10 laps from end, lowering lap record *en route*, after BRMs led opening laps.

1-5-72 SPANISH GP,
Jarama, Madrid – 90 laps, 190.15 miles
1. Emerson Fittipaldi (Lotus 72 R7), 90 laps in 2:03;41.23, 92.35 mph.
2. Jacky Ickx (Ferrari 312B2 006), 90 in 2:04;00.15.
3. Clay Regazzoni (Ferrari 312B2 008), 89.
4. Andrea de Adamich (Surtees TS9-004), 89.
5. Peter Revson (McLaren M19A/2), 89. 6. Carlos Pace (March 711/3), 89.
PP – Ickx, 1;18.43; FL – Ickx, 1;21.01, 94.00 mph.
Fittipaldi qualified on front row, passed Stewart's leading Tyrrell on lap 19 and dominated thereafter.

14-5-72 MONACO GP,
Monte Carlo – 80 laps in 156.32 miles
1. Jean-Pierre Beltoise (BRM V12 P160-01), 80 laps in 2:26;54.7, 63.85 mph.
2. Jacky Ickx (Ferrari 312B2 006), 80 in 2:27;32.9.
3. Emerson Fittipaldi (Lotus 72 R7), 79. 4. Jackie Stewart (Tyrrell 004), 78. 5. Brian Redman (McLaren M19A/2), 77. 6. Chris Amon (Matra V12 MS120-04), 77.
PP – Fittipaldi, 1;21.4; FL – Beltoise, 1;40.0, 70.35 mph.
In heavy rain Beltoise and BRM triumphed, leading from start to finish, only Ickx's Ferrari in same class that day.

29-5-72 International Gold Cup,
Oulton Park, GB – 40 laps, 110.44 miles
1. Denny Hulme (McLaren M19A/1), 40 laps in

57;15.6, 115.17 mph.
2. Emerson Fittipaldi (Lotus 72 R5), 40 in 57;53.0.
3. Tim Schenken (Surtees TS9-006), 39. **4.** Brian Redman (Chevron-Chevrolet B24 72-01 Formula 5000), 39. **5.** Vern Schuppan (BRM V12 P153-06), 39. **6.** Ray Allen (McLaren-Chevrolet M18 500-05 Formula 5000), 38.
PP – Peter Gethin (BRM (P160-03), 1;24.6; FL – Redman, 1;25.8, 115.85 mph.
Comfortable McLaren win at record pace against thin F1 field, Fittipaldi's Lotus handicapped by poor tyre choice.

4-6-72 BELGIAN GP, Nivelles, Brussels – 85 laps, 196.69 miles
1. Emerson Fittipaldi (Lotus 72 R7), 85 laps in 1:44;06.7, 113.35 mph.
2. François Cevert (Tyrrell 002), 85 in 1:44;33.3.
3. Denny Hulme (McLaren M19C/1), 85. **4.** Mike Hailwood (Surtees TS9-005), 85. **5.** Carlos Pace (March 711/3), 84. **6.** Chris Amon (Matra V12 MS120-06), 84.
PP – Fittipaldi, 1;11.43; FL – Amon, 1;12.12, 115.38 mph.
Regazzoni's Ferrari led first 8 laps, then the Lotus 72 was simply driven away from everyone else – the Ferrari went out in collision with the new flat-12 Tecno.

18-6-72 Gran Premio Republica Italiana, Vallelunga, Rome, I – 80 laps, 159.04 miles
1. Emerson Fittipaldi (Lotus 72 R5), 80 laps in 1:37;31.9, 97.85 mph.
2. Andrea de Adamich (Surtees TS9-004), 80 in 1:38;04.7.
3. Nanni Galli (Tecno flat-12 PA123-T-001), 79. **4.** Mike Beuttler (March 721G/1), 79. UNC **'5th'**. Howden Ganley (BRM V12 P160-05), 59.
No other finishers.
PP – Fittipaldi 1;9.82; FL – Fittipaldi, 1;11.06, 99.98 mph.
Inconsequential race, fodder for Fittipaldi's Lotus which led start to finish.

2-7-72 FRENCH GP, Clermont-Ferrand – 38 laps, 190.19 miles
1. Jackie Stewart (Tyrrell 003), 38 laps in 1:52;21.5, 101.56 mph.
2. Emerson Fittipaldi (Lotus 72 R7), 1:52;49.2.
3. Chris Amon (Matra V12 MS120-07), 38. **4.** François Cevert (Tyrrell 002), 38. **5.** Ronnie Peterson (March 721G/3), 38. **6.** Mike Hailwood (Surtees TS9-005), 38.
PP – Amon, 2;53.4; FL – Amon, 2;53.9, 103.61 mph.
Stewart and Tyrrell back on form but superb Amon performance in new Matra leading 20 laps until tyre deflated. Eight cars delayed by punctures.

15-7-72 BRITISH GP, Brands Hatch – 76 laps, 201.32 miles
1. Emerson Fittipaldi (Lotus 72 R7), 76 laps in 1:47;50.2, 112.06 mph.
2. Jackie Stewart (Tyrrell 003), 76 in 1:47;54.3.
3. Peter Revson (McLaren M19A/1), 76. **4.** Chris Amon (Matra V12 MS120-04), 75. **5.** Denny Hulme (McLaren M19C/1), 75. **6.** Arturo Merzario (Ferrari 312B2 007), 75.
PP – Jacky Ickx (Ferrari 312B2 005), 1;22.6; FL – Stewart, 1;24.00, 113.84 mph.
Ickx's Ferrari led 48 laps until oil cooler punctured, Fittipaldi had won duel with Stewart and led until finish.

30-7-72 GERMAN GP, Nürburgring – 14 laps, 198.64 miles
1. Jacky Ickx (Ferrari 312B2 005), 14 laps in 1:42;12.3, 116.60 mph.
2. Clay Regazzoni (Ferrari 312B2 007), 14 in 1:43;00.6.
3. Ronnie Peterson (March 721G/3), 14. **4.** Howden Ganley (BRM V12 P160-06), 14. **5.** Brian Redman (McLaren M19A/1), 14. **6.** Graham Hill (Brabham BT37/1), 14.
PP – Ickx, 7;07.0; FL – Ickx, 7;13.6, 117.81 mph.
Ickx took 12 secs off record in practice, led race throughout; Fittipaldi's Lotus lost 2nd place late in race when gearbox broke, Stewart collided with Regazzoni and crashed on last lap.

13-8-72 AUSTRIAN GP, Österreichring – 54 laps, 198.34 miles
1. Emerson Fittipaldi (Lotus 72 R5), 54 laps in 1:29;16.66, 133.32 mph.
2. Denny Hulme (McLaren M19C/1), 54 in 1;29;17.84.
3. Peter Revson (McLaren M19C/2), 54. **4.** Mike Hailwood (Surtees TS9-005), 54. **5.** Chris Amon (Matra V12 MS120-07), 54. **6.** Howden Ganley (BRM V12 P160-06), 54.
PP – Fittipaldi, 1;35.97; FL – Hulme, 1;38.32, 134.50 mph.
Stewart's new Tyrrell 005 led until lap 24 when Fittipaldi went by in spare Lotus 72, Tyrrell's handling deteriorated and McLarens closed on leader near end.

10-9-72 ITALIAN GP, Monza – 55 laps, 196.35 miles
1. Emerson Fittipaldi (Lotus 72 R5), 55 laps in 1:29;58.4, 131.61 mph.
2. Mike Hailwood (Surtees TS9-005), 55 in 1:30;12.9.
3. Denny Hulme (McLaren M19C/1), 55. **4.** Peter Revson (McLaren M19C/2), 55. **5.** Graham Hill (Brabham BT37/1), 55. **6.** Peter Gethin (BRM V12 P160-05), 55.
PP – Jacky Ickx (Ferrari 312B2 005), 1;35.65; FL – Ickx, 1;36.3, 134.14 mph.
Fittipaldi and Lotus clinch titles, after tense battle with Ickx's Ferrari faded 10 laps from end due to Ferrari electrical fault.

24-9-72 CANADIAN GP, Mosport Pk, Toronto – 80 laps, 196.72 miles
1. Jackie Stewart (Tyrrell 005), 80 laps in 1:43;16.9, 114.28 mph.
2. Peter Revson (McLaren M19C/2), 80 in 1:44·05.1.
3. Denny Hulme (McLaren M19C/1), 80. **4.** Carlos Reutemann (Brabham BT37/2), 80. **5.** Clay Regazzoni (Ferrari 312B2 007), 80. **6.** Chris Amon (Matra V12 MS120-07), 79.
PP – Revson, 1;13.6; FL – Stewart, 1;15.7, 117.57 mph.
50th GP win for Cosworth DFV engine, 20th for Stewart the driver. Peterson's March led initially, ran second before collision with Hill's Brabham when lapping it on lap 50; Fittipaldi lost time after nose-fin knocked awry when challenging for third place.

8-10-72 UNITED STATES GP, Watkins Glen, NY – 59 laps, 199.24 miles
1. Jackie Stewart (Tyrrell 005), 59 laps in 1:41;45.354, 117.48 mph.
2. François Cevert (Tyrrell 006), 59 in 1:42;17.622.
3. Denny Hulme (McLaren M19C/1), 59. **4.** Ronnie Peterson (March 721G/3), 59. **5.** Jacky Ickx (Ferrari 312B2 005), 59. **6.** Mario Andretti (Ferrari 312B2 006), 58.
PP – Stewart, 1;40.481; FL – Stewart, 1;41.644, 119.61 mph.
New Tyrrells dominant, Stewart leading throughout while Cevert disposed of Hulme's McLaren for 2nd place.

22-10-72 World Championship Victory Race, Brands Hatch, GB – 40 laps, 105.96 miles
1. Jean-Pierre Beltoise (BRM V12 P180-02), 40 laps in 59;47.8, 106.36 mph.
2. Carlos Pace (Surtees TS9-006), 40 in 59;54.4.
3. Andrea de Adamich (Surtees TS9-004), 40. **4.** Vern Schuppan (BRM V12 P160-05), 39. **5.** Peter Gethin (BRM V12 P160-06), 39. **6.** John Watson (March 721/4), 39.
PP – Emerson Fittipaldi (Lotus 72 R7), 1;20.8; FL – Fittipaldi, 1;23.8, 113.84 mph.
Wet-dry race gave BRM edge when Beltoise's crew chose dry tyres and track dried out; front-runners Peterson (March), Hailwood (Surtees) and Fittipaldi all started on wets and forced to change tyres.

1973

28-1-73 ARGENTINE GP, Buenos Aires – 96 laps, 199.56 miles
1. Emerson Fittipaldi (Lotus 72 R7), 96 laps in 1:56;18.22, 104.84 mph.
2. François Cevert (Tyrrell 006), 96 in 1:56;22.91.
3. Jackie Stewart (Tyrrell 005), 96. **4.** Jacky Ickx (Ferrari 312B2 005), 96. **5.** Denny Hulme (McLaren M19C/1), 95. **6.** Wilson Fittipaldi (Brabham BT37/1), 95.
PP – Clay Regazzoni (BRM V12 P160-01), 1;10.54; FL – Fittipaldi, 1;11.22, 104.84 mph.
Regazzoni pole for BRM and led 30 laps before tyres overheated, Cevert took over lead while Stewart, bothered by tyre problems, tried in vain to hold off Lotuses of Fittipaldi and Peterson. The latter retired with engine failure, Fittipaldi made charge and caught Cevert for lead with only 10 laps to run.

11-2-73 BRAZILIAN GP, Interlagos – 40 laps, 197.84 miles
1. Emerson Fittipaldi (Lotus 72 R7), 40 laps in 1:43;55.6, 114.24 mph.
2. Jackie Stewart (Tyrrell 005), 40 in 1:44;09.1.
3. Denny Hulme (McLaren M19C/1), 40. **4.** Arturo Merzario (Ferrari 312B2 008), 39. **5.** Jacky Ickx (Ferrari 312B2 005), 39. **6.** Clay Regazzoni (BRM V12 P160-01), 39.
PP – Ronnie Peterson (Lotus 72 R8), 2;30.5; FL – Fittipaldi & Hulme, 2;35.0, 114.88 mph.
One of Fittipaldi's easiest victories, led from first corner, never challenged while heat claimed many. Lotus 72 still the car to beat, dominated qualifying and race though Peterson had rear wheel break when challenging Stewart for 2nd place. Beltoise's BRM 4th until flying stone damaged its electrics.

3-4-73 SOUTH AFRICAN GP, Kyalami – 79 laps, 201.45 miles
1. Jackie Stewart (Tyrrell 006), 79 laps in 1:43;11.07, 117.14 mph.
2. Peter Revson (McLaren M19C/2), 79 in 1:43;35.62.
3. Emerson Fittipaldi (Lotus 72 R7), 79. **4.** Arturo Merzario (Ferrari 312B2 005), 78. **5.** Denny Hulme (McLaren M23/1), 77. **6.** George Follmer (Shadow DN1-1A), 77.
PP – Hulme, 1;16.28; FL – Fittipaldi, 1;17.10, 119.07 mph.
Stewart crashed regular Tyrrell in practice, took over Cevert's car for race and won controversially amidst allegations of passing under yellow flag. Promising McLaren M23 debut.

17-3-73 Race of Champions, Brands Hatch, GB – 40 laps, 105.96 miles
1. Peter Gethin (Chevron-Chevrolet B24 72-05 Formula 5000), 40 laps in 57;22.9, 110.34 mph.
2. Denny Hulme (McLaren M23/1), 40 in 57;26.3.
3. James Hunt (Surtees TS9-006), 40. **4.** Tony Trimmer (Williams FX3/1), 40. **5.** Tony Dean (Chevron-Chevrolet B24 72-02 Formula 5000), 39. **6.** Jean-Pierre Beltoise (BRM V12 P160-03), 39.
PP – Beltoise, 1;21.1; FL – Beltoise, Niki Lauda (BRM V12 P160-01) & Ronnie Peterson (Lotus 72 R6), 1;23.0, 114.94 mph.
Gethin's F5000 beat F1s as they dropped like flies, BRM P160s on front of grid. Peterson led until retirement at 18 laps, Beltoise's BRM punctured, Hailwood's Surtees led and crashed, Hulme first with five laps to go but clutch failed and Gethin passed with one lap to go.

8-4-73 BRDC International Trophy, Silverstone, GB – 40 laps, 117.08 miles
1. Jackie Stewart (Tyrrell 006/2), 40 laps in 52;53.2, 132.82 mph.
2. Ronnie Peterson (Lotus 72 R8), 40 in 53;03.6.
3. Clay Regazzoni (BRM V12 P160-07), 40. **4.** Peter Revson (McLaren M23/2), 40. **5.** Niki Lauda (BRM V12 P160-01), 40. **6.** George Follmer (Shadow DN1/2A), 39.
PP – Emerson Fittipaldi (Lotus 72 R5), 1;16.4; FL – Peterson, 1;17.5, 135.96 mph.
Victorious debut of new Tyrrell deformable structure car, Stewart spun out of initial lead, Peterson's Lotus took over, Stewart closed again and Swede spun in snow shower!

29-4-73 SPANISH GP, Montjuich Pk, Barcelona – 75 laps, 176.654 miles
1. Emerson Fittipaldi (Lotus 72 R5), 75 laps in 1:48;18.7, 97.86 mph.
2. François Cevert (Tyrrell 006), 75 in 1:49;01.4.
3. George Follmer (Shadow DN1/2A), 75. **4.** Peter Revson (McLaren M23/2), 74. **5.** Jean-Pierre Beltoise (BRM V12 P160-03), 74. **6.** Denny Hulme (McLaren M23/1), 74.
PP – Ronnie Peterson (Lotus 72 R8), 1;21.8; FL – 1;23.8, 101.19 mph.
Peterson's Lotus led again for 18 laps until gearbox failed, Stewart's Tyrell had brake problems and Fittipaldi drove final 25 laps on deflating rear tyre to score Lotus's 50th GP win.

20-5-73 BELGIAN GP, Zolder – 70 laps, 183.54 miles
1. Jackie Stewart (Tyrrell 006/2), 70 laps in 1:42;13.43, 107.73 mph.
2. François Cevert (Tyrrell 006), 70 in 1:42;45.27.
3. Emerson Fittipaldi (Lotus 72 R7), 70. **4.** Andrea de Adamich (Brabham BT37/2), 69. **5.** Niki Lauda (BRM V12 P160-08), 69. **6.** Chris Amon (Tecno flat-12 PA123/B 006), 67.
PP – Ronnie Peterson (Lotus 72 R6), 1;22.46; FL – Cevert, 1;25.42, 110.51 mph.
Track surface broke up, Cevert led 18 laps, spun and regained ground, Fittipaldi led five laps, Stewart remainder; many accidents on loose surface.

3-6-73 MONACO GP, Monte Carlo – 78 laps, 158.87 miles
1. Jackie Stewart (Tyrrell 006/2), 78 laps in 1:57;44.3, 80.96 mph.
2. Emerson Fittipaldi (Lotus 72 R7), 78 in 1:57;45.6.
3. Ronnie Peterson (Lotus 72 R6), 77. **4.** François Cevert (Tyrrell 006), 77. **5.** Peter Revson (McLaren M23/2), 76. **6.** Denny Hulme (McLaren M23/1).
PP – Stewart, 1;27.5; FL – Fittipaldi, 1;28.1, 83.23 mph.
Stewart's 25th GP win to equal Clark's record, close and hard-fought battle throughout with Fittipaldi – see winning margin! Cevert and Peterson led early on.

17-6-73 SWEDISH GP, Anderstorp – 80 laps, 199.61 miles
1. Denny Hulme (McLaren M23/1), 80 laps in 1:56;46.049, 102.65 mph.
2. Ronnie Peterson (Lotus 72 R6), 80 in 1:56;50.088.
3. François Cevert (Tyrrell 006), 80. **4.** Carlos Reutemann (Brabham BT42/3), 80. **5.** Jackie Stewart (Tyrrell 006/2), 80. **6.** Jacky Ickx (Ferrari 312B3 010), 79.
PP – Peterson, 1;23.810; FL – Hulme, 1;26.146, 104.04 mph.
Peterson led 79 of the 80 laps, staving off Fittipaldi and Stewart who slowed with brake problems, Hulme emerged in final 20 laps and won when Lotus rear tyre deflated.

1-7-73 FRENCH GP, Ricard-Castellet – 54 laps, 194.61 miles
1. Ronnie Peterson (Lotus 72 R6), 54 laps in 1:41;36.52, 115.17 mph.
2. François Cevert (Tyrrell 006), 54 in 1:42;17.44.
3. Carlos Reutemann (Brabham BT42/3), 54. **4.** Jackie Stewart (Tyrrell 006/2), 54. **5.** Jacky Ickx (Ferrari 312B3 010), 54. **6.** James Hunt (March 731/3), 54.
PP – Stewart, 1;48.37; FL – Hulme, 1;50.99, 117.51 mph.
Peterson's long-overdue first GP win, but newcomer Scheckter's McLaren led dominantly up to lap 41 when Fittipaldi tried to go by and their cars collided, Peterson then leading from lap 42 to finish.

14-7-73 BRITISH GP, Silverstone – 67 laps, 196.11 miles*
**Race stopped after two laps, due to multiple accident, restarted over original distance.*
1. Peter Revson (McLaren M23/2), 67 laps in 1:29;18.5, 131.75 mph.
2. Ronnie Peterson (Lotus 72 R6), 67 in 1:29;21.3.
3. Denny Hulme (McLaren M23/1), 67. **4.** James Hunt (March 731/3), 67. **5.** François Cevert (Tyrrell 006), 67. **6.** Carlos Reutemann (Brabham BT42/3), 67.
PP – Peterson, 1;16.3; FL – Hunt, 1;18.6, 134.06 mph.
Farcical event, massive pile-up ended first attempt. After restart Peterson led, Stewart spun from threatening second place, Revson finally displaced ill-handling Lotus 72 for lead on lap 39.

29-7-73 DUTCH GP, Zandvoort – 72 laps, 189.06 miles
1. Jackie Stewart (Tyrrell 006/2), 72 laps in 1:39;12.45, 114.35 mph.
2. François Cevert (Tyrrell 006), 72 in 1:39;28.28.
3. James Hunt (March 731/3), 72. **4.** Peter Revson (McLaren M23/2), 72. **5.** Jean-Pierre Beltoise (BRM V12 P160-07), 72. **6.** Gijs van Lennep (Williams FX4/1), 70.
PP – Ronnie Peterson (Lotus 72 R6), 1;19.47; FL – Peterson, 1;20.31, 117.71 mph.
Peterson led from start until lap 64 when gearbox failed, handing Stewart his record-breaking 26th GP win and Tyrrell a fine 1-2; race marred by fatal accident to Roger Williamson in March 731.

5-8-73 GERMAN GP, Nürburgring – 14 laps, 198.64 miles
1. Jackie Stewart (Tyrrell 006/2), 14 laps in 1:42;03.0, 116.82 mph.
2. François Cevert (Tyrrell 006), 14 in 1:42;04.6.
3. Jacky Ickx (McLaren M23/4), 14. **4.** Carlos Pace (Surtees TS14-05), 14. **5.** Wilson Fittipaldi (Brabham BT42/2), 14. **6.** Emerson Fittipaldi (Lotus 72 R7), 14.
PP – Stewart, 7;07.8; FL – Pace, 7;11.4, 118.43 mph.
Tyrrell race from start to finish, only Ickx's freelance McLaren drive offering any challenge. Pace showed his class in Surtees.

19-8-73 AUSTRIAN GP, Österreichring – 54 laps, 198.34 miles
1. Ronnie Peterson (Lotus 72 R6), 54 laps in 1:28;48.78, 133.50 mph.
2. Jackie Stewart (Tyrrell 006/2), 54 in 1:28;57.79.
3. Carlos Pace (Surtees TS14-05), 54. **4.** Carlos Reutemann (Brabham BT42/3), 54. **5.** Jean-Pierre Beltoise (BRM V12 P160-07), 54. **6.** Clay Regazzoni (BRM V12 P160-09), 54.
PP – Emerson Fittipaldi (Lotus 72 R7), 1;34.98; FL – Pace, 1;37.29, 135.91 mph.
Lotus 72s back to the fore, Peterson waved Fittipaldi ahead on lap 16 but fuel line failed five laps from end leaving Peterson to win from Stewart. Pace challenged Stewart until fuel pressure fell.

9-9-73 ITALIAN GP, Monza – 55 laps, 197.34 miles
1. Ronnie Peterson (Lotus 72 R6), 55 laps in 1:29;17.0, 132.63 mph.
2. Emerson Fittipaldi (Lotus 72 R7), 55 in 1:29;17.8.
3. Peter Revson (McLaren M23/4), 55. **4.** Jackie Stewart (Tyrrell 006/2), 55. **5.** François Cevert (Tyrrell 006), 55. **6.** Carlos Reutemann (Brabham BT42/3), 55.
PP – Peterson, 1;34.80; FL – Stewart, 1;35.3, 135.55 mph.
Lotus 72s utterly dominant, but Stewart stopped Tyrrell when 4th in early stages as tyre deflated, rejoined with new tyre in 19th place almost one lap down and soared through field, setting lap record.

23-9-73 CANADIAN GP, Mosport Pk, Toronto – 80 laps, 196.72 miles
1. Peter Revson (McLaren M23/4), 80 laps in 1:59;04.083, 99.13 mph.
2. Emerson Fittipaldi (Lotus 72 R7), 80 in 1:59;36.817.
3. Jack Oliver (Shadow DN1/6A), 80. **4.** Jean-Pierre Beltoise (BRM V12 P160-07), 80. **5.** Jackie Stewart (Tyrrell 006/2), 79. **6.** Howden Ganley (Williams FX4/2), 79.
PP – Ronnie Peterson (Lotus 72 R6), 1;13.697; FL – Fittipaldi, 1;15.496, 117.77 mph.
Yet another controversial race won by McLaren, this time rain shower before start put nearly everyone on wet tyres. Lauda's BRM built lead for 20 laps, then track dried and spate of tyre stops commenced. Accident brought out pace car for first time to shepherd field but went ahead of the wrong car – chaos ensued and lap charting went awry; Oliver's Shadow led race at one stage, as did Beltoise's BRM.

7-10-73 UNITED STATES GP, Watkins Glen, NY – 59 laps, 199.24 miles
1. Ronnie Peterson (Lotus 72 R6), 59 laps in 1:41;15.779, 118.06 mph.
2. James Hunt (March 731/3), 59 in 1:41;16.467.
3. Carlos Reutemann (Brabham BT42/3), 59. **4.** Denny Hulme (McLaren M23/1), 59. **5.** Peter Revson (McLaren M23/4), 59. **6.** Emerson Fittipaldi (Lotus 72 R7), 59.
PP – Peterson, 1;39.657; FL – Hunt, 1;41.652, 119.60 mph.
Cevert killed in practice, Tyrrell team withdrew, end of Stewart's career. Peterson led start to finish staving off fearsome challenge from Hunt's private March. Note winning margin.

1974

13-1-74 ARGENTINE GP, Buenos Aires – 53 laps, 196.55 miles
1. Denny Hulme (McLaren M23/6), 53 laps in 1:41;02.01, 116.72 mph.
2. Niki Lauda (Ferrari 312B3 012), 53 in 1:41;11.28.
3. Clay Regazzoni (Ferrari 312B3 011), 53. **4.** Mike Hailwood (McLaren M23/1), 53. **5.** Jean-Pierre Beltoise (BRM V12 P160-09), 53. **6.** Patrick Depailler (Tyrrell 005), 53.
PP – Ronnie Peterson (Lotus 72 R8), 1;50.78; FL – Regazzoni, 1;52.10, 119.09 mph.
Local hero Carlos Reutemann dominated in Brabham BT44 until engine airbox worked loose then ran out of fuel after 51 of 53 laps; promising debut for Ferrari B3/74s.

27-1-74 BRAZILIAN GP, Interlagos – 40 laps, 197.84 miles*
**Race stopped due to heavy rain after only Fittipaldi and Regazzoni completed 31 laps and were into their 32nd.*
1. Emerson Fittipaldi (McLaren M23/5), 32 laps in 1:24;37.06, 112.24 mph.
2. Clay Regazzoni (Ferrari 312B3 011), 32 in 1:24;50.63.
3. Jacky Ickx (Lotus 72 R5), 31. **4.** Carlos Pace (Surtees TS16-02), 31. **5.** Mike Hailwood (McLaren M23/1), 31. **6.** Ronnie Peterson (Lotus 72 R8), 31.
PP – Fittipaldi, 2;32.97; FL – Regazzoni, 2;36.05, 114.11 mph.
Early duel between Fittipaldi and Peterson ended when Lotus's tyre deflated; Reutemann's Brabham led briefly at start until front tyres lost grip.

3-2-74 Grande Prêmio Presidente Medici, Brasilia, BRA – 40 laps, 136.09 miles
1. Emerson Fittipaldi (McLaren M23/5), 40 laps in 1:15;22.75, 108.27 mph.
2. Jody Scheckter (Tyrrell 006/2), 40 in 1:15;35.15.
3. Arturo Merzario (Williams FX4/1), 40. **4.** Jochen Mass (Surtees TS16-03), 40. **5.** Wilson Fittipaldi (Brabham BT44/2), 39. **6.** Howden Ganley (March 741/2), 39.
PP – Carlos Reutemann (Brabham BT44/1),

1;51.18; FL – E. Fittipaldi, 1;51.62, 109.30 mph.
Reutemann's Brabham form continued, led from pole until piston failed; Scheckter slowed when balance weight fell off wheel, unable to challenge for lead.

17-3-74 Race of Champions, Brands Hatch, GB – 40 laps, 105.96 miles
1. Jacky Ickx (Lotus 72 R5), 40 laps in 1:03;37.6, 99.96 mph.
2. Niki Lauda (Ferrari 312B3 011), 40 in 1:03;39.1. **3.** Emerson Fittipaldi (McLaren M23/4), 40. **4.** Mike Hailwood (McLaren M23/1), 40. **5.** Clay Regazzoni (Ferrari 312B3 012), 40. **6.** Peter Revson (Shadow DN3/1A), 39.
PP – James Hunt (Hesketh 308-1), 1;21.5; FL – Ickx, 1;33.8, 102.80 mph.
Lauda dominated most of race in driving rain, until Ickx passed on outside of difficult Paddock Hill Bend with just five laps to run. Reutemann crashed due to brake trouble after brief initial lead.

30-3-74 SOUTH AFRICAN GP, Kyalami – 78 laps, 198.80 miles
1. Carlos Reutemann (Brabham BT44/1), 78 laps in 1:42;40.96, 116.24 mph.
2. Jean-Pierre Beltoise (BRM V12 P201-01), 78 in 1:43;14.90.
3. Mike Hailwood (McLaren M23/1), 78. **4.** Patrick Depailler (Tyrrell 005), 78. **5.** Hans Stuck Jr (March 741/1), 78. **6.** Arturo Merzario (Williams FX4/1), 78.
PP – Niki Lauda (Ferrari 312B3 012), 1;16.58; FL – Reutemann, 1;18.16, 117.47 mph.
Brabham luck changed at last – Reutemann took lead from Lauda end of lap 10, and held off Ferrari until it retired with electrical trouble four laps from end; new BRM finished well while others retired.

7-4-74, BRDC International Trophy, Silverstone, GB – 40 laps, 117.08 miles
1. James Hunt (Hesketh 308-1), 40 laps in 52;35.4, 133.58 mph.
2. Jochen Mass (Surtees TS16-03), 40 in 53;12.4.
3. Jean-Pierre Jarier (Shadow DN3/2A), 40.
4. Henri Pescarolo (BRM V12 P160-10), 40.
5. François Migault (BRM V12 P160-05), 40.
6. John Nicholson (Lyncar F1-007), 39.
PP – Hunt, 1;16.7; FL – Hunt, 1;17.6, 135.79 mph.
Hunt and Hesketh emerged to take lead from Peterson's Lotus on lap 28.

28-4-74 SPANISH GP, Jarama, Madrid – 90 laps, 190.15 miles*
**Race stopped after two hours under CSI regulation since heavy rain had slowed pace.*
1. Niki Lauda (Ferrari 312B3 015), 84 laps in 2:00;29.56, 88.48 mph.
2. Clay Regazzoni (Ferrari 312B3 014), 84 in 2:01;05.17.
3. Emerson Fittipaldi (McLaren M23/5), 83. **4.** Hans Stuck Jr (March 741/1), 82. **5.** Jody Scheckter (Tyrrell 007-1), 82. **6.** Denny Hulme (McLaren M23/4), 82.
PP – Lauda, 1;18.44; FL – Lauda, 1;20.83, 94.20 mph.
Lauda's first GP win, Ferrari's 50th. Peterson's Lotus 76 led first 20 laps before pit stop to change from wet to dry tyres as track dried.

12-5-74 BELGIAN GP, Nivelles, Brussels – 85 laps, 196.69 miles
1. Emerson Fittipaldi (McLaren M23/5), 85 laps in 1:44;20.57, 114.10 mph.
2. Niki Lauda (Ferrari 312B3 012), 85 in 1:44;20.92.
3. Jody Scheckter (Tyrrell 007-1), 85. **4.** Clay Regazzoni (Ferrari 312B3 011), 85. **5.** Jean-Pierre Beltoise (BRM V12 P201-01), 85. **6.** Denny Hulme (McLaren M23/6), 85.
PP – Regazzoni, 1;09.82; FL – Hulme, 1;11.31, 116.82 mph.
Fittipaldi first driver to win two GPs this season, Scheckter true pole time disallowed, Regazzoni led until lap 39, only lost 3rd as tanks dried on run-in to line; awful new circuit.

26-5-74 MONACO GP, Monte Carlo – 78 laps, 158.87 miles
1. Ronnie Peterson (Lotus 72 R8), 78 laps in 1:58;03.7, 80.74 mph.
2. Jody Scheckter (Tyrrell 007-1), 78 in 1:58;32.5.
3. Jean-Pierre Jarier (Shadow DN3/2A), 78.
4. Clay Regazzoni (Ferrari 312B3 014), 78.
5. Emerson Fittipaldi (McLaren M23/5), 77. **6.** John Watson (Brabham BT42/2), 77.
PP – Niki Lauda (Ferrari 312B3 010), 1;26.3; FL – Peterson, 1;27.9, 83.42 mph.
Lauda led until electrical trouble on lap 33 allowed Peterson to take over in old faithful Lotus 72, replacing failed new model.

9-6-74 SWEDISH GP, Anderstorp – 80 laps, 199.61 miles
1. Jody Scheckter (Tyrrell 007-1), 80 laps in 1:58;31.391, 101.11 mph.
2. Patrick Depailler (Tyrrell 007-2), 80 in 1:58;31.771.
3. James Hunt (Hesketh 308-2), 80. **4.** Emerson Fittipaldi (McLaren M23/4), 80. **5.** Jean-Pierre Jarier (Shadow DN1/2A), 80. **6.** Graham Hill (Lola T370 HU-2), 79.
PP – Depailler, 1;24.758; FL – Depailler, 1;27.262, 103.01 mph.
Utter Tyrrell domination, 007s shared front row, Peterson's Lotus split them briefly in second place.

23-6-74 DUTCH GP, Zandvoort – 75 laps, 196.95 miles
1. Niki Lauda (Ferrari 312B3 015), 75 laps in 1:43;00.35, 114.72 mph.
2. Clay Regazzoni (Ferrari 312B3 014), 75 in 1:43;08.60.
3. Emerson Fittipaldi (McLaren M23/5), 75. **4.** Mike Hailwood (McLaren M23/7), 75. **5.** Jody Scheckter (Tyrrell 007-1), 75. **6.** Patrick Depailler (Tyrrell 007-2), 75.
PP – Lauda, 1;18.31; FL – Ronnie Peterson (Lotus 72 R8), 1;21.44, 116.08 mph.
Ferrari's turn, sharing front row, Regazzoni briefly bothered by Hailwood's McLaren on opening lap but Italian cars dominant thereafter.

7-7-74 FRENCH GP, Dijon-Prenois – 80 laps, 163.50 miles
1. Ronnie Peterson (Lotus 72 R8), 80 laps in 1:21;55.02, 119.75 mph.
2. Niki Lauda (Ferrari 312B3 012), 80 in 1:22;15.38.
3. Clay Regazzoni (Ferrari 312B3 014), 80. **4.** Jody Scheckter (Tyrrell 007-1), 80. **5.** Jacky Ickx (Lotus 72 R5), 80. **6.** Denny Hulme (McLaren M23/6), 80.
PP – Lauda, 00;58.79 (very short lap distance); FL – Scheckter, 1;00.00, 122.62 mph.
Peterson Lotus *tour de force*, disposing of Lauda's more powerful Ferrari and keeping ahead on dizzy little circuit.

20-7-74 BRITISH GP, Brands Hatch – 75 laps, 198.75 miles
1. Jody Scheckter (Tyrrell 007-1), 75 laps in 1:43;02.2, 115.73 mph.
2. Emerson Fittipaldi (McLaren M23/8), 75 in 1:43;17.5.
3. Jacky Ickx (Lotus 72 R5), 75. **4.** Clay Regazzoni (Ferrari 312B3 014), 75. **5.** Niki Lauda (Ferrari 312B3 015), 74. **6.** Carlos Reutemann (Brabham BT44/1), 74.
PP – Lauda, 1;19.7; FL – Lauda, 1;21.1, 117.63 mph.
Lauda led from start but delayed pit stop too late to replace punctured tyre and was trapped in pit lane by organizational failure at finish, allowing Scheckter lucky win; processional race, last-minute farce.

4-8-74 GERMAN GP, Nürburgring – 14 laps, 198.64 miles
1. Clay Regazzoni (Ferrari 312B3 016), 14 laps in 1:41;35.0, 117.33 mph.
2. Jody Scheckter (Tyrrell 007-1), 14 in 1:42;25.7.
3. Carlos Reutemann (Brabham BT44/1), 14.
4. Ronnie Peterson (Lotus 76 R10), 14. **5.** Jacky Ickx (Lotus 72 R5), 14. **6.** Tom Pryce (Shadow DN3/5A), 14.
PP – Niki Lauda (Ferrari 312B3 012), 7;00.8; FL – Scheckter, 7;11.1, 118.49 mph.
Young Hunt had said Regazzoni was over the hill, so he was at the Ring, leading start to finish after Lauda immaturity crashed pole Ferrari on second corner – record-breaking Scheckter drive into good second couldn't challenge Ferrari, or Regazzoni.

18-8-74 AUSTRIAN GP, Österreichring – 54 laps, 198.34 miles
1. Carlos Reutemann (Brabham BT44/1), 54 laps in 1:28;44.72, 134.10 mph.
2. Denny Hulme (McLaren M23/6), 54 in 1:29;27.64.
3. James Hunt (Hesketh 308-3), 54. **4.** John Watson (Brabham BT44/4), 54. **5.** Clay Regazzoni (Ferrari 312B3 014), 54. **6.** Vittorio Brambilla (March 741/2), 54.
PP – Niki Lauda (Ferrari 312B3 015), 1;35.40; FL – Regazzoni, 1;37.22, 136.01 mph.
Brabham start to finish win, team-mate Pace out with fuel leak losing hard-won second place on lap 41, Lauda engine failure, 3-4-5 all had to change blistered or deflating tyres.

8-9-74 ITALIAN GP, Monza – 52 laps, 186.76 miles
1. Ronnie Peterson (Lotus 72 R8), 52 laps in 1:22;56.6, 135.41 mph.
2. Emerson Fittipaldi (McLaren M23/8), 52 in 1:22;57.4.
3. Jody Scheckter (Tyrrell 007-1), 52. **4.** Arturo Merzario (Williams FX4/3), 52. **5.** Carlos Pace (Brabham BT44/2), 51. **6.** Denny Hulme (McLaren M23/6), 51.
PP – Niki Lauda (Ferrari 312B3 015), 1;33.16; FL – Pace, 1;34.2, 137.26 mph.
Lauda's 9th pole of season but both Ferraris failed when leading, Peterson inherited lead on lap 39, Fittipaldi headed him for a few yards on one lap, but Lotus held on.

22-9-74 CANADIAN GP, Mosport Pk, Toronto – 80 laps, 196.72 miles
1. Emerson Fittipaldi (McLaren M23/8), 80 laps in 1:40;26.136, 117.52 mph.
2. Clay Regazzoni (Ferrari 312B3 016), 80 in 1:40;39.170.
3. Ronnie Peterson (Lotus 72 R8), 80. **4.** James Hunt (Hesketh 308-2), 80. **5.** Patrick Depailler (Tyrrell 007-4), 80. **6.** Denny Hulme (McLaren M23/6), 79.
PP – Fittipaldi, 1;13.188; FL – Niki Lauda (Ferrari 312B3 015), 1;13.659, 120.18 mph.
Lauda again led from start but this time hit soil scattered on track by incident and crashed on lap 69, allowing Fittipaldi win to take Championship on into final round, between Fittipaldi, Regazzoni and Scheckter; McLaren, Ferrari, Tyrrell.

6-10-74 UNITED STATES GP, Watkins Glen, NY – 59 laps, 199.24 miles
1. Carlos Reutemann (Brabham BT44/1), 59 laps in 1:40;21.439, 119.12 mph.
2. Carlos Pace (Brabham BT44/2), 59 in 1:40;32.174.
3. James Hunt (Hesketh 308-2), 59. **4.** Emerson Fittipaldi (McLaren M23/8), 59. **5.** John Watson (Brabham BT44/4), 59. **6.** Patrick Depailler (Tyrrell 007-4), 59.
PP – Reutemann, 1;38.978; FL – Pace, 1;40.608, 120.84 mph.
Brabham all the way for superb 1-2 finish, Hunt shone until Hesketh brakes faded, Ferrari a shambles, Tyrrell failed so McLaren (Fittipaldi) earned titles.

1975

12-1-75 ARGENTINE GP, Buenos Aires – 53 laps, 196.55 miles
1. Emerson Fittipaldi (McLaren M23/9), 53 laps in 1:39;26.29, 118.60 mph.
2. James Hunt (Hesketh 308-3), 53 in 1:39;32.20.
3. Carlos Reutemann (Brabham BT44B/1), 53.
4. Clay Regazzoni (Ferrari 312B3 014), 53.
5. Patrick Depailler (Tyrrell 007-4), 53. **6.** Niki Lauda (Ferrari 312B3 020), 53.
PP – Jean-Pierre Jarier (Shadow DN5/1A), 1;49.21; FL – Hunt, 1;50.91, 120.37 mph.
Hunt's Hesketh got best of initial battle with Brabhams, but Fittipaldi's new McLaren pressured him into mistake on lap 35 and went on to win, Shadow pole but diff failed on warm-up lap!

26-1-75 BRAZILIAN GP, Interlagos – 40 laps, 197.84 miles
1. Carlos Pace (Brabham BT44B/2), 40 laps in 1:44;41.17, 113.39 mph.
2. Emerson Fittipaldi (McLaren M23/9), 40 in 1:44;46.96.
3. Jochen Mass (McLaren M23/8), 40. **4.** Clay Regazzoni (Ferrari 312B3 014), 40. **5.** Niki Lauda (Ferrari 312B3 020), 40. **6.** James Hunt (Hesketh 308-3), 40.
PP – Jean-Pierre Jarier (Shadow DN5/1A), 2;29.88; FL – Jarier, 2;34.16, 115.51 mph.
Reutemann led to lap 5, impressive Jarier Shadow thereafter building big lead until metering unit seized with 8 laps to run, allowing Pace home victory for Brabham.

1-3-75 SOUTH AFRICAN GP, Kyalami – 78 laps, 198.90 miles
1. Jody Scheckter (Tyrrell 007-2), 78 laps in 1:43;16.90, 115.51 mph.
2. Carlos Reutemann (Brabham BT44B/1), 78 in 1:43;20.64.
3. Patrick Depailler (Tyrrell 007-4), 78. **4.** Carlos Pace (Brabham BT44B/2), 78. **5.** Niki Lauda (Ferrari 312T 018), 78. **6.** Jochen Mass (McLaren M23/8), 78.
PP – Pace, 1;16.41; FL – Pace, 1;17.20, 118.92 mph.
Fine victory in spare Tyrrell with untried spare engine, Scheckter taking home-race lead from lap 3 and holding off Reutemann thereafter.

16-3-75 Race of Champions, Brands Hatch, GB – 40 laps, 105.96 miles
1. Tom Pryce (Shadow DN5/2A), 40 laps in 55;53.5, 113.79 mph.
2. John Watson (Surtees TS16-04), 40 in 56;24.0.
3. Ronnie Peterson (Lotus 72 R9), 40. **4.** Jacky Ickx (Lotus 72 R5), 39. **5.** Emerson Fittipaldi (McLaren M23/9), 39. **6.** Bob Evans (BRM P201-05), 38.
PP – Pryce, 1;34.9; FL – Pryce, 1;21.1, 117.63 mph.
Scheckter had race in bag for Tyrrell, but Pryce's Shadow then closed rapidly and Tyrrell engine failed on brink of anticipated battle giving Pryce Shadow's first F1 victory.

13-4-75 BRDC International Trophy, Silverstone, GB – 40 laps, 117.08 miles
1. Niki Lauda (Ferrari 312T 022), 40 laps in 52;17.6, 134.33 mph.
2. Emerson Fittipaldi (McLaren M23/4), 40 in 52;17.7.
3. Mario Andretti (Parnelli VPJ4-002), 40. **4.** John Watson (Surtees TS16-04), 40. **5.** Patrick Depailler (Tyrrell 007-4), 40. **6.** Mark Donohue (Penske PC1-002), 40.
PP – James Hunt (Hesketh 308-2), 1;17.3; FL – Hunt & Fittipaldi, 1;17.7, 135.61 mph.
Hunt's Hesketh led until lap 25 when engine blew, leaving Ferrari/McLaren duel for lead and close finish.

27-4-75 SPANISH GP, Montjuich Pk, Barcelona – 75 laps, 176.65 miles*
**Race stopped after 29 laps due to accident.*
1. Jochen Mass (McLaren M23/8), 29 laps in 42;53.7, 95.54 mph.
2. Jacky Ickx (Lotus 72 R5), 29 in 42;54.8.
3. Carlos Reutemann (Brabham BT44B/1), 28.
4. Jean-Pierre Jarier (Shadow DN5/1A), 29**.
5. Vittorio Brambilla (March 751/3), 28. **6.** Lella Lombardi (March 751/2), 27.
***One place penalty for overtaking under yellow caution flag.*
PP – Niki Lauda (Ferrari 312T 022), 1;23.4; FL – Mario Andretti (Parnelli VPJ4-002) 1;25.1, 99.64 mph.
Circuit safety worries persuaded Fittipaldi to boycott race, the Ferraris rammed each other in first corner, Hunt led briefly but crashed on spilled oil. Andretti took over in new Parnelli until lap 22 crash, then Stommelen's Hill led until rear wing strut failed and car went into bystanders, killing 5, on lap 26 – Pace crashed in avoidance leaving Mass victory as race was stopped.

11-5-75 MONACO GP, Monte Carlo – 78 laps, 158.87 miles*
**Race stopped after 75 laps to comply with two-hour rule.*
1. Niki Lauda (Ferrari 312T 023), 75 laps in 2:01;21.31, 75.55 mph.
2. Emerson Fittipaldi (McLaren M23/9), 75 in 2:01;24.09.
3. Carlos Pace (Brabham BT44B/2), 75. **4.** Ronnie Peterson (Lotus 72 R9), 75. **5.** Patrick Depailler (Tyrrell 007-4), 75. **6.** Jochen Mass (McLaren M23/8), 75.
PP – Lauda, 1;26.40; FL – Depailler, 1;28.67, 82.71 mph.
Wet-dry race saw everyone changing to dry tyres after 20 laps or so, Lauda led all but one lap in Ferrari demonstration.

25-5-75 BELGIAN GP, Zolder – 70 laps, 185.38 miles
1. Niki Lauda (Ferrari 312T 023), 70 laps in 1:43;53.98, 107.06 mph.
2. Jody Scheckter (Tyrrell 007-2), 70 in 1:44;13.20.
3. Carlos Reutemann (Brabham BT44B/1), 70.
4. Patrick Depailler (Tyrrell 007-4), 70. **5.** Clay Regazzoni (Ferrari 312T 022), 70. **6.** Tom Pryce (Shadow DN5/2A), 70.
PP – Lauda, 1;25.43; FL – Regazzoni, 1;26.76, 109.90 mph.
Lauda won from his 12th pole since joining Ferrari previous year, first five laps saw battle for lead with Pace's Brabham and Brambilla's March.

8-6-75 SWEDISH GP, Anderstorp – 80 laps, 199.76 miles
1. Niki Lauda (Ferrari 312T 023), 80 laps in 1:59;18.319, 100.41 mph.
2. Carlos Reutemann (Brabham BT44B/1), 80 in 1:59;24.607.
3. Clay Regazzoni (Ferrari 312T 021), 80. **4.** Mario Andretti (Parnelli VPJ4-001), 80. **5.** Mark Donohue (Penske PC1-01), 80. **6.** Tony Brise (Hill GH-1/1), 79.
PP – Vittorio Brambilla (March 751/3), 1;24.360; FL – Lauda, 1;28.267, 101.82 mph.
Brambilla's on-form March led first 15 laps until tyre trouble, Reutemann's Brabham led until front tyres deteriorated, Lauda taking lead with 10 laps to run.

22-6-75 DUTCH GP, Zandvoort – 75 laps, 196.95 miles
1. James Hunt (Hesketh 308-2), 75 laps in 1:46;57.40, 110.49 mph.
2. Niki Lauda (Ferrari 312T 022), 75 in 1:46;58.46.
3. Clay Regazzoni (Ferrari 312T 021), 75. **4.** Carlos Reutemann (Brabham BT44B/1), 75. **5.** Carlos Pace (Brabham BT44B/2), 74. **6.** Tom Pryce (Shadow DN5/2A), 74.
PP – Lauda, 1;20.29; FL – Lauda, 1;21.54, 115.91 mph.
Another wet-dry tyre race, Hesketh timed Hunt's stop right, and he held off early leader Lauda by might and main.

6-7-75 FRENCH GP, Ricard-Castellet – 54 laps, 194.61 miles
1. Niki Lauda (Ferrari 312T 022), 54 laps in 1:40;18.84, 116.60 mph.
2. James Hunt (Hesketh 308-2), 54 in 1:40;20.43.
3. Jochen Mass (McLaren M23/6), 54. **4.** Emerson Fittipaldi (McLaren M23/9), 54. **5.** Mario Andretti (Parnelli VPJ4-001), 54. **6.** Patrick Depailler (Tyrrell 007-4), 54.
PP – Lauda, 1;47.82; FL – Mass, 1;50.60, 117.51 mph.
Lauda's race throughout, built large mid-race lead and let it shrink comfortably to final winning margin, Hunt and Mass both very competitive this day.

19-7-75 BRITISH GP, Silverstone – 67 laps, 196.44 miles*
**Race stopped after 56 laps due to multiple crashes in rainstorm.*
1. Emerson Fittipaldi (McLaren M23/9), 56 laps in 1:22;05.0, 120.01 mph.
2. Carlos Pace (Brabham BT44B/2), 55.
3. Jody Scheckter (Tyrrell 007-6), 55. **4.** James Hunt (Hesketh 308-2), 55. **5.** Mark Donohue (March 751/5), 55. **6.** Vittorio Brambilla (March 751/3), 55.
PP – Tom Pryce (Shadow DN5/2A), 1;19.36; FL – Clay Regazzoni (Ferrari 312T 024), 1;20.9, 130.47 mph.
Pace led until lap 13 when Regazzoni went by only to spin five laps later in first rain shower, Pryce's Shadow led for one lap before crashing; some changed to wet tyres, some didn't. Scheckter did and built huge lead only for track to dry, and he stopped again to change to dries. Jarier's Shadow led two laps before inevitable crash, Hunt seven laps until exhaust broke, Fittipaldi inherited lead; 12 laps later storm broke and nine more crashed as another British GP collapsed in farce.

3-8-75 GERMAN GP, Nürburgring – 14 laps, 198.64 miles
1. Carlos Reutemann (Brabham BT44B/1), 14 laps in 1:41;14.1, 117.73 mph.
2. Jacques Laffite (Williams FX4 IR-03), 14 in 1:42;51.8.
3. Niki Lauda (Ferrari 312T 022), 14. **4.** Tom Pryce (Shadow DN5/2A), 14. **5.** Alan Jones (Hill GH1-3), 14. **6.** Gijs van Lennep (Ensign N175 MN-04), 14.
PP – Lauda, 6;58.6; FL – Clay Regazzoni (Ferrari 312T 021), 7;06.4, 119.79 mph.
Yet another daffy-duck race as flints on track caused spate of punctures; Lauda led first nine laps, Reutemann thereafter, and Laffite rising through field as faster runners delayed.

17-8-75 AUSTRIAN GP, Österreichring – 54 laps, 198.34 miles*
**Race stopped after 29 laps due to rainstorm.*
1. Vittorio Brambilla (March 751/3), 29 laps in 57;56.69, 111.23 mph.
2. James Hunt (Hesketh 308-2), 29 in 58;23.72.
3. Tom Pryce (Shadow DN5/2A), 29. **4.** Jochen Mass (McLaren M23/6), 29. **5.** Ronnie Peterson (Lotus 72 R9), 29. **6.** Niki Lauda (Ferrari 312T 022), 29 laps.
PP – Lauda, 1;34.85; FL – Brambilla, 1;53.90, 116.08 mph.
Hat-trick of strange GPs – Lauda led in Ferrari set-up in hope track would dry, but rain increased and Hunt took lead on lap 15 with works March in contact and taking lead on lap 19 as Hesketh went onto 7 cylinders. Stuck's works March also very fast, Mark Donohue fatally injured in pre-race March crash.

24-8-75 'Swiss GP,' Dijon-Prenois, F – 60 laps, 122.63 miles
1. Clay Regazzoni (Ferrari 312T 021), 60 laps in 1:01;25.34, 120.61 mph.
2. Patrick Depailler (Tyrrell 007-4), 60 in 1:01;33.69.
3. Jochen Mass (McLaren M23/6), 60. **4.** Ronnie Peterson (Lotus 72 R9), 60. **5.** John Watson (Surtees TS16-05), 60. **6.** Carlos Pace (Brabham BT44B/3), 60.
PP – Jean-Pierre Jarier (Shadow DN5/4A), 59.25; FL – Jarier, 1;00.44, 121.73 mph.
Jarier's Shadow led handsomely until gearbox failed, leaving easy if minor victory to Regazzoni and Ferrari; only 16 starters, which would have been a big field in '50s Formula 1!

THE RACING RECORD

7-9-75 ITALIAN GP,
Monza – 52 laps, 186.76 miles
1. Clay Regazzoni (Ferrari 312T 024), 52 laps in 1;22;42.6, 135.48 mph.
2. Emerson Fittipaldi (McLaren M23/10), 52 in 1;22;59.2.
3. Niki Lauda (Ferrari 312T 023), 52. **4.** Carlos Reutemann (Brabham BT44B/1), 52. **5.** James Hunt (Hesketh 308C-1), 52. **6.** Tom Pryce (Shadow DN5/2A), 52.
PP – Lauda, 1;32.24; FL – Regazzoni, 1;33.1, 138.87 mph.
Repeat of Regazzoni's 1970 Ferrari triumph on their home soil, led start to finish, Lauda deposed late on by Fittipaldi for second place.

5-10-75 UNITED STATES GP,
Watkins Glen, NY – 59 laps, 199.24 miles
1. Niki Lauda (Ferrari 312T 023), 59 laps in 1;42;.58.175, 116.10 mph.
2. Emerson Fittipaldi (McLaren M23/10), 59 in 1;43;03.118.
3. Jochen Mass (McLaren M23/6), 59. **4.** James Hunt (Hesketh 308C-1), 59. **5.** Ronnie Peterson (Lotus 72 R9), 59. **6.** Jody Scheckter (Tyrrell 007-9), 59.
PP – Lauda, 1;42.003; FL – Fittipaldi, 1;43.374, 117.60 mph.
Lauda all the way, fastest in all four practice sessions and held off Fittipaldi for first 20 laps in close duel until lapping delayed Regazzoni and he blocked the McLaren, costing Fittipaldi 13 secs in next five laps, being black-flagged but effectively ruining race, Jarier's Shadow strong third until wheel bearing collapsed after 19 laps.

1976

25-1-76 BRAZILIAN GP,
Interlagos – 40 laps, 197.84 miles
1. Niki Lauda (Ferrari 312T 023), 40 laps in 1;45;16.78, 112.76 mph.
2. Patrick Depailler (Tyrrell 007-4), 40 in 1;45;38.25.
3. Tom Pryce (Shadow DN5/5A), 40. **4.** Hans Stuck Jr (March 761/2), 40. **5.** Jody Scheckter (Tyrrell 007-6), 40. **6.** Jochen Mass (McLaren M23/6), 40.
PP – James Hunt (McLaren M23/8), 2;32.50; FL – Jean-Pierre Jarier (Shadow DN5/6A), 2;35.07, 114.83 mph.
Beaten for pole by Hunt's McLaren, Lauda took lead from team-mate Regazzoni after 9 laps, pulled away until Jarier's Shadow closed to within 2 secs before sliding off on oil – Pryce's Shadow only lost second place due to brake problems towards end.

6-3-76 SOUTH AFRICAN GP,
Kyalami – 78 laps, 198.90 miles
1. Niki Lauda (Ferrari 312T 023), 78 laps in 1;42;18.4, 116.58 mph.
2. James Hunt (McLaren M23/8), 78 in 1;42;19.7.
3. Jochen Mass (McLaren M23/6), 78. **4.** Jody Scheckter (Tyrrell 007-6), 78. **5.** John Watson (Penske PC3-01), 77. **6.** Mario Andretti (Parnelli VPJ4-002), 77.
PP – Hunt, 1;16.10; FL – Lauda, 1;17.94, 117.72 mph.
Hunt's McLaren on pole again but Lauda's race throughout, despite deflating tyre in latter stages; Pryce's Shadow again impressive, losing fourth place due to puncture.

14-3-76 Race of Champions,
Brands Hatch, GB – 40 laps, 105.96 miles
1. James Hunt (McLaren M23/8), 40 laps in 58;01.23, 107.96 mph.
2. Alan Jones (Surtees TS19-02), 40 in 58;19.65.
3. Jacky Ickx (Hesketh 308C/3), 40. **4.** Vittorio Brambilla (March 761/1), 40. **5.** Chris Amon (Ensign N174 MN-02), 39. **6.** Tom Pryce (Shadow DN5/5A), 39.
PP – Jody Scheckter (Tyrrell 007-6), 1;20.42; FL – Hunt, 1;23.78, 112.15 mph.
Sensational Surtees debut for Alan Jones, taking lead on first lap, Hunt going by and pulling away to 18 sec win as Jones baulked by back-marker.

28-3-76 UNITED STATES GP WEST,
Long Beach, California – 99 laps, 199.98 miles
1. Clay Regazzoni (Ferrari 312T 024), 80 laps in 1;53;18.471, 85.57 mph.
2. Niki Lauda (Ferrari 312T 023), 80 in 1;54;00.885.
3. Patrick Depailler (Tyrrell 007-4), 80. **4.** Jacques Laffite (Ligier-Matra V12 JS5-01), 80. **5.** Jochen Mass (McLaren M23/6), 80. **6.** Emerson Fittipaldi (Fittipaldi FD04-1), 79.
PP – Regazzoni, 1;23.099; FL – Regazzoni, 1;23.076, 87.53 mph.
Utter domination for Regazzoni – pole, led whole distance, fastest lap. Lauda hampered by 'transmission vibration', Depailler pushed Hunt's McLaren out of race on lap 3 . . . Hunt *was* cross.

11-4-76 BRDC International Trophy,
Silverstone, GB – 40 laps, 117.28 miles
1. James Hunt (McLaren M23/9), 40 laps in 53;04.57, 132.58 mph.
2. Vittorio Brambilla (March 761/3), 40 in 53;15.81.
3. Jody Scheckter (Tyrrell 007-6), 40. **4.** Tom Pryce (Shadow DN5/5A), 40. **5.** Jean-Pierre Jarier (Shadow DN5/4A), 40. **6.** Gunnar Nilsson (Lotus 77 R2), 40.
PP – Hunt, 1;17.91; FL – Hunt, 1;18.81, 133.93 mph.
Dull minor event, Hunt's McLaren led superbly entire distance.

2-5-76 SPANISH GP,
Jarama, Madrid – 75 laps, 158.63 miles
1. James Hunt (McLaren M23/8-2), 75 laps in 1;42;20.43, 92.95 mph.
2. Niki Lauda (Ferrari 312T 026), 75 in 1;42;51.40.
3. Gunnar Nilsson (Lotus 77 R2), 75. **4.** Carlos Reutemann (Brabham-Alfa Romeo f12 BT45/1), 74. **5.** Chris Amon (Ensign N176 MN-05), 74. **6.** Carlos Pace (Brabham-Alfa Romeo f12 BT45/3), 74.
PP – Hunt, 1;18.52; FL – Jochen Mass (McLaren M23/9), 1;20.93, 94.04 mph.
First race for new airbox, wing, cockpit hoop regs. Lauda/Hunt duel resolved when McLaren took lead on lap 32, Lauda handicapped by rib injury but decisive win for McLaren until post-race disqualification for too-wide rear track (decision later reversed by FIA appeal). Lotus 77s impressive, 6-wheel Tyrrell P34 debut.

16-5-76 BELGIAN GP,
Zolder – 70 laps, 185.38 miles
1. Niki Lauda (Ferrari 312T2 026), 70 laps in 1;42;53.23, 108.11 mph.
2. Clay Regazzoni (Ferrari 312T2 025), 70 in 1;42;56.69.
3. Jacques Laffite (Ligier-Matra V12 JS5-01), 70. **4.** Jody Scheckter (Tyrrell P34/3), 70. **5.** Alan Jones (Surtees TS19-02), 69. **6.** Jochen Mass (McLaren M23/9), 69.
PP – Lauda, 1;26.55; FL – Lauda, 1;25.98, 110.87 mph.
12-cylinders dominant, Ferrari 1-2 from lap 7, Lauda led throughout. Scheckter's first Cosworth car home had broken rear suspension pick-up and was only a length clear of being lapped by winner! Hunt's McLaren fell back from good start, convincing critics its post-Spanish 'legalization' mods had removed its 'cheating' competitiveness . . . they were mistaken.

30-5-76 MONACO GP,
Monte Carlo – 78 laps, 160.52 miles
1. Niki Lauda (Ferrari 312T2 026), 78 laps in 1;59;51.47, 80.36 mph.
2. Jody Scheckter (Tyrrell P34/3), 78 in 2:00;02.60.
3. Patrick Depailler (Tyrrell P34/2), 78. **4.** Hans Stuck Jr (March 761/2), 77. **5.** Jochen Mass (McLaren M23/9), 77. **6.** Emerson Fittipaldi (Fittipaldi FD04-1), 77.
PP – Lauda, 1;29.65; FL – Lauda, 1;30.36, 81.99 mph.
Ferrari's fifth win of season for Lauda, leading throughout; Tyrrells impressed though Depailler finished with another broken rear suspension pick-up; Peterson's March started 3rd, ran 2nd until crashed; Regazzoni crashed Ferrari when challenging Scheckter for 2nd place four laps from finish.

13-6-76 SWEDISH GP,
Anderstorp – 72 laps, 179.78 miles
1. Jody Scheckter (Tyrrell P34/3), 72 laps in 1;46;53.729, 100.85 mph.
2. Patrick Depailler (Tyrrell P34/2), 72 in 1;47;13.495.
3. Niki Lauda (Ferrari 312T2 026), 72. **4.** Jacques Laffite (Ligier-Matra V12 JS5-01), 72. **5.** James Hunt (McLaren M23/8-2), 72. **6.** Clay Regazzoni (Ferrari 312T2 027), 72.
PP – Scheckter, 1;25.659; FL – Mario Andretti (Lotus 77 R1), 1;28.002, 102.13 mph.
Andretti's Lotus 77 started from front row and led 45 laps until engine failed, leaving Tyrrell 6-wheelers triumphant; Amon's Ensign 3rd fastest in practice, ran comfortable 4th until lap 38 crash.

4-7-76 FRENCH GP,
Ricard-Castellet – 54 laps, 194.61 miles
1. James Hunt (McLaren M23/8-2), 54 laps in 1;40;58.60, 115.84 mph.
2. Patrick Depailler (Tyrrell P34/2), 54 in 1;41;11.30.
3. John Watson (Penske PC4-001), 54. **4.** Carlos Pace (Brabham-Alfa Romeo f12 BT45/3), 54. **5.** Mario Andretti (Lotus 77 R1), 54. **6.** Jody Scheckter (Tyrrell P34/3), 54.
PP – Hunt, 1;47.89; FL – Niki Lauda (Ferrari 312T2 026), 1;51.0, 117.09 mph.
Both Ferraris retired with engine seizures one-third distance, Hunt's most dominant win thereafter. Peterson 3rd for March until fuel metering unit failure three laps from end, Watson's Penske disqualified for alleged wing height infringement, later reinstated.

18-7-76 BRITISH GP,
Brands Hatch – 76 laps, 201.40 miles*
**Race stopped after first-corner multiple collision; restarted over full distance, controversially allowing spare cars to be used.*
1. Niki Lauda (Ferrari 312T2 028), 76 laps in 1;44;19.66, 114.82 mph**.
2. Jody Scheckter (Tyrrell P34/3), 76 in 1;44;35.84.
3. John Watson (Penske PC4-001), 75. **4.** Tom Pryce (Shadow DN5/5A), 75. **5.** Alan Jones (Surtees TS19-02), 75. **6.** Emerson Fittipaldi (Fittipaldi FD04-3), 74.
PP – Lauda, 1;19.35; FL – James Hunt (McLaren M23/8-2), 1;19.82, 117.71 mph.
***First on road was Hunt, 76 laps in 1;43;27.61, 115.19 mph, later disqualified by FIA appeal hearing.*
Yet another silly British GP: Ferraris collided in first corner, involving others, including Hunt's McLaren – race restarted with Hunt in prime car; he took lead from Lauda after 43 laps, pulled away to dominant win, only 10 cars running at finish. Ferrari protested McLaren's restart car, and won.

1-8-76 GERMAN GP,
Nürburgring – 14 laps, 198.64 miles
1. James Hunt (McLaren M23/6), 14 laps in 1;41;42.7, 117.18 mph.
2. Jody Scheckter (Tyrrell P34/3), 14 in 1;42;10.4.
3. Jochen Mass (McLaren M23/9), 14. **4.** Carlos Pace (Brabham-Alfa Romeo f12 BT45/4), 14. **5.** Gunnar Nilsson (Lotus 77 R2), 14. **6.** Rolf Stommelen (Brabham-Alfa Romeo f12 BT45/1), 14.
PP – Hunt, 7;06.5; FL – Scheckter, 7;10.8, 118.57 mph.
Hunt's third successive on-road GP win, but Lauda crashed and was burned on lap 2; race stopped and restarted, Hunt's task eased when Regazzoni spun off when 2nd.

15-8-76 AUSTRIAN GP,
Österreichring – 54 laps, 198.34 miles
1. John Watson (Penske PC4-001), 1;30;07.86, 132.03 mph.
2. Jacques Laffite (Ligier-Matra V12 JS-02), 54 in 1;30;18.65.
3. Gunnar Nilsson (Lotus 77 R2), 54. **4.** James Hunt (McLaren M23/8-2), 54. **5.** Mario Andretti (Lotus 77 R3), 54. **6.** Ronnie Peterson (March 761/6), 54.
PP – Hunt, 1;35.02; FL – Hunt, 1;35.91, 137.83 mph.
Ferrari cancelled entries, fine race ensued. Peterson (March)/Watson/Scheckter (Tyrrell)/Nilsson (Lotus) battle resolved as Tyrrell broke suspension and crashed and March brakes faded, Nilsson slowed by fluctuating oil pressure at end, allowing Laffite by.

29-8-76 DUTCH GP,
Zandvoort – 75 laps, 196.95 miles
1. James Hunt (McLaren M23/8-2) 75 laps in 1;44;52.09, 112.69 mph.
2. Clay Regazzoni (Ferrari 312T2 027), 75 in 1;44;53.01.
3. Mario Andretti (Lotus 77 R1), 75. **4.** Tom Pryce (Shadow DN8/1A), 75. **5.** Jody Scheckter (Tyrrell P34/4), 75. **6.** Vittorio Brambilla (March 761/1), 75.
PP – Ronnie Peterson (March 761/6), 1;21.31; FL – John Watson (Penske PC4-001), 1;23.10, 113.76 mph.
'Drive as you would normally, don't think for one minute the honour of Ferrari and of Italy rests with you' – Mr Ferrari to Regazzoni. Peterson's March and Watson's Penske both led early on, Peterson's engine failed, 30-lap Hunt/Watson battle ended with Penske gearbox failure after 48 laps, Regazzoni started his charge just too late . . . Ferrari disapproved.

12-9-76 ITALIAN GP,
Monza – 52 laps, 187.41 miles
1. Ronnie Peterson (March 761/6), 52 laps in 1;30;35.6, 124.12 mph.
2. Clay Regazzoni (Ferrari 312T2 027), 52 in 1;30;37.9.
3. Jacques Laffite (Ligier-Matra V12 JS5-02), 52. **4.** Niki Lauda (Ferrari 312T2 026), 52. **5.** Jody Scheckter (Tyrrell P34/4), 52. **6.** Patrick Depailler (Tyrrell P34/2), 52.
PP – Laffite, 1;41.35; FL – Peterson, 1;41.3, 128.08 mph.
McLaren and Penske practice times disallowed after dubious fuel analysis, steamy Hunt went off when brake-tested by Pryce's Shadow in race, Peterson's March passed Scheckter for lead on lap 11 and was never headed thereafter, Lauda's stunning come-back from injury.

3-10-76 CANADIAN GP,
Mosport Pk, Toronto – 80 laps, 196.72 miles
1. James Hunt (McLaren M23/8-2), 80 laps in 1;40;09.626, 117.843 mph.
2. Patrick Depailler (Tyrrell P34/2), 80 in 1;40;15.957.
3. Mario Andretti (Lotus 77 R1), 80. **4.** Jody Scheckter (Tyrrell P34/4), 80. **5.** Jochen Mass (McLaren M23/9), 80. **6.** Clay Regazzoni (Ferrari 312T2 027), 80.
PP – Hunt, 1;12.389; FL – Depailler, 1;13.817, 119.92 mph.
Early bid from Peterson faded leaving Hunt dominant win.

10-10-76 UNITED STATES GP,
Watkins Glen, NY – 59 laps, 199.24 miles
1. James Hunt (McLaren M23/8-2), 59 laps in 1;42;40.741, 116.43 mph.
2. Jody Scheckter (Tyrrell P34/4), 59 in 1;42;48.771.
3. Niki Lauda (Ferrari 312T2 026), 59. **4.** Jochen Mass (McLaren M23/9), 59. **5.** Hans Stuck Jr (March 761/2), 59. **6.** John Watson (Penske PC4-02), 59.
PP – Hunt, 1;43.622; FL – Hunt, 1;42.851, 118.20 mph.
Great race between Hunt and Scheckter, McLaren led only 18 of 59 laps, Tyrrell 6-wheeler also second on grid – Hunt now within three points of Lauda's Championship lead.

24-10-76 JAPANESE GP,
Fuji – 73 laps, 197.72 miles
1. Mario Andretti (Lotus 77 R1), 73 laps in 1;43;58.86, 114.09 mph.
2. Patrick Depailler (Tyrrell P34/3), 72.
3. James Hunt (McLaren M23/8-2), 72. **4.** Alan Jones (Surtees TS19-04), 72. **5.** Clay Regazzoni (Ferrari 312T2 027), 72. **6.** Gunnar Nilsson (Lotus 77 R2), 72.
PP – Andretti, 1;12.77; FL – Masahiro Hasemi (Kojima KE007/1), 1;18.23, 124.62 mph.
Championship clincher for Hunt, Lauda abandoned race and title in heavy rain. Hunt led to lap 61 when wet tyres failed as track dried, Depailler led two laps before stopping, Andretti ran out winner while Hunt charged back to title-winning third-place finish.

1977

9-1-77 ARGENTINE GP,
Buenos Aires – 53 laps, 196.55 miles
1. Jody Scheckter (Wolf WR1), 53 laps in 1;40;11.19, 117.71 mph.
2. Carlos Pace (Brabham-Alfa Romeo f12 BT45/5), 53 in 1;40;54.43.
3. Carlos Reutemann (Ferrari 312T2 029), 53. **4.** Emerson Fittipaldi (Fittipaldi FD04-3), 53. **5.** Mario Andretti (Lotus 78 R1), 51. **6.** Clay Regazzoni (Ensign N177 MN-06), 51.
PP – James Hunt (McLaren M23/10), 1;48.68; FL – Hunt, 1;51.06, 120.21 mph.
Lucky debut win for Wolf – early leader Watson retired now-competitive Brabham-Alfa when gearbox mounting bolts failed, Hunt's McLaren led comfortably until suspension failure, Pace's Brabham-Alfa led laps 35-47, driver unwell and Scheckter won; Andretti's Lotus should have placed second but rear wheel bearing seized.

23-1-77 BRAZILIAN GP,
Interlagos – 40 laps, 197.84 miles
1. Carlos Reutemann (Ferrari 312T2 029), 40 laps in 1:45;07.72, 112.92 mph.
2. James Hunt (McLaren M23/10), 40 in 1;45;18.43.
3. Niki Lauda (Ferrari 312T2 026), 40. **4.** Emerson Fittipaldi (Fittipaldi FD04-3), 39. **5.** Gunnar Nilsson (Lotus 78 R1), 39. **6.** Renzo Zorzi (Shadow DN5/5A), 39.
PP – Hunt, 2;30.11; FL – Hunt, 2;34.55, 115.21 mph.
Brabham-Alfas potent again, Pace led six laps until collision with Hunt, whose McLaren wore out both front tyres after 24 laps, had to stop to replace them; eight cars crashed on disintegrating track surface.

5-3-77 SOUTH AFRICAN GP,
Kyalami – 78 laps, 198.90 miles
1. Niki Lauda (Ferrari 312T2 030), 78 laps in 1;42;21.6, 116.59 mph.
2. Jody Scheckter (Wolf WR1), 78.
3. Patrick Depailler (Tyrrell P34/2), 78. **4.** James Hunt (McLaren M23/11), 78. **5.** Jochen Mass (McLaren M23/6), 78. **6.** John Watson (Brabham-Alfa Romeo f12 BT45/3), 78.
PP – Hunt, 1;15.96; FL – Watson, 1;17.63, 118.26 mph.
Lauda from lap 7 to finish despite running over debris from tragic Tom Pryce fatal accident, damaging coolers; fine Wolf performance.

20-3-77 Race of Champions,
Brands Hatch, GB – 40 laps, 105.96 miles
1. James Hunt (McLaren M23/10), 40 laps in 53;54.35, 116.36 mph.
2. Jody Scheckter (Wolf WR1), 40 in 54;17.87.
3. John Watson (Brabham-Alfa Romeo f12 BT45/1), 40. **4.** Brian Henton (March 761 Spl), 39. **5.** Jack Oliver (Shadow DN8/1A), 39. **6.** David Purley (LEC Pilbeam R21-01), 39.
PP – Watson, 1;19.05; FL – Hunt, 1;19.48, 118.38 mph.
Andretti's Lotus 78 led for 34 laps until electrical failure, Hunt inheriting win, Watson delayed from pole start by stop to change blistered front tyre.

3-4-77 UNITED STATES GP WEST,
Long Beach, California – 80 laps, 161.60 miles
1. Mario Andretti (Lotus 78 R3), 80 laps in 1;51;35.470, 89.89 mph.
2. Niki Lauda (Ferrari 312T2 030), 80 in 1;51;36.243.
3. Jody Scheckter (Wolf WR1), 80. **4.** Patrick Depailler (Tyrrell P34/2), 80. **5.** Emerson Fittipaldi (Fittipaldi FD04-3), 80. **6.** Jean-Pierre Jarier (ATS Penske PC4-002), 79.
PP – Lauda, 1;21.630; FL – Lauda, 1;21.650, 89.09 mph.
Classic race, first-corner collisions, Scheckter led 77 laps with Lotus and Ferrari in close contact before slow puncture let them by.

8-5-77 SPANISH GP,
Jarama, Madrid – 75 laps, 158.65 miles
1. Mario Andretti (Lotus 78 R3), 75 laps in 1;42;52.22, 91.79 mph.
2. Carlos Reutemann (Ferrari 312T2 029), 75 in 1;43;08.07.
3. Jody Scheckter (Wolf WR2), 75. **4.** Jochen Mass (McLaren M23/12), 75. **5.** Gunnar Nilsson (Lotus 78 R2), 75. **6.** Hans Stuck Jr (Brabham-Alfa Romeo f12 BT45/1), 74.
PP – Andretti, 1;18.70; FL – Jacques Laffite (Ligier-Matra V12 JS7-02), 1;20.81, 94.24 mph.
Lotus 78 dominance begins, though Brabham-Alfas will shine mid-season. Andretti fastest in three practice sessions, led start to finish, only Laffite's Ligier-Matra could keep Lotus in sight but stopped after 12 laps for loose rear wheel to be tightened, miserable McLaren M26 debut for Hunt, Lauda did not start.

22-5-77 MONACO GP,
Monte Carlo – 76 laps, 156.44 miles
1. Jody Scheckter (Wolf WR1), 76 laps in 1;57;52.77, 79.61 mph.
2. Niki Lauda (Ferrari 312T2 030), 76 in 1:57;53.66.
3. Carlos Reutemann (Ferrari 312T2 029), 76.
4. Jochen Mass (McLaren M23/12), 76. **5.** Mario Andretti (Lotus 78 R3), 76. **6.** Alan Jones (Shadow DN8/3A), 76.
PP – John Watson (Brabham-Alfa Romeo f12 BT45/5), 1;29.86; FL – Scheckter, 1;31.07, 81.35 mph.
Wolf throughout for Cosworth's 100th GP win, Watson's Brabham-Alfa challenged but slowed with brake then terminal gearbox trouble, Scheckter eased off to final winning margin.

5-6-77 BELGIAN GP,
Zolder – 70 laps, 185.38 miles
1. Gunnar Nilsson (Lotus 78 R2), 70 laps in 1;55;05.71, 96.64 mph.
2. Niki Lauda (Ferrari 312T2 030), 70 in 1;55;19.90.
3. Ronnie Peterson (Tyrrell P34/5), 70. **4.** Vittorio Brambilla (Surtees TS19-06), 70. **5.** Alan Jones (Shadow DN8/3A), 70. **6.** Hans Stuck Jr (Brabham-Alfa Romeo f12 BT45/1), 69.
PP – Mario Andretti (Lotus 78 R3), 1;24.64; FL – Nilsson 1;27.54, 108.96 mph.
Very wet race, Andretti/Watson collision on first lap, Nilsson showed Lotus 78 potential by catching Lauda's leading Ferrari after tardy stop to fit dry tyres, took lead with 20 laps to run.

19-6-77 SWEDISH GP,
Anderstorp – 72 laps, 179.78 miles
1. Jacques Laffite (Ligier-Matra V12 JS7-02), 72 laps in 1;46;55.520, 100.85 mph.
2. Jochen Mass (McLaren M23/12), 72 in 1;47;03.969.
3. Carlos Reutemann (Ferrari 312T2 029), 72.
4. Patrick Depailler (Tyrrell P34/7), 72. **5.** John Watson (Brabham-Alfa Romeo f12 BT45/6), 72.
6. Mario Andretti (Lotus 78 R3), 72.
PP – Andretti, 1;25.404; FL – Andretti, 1;27.607, 102.61 mph.

Lucky but popular V12 win. Andretti's Lotus 78 took lead from Watson on lap 2 but metering unit flopped onto 'full rich' and forced fuel top-up stop two laps from end, giving Laffite victory; Watson/Wolf collision, Hunt's M26 delayed by stop for tyres.

3-7-77 FRENCH GP,
Dijon-Prenois – 80 laps, 188.89 miles
1. Mario Andretti (Lotus 78 R3), 80 laps in 1:39;40.13, 113.71 mph.
2. John Watson (Brabham-Alfa Romeo f12 BT45/6), 80 in 1:39;41.68.
3. James Hunt (McLaren M26/2), 80. **4.** Gunnar Nilsson (Lotus 78 R2), 80. **5.** Niki Lauda (Ferrari 312T2 031), 80. **6.** Carlos Reutemann (Ferrari 312T2 029), 79.
PP – Andretti, 1;12.21; FL – Andretti, 1;13.75, 115.34 mph.
Watson Brabham-Alfa should have won brilliant victory but fuel dried on final lap, having led from lap 3; Andretti had settled for 2nd place but given very lucky win.

16-7-77 BRITISH GP,
Silverstone – 68 laps, 199.58 miles
1. James Hunt (McLaren M26/2), 68 laps in 1:31;46.06, 130.36 mph.
2. Niki Lauda (Ferrari 312T2 031), 68 in 1:32;04.37.
3. Gunnar Nilsson (Lotus 78 R2), 68. **4.** Jochen Mass (McLaren M26/3), 68. **5.** Hans Stuck Jr (Brabham-Alfa Romeo f12 BT45/3), 68. **6.** Jacques Laffite (Ligier-Matra V12 JS7-01), 67.
PP – Hunt, 1;18.49; FL – Hunt, 1;19.60, 132.60 mph.
Watson and Brabham-Alfa again dominant for 50 laps, first from Lauda, then Hunt, until fuel pick-up then engine problems sidelined it; Andretti engine failure, M26's maiden win. Renault turbo debut.

31-7-77 GERMAN GP,
Hockenheim – 47 laps, 198.25 miles
1. Niki Lauda (Ferrari 312T2 031), 47 laps in 1:31;48.62, 129.48 mph.
2. Jody Scheckter (Wolf WR2), 47 in 1:32;02.95.
3. Hans Stuck Jr (Brabham-Alfa Romeo f12 BT45/3), 47. **4.** Carlos Reutemann (Ferrari 312T2 029), 47. **5.** Vittorio Brambilla (Surtees TS19-06), 47.
6. Patrick Tambay (Ensign N177 MN-08), 47.
PP – Scheckter, 1;53.07; FL – Lauda, 1;55.99, 130.83 mph.
Wolf led 12 laps before Lauda got by, then handicapped by fuel pick-up problems; Brabham-Alfa again thirsty, Stuck coasting over line with engine dead; Lotus 78 engine failures.

14-8-77 AUSTRIAN GP,
Österreichring – 54 laps, 199.39 miles
1. Alan Jones (Shadow DN8/4A), 54 laps in 1:37;16.49, 122.99 mph.
2. Niki Lauda (Ferrari 312T2 031) 54 in 1:37;36.62.
3. Hans Stuck Jr (Brabham-Alfa Romeo f12 BT45/3), 54. **4.** Carlos Reutemann (Ferrari 312T2 029), 54. **5.** Ronnie Peterson (Tyrrell P34/6), 54.
6. Jochen Mass (McLaren M26/1), 53.
PP – Lauda, 1;39.32; FL – John Watson (Brabham-Alfa Romeo f12 BT45/5), 1;40.96, 137.83 mph.
Wet start saw Andretti's Lotus 78 lead 10 laps before engine blew; team-mate Nilsson changed onto slicks when 2nd, rocketed back up to third behind Hunt's leading M26 then engine failed; Hunt's leading M26 also blew, leaving maiden victory to Jones and Shadow.

28-8-77 DUTCH GP,
Zandvoort – 75 laps, 196.65 miles
1. Niki Lauda (Ferrari 312T2 030), 75 laps in 1:41;45.93, 116.12 mph.
2. Jacques Laffite (Ligier-Matra V12 JS7-02), 75 in 1:41;47.82.
3. Jody Scheckter (Wolf WR2), 74. **4.** Emerson Fittipaldi (Fittipaldi F5/2), 74. **5.** Patrick Tambay (Ensign N177 MN-08), 73. **6.** Carlos Reutemann (Ferrari 312T2 029), 73.
PP – Mario Andretti (Lotus 78 R3), 1;18.65; FL – Niki Lauda, 1;19.99, 118.18 mph.
Hunt's M26 led five laps until Andretti passed round outside at Tarzan and cars collided, Hunt going out; Andretti's engine broke nine laps later, Lauda consolidated Championship lead.

11-9-77 ITALIAN GP,
Monza – 52 laps, 187.41 miles
1. Mario Andretti (Lotus 78 R3), 52 laps in 1:27;50.30, 128.01 mph.
2. Niki Lauda (Ferrari 312T2 031), 52 in 1:28;07.26.
3. Alan Jones (Shadow DN8/4A), 52. **4.** Jochen Mass (McLaren M26/3), 52. **5.** Clay Regazzoni (Ensign N177 MN-07), 52. **6.** Ronnie Peterson (Tyrrell P34/6), 52.
PP – James Hunt (McLaren M26/2), 1;38.08; FL – Andretti, 1;39.10, 130.92 mph.
Scheckter's Wolf led 10 laps, Andretti went by to dominant victory, Wolf's engine blew in attempt to keep Lotus 78 in sight, Hunt spun when 3rd early on, later retired with brake problems.

2-10-77 UNITED STATES GP,
Watkins Glen, NY – 59 laps, 199.24 miles
1. James Hunt (McLaren M26/2), 59 laps in 1:58;23.267, 100.98 mph.
2. Mario Andretti (Lotus 78 R3), 59 in 1:58;25.293.
3. Jody Scheckter (Wolf WR1), 59. **4.** Niki Lauda (Ferrari 312T2 031), 59. **5.** Clay Regazzoni (Ensign N177 MN-07), 59. **6.** Carlos Reutemann (Ferrari 312T2 030), 58.
PP – Hunt, 1;40.863; FL – Ronnie Peterson (Tyrrell P34/6), 1;51.854, 108.69 mph.
Very wet race dominated by superb Hans Stuck Brabham-Alfa drive until lap 14 crash when clutchless car jumped out of gear; Hunt won from Andretti closing all the time, Lauda's 4th place clinched his title.

9-10-77 CANADIAN GP,
Mosport Pk, Toronto – 80 laps, 196.72 miles
1. Jody Scheckter (Wolf WR1), 80 laps in 1:40;00.00, 118.03 mph.
2. Patrick Depailler (Tyrrell P34/7), 80 in 1:40;06.77.
3. Jochen Mass (McLaren M26/3), 80. **4.** Alan Jones (Shadow DN8/5A), 80. **5.** Patrick Tambay (Ensign N177 MN-08), 80. **6.** Vittorio Brambilla (Surtees TS19-06), 78.
PP – Mario Andretti (Lotus 78 R3), 1;11.385; FL – Andretti, 1;13.299, 120.94 mph.
Andretti's dominant Lotus 78 slowed so much that Scheckter had just unlapped himself in 2nd place when Lotus engine blew. Earlier on, Hunt's narrowly leading McLaren had been inadvertently put out by team-mate Mass while lapping him.

23-10-77 JAPANESE GP,
Fuji – 73 laps, 197.72 mph
1. James Hunt (McLaren M26/3), 73 laps in 1:31;51.68, 129.15 mph.
2. Carlos Reutemann (Ferrari 312T2 029), 73 in 1:32;54.13.
3. Patrick Depailler (Tyrrell P34/7), 73. **4.** Alan Jones (Shadow DN8/5A), 73. **5.** Jacques Laffite (Ligier-Matra V12 JS7-02), 72. **6.** Riccardo Patrese (Shadow DN8/3A), 72.
PP – Mario Andretti (Lotus 78 R3), 1;12.23; FL – Jody Scheckter (Wolf WR3), 1;14.30, 131.24 mph.
Hunt's McLaren all the way; Andretti out in 2nd-lap collision while chasing Hunt, Mass's M26 2nd until lap 28 engine breakage, Regazzoni's Ensign then 2nd until engine failure, Laffite's turn then in Ligier-Matra but out of fuel on last lap, giving Ferrari lucky placing.

1978

15-1-78 ARGENTINE GP,
Buenos Aires – 53 laps, 196.55 miles
1. Mario Andretti (Lotus 78 R3), 52 laps in 1:37;04.47, 119.19 mph.
2. Niki Lauda (Brabham-Alfa Romeo f12 BT45/7), 52 in 1:37;17.68.
3. Patrick Depailler (Tyrrell 008-1), 52. **4.** James Hunt (McLaren M26/4), 52. **5.** Ronnie Peterson (Lotus 78 R2), 52. **6.** Patrick Tambay McLaren M26/3), 52.
PP – Andretti, 1;47.75; FL – Gilles Villeneuve (Ferrari 312T2 027), 1;49.76, 121.63 mph.
Andretti's Lotus from start to finish; brief challenge from Watson's Brabham-Alfa.

29-1-78 BRAZILIAN GP,
Jacarepaguá, Rio de Janeiro – 63 laps, 196.94 miles
1. Carlos Reutemann (Ferrari 312T2 031) 63 laps in 1:49;50.86, 107.43 mph.
2. Emerson Fittipaldi (Fittipaldi F5A/1), 63 in 1:50;48.99.
3. Niki Lauda (Brabham-Alfa Romeo f12 BT45/7), 63. **4.** Mario Andretti (Lotus 78 R3), 63. **5.** Clay Regazzoni (Shadow DN8/5A), 62. **6.** Didier Pironi (Tyrrell 008-2), 62.
PP – Ronnie Peterson (Lotus 78 R2), 1;40.45; FL – Reutemann, 1;43.07, 109.19 mph.
Michelin's first modern GP victory on dominant Ferrari in terrific heat, Fittipaldi's best finish in family F1 car, Andretti lost 2nd place with gearbox trouble.

4-3-78 SOUTH AFRICAN GP,
Kyalami – 78 laps, 198.90 miles
1. Ronnie Peterson (Lotus 78 R2), 78 laps in 1;42;15.76, 116.70 mph.
2. Patrick Depailler (Tyrrell 008-3), 78 in 1:42;16.23.
3. John Watson (Brabham-Alfa Romeo f12 BT46/3), 78. **4.** Alan Jones (Williams FW06/1), 78.
5. Jacques Laffite (Ligier-Matra V12 JS7-01), 78.
6. Didier Pironi (Tyrrell 008-2), 77.
PP – Niki Lauda (Brabham-Alfa Romeo f12 BT46/4), 1;14.65; FL – Mario Andretti (Lotus 78 R3), 1;17.09, 119.08 mph.
Classic race with Patrese's new Arrows taking lead on less critical tyre combination then leading Andretti/Scheckter/Lauda group, engine blew 14 laps to go. Depailler led Andretti and Peterson, Mario fuel stop four laps to go, Tyrrell fuel pick-up hiccup into last lap and Peterson just squeezed by; Watson had spun on oil when leading Peterson towards end.

19-3-78 BRDC International Trophy,
Silverstone, GB – 40 laps, 117.40 miles
1. Keke Rosberg (Theodore TR1/2), 40 laps in 1:12;49.02, 96.64 mph.
2. Emerson Fittipaldi (Fittipaldi F5A/2), 40 in 1:12;50.90.
3. Tony Trimmer (McLaren M23/14), 37. **4.** Brett Lunger (McLaren M23/11), 37. UNC **'5th'** Rupert Keegan (Surtees TS19-07), 31. UNC **'6th'** Hans Stuck Jr (Shadow DN9/1A), 25.
PP – Ronnie Peterson (Lotus 78 R2), 1;16.07; FL – Fittipaldi, 1;38.63, 107.02 mph.
Flooded race, Daly's Hesketh 308E led, new Lotus 79 one of many cars to crash, after dozen laps Rosberg's 'no-hoper' established in winning lead – a day for sheer wet-weather control.

2-4-78 UNITED STATES GP WEST,
Long Beach, California – 80 laps, 162.89 miles
1. Carlos Reutemann (Ferrari 312T3 032), 80 laps in 1:52;01.301, 87.10 mph.
2. Mario Andretti (Lotus 78 R3), 80 in 1:52;12.362.
3. Patrick Depailler (Tyrrell 008-1), 80. **4.** Ronnie Peterson (Lotus 78 R2), 80. **5.** Jacques Laffite (Ligier-Matra V12 JS7-03), 80. **6.** Riccardo Patrese (Arrows FA1/2), 79.
PP – Reutemann, 1;20.636; FL – Alan Jones (Williams FW06/2), 1;22.215, 88.45 mph.
38 laps led by Villeneuve's Ferrari before he ran into back-marker, Reutemann then challenged hard by Jones's Williams until its nose aerofoils collapsed and fuel pick-up faltered.

7-5-78 MONACO GP,
Monte Carlo – 75 laps, 154.35 miles
1. Patrick Depailler (Tyrrell 008-3), 75 laps in 1:55;14.66, 80.36 mph.
2. Niki Lauda (Brabham-Alfa Romeo f12 BT46/4), 75 in 1:55;37.11.
3. Jody Scheckter (Wolf WR1), 75. **4.** John Watson (Brabham-Alfa Romeo f12 BT46/3), 75. **5.** Didier Pironi (Tyrrell 008-4), 75. **6.** Riccardo Patrese (Arrows FA1/2), 75.
PP – Carlos Reutemann (Ferrari 312T3 032), 1;28.34; FL – Lauda, 1;28.65, 83.67 mph.
Depailler's maiden win in six years of F1, beat off Brabhams when Watson's brakes wore and Lauda forced to change deflating tyre. Wolf lost 2nd place only in last three laps when gearbox lost 2nd gear, Ferrari practice promise foiled by collision and crash in race.

21-5-78 BELGIAN GP,
Zolder – 70 laps, 185.38 miles
1. Mario Andretti (Lotus 79 R2), 70 laps in 1:39;52.02, 111.31 mph.
2. Ronnie Peterson (Lotus 78 R2), 70 in 1;40;01.92.
3. Carlos Reutemann (Ferrari 312T3 033), 70.
4. Gilles Villeneuve (Ferrari 312T3 034), 70.
5. Jacques Laffite (Ligier-Matra V12 JS79-01), 69.
6. Didier Pironi (Tyrrell 008-4), 69.
PP – Andretti, 1;20.90; FL – Peterson, 1;23.13, 114.66 mph.
Colin Chapman's 50th birthday Lotus 1-2, Andretti undisputedly superior in 79, Peterson 2nd in 78 after chase through field following stop to change front tyres. Villeneuve delayed when front tyre deflated, drove lap on rim; Reutemann slowed by persistent understeer. Hunt, Lauda, Scheckter hopes end in startline shunt.

4-6-78 SPANISH GP,
Jarama, Madrid – 75 laps, 158.65 miles
1. Mario Andretti (Lotus 79 R3), 75 laps in 1:41;47.06, 93.53 mph.
2. Ronnie Peterson (Lotus 79 R2), 75 in 1:42;06.62.
3. Jacques Laffite (Ligier-Matra JS9-01), 75.
4. Jody Scheckter (Wolf WR5), 75. **5.** John Watson (Brabham-Alfa Romeo f12 BT46/4), 75. **6.** James Hunt (McLaren M26/3), 74.
PP – Andretti, 1;16.39; FL – Andretti, 1;20.06, 95.10 mph.
Lotus 79s 1-2, Hunt's M26 on sticky tyres led five laps, lay 2nd for 50 before stop for fresh tyres, Peterson recovered from dreadful start.

17-6-78 SWEDISH GP,
Anderstorp – 70 laps, 175.33 miles
1. Niki Lauda (Brabham-Alfa Romeo f12 BT46B/6), 70 laps in 1:41;00.606, 104.14 mph.
2. Riccardo Patrese (Arrows FA1/4), 70 in 1;41;34.625.
3. Ronnie Peterson (Lotus 79 R2), 70 in 1:41;34.711. **4.** Patrick Tambay (McLaren M26/5), 69. **5.** Clay Regazzoni (Shadow DN9/4A), 69.
6. Emerson Fittipaldi (Fittipaldi F5A/3), 69.
PP – Mario Andretti (Lotus 79 R3), 1;22.058; FL – Lauda, 1;24.836, 106.25 mph.
Ingenious Brabham fan-cars triumphant; Andretti held off Lauda for 40 laps until fan-car exploited advantage on oily surface, Lotus's engine blew on lap 46. Patrese muscled-out Peterson's efforts to take 2nd place after early Lotus stop to replace punctured rear tyre, Watson's fan-car spun in 4th place, sand clogging throttle slides causing retirement.

1-7-78 FRENCH GP,
Ricard-Castellet – 54 laps, 194.95 miles
1. Mario Andretti (Lotus 79 R3), 54 laps in 1:38;51.92, 118.31 mph.
2. Ronnie Peterson (Lotus 79 R2), 54 in 1:38;54.85.
3. James Hunt (McLaren M26/3), 54. **4.** John Watson (Brabham-Alfa Romeo BT46/4), 54.
5. Alan Jones (Williams FW06/1), 54. **6.** Jody Scheckter (Wolf WR5), 54.
PP – Watson, 1;44.41; FL – Carlos Reutemann (Ferrari 312T3 036), 1;48.56, 119.67 mph.
Hunt kept dominant 79s in sight after Watson led first half-lap, in non-fan Brabham – Hunt spun on last lap, physically sick with effort.

16-7-78 BRITISH GP,
Brands Hatch – 76 laps, 198.36 miles
1. Carlos Reutemann (Ferrari 312T3 033), 76 laps in 1:42;12.39, 116.61 mph.
2. Niki Lauda (Brabham-Alfa Romeo f12 BT46/6), 76 in 1:42;13.62.
3. John Watson (Brabham-Alfa Romeo f12 BT46/5), 76. **4.** Patrick Depailler (Tyrrell 008-3), 76.
5. Hans Stuck Jr (Shadow DN9/1A), 75. **6.** Patrick Tambay (McLaren M26/5), 75.
PP – Ronnie Peterson (Lotus 79 R2), 1;16.80; FL – Lauda, 1;18.60, 119.71 mph.
79s dominated practice, drew away one second per lap in race before Peterson fuel pump failure and Andretti puncture. New Wolf WR5 wing-car led up to lap 39 when gearbox failed; Lauda inherited lead, caught by Reutemann who got by when back-marker baulked Brabham-Alfa on lap 60.

30-7-78 GERMAN GP,
Hockenheim – 45 laps, 189.81 miles
1. Mario Andretti (Lotus 79 R3), 45 laps in 1:28;00.90, 129.39 mph.
2. Jody Scheckter (Wolf WR5), 45 in 1:28;16.25.
3. Jacques Laffite (Ligier-Matra V12 JS9-01), 45.
4. Emerson Fittipaldi (Fittipaldi F5A/1), 45.
5. Didier Pironi (Tyrrell 008-2), 45. **6.** Hector Rebaque (Lotus 78 R4), 45.
PP – Andretti, 1;51.90; FL – Ronnie Peterson (Lotus 79 R2), 1;55.62, 131.33 mph.
Peterson led five laps, let Andretti by but later stuck in 4th gear before transmission failed; Scheckter last but one due to early fuel vaporization but recovered to take 2nd; Jones's Williams 3rd behind 79s until lap 31 retirement with fuel vapourization.

13-8-78 AUSTRIAN GP,
Österreichring – 54 laps, 199.39 miles*
**Race stopped after seven laps due to torrential rain, restarted over remaining 47 laps.*
PART ONE: 1. Peterson; **2.** Depailler; **3.** Watson; **4.** Laffite; **5.** Jones; **6.** Lauda.
PART TWO: 1. Peterson; **2.** Depailler; **3.** Villeneuve; **4.** Fittipaldi; **5.** Brambilla; **6.** Laffite.

AGGREGATE:
1. Ronnie Peterson (Lotus 79 R2), 54 laps in 1:41;21.50, 118.03 mph.
2. Patrick Depailler (Tyrrell 008-3), 54 in 1:42;09.00.
3. Gilles Villeneuve (Ferrari 312T3 034), 54.
4. Emerson Fittipaldi (Fittipaldi F5A/1), 53.
5. Jacques Laffite (Ligier-Matra V12 JS9-02), 53.
6. Vittorio Brambilla (Surtees TS20-02), 53.
Drivers placed in races but not in final aggregate drove following cars; John Watson (Brabham-Alfa Romeo f12 BT46/5); Didier Pironi (Tyrrell 008-2); Niki Lauda (Brabham-Alfa Romeo f12 BT46/6).
PP – Peterson, 1;37.71; FL – Race 2, Peterson, 1;43.12, 128.91 mph.
Peterson spun off on lap 8 only to find race had been stopped ending lap 7. Track dried in Part Two, everyone changed onto slicks, Andretti crashed lap 1 of first race, Peterson easy winner overall.

27-8-78 DUTCH GP,
Zandvoort – 75 laps, 196.65 miles
1. Mario Andretti (Lotus 79 R4), 75 laps in 1:41;04.23, 116.92 mph.
2. Ronnie Peterson (Lotus 79 R2), 75 in 1:41;04.55.
3. Niki Lauda (Brabham-Alfa Romeo f12 BT46/7), 75. **4.** John Watson (Brabham-Alfa Romeo f12 BT46/5), 75. **5.** Emerson Fittipaldi (Fittipaldi F5A/1), 75. **6.** Gilles Villeneuve (Ferrari 312T3 034), 75.
PP – Andretti, 1;16.36; FL – Lauda, 1;19.57, 118.81 mph.
Fourth Lotus 1-2 of year, led Lauda throughout, record eight Lotus GP wins in season.

10-9-78 ITALIAN GP,
Monza – 52 laps, 187.41 miles*
**Race stopped after first-lap multiple collision, restarted over 40 laps, 144.16 miles*
1. Niki Lauda (Brabham-Alfa Romeo f12 BT46/7), 40 laps in 1:07;04.54, 128.95 mph.
2. John Watson (Brabham-Alfa Romeo f12 BT46/5), 40 in 1:07;06.02.
3. Carlos Reutemann (Ferrari 312T3 035), 40.
4. Jacques Laffite (Ligier-Matra V12 JS9-02), 40.
5. Patrick Tambay (McLaren M26/3), 40. **6.** Mario Andretti (Lotus 79 R4), 40**.
***Time of 1:07;50.87 includes 60 sec penalty for jumping start; actually first on road with true time of 1:06;50.87, 16 secs ahead of Lauda's Brabham.*
PP – Andretti, 1;37.520; FL – Andretti, 1;38.23, 132.08 mph.
Tragic race, fatal Peterson multiple accident. Late afternoon restart saw Villeneuve/Andretti battle resolved five laps from end as Ferrari tyres faded and Andretti easily drove past, both penalized for jumping start leaving cheerless Brabham-Alfa 1-2. Andretti wins World title.

1-10-78 UNITED STATES GP,
Watkins Glen, NY – 59 laps, 199.24 miles
1. Carlos Reutemann (Ferrari 312T3 035), 59 laps in 1:40;48.800, 118.58 mph.
2. Alan Jones (Williams FW06/1), 59 in 1:41;08.539.
3. Jody Scheckter (Wolf WR6), 59. **4.** Jean-Pierre Jabouille (Renault turbo V6 RS01/2), 59.
5. Emerson Fittipaldi (Fittipaldi F5A/2), 59.
6. Patrick Tambay (McLaren M26/7), 59.
PP – Andretti, 1;38.114; FL – Jean-Pierre Jarier (Lotus 79 R1), 1;39.537, 112.11 mph.
Andretti on pole by second, but stub axle sheared on race morning, had to take second 79, held off Ferraris for lap then dropped back until engine blew. Villeneuve 2nd in dominant Ferrari 1-2 until lap 22 engine failure, good Williams and turbo Renault performances, Jarier in second Lotus out of fuel when 3rd with three laps to run. Renault's first points.

8-10-78 CANADIAN GP,
Ile Notre Dame, Montreal – 70 laps, 195.73 miles
1. Gilles Villeneuve (Ferrari 312T3 034), 70 laps in 1:57;49.196, 99.67 mph.
2. Jody Scheckter (Wolf WR6), 70 in 1:58;02.568.
3. Carlos Reutemann (Ferrari 312T3 035), 70.
4. Riccardo Patrese (Arrows A1/3), 70. **5.** Patrick Depailler (Tyrrell 008-3), 70. **6.** Derek Daly (Ensign N177 MN-06), 70.
PP – Jean-Pierre Jarier (Lotus 79 R3), 1;38.015; FL – Alan Jones (Williams FW06/1), 1;38.077, 102.64 mph.
Jarier confirmed 79's class by leading decisively until major oil leak after 49 laps; Andretti/Watson collision in early stages.

1979

21-1-79 ARGENTINE GP,
Buenos Aires – 53 laps, 196.55 miles*
**Race stopped after first-lap multiple accident, restarted over full distance.*
1. Jacques Laffite (Ligier JS11-02), 53 laps in 1:36;03.21, 122.78 mph.
2. Carlos Reutemann (Lotus 79 R2), 53 in 1:36;18.15.
3. John Watson (McLaren M28/2), 53. **4.** Patrick Depailler (Ligier JS11-03), 53. **5.** Mario Andretti (Lotus 79 R4**), 52. **6.** Emerson Fittipaldi (Fittipaldi F5A/1), 52.
***Used spare car in restart after damaging 79 R3 in 'first race' accident.*
PP – Laffite, 1;44.20; FL – Laffite, 1;28.76, 118.40 mph.
Brilliant Ligier-Cosworth ground-effects car debut, 1-2 on grid, restarted race had 20 starters; Depailler led before fuel pressure misfire, Laffite taking over from lap 11.

4-2-79 BRAZILIAN GP,
Interlagos – 40 laps, 197.84 miles
1. Jacques Laffite (Ligier JS11-02), 40 laps in 1:40;09.64, 117.23 mph.
2. Patrick Depailler (Ligier JS11-03), 40 in 1:40;14.92.
3. Carlos Reutemann (Lotus 79 R2), 40. **4.** Didier Pironi (Tyrrell 009-2), 40. **5.** Gilles Villeneuve (Ferrari 312T3 034), 39. **6.** Jody Scheckter (Ferrari 312T3 035), 39.

PP – Laffite, 2;23.07; FL – Laffite, 2;28.76, 118.40 mph.
Ligiers shine again, Fittipaldi's F5A challenged Reutemann's position in early stages before stop to fix loose rear wheel.

3-3-79 SOUTH AFRICAN GP,
Kyalami – 78 laps, 198.90 miles
1. Gilles Villeneuve (Ferrari 312T4 037), 79 laps in 1:41;.49.96, 117.19 mph.
2. Jody Scheckter (Ferrari 312T4 038), 78 in 1:41;53.38.
3. Jean-Pierre Jarier (Tyrrell 009-3), 78. **4.** Mario Andretti (Lotus 79 R5), 78. **5.** Carlos Reutemann (Lotus 79 R2), 78. **6.** Niki Lauda (Brabham-Alfa Romeo V12 BT48/2), 77.
PP – Jean-Pierre Jabouille (Renault turbo V6 RS01-02), 1;11.80; FL – Villeneuve; 1;14.412, 123.37 mph.
Debut race dominance for Ferrari T4s, race stopped after three laps due to rainstorm when turbo Renaults and Ferraris fighting torrid duel. Race restarted over 76 laps balance, track still wet; Villeneuve on wets, stopped for slicks as track dried at 15 laps; Scheckter led up to lap 52 when he changed slicks, leaving team-mate to win while he recovered 2nd place.

8-4-79 UNITED STATES GP WEST,
Long Beach – 80 laps, 161.52 miles
1. Gilles Villeneuve (Ferrari 312T4 037), 80 laps in 1:50;04.00, 87.81 mph.
2. Jody Scheckter (Ferrari 312T4 038), 80 in 1:50;18.00.
3. Alan Jones (Williams FW06/04), 80. **4.** Mario Andretti (Lotus 79 R5), 80. **5.** Patrick Depailler (Ligier JS11-03), 80. **6.** Jean-Pierre Jarier (Tyrrell 009-3), 79.
PP – Villeneuve, 1;18.825; FL – Villeneuve, 1;21.200, 89.56 mph.
Villeneuve and Ferrari demonstration and fine drive from Jones keeping 'T4s in sight.

15-4-79 Race of Champions,
Brands Hatch, GB – 40 laps, 104.54 miles
1. Gilles Villeneuve (Ferrari 312T3 033), 40 laps in 53;17.12, 117.72 mph.
2. Nelson Piquet (Brabham-Alfa Romeo V12 BT48/1), 40 in 53;31.19.
3. Mario Andretti (Lotus 79 R4), 40. **4.** Jochen Mass (Arrows A1/2A), 40. **5.** Niki Lauda (Brabham-Alfa Romeo V12 BT48/2), 39. **6.** Elio de Angelis (Shadow DN9/4B), 39.
PP – Andretti, 1;17.52; FL – Piquet, 1;17.46, 121.47 mph.
Lauda led in BT48 ground-effects car until wrong-choice tyres blistered, lap 8; Villeneuve's elderly 'T3 led one lap before Andretti passed but Lotus tyre/gearbox/brake problems allowed Villeneuve through again on lap 28 for third F1 win in a row; promising Piquet 2nd after changing blistered tyre.

29-4-79 SPANISH GP,
Jarama, Madrid – 75 laps, 158.65 miles
1. Patrick Depailler (Ligier JS11-03), 75 laps in 1;39;11.84, 95.97 mph.
2. Carlos Reutemann (Lotus 79 R2), 75 in 1:39;32.78.
3. Mario Andretti (Lotus 80 R1), 75. **4.** Jody Scheckter (Ferrari 312T4 039), 75. **5.** Jean-Pierre Jarier (Tyrrell 009-3), 75. **6.** Didier Pironi (Tyrrell 009-1), 75.
PP – Jacques Laffite (Ligier JS11-02), 1;14.50; FL – Gilles Villeneuve (Ferrari 312T4 037), 1;16.44, 99.61 mph.
Another Ligier 1-2 looked set until Laffite missed gear on lap 16 and blew engine; Depailler led throughout, Andretti impressive in Lotus 80 debut beat Scheckter and Jarier in close battle.

13-5-79 BELGIAN GP,
Zolder – 70 laps 185.38 miles
1. Jody Scheckter (Ferrari 312T4 040), 70 laps in 1:39;59.53, 111.24 mph.
2. Jacques Laffite (Ligier JS11-02), 70 in 1:40;14.89.
3. Didier Pironi (Tyrrell 009-1), 70. **4.** Carlos Reutemann (Lotus 79 R2), 70. **5.** Riccardo Patrese (Arrows A1/6A), 70. **6.** John Watson (McLaren M28/2), 70.
PP – Laffite, 1;21.13; FL – Scheckter, 1;22.39, 115.72 mph.
Scheckter victory through survival rather than pacemaking, as team-mate Villeneuve raced back through field after early delay only to run out of fuel on last lap; Jones's superb new Williams FW07 led comfortably before retiring with electrical failure.

27-5-79 MONACO GP,
Monte Carlo – 76 laps, 155.41 miles
1. Jody Scheckter (Ferrari 312T4 040), 76 laps in 1:55;22.48, 81.34 mph.
2. Clay Regazzoni (Williams FW07/2), 76 in 1:55;22.92.
3. Carlos Reutemann (Lotus 79 R4), 76. **4.** John Watson (McLaren M28/3), 76. **5.** Patrick Depailler (Ligier JS11-03), 74. **6.** Jochen Mass (Arrows A1/5A), 69.
PP – Scheckter, 1;26.43; FL – Depailler, 1;28.82, 83.41 mph.
Scheckter's Ferrari all the way from pole but Regazzoni closed to within a half-second at finish after final 15-lap charge; Villeneuve looked stronger challenger for lead, tracking team-mate until transmission failure late in race; Jones's FW07 bent steering arm against barrier when pressing both Ferraris hard.

1-7-79 FRENCH GP,
Dijon-Prenois – 80 laps, 188.90 miles
1. Jean-Pierre Jabouille (Renault turbo V6 RS10-02*), 80 laps in 1:35;20.42, 118.88 mph.
2. Gilles Villeneuve (Ferrari 312T4 041), 80 in 1:35;35.01.
3. René Arnoux (Renault turbo V6 RS10-03*), 80 in 1:35;35.25. **4.** Alan Jones (Williams FW07/3), 80. **5.** Jean-Pierre Jarier (Tyrrell 009-3), 80. **6.** Clay Regazzoni (Williams FW07/2), 80.

**These individual cars are also known as RS11 and RS12, respectively.*
PP – Jabouille, 1;07.19 ; FL – Arnoux, 1;09.16, 122.91 mph.
Renault's great day; both cars on front row but Villeneuve led from start, Jabouille took lead lap 46, Villeneuve's tyres badly worn so fell back into wheel-banging last-lap ruckus with Arnoux – turbo 1.5's maiden win.

14-7-79 BRITISH GP,
Silverstone – 68 laps, 199.38 miles
1. Clay Regazzoni (Williams FW07/2), 68 laps in 1:26;11.17, 138.80 mph.
2. René Arnoux (Renault RS10-03), 68 in 1:26;35.45.
3. Jean-Pierre Jarier (Tyrrell 009-3), 67. **4.** John Watson (McLaren M29/1), 67. **5.** Jody Scheckter (Ferrari 312T4 039), 67. **6.** Jacky Ickx (Ligier JS11-01), 67.
PP – Alan Jones (Williams FW07/1), 1;11.88; FL – Regazzoni, 1;14.40, 141.87 mph.
Great day for Williams – Jones's FW07 set fantastic pace, engine failed after water pump crack leaked coolant away, Regazzoni took over for Williams's maiden GP win, only Jabouille challenged Jones early on before multiple Renault problems; both Brabhams failed.

29-7-79 GERMAN GP,
Hockenheim – 45 laps, 189.81 miles
1. Alan Jones (Williams FW07/4), 45 laps in 1:24;48.83, 134.27 mph.
2. Clay Regazzoni (Williams FW07/2), 45 in 1:24;51.74.
3. Jacques Laffite (Ligier JS11-04), 45. **4.** Jody Scheckter (Ferrari 312T4 040), 45. **5.** John Watson (McLaren M29/1), 45. **6.** Jochen Mass (Arrows A2/2), 44.
PP – Jean-Pierre Jabouille (Renault turbo V6 RS10/02), 1;48.48; FL – Gilles Villeneuve (Ferrari 312T4 041), 1;51.89, 135.71 mph.
Jones beat Jabouille from start but couldn't shake him off until lap 8 driver error spun and stalled Renault. Jones bugged by high-speed misfire and deflating tyre in latter stages but scraped home 3 secs clear of team-mate for fine Williams 1-2.

12-8-79 AUSTRIAN GP,
Österreichring – 54 laps, 199.39 miles
1. Alan Jones (Williams FW07/4), 54 laps in 1:27;38.01, 136.52 mph.
2. Gilles Villeneuve (Ferrari 312T4 041), 54 in 1:28;14.06.
3. Jacques Laffite (Ligier JS11-04), 54. **4.** Jody Scheckter (Ferrari 312T4 040), 54. **5.** Clay Regazzoni (Williams FW07/1), 54. **6.** René Arnoux (Renault turbo V6 RS10-03), 53.
PP – Arnoux, 1;34.07; FL – Arnoux, 1;35.77, 138.80 mph.
Williams team hat-trick, Jones's second successive win. Villeneuve led two laps, Renaults both ran 2nd before trouble, Arnoux stopping for fuel only four laps from end, Jabouille stopped by clutch problem.

26-8-79 DUTCH GP,
Zandvoort – 75 laps, 196.94 miles
1. Alan Jones (Williams FW07/1), 75 laps in 1:41;19.775, 116.62 mph.
2. Jody Scheckter (Ferrari 312T4 040), 75 in 1:41;41.558.
3. Jacques Laffite (Ligier JS11-04), 75. **4.** Nelson Piquet (Brabham-Alfa Romeo V12 BT48/2), 74. **5.** Jacky Ickx (Ligier JS11-01), 74. **6.** Jochen Mass (Arrows A2/2), 73.
PP – René Arnoux (Renault turbo V6 RS10-03), 1;15.461; FL – Gilles Villeneuve (Ferrari 312T4 041), 1;19.438, 119.00 mph.
Four for Williams, hat-trick for Jones – he took early control of race but gearbox problems allowed Villeneuve ahead lap 11, Ferrari 1st until lap 47 spin, two laps later tyre collapsed and off again, driver destroying suspension in brainless but classic high-speed three-wheeled run back to pits . . .

9-9-79 ITALIAN GP,
Monza – 50 laps, 180.20 miles
1. Jody Scheckter (Ferrari 312T4 040), 50 laps in 1:22;00.22, 131.85 mph.
2. Gilles Villeneuve (Ferrari 312T4 038), 50 in 1:22;00.68.
3. Clay Regazzoni (Williams FW07/1), 50. **4.** Niki Lauda (Brabham-Alfa Romeo V12 BT48/4), 50. **5.** Mario Andretti (Lotus 79 R5), 50. **6.** Jean-Pierre Jarier (Tyrrell 009-3), 50.
PP – Jean-Pierre Jabouille (Renault turbo V6 RS10-02), 1;34.580; FL – Regazzoni, 1;35.60, 135.71 mph.
Convincing title-winning drive by Scheckter and fine, very close Ferrari 1-2 finish. Arnoux's Renault led laps 2-12, fell away to retire with misfire, Scheckter untroubled thereafter; Laffite with outside chance of title lost third place with brake/clutch troubles, finally over-revving engine; Jones, delayed by stop to replace dud battery, tore back but only ninth at finish.

16-9-79 Gran Premio Dino Ferrari,
Imola, I – 40 laps, 124.99 miles
1. Niki Lauda (Brabham-Alfa Romeo V12 BT48/4), 40 laps in 1:03;55.89, 117.31 mph.
2. Carlos Reutemann (Lotus 79 R2), 40 in 1:04;02.98.
3. Jody Scheckter (Ferrari 312T4 040), 40. **4.** Riccardo Patrese (Arrows A1/5A), 40. **5.** Jean-Pierre Jarier (Tyrrell 009-5), 40. **6.** Keke Rosberg (Wolf WR8), 40.
PP – Gilles Villeneuve (Ferrari 312T4 038), 1;32.91; FL – Villeneuve, 1;33.61, 120.17 mph.
Brabham-Alfa swansong victory as Cosworth BT49 imminent; duel with Villeneuve's Ferrari ended when 'T4 rammed Lauda's tail under braking, stopping for new nosepiece. This minor race a rehearsal for staging 1980 Italian GP at Imola.

30-9-79 CANADIAN GP,
Ile Notre Dame, Montreal – 72 laps, 201.32 miles
1. Alan Jones (Williams FW07/4), 72 laps in 1:52;06.892, 105.96 mph.
2. Gilles Villeneuve (Ferrari 312T4 041), 72 in 1:52;07.972.
3. Clay Regazzoni (Williams FW07/1), 72. **4.** Jody Scheckter (Ferrari 312T4 040), 71. **5.** Didier Pironi (Tyrrell 009-6), 71. **6.** John Watson (McLaren M29/3), 70.
PP – Jones, 1;29.892; FL – Jones, 1;32.272, 107.95 mph.
Very hard race between Jones and Villeneuve, Ferrari leading 51 laps until ever-present Jones slipped ahead; impressive new Piquet Brabham-Cosworth BT49 chased leaders hard until gearbox failed, leaving place to Regazzoni.

7-10-79 UNITED STATES GP,
Watkins Glen, NY – 59 laps, 199.24 miles
1. Gilles Villeneuve (Ferrari 312T4 041), 59 laps in 1:52;17.734, 106.46 mph.
2. René Arnoux (Renault turbo V6 RS10-03), 59 in 1:53;06.521.
3. Didier Pironi (Tyrrell 009-6), 59. **4.** Elio de Angelis (Shadow DN9/1B), 59. **5.** Hans Stuck Jr (ATS D3-01), 59. **6.** John Watson (McLaren M29/3), 58.
PP – Alan Jones (Williams FW07/4), 1;35.615; FL – Nelson Piquet (Brabham BT49/2), 1;40.054, 121.50 mph.
Villeneuve won as Williams fudged Jones pit stop – 'T4 led in heavy rain on Michelin wets until track dried, lightning Ferrari stop put Villeneuve back out half-minute behind Williams, but Jones lost wheel after his tyre change, leaving Villeneuve comfortable win despite fading oil pressure.

1980

13-1-80 ARGENTINE GP,
Buenos Aires – 53 laps, 196.55 miles
1. Alan Jones (Williams FW07/4), 53 laps in 1:43;24.38, 113.98 mph.
2. Nelson Piquet (Brabham BT49/4), 53 in 1:43;48.97.
3. Keke Rosberg (Fittipaldi F7/2), 53. **4.** Derek Daly (Tyrrell 009-6), 53. **5.** Bruno Giacomelli (Alfa Romeo 179-004*), 52. **6.** Alain Prost (McLaren M29/1B), 52.
**All Alfa Romeo chassis numbers are open to doubt as Autodelta indulged in unparalleled chassis-plate swopping between cars.*
PP – Jones, 1;44.17; FL – Jones, 1;50.45, 120.87 mph.
Despite three spins and a stop to remove plastic bag debris blanking Williams's radiator, Jones won 5th GP from last 7. Longer-underwing FW07B version flopped in practice, as did long-underwing Brabhams; floors stripped off for race; BT49 a real threat.

27-1-80 BRAZILIAN GP,
Interlagos – 40 laps, 197.84 miles
1. René Arnoux (Renault turbo V6 RE21), 40 laps in 1:40;01.35, 117.40 mph.
2. Elio de Angelis (Lotus 81 R1), 40 in 1:40;23.19.
3. Alan Jones (Williams FW07/6), 40. **4.** Didier Pironi (Ligier JS11-04), 40. **5.** Alain Prost (McLaren M29/1B), 40. **6.** Riccardo Patrese (Arrows A3/1), 39.
PP – Jean-Pierre Jabouille (Renault RE22), 2;21.40; FL – Arnoux, 2;27.311, 119.57 mph.
Arnoux's maiden win; car ran out of fuel on slowing-down lap. From end of lap 2 Renaults split by Ligiers but the latter had skirt stick (Pironi) and engine cut (Laffite) leaving Renault turbos 1-2 before Jabouille's turbo failed lap 25. De Angelis coped well with ill-handling Lotus.

1-3-80 SOUTH AFRICAN GP,
Kyalami – 78 laps, 198.90 miles
1. René Arnoux (Renault turbo V6 RE21), 78 laps in 1:36;52.54, 123.19 mph.
2. Jacques Laffite (Ligier JS11-03), 78 in 1;37;26.61.
3. Didier Pironi (Ligier JS11-04), 78. **4.** Nelson Piquet (Brabham BT49/4), 78. **5.** Carlos Reutemann (Williams FW07/5), 77. **6.** Jochen Mass (Arrows A3/4), 77.
PP – Jean-Pierre Jabouille (Renault turbo V6 RE23), 1;10.00; FL – Arnoux, 1;13.15, 125.49 mph.
Turbo advantage at altitude; Jones and Laffite mounted brief challenges but Renaults unmatched, luckless Jabouille tyre deflation 18 laps from end left Arnoux to 2nd consecutive win. French drivers 1-2-3 as Pironi won late-stages dice with Piquet.

30-3-80 UNITED STATES GP WEST,
Long Beach, California – 80.5 laps, 161.52 miles
1. Nelson Piquet (Brabham BT49/6), 80 laps in 1:50;18.550, 88.47 mph.
2. Riccardo Patrese (Arrows A3/3), 80 in 1:51;07.762.
3. Emerson Fittipaldi (Fittipaldi F7/1), 80. **4.** John Watson (McLaren M29/2C), 79. **5.** Jody Scheckter (Ferrari 312T5 046), 79. **6.** Didier Pironi (Ligier JS11-04), 79.
PP – Piquet, 1;17.694; FL – Piquet, 1;19.830, 91.09 mph.
Piquet's maiden win proved class of driver and BT49 car – led throughout. Patrese and Fittipaldi finished well, Ensign crash injuries ended Regazzoni's career.

4-5-80 BELGIAN GP,
Zolder – 72 laps, 190.66 miles
1. Didier Pironi (Ligier JS11-04), 72 laps in 1:38;46.51, 115.82 mph.
2. Alan Jones (Williams FW07B/7), 72 in 1:39;33.88.
3. Carlos Reutemann (Williams FW07B/5), 72. **4.** René Arnoux (Renault turbo V6 RE24), 71. **5.** Jean-Pierre Jarier (Tyrrell 010/1), 71. **6.** Gilles Villeneuve (Ferrari 312T5 045), 71.
PP – Jones, 1;19.12; FL – Jacques Laffite (Ligier JS11-03), 1;20.88, 117.88 mph.
Debut of definitive Williams FW07Bs but Ligier dominated, Pironi's performance superb.

18-5-80 MONACO GP,
Monte Carlo – 76 laps, 156.41 miles
1. Carlos Reutemann (Williams FW07B/5), 76 laps in 1:55;34.365, 81.20 mph.
2. Jacques Laffite (Ligier JS11-03), 76 in 1:56;47.994.
3. Nelson Piquet (Brabham BT49/7), 76. **4.** Jochen Mass (Arrows A3/4), 75. **5.** Gilles Villeneuve (Ferrari 312T5 045), 75. **6.** Emerson Fittipaldi (Fittipaldi F7/1), 74.
PP – Didier Pironi (Ligier JS11-04), 1;24.813; FL – Riccardo Patrese (Arrows A3/5), 1;26.058, 86.09 mph.
Pironi looked set to repeat Zolder win, leading from pole, holding off Jones until Williams transmission failed, then Ligier slid into barrier leaving race to Reutemann's Williams on damp and slippery street circuit – first-corner pile-up starred Daly's aviating Tyrrell.

1-6-80 Spanish GP*,
Jarama, Madrid – 80 laps, 164.74 miles
**Race declared non-Championship after being organized as Round 7 of the 1980 series.*
1. Alan Jones (Williams FW07B/7), 80 laps in 1:43;14.076, 95.69 mph.
2. Jochen Mass (Arrows A3/4), 80 in 1:44;05.016.
3. Elio de Angelis (Lotus 81 R3), 80. **4.** Jean-Pierre Jarier (Tyrrell 010/1), 79. **5.** Emerson Fittipaldi (Fittipaldi F7/1), 79. **6.** Patrick Gaillard (Ensign N180 MN-14), 75.
PP – Jacques Laffite (Ligier JS11-03, 1;12.647; FL – Jones, 1;15.467, 98.17 mph.
Race declared illegal by FISA after drivers refused to pay summary fines from Zolder dispute; Ferrari, Renault, Alfa boycotted race. Jones initially 2nd to Reutemann, missed gearchange and fell to 5th, then car overheated but Reutemann and Laffite collided, Piquet's Brabham broke gearbox, Pironi lost wheel after inheriting lead and Jones couldn't believe his luck. . .

29-6-80 FRENCH GP,
Ricard-Castellet – 54 laps, 194.95 miles
1. Alan Jones (Williams FW07B/7), 54 laps in 1:32;43.42, 126.65 mph.
2. Didier Pironi (Ligier JS11-04), 54 in 1:32;47.94.
3. Jacques Laffite (Ligier JS11-01), 54. **4.** Nelson Piquet (Brabham BT49/8), 54. **5.** René Arnoux (Renault turbo V6 RE24), 54. **6.** Carlos Reutemann (Williams FW07B/5), 54.
PP – Laffite, 1;38.88; FL – Jones, 1;41.45, 128.11 mph.
Brits beat French – after Spanish upset and loss of points, Williams team determined to beat them on their home soil. Ligiers and Renault turbo faster in practice but Jones had fine race set-up in FW07B and battled ahead of Ligiers with 20 laps to go.

13-7-80 BRITISH GP,
Brands Hatch – 76 laps, 198.63 miles
1. Alan Jones (Williams FW07B/7), 76 laps in 1:34;49.228, 125.69 mph.
2. Nelson Piquet (Brabham BT49/8), 76 in 1:35;00.235.
3. Carlos Reutemann (Williams FW07B/5), 76. **4.** Derek Daly (Tyrrell 010/2), 75. **5.** Jean-Pierre Jarier (Tyrrell 010/4), 75. **6.** Alain Prost (McLaren M29/4C), 75.
PP – Didier Pironi (Ligier JS11-04), 1;11.004; FL – Pironi, 1;12.368, 130.02 mph.
Ligiers dominant until rim trouble put Pironi into pits for tyre change, Laffite off road and Jones inherited lead he held thereafter – Pironi rejoined but brilliant recovery drive foiled by another tyre deflation.

10-8-80 GERMAN GP,
Hockenheim – 45 laps, 189.79 miles
1. Jacques Laffite (Ligier JS11-04), 45 laps in 1:22;59.73, 137.26 mph.
2. Carlos Reutemann (Williams FW07B/5), 45 in 1:23;02.32.
3. Alan Jones (Williams FW07B/9), 45. **4.** Nelson Piquet (Brabham BT49/8), 45. **5.** Bruno Giacomelli (Alfa Romeo 179-03), 45. **6.** Gilles Villeneuve (Ferrari 312T5 048), 45.
PP – Jones, 1;45.85; FL – Jones, 1;48.49, 139.96 mph.
Lucky Ligier win; Jabouille and Jones disputed lead, Williams unable to do much about Renaults until both turbos burned valves. Williams pair ran 1-3 sandwiching Laffite until five laps from end when Jones's left front tyre punctured; Jones just held off Piquet for third after tyre change.

17-8-80 AUSTRIAN GP,
Österreichring – 54 laps, 199.39 miles
1. Jean-Pierre Jabouille (Renault turbo V6 RE23), 54 laps in 1:26;15.73, 138.69 mph.
2. Alan Jones (Williams FW07B/9), 54 in 1:26;16.55.
3. Carlos Reutemann (Williams FW07B/8), 54. **4.** Jacques Laffite (Ligier JS11-03), 54. **5.** Nelson Piquet (Brabham BT49/7), 54. **6.** Elio de Angelis (Lotus 81 R3), 54.
PP – René Arnoux (Renault turbo V6 RE25), 1;30.27; FL – Arnoux 1;32.53, 143.66 mph.
Jones from start before Renaults powered past, Arnoux stopped for tyre change while Jabouille paced Jones to finish, fighting real battle only in last few laps; both set their fastest laps on final tour.

31-8-80 DUTCH GP,
Zandvoort – 72 laps, 190.23 miles
1. Nelson Piquet (Brabham BT49/7), 72 laps in 1:38;13.83, 116.19 mph.
2. René Arnoux (Renault turbo V6 RE25), 72 in 1:38;26.76.
3. Jacques Laffite (Ligier JS11-03), 72. **4.** Carlos Reutemann (Williams FW07B/8), 72. **5.** Jean-Pierre Jarier (Tyrrell 010-5), 72. **6.** Alain Prost (McLaren M30/1), 72.
PP – Arnoux, 1;17.44; FL – Arnoux, 1;19.35, 119.87 mph.
Jones built big lead too fast, damaged skirt on kerb and had to stop for it to be changed, allowing Championship rival Piquet to score for

Brabham; Laffite robbed of 2nd place right at end when caught napping by Arnoux's late charge.

14-9-80 ITALIAN GP,
Imola – 60 laps, 187.92 miles
1. Nelson Piquet (Brabham BT49/9), 60 laps in 1:38;07.52, 113.98 mph.
2. Alan Jones (Williams FW07B/9), 60 in 1:38;36.45.
3. Carlos Reutemann (Williams FW07B/8), 60. **4.** Elio de Angelis (Lotus 81 R3), 59. **5.** Keke Rosberg (Fittipaldi F8/1), 59. **6.** Didier Pironi (Ligier JS11-04), 59.
PP – René Arnoux (Renault turbo V6 RE25), 1;33.988); FL – Jones, 1;36.089, 116.40 mph.
Piquet disposed of Renaults in first three laps, Jones hampered by indifferent braking had to settle for 2nd, losing Championship lead to Piquet by one point, game drive by Reutemann having lost clutch and 4th gear. Both Ferrari drivers suffered major accidents – Scheckter in practice, Villeneuve a mightier moment in race.

28-9-80 CANADIAN GP,
Ile Notre Dame, Montreal – 70 laps, 191.90 miles
1. Alan Jones (Williams FW07B/9), 70 laps in 1:46;45.53, 110.00 mph.
2. Carlos Reutemann (Williams FW07B/8), 70 in 1:47;01.07.
3. Didier Pironi (Ligier JS11-04), 70. **4.** John Watson (McLaren M29/2C), 70. **5.** Gilles Villeneuve (Ferrari 312T4 044), 70. **6.** Hector Rebaque (Brabham BT49/6), 69.
PP – Nelson Piquet (Brabham BT49/9), 1;27.328; FL – Pironi, 1;28.769, 113.40 mph.
Jones/Piquet first-corner collision sparked multiple which stopped race. Piquet restarted in spare car still fitted with practice 'screamer' engine, predictably led until it blew on lap 24; Pironi penalized one minute for jumped start took lead on road and Jones sat back to finish 2nd on road, 1st overall, clinching World title; Watson 4th marked McLaren resurgence.

5-10-80 UNITED STATES GP,
Watkins Glen, NY – 59 laps, 199.24 miles
1. Alan Jones (Williams FW07B/9), 59 laps in 1:34;36.05, 126.37 mph.
2. Carlos Reutemann (Williams FW07B/8), 59 in 1:34;40.26.
3. Didier Pironi (Ligier JS11-02), 59. **4.** Elio de Angelis (Lotus 81 R2), 59. **5.** Jacques Laffite (Ligier JS11-03), 58. **6.** Mario Andretti (Lotus 81 R3), 58.
PP – Bruno Giacomelli (Alfa Romeo 179-06), 1;33.291; FL – Jones, 1;34.068, 129.24 mph.
Fine Williams 1-2 to emphasize Championship success but Giacomelli's Alfa was the star: pole position and led going away until electrics failed at half-distance. Jones left road at first corner, resumed 12th, took 3rd when Piquet spun, overtook team-mate for 2nd then inherited 1st as Alfa failed. Both Lotuses in points for first time in season.

1981

7-2-81 South African GP,
Kyalami – 77 laps, 196.35 miles
1. Carlos Reutemann (Williams FW07B/10), 77 laps in 1:44;54.03, 112.31 mph.
2. Nelson Piquet (Brabham BT49B/10), 77 in 1:45;14.17.
3. Elio de Angelis (Lotus 81 R3), 77. **4.** Keke Rosberg (Fittipaldi F8C/3), 76. **5.** John Watson (McLaren M29C/4), 76. **6.** Riccardo Patrese (Arrows A3/3), 76.
PP – Piquet, 1;12.78; FL – Reutemann, 1:13.61, 124.71 mph.
Another pointless race boycotted by *Grande Costruttori* after FOCA ran skirted rules – excluded from Championship. Great Reutemann drive on slicks from wet weather start while others stopped to change from wets as track dried; Piquet early leader, close Rosberg/Watson battle.

15-3-81 UNITED STATES GP WEST,
Long Beach, California – 80.5 laps, 162.61 miles
1. Alan Jones (Williams FW07C/11), 80 laps in 1:50;41.33, 87.60 mph.
2. Carlos Reutemann (Williams FW07C/12), 80 in 1:50;50.52.
3. Nelson Piquet (Brabham BT49C/11), 80.
4. Mario Andretti (Alfa Romeo 179-02), 80.
5. Eddie Cheever (Tyrrell 010-3), 80. **6.** Patrick Tambay (Theodore TR-3), 79.
PP – Riccardo Patrese (Arrows A3/3), 1;19.399; FL – Jones, 1;20.901, 89.89 mph.
Redesigned cars after skirts ban still saw Williams dominant but Patrese's new Arrows A3 dominated practice and early stages until fuel filter blocked one-third distance; new turbo Ferraris promising before retirements, only eight finished. 'Twin-chassis' Lotus 88 excluded in practice controversy. Turbo Ferrari debut.

29-3-81 BRAZILIAN GP,
Jacarepaguá – 62 laps, 193.82 miles*
**Race flagged one lap short of scheduled 63 under two-hour rule due to heavy rain slowing pace.*
1. Carlos Reutemann (Williams FW07C/12), 62 laps in 2:00;23.66, 96.59 mph.
2. Alan Jones (Williams FW07C/11), 62 in 2:00;28.10.
3. Riccardo Patrese (Arrows A3/3), 62. **4.** Marc Surer (Ensign N180 MN-15) 62. **5.** Elio de Angelis (Lotus 81 R3), 62. **6.** Jacques Laffite (Ligier-Matra V12 JS17-02), 62.
PP – Nelson Piquet (Brabham BT49C/11), 1;35.079; FL – Surer, 1;54.302, 98.46 mph.
Williams dominant but Reutemann accused of disregarding pit direction to allow Jones by. Fine drives by Patrese and Surer in unfashionable cars, Ferrari's turbos luckless, controversial debut of Brabham lowering suspension.

12-4-81 ARGENTINE GP,
Buenos Aires – 53 laps, 196.55 miles
1. Nelson Piquet (Brabham BT49C/11), 53 laps in 1:34;32.74, 124.67 mph.
2. Carlos Reutemann (Williams FW07C/12), 53 in 1:34;59.35.
3. Alain Prost (Renault turbo V6 RE22B), 53.
4. Alan Jones (Williams FW07C/11), 53. **5.** René Arnoux (Renault turbo V6 RE27B), 53. **6.** Elio de Angelis (Lotus 81 R3), 52.
PP – Piquet, 1;42.665; FL – Piquet, 1;45.287, 126.80 mph.
Superior Brabham suspension ploy led start-to-finish, number 2 driver Rebaque passing Williams pair for second behind Piquet in mid-race until rotor arm broke; good day for Renault.

3-5-81 'SAN MARINO' GP,
Imola, I – 60 laps, 187.92 miles.
1. Nelson Piquet (Brabham BT49C/11), 60 laps in 1:51;23.97, 101.20 mph.
2. Riccardo Patrese (Arrows A3/5), 60 in 1:51;28.55.
3. Carlos Reutemann (Williams FW07C/12), 60.
4. Hector Rebaque (Brabham BT49C/12), 60.
5. Didier Pironi (Ferrari turbo V6 126C 051), 60.
6. Andrea de Cesaris (McLaren M29F/4), 60.
PP – Gilles Villeneuve (Ferrari turbo V6 126C 052), 1;48.064, 104.33 mph.
Piquet's second successive win but opposed strongly by Reutemann, Arrows and, surprisingly, Ferrari. Villeneuve led first 14 laps in wet before changing to dry tyres, Pironi in command before broken skirt and worn tyres, Piquet took lead with 13 laps to go. Watson's new McLaren 2nd fastest in race but early error; Jones collided with team-mate on first lap.

17-5-81 BELGIAN GP,
Zolder – 70 laps, 185.36 miles
1. Carlos Reutemann (Williams FW07C/12), 54 laps in 1:16;31.61, 112.12 mph.
2. Jacques Laffite (Ligier-Matra V12 JS17-02), 54 in 1:17;07.67.
3. Nigel Mansell (Lotus 81 R1), 54. **4.** Gilles Villeneuve (Ferrari turbo V6 126C 050), 54. **5.** Elio de Angelis (Lotus 81 R3), 54. **6.** Eddie Cheever (Tyrrell 010-3), 54.
PP – Reutemann, 1;22.28; FL – Reutemann, 1;23.30, 114.45 mph.
Race shambles as start accident injured mechanic on grid as lights changed. Restart saw Pironi lead, Piquet and Jones got by, Brabham barged off road, Jones crashed when leading leaving Reutemann to win in 14th consecutive points-scoring finish – including Kyalami – race stopped early as drizzle fell.

31-5-81 MONACO GP,
Monte Carlo – 76 laps, 156.41 miles
1. Gilles Villeneuve (Ferrari turbo V6 126C 052), 76 laps in 1:54;23.38, 82.04 mph.
2. Alan Jones (Williams FW07C/15), 76 in 1:55;.03.29.
3. Jacques Laffite (Ligier-Matra V12 JS17-02), 76.
4. Didier Pironi (Ferrari turbo V6 126C 050), 75.
5. Eddie Cheever (Tyrrell 010-3), 74. **6.** Marc Surer (Ensign N190 MN-15), 74.
PP – Nelson Piquet (Brabham BT49C/11), 1;25.710; FL – Jones, 1;27.470, 84.70 mph.
Piquet still rattled by Zolder incident with Jones, pressured into mistake by Williams driver when leading, crashed and gave lead to Jones, who stayed in front until lap 66 when slowed by fuel pick-up problem. Villeneuve inherited win after never-say-die drive in difficult turbo Ferrari.

21-6-81 SPANISH GP,
Jarama, Madrid – 80 laps, 164.64 miles
1. Gilles Villeneuve (Ferrari turbo V6 126C 052), 80 laps in 1:46;35.01, 92.68 mph.
2. Jacques Laffite (Ligier-Matra V12 JS17-04), 80 in 1:46;35.23.
3. John Watson (McLaren MP4/1-2), 80 in 1:46;35.59. **4.** Carlos Reutemann (Williams FW07C/12), 80 in 1:46;36.02. **5.** Elio de Angelis (Lotus 87 R2), 80 in 1:46;36.25. **6.** Nigel Mansell (Lotus 87 R1), 80.
PP – Laffite, 1;13.754; FL – Jones, 1;17.818, 95.21 mph.
Jones threw race away by driver error when well ahead, leaving Villeneuve to block off pursuers after searing start – superficially looked fabulous race but really a case of speed on straight and blocking 'em all through corners.

5-7-81 FRENCH GP,
Dijon-Prenois – 80 laps, 188.88 miles*
**Race stopped due to torrential rain shower after 58 laps and converted into two-part event with second section covering 22 laps.*
PART ONE: 1. Piquet; **2.** Prost; **3.** Watson; **4.** Reutemann; **5.** Arnoux; **6.** Rebaque.
PART TWO: 1. Prost; **2.** Watson; **3.** Arnoux; **4.** Pironi; **5.** Piquet; **6.** de Cesaris.
AGGREGATE:
1. Alain Prost (Renault turbo V6 RE30-2), 80 laps in 1:35;48.13, 118.30 mph.
2. John Watson (McLaren MP4/1-2), 80 in 1:35;50.42.
3. Nelson Piquet (Brabham BT49C/11), 80.
4. René Arnoux (Renault turbo V6 RE30-3), 80.
5. Didier Pironi (Ferrari turbo V6 126C 053) 79.
6. Elio de Angelis (Lotus 87 R2), 79.
Drivers placed in 'heats' but not in overall aggregate result drove the following cars. Carlos Reutemann (Williams FW07C/12); Hector Rebaque (Brabham BT49C/12); Andrea de Cesaris (McLaren MP4/1-1).
PP – Part One, Arnoux, 1;05.95; Part Two, result of Part One. FL – Overall, Prost, 1;09.14, 122.94 mph.
Goodyear servicing Williams and Brabham again for first time since their withdrawal at end of 1980, their race tyres better than result suggests, though Michelin qualifiers better – sticky Michelins on Renaults for restart gave them big advantage in unrealistic race.

18-7-81 BRITISH GP,
Silverstone – 68 laps, 199.38 miles
1. John Watson (McLaren MP4/1-2), 68 laps in 1:26;54.80, 137.64 mph.
2. Carlos Reutemann (Williams FW07C/12), 68 in 1:27;35.45.
3. Jacques Laffite (Ligier-Matra V12 JS17-04;, 67.
4. Eddie Cheever (Tyrrell 010-2), 67. **5.** Hector Rebaque (Brabham BT49C/12), 67. **6.** Slim Borgudd (ATS D5-01), 67.
PP – René Arnoux (Renault turbo V6 RE30-3), 1;11.00; FL – Arnoux, 1;15.067, 140.61 mph.
Villeneuve lost Ferrari lap 4 at Woodcote chicane, taking out Jones, Watson, de Cesaris. Watson rejoined 10th as Renaults extended lead; Piquet crashed 3rd place Brabham when tyre failed, Prost out with burned valves, Arnoux led Watson for 30 laps up to lap 50 when Renault engine began to falter. First win for carbon-fibre McLaren – high retirement rate.

2-8-81 GERMAN GP,
Hockenheim – 45 laps, 189.79 miles
1. Nelson Piquet (Brabham BT49C/14), 45 laps in 1:25;55.60, 132.53 mph.
2. Alain Prost (Renault turbo V6 RE30-2), 45 in 1:26;07.12.
3. Jacques Laffite (Ligier-Matra V12 JS17-04), 45.
4. Hector Rebaque (Brabham BT49C/12), 45.
5. Eddie Cheever (Tyrrell 011-1), 45. **6.** John Watson (McLaren MP4/1-2), 44.
PP – Prost, 1;47.50; FL – Alan Jones (Williams FW07C/16), 1;52.42, 135.07 mph.
Early Renault/Williams battle until Jones's Monaco misfire returned; Reutemann's engine failed and Piquet caught Prost despite damaged Brabham skirt. Good drive by Rebaque; Watson unhappy with spare McLaren's ride.

16-8-81 AUSTRIAN GP,
Österreichring – 53 laps, 195.69 miles
1. Jacques Laffite (Ligier-Matra V12 JS17-04), 53 laps in 1:27;36.47, 134.03 mph.
2. René Arnoux (Renault turbo V6 RE30-3), 53 in 1:27;41.64.
3. Nelson Piquet (Brabham BT49C/14), 53. **4.** Alan Jones (Williams FW07C/16), 53. **5.** Carlos Reutemann (Williams FW07C/14), 53. **6.** John Watson (McLaren MP4/1-3), 53.
PP – Arnoux, 1;32.018; FL – Laffite, 1;37.62, 136.17 mph.
New Ligier team manager Jabouille earmarked Michelin tyre as ideal for Austria during Zandvoort tyre tests – Laffite used it brilliantly to beat Arnoux's Renault in closing stages. Villeneuve led until brake trouble, then Renault monopoly before Prost crashed through suspension failure, and Arnoux fighting understeer was caught by Laffite.

30-8-81 DUTCH GP,
Zandvoort – 72 laps, 190.23 miles
1. Alain Prost (Renault turbo V6 RE30-4), 72 laps in 1:40;22.43, 113.71 mph.
2. Nelson Piquet (Brabham BT49C/14), 72 in 1:40;30.67.
3. Alan Jones (Williams FW07C/16), 72. **4.** Hector Rebaque (Brabham BT49C/12), 71. **5.** Elio de Angelis (Lotus 87 R3), 71. **6.** Eliseo Salazar (Ensign N180 MN-15), 70.
PP – Prost, 1;18.176; FL – Jones, 1;21.83, 116.23 mph.
Fierce Jones/Prost duel decided in Renault's favour when Williams tyres 'went off'; Piquet's Brabham took title lead as Reutemann collided with Laffite's Ligier when disputing 4th place.

13-9-81 ITALIAN GP,
Monza – 52 laps, 187.41 miles
1. Alain Prost (Renault turbo V6 RE30-4), 52 laps in 1:26;33.897, 129.89 mph.
2. Alan Jones (Williams FW07D/16), 52 in 1:26;56.072.
3. Carlos Reutemann (Williams FW07C/17), 52.
4. Elio de Angelis (Lotus 87 R3), 52. **5.** Didier Pironi (Ferrari turbo V6 126C 049), 52. **6.** Nelson Piquet (Brabham BT49C/14), 51.
PP – René Arnoux (Renault turbo V6 RE30-3), 1;33.467; FL – Reutemann, 1;37.528, 133.03 mph.
Difficult race on damp surface. Prost supreme, Piquet lost 3rd place on last lap when engine blew, Jones overcame handicap of driving with broken finger. Reutemann fast in practice, set car up for dry, hard drive into 3rd place, led Championship since Brazil.

27-9-81 CANADIAN GP,
Ile Notre Dame, Montreal – 70 laps, 191.90 miles*
**Race affected by rain, stopped after regulation two hours at 63 laps.*
1. Jacques Laffite (Ligier-Matra V12 JS17-05), 63 laps in 2:01;25.205, 85.25 mph.
2. John Watson (McLaren MP4/1-4), 63 in 2:01;31.438.
3. Gilles Villeneuve (Ferrari turbo V6 126C 052), 63. **4.** Bruno Giacomelli (Alfa Romeo 179-04), 62.
5. Nelson Piquet (Brabham BT49C/15), 62. **6.** Elio de Angelis (Lotus 87 R3), 62.
PP – Piquet, 1;29.211; FL – Watson, 1;49.475, 90.11 mph.
Appallingly wet conditions, Michelin rain tyres supreme. Jones spun off when leading, Prost lost lead with locking brakes and Laffite raced home to have an outside chance of winning World Championship in Vegas!

17-10-81 CAESAR'S PALACE GP,
Las Vegas, USA – 75 laps, 169.50 miles
1. Alan Jones (Williams FW07D/16), 75 laps in 1:44;09.077, 97.90 mph.
2. Alain Prost (Renault turbo V6 RE30-4), 75 in 1:44;29.125.
3. Bruno Giacomelli (Alfa Romeo 179-04), 75.
4. Nigel Mansell (Lotus 87 R5), 75. **5.** Nelson Piquet (Brabham BT49C/15), 75. **6.** Jacques Laffite (Ligier-Matra V12 JS17-03), 75.
PP – Carlos Reutemann (Williams FW07C/17), 1;17.821; FL – Didier Pironi (Ferrari turbo V6 126C 049), 1;20.156, 101.86 mph.
Reutemann freaked out of Championship, Jones rubbed-in his abilities in farewell race, Laffite rose to 2nd before tyre stop; Watson 7th not enough to deny Piquet title.

1982

23-1-82 SOUTH AFRICAN GP,
Kyalami – 77 laps, 196.35 miles
1. Alain Prost (Renault turbo V6 RE30B-6), 77 laps in 1:32;08.401, 127.86 mph.
2. Carlos Reutemann (Williams FW07D/16), 77 in 1:32;23.347.
3. René Arnoux (Renault turbo V6 RE30B-5), 77.
4. Niki Lauda (McLaren MP4/1-4), 77. **5.** Keke Rosberg (Williams FW07C/15), 77. **6.** John Watson (McLaren MP4/1-5), 77.
PP – Arnoux, 1;06.351; FL – Prost, 1;08.278, 134.45 mph.
Seven turbos on grid – Renaults, Ferraris, Brabham-BMWs and lone Toleman-Hart – 6 of 7 filled first three grid rows. Piquet crashed, Patrese and Villeneuve blew turbos in first quarter, six laps later Pironi in pits. Renaults dominated from Williams pair until Prost had puncture, rejoined 8th, brilliant drive into lead after only 26 laps as Pironi regained 2nd before engine misfire; Arnoux lost lead to Prost as tyres wore.

21-3-82 BRAZILIAN GP,
Jacarepaguá, Rio de Janeiro – 63 laps, 196.94 miles
1. Alain Prost (Renault turbo V6 RE30B-6), 63 laps in 1:44;33.134, 112.97 mph*.
2. John Watson (McLaren MP4/1-5), 63 in 1:44;36.124.
3. Nigel Mansell (Lotus 91 R7), 63. **4.** Michele Alboreto (Tyrrell 011/4), 63. **5.** Manfred Winkelhock (ATS D5/3), 62. **6.** Didier Pironi (Ferrari turbo V6 126C2 056), 62.
PP – Prost, 1;28.808; FL – Nelson Piquet (Brabham BT49/16), 1;36.582, 116.52 mph.
**Elevated to 1st place after disqualification of:*
1. Nelson Piquet (Brabham BT49D/16), 63 laps in 1:43;53.760, 114.08 mph.
2. Keke Rosberg (Williams FW07C/17), 63 in 1:44;05.737.
Like Spain '81, as Villeneuve's turbo power held off lightweight cars of Piquet and Rosberg along straights for 29 laps until Ferrari crashed. Piquet won comfortably as Williams tyres were shot, Prost handicapped by misfire, Reutemann collided with Lauda then later Arnoux, putting them out. 'Brake cooling' ballast ploy judged illegal so first two later disqualified, rest elevated.

4-4-82 UNITED STATES GP WEST,
Long Beach, Calif. – 75.5 laps, 160.91 miles
1. Niki Lauda (McLaren MP4/1-4), 75 laps in 1:58;25.318, 81.40 mph.
2. Keke Rosberg (Williams FW07C/15), 75 in 1:58;39.978.
3. Riccardo Patrese (Brabham BT49C/15), 75.
4. Michele Alboreto (Tyrrell 011-4), 75. **5.** Elio de Angelis (Lotus 91 R6), 74. **6.** John Watson (McLaren MP4/1-2), 74.
PP – Andrea de Cesaris (Alfa Romeo V12 182/2), 1;27.316; FL – Lauda, 1:30.831, 84.42 mph.
Lauda looked set for pole until last-moment effort by de Cesaris won it for Alfa. Italian led until brush with wall after Lauda got by in clinical charge through field; remade track broke up in places.

25-4-82 'SAN MARINO' GP,
Imola, I – 60 laps, 187.92 miles
1. Didier Pironi (Ferrari turbo V6 126C2 056), 60 laps in 1:36;38.887, 116.66 mph.
2. Gilles Villeneuve (Ferrari turbo V6 126C2 058), 60 in 1:36;39.253.
3. Michele Alboreto (Tyrrell 011-5), 60. **4.** Jean-Pierre Jarier (Osella FA1/003), 59. **5.** Eliseo Salazar (ATS D5/3), 57.
UNC **'6th'.** Teo Fabi (Toleman-turbo 4 Hart TG181-07), 52.
PP – René Arnoux (Renault turbo V6 RE30B-7), 1;29.765; FL – Pironi, 1;35.036, 118.63 mph.
Ten FOCA teams boycotted race in ill-judged move marking end of FOCA's dominant power; 14 starters. Ferrari show went wrong as Pironi ignored pit signals and tore lead from aggrieved – if naïve – Villeneuve.

9-5-82 BELGIAN GP,
Zolder – 70 laps, 185.36 miles
1. John Watson (McLaren MP4/1-2), 70 laps in 1:35;41.995, 116.20 mph.
2. Keke Rosberg (Williams FW08/3), 70 in 1:35;49.263.
3. Eddie Cheever (Ligier-Matra V12 JS17-06), 69.
4. Elio de Angelis (Lotus 91 R6), 68. **5.** Nelson Piquet (Brabham-turbo 4 BMW BT50/3), 67.
6. Chico Serra (Fittipaldi F8D/3), 67.
PP – Alain Prost (Renault turbo V6 RE30B-8) 1;15.701; FL – Watson, 1;20.214, 118.85 mph.
Villeneuve killed in practice crash, Pironi DNS. Rosberg looked set to win from Lauda but tyre trouble for both let Watson win on penultimate lap, running perfect set-up; Lauda 3rd on road, disqualified as car underweight when scrutineered.

23-5-82 MONACO GP,
Monte Carlo – 76 laps, 156.41 miles
1. Riccardo Patrese (Brabham BT49D/17), 76 laps in 1:54;11.259, 82.21 mph.
2. Didier Pironi (Ferrari turbo V6 126C2 059), 75 out of fuel.
3. Andrea de Cesaris (Alfa Romeo V12 182/4), 75 out of fuel. **4.** Nigel Mansell (Lotus 91 R7), 75.
5. Elio de Angelis (Lotus 91 R6), 75. **6.** Derek Daly (Williams FW08/4) 74 crash damage.
PP – René Arnoux (Renault turbo V6 RE30B-7), 1;23.281; FL – Patrese, 1;29.354, 85.79 mph.
Arnoux spun and stalled lap 15, Prost took over with Patrese challenging but tried too hard on damp track and crashed lap 73; lap 75 Patrese spun, Pironi led then ran out of fuel. Daly's Williams potential winner but damaged rear

end in spin; de Cesaris's Alfa out of fuel, so Patrese won extraordinary event.

6-6-82 DETROIT GP,
Michigan, USA – 62 laps, 160.58 miles
1. John Watson (McLaren MP4/1-5), 62 laps in 1:58;41.043, 78.20 mph.
2. Eddie Cheever (Ligier-Matra V12 JS17-06), 62 in 1:58;56.769.
3. Didier Pironi (Ferrari turbo V6 126C2 056), 62. **4.** Keke Rosberg (Williams FW08/3), 62. **5.** Derek Daly (Williams FW08/4), 62. **6.** Jacques Laffite (Ligier-Matra V12 JS17-04), 61.
PP – Alain Prost (Renault turbo V6 RE30B-6), 1;48.537; FL – Prost, 1;50.438, 81.28 mph.
Race stopped after minor accident lap 7, restarted with McLarens on harder Michelins, Watson tigered through pack to brilliant win. Good drive by Cheever to pass Pironi, Prost/Rosberg led and broke, Lauda crashed when 2nd, spoiling McLaren 1-2.

13-6-82 CANADIAN GP,
Ile Notre Dame, Montreal – 70 laps, 191.90 miles*
**Race stopped on first lap by startline collision, fatal to Ricardo Paletti; restarted with Pironi in spare Ferrari.*
1. Nelson Piquet (Brabham-turbo 4 BMW BT50/3), 70 laps in 1:46;39.577, 107.93 mph.
2. Riccardo Patrese (Brabham BT49D/18), 70 in 1:46;53.376.
3. John Watson (McLaren MP4/1-5), 70. **4.** Elio de Angelis (Lotus 91 R6), 69. **5.** Marc Surer (Arrows A4/1), 69. **6.** Andrea de Cesaris (Alfa Romeo V12 182/3), 68.
PP – Didier Pironi (Ferrari turbo V6 126C2 057), 1;27.509; FL – Pironi (Ferrari turbo V6 126C2 059), 1;28.323, 111.68 mph.
Brabham logistical triumph with different types of car 1-2, BMW turbo coming of age. Pironi's new pullrod suspension Ferrari stalled on pole, rammed fatally by Ricardo Paletti's Osella; restart with Pironi in spare car. Another disastrous Renault showing.

3-7-82 DUTCH GP,
Zandvoort – 72 laps, 190.23 miles
1. Didier Pironi (Ferrari turbo V6 126C2 060), 72 laps in 1:38;03.254, 116.40 mph.
2. Nelson Piquet (Brabham-turbo 4 BMW BT50/3), 72 in 1:38;24.903.
3. Keke Rosberg (Williams FW08/5), 72. **4.** Niki Lauda (McLaren MP4/1-6), 72. **5.** Derek Daly (Williams FW08/4), 71. **6.** Mauro Baldi (Arrows A4/2), 71.
PP – René Arnoux (Renault turbo V6 RE30B-7), 1;14.233; FL – Derek Warwick (Toleman-turbo 4 Hart TG181-06), 1;19.780, 119.22 mph.
Renault front row for third successive year, both retired. Pironi dominant for Ferrari on Goodyear race tyres, Arnoux crashed heavily in Renault.

18-7-82 BRITISH GP,
Brands Hatch – 76 laps, 198.63 miles
1. Niki Lauda (McLaren MP4/1-6), 76 laps in 1:35;33.812, 124.70 mph.
2. Didier Pironi (Ferrari turbo V6 126C2 060), 76 in 1:35;59.538.
3. Patrick Tambay (Ferrari turbo V6 126C2 061), 76. **4.** Elio de Angelis (Lotus 91 R8), 76. **5.** Derek Daly (Williams FW08/4), 76. **6.** Alain Prost (Renault turbo V6 RE30B-6), 76.
PP – Keke Rosberg (Williams FW08/5), 1;09.540; FL – Brian Henton (Tyrrell 011-2), 1;13.028, 128.84 mph.
Rosberg failed to start on pole, Patrese startline collision removed Arnoux; Piquet pulled away on light tanks towards scheduled refuelling stop but was out at 9 laps, Lauda taking 19th GP win of career.

25-7-82 FRENCH GP,
Ricard-Castellet – 54 laps, 194.94 miles
1. René Arnoux (Renault turbo V6 RE30B-8), 54 laps in 1:33;33.217, 124.99 mph.
2. Alain Prost (Renault turbo V6 RE30B-6), 54 in 1:33;50.525.
3. Didier Pironi (Ferrari turbo V6 126C2 060), 54. **4.** Patrick Tambay (Ferrari turbo V6 126C2 061), 54. **5.** Keke Rosberg (Williams FW08/5), 54. **6.** Michele Alboreto (Tyrrell 011/5), 54.
PP – Arnoux, 1;34.406; FL – Riccardo Patrese (Brabham-turbo 4 BMW BT50/4), 1;40.075, 129.87 mph.
Renault intended Prost to win, bolstering outside chance of Championship, but as Arnoux pulled out 20 sec lead he wasn't about to give it up. Brabham-BMWs slaughtered all opposition on half-tanks and soft tyres in early stages, both broke before scheduled stops. Potentially catastrophic lap 11 accident put Mass's March into spectator area, ground-effects safety questions highlighted.

8-8-82 GERMAN GP,
Hockenheim – 45 laps, 189.86 miles
1. Patrick Tambay (Ferrari turbo V6 126C2 061), 45 laps in 1:27;25.178, 130.43 mph.
2. René Arnoux (Renault turbo V6 RE30B-8), 45 in 1:27;41.557.
3. Keke Rosberg (Williams FW08/1), 44. **4.** Michele Alboreto (Tyrrell 011-5), 44. **5.** Bruno Giacomelli (Alfa Romeo V12 182/3), 44. **6.** Marc Surer (Arrows A4/1), 44.
PP – Didier Pironi (Ferrari turbo V6 126C2 061), 1;47.947; FL – Nelson Piquet (Brabham-turbo 4 BMW BT50/3), 1;54.035, 133.33 mph.
Pironi's career ended by ghastly practice accident; Tambay underlined Ferrari potential after Piquet collided with back-marker and took up boxing, Prost slowed with injection trouble, Arnoux unable to respond, Watson crashed when suspension broke. Lauda DNS, injured wrist in practice.

15-8-82 AUSTRIAN GP,
Österreichring – 53 laps, 195.69 miles
1. Elio de Angelis (Lotus 91 R8), 53 laps in 1:25;02.212, 138.07 mph.
2. Keke Rosberg (Williams FW08/1), 53 in 1:25;02.262.
3. Jacques Laffite (Ligier-Matra V12 JS19-03), 52. **4.** Patrick Tambay (Ferrari turbo V6 126C2 061), 52. **5.** Niki Lauda (McLaren MP4/1-6), 52. **6.** Mauro Baldi (Arrows A4/2), 52.
PP – Nelson Piquet (Brabham-turbo 4 BMW BT50/3), 1;27.612; FL – Piquet, 1;33.699, 141.87 mph.
Brabham pit stops reached for first time, cars still broke; Prost left leading in last turbo until injection failed five laps from end, de Angelis just held off Rosberg who made up 4 secs in those last few laps as Lotus misfired. 150th Cosworth victory, de Angelis was just 9 years old when Clark won first in 1967.

29-8-82 'SWISS GP',
Dijon-Prenois, F – 80 laps, 188.88 miles
1. Keke Rosberg (Williams FW08/5), 80 laps in 1:32;41.087, 122.29 mph.
2. Alain Prost (Renault turbo V6 RE30B-10), 80 in 1:32;45.529.
3. Niki Lauda (McLaren MP4/1-7), 80. **4.** Nelson Piquet (Brabham-turbo 4 BMW BT50/5), 79. **5.** Riccardo Patrese (Brabham-turbo 4 BMW BT50/4), 79. **6.** Elio de Angelis (Lotus 91 R8), 79.
PP – Prost, 1;01.380; FL – Prost, 1;07.477, 125.97 mph.
No Ferraris, Tambay withdrawn due to pinched nerve. Prost dominant first 10 laps until oil went down on track when Prost eased to save car and tyres; Arnoux set to inherit lead when injection trouble intervened, Rosberg fastest on track at end. Organizers almost ended race two laps short with Prost still leading, when Williams management intervened; confusion saw 81 laps run instead of 80! Brabham-BMWs off pace.

12-9-82 ITALIAN GP,
Monza – 52 laps, 187.40 miles
1. René Arnoux (Renault turbo V6 RE30B-5), 52 laps in 1:22;25.734, 136.39 mph.
2. Patrick Tambay (Ferrari turbo V6 126C2 062), 52 in 1:22;39.39.
3. Mario Andretti (Ferrari turbo V6 126C2 061), 52. **4.** John Watson (McLaren MP4/1-5), 52. **5.** Michele Alboreto (Tyrrell 011-6), 51. **6.** Eddie Cheever (Ligier-Matra V12 JS19-01), 51.
PP – Andretti, 1;28.473; FL – Arnoux, 1;33.619, 138.59 mph.
Arnoux took lead from Tambay ending lap 1 and was never headed, Brabham challenge fizzled out, Prost lost 3rd with turbo failure.

25-9-82 CAESAR'S PALACE GP,
Las Vegas, USA – 75 laps, 170.10 miles
1. Michele Alboreto (Tyrrell 011-6), 75 laps in 1:41;56.888, 100.10 mph.
2. John Watson (McLaren MP4/1-5), 75 in 1:42;24.180.
3. Eddie Cheever (Ligier-Matra V12 JS19-01), 75. **4.** Alain Prost (Renault turbo V6 RE30B-10), 75. **5.** Keke Rosberg (Williams FW08/5), 75. **6.** Derek Daly (Williams FW08/6), 74.
PP – Prost, 1;16.356; FL – Alboreto, 1;19.639, 102.52 mph.
Rosberg Champion in steady, heady drive, Watson's outside chance taken brilliantly but not lucky enough, Renault again in trouble after leading. Alboreto inherited good lead, cretinous circuit but ideal for Tyrrell and driver – no offence meant.

1983

13-3-83 BRAZILIAN GP,
Jacarepaguá, Rio de Janeiro – 63 laps, 196.945 miles
1. Nelson Piquet (Brabham-turbo 4 BMW BT52/3), 63 laps in 1:48;27.731, 108.926 mph.
2. Keke Rosberg (Williams FW08C/7), 63 in 1:48;48.362*.
3. Niki Lauda (McLaren MP4/1-7), 63 in 1:49;19.614. **4.** Jacques Laffite (Williams FW08C/8), 63. **5.** Patrick Tambay (Ferrari turbo V6 126C2B 063), 63. **6.** Marc Surer (Arrows A6/2), 63.
**Disqualified for alleged push-start, elevating slower finishers including Alain Prost (Renault turbo V6 RE30C-12), 62 laps.*
PP – Rosberg, 1;34.526; FL – Piquet, 1;39.829, 112.733 mph.
First 'flat-bottom' race. Rosberg displaced from early lead by Piquet, brief pit fire delayed Williams in team's first refuelling stop, McLarens strong, Watson out when engine seized while setting up challenge for lead, Prost Renault handicapped by rear tyre vibration.

27-3-83 UNITED STATES GP WEST,
Long Beach, Calif. – 75 laps, 152.625 miles
1. John Watson (McLaren MP4/1-6), 75 laps in 1:53;34.889, 80.6 mph.
2. Niki Lauda (McLaren MP4/1-7), 75 in 1:54;02.882.
3. René Arnoux (Ferrari 126C2B 064), 75. **4.** Jacques Laffite (Williams FW08C/8), 74. **5.** Marc Surer (Arrows A6/3), 74. **6.** Johnny Cecotto (Theodore N183-18), 74.
PP – Tambay, (Ferrari 126C2B 063), 1;26.117; FL – Lauda, 1;28.33, 82.939 mph.
McLaren classic, 22-23 on grid, ideal race set-up on Michelin tyres. Tambay Ferrari rammed by Rosberg Williams to lose lead, McLarens took lead lap 45, lapped Laffite by lap 75.

10-4-83 Race of Champions,
Brands Hatch, GB – 40 laps, 104.544 miles
1. Keke Rosberg (Williams FW08C/6), 40 laps in 53;15.253, 117.886 mph.
2. Danny Sullivan (Tyrrell 011-2), 40 in 53;15.743.
3. Alan Jones (Arrows A6/3), 40. **4.** Brian Henton (Theodore N183-18), 40. **5.** Raul Boesel (Ligier JS21-03), 40. **6.** Jean-Louis Schlesser (March-RAM 01-02), 39.
PP – Rosberg, 1;15.766; FL – René Arnoux (Ferrari turbo V6 126C2B 063), 1;17.826, 120.897 mph.
Sullivan shone in inconsequential minor race, Rosberg slowed by badly blistered tyre.

17-4-83 FRENCH GP,
Ricard-Castellet – 54 laps, 194.95 miles
1. Alain Prost (Renault turbo V6 RE40-01), 54 laps in 1:34;13.913, 124.191 mph.
2. Nelson Piquet (Brabham-turbo 4 BMW BT52/3), 54 in 1:34;43.633.
3. Eddie Cheever (Renault turbo V6 RE40-02), 54. **4.** Patrick Tambay (Ferrari turbo V6 126C2B 065), 54. **5.** Keke Rosberg (Williams FW08C/7), 53. **6.** Jacques Laffite (Williams FW08C/8), 53.
PP – Prost, 1;36.672; FL – Prost, 1;42.695, 126.555 mph.
Ferrari and Goodyear problems, Renault dominant on Michelins; Brabham-BMWs matched Renault power but not handling, non-turbo Williams drivers drove their hearts out in hopeless task.

1-5-83 'SAN MARINO' GP,
Imola, I – 60 laps, 187.90 miles
1. Patrick Tambay (Ferrari turbo V6 126C2B 065), 60 laps in 1:37;52.460, 115.251 mph.
2. Alain Prost (Renault turbo V6 RE40-03), 59.
4. Keke Rosberg (Williams FW08C/7), 59. **5.** John Watson (McLaren MP4/1-6), 59. **6.** Marc Surer (Arrows A6/2), 59.
PP – René Arnoux (Ferrari 126C2B 064), 1;31.238; FL – Riccardo Patrese (Brabham-turbo 4 BMW BT52/4), 1;34.437, 119.383 mph.
Brabham-BMW dominant, yet Piquet stalled on line, Arnoux lost lead to Patrese lap 6, slow pit stop left Patrese 2nd, he retook lead then crashed, Tambay left to win. Cosworth cars now outclassed even on slower circuits.

15-5-83 MONACO GP,
Monte Carlo – 76 laps, 156.406 miles
1. Keke Rosberg (Williams FW08C/7), 76 laps in 1:56;38.121, 80.521 mph.
2. Nelson Piquet (Brabham-turbo 4 BMW BT52/3), 76 in 1:56;56.596.
3. Alain Prost (Renault turbo V6 RE40-03), 76. **4.** Patrick Tambay (Ferrari turbo V6 126C2B 065), 76. **5.** Danny Sullivan (Tyrrell 011-5), 74. **6.** Mauro Baldi (Alfa Romeo turbo V8 183T-04), 74.
PP – René Arnoux (Ferrari 126C2B 064), 1;25.182; FL – Piquet, 1;27.283, 84.881 mph.
Wet race won by Rosberg's brilliant natural car control, Laffite's sister Williams lost 2nd place with gearbox trouble.

22-5-83 BELGIAN GP,
Spa-Francorchamps – 40 laps, 173.127 miles
1. Alain Prost (Renault turbo V6 RE40-03), 40 laps in 1:27;11.502, 119.135 mph.
2. Patrick Tambay (Ferrari turbo V6 126C2B 065), 40 in 1:27;34.684.
3. Eddie Cheever (Renault turbo V6 RE40-02), 40. **4.** Nelson Piquet (Brabham turbo 4 BMW BT52/3), 40. **5.** Keke Rosberg (Williams FW08C/7), 40. **6.** Jacques Laffite (Williams FW08C/8), 40.
PP – Prost, 2;04.615; FL – Andrea de Cesaris (Alfa Romeo turbo V8 183T/02), 2;07.493, 121.923 mph.
F1 return to Spa after 13 years, new circuit still put premium on power. Alfa controlled race until pit stop but injection failed 15 laps from end, Prost stroked home, Piquet fell 2nd to 4th when lost 5th gear, Williams consistency paid minor dividends.

5-6-83 DETROIT GP,
Michigan, USA – 60 laps, 150 miles
1. Michele Alboreto (Tyrrell 011-4), 60 laps in 1:50;53.669, 81.158 mph.
2. Keke Rosberg (Williams FW08C/7), 60 in 1:51;01.371.
3. John Watson (McLaren MP4/1C-8), 60. **4.** Nelson Piquet (Brabham-turbo 4 BMW BT52/3), 60. **5.** Jacques Laffite (Williams FW08C/8), 60. **6.** Nigel Mansell (Lotus 92 R10), 59.
PP – René Arnoux (Ferrari turbo V6 126C2B 064), 1;44.734; FL – Watson, 1;47.668, 83.590 mph.
Brabham quietly planned to run non-stop but Piquet lost lead with puncture 10 laps from end; Cosworth cars lucky to take five of top six places. Cosworth V8's 155th and last F1 victory.

12-6-83 CANADIAN GP,
Ile Notre Dame, Montreal – 70 laps, 191.82 miles
1. René Arnoux (Ferrari turbo V6 126C2B 064), 70 laps in 1:48;31.838, 106.044 mph.
2. Eddie Cheever (Renault turbo V6 RE40-02), 70 in 1:49;13.867.
3. Patrick Tambay (Ferrari turbo V6 126C2B 065), 70. **4.** Keke Rosberg (Williams FW08C/7), 70. **5.** Alain Prost (Renault turbo V6 RE40-03), 69. **6.** John Watson (McLaren MP4/1C-8), 69.
PP – Arnoux, 1;28.729; FL – Tambay, 1;30.851, 108.583 mph.
Faultless Ferrari win, Arnoux only gave up lead in refuelling stop, Piquet retired when 3rd, Prost's Renault down on power and suffering puncture, Patrese 2nd until gearbox failed.

16-7-83 BRITISH GP,
Silverstone – 67 laps, 196.44 miles
1. Alain Prost (Renault turbo V6 RE40-05), 67 laps in 1:24;39.780, 139.218 mph.
2. Nelson Piquet (Brabham-turbo 4 BMW BT52B/5), 67 in 1:24;58.941.
3. Patrick Tambay (Ferrari turbo V6 126C3 067), 67. **4.** Nigel Mansell (Lotus-Renault turbo V6 94T R2), 67. **5.** René Arnoux (Ferrari turbo V6 126C3 066), 67. **6.** Niki Lauda (McLaren MP4/1C-7) 66.
PP – Arnoux, 1;09.462; FL – Prost, 1;14.212, 142.23 mph.
New Ferraris led 20 laps until tyres lost edge, Prost's Renault took over with Piquet emphasizing Michelin dominance, taking 2nd on lap 31, leading when Prost stopped but later settling for 2nd after his own stop. Much fuss over pace of new Lotuses; Honda returned to F1 with turbo V6 engine in Spirit 201; Lauda's McLaren won 'Cosworth class'.

17-8-83 GERMAN GP,
Hockenheim – 45 laps, 190.055 miles
1. René Arnoux (Ferrari turbo V6 126C3 066), 45 laps in 1:27;10.319, 130.813 mph.
2. Andrea de Cesaris (Alfa Romeo turbo V8 183T/03), 45 in 1:28;20.971.
3. Riccardo Patrese (Brabham-turbo 4 BMW BT52B/6), 45. **4.** Alain Prost (Renault turbo V6 RE40-05), 45. **5.** *Niki Lauda (McLaren MP4/1C-7), 44. **5.** John Watson (McLaren MP4/1C-2), 44. **6.** Jacques Laffite (Williams FW08C/8), 44.
**Disqualified for reversing in pit lane after overshooting refuelling marks.*
PP – Patrick Tambay (Ferrari turbo V6 126C3 067), 1;49.328; FL – Arnoux, 1;53.938, 133.444 mph.
Tambay led two laps, Arnoux the rest save for refuelling stop; Piquet secure 2nd with three laps to go when fuel filter cracked, fire retired Brabham-BMW, Cheever Renault broke fuel pump drive giving de Cesaris Alfa's best result in modern F1; Prost Renault handicapped by loss of 5th gear.

24-8-83 AUSTRIAN GP,
Österreichring – 53 laps, 195.699 miles
1. Alain Prost (Renault turbo V6 RE40-05), 53 laps in 1:24;32.745, 138.872 mph.
2. René Arnoux (Ferrari turbo V6 126C3 068), 53 in 1:24;39.580.
3. Nelson Piquet (Brabham-turbo 4 BMW BT52B/5), 53. **4.** Eddie Cheever (Renault turbo V6 RE40-04), 53. **5.** Nigel Mansell (Lotus-Renault turbo V6 94T R2), 52. **6.** Niki Lauda (McLaren MP4/1C-7), 51.
PP – Patrick Tambay (Ferrari turbo V6 126C3 067), 1;29.871; FL – Prost, 1;33.961, 141.461 mph.
Ferrari front row, Tambay led until baulked by Jarier's Ligier letting Arnoux and Piquet by; Arnoux gearbox trouble allowed Prost to catch and pass with six laps to run. Cheever, handicapped by wrong tyre choice, almost caught Piquet (losing revs) on line. Lauda McLaren won 'Cosworth class' again.

28-8-83 DUTCH GP,
Zandvoort – 72 laps, 190.228 miles
1. René Arnoux (Ferrari turbo V6 126C3 066), 72 laps in 1:38;41.950, 115.640 mph.
2. Patrick Tambay (Ferrari turbo V6 126C3 067), 72 in 1:39;02.789.
3. John Watson (McLaren MP4/1C-2), 72. **4.** Derek Warwick (Toleman-turbo 4 Hart TG183B-04), 72. **5.** Mauro Baldi (Alfa Romeo turbo V8 183T/04), 72. **6.** Michele Alboreto (Tyrrell 012-1), 71.
PP – Nelson Piquet (Brabham-turbo 4 BMW BT52B/5), 1;15.630; FL – Arnoux, 1;19.863, 119.097 mph.
Tambay, alongside Piquet on grid, muffed start and fell to 21st – Arnoux won from 10th on grid, Tambay fought through to form Ferrari 1-2. Prost/Piquet collision when disputing lead on lap 42, Lauda debut of McLaren MP4/1E TAG-Porsche turbo V6 niggled Watson in old Cosworth car, superb drive to 3rd place, so McLaren won class in their Cosworth swan-song.

11-9-83 ITALIAN GP,
Monza – 52 laps, 187.403 miles
1. Nelson Piquet (Brabham-turbo 4 BMW BT52B/5), 52 laps in 1:23;10.880, 135.178 mph.
2. René Arnoux (Ferrari turbo V6 126C3 066), 52 in 1:23;21.092.
3. Eddie Cheever (Renault turbo V6 RE40-04), 52. **4.** Patrick Tambay (Ferrari turbo V6 126C3 069), 52. **5.** Elio de Angelis (Lotus-Renault turbo V6 94T R1), 52. **6.** Derek Warwick (Toleman-turbo 4 Hart TG183B-04), 52.
PP – Riccardo Patrese (Brabham-turbo 4 BMW BT52B/6), 1;29.122; FL – Piquet, 1;34.431, 137.393 mph.
Championship leader Prost's race ended in turbo failure, Patrese blew engine lap 3, Piquet led thereafter. First race to see turbocharged cars filling first six places.

25-9-83 EUROPEAN GP,
Brands Hatch, GB – 76 laps, 198.63 miles
1. Nelson Piquet (Brabham-turbo 4 BT52B/5), 76 laps in 1:36;45.865, 123.165 mph.
2. Alain Prost (Renault turbo V6 RE40-05), 76 in 1:36;52.436.
3. Nigel Mansell (Lotus-Renault turbo V6 94T R2), 76. **4.** Andrea de Cesaris (Alfa Romeo turbo V8 183T/05, 76. **5.** Derek Warwick (Toleman-turbo 4 Hart TG183B-04), 76. **6.** Bruno Giacomelli (Toleman-turbo 4 Hart TG183B-03), 76.
PP – Elio de Angelis (Lotus-Renault turbo V6 94T R1), 1;12.092; FL – Mansell, 1;14.342, 126.563 mph.
Ferrari débâcle – Arnoux 9th, Tambay crashed with brake failure when 4th. De Angelis 1st pole in Lotus but collided with Patrese in early duel for lead, fine Warwick drive delayed by fire extinguisher discharging into cockpit; Piquet unmatchable overall.

15-10-83 SOUTH AFRICAN GP,
Kyalami – 77 laps, 196.35 miles
1. Riccardo Patrese (Brabham-turbo 4 BMW BT52B/6), 77 laps in 1:33;25.708, 126.100 mph.
2. Andrea de Cesaris (Alfa Romeo turbo V8 183T/03), 77 in 1:33;35.027.
3. Nelson Piquet (Brabham-turbo 4 BMW BT52B/5), 77. **4.** Derek Warwick (Toleman-turbo 4 Hart TG183B-02), 76. **5.** Keke Rosberg (Williams-turbo V6 Honda FW09/1), 76. **6.** Eddie Cheever (Renault turbo V6 RE40-04), 76.
PP – Patrick Tambay (Ferrari 126C3 069), 1;06.554; FL – Piquet, 1;09.948, 131.245 mph.
Championship decided as Piquet started very light, tore away from field with team-mate 2nd, stopped early for conservative hard tyres and refuelling then settled back for Champion finish as Prost lost 4th place and title in turbo failure on lap 35. Lauda lost 2nd place after charge from 12th in new McLaren turbo when electrics failed six laps from end; promising debut practice for new Williams-Hondas.

1984

25-3-84 BRAZILIAN GP,
Jacarepaguá, Rio de Janeiro – 61 laps, 190.692 miles
1. Alain Prost (McLaren-turbo V6 TAG-Porsche MP4/2-2), 61 laps in 1:42;34.492, 111.543 mph.

2. Keke Rosberg (Williams-turbo V6 Honda FW09/4), 61 in 1:43;15.006.
3. Elio de Angelis (Lotus-turbo V6 Renault 95T R3), 61. **4.** Eddie Cheever (Alfa Romeo turbo V8 184T/01), 60. **5.** Martin Brundle (Tyrrell 012-3), 60. **6.** Patrick Tambay (Renault turbo V6 RE50-03), 59.
PP – de Angelis, 1;28.392; FL – Prost, 1;36.499, 116.622 mph.
New 220-litre race fuel restriction serious worry for all but TAG-Porsche. Alboreto's Ferrari spun from lead lap 12, Lauda took over until lap 38 electrical failure, Warwick inherited lead for Renault before front suspension failed following earlier nudge from Lauda, allowing Prost win in largely untested new turbo McLaren.

7-4-84 SOUTH AFRICAN GP,
Kyalami – 75 laps, 191.247 miles
1. Niki Lauda (McLaren-turbo V6 TAG-Porsche MP4/2-1), 75 laps in 1:29;43.430, 126.367 mph.
2. Alain Prost (McLaren-turbo V6 TAG-Porsche MP4/2-3), 75 in 1:30;29.380.
3. Derek Warwick (Renault turbo V6 RE50/04), 74. **4.** Riccardo Patrese (Alfa Romeo turbo V8 184T/02), 73. **5.** Andrea de Cesaris (Ligier-turbo V6 Renault JS23-03), 73. **6.** Ayrton Senna (Toleman-turbo 4 Hart TG183B-05), 72.
PP – Nelson Piquet (Brabham-turbo 4 BMW BT53/5), 1;04.871; FL – Patrick Tambay (Renault turbo V6 RE50/03), 1;08.877, 133.279 mph.
McLarens utterly dominant with brilliant race set-up despite Prost having to race spare car at last moment, not properly adjusted to his needs; superb drive from back of field to team 1-2.

29-4-84 BELGIAN GP,
Zolder – 70 laps, 185.38 miles
1. Michele Alboreto (Ferrari turbo V6 126C4/074), 70 laps in 1:36;32.048, 115.221 mph.
2. Derek Warwick (Renault turbo V6 RE50/04), 70 in 1:37;14.434.
3. René Arnoux (Ferrari turbo V6 126C4/073), 70. **4.** Keke Rosberg (Williams-turbo V6 Honda FW09/4), 69. **5.** Elio de Angelis (Lotus-turbo V6 Renault 95T R3), 69. **6.** Stefan Bellof (Tyrrell 012-2), 69.
PP – Alboreto, 1;14.846; FL – Arnoux, 1;19.294, 120.233 mph.
Alboreto's first Ferrari pole as McLaren and BMW suffered many practice blow-ups, Rosberg bad start followed by meteoric drive into 3rd place at price of running out of fuel last lap, 1st win for Italian Ferrari driver since Monza 1966.

6-5-84 'SAN MARINO' GP,
Imola, I – 60 laps, 187.90 miles
1. Alain Prost (McLaren-turbo V6 TAG-Porsche MP4/2-3), 60 laps in 1:36;53.679, 116.354 mph.
2. René Arnoux (Ferrari turbo V6 126C4/073), 60 in 1:37;07.095.
3. Elio de Angelis (Lotus-turbo V6 Renault 95T R3), 59. **4.** Derek Warwick (Renault turbo V6 RE50/04), 59. **5.** Stefan Bellof (Tyrrell 012-1), 59. **6.** Thierry Boutsen (Arrows A6/4), 59.
PP – Nelson Piquet (Brabham-turbo 4 BMW BT53/5), 1;28.517; FL – Piquet, 1;33.275, 120.869 mph.
Prost led from start, through spin, through refuelling stop; Lauda delayed at start, challenging for 3rd when piston failed; worst Williams race since 1978, both retiring; Brabham BMWs burned turbos.

20-5-84 FRENCH GP,
Dijon-Prenois – 79 laps, 186.535 miles
1. Niki Lauda (McLaren-turbo V6 TAG-Porsche MP4/2-1), 79 laps in 1:31;11.951, 125.531 mph.
2. Patrick Tambay (Renault turbo V6 RE50/05), 79 in 1:31;19.105.
3. Nigel Mansell (Lotus-turbo V6 Renault 95T R2), 79. **4.** René Arnoux (Ferrari turbo V6 126C4/073), 79. **5.** Elio de Angelis (Lotus-turbo V6 Renault 95T R3), 79. **6.** Keke Rosberg (Williams-turbo V6 Honda FW09/5, 78.
PP – Tambay, 1;02.200; FL – Alain Prost (McLaren-turbo V6 TAG-Porsche MP4/2-2), 1;05.257, 133.242 mph.
First Renault pole in almost a year, Lauda win after Prost delayed by loose wheel, Renault misfortune and major work by Porsche to rush fresh engines from Weissach overnight pre-race after spate of practice problems.

3-6-84 MONACO GP,
Monte Carlo – 31 laps, 63.797 miles*
**Rain shortened race from scheduled 78 laps.*
1. Alain Prost (McLaren-turbo V6 TAG-Porsche MP4/2-2), 31 laps in 1:01;07.740, 62.619 mph.
2. Ayrton Senna (Toleman-turbo 4 Hart TG184-02), 31 in 1:01;15.186.
3. Stefan Bellof (Tyrrell 012-4), 31. **4.** René Arnoux (Ferrari turbo V6 126C4/074), 31. **5.** Keke Rosberg (Williams-turbo V6 Honda FW09/5), 31. **6.** Elio de Angelis (Lotus-turbo V6 Renault 95T R3), 31.
PP – Prost, 1;22.661; FL – Senna, 1;54.334, 64.798 mph.
Flooded track; Mansell Lotus lead after front-row start before crashing through driver error. Prost lead gobbled up by Senna's Toleman which was bound to take lead when red flag abruptly stopped race, saving very lucky Prost McLaren win. Renault first-corner collision débâcle injured Tambay, Lauda spun out later.

17-6-84 CANADIAN GP,
Ile Notre Dame, Montreal – 70 laps, 191.82 miles
1. Nelson Piquet (Brabham-turbo 4 BMW BT53/5), 70 laps in 1:46;23.748, 108.171 mph.
2. Niki Lauda (McLaren-turbo V6 TAG-Porsche MP4/2-1), 70 in 1:46;26.360.
3. Alain Prost (McLaren-turbo V6 TAG-Porsche MP4/2-2), 70. **4.** Elio de Angelis (Lotus-turbo V6 Renault 95T R3), 69. **5.** René Arnoux (Ferrari turbo V6 126C4/075), 68. **6.** Nigel Mansell (Lotus-turbo V6 Renault 95T R2), 68.
PP – Piquet, 1;25.422; FL – Piquet, 1;28.763, 111.691 mph.
Despite burned foot due to new nose oil-cooler, altered weight-distribution Brabham ran superbly for Piquet win; McLarens still 1-2 as usual, only this time Brabham-BMW survived to finish ahead of them!

24-6-84 DETROIT GP,
Michigan, USA – 63 laps, 157.50 miles
1. Nelson Piquet (Brabham-turbo 4 BMW BT53/3), 63 laps in 1:55;41.842, 81.679 mph.
2. Martin Brundle (Tyrrell 012-2), 63 in 1:55;42.679*.
3. Elio de Angelis (Lotus-turbo V6 Renault 95T R3), 63. **4.** Teo Fabi (Brabham-turbo 4 BMW BT53/2), 63. **5.** Alain Prost (McLaren-turbo V6 TAG-Porsche MP4/2-2), 63. **6.** Jacques Laffite (Williams-turbo V6 Honda FW09/3), 62.
**Subsequently disqualified for alleged technical infringement.*
PP – Piquet, 1;40.980; FL – Derek Warwick (Renault turbo V6 RE50), 1;46.221, 84.729 mph.
Mansell Lotus sparked first-start collision. Restart with Piquet in spare car still leading start to finish, eased up allowing Brundle to close apparently dramatically near finish in car suiting street circuit.

8-7-84 DALLAS GP,
Fair Park, Texas, USA – 67 laps, 162.408 miles
1. Keke Rosberg (Williams-turbo V6 Honda FW09/5), 67 laps in 2:01;22.617, 80.283 mph.
2. René Arnoux (Ferrari turbo V6 126C4/075), 67 in 2:01;45.081.
3. Elio de Angelis (Lotus-turbo V6 Renault 95T R3), 66. **4.** Jacques Laffite (Williams-turbo V6 Honda FW09/3), 65. **5.** Piercarlo Ghinzani (Osella-turbo V8 Alfa Romeo FA1F-02), 65. **6.** Nigel Mansell (Lotus-turbo V6 Renault 95T R2), 64.
PP – Mansell, 1;37.041; FL – Niki Lauda (McLaren-turbo V6 TAG-Porsche MP4/2-1), 1;45.353, 82.830 mph.
Long hot race on crumbling circuit; 4-5 car battle for lead, Warwick's Renault and McLarens all retired. Mansell led from pole for half race but damaged car, collapsed exhausted in ill-advised and now illegal attempt to push across line at finish; classic drives by Rosberg and Arnoux.

22-7-84 BRITISH GP,
Brands Hatch – 71 laps, 185.566 miles
1. Niki Lauda (McLaren-turbo V6 TAG-Porsche MP4/2-1), 71 laps in 1:29;28.532, 124.406 mph.
2. Derek Warwick (Renault turbo V6 RE50/08), 71 in 1:30;10.655.
3. Ayrton Senna (Toleman-turbo Hart TG184-02), 71. **4.** Elio de Angelis (Lotus-turbo V6 Renault 95T R3), 70. **5.** Michele Alboreto (Ferrari turbo V6 126C4/076), 70. **6.** René Arnoux (Ferrari turbo V6 126C4/075), 70.
PP – Nelson Piquet (Brabham-turbo 4 BMW BT53/4), 1;10.869; FL – Lauda, 1;13.191, 128.523 mph.
Initial Piquet/McLarens battle ended when race stopped after 11 laps by Palmer RAM crash. After restart Piquet lost boost pressure, Prost's gearbox failed; Lauda's day, and Warwick's, and Senna's . . .

5-8-84 GERMAN GP,
Hockenheim – 44 laps, 185.83 miles
1. Alain Prost (McLaren-turbo V6 TAG-Porsche MP4/2-3), 44 laps in 1:24;43.210, 131.608 mph.
2. Niki Lauda (McLaren-turbo V6 TAG-Porsche MP4/2-1), 44 in 1:24;46.359.
3. Derek Warwick (Renault turbo V6 RE50/08), 44. **4.** Nigel Mansell (Lotus-turbo V6 Renault 95T R2), 44. **5.** Patrick Tambay (Renault turbo V6 RE50/09), 44. **6.** René Arnoux (Ferrari turbo V6 126C4/075), 43.
PP – Prost, 1;47.012; FL – Prost, 1;53.538, 133.915 mph.
Boring race – de Angelis Lotus led seven laps until Renault engine blew, Piquet led until transmission failed, then McLarens all the way; Senna crashed Toleman when wing fell off after fast start.

19-8-84 AUSTRIAN GP,
Österreichring – 51 laps, 188.313 miles
1. Niki Lauda (McLaren-turbo V6 TAG-Porsche MP4/2-1), 51 laps in 1:21;12.851, 139.11 mph.
2. Nelson Piquet (Brabham-turbo 4 BMW BT53/4), 51 in 1:21;36.376.
3. Michele Alboreto (Ferrari turbo V6 126C4/076), 51. **4.** Teo Fabi (Brabham-turbo 4 BMW BT53/5), 51. **5.** Thierry Boutsen (Arrows-turbo 4 BMW A7/2), 50. **6.** Marc Surer (Arrows-turbo 4 BMW A7/3), 50.
PP – Piquet, 1;26.173; FL – Lauda, 1;32.882, 143.105 mph.
Prost spun off when leading, Piquet lost lead due to worn rear Michelins as Lauda rushed by with 11 laps to go, then 4th gear broke, but McLaren kept running. Lauda nursed it home and Piquet unsuspectingly stroked home to distant 2nd instead of mounting last-laps attack to repass crippled car.

26-8-84 DUTCH GP,
Zandvoort – 71 laps, 187.586 miles
1. Alain Prost (McLaren-turbo V6 TAG-Porsche MP4/2-2), 71 laps in 1:37;21.468, 115.606 mph.
2. Niki Lauda (McLaren-turbo V6 TAG-Porsche MP4/2-1), 71 in 1:37;31.751.
3. Nigel Mansell (Lotus-turbo V6 Renault 95T R2), 71. **4.** Elio de Angelis (Lotus-turbo V6 Renault 95T R3), 70. **5.** Teo Fabi (Brabham-turbo 4 BMW BT53/5), 70. **6.** Patrick Tambay (Renault turbo V6 RE50/09), 70.
PP – Prost, 1;13.567; FL – René Arnoux (Ferrari turbo V6 126C4/077), 1;19.465, 119.693 mph.
Prost pulled away from team-mate, though Piquet led first 10 laps before oil union pulled apart; fine Mansell drive, Rosberg Williams-Honda 3rd at one stage but ran out of fuel near end.

9-9-84 ITALIAN GP,
Monza – 51 laps, 183.801 miles
1. Niki Lauda (McLaren-turbo V6 TAG-Porsche MP4/2-1), 51 laps in 1:20;29.065, 137.021 mph.
2. Michele Alboreto (Ferrari turbo V6 126C4/076), 51 in 1:20;53.314.
3. Riccardo Patrese (Alfa Romeo turbo V8 184T/04), 50. **4.** Stefan Johansson (Toleman-turbo 4 Hart TG184-05), 49. **5.** Jo Gartner (Osella-turbo V8 Alfa Romeo FA1F-04), 49. **6.** Gerhard Berger (ATS-turbo 4 BMW D7/02), 49.
PP – Nelson Piquet (Brabham-turbo 4 BMW BT53/4), 1;26.584; FL – Lauda, 1;31.912, 141.158 mph.
Prost engine broke lap 4, Lauda drove usual fine race despite slipped disc in back. Piquet of course led initially until BMW engine wilted due to coolant loss from split radiator; Tambay led Lauda and Fabi Brabham; at lap 40 Lauda 2nd and on lap 43 took lead from Tambay. Fabi stopped out of oil, Tambay throttle linkage parted, leaving Lauda to cruise away from Alboreto's lucky Ferrari.

7-10-84 EUROPEAN GP,
ersatz-Nürburgring, D – 67 laps, 189.091 miles
1. Alain Prost (McLaren-turbo V6 TAG-Porsche MP4/2-2), 67 laps in 1:35;13.284, 119.148 miles.
2. Michele Alboreto (Ferrari turbo V6 126C4/M2-074), 67 in 1:35;37.195.
3. Nelson Piquet (Brabham-turbo 4 BMW BT53/6), 67. **4.** Niki Lauda (McLaren-turbo V6 TAG-Porsche MP4/2-1), 67. **5.** René Arnoux (Ferrari turbo V6 126C4/M2-077), 67. **6.** Riccardo Patrese (Alfa Romeo turbo V8 184T/04), 66.
PP – Piquet, 1;18.871; FL – Piquet & Alboreto, 1;23.146, 122.196 mph.
Prost survived pre-race crash to lead start to finish; Piquet hampered by baulky gearbox, Tambay robbed by engine misfire, both Piquet and Alboreto cars out of fuel on last lap. Lauda spun mid-race yet could easily have finished 2nd if race was only half a lap longer . . .

21-10-84 PORTUGUESE GP,
Estoril – 70 laps, 189.207 miles
1. Alain Prost (McLaren-turbo V6 TAG-Porsche MP4/2-2), 70 laps in 1:41;11.753, 112.182 mph.
2. Niki Lauda (McLaren-turbo V6 TAG-Porsche MP4/2-1), 70 in 1:41;25.178.
3. Ayrton Senna (Toleman-turbo 4 Hart TG184-05), 70. **4.** Michele Alboreto (Ferrari turbo V6 126C4/M2-074), 70. **5.** Elio de Angelis (Lotus-turbo V6 Renault 95T R3), 70. **6.** Nelson Piquet (Brabham-turbo 4 BMW BT53/6), 69.
PP – Piquet, 1;21.703; FL – Lauda, 1;22.996, 117.242 mph.
Prost won seven GPs in season yet missed Drivers' title again, Lauda's five wins plus placings taking it. Piquet spun from lead on first lap, Rosberg fought Williams FW09 round eight laps in lead, Senna and Johansson shone, Mansell good 2nd in Lotus until brake failure in lap 52. McLaren 1-2, typifying whole season, for last 18 laps. Lauda's title by half-point was narrowest margin in competition's 35 seasons. McLaren team domination of season unprecedented in modern times .

1985

7-4-85 BRAZILIAN GP,
Jacarepaguá – 61 laps, 190.692 miles
1. Alain Prost (McLaren-turbo V6 TAG Turbo-Porsche MP4/2B-5), 61 laps in 1:41;26.115, 112.795 mph.
2. Michele Alboreto (Ferrari turbo V6 156/85 079), 61 in 1:41;29.374.
3. Elio de Angelis (Lotus-turbo V6 Renault 97T-2), 60. **4.** René Arnoux (Ferrari turbo V6 156/85 080), 59. **5.** Patrick Tambay (Renault turbo V6 RE60-2), 59. **6.** Jacques Laffite (Ligier-turbo V6 Renault JS25-02), 59.
PP – Alboreto, 1;27.768; FL – Prost, 1;36.702, 116.378 mph.
The rest had closed gap on McLaren, but race lasted only 18 laps between Rosberg's new carbon-tub Williams-Honda and Alboreto, handicapped after first-corner contact with Mansell's Williams. When Rosberg lost a turbo, Alboreto could not resist Prost's charge in updated McLaren.

21-4-85 PORTUGUESE GP,
Estoril – 67 laps, 181.098 miles
Wet race scheduled for 69 laps, but shortened in accordance with two-hour rule.
1. Ayrton Senna (Lotus-turbo V6 Renault 97T-2), 67 laps in 2:00;28.006, 90.198 mph.
2. Michele Alboreto (Ferrari turbo V6 156/85 079), 67 in 2:01;30.984.
3. Patrick Tambay (Renault turbo V6 RE60-4), 66. **4.** Elio de Angelis (Lotus-turbo V6 Renault 97T-3) 66. **5.** Nigel Mansell (Williams-turbo V6 Honda FW10-2), 65. **6.** Stefan Bellof (Tyrrell 012-7), 65.
PP – Senna, 1;21.007; FL – Senna, 1;44.121, 93.455 mph.
Senna proved his class with the perfect motor racing performance: pole, led throughout, fastest lap. Prost and Rosberg crashed; Renault picked up early-season points without ever looking competitive.

5-5-85 SAN MARINO GP,
Imola, I – 60 laps, 187.90 miles
1.* Elio de Angelis (Lotus-turbo V6 Renault 97T-3), 60 laps in 1:34;35.955, 119.177 mph.
2. Thierry Boutsen (Arrows-turbo 4 BMW A8-4), 59 laps.
3. Patrick Tambay (Renault turbo V6 RE60-4), 59. **4.** Niki Lauda (McLaren-turbo V6 TAG Turbo-Porsche MP42B/4), 59. **5.** Nigel Mansell (Williams-turbo V6 Honda FW10-2), 58. **6.** Stefan Johansson (Ferrari turbo V6 156/85 079), 57.**
**First on road was Alain Prost (McLaren-turbo V6 TAG Turbo-Porsche MP4/2B-5), who completed 60 laps in 1:33;57.118 but car disqualified for being under minimum weight at post-race scrutineering.*
***Out of fuel, not running at finish*
PP – Ayrton Senna (Lotus-turbo V6 Renault 97T-2), 1;27.327; FL – Michele Alboreto (Ferrari turbo V6 156/85 081), 1;30.961, 123.945 mph.
Senna dominant again but out of fuel with four laps to run; Johansson inherited lead but ran out of fuel; Prost first but McLaren disqualified; de Angelis's lucky day!

19-5-85 MONACO GP,
Monte Carlo – 78 laps, 160.522 miles
1. Alain Prost (McLaren-turbo V6 TAG Turbo-Porsche MP4/2B-5), 78 laps in 1:51;58.034, 89.654 mph.
2. Michele Alboreto (Ferrari turbo V6 156/85 081), 78 in 1:52;05.575.
3. Elio de Angelis (Lotus-turbo V6 Renault 97T-3), 78 laps. **4.** Andrea de Cesaris (Ligier-turbo V6 Renault JS25-04), 77. **5.** Derek Warwick (Renault turbo V6 RE60-3), 77. **6.** Jacques Laffite (Ligier-turbo V6 Renault JS25-03), 77.
PP – Ayrton Senna (Lotus-turbo V6 Renault 97T-2), 1;20.450; FL – Alboreto, 1;22.637, 89.654 mph.
Senna led until engine broke on lap 13, Prost/Alboreto battle resolved by Ferrari slide on oil spilled in spectacular Piquet/Patrese collision; Italian retook lead, lost it finally with puncture but tigered home second after pit stop. De Angelis led Drivers' Championship.

2-6-85 BELGIAN GP,
Spa-Franchorchamps
Race postponed, lifting track surface unsafe

16-6-85 CANADIAN GP,
Ile Notre Dame, Montreal – 70 laps, 191.82 miles
1. Michele Alboreto (Ferrari turbo V6 156/85 081), 70 laps in 1:46;01.813, 108.544 mph.
2. Stefan Johansson (Ferrari turbo V6 156/85 082), 70 in 1:46;03.770.
3. Alain Prost (McLaren-turbo V6 TAG Turbo-Porsche MP4/2B-5), 70. **24.** Keke Rosberg (Williams-turbo V6 Honda FW10-4), 70. **5.** Elio de Angelis (Lotus-turbo V6 Renault 97T-3), 70. **6.** Nigel Mansell (Williams-turbo V6 Honda FW10-2), 70.
PP – De Angelis 1;24.567; FL – Ayrton Senna (Lotus-turbo V6 Renault 97T-2), 1;27.445, 112.812 mph.
First Ferrari 1-2 since Zandvoort 1983. All-Lotus front row but Senna delayed by early turbo problem, de Angelis led 15 laps but faded. Ferrari fuel economy held off Prost, and his late-charge plans were foiled by de Cesaris's Ligier in his path. New Honda E-Type engine shone in otherwise troubled Williams cars.

23-6-85 DETROIT GP,
Michigan, USA – 63 laps, 157.500 miles
1. Keke Rosberg (Williams-turbo V6 Honda FW10-4), 63 laps in 1:55;39.851, 81.702 mph.
2. Stefan Johansson (Ferrari turbo V6 156/85 082), 63 in 1:56;37.400.
3. Michele Alboreto (Ferrari turbo V6 156/85 081), 63. **4.** Stefan Bellof (Tyrrell 012-7), 63. **5.** Elio de Angelis (Lotus-turbo V6 Renault 97T-3), 63. **6.** Nelson Piquet (Brabham-turbo 4 BMW BT54-6), 62.
PP – Ayrton Senna (Lotus-turbo V6 Renault 97T-2), 1;42.051; FL – Senna, 1;45.612, 85.217 mph.
Senna led seven laps but, like Mansell, Tambay and Prost, crashed. Brundle's Tyrrell-DFY fourth when put out by back-marker. Second US street circuit Rosberg Williams-Honda win after Dallas '84.

7-7-85 FRENCH GP,
Ricard-Castellet – 53 laps, 191.337 miles
1. Nelson Piquet (Brabham-turbo V6 BMW 4 BT54-6), 53 laps in 1:31;46.266, 125.096 mph.
2. Keke Rosberg (Williams-turbo V6 Honda FW10-4), 53 in 1:31;52.926.
3. Alain Prost (McLaren-turbo V6 TAG Turbo-Porsche MP4/2B-5), 53. **4.** Stefan Johansson (Ferrari turbo V6 156/85 081), 53. **5.** Elio de Angelis (Lotus-turbo V6 Renault 97T-3), 53. **6.** Patrick Tambay (Renault turbo V6 RE60B-6), 53.
PP – Rosberg, 1;32.462; FL – Rosberg, 1;39.914, 130.077 mph.
Heat-wave suited Brabham's latest Pirellis, and Piquet drove away when heat and Honda power overwhelmed Williams's Goodyears after Rosberg had led first 10 laps. Senna crashed on own oil after engine blew – Mansell non-started after heavy practice crash.

21-7-85 BRITISH GP
Silverstone – 65 laps, 190.580 miles
1. Alain Prost (McLaren-turbo V6 TAG Turbo-Porsche MP4/2B-2), 65 laps in 1:18;10.436, 146.274 mph.
2. Michele Alboreto (Ferrari turbo V6 156/85 081), 64 laps.
3. Jacques Laffite (Ligier-turbo V6 Renault JS25-05), 64. **4.** Nelson Piquet (Brabham-turbo 4 BMW BT54-6), 64. **5.** Derek Warwick (Renault turbo V6 RE60B-7), 64. **6.** Marc Surer (Brabham-turbo 4 BMW BT54-3), 63.
PP – Rosberg (Williams-turbo V6 Honda FW10-4), 1;05.591; FL – Prost, 1;09.886, 151.035 mph.
Senna dominant but electronic management failure over-enriched mixture, so fuel ran out after 57 straight laps in lead, with one more after Prost had gone by. Senna recaught, then Lotus coughed, cleared and finally retired with 5 laps to go. Ferraris not competitive, Hondas failed after blinding qualifying speed. Flag shown a lap early otherwise Piquet would have displaced out-of-fuel Laffite. Alboreto two points clear of Prost for Drivers' title.

4-8-85 GERMAN GP,
***ersatz* Nürburgring – 67 laps, 189.091 mph**
1. Michele Alboreto (Ferrari turbo V6 156/85 080), 67 laps in 1:35;31.337, 118.773 mph.
2. Alain Prost (McLaren-turbo V6 TAG Turbo-Porsche MP4/2B-2), 67 in 1:35;42.998.
3. Jacques Laffite (Ligier-turbo V6 Renault JS25-05), 67. **4.** Thierry Boutsen (Arrows-turbo 4 BMW A8-4), 67. **5.** Niki Lauda (McLaren-turbo V6 TAG Turbo-Porsche MP4/2B-4), 67. **6.** Nigel Mansell (Williams-turbo V6 Honda FW10-6), 67.
PP – Teo Fabi (Toleman-turbo 4 Hart TG185-3*), 1;17.429; FL – Lauda, 1;22.806, 122.698 mph.
**Pole chassis are numbered as used in race, not necessarily reflecting that used to set pole time.*
Ferraris well matched to course in race trim but Alboreto hit Johansson in first corner, preventing a potential Ferrari 1-2 but Rosberg led 33 laps, broken for 11 laps by Senna before Lotus driveshaft problem; Williams brake trouble then gave Alboreto victory. Fabi's Toleman-Hart first-day pole time survived when rain slowed later session.

18-8-85 AUSTRIAN GP,
Österreichring – 52 laps, 191.993 mph
1. Alain Prost (McLaren-turbo V6 TAG Turbo-Porsche MP4/2B-3), 52 laps in 1:20:12.583, 143.618 mph. **2.** Ayrton Senna (Lotus-turbo V6 Renault 97T-4), 52 in 1:20:42.585.
3. Michele Alboreto (Ferrari turbo V6 156/85 080), 52. **4.** Stefan Johansson (Ferrari turbo V6 156/85 079), 52. **5.** Elio de Angelis (Lotus-turbo V6 Renault 97T-3), 52. **6.** Marc Surer (Brabham-turbo 4 BMW BT54-8), 51.
PP – Prost, 1;25.490; FL – Prost, 1;29.241, 148.943 mph.
Four-car grid pile-up stopped race, spare cars used in restart, utter McLaren domination once Honda bottom-end troubles hit Williams. Prost led first 26 laps, then Lauda's McLaren 13 before engine failure. Prost tied with Alboreto for Drivers' Championship lead, Ferrari 72 points to McLaren 55 in Constructors' Cup.

25-8-85 DUTCH GP,
Zandvoort – 70 laps, 184.944 mph
1. Niki Lauda (McLaren-turbo V6 TAG Turbo-Porsche MP4/2B-4), 70 laps in 1:32:29.263, 119.979 mph.
2. Alain Prost (McLaren-turbo V6 TAG Turbo-Porsche MP4/2B-3), 70 in 1:32;29.495.
3. Ayrton Senna (Lotus-turbo V6 Renault 97T-4) 70. **4.** Michele Alboreto (Ferrari turbo V6 156/85 080), 70. **5.** Elio de Angelis (Lotus-turbo V6 Renault 97T-3), 69. **6.** Nigel Mansell (Williams-turbo V6 Honda FW10-6), 69.
PP – Nelson Piquet (Brabham-turbo 4 BMW BT54-6), 1;11.074; FL – Prost 1;16.538, 124.270 mph.
Abrasive track made tyre changes necessary – Lauda's stop-early tactic paid off, just pipped team-mate to finish, but Rosberg's Williams-Honda led 32 laps before engine failure. Lauda and Prost now had 45 career wins between them, other 24 drivers in field aggregated only 35 between them!

8-9-85 ITALIAN GP,
Monza – 51 laps, 183.801 miles
1. Alain Prost (McLaren-turbo V6 TAG Turbo-Porsche MP4/2B-5), 51 laps in 1:17:59.451, 141.402 mph.
2. Nelson Piquet (Brabham-turbo 4 BMW BT54-6), 51 in 1:18:51.086.
3. Ayrton Senna (Lotus-turbo V6 Renault 97T-4), 51. **4.** Marc Surer (Brabham-turbo 4 BMW BT54-8), 51. **5.** Stefan Johansson (Ferrari turbo V6 156/85 083), 50. **6.** Elio de Angelis (Lotus-turbo V6 Renault 97T-3), 50.
PP – Senna, 1;25.084; FL – Nigel Mansell (Williams-turbo V6 Honda FW10-6), 1;28.283, 146.961 mph.
Ferrari trounced on home ground; Rosberg's race, lost lead in tyre-change stop, retook it before engine bottom-end failed again 8 laps from home. Senna underpowered in race, Mansell's Williams-Honda fastest on track after early stop. Prost led 19 of 51 laps, displaced Alboreto, and McLaren displaced Ferrari, in respective Championships.

15-9-85 BELGIAN GP,
Spa-Francorchamps – 43 laps, 185.669 miles
1. Ayrton Senna (Lotus-turbo V6 Renault 97T-4), 43 laps in 1:34;19.893, 117.943 mph.
2. Nigel Mansell (Williams-turbo V6 Honda FW10-6), 43 in 1:34:48.315.
3. Alain Prost (McLaren-turbo V6 TAG Turbo-Porsche MP4/2B-5), 43. **4.** Keke Rosberg (Williams-turbo V6 Honda FW10-7), 43. **5.** Nelson Piquet (Brabham-turbo 4 BMW BT54-6), 42. **6.** Derek Warwick (Renault V6 RE60B-3), 42.
PP – Prost, 1;55.306; FL – Prost 2;01.730, 127.531 mph.
Ferraris blew up early, Senna lost lead only in tyre-change stop for pre-heated slicks after part-wet race, thereafter uncatchable. Williams-Hondas and McLaren both strong. Lauda injured wrist in practice crash, non-started.

6-10-85 EUROPEAN GP,
Brands Hatch – 75 laps, 196.050 miles
1. Nigel Mansell (Williams-turbo V6 Honda FW10-6), 75 laps in 1:32:58.109, 126.527 mph.
2. Ayrton Senna (Lotus-turbo V6 Renault 97T-4), 75 in 1:33;19.505.
3. Keke Rosberg (Williams-turbo V6 Honda FW10-7), 75. **4.** Alain Prost (McLaren-turbo V6 TAG Turbo-Porsche MP4/2B-2), 75. **5.** Elio de Angelis (Lotus-turbo V6 Renault 97T-3), 74. **6.** Thierry Boutsen (Arrows-turbo 4 BMW A8-4), 73.
PP – Senna, 1;07.169; FL – Jacques Laffite (Ligier-turbo V6 Renault JS25-05), 1;11.526, 131.566 mph.
Senna Lotus battle with both Williams cars resolved when Rosberg spun and Piquet rammed him, Rosberg rejoined after stop ahead of Senna and gave Mansell chance to pass them both for lead he never lost. Ferrari flopped again, Brabham and Ligier shone on Pirellis, Prost Champion. Watson, deputizing for Lauda, seventh.

19-10-85 SOUTH AFRICAN GP,
Kyalami – 75 laps, 191.247 miles
1. Nigel Mansell (Williams-turbo V6 Honda FW10-6), 75 laps in 1:28:22.866, 129.840 mph.
2. Keke Rosberg (Williams-turbo V6 Honda FW10-7), 75 in 1:28;30.438.
3. Alain Prost (McLaren-turbo V6 TAG Turbo-Porsche MP4/2B-6), 75. **4.** Stefan Johansson (Ferrari turbo V6 156/85 086), 74. **5.** Gerhard Berger (Arrows-turbo 4 BMW A8-2), 74. **6.** Thierry Boutsen (Arrows-turbo 4 BMW A8-4), 74.
PP – Mansell, 1;02.366; FL – Rosberg, 1;08.149, 134.710 mph.
Flawless Mansell drive under pressure from Prost but Rosberg blindingly fast after spin into sand-trap and two tyre-stops to Mansell's one, Williams-Honda clearly in new class.

3-11-85 AUSTRALIAN GP,
Adelaide – 82 laps, 192.498 miles
1. Keke Rosberg (Williams-turbo V6 Honda FW10-7), 82 laps in 2:00;40.473, 95.71 mph.
2. Jacques Laffite (Ligier-turbo V6 Renault JS25-05), 82 in 2:01;26.603.
3. Philippe Streiff (Ligier-turbo V6 Renault JS25-04), 82. **4.** Ivan Capelli (Tyrrell-turbo V6 Renault 014-2), 81. **5.** Stefan Johansson (Ferrari turbo V6 156/85 086), 81. **6.** Gerhard Berger (Arrows-turbo 4 BMW A8-2), 81.
PP – Ayrton Senna (Lotus-turbo V6 Renault 97T-4), 1;19.843; FL – Rosberg, 1;23.758, 100.899 mph.
Sensational new race, Rosberg/Senna battle included multiple tyre-stops and incidents until Lotus finally blew engine. Lauda led his final GP for two laps before brake failure and crash; Rosberg won despite *three* stops; Ligier team-mates squabbled near finish, Streiff wrecking his left-front suspension on Laffite car's rear wheel. McLaren retained Constructor's Cup from Ferrari, Williams displaced Lotus third.

Whatever the technicalities, the name of the game is simply WINNING.